THE HISTORY OF

YORKSHIRE
COUNTY
CRICKET CLUB

THE CHRISTOPHER HELM
COUNTY CRICKET HISTORIES

Series Editors:
Peter Arnold and Peter Wynne-Thomas

DERBYSHIRE
John Shawcroft, with a personal view by Bob Taylor

GLAMORGAN
Andrew Hignell, with a personal view by Tony Lewis

HAMPSHIRE
Peter Wynne-Thomas with a personal view by John Arlott

KENT
Dudley Moore, with a personal view by Derek Underwood

LANCASHIRE
Peter Wynne-Thomas, with a personal view by Brian
Statham

MIDDLESEX
David Lemmon, with a personal view by Denis Compton

SURREY
David Lemmon, with a personal view by Peter May

WORCESTERSHIRE
David Lemmon, with a personal view by Basil D'Oliveira

THE HISTORY OF

YORKSHIRE
COUNTY
CRICKET CLUB

Anthony Woodhouse

With a personal view by
SIR LEONARD HUTTON

CHRISTOPHER HELM

London

© 1989 A. Woodhouse
Christopher Helm (Publishers) Ltd, Imperial House,
21–25 North Street, Bromley, Kent BR1 1SD

ISBN 0-7470-3408-7

A CIP catalogue record for this book is available from the British Library

Typeset by Cotswold Typesetting Ltd, Gloucester
Printed and bound by Biddles Ltd, Guildford, Surrey

CONTENTS

A PERSONAL VIEW
Sir Leonard Hutton

IN MY TRAVELS OVERSEAS I have always been impressed with the reputation and regard in which Yorkshire Cricket is held by those who have never visited our shores. A few years ago Yorkshire were at the foot of the Championship table. This, to our overseas supporters and to many English Yorkshire followers, was almost impossible to comprehend bearing in mind the staggering success which the Yorkshire Club had enjoyed for so long since its formation in 1863.

It was in 1929 as a 13-year-old schoolboy that I first saw the Yorkshire team at what I call very close quarters. The match was in aid of Herbert Sutcliffe's benefit and played on the Pudsey St Lawrence Ground. All the stars of the Yorkshire team of the 1920s were present, all heroes of mine from a small boy: Sutcliffe, Rhodes, Leyland, Robinson, Oldroyd, Holmes. Sir William Worsley was captain.

It was an evening game and the ground was full – very full – but I managed to find a spot very near to the Yorkshire dressing rooms. I could hear what the giants of cricket said as they prepared to do battle against the Pudsey and District Fifteen. Yorkshire were playing at Park Avenue at the time and were having a rather rough time against a southern county; they were struggling and in danger of defeat. A gentleman standing very close to me asked Wilfred Rhodes about the match at Park Avenue. Wilfred, in his quiet manner, informed the gentleman not to worry, Yorkshire would not lose and they did not lose.

I was asked to join the Yorkshire team as 12th man at Leicester in 1933. This was a great occasion for me. To share the same dressing room with Sutcliffe, Leyland, Bowes and Verity was to be for me a never-to-be-forgotten thrill. The size of their cricket bags – too heavy to lift – filled the floor of the dressing room. Sutcliffe carried three bats. Bill Bowes just had the one bat which he used throughout his career. Sutcliffe and Leyland carried suit cases which contained white trousers and shirts. Most of the players had a special pair of trousers which they used for batting. My small bag looked very much out of place in that Leicester dressing room.

I really could not believe my luck at being at the heart of Yorkshire cricket. This Championship team of cricketers were household names. Strange to recall that the weather was very hot for my first occasion with the team, so hot that it was decided to take drinks at 3.15 on the field. Beforehand I was certain Yorkshire cricketers kept their minds on cricket during the day's play. This was not so, as I was asked by George Macaulay to take out to him on the field at drinks time the winner of the 2.30 at Thirsk. I had never spoken to Mac before, but with the help of Frank Stainton of the *Sheffield Telegraph* I was able to supply Mac with the required information promptly at 3.15 pm.

Before he retired in 1935 I had several of what I thought were amusing little incidents with Mac. On one occasion at Lord's I was fielding in the leg trap to Mac's bowling; Patsy Hendren was batting and looked in great form. A particular ball found the edge of

Patsy's bat, giving a possible catch to Cyril Turner and myself stationed in the close-to-the-wicket positions. I made no move, and neither did Cyril Turner, as each of us decided to leave the chance to the other. We both looked at Macaulay, who glared back at the two of us and said: 'I'll get you two in Madame Tussauds'.

Macaulay, on a wicket with a little help, was dynamite; his off-spinners and medium-pace inswingers and outswingers made him one of the finest bowlers in England in his prime. If you wanted to speak to Mac at the end of the day's play you had to be quick – I have never known any cricketer who could change into his street clothes quicker than the former bank clerk from Thirsk.

It was during the match at Leicester that I became close to Bill Bowes and Hedley Verity. They both talked to me and we became good friends as the years slipped by. I do not remember any other member of the Yorkshire team showing much interest in me. Macaulay had of course asked me to find out what had won the 2.30 at Thirsk – apart from that my heroes had nothing to say.

I myself said little or nothing in those days. It was a wonderful experience just to watch and listen to cricketers whose knowledge was the finest of any cricket team the world over.

Long before I first met Bill Bowes I was one of his great admirers, I simply could not understand why he was not one of the early selections for the 'bodyline' tour of 1932–33. In actual fact Bill was one of the the last selections, just scraping in at the last moment. His figures for the 1932 English season were outstanding – he was at the top or near the top of the averages pretty well most of the season.

During the early 1930s Bill Bowes was the main strike force in the Yorkshire attack; it was mainly due to his accurate bowling over long spells which enabled Yorkshire to become the outstanding team of the decade.

It was in the Yorkshire *v* Australia match at Sheffield when I made one of my biggest mistakes in my cricket career. I think this dropped slip catch cost Yorkshire the match. The bowling of Bowes during the Australian second innings to Don Bradman was magnificent. With his score under double figures Bradman edged an outswinger to me at second slip, but the easiest of slip catches was put down. I was so upset that Bill made a special point of saying to me: 'Don't worry, Len.' No black looks, no angry words from this great bowler. This was the only occasion that I saw Don Bradman made to look like a second rater. Now, 50 years later, this spell of bowling by Bowes and the luck which enabled Bradman to make over 40 runs, remain as clear as a bell in my memory.

Yes, a dropped slip catch, the easiest of chances, cost Yorkshire this game. We wanted 67 to win with seven wickets standing when rain put an end to the match, preventing Yorkshire from gaining their first victory against Australia since 1902.

Anthony Woodhouse remarks in this history on the opening batsmen of Yorkshire. In Holmes and Sutcliffe they had a magnificent pair. Their partnerships became classic displays of batsmanship on all types of wickets. Percy Holmes was most attractive to watch. The quickness of his feet enabled him to play shots all round the wicket. I did, however, have the opportunity to study Herbert at closer quarters sharing 15 century partnerships with him. On one occasion we were on 315 at the tea interval against Leicester at Hull. On the way to the wicket after tea Herbert said to me we will go for

556. Herbert, with Percy Holmes, was the holder of the world record opening score of 555, made in 1932. Without adding to my score I was bowled out, much to the disgust of Herbert who gave me one of his famous black looks as I passed him on my way to the pavilion.

It was impossible not to improve, playing with Herbert. He was the finest opening batsman whom I played with. He did, however, say to me several times that he was not so good as he used to be — but he remained a very fine player to his last season.

What I found of great interest, having studied many books on how to play cricket as a schoolboy, was the different techniques used by the outstanding cricketers of different generations. I never saw anyone hold the bat as Herbert Sutcliffe did. Very few batsmen picked the bat up perfectly straight, but most of them managed to bring the bat down pretty straight. Wilfred Barber was an exception — no one picked the bat up straighter than he.

Wilfred Rhodes stood at the wicket with his left shoulder pointing towards mid-on. Edgar Oldroyd had a similar stance — he was a very good puller of the ball, one of the best I have seen.

Maurice Leyland used a very heavy bat — to me it always had the look of a railway sleeper. His forearms were as thick as my thighs. During his great innings at The Oval in 1938 against Australia, Maurice called me to the centre of the pitch and said: 'I have got Bill O'Reilly taped' — and: 'I'll tell you something else as well; he knows it.'

Arthur Mitchell struck me in my early days as the most difficult man in the Yorkshire team. He once said to me: 'I know how to do it but I can't do it.' He was talking about cricket — in later years he became the Yorkshire coach. Mitchell was funny, very humourous in a way which took me a couple of years to appreciate. In my first match at The Oval, one of the largest grounds in England, Surrey won the toss and proceeded to make a huge score batting all day. At close of play, while I was sitting in the dressing room resting my tired legs and aching feet, Mitchell turned to me and said: 'Where as tha been all day?' There was a pause then came his follow-up remark: 'Hast ter got six-inch nails in thee boots?'

I had run and thrown for six hours on a ground baked hard in the August sun. Some might have said well fielded, but not Mitchell. He never said well done to anyone. He was funny, but knowledge of the Yorkshire dialect was essential.

*　*　*

There are times in all our lives when we look back, and wish we had the chance again to make amends for missed opportunities. Anyone who has followed Yorkshire cricket for 60 years, as I have, will know of George Herbert Hirst and Wilfred Rhodes. Both came from Kirkheaton, near Huddersfield, and both learnt their cricket in what might be called an industrial village, cricket being the game to play and the cricket ground the meeting place for all during the summer months.

When I was playing in the Huddersfield area I would hear supporters say, have you seen George Herbert, never George Hirst, always George Herbert. When I was in the company of these two giants of cricket, which I might add was frequent, I wanted to ask them so many questions but suffered from shyness, and became almost speechless. On one occasion I was with George Herbert, on the tramcar travelling from Headingley to

3

City Square in Leeds. I was a 15-year-old at the time, and George placed his hand on my arm and said: 'Whatever you do, don't become like Victor Trumper'.

This remark almost knocked me for six. 'Why?' I asked. George said that Victor Trumper was so superstitious that he made his life a misery. He wore the same trousers to bat in all his life, so that little remained of the original pair – the patches had become the main feature of the garment.

In my early days I spent a great deal of time with George Herbert. On one occasion I helped him with the coaching session for schoolboys, which was most interesting. To hear George talk to the boys was quite a revelation. He said to me: 'I don't think I will say anything more to this boy. You see, Len, when I say anything to him he always says, "I know"'.

Wilfred Rhodes was very different to George Herbert – nowhere near the generous, cheerful and kind George. All the best Wilfred would say of Bradman was that he was a good player. When asked if he played against Bradman, Wilfred said 'On one occasion only. I would have had him out when he was ten, if my mid-off had been any good'. Wilfred was asked who his mid-off was at the time. 'R. E. S. Wyatt', he replied.

This particular match was MCC against Australia at Scarborough in 1930. I have asked Bob Wyatt about this incident, who said to me: 'Yes, it was a chance. Unfortunately, I did not see the ball early enough to get into position to make the catch. It is very difficult to see the ball on many grounds when the sun is shining, and the crowd is big.' This little story amuses Bob Wyatt, who has a great sense of humour, very much. Wilfred was playing in his last match of importance and was just as keen to get Bradman out as he was to get wickets when playing for Yorkshire and England at the turn of the century.

During one of our little chats together Wilfred confided to me that he had bowled against some fine players, but Bradman was the best he had ever bowled against.

There was, however, one man who Wilfred thought was supreme. The only man whom Wilfred would take off his cap to was Colin Blythe of Kent. He must have been good for Wilfred to say that to me about him.

On one of my MCC tours of Australia, I received a message to say a lady would like to see me in the foyer of the hotel. I found an elderly lady waiting for me carrying a small package. This lady said to me that her husband came from Kirkheaton, and was brought out to Australia by his parents when he was a small boy. She said that her husband, who had passed away a year or so previously, always remained a Yorkshireman, and had become a friend of Wilfred's and would spend a lot of time with Wilfred whenever the MCC were playing in Melbourne. She then opened the package she was carrying, and produced a cricket ball. She said this was the ball which was used in the Test match there in 1904 when Wilfred took eight wickets for 68 runs. 'Would you kindly take this back to England and give it to Wilfred', she asked me, and this I did. I repeated the story to Wilfred, and as he opened the package and held the ball in his hand a delightful smile came over his face. His thoughts were I am sure of Melbourne in January 1904, 50 years earlier, when he took 15 wickets in the match, seven in the first innings and eight in the second.

Mr Woodhouse gives on the following pages some excellent pen pictures of so many Yorkshire cricketers. Some are almost forgotten, but I shall always remember them not as players but as visitors to the Yorkshire dressing room in my early days. Bobby Peel and David Denton were frequent visitors, and Arthur Dolphin was often to be seen and heard in the dressing room.

Wilfred Rhodes was a regular visitor and on one occasion at Bramall Lane I asked him if he would bowl to me in the nets. We walked out to the practice ground near to the pavilion, which is now sadly gone. On this pitch Wilfred took his jacket off, and in his braces and street shoes he bowled at me for at least 20 minutes.

This was the most remarkable net practice which I ever had in my cricketing life. I knew Wilfred could flight and spin the ball, but such accuracy was quite remarkable. It was then that I realised why Wilfred had taken over 4,000 wickets in first-class cricket.

I had a similar experience in Perth, Western Australia, when Clarrie Grimmett kindly bowled to me at the start of the 1946–47 Australian tour. His accuracy was truly amazing as he bowled his leg-breaks and googlies.

* * *

In Yorkshire, we had a very useful young fast bowler called Bert Hargreaves, from Sheffield. His first match was against Kent at Maidstone in 1934. Kent won the toss, and Hargreaves opened the bowling to Frank Woolley, who was opening the innings for Kent at that time. The first ball that Bert Hargreaves bowled in first-class cricket was pulled just behind square for six by Frank Woolley. This was a fine stroke to a ball just short of a length. As the ball soared over the pavilion I looked at Bert Hargreaves, who looked as though he had received a severe shock. Frank Woolley could do this sort of thing without any hint of aggression. Woolley could hit you for six without offending you. Of all the batsmen whom I played against, Woolley was the most graceful. He once hit me for six without rousing any resentment in me at all.

* * *

I have always thought that the excellent work of Cyril Turner with Yorkshire cricket was not fully appreciated. Figures and averages gave no indication of the value he gave to Yorkshire. So often he would go to the wicket when quick runs were required, and at other times a rain-affected wicket would be his lot. Again, when bowling so often he would be required when Bowes and Verity could find no help from the plumb wickets to be seen at Sheffield, Headingley and elsewhere. Some of the excellent catches which he made fielding in the gully position were really outstanding, but little or nothing is to be seen in the record books to tell you that Cyril was one of the safest catchers in first-class cricket.

There was another thing about the man from Wath-on-Dearne – he was one of the nicest chaps who ever played for Yorkshire. He worked well with young cricketers, and his companionship towards me was invaluable at a very important period of my cricketing life. Cyril Turner was a good man. I spent many very happy hours with him on and off the field. He was an excellent coach and adviser to all young cricketers. I myself have a lot to thank Cyril for – 'they don't make 'em like him any more'.

* * *

Being captain of Yorkshire is not an easy task, and harder these days than perhaps in the whole history of the Club.

One skipper who I think was unlucky not to have three Championships during his period as captain was Norman Yardley. Norman had to build a new team in 1947, as just one or two players remained who were of pre-war vintage. He had a harder task than any Yorkshire captain in the history of the Club.

I have heard it said that it takes three years for a young cricketer really to become accustomed to first-class cricket. This I found myself. The difference between club and 2nd XI cricket is considerable. Playing six days a week is vastly different to playing club cricket. To bowl in first-class cricket requires good legs – the strain on a fast bowler is considerable.

I very much admired the way in which Yardley handled the promising young Yorkshire cricketers in the period 1947 to 1955. Wardle came along at this time, and a little later Trueman and Close made their appearance. All developed into England players, as did Frank Lowson, who unfortunately suffered from varicose veins. During this period Alex Coxon was a very useful member of the side. I was sorry to hear of his resignation when I was in Colombo, whilst on the 1950–51 tour of Australia. Coxon was sadly missed during the 1951 season; he was a great team man and a great trier.

The young cricketers prospered under the careful leadership of Norman Yardley. Fred Trueman from time to time looked full of promise, but was not to develop into the great bowler he became, until both Norman and myself had retired.

Perhaps the greatest joy to all of us was to see the arrival of Bob Appleyard, who met with instant success. This is most unusual. He was within a very short time a Test match prospect. He was the best bowler of his type in the country when he was stricken with the illness which cut his progress in cricket considerably. Bob was the great discovery of post-war Yorkshire cricket; he took 637 wickets for Yorkshire in what was a very short period of time.

Looking back on the years of Norman Yardley's captaincy of Yorkshire and England, I consider Norman was unlucky. He struck in 1948 perhaps the finest Australian side ever to visit these shores. This was the best team I played against. No cricketer could hope to play under a more knowledgeable or nicer man than Norman. Never did I see him do or say anything which was unsporting. He played the game as it was intended to be played.

* * *

In the early 1930s Yorkshire had two outstanding fast bowlers, Bill Bowes and Sandy Jacques, a farmer from Selby. Jacques had one of the finest actions seen on a cricket field – I have never seen a fast bowler with a better action. Unfortunately, he suffered from leg trouble. He found playing six days a week too big a strain and this was the reason why we saw so little of him. On such things do great careers in cricket rest.

These are a few of my personal views of a lifetime commitment to Yorkshire cricket, every moment of which I have enjoyed.

IDDISON IN CHARGE

THOMAS LORD, THE FOUNDER OF LORD'S was the first professional cricketer produced by Yorkshire. He founded Lord's in 1787 and started playing important cricket in that same year. Admittedly it was more or less an accident that he was born in the town of Thirsk; but the house where he was born still exists and is a cricket museum. Whether he ever played before leaving for Diss in Norfolk seems very doubtful. Other cricketers who had loose connections with Yorkshire were the Hon Brudenell and Captain Beckett as we move into the 19th century to be followed by the London-born George Osbaldeston, who spent most of his life in the Scarborough area when not hunting, or cricketing or taking part in other sports. Sheffield was becoming noted in cricket circles and the game appeared to develop in that city on a slightly more organised basis than in the rest of Yorkshire, where it spread very slowly in rural areas without receiving much recognition in the newspapers.

Yorkshire first took the field under that name in 1833 on the Hyde Park Ground at Sheffield and the side consisted of 11 Sheffield cricketers, one of whom, T. R. Barker, was a native of Bakewell and so had the distinction of being the first 'foreigner' to represent the County. From that 1833 match, which Yorkshire won against a Norfolk team containing Fuller Pilch, until 1862 the county played 28 matches without the side being organised in any way.

The first attempt to place Yorkshire county cricket on an organised footing came in 1861, when the Sheffield Public Match Fund Committee was set up on 7 March at Henry Sampson's home, the Adelphi Hotel in Sheffield. This resolution was unanimously adopted:

> That immediate steps be taken to raising a Public Match Fund to defray the expenses of playing County and Public Matches that may be played on the Bramall Lane Ground in Sheffield and that the offices of the various clubs of the Town be requested to lend their cordial assistance towards raising such Funds and forming a Committee for carrying out the same.

Certainly the committee made efforts to produce fixtures during the 1861 and 1862 seasons when six games were played against Kent and Surrey. The local clubs in Sheffield certainly gave their financial assistance. The larger towns who were hoping to play county matches gave their support in due course although there was always a feeling that Sheffield might dominate matters too much. The Bramall Lane ground was certainly a first-class venue with few superior in the country, and as the game advanced in the county and large crowds were willing to attend the big matches other towns followed suit and built their own 'county' grounds. Bradford was a typical example of a club that would perhaps have preferred to have taken matters into their own hands, and there was in later seasons something of a split in the county, with the make-up teams appearing to be taken out of the Sheffield Club's hands.

On 8 January 1863 the following resolution was passed:

> That a County Club be formed, the Annual Subscription to be not less than 10/6d [52½ p] per member.

Before the season opened, the Club was formed, and officers and committee were all named and rules set down by 28 April. At the same meeting a team was chosen to play against Surrey in June. The Yorkshire County Cricket Club had been set in motion; it was to be a momentous journey, beset by problems on and off the field; yet the days of success have been many and probably no Club in any period has had such a devoted and faithful set of members dedicated to its success.

Yorkshire took the field for the first time at The Oval on 4, 5 and 6 June 1863 with rain affecting the play on all three days, the result being a draw. The side was as follows: R. Iddison (captain), John Thewlis, John Berry, J. Rowbotham, E. Stephenson, E. Dawson, G. Anderson, Mr B. W. Waud, G. R. Atkinson, I. Hodgson and W. Slinn. Three of the players came from Sheffield and three from Huddersfield, while two came from Bedale.

Roger Iddison, the first captain of Yorkshire County Cricket Club, was a powerful hitter with a free, forward style as well as being a fast round-arm bowler and occasionally successful slow lob bowler who excelled at point. He started to play in important cricket in 1853 and continued to play for Yorkshire until 1876, also assisting Lancashire in 1865–70, obtaining centuries for both Counties and meeting with all-round success for them. He also assisted the Players against the Gentlemen and helped to form the United North of England XI along

Yorkshire's first captain, Roger Iddison, was also in the first touring team to Australia in 1861–62.

with George Freeman, playing their first match in 1883. He also assisted the United England XI and toured Australia on the first tour there in 1862 when he took 103 wickets at 6.59 each. Roger Iddison also started the ill-fated Yorkshire United CC in 1874. A short, stout, red-faced man, he developed diabetes and consumption just before his death at York in 1890 aged 55.

John Thewlis senior, was born at Kirkheaton in 1828 but moved to Lascelles Hall when eight years old. Possessing white hair, he refused to go to school but taught himself to read and write and to play cricket. He played his first match for Lascelles Hall on Birkenshaw Moor and would not take his coat off as his shirt was full of holes. He played for Yorkshire in 1863–75 and was the only player not to miss a match in the County Club's first three seasons. He scored the Club's first-ever century in 1868 against Surrey. A sound, steady right-hand batsman, and brilliant long-stop, he was 34 years of age when the County Club was formed, and appeared in important matches only from 1862. He represented the Players *v* Gentlemen in 1868. Latterly he fell on evil times and was discovered by the *Yorkshire Evening Post* trudging on foot with washing while walking from Manchester to his home in Failsworth. In the 1880s he was an umpire and still living in Lascelles Hall, but after being found in poor circumstances he became groundsman to the Greenfield Club and was granted 10/– (50p) per week by the Yorkshire CCC.

John Berry, a nephew of George Berry, was 40 years old when he appeared for Yorkshire in 1863. A hard-hitting batsman with a good defence and very useful roundarm medium-pace bowler, he was a leading member of the then powerful Dalton side from 1842 until he left there in 1852 when he became a professional in Sheffield. He acquitted himself well in important matches from 1847 with both bat and ball and he continued to play for Yorkshire until 1867. From 1852 he acted as a servant to Mr M. J. Ellison, the famous Treasurer of the Yorkshire CCC and he continued to play in local cricket until 1883 and his last engagement was at Accrington. A typical Yorkshireman, he was a fancy weaver by trade and in 1842 when aged only 18 he took all 10 wickets for Dalton against Bradford. He also appeared for North *v* South at The Oval. He died at Haslingden in 1895, aged 72.

Joseph Rowbotham (irreverently called 'Old Tarpot') was born near Bramall Lane in 1831 and was originally a saw-maker by trade. A fine batsman with an attractive style, he began to play in important matches in 1854 and assisted Yorkshire up to 1876. He took part in the first ever match at Bramall Lane and helped to cut sods for the first wicket to be laid there. A short, heavily built man he excelled at point and long-stop and could also keep wicket. He played in many of the early Sheffield matches and represented the Players *v* Gentlemen in

1864–69. The Yorkshire *v* Gloucestershire game in 1873 was played for his benefit and was a success as he was very popular and greatly respected in Sheffield.

Edwin ('Ned') Stephenson was a free hard-hitting batsman, a right-arm round-arm bowler and fine wicket-keeper. He took part in important matches from 1851 and he continued to play for Yorkshire until 1873 although Pinder had started to take over the wicket-keeping role from 1867. At one time he was considered inferior only to Lockyer as a wicket-keeper. In 1870 he became the first Yorkshire cricketer to obtain a benefit from the County Club but in later years he fell into straitened circumstances.

Brian Waud, known as 'The Major', was a stylish batsman and fine wicket-keeper who was in the Eton XI of 1855 and the Oxford University XI in 1857–60. He appeared for Yorkshire in 1862–64, and represented the Gentlemen against the Players. He had been a member of the Yorkshire Gentlemen's Cricket Club from its formation in 1864. He went to Canada and in 1881 appeared for Canada against the USA. A barrister and later a journalist by profession, he went insane just prior to his death in Toronto in 1889 aged 51.

George Anderson, one of the best batsmen of his day in the north of England, played in important matches from 1850 onwards and last appeared for Yorkshire in 1869. A tall upright batsman, he was a very powerful driver, especially strong in front of the wicket. He possessed two portraits of himself, one sketched by Felix and one taken when he was in Melbourne during the 1863–64 tour, on which he was not very successful owing to illness. He kept a diary on that tour which is now in the possession of the MCC at Lord's. He did not receive a benefit from Yorkshire until long after his retirement owing to his having declined to play for his County against Surrey, who had induced Lillywhite to no-ball Willsher. His benefit in 1895 realised the sum of £300, but towards the end of his life he was rather hard up.

William Slinn, a right-arm round-arm fast bowler, was a member of the famous bowling partnership of 'Hodgson and Slinn'. He played in important matches between 1859 and 1865, when he last played for Yorkshire. A fine bowler with a graceful delivery, he was a very poor fielder and batsman. He and Hodgson were the first great pair of bowlers produced by the County. Although he never played for the Players against the Gentlemen, Slinn, a scissor-smith by trade, took some 600 wickets for local 22s against England Elevens between 1859 and 1870. In 1862 he took eight for 33 for Yorkshire against Surrey at Sheffield and was a regular attender at Bramall Lane to the end of his life.

Isaac ('Ikey') Hodgson was an excellent left-handed round-arm slow bowler who played once for Players *v* Gentlemen in 1863 and was best-known for his combination with William Slinn in matches for local 22s against England Elevens. He played in important matches from 1847 and last played for Yorkshire in 1864 when he gave up the game owing to consumption, from which he died in the following year. He was also a noted knurr and spell player.

That opening drawn match of the new Club with Surrey saw Hodgson in good form as he took four for 96 in the home side's total of 315 and followed that up with five for 27 as Surrey collapsed to 60, the match finishing at the interesting stage of Yorkshire requiring 118 to win in the fourth innings. With an unchanged team Yorkshire met Nottinghamshire on the old Horton Road Ground and began well by bowling out their illustrious opponents for 128. Nottinghamshire were dismissed mainly through their own shortcomings as no less than four batsmen were run out including the top scorer, Richard Daft, for 27. Thanks mainly to Thewlis (46) Yorkshire passed the Nottinghamshire score by 16 runs. Nottinghamshire batted even worse in their second innings as Iddison, the skipper, took seven for 30 in a remarkable spell of bowling. B. W. Waud with 34 not out was mainly responsible for Yorkshire's eight-wicket win.

Yorkshire's next match was the return with Nottinghamshire at Trent Bridge when B. W. Waud and Atkinson were replaced by Ashley Walker and John Hall. Atkinson refused to play, leading to eight of the Yorkshire team signing a statement to the effect that they would not play in the next game if Atkinson was chosen. Yorkshire scored 243, their chief run-getter being George Anderson, who made 82. Nottinghamshire were dismissed for 162 and as they were over 80 behind on the first innings they were bound to follow on. Nottinghamshire did rather better in the second innings, reaching 181 with Slinn taking five for 52. Set 101 to win, Yorkshire were in a good position at 60 for two, collapsed and Nottinghamshire won an exciting match by six runs.

Ashley Walker was a right-handed batsman and round-arm bowler who was in the Westminster XI in 1860–62 and the Cambridge University XI in 1864–66. A stylish, free-scoring batsman and useful slow bowler, he played several times for Yorkshire between 1863 and 1870 with little success. From 1876 he served in Ceylon (now Sri Lanka) and did much for cricket there, captaining teams to Madras and to Bombay.

John Hall had the distinction of being the first non-Yorkshireman to play for the new County Club, as well as being born earlier than any other Yorkshire player who played from 1863 onwards. He was born at Nottingham in 1815 and was therefore 47 years old when he turned out at Trent Bridge. He never played for Yorkshire again.

At Bramall Lane, Yorkshire faced Surrey who batted first and scored 201. Yorkshire, thanks to Iddison's 51, came to within 29 runs of Surrey's total and then Hodgson and Slinn bowled out Surrey for 144. Yorkshire, needing 174 to win, lost four wickets for 9 before Iddison (53) and Rowbotham (65) combined in a big stand and Yorkshire went on to win by three wickets.

Thomas Brownhill, a right-handed batsman and a fine cover-point and outfielder, appeared in this match for Yorkshire and went on to play for Yorkshire until 1871, later becoming a first-class umpire.

Yorkshire had made a good if modest start as a county, with two wins and one defeat in a four-match programme. They were to extend their fixture list to seven matches in 1864. They won two and lost four, drawing the seventh.

The draw came in the first match against Surrey, for whom Jupp made 110, Thomas Darnton appeared in this match, becoming the second non-Yorkshireman to play for the County, as did Luke Greenwood, a right-hand hard-hitting batsman and very fine straight round-arm bowler, who played for Yorkshire from 1861 to 1874. His benefit match *v* Gloucestershire that year realised £300. An honest, hardworking, strong level-headed cricketer, it was reckoned that he took over 300 wickets in 1867. He became a first-class umpire after leaving Yorkshire and he stood in the famous Oval Test in 1882 (the 'Ashes' Test). He fell upon bad times in the 1890s and was given a pension of 10/- (50p) per week by the Yorkshire CCC.

Yorkshire came on top in their next match at Trent Bridge against Nottinghamshire, leading by one run on the first innings, and eventually winning by 99. Slinn took six for 19 and six for 34. A fine innings of 99 not out by George Anderson changed the game in Yorkshire's favour.

Brownhill replaced B. W. Waud for the next match at Parker's Piece, Cambridge for the first meeting of Cambridgeshire and Yorkshire; the game being played for the benefit of the home players, Hayward, Carpenter and Tarrant. Cambridgeshire won with only three wickets to spare.

Yorkshire also lost the return match at Bramall Lane by 55 runs. Requiring 199 to win, at no time did Yorkshire look like scoring them.

Charles Henry Prest, a member of a well-known brotherhood, was a right-handed batsman who was an outstanding fielder as well as being a sprinter of note. He only played twice for Yorkshire in 1864 but also played for the Yorkshire Gentlemen and had appeared for the Gentlemen of the North *v* Gentlemen of the South in 1861. A solicitor by profession in London, he achieved fame as an actor in the capital and was a great favourite under the name of 'Mr Peveril', later turning professional on the stage. He died in 1875 aged only 33.

After Surrey had gained a hard-fought victory by 62 runs at The Oval, Yorkshire suffered yet another defeat; this time at Bradford by Nottinghamshire, who won by seven wickets. Iddison took five for 84 in the first innings, Stephenson stumping four batsmen off him, but in Yorkshire's second innings Anderson had to retire hurt while Atkinson could not bat at all as he had been badly injured by a Richard Daft drive that rendered him unconscious. Nottinghamshire were set the easy task of scoring 33 to win.

Yorkshire's final match of the season took place at Middlesbrough against Kent. It was probably aranged by Mr Vaughan, a patron of cricket in the north-east, in conjunction with the Yorkshire players and the game may have no direct links with Yorkshire CCC. This was the case in many such matches in the 1860s, especially games that were not played in Sheffield. How representative the Yorkshire side was in some of these games it is impossible to conjecture. Luke Greenwood was probably ill, but Hodgson and Slinn's absence must have weakened the Yorkshire side and neither appeared to have been playing anywhere else at the time. It was 19 September before the game began. Yorkshire passed Kent's first innings total by 17 runs, and eventually needed only 94 to win, which they obtained for the loss of six wickets.

Yorkshire opened the 1865 season with a match at Bradford against Cambridgeshire which was arranged by the Committee of the Bradford Club. On paper the side appeared to be at full strength with only Slinn, who was never to play for Yorkshire again, missing from the list of possibles. Cambridgeshire batted first and scored 199, Atkinson taking four for 78. Yorkshire were all out for 114. Following on Ned Stephenson opened the innings and scored 52 and with Iddison and Anderson reaching 20 Yorkshire finally totalled 174, to set the opposition 90 to win. Cambridgeshire just got home by three wickets, Atkinson taking three for 28 in 40 overs and being presented with an inscribed ball for his performance.

Five of Yorkshire's leading players refused to play against Surrey at Bramall Lane; Anderson, Atkinson, Iddison, Rowbotham and Stephenson. They were alleged to be in dispute with players from the south, and Surrey in particular, as the latter club were supposed to have given instructions for Willsher to be no-balled when playing for the All-England Eleven, of which side Anderson was also a member. That was back in 1862, and they had not played against Surrey since then. One member of the Sheffield Committee stated that none of the five should ever play at Bramall Lane again. A benefit match for the five members concerned was arranged to take place in September in Sheffield in opposition to that view. The real truth about this matter is unlikely to ever come out, the minutes of the Yorkshire CCC saying nothing. George Anderson was a little different from the run of the mill professional of his period, working in the Savings Bank at Bedale for many years. He was one of Yorkshire's earliest rebels. (It should be pointed out that four of the five strikers all appeared in an AEE match at Mirfield on the same day).

Yorkshire won the toss and scored 188 with Luke Greenwood top scorer with 83, but Surrey reached a formidable 327 and went on to win by ten wickets.

A. J. A Wilkinson – father of the Surrey captain of 1914–20 – was born at Mount Oswald in County Durham in 1835 and thus became the third non-Yorkshireman to play for Yorkshire. He opened Yorkshire's innings in the match with Surrey with Thomas Darnton, this being the first pair to open for Yorkshire neither of whom had been born in the county – it was also the first time that a Yorkshire team had contained two 'foreigners'. A good steady batsman and useful slow bowler, he played in a few matches for Yorkshire in 1865–68 and also appeared for Middlesex between 1864 and 1874. He also played for Durham and Lincolnshire and chaired the meeting in 1874 when the Durham CCC was founded.

Yorkshire came back to full strength against Nottinghamshire at Bradford where Richard Daft's batting looked a class above anything else seen in the match. He scored 66 as Notinghamshire reached 233 and this was far too many for Yorkshire, who could not avoid the follow-on, losing by an innings and 30 runs.

At Bramall Lane, Yorkshire met the All England Eleven but the match aroused very little interest as the five 'strikers' were not allowed to play by the Sheffield Committee. The All England Eleven scored 524, with Hayward and Carpenter each scoring centuries. Yorkshire were dismissed for 125 and 144, with Thomas Darnton making 81 not out in the second innings as George Wootton took all ten wickets.

Gideon Holgate, who played against the All England Eleven, was an excellent wicket-keeper and capable batsman who assisted Yorkshire in 1865–67 and also Lancashire in 1886–67. He was a participant in the strikes that afflicted cricket in the 1860s, and for one season he kept wicket for the United England Eleven before his retirement in 1868.

At Trent Bridge, Iddison and his four recalcitrant comrades returned to the side. It is by no means clear from the committee minutes why they returned, because for the return game at The Oval, the Committee had already replaced them. If the Committee were insisting on punishing the five by not playing them against Surrey, why choose them for the Nottinghamshire game? It is possible that the players chose that side. On 6 April 1865, according to the minutes, an invitation was made to Anderson to captain the Yorkshire side. In fact

Iddison continued to lead the Yorkshire team and there was no further mention of Anderson in the minutes.

After Nottinghamshire put on 71 for the first wicket, Luke Greenwood proved unplayable, taking seven for 43 as Nottinghamshire were dismissed for 117. Iddison then played a captain's innings of 53 and Yorkshire gained a lead of 74 runs on the first innings. George Parr with 58 and Jackson 55 then took Nottinghamshire to 182, leaving the visitors with 109 runs to win. Shaw proved irresistable and had the remarkable analysis of 37.3-22-32-6, and Yorkshire were well beaten by 55 runs.

Defeat at The Oval by five wickets was no disgrace as Luke Greenwood had to be replaced as he was taken ill, Bocking, the umpire, coming into his place. Bocking umpired on the first day, the second was blank, and he played in the third. A drawn match followed against Kent at Gravesend, where Yorkshire gained a lead of 66 runs on the first innings with 283, and then Kent were dismissed again for 194. But there was no further play as showers had interrupted the game from time to time.

John Smith of Yeadon played in just these two games for Yorkshire. He was a good batsman and left-arm medium-pace bowler who had many professional engagements in Scotland, Lancashire and Yorkshire before moving to Marlborough in 1874 as groundsman and coach. In 1883 he moved to Worcestershire as professional. He also appeared for Lancashire in 1865–69.

The return match with Kent took place at Bramall Lane and the weakened Yorkshire side suffered defeat by an innings and 70. Edgar Willsher was Kent's hero with the bat scoring 37 out of his side's 159, and then Yorkshire were dismissed for 59 and 30. Willsher followed up his good batting by taking six for 19 and six for 9, bowling 38 overs in all. He and George Bennett bowled unchanged and Yorkshire's ignominious defeat occurred after they had put Kent into bat.

Yorkshire's next match was at Ashton-under-Lyne against Cambridgeshire; the venue being switched from Old Trafford as the game between Cambridgeshire and Nottinghamshire at that ground had not been a financial success. The game was drawn with Yorkshire still needing 96 for victory with the last two batsmen at the crease.

This was George Freeman's first match for Yorkshire. He had a short, mercurial career for the County and it was largely due to him that Yorkshire were declared the 'Champion County' in 1867 and 1870. A genuinely fast bowler (Yorkshire have had very few during their distinguished existence) he took 209 wickets for Yorkshire in a regular career from 1867 to 1870 although he did play in odd matches in 1865 and 1866 and from 1871 to 1880, when his business as an auctioneer allowed. He was born in Boroughbridge in 1843 and his

George Freeman, a round-arm bowler, was regarded for about five seasons as the greatest fast bowler of his time.

first match of note was in 1857 for 10 Boys of Boroughbridge against 10 Boys of Sessay. He moved to Leeds in 1860, and then in 1863 to Edinburgh, as cricket tutor and clerk to Mr Dalgleish at Grange House School. In 1865 he returned to Malton and was professional to the Malton CC where he began to make a name as fast bowler. He was soon engaged by George Parr for the AEE. A powerfully built, handsome man, he played regularly in big matches until 1871 when he practically retired, having become a successful auctioneer in Thirsk in 1869. Considered by W. G. Grace the best fast bowler that he ever faced, Freeman toured America in 1868–69 with considerable success under the leadership of Edgar Willsher. In 1869 he was joint secretary of the United North of England Eleven with R. Iddison, and he appeared once for Players *v* Gentlemen in 1870. In 1867 he took seven for 10 *v* Lancashire and in 1868 eight for 11 against the same opponents.

It must have been a relief to all – players and committee – to get the 1865 season out of the way. Yorkshire had drawn two of their nine matches and lost all the others. There was a serious effort made to solve the problems of the five 'absentees' at a meeting on 21 December 1865, to which the players all wrote letters explaining why they would not play against Surrey. The correspondence to and from the players filled 12½ pages in the minutes book, after which a special meeting of members was held in which it was agreed that the argument between the Surrey players and the Yorkshire players would be decided by arbitration by the Marylebone Cricket Club.

A strange decision was made by the general committee at their next meeting on 28 February 1866, as follows:

> That it be left to the discretion of the Committee to determine whether any and what Matches shall be played during the ensuing season but that it be a distinct instruction to the Committee that Anderson, Atkinson, Rowbotham and Stephenson be excluded from any Match which the Committee may make.

The next meeting of the Committee did not take place until 7 March 1867, so we can assume that the three matches arranged to be played and accepted as Yorkshire matches in 1866 had nothing to do with the county committee.

Cambridgeshire were Yorkshire's first visitors to Bradford to the Great Horton Road ground and winning the toss batted almost the whole of the first day to score 224. Thomas Hayward with 78 and Robert Carpenter (97 not out) put on 156 for the fourth wicket, with Hodgson taking six for 63 and Atkinson four for 68. Yorkshire were caught on a wet wicket but they batted very poorly in both innings and lost the match by an innings and 67 runs. Apart from John Thewlis who was injured, Yorkshire were at full strength.

The next game against Nottinghamshire was also at Bradford but rain washed out play on the first two days and in order to give the spectators some cricket play on the third went on until 8.20, Nottinghamshire scoring 103 for six. The return match with Nottinghamshire at Trent Bridge saw Yorkshire go down heavily by nine wickets, but Tom Emmett in his first match took five for 33.

Thomas Emmett, an attacking left-handed batsman and left-arm fast bowler who had a tendency to be erratic, was a regular member of the Yorkshire team until 1887, by when he had missed only 14 of his

Tom Emmett, the doyen of Yorkshire cricket characters. (Marylebone CC)

County's matches. He also played in two games in 1888. He had a remarkable career. He was the first Yorkshire bowler to take 1,000 wickets for the County, and he obtained them at a cheaper rate than any other bowler – 1,216 at 12.71. He also scored over 6,000 runs. Tom Emmett was born at Halifax and lived at Illingworth where he played with the local club. He was spotted by Halifax who paid him 2s 6d (12½p) per match. He was purely a fast bowler at first but later developed a slower 'break-back' which he called his 'sosteneuter' which caused him to have many victims caught on the off-side. Beloved by the Yorkshire crowds, he took a lot of his wickets with sheer guile. The stories about Tom Emmett, perhaps cricket's greatest character, are legion. Captain of Yorkshire from 1878 until 1882, he

18

was probably too easygoing to make a success of such a task. He three times toured Australia, taking 137 wickets on the 1878–79 tour. From 1889 he was coach at Rugby for a time, where he helped to bring out P. F. Warner. He also acted as groundsman, and was later coach at Leicestershire where he lived with his son Arthur, who appeared for Leicestershire in 1902. He died at Leicester in 1904 after a fit of apoplexy at the age of 62.

Early in April 1867 the committee of the Yorkshire CCC were obviously in charge of team selection again as the minutes state that 'J. Rowbotham, R. Iddison, L. Greenwood, G. Freeman, G. Holgate should be engaged for the matches against Surrey'. There was no mention of Stephenson, Anderson and Atkinson, although Stephenson did subsequently write a note to the Club expressing his 'regret for his conduct' and he was reinstated for the return match with Surrey.

The match at The Oval proved to be an easy victory for the visitors who won by an innings and 111 runs. A. J. A. Wilkinson with 53 was top scorer for Yorkshire who recovered from 112 for seven (Holgate 38) to a score of 265 all out with Emmett scoring 38 and Freeman 22. Only Thomas Humphrey (28) made any progress against Yorkshire's new attack in which Freeman (three for 39 and five for 34) bowled unchanged with Luke Greenwood (six for 43 and five for 28).

George Pinder made his first appearance for Yorkshire in the above match and he went on to become Yorkshire's regular wicket-keeper from 1870 to 1880. He was considered to be the best wicket-keeper ever to have been produced by Yorkshire. Born at Ecclesfield in 1841, he was brought up in the same street as Ned Stephenson, whom he copied in style. He was a bowler in early days and kept wicket for the first time in an emergency when aged 18. In 1863 he assisted 22 of Sheffield Shrewsbury against the AEE and when he got into the County side only Pilling was his rival as a wicket-keeper. Pinder claimed to have been the first wicket-keeper to have stood up to fast bowling, which he did when representing the North against the South at Lord's when keeping to Morley and Emmett. Pinder received a benefit match in 1880 with the game against Lascelles Hall, which brought in £300, but he was dropped by the County after that season and he fell on hard times. He died at his daughter's house at Hickleton in 1903 aged 61 having been in poor health for some time. His real name was George Pinder Hattersley. He was also a useful right-hand batsman and his lobs were occasionally successful in first-class cricket.

On 20 June Yorkshire met Lancashire at Whalley and defeated them by an innings and 56 runs. Anderson, Atkinson, and Stephenson were included in the Yorkshire side which had certainly nothing to do with the Yorkshire CCC committee. Ned Stephenson made the top score for Yorkshire with 54 from 188. Lancashire, who included Holgate in their ranks, were dismissed for 57 and 75 with Freeman (seven for 10 and five for 41) and Greenwood (three for 44 and four for 32) proving far too good for them.

The return match with Surrey saw Yorkshire's miscreants replaced once again as the wishes of the committee ruled at Bramall Lane. It made little difference on the field of play, as once again Yorkshire triumphed by 184 runs. Joseph Rowbotham was Yorkshire's leading run-maker with 27 out of his side's first-innings 114, with F. Roberts taking seven for 72 for Surrey in 42.3 overs. A fast round-arm bowler, he played in four matches for Surrey but never took a wicket for them in any other game but this one. In reply Surrey scored only 96 with George Freeman taking seven for 29 in 33.3 overs, while Emmett took two for 15. In their second innings Yorkshire batted much better to total 242, with skipper Roger Iddison scoring 60 and Tom Emmett 41. At 70 for one Surrey appeared to be in with a chance but Emmett came on and had the remarkable analysis of 12-8-7-6, while Freeman took three for 29 in an overwhelming victory.

A visit to Old Trafford – Yorkshire's second away match of the season with the old enemy – seemed to be regarded as of little importance by the players or public. It was of no concern to the County committee, whose interest in Yorkshire cricket seemed to be confined purely to the matches that had been arranged for Sheffield and to any corresponding away match. One can suppose that the person who would take the most interest in the Yorkshire fixtures that were played away from Sheffield would be the captain, Roger Iddison, himself. There was no mention of his captaincy in the Yorkshire minutes and yet he continued to lead the side in all matches apart from the five that he missed in 1865; in fact he did not miss another Yorkshire match until 1869.

For the Old Trafford game he had to make six changes from the previous Surrey match, bringing in two new players in E. B. Rawlinson and G. G. Lynas. Yorkshire batted first and were all out for 149 with John Thewlis (44) and Gideon Holgate (35) opening with a good partnership and later the skipper added a valuable 34. Lancashire did very well to gain a lead of ten runs. Cuttell was Yorkshire's best bowler with four for 38. Yorkshire did even better to score 273 in their second innings, thanks mainly to William Smith (60) and Tom Emmett (61), but Iddison again batted well with 38 as did Holgate and Darnton. Needing 264 to win, Lancashire were dismissed for 98, with Both Emmett and Cuttell taking five for 46.

Yorkshire met Cambridgeshire at Wisbech with Anderson back in the side and once again Freeman (five for 36) and Greenwood (five for 46) bowled out the home side for 86. But Tarrant (six for 27) was in even better form as Yorkshire were bowled out for 70, with

Rowbotham top scorer with 34. Tarrant (29) also batted well as Cambridge failed once again to be dismissed for 74, with Emmett taking six for 43 and Freeman three for 24. Then came a rare battle for Yorkshire to score 91 to win. Again it was a tussle between Rowbotham and Tarrant. The latter finished with seven for 33 in 51.3 overs (36 maidens) but the Sheffield player was there until the end with 34 not out as Yorkshire triumphed by one wicket. After the match there was 'a dispute about a decision of the Yorkshire umpire'.

The return match with Cambridgeshire was played at Savile Town, Dewsbury. It is thought that this match had been arranged between the Cambridge players and the Yorkshire players as it seems that the Cambridge players had refused to come to a match arranged by the Yorkshire committee at Bramall Lane. (That match was supposed to take place in July but no dates are mentioned in the Yorkshire CCC minutes). Yorkshire again triumphed in a close match by four wickets with Luke Greenwood having the remarkable analysis in the first innings of 47-25-35-8. Even so, Yorkshire trailed by five. Cambridgeshire scored 105 as Emmett took six for 26 in 40 overs, and Yorkshire required 111 to win. George Freeman came good with the bat as he scored 32 not out, and receiving help from Ned Stephenson (28) he saw Yorkshire win through by four wickets.

Yorkshire met Lancashire for a third time at Middlesbrough and recorded their third win over their main rivals. Freeman (four for 48) and Emmett (six for 41) bowled out the opposition for 97 and in reply William Smith of Middlesbrough scored 90 of his side's 205 after Darnton and Stephenson had opened with a stand of 55. In their second innings Lancashire were dismissed for 68 with Freeman taking five for 25 and Emmett four for 25. Yorkshire had now gone through the season undefeated and were declared to be 'Champion County' in the sporting press. It was a remarkable up-turn in fortunes after two depressing seasons without a win.

Yorkshire's first match in 1868 was at Bramall Lane against Surrey in a match arranged by the Yorkshire committee. Surrey won the toss and scored 222 with Henry Jupp carrying his bat through the innings for a splendid innings of 90 not out. Yorkshire then gave a very poor display of batting to be dismissed for 71 and 145 to lose by an innings and six runs, James Southerton taking six for 39 and five for 86.

When in this match Harry Verelst became the fifth non-native to play for Yorkshire, it is interesting to note that four of the five had been chosen by the Yorkshire committee and not by the other ground authorities or by the captain or by anybody else who might have been responsible for picking the teams outside the Sheffield-based committee.

Yorkshire's visit to Trent Bridge saw them compile 213 on the first day with George Freeman, surprisingly, opening the innings and making top score of 53. Freeman was then quite unplayable with the ball as he took five for 25 in the home side's total of 60, and though he failed to take a wicket when Nottinghamshire followed on. Iddison completed match figures of six for 43 and Emmett nine for 61 as Nottinghamshire went down by nine wickets.

Alfred Farrar Smith played in this match and one other in 1868 and made one further apperance in 1871 before playing regularly for the county in 1873 and 1874, in which years he was one of the most dependable batsmen in the Yorkshire team. He retired from cricket after the 1874 season due to domestic and business reasons.

At Holbeck, Lancashire, with a very weak side, were thrashed by Yorkshire by an innings and 186 runs. Lancashire were dismissed for 30 by Freeman, who took eight for 11 and in reply Yorkshire made 250 with G. Savile scoring 65 and R. Iddison 57. In their second innings, Lancashire managed to obtain 34; this time George Freeman took four for 12 and Tom Emmett six for 13. John West made his debut in this match. He was a left-handed medium-fast bowler and useful left-handed batsman who played for Yorkshire with some success from 1868 to 1876 and served on the groundstaff at Lord's for 20 years. He was born at Little Sheffield in 1845 and died there at his home in 1890 aged 44. His benefit in 1889 at Lord's between North and South was a washout and he died before the match could be replayed in the following season.

The next match at Bramall Lane was against Middlesex who won the toss and were dismissed for 79. Only I. D. Walker and his brother V.E., the skipper, made much impression against the remarkable pace attack of Freeman (seven for 29) and Emmett (three for 12) and Yorkshire were 62 in front by the end of the first day. They were all out for 162, and in their second innings Middlesex collapsed again for 59. Freeman took five for 32 and Emmett three for 16 as Yorkshire won by an innings and 24 runs. In this match Freeman performed the hat-trick for the second time in five days.

At Dewsbury, Nottinghamshire gained a handsome victory by 108 runs. Winning the toss, they made 162, Freeman taking six for 64 and Emmett four for 63. But only Iddison and Stephenson batted well for Yorkshire and Nottinghamshire had a lead of 77. In the second innings Emmett had the outstanding analysis of 40.1-26-34-9 as Nottinghamshire were bowled out for 107 but Yorkshire were well beaten when dismissed for 76.

An accident prevented Luke Greenwood turning out at Islington against Middlesex while George Freeman sprained his ankle after bowling 11 overs for three runs. This was after Yorkshire had been bowled out for 60. But Emmett replied by taking seven for 43 as

Middlesex were restricted to a 26-run lead. When Yorkshire batted again, Rowbotham made 42 and Atkinson 27 as they hoisted 138 on the board, leaving the home side with 113 to win. Middlesex were soon in trouble at 38 for five but went on to win a hard-fought match by three wickets.

Yorkshire's visit to The Oval provided a remarkable victory for the Yorkshire team. Surrey, winning the toss, collapsed against Tom Emmett (five for 65) and John West (three for 45) for 195 all out after being 177 for three. At the close of play, Yorkshire were 109 for no wicket. The opening pair were John Thewlis and his nephew Ephraim Lockwood, who cut a comical figure to The Oval crowd, but soon convinced them that he was no simple country lad by the style and authority of his batsmanship. The following day the pair took their opening partnership to 176 before Lockwood was out for 91; his uncle continued to 108. Iddison (38) and Atkinson (44) continued to defy the Surrey attack, and Yorkshire batted the rest of the day before being dismissed for 389 on the last morning. When Surrey batted again they were rattled out for 52, with Atkinson taking six for 19 overs and Emmett four for 28.

Ephraim Lockwood, a right-hand batsman and round-arm medium-pace bowler, was born at Lascelles Hall in 1845 and made his first appearance for Yorkshire in this match. A very fine batsman, strong in defence and with one of the handsomest cuts in cricket, he

An early photograph of Ephraim Lockwood, a sound batsman who later captained Yorkshire.

was without doubt one of the finest batsmen to have been produced by the County. He scored over 12,500 runs in first-class cricket at an average of 23, including eight centuries, and toured North America in 1879. He twice turned down tours to Australia. Lockwood's first engagement was with Kirkburton in 1864 and he was with Cheetham Hill when called up by Yorkshire. He captained Yorkshire in 1876 and 1877 but was not cut out for the job as he tried to please too many of his colleagues. His benefit in 1882 realised £591. A quiet, reticent type with an unassuming disposition, his nickname was 'Mary-Anne'.

Yorkshire's first match in 1869 was at Trent Bridge. Iddison was injured so he took over the umpiring position. Pinder was also unavailable. Nottinghamshire were bowled out for 111 with Emmett taking five for 59 and Freeman three for 34. Yorkshire batted both badly and slowly to be out for 43, and Nottinghamshire took their second innings to 204 to be in a strong position at the end of the second day. Needing 273 to win, Rawlinson offered stout resistance, scoring 55, but Nottinghamshire won comfortably by 101 runs.

Andrew Greenwood, who made his debut in the match, was a nephew of Luke's and son of Job Greenwood. He was a capable right-hand batsman who played regularly for Yorkshire until 1878 and one further match in 1880. He twice toured Australia, in 1873–4 and in 1876–7, and appeared in two Test matches, yet his overall batting average was only 18. He was a fine outfielder.

Yorkshire's next match was at Bramall Lane against Surrey; the match being played in gloomy conditions with the bowlers very much on top. Yorkshire put Surrey in to bat and in 70 overs bowled them out for 52. Pooley was top scorer with 17 and both he and Stephenson were run out, with Freeman taking all the other eight wickets for 29 runs. Yorkshire headed that total by 30 after being 36 for seven at one time before Freeman (31) and Iddison (15) added 32 valuable runs. Going in again Surrey fared only a little better with J. Street making the top score of 18. Freeman (five for 31) again bowled unchanged with Emmett who in this innings had better fortune to take five for 33. Yorkshire obtained the 40 required to win the match by six wickets.

At Woodhouse Hill, Hunslet, Yorkshire met Cambridgeshire in a game got up by the Cambridgeshire skipper Robert Carpenter after his county club had been dissolved in the previous March. Yorkshire made the very presentable score of 352 after being 294 for nine at the end of the first day with Roger Iddison 94 not out. Iddison batted for $5\frac{1}{2}$ hours for his fine 112 which included 15 threes and he was presented with £5. Tom Emmett (47 not out) partnered him in a last wicket stand of 72. Owing to an attack of pleurisy, George Tarrant was unable to play for the visitors and his bowling was sadly missed.

Freeman (three for 16 and one for 15) and Emmett (seven for 15 and nine for 23) again bowled unchanged and the latter held three catches as well as the opposition were bowled out for 40 and 46.

Yorkshire finished the first day only 16 runs behind on the first innings with nine wickets in hand against Surrey at The Oval. Surrey scored 187 with Henry Jupp dominating the innings with a fine 96 before being run out. Joseph Rowbotham (101) then opened with a remarkable 166 stand with Ephraim Lockwood, who went on to score 103 on the next morning adding 79 with George Freeman, who scored 53. Yorkshire went on to score 284 before dismissing Surrey for 176 and obtained 81 for three to win one watch by seven wickets with Lockwood again prominent with 34 not out.

Yorkshire's last match of the season took place at Bramall Lane against Nottinghamshire who won the toss and spent most of the first day compiling 213 in 156.3 overs. Richard Daft (50) and F. Wild (47) held the Nottinghamshire batting together while Emmett took five for 76 and Freeman three for 59 in 48 overs. Overnight 13 for one, Yorkshire went on to score 205, being indebted to Joseph Rowbotham who batted three hours for his 100. Nottinghamshire were 44 for six at the close of play on the second day, Emmett sending a bail 47 yards when he bowled Bignall. Only Daft with 31 not out was able to withstand the onslaught of Tom Emmett who took seven for 35 in 38 overs while his partner Freeman took three for 40. Requiring 88 to win Yorkshire got home by five wickets. According to *Lillywhite's Companion*, Yorkshire could claim an equal right (with Nottinghamshire) to the title of Champion County.

At the end of the season both Stephenson and Iddison applied to have a benefit during the 1870 season and as Stephenson was retiring he was given preference and became the first beneficiary of the Yorkshire County Cricket Club. Iddison's followed in 1872. There was one other item in the minutes of the meeting of 3 February 1870 – the first during that particular year – and it read as follows: 'That the sum of £1,000 per year be paid to Mr J. B. Wostinholm as secretary.'

Yorkshire's first match in 1870 was a visit to Lord's where the MCC were beaten in an exciting finish by one wicket. It was the first time that the sides had met but as there is no mention of the game in the club minutes one must assume the match was arranged by some other agency. Freeman (six for 26) and Emmett (four for 38) were unplayable as the MCC were dismissed for 73, but Yorkshire did little better, gaining a lead of 18 only because George Pinder scored 31. At the end of the first day, W. G. Grace had completed his 50 out of 127 for five and finally scored 66, with C. E. Green contributing 51. Emmett this time took five for 65 and Freeman four for 38, leaving

Yorkshire with 144 to win. At 94 for eight, Yorkshire's chances seemed remote but Luke Greenwood batted very well to score 44 before being run out with the sides level, and Tom Emmett obtained the winning run.

Nottinghamshire were below strength at Trent Bridge where another exciting match went Yorkshire's way by the narrow margin of two runs. Nottinghamshire were without Biddulph and Wootton who the MCC refused to release, but Yorkshire were dismissed for 108. Pinder batted well with 47 but Nottinghamshire made a hash of their innings with three run outs not helping in a score of 56 all out. Yorkshire were on the road to victory, and in their second innings, Lockwood with 44 helped the side to a lead of 174. Rain then altered the state of the pitch with very little play on the second day. needing 175 to win, Nottinghamshire began well with 65 for the first wicket but fell just short as Iddison took four for 55 and Lockwood two for 5.

Yorkshire were without Iddison, Luke Greenwood and George Freeman (owing to a bad arm) and so introduced three new players into the team for the visit of Surrey to Bramall Lane. Surrey won the toss and apart from Pooley (25) failed completely against West, who had the impressive analysis of 11.3-8-3-5. Clayton took four for 36. Yorkshire were well into the lead by the end of the first day and led on the first innings by 79. Surrey's second innings was similar to the first with West and Clayton taking four wickets each and Yorkshire knocked off the 26 needed for victory for the loss of three wickets.

Robert Clayton, who did so well in his first match at the age of 26, was a right-handed batsman and right-arm medium-fast bowler. He was considered one of the best fast bowlers in the country but never quite realised his early promise. He continued to play regularly for Yorkshire until 1877 and played in one further match in 1879 but his total of 154 wickets for Yorkshire was very disappointing in view of his good start. In 1871 he was considered good enough to assist the North against the South and in 1892 the Married v Single Match was played for his benefit. He also umpired for several seasons. In 1872 he joined the MCC groundstaff at Lord's and at the time of his death he had been there longer than anyone else apart from Frank Farrands.

Kent scored 168 at the Bat and Ball ground at Gravesend with Emmett taking five for 82, and at the close of play Yorkshire were 112 for three. On the following day, Rawlinson went on to make 52 while skipper Iddison batted through to be 48 not out when the Yorkshire side were all out for 229. In their second innings Kent were all out for 94, Freeman taking five for 27 and Iddison five for 33. Yorkshire won the match by eight wickets inside two days. The return match took place at Dewsbury and after winning the toss Yorkshire were all out for 122. After Charles Payne was caught and bowled by Freeman for

27, Kent lost wickets quickly and were all out for 98 with Freeman taking five for 28 in 35 overs and Emmett four for 33. In their second innings, Rawlinson made 42 and Iddison 34 as Yorkshire took their score to 139. E. Henty opened Kent's second innings as they set about their task of obtaining 164 to win and he succeeded in carrying his bat through the innings for 32 not out. Alas for Kent, no one else reached double figures as Kent were dismissed for 81. Freeman finished with five for 14 and Emmett three for 44.

The return game with Nottinghamshire at Trent Bridge turned out to be an excellent game of cricket although *Lillywhite's Companion* stated 'the loss of time was most reprehensible'. Nottinghamshire won the toss and were dismissed for 146 on a pitch that was decidedly rough, with Freeman taking six for 55. In reply Yorkshire took a lead of one run. At the end of the second day Nottinghamshire had taken their score to 68 for five and Daft (46) and Wild (33) took their sixth-wicket stand to 72 before Wild was badly run out by his partner with the score on 105. Nottinghamshire finally scored 142 to set Yorkshire 142 to win. Lockwood and Pinder put on 29 for the first wicket but Yorkshire spent 92 overs over their innings of 107 for six and were quite content to bat out time.

Yorkshire's last match was at The Oval and winning the toss they scored 114 with Southerton taking seven for 61 in 53.2 overs and Pooley taking six victims behind the stumps. Pooley also made top score in Surrey's first innings, making 26 as Surrey were dismissed for 60. Freeman took five for 15 in 35 overs and Emmett took four for 41. Roger Iddison was in fine form when Yorkshire batted again dominating the whole innings to score 77 out of his side's 170. When Surrey went in again to attempt to obtain 225 to win, they were hustled out once again for only 87, Freeman and Emmett bowling unchanged to take five for 28 and five for 51 respectively. Iddison won a silver cup for his all-round cricket. Yorkshire finished the season with an unbeaten record to be again considered the 'Champion County'. The records of their two famous bowlers are well worth looking at during these four seasons when Tom Emmett missed only one match and George Freeman three.

Freeman	Wkts	Runs	Avge	Emmett	Wkts	Runs	Avge
1867	51	380	7.45	1867	38	260	6.84
1968	37	360	9.72	1868	56	455	8.12
1869	27	291	10.77	1869	32	294	9.18
1870	50	327	6.54	1870	42	627	14.92

Yorkshire visited Lord's for the first match of the 1871 season. George Freeman had just got married so he was replaced by Allen Hill, who made his first appearance for his County. The MCC, after putting on 42 for the first wicket, were dismissed for 116 with Clayton taking five for 36. Despite Ephraim Lockwood's 35, Yorkshire did even worse and were all out for 100. When they batted again the MCC had W. G. Grace to thank for their improved score, as he made 98 before being run out, the home side reaching 173. Clayton again bowled well with five for 58 but Yorkshire, in their second innings, could score only 134, and the MCC won by 55 runs.

Allen Hill, a right-handed attacking batsman, and a medium-fast bowler with a beautiful action, bowled fast from a surprisingly short run which occasionally took batsmen unawares. He gained a place in the Yorkshire side in 1872 and remained a regular member of the team until 1882 when he retired. In 1884 he made his last appearance at Birmingham when he broke his collar-bone. He was 27 when he made his debut and took around 750 wickets in first-class cricket during a successful career. He had the distinction of taking the first wicket in Test cricket and also taking the first catch in Test cricket. He was a quiet, unassuming man, perhaps prone to injury, and although a hard-working cricketer and bowler and proud of his profession he lacked the staying power of Tom Emmett and was not as dangerous as Freeman.

In poor weather and bad light, Surrey won the toss at Bramall Lane and put Yorkshire in to bat. George Freeman batted well to score 46 but Yorkshire could score only 107 with Southerton having an analysis of 51.2-20-50-5. Surrey, thanks to Thomas Humphrey (60 not out) and his younger brother Richard Humphrey (80) enabled Surrey to score 165, George Freeman taking seven for 74. Yorkshire batted much better in their second innings to total 218, thanks to 89 from Lockwood and 40 from skipper Rowbotham. Surrey finished the match with the score at 0 for no wicket.

At Trent Bridge, Yorkshire won the toss and batted, and when in their turn Nottinghamshire found Freeman quite devastating as he clean bowled six of his seven victims at the cost of 30 runs, the lace county found themselves 39 in arrears. Yorkshire then lost five wickets for only 19 runs before recovering to 101. Needing 141 to win, Nottinghamshire were 37 for one when the third day commenced, but lost six for 88 before Richard Daft (50 not out) steered Nottinghamshire to a fine victory.

A weak Lancashire team were summarily dispatched by 222 runs at Old Trafford. George Freeman's 51 was the only score of note when Yorkshire batted first to score 142. Lancashire were 53 for two at the close of play when honours were even, but there came a swift collapse to 90 all out with Emmett taking five for 34 and Yorkshire put themselves out of reach by the end of the second day. Andrew

Greenwood who had scored 21 not out in the first innings opened this time to score the highest score of the game with 50 while Freeman made a useful 37. George Pinder (35) and Emmett (48) then added 48 for the eighth wicket and Yorkshire totalled 265. Lancashire were dismissed for only 95, and Freeman (four for 27) and Emmett (six for 51) bowled unchanged throughout the match.

There were four changes in the Lancashire side when they appeared for the return game at Bramall Lane, where Yorkshire lacked Freeman. The home side were completely outplayed by their rivals who batted the whole of the first day for 253 for eight. Alfred Appleby, who had the misfortune to be out for 99, and put on 111 for the ninth wicket before Hickton was out for 55, and Lancashire reached 343. Clayton bowled well to take six for 92. Yorkshire recovered from 96 for eight thanks to Roger Iddison (54 not out) but were finally dismissed for 191 and, following on, were soon in trouble again. All out for 171 they provided Lancashire with a most satisfactory ten-wicket win.

Yorkshire's visit to The Oval saw a return to form with Allen Hill in particular doing well as he took six for 33 and six for 24 in the match. Only Richard Humphrey, with 30 and 35, played Hill with any confidence as Surrey were dismissed for 111 and 72, Emmett taking four for 74 and four for 39, bowling unchanged with Hill. Allen Hill also shone with the bat, scoring 28 as Yorkshire totalled only 100, but in the second innings Luke Greenwood (33 not out) and Joseph Rowbotham (48 not out) knocked off the 85 needed without losing a wicket. Silver cups were presented to Greenwood, Rowbotham and Hill for their performances by a London-based Yorkshire follower.

Huge crowds who attended the return match with Nottinghamshire at Bramall Lane saw Yorkshire struggle to 171 all out in the face of good bowling from Jemmy Shaw, who took six for 68, but by the close of play Nottinghamshire themselves were struggling at 31 for three. Yorkshire took an 18 runs lead on the first innings. Emmett took five for 59 and he followed that up with a splendid 64 not out after Yorkshire were reduced to 86 for seven, adding 84 for the eighth wicket with John West (36). In reply to Yorkshire's 199 Nottinghamshire had 30 on the board without loss but then collapsed to 77 all out, with Emmett again in irresistible form with 33.1-24-31-8. He had had a magnificent match.

Yorkshire made their first visit to Prince's on 23 May 1872 to face a strong-looking Middlesex side. Tom Hearne gave the home side a good start by scoring 54 but Emmett with six for 56 proved too good for the other batsmen as Middlesex were dismissed for 152. Hill, Greenwood and Emmett all reached 30 to give Yorkshire a lead of 20 on the first innings. The home side batted rather better in their second innings to obtain 175, George Freeman taking six for 59. Requiring 156 to win, Yorkshire made steady progress towards their target and achieved a two-wicket victory.

Yorkshire remained in London as the next match was at Lord's against the MCC, for whom W. G. Grace scored 101 and 43 not out and had much to do with the home team's easy win by eight wickets. The MCC totalled 215 with Allen Hill taking five for 66 but Yorkshire gave a poor batting performance and were bowled out for 96. Following on, Yorkshire's batting improved considerably with Andrew Greenwood scoring 56, Rowbotham 35 and Iddison 33, but MCC obtained 82 for two in 55 minutes to secure an eight-wicket victory.

Another defeat at Old Trafford was Yorkshire's next fall from grace. Lancashire won the toss and scored 157, with Emmett taking six for 57 but in reply Yorkshire's batting failed completely. More good bowling by Clayton (five for 32) and Emmett (five for 42) set Yorkshire only 144 to win but they were bowled out for 100 and well beaten.

At Bramall Lane, a weak Yorkshire team turned out against Surrey. Emmett was engaged at Middlesbrough, Clayton was ill and Freeman could no longer be expected to play because of business. John Thewlis returned to the side and there were two other newcomers. Surrey won the toss and scored 147 with Richard Humphrey scoring 45 and Pooley 30 with Lockwood having the best bowling figures with three for 32. He was also the star batsman for Yorkshire with 64 not out, adding 60 for the ninth wicket with Allen Hill (36). Yorkshire led by five, and Surrey were then dismissed for 106, with West taking five for 27. Yorkshire needed only 102 to win but after being 69 for three at one stage, with Ephraim Lockwood on 30, Yorkshire collapsed to 83 all out before Southerton.

Nottinghamshire won the toss at Trent Bridge and in a slow day's play of keenly contested cricket were dismissed for 102 in 97 overs. F. Wild scored a patient 42 with Hill taking five for 21 in 30 overs. At the close of play Yorkshire were struggling at 58 for seven. The following day the innings finished at 76. The second Nottinghamshire wicket did not fall until 106 was hoisted on the board in the second innings and they went on to score 161, with West taking five for 43, setting Yorkshire 188 to win. Yorkshire fought hard and opener Tom Emmett made 45 before being run out as he and Iddison (20) took the score to 57 after Yorkshire had lost Rawlinson without scoring. Lockwood was again Yorkshire's best batsman with 50 but Yorkshire collapsed sadly from 128 for four to 137 all out, after batting for 132.2 overs.

Facing Lancashire at Bramall Lane, Yorkshire were by no means at full strength but managed to dismiss the visitors for 89. Emmett taking five for 32. Only Lockwood and Andrew Greenwood made double figures for Yorkshire and the side was all out for 55. On the second day Lockwood again surprised his admirers by taking five for 29 (nine for 69 in the match) as Lancashire struggled to 76. Yorkshire needed 111 to win, but were always struggling and were finally out for 68. McIntyre took six for 19 to complete marvellous match figures of 37-18-31-11.

At Prince's, Yorkshire met Nottinghamshire in a match that was supposed to be a combination of the two sides against an England eleven but the gathering of the latter did not materialise so this game was substituted. It proved an exciting game with Nottinghamshire winning the toss and scoring 160. Emmett took five for 72 and Lockwood four for 56. In reply Yorkshire were 79 for six at the end of the first day and lost their seventh wicket at 80 before Iddison (69 not out) was joined by Pinder (41). A stand of 82 was forthcoming and with John West scoring 18, Yorkshire had a lead of 49 on the first innings. Useful scores took Nottinghamshire to 173 in the second knock, leaving Yorkshire 125 to win. With six down for 35, Yorkshire looked well beaten but Pinder (23) and Kaye (20) rallied Yorkshire to 79 for seven and with John West making 14 not out Yorkshire narrowed the gap to six runs before losing their last wicket.

Large attendances came to Bramall Lane for the visit of Gloucestershire for Roger Iddison's benefit match. The popular Yorkshire all-rounder had been a member of the County side since 1855 and there was nobody more popular with the public. The match was dominated from beginning to end by the presence of W. G. Grace. Opening the innings with T. G. Matthews (85) he helped put on 238 for Gloucestershire's first wicket and went on to make 150 in 3½ hours. Freeman took five for 97. When Yorkshire batted, W. G. Grace took eight for 33 as Yorkshire were dismissed for 66, and following on they scored 116 with E. B. Rawlinson making 47 and R. Iddison 34, with W. G. Grace this time taking seven for 46.

At The Oval, Surrey made 194 against Yorkshire with Richard Humphrey making top score of 70, but Lockwood put Yorkshire in a strong position with a fine 121 in three hours, H. Kaye (33) helping him to put on 80 for the second wicket. Emmett scored 39, J. West 31 and Pinder 42 not out as Yorkshire scored 345. In the second innings, H. Jupp (64) and R. Humphrey (70) led off with 110 for the first wicket but the rest of the side could take Surrey only to 172, and Yorkshire won easily enough by ten wickets.

Yorkshire's final match of the season was at Bramall Lane against Nottinghamshire, who were without Alfred Shaw (ill with bronchitis). Yorkshire won the toss and scored 160 with Lockwood the top scorer with 67 not out. He batted very steadily against an accurate attack. Nottinghamshire finished 13 in arrears on the first innings, Hill taking five for 56. George Pinder opened in the second knock and went on to score 55, but Yorkshire were dismissed for 156. Somewhat surprisingly Richard Daft was the best Nottinghamshire bowler taking six for 59 with his lobs. Nottinghamshire, after losing four wickets for 34 could do no more than play for a draw and finished at 81 for seven with Daft 21 not out.

Thomas Armitage played in this match. A useful right-hand bat and round-arm bowler who also bowled lobs, he was a portly figure, who continued to play for Yorkshire until 1878 but was a regular for only his last three seasons. In 1876–77 he toured Australia as a lob bowler without having much success. In all he took 119 wickets for Yorkshire at 14.08 each and also notched over a thousand runs for them. His best performance was to take 13 for 46 for Yorkshire *v* Surrey in 1876. He went to live in the USA in 1894, coaching and becoming groundsman at Pullman CC in 1902. On going to the States, he had become an inmate of Kinwakee Asylum, for a while acting as a waiter, being normal in most things until his recovery in 1897.

Yorkshire had finished the 1872 season with two wins, seven losses and one draw; the season saw the end of Roger Iddison's captaincy after ten years. He had been captain since the Club was formed, although the Club records give the impression that Rowbotham was captain in 1871 and 1872. Iddison's last successful season was 1870, so it was quite probable that a change was due with him now being 39 years old. He had missed only seven matches during his term of captaincy and five of those were during the 'strike' season of 1865. What influence he had on Yorkshire cricket is hard to estimate. He was a successful captain and in his various capacities as secretary of this and that organisation he must have been a man of influence and of some substance. He may have had a quick temper and been a little too forthright at times. It is doubtful whether he could ever gain the full approval of the Yorkshire committee, to whom he appeared not to exist, let alone to have any sphere of influence whatsoever. If ever a biography of a cricketer was needed it is his, and historians should consider Iddison before any other 19th century player. His leadership and influence on that 1860s side must have been immense. There was a world of difference between the Sheffield contingent that purported to run Yorkshire cricket and the man from Bedale, both in terms of ability and the difference between the gentleman and the professional cricketer.

THE OLD PROS IN CHARGE

IN THE MINUTES OF 20 FEBRUARY 1873, the following entries were noted:

It was resolved – that it is desirable that the Captaincy of the County Eleven be changed for the ensuing season.

That J. Rowbotham be Captain for the ensuing season.

Yorkshire started the new season with a match at Prince's, scoring 163, the top scorer being Louis Hall with 37 on his debut. Middlesex took a lead of 52 runs. Emmett took four for 42, and then scored 30 not out from Yorkshire's poor second innings performance of 118. Middlesex knocked off their modest target of 67 without loss.

Louis Hall joined Yorkshire from the Batley CC and made nine appearances in 1873 but at the end of the season he was dropped until 1878 as his performances had been very poor, and this innings of 37 against Middlesex was his best effort. He was recalled to the Yorkshire side after scoring 79 for XVIII of Hunslet against the Australians and went from strength to strength after that. A noted stonewaller, he carried his bat through an innings on 14 occasions for Yorkshire and with Ulyett formed an opening partnership that was almost as famous as Hornby and Barlow. Hall was a sober-minded teetotaller who often captained Yorkshire when Lord Hawke was absent from the side and he continued to play for Yorkshire until his retirement in 1892 (but returned for one match in 1894). Hall, a life-long Methodist, was in contrast to most of his colleagues in the Yorkshire team. He continued to play for Batley long after his first-class career was over and was also the honorary secretary of Batley RU Club from the early 1880s.

At Lord's, Yorkshire lost to the MCC by an innings and 12 runs with A. F. Smith (32 not out) being top scorer when Yorkshire were bowled out for 68 and 64. Allen Hill took six for 40.

On a pitch that always gave some assistance to the bowler at Old Trafford, Lancashire won the toss and were dismissed by Emmett (seven for 29) and Hill (three for 23) for only 58. It was a modest total but Yorkshire did not pass it until seven wickets were down. In the end they reached 98. In their second innings, after losing seven for 47, Lancashire recovered to score 82. Hill took five for 24 and Emmett four for 53. Yorkshire knocked off the 43 needed for victory for the loss of Ullathorne with Lockwood 25 not out.

The trip to Trent Bridge resulted in a real drubbing for Yorkshire by an innings and 120 runs. At the end of the first day Nottinghamshire had dismissed Yorkshire for 65, and replied with 228 for four. On the second day, Richard Daft went on to score 161 as Nottinghamshire totalled 355. In their second innings Yorkshire scored 170.

At Bramall Lane, Yorkshire defeated Surrey by eight wickets. It was a game in which Pooley was accused of placing a bet of £50 on Surrey losing the game and though he denied the charge he did not play for Surrey again during the season and was suspended from playing for the United South of England Eleven. Surrey won the toss and were dismissed for only 79, with Emmett taking four for 46 and Hill four for 23. Yorkshire did even worse, scoring only 54, Andrew Greenwood making 22 of them with Southerton taking six for 24. When Surrey batted again they recovered from 52 for eight to total 84. Emmett this time took six for 46 and Hill four for 23 again. Yorkshire needed 110 for victory. Emmett opened the innings and scored 41, putting on 64 for the second wicket with Lockwood (30 not out) and the latter and A. F. Smith (25 not out) took Yorkshire to a creditable victory.

Another comfortable win at Bramall Lane followed against Lancashire, who were lacking A. N. Hornby. Yorkshire scored only 63 with Andrew Greenwood making 20. Lancashire lost seven wickets for 26 before J. R. Hillkirk (56 not out) took them to 94. Emmett took six for 45 and Clayton three for 29 – Hill being injured and Pinder unwell. At 78 for seven Yorkshire were hardly back into the game until Rowbotham played a resolute innings of 33 and Clayton hit well to score 19 not out in a last wicket stand that took the score to 142, setting their opponents 112 to win. At no time did Lancashire give the

George Ulyett was a great all-rounder who opened the batting and who was regarded at the turn of the century as the best batsman to have played for Yorkshire.

impression that they might make a fight of it as they lost six wickets for 19. Emmett (five for 19) and Clayton (five for 27) saw Yorkshire home by 64 runs.

Yorkshire's first encounter with Sussex since the formation of the Club took place at Bramall Lane on 14 July and finished in a win by an innings and 62 runs. Yorkshire scored 200 with Andrew Greenwood making the highest score of 68. At the close of play on the first day, Sussex were 12 for three and in the end were dismissed for 91. Hill took four for 39 and newcomer Ulyett three for 21, and following on Sussex did even worse to be dismissed for 47. Hill took four for 16, all clean bowled, while John West took three for 8.

George Ulyett thus began his career with Yorkshire when only 21 years old, and he maintained his place in the side until he retired after the 1893 season, when Yorkshire officially won the Championship for the first time. He was born at Crabtree, Pitsmoor, Sheffield in 1851 and as a boy played cricket for Crabtree. When 16 he represented the old Pitsmoor CC, following his elder brother Jack (after whom George got his nickname 'Happy Jack' and who became groundsman at Bramall Lane). An attacking right-handed opening batsman, a true foil for Louis Hall, and a large strong man with a preference for the drive, he was also a fast bowler of merit, good enough to take almost 50 wickets against Australia in Test cricket. He was also a fine and enthusiastic fielder anywhere and he was very popular throughout Yorkshire, especially in his native Sheffield. He toured Australia five times and South Africa and North America once each. He also represented the Players against the Gentlemen on 37 occasions between 1875 and 1892 and he was the first Yorkshire professional to receive a benefit of £1,000 in 1887. He also played in goal for Sheffield Wednesday until he retired in 1883. He died in 1898 aged 46 after catching cold at the Yorkshire v Kent match at Bramall Lane and he died at Pitsmoor; over 4,000 attending his funeral at Burngreave Cemetery.

The return match at Hove against Sussex saw the home side give a much better account of themselves after Yorkshire had dismissed them for 63 (Emmett four for 22 and Hill five for 35). Andrew Greenwood with 36 put Yorkshire on the way to a substantial lead and Rowbotham made 50 not out as Yorkshire totalled 179. In the second innings Sussex were 125 for seven at one stage, but finally obtained 224 and set Yorkshire 109 to win. Yorkshire had to struggle to obtain their target but Andrew Greenwood stood secure and was 43 not out when victory came by three wickets.

At Bramall Lane, the Gloucestershire match was played for the benefit of Joseph Rowbotham and large crowds watched on all three days. A. F. Smith (27) and Andrew Greenwood (23) started off with a partnership of 44 but Ulyett with 24 not out was the only other Yorkshire batsman to have any success and the innings ended at 113, with three of the players run out. At the end of the day Gloucestershire had replied with 129 for three with W. G. Grace out for 79. Frank Townsend went on to make 88 and G. F. Grace 29 before the innings ended on 282. At the end of the second day Yorkshire had replied with 101 for one. On the final day, Andrew Greenwood (89) helped Yorkshire to 247. This left Gloucestershire with 79 to win and they obtained these without much difficulty for four wickets.

At The Oval, Yorkshire scored 258 after losing six wickets for 75, with Greenwood making 38 of those. Rowbotham (113) and John Thewlis (50) came together to add 148 for the seventh wicket. Rowbotham's innings was described as 'a great display of resolute hitting and fast scoring'. It was his third century for Yorkshire. Southerton took eight for 113. Surrey could only muster 131 in reply and although in their second innings Jupp (54) and Richard Humphrey (30) opened with 46 for the first wicket, Hill bowled exceptionally well to take six for 66 in 56 overs as Surrey were dismissed for 162. Yorkshire went on to win by nine wickets.

At Clifton College, the return match with Gloucestershire saw the home side occupy the wickets for the whole of the first day to score 344 for eight with E. M. Grace scoring 64 and T. G. Matthews 76, adding 101 for the second wicket. G. F. Grace was 120 not out at the end of the day and he went on to score 165 not out in less than four hours. Yorkshire were then dismissed for 182 with Ephraim Lockwood scoring 55 and A. F. Smith 41. In their second innings, Tom Emmett opened the innings and scored 104 – his only century for the County – while newcomer Betts scored 44 not out and 287 was a great improvement on their first innings. W. G. Grace took four for 88 and then scored 25 as Gloucestershire, needing 66 to win, won comfortably enough by five wickets.

A rain-ruined match took place at Bramall Lane against Nottinghamshire who needed 148 to win at the close with all their second innings wickets standing. A. Greenwood scored 42 out of 102 and Nottinghamshire were bowled out for 79 by Emmett (five for 35) and Hill (five for 41). Joseph Rowbotham (47) and Clayton (22) added 60 for the ninth wicket and rescued Yorkshire after they were 67 for eight and they were all out for 136.

Yorkshire played a third match against Nottinghamshire at the end of the season at Fartown which was not sanctioned by the Nottinghamshire committee. A. F. Smith with 89 dominated the Yorkshire innings as he showed the quality of his defensive powers in Yorkshire's score of 194. With rain affecting the pitch, Nottinghamshire had little chance in the conditions and collapsed twice for 104 and

66, with Ulyett taking five for 17 in the first innings and Hill having match figures of eight for 63 and Luke Greenwood, now aged 39, six for 65. Yorkshire had finished a satisfactory season with seven wins, five defeats and one draw. Before the 1874 season started, Luke Greenwood was appointed to the captaincy in place of Rowbotham, in what was to be his last season for Yorkshire. In fact Greenwood had not been a regular member of the side since 1870. Yorkshire began at Prince's with a five-wicket win over Middlesex. There was a sensation at the start of the match when Middlesex objected to Yorkshire's choice of H. S. Reynolds in the side. Reynolds was engaged at Middlesbrough but was a native of Ollerton in Nottinghamshire and Middlesex claimed he was not properly qualified. Yorkshire countered by objecting to W. C. Wheeler appearing for Middlesex on the same grounds. Both objections were upheld. There was no mention of Reynolds in the Yorkshire minutes, but owing to late injuries, late replacements had to be found and R. Baker and G. A. B. Leatham were drafted into the side for the first time.

Middlesex won the toss and made a good start but were bowled out for 112 with Emmett taking five for 40 and Hill five for 50. Yorkshire gained the lead on first innings only by six runs with Allen Hill making 42. More good bowling from Emmett (six for 43) restricted Middlesex to a second-innings 111, so Yorkshire needed 106 to win. Five wickets were down for 78 before they knocked off the balance for a five-wicket win.

Gerald Arthur Buxton Leatham was a right-hand batsman and very fine amateur wicket-keeper who continued to play occasionally for the County until 1886. Educated at Uppingham he failed to get into the eleven, but appeared for Gentlemen v Players in 1882 at Lord's and also appeared for the Yorkshire Gentlemen's CC. A fine golfer, he was captain of Portmarnock Club and was honorary secretary and treasurer to the Bramham Moor Hunt. There were two views of his connection with Yorkshire cricket. Some claimed that he should have been used more often and others said that he robbed Pinder and Joseph Hunter of their means of earning a living.

At Trent Bridge, Yorkshire won the toss, scored 208 and went on to defeat their illustrious opponents by an innings and 13 runs. Emmett and Lockwood each scored 46 for Yorkshire. Nottinghamshire made 104 and 91. Hill (six for 44 and four for 52) and Emmett (four for 54 and five for 33) bowled unchanged throughout.

At Bramall Lane, Yorkshire again won the toss and batted against Surrey, with 206 a satisfactory total. Andrew Greenwood scored 77. Surrey were soon 59 for six but finally obtained 138. Emmett took five for 57 and Hill four for 59. In their second innings Yorkshire compiled a formidable 251 with Walker Smith (59) and Tom Emmett (69) adding 105 for the fifth wicket. Surrey had very little hope of reaching 320, especially when the first five wickets fell for 19. They were dismissed for 121 to lose by 198 runs. Hill took seven for 62 (six bowled).

The United South of England XI visited Bradford on 22 June where an interesting game resulted in a win for Yorkshire by 26 runs. Yorkshire scored only 64. The South of England made 147, Ulyett taking seven for 82 (all the batsmen were bowled) and Hill three for 58. In their second innings Yorkshire again struggled but Lockwood with 38 and Tom Armitage 25 enabled them to reach 148 which left the South with only 66 to win. Only W. G. Grace with 15 reached double figures for the Eleven and they were bowled out for 39, with Allen Hill having the following outstanding analysis: 15-7-9-6. Ulyett took three for 26.

At Old Trafford, Lancashire put Yorkshire in to bat and succeeded in bowling them out for 96, but this was followed by a poor Lancashire display as they collapsed to 39 all out, Emmett taking five for 24 and Hill four for 11. Yorkshire then scored 96 again, Tom Emmett making 29. Set 154 to win, Lancashire were never in with a chance and were dismissed for 87. Yorkshire therefore were worthy winners by 66 runs with Hill taking six for 27 in 29.3 overs and Emmett three for 50.

At Bramall Lane, Sussex gave Yorkshire a good game before the latter proved victorious by 67 runs. Winning the toss, Yorkshire scored 121 with Rowbotham making the highest score of 26 before Sussex compiled 190 and a lead of 69 runs. When Yorkshire batted again Lockwood batted well to obtain 69 adding 68 for the third wicket with Andrew Greenwood (41) and Yorkshire went on to score 184 leaving Sussex with 116 to win. Their batting was very poor as they collapsed for 48. Hill took five for 25 in 25.3 overs and Emmett five for 18 in 25 overs.

At Huddersfield, Yorkshire beat the All England Eleven by an innings and 11 runs. Once again winning the toss, Yorkshire scored 236 with Joseph Rowbotham batting very well for 70. All out for 131, the AEE followed on and scored only 94 in their second innings on a pitch that was deteriorating. Hill (four for 55) and Emmett (four for 43) were the wicket-takers.

The first match played by the Yorkshire United Cricket Club took place against Derbyshire on 2 July 1874. This Club had been formed at York on 24 January with Lord Londesborough as its president, C. D. Barstow as secretary and Roger Iddison as assistant secretary. It was formed 'for the purpose of generally advancing the interest of cricket in the county'. It did not exist for long and none of its matches were considered to be of first-class status. The name of Iddison among its officers is of interest; he continued to assist Yorkshire during 1875 and 1876 and the game in the latter year in which he played against Middlesex was certainly arranged by the Yorkshire CCC.

At Bramall Lane, Gloucestershire won the toss and batted all day in a match well attended partly because of the visit of W.G. and partly because it was Luke Greenwood's benefit match. W. G. Grace did not disappoint those who had come to see him bat as he scored 167 of his side's 314. F. Townsend managed to score 66 and G. F. Grace 30 while the two pace bowlers Clayton (five for 91) and Ulyett (five for 126) took all the wickets. Hill had broken down after bowling 16 overs; Pinder could not keep wicket and Emmett had another engagement. Yorkshire were then dismissed for 117 and 103 in a very poor display of batting with Pinder making top score (28) in each innings. Luke Greenwood also scored 20 not out in the first innings. W. G. Grace completed a remarkable match by taking four for 57 and seven for 44 and brother G.F. took four for 53 and two for 43. Hill did not bat for Yorkshire in either innings.

Yorkshire faced Lancashire at Bradford without the services of Hill and Rowbotham and a heavy defeat awaited them. Lancashire won the toss and were dismissed for 209. Emmett took four for 61 in 61 overs and Ulyett three for 35. Ulyett also made top score when Yorkshire batted being run out for 26 but no one else reached 20. Following on Yorkshire failed completely to be put out for 69 and lost by an innings and 33 runs.

The Graces were more dominant than ever in their innings win over Yorkshire at Clifton, where Yorkshire, who were already without Hill and Pinder, lost Rowbotham injured too and were compelled to play only ten men. W. G. and E. M. Grace opened with a partnership of 133 before the elder brother was dismissed for 51. A fourth-wicket stand with G. F. Grace took the score to 216 before W.G. left for 127, and G.F. went on to score 81 as Gloucestershire were all out for 316. A. F. Smith with 31 and Andrew Greenwood 34 both batted well for Yorkshire but the rest batted poorly and the side was all out for 87, with W. G. Grace taking five for 44 and G. F. Grace four for 43. When they followed on an innings of 78 not out by Andrew Greenwood, who carried his bat through the innings, was some consolation for Yorkshire who were dismissed for 151. W. G. Grace took five for 77 as Yorkshire lost by an innings and 78 runs.

At The Oval, John Thewlis (50) and Ephraim Lockwood (96) put on 96 for Yorkshire's second wicket, both batsmen playing on their favourite ground, but the County was all out for 187. When Surrey batted, Henry Jupp carried his bat for 43 not out in an innings lasting $2\frac{1}{4}$ hours as Surrey were out for 95. Ulyett took five for 52 and Emmett four for 36. Jupp performed even more remarkably in the second innings as he once again carried his bat to score 109 not out from a total of 193. Emmett this time took five for 64 and Ulyett four for 69, and Yorkshire needed 102 to win. John Thewlis (38) and Tom Emmett (32) put Yorkshire on the road to victory with a stand of 51 and Andrew Greenwood steered them home with 22 not out as Yorkshire won by four wickets.

At Hove, Yorkshire gained a comfortable win against Sussex by 132 runs, Emmett making 65 not out and taking part in a useful stand with Ulyett (26) and Ullathorne (21) as Yorkshire compiled 188. Ulyett with six for 46 and Emmett (four for 69) then bowled out Sussex for 136. When Yorkshire batted again, John Thewlis batted well to score 62 of his side's 175. Sussex were then dismissed for 95 with Emmett taking four for 42.

At Bramall Lane, Yorkshire defeated their chief rivals, Nottinghamshire, by 188 runs. Winning the toss Lockwood 36 and Rowbotham 31 were the only Yorkshire players to bat well as they reached 115. Nottinghamshire were then dismissed in 90 overs for 77 with Emmett having the analysis 45-28-35-5 and Ulyett 45-31-28-5. In their second innings, Yorkshire had three wickets down for 37 but when Rowbotham joined Lockwood they added 101 for the fourth wicket before Rowbotham went for 53. Lockwood went on to 90 before he was run out and Yorkshire finished with 251. Nottinghamshire could make only 101, Lockwood completing a fine match by taking six for 43.

Yorkshire finished their season with a draw at Scarborough against Middlesex. Playing under the patronage of Lord Londesborough, the Yorkshire side was hardly at full strength but at the end of the first day they were well in command with 172 (A. F. Smith 51) while Middlesex replied with 54 for seven. Middlesex were all out for 60 with Emmett taking six for 21. On the final day, due to rain, play could not commence until 3.15 when Middlesex took their follow-on score to 240 in 192.2 overs, hardly festival cricket for the Scarborough holiday-makers. Emmett took six for 89 in 74 overs and W. E. Bosomworth had this analysis: 59-38-37-2. At the close Yorkshire were 9 for two.

Yorkshire thus had a playing record of ten matches won, three lost and the other match drawn. Only Gloucestershire had a better record and they thrashed Yorkshire twice. It had also been a very successful season financially, and the committee had spent a large amount of money on improving the facilities for members at Bramall Lane. Taking into consideration the costs of maintenance and improvements the season had still resulted in a profit of £500 for the Club.

The new season of 1875 would begin with Joseph Rowbotham as captain although there is no mention of that in the committee minutes.

Luke Greenwood had now retired and would not play again for the County, and A. F. Smith was also unavailable.

Yorkshire's first match of the season at Prince's against Middlesex was ruined by the rain, there being very little play on the first day. Yorkshire won the toss and batted, and at 140 for nine R. Clayton (62) was joined by Allen Hill (39 not out) and the last pair took the score to 229. Middlesex made 216. Yorkshire batted the rest of the match out, making 280 with Andrew Greenwood scoring 50 and Lockwood 49.

At Lord's the MCC defeated Yorkshire by 139 runs with Yorkshire failing to reach 100 in either innings. W. G. Grace took eight for 75 and A. Shaw seven for 62 in the match, W.G. having scored 71 in the MCC second innings.

Yorkshire won the toss against Nottinghamshire at Bramall Lane and were dismissed for 89 with Ulyett scoring 26. Arthur Shrewsbury also played very soundly to obtain 26 when Nottinghamshire batted and were dismissed for five runs short of the opposition. Going in again Yorkshire struggled for runs with skipper Rowbotham scoring 27 and Lockwood 21. Nottinghamshire required 113 to win, and a second-wicket stand between A. Shrewsbury (26) and F. Wild (61) added 73, allowing them eventually to get home by six wickets. When Oscroft was run out for nine following a throw from Hill there was an unseemly incident as the batsman disputed umpire Coward's decision; a discussion lasting half-an-hour being carried out on the pitch.

Henry Jupp was again in fine form for Surrey against Yorkshire with top scores of 60 and 30, with Hill having a match analysis of seven for 111 and Ulyett eight for 52. Andrew Greenwood also batted well in each innings to score 61 and 40 not out as Yorkshire led by 47 on the first innings. Needing only 75 to win, Yorkshire won through by four wickets.

Yorkshire's visit to Old Trafford was not lucrative as they went down by ten wickets. They were bowled out for 83 and Lancashire passed that total with only five wickets down and went on to lead by 71 runs. George Ulyett (50) and Tom Emmett (39) were the chief Yorkshire run-getters as they obtained 216 in the second innings, which left Lancashire with 146 to win. A fine display of batting by the legendary Hornby (78 not out) and Barlow (50 not out) took Lancashire to a fine win by ten wickets.

The return match at Bramall Lane took a quite different course. After Hornby (20) and Barlow (22) had put on 34 for Lancashire's first wicket, no other pair of batsmen did as well for the visitors as they collapsed in both innings for only 112 and 100. Allen Hill took eight for 88 in the match and Clayton seven for 69 with Yorkshire's 218 taking them to victory by an innings and six runs. Clayton (44) and Lockwood (43) both batted well for Yorkshire.

The next match at Bramall Lane was John Thewlis's benefit game against Gloucestershire, who because of W.G's presence were popular as benefit opponents. Once again the great batsman came good scoring 111 out of his side's score of 194. After Yorkshire had lost two wickets without a run, Andrew Greenwood (52) and Ephraim Lockwood (74) took Yorkshire to 117 and with Clayton hitting well for 24, Yorkshire gained a lead of 17 on the first innings, with W. G. Grace taking five for 64. In their second innings W.G.(43) and T. G. Matthews (23) gave Gloucestershire a good start with 43 for the first wicket but the rest of the side soon capitulated and were all out for 107, with Hill taking six for 38 and Emmett four for 28 in 34 overs. Needing 93 to win, Yorkshire soon lost three for 21 before Greenwood (24 not out) and Lockwood (39 not out) won the game with an unfinished partnership of 72 runs.

At Bramall Lane, Yorkshire scored 149 with George Ulyett top scorer on 40. W. H. Hadow bowled well to take seven for 64 and followed that up by making top score (58) out of Middlesex's 129. Hill was steadiness personified as he finished with this analysis: 45-30-34-6. In their second innings, Yorkshire, on a rain-affected wicket were dismissed for 93 with the newcomer H. M. Sims making the top score of 35 not out. Middlesex were then bowled out for 61 with Lockwood taking six for 26 and Hill four for 32 and Yorkshire won by 52 runs.

W. G. Grace again made top score (37) when Gloucestershire met Yorkshire at Clifton College and then his brother G.F. (25) added 55 for the fourth wicket with G. N. Wyatt (30) as they took the score to 107, only for the last six wickets to fall for 29 runs. Emmett took five for 21 but Yorkshire could only reply with 99, Clayton with 29 being the top scorer. W. G. Grace took six for 51. In their second innings it was G. F. Grace with 56 and F. Townsend 30 who took Gloucestershire to 168 as Yorkshire were set 206 to win. With W. G. Grace taking seven for 47 and G.F. two for 33 in 40 overs, Yorkshire were all out for 83.

At The Oval a good contest against Surrey saw the home side bowled out for 182 with Clayton being Yorkshire's best bowler with five for 38. Hicks with 66 did well for Yorkshire who replied with 161. Walter Read with 49 not out was the only Surrey player to bat well in the second innings which closed at 105, with Emmett taking four for 14 and Lockwood three for 19. Thanks to Tom Armitage who played one of the best innings of his career with his 68 not out, Yorkshire won by eight wickets.

Yorkshire surprised Nottinghamshire at Trent Bridge but no one made double figures in the first innings as Yorkshire won the toss, batted first and were dismissed for 49. It took Nottinghamshire 95 overs to compile 87 in reply, with Clayton finishing with six for 36 in

48 overs. Yorkshire batted much more consistently in their second innings with H. M. Sims scoring 31 and Clayton 26 and Yorkshire's final total amounted to 183. Nottinghamshire needed only 146 for victory but after losing three wickets for 3 runs they were completely dumbfounded by the lobs of Tom Armitage, who had four of his five victims stumped by Pinder and finished with five for 8 in 4.1 overs. In spite of their defeat, Nottinghamshire were declared the Champion County.

On the Castle Hill ground at Scarborough, Yorkshire finished the season with a drawn match against the MCC, who won the toss and were dismissed for 160. Lockwood scored 40 as Yorkshire reached 121, and then Hill, bowling at a lively pace, took seven for 39 as the MCC were dismissed for 87. Lockwood was 44 not out and Greenwood 24 not out when rain stopped play for the end of the game as Yorkshire were chasing 127. According to Haygarth, 1/– was charged for admission in order to pay off the debt incurred in building the pavilion which is neither a commodious nor imposing structure.

Yorkshire finished the 1875 season with six wins; four losses and two draws; by no means as successful as the previous season but at their best they were a strong side. For the 1876 season Ephraim Lockwood was appointed captain. John Thewlis, E. B. Rawlinson and C. Ullathorne had all played their last games for the County.

Yorkshire's first match in 1876 took place at Prince's with Middlesex making a modest 82 (Hill six for 25) Yorkshire went on to make 167 with Andrew Greenwood scoring 43 and Allen Hill 42 not out. When Middlesex batted again they made 118. Yorkshire scored 36 for seven to win the match with Lockwood playing a steady role of 12 not out.

Revd Edmund ('Teddy') Sardinson Carter, an unorthodox right-hand batsman, fast bowler, lob bowler and wicket-keeper, made his first appearance for Yorkshire in this match and did only moderately in the 14 games that he assisted the County up to 1881. In 1869 he had visited Australia for eight weeks while convalescing after a bout of pleurisy and appeared for both Melbourne CC and Victoria. He played for the Yorkshire Gentlemen in 1864–1900, being considered the life and soul of the club. He it was who invited Lord Hawke to play for Yorkshire and also introduced Peate to the side. He served on the Yorkshire committee for many years and had a fund of cricket stories second only to E. M. Grace.

The MCC match at Lord's was drawn – the third day of the game being Derby Day, it was decided not to play on that day. MCC made a very useful total of 196. Lockwood (58) and Andrew Greenwood (34) were the only Yorkshire batsmen to shine as 91 for two changed to 164 all out. In the MCC second innings total of 159, Lockwood took four for 12, and he was 63 not out with Yorkshire at 113 for four at the close.

Huge crowds watched the two day's play against Surrey, who won the toss and were dismissed for 74, Henry Jupp carrying his bat through the innings for exactly half of those. Surprisingly it was Thomas Armitage's lobs that carried the day for Yorkshire to the delight of the Bramall Lane crowd as he took six for 20, and when Surrey batted again, he did better with seven for 26 as Surrey capitulated to 41 all out. In between the two innings, Yorkshire totalled 173 with top scorer none other than the portly Tom with 47.

At Old Trafford, Yorkshire completely outplayed the home side to win by nine wickets. A. N. Hornby carried his bat through Lancashire's innings of 56 scoring 23 not out in 24 overs. Hill took six for 24 and Armitage, with his lobs, four for 30. At the end of the day Yorkshire had been dismissed for 138. On the next day Hornby again batted very well to score 43 before falling to Ulyett, who finished with four for 14 as Lancashire were dismissed for 98.

A big crowd turned up for the Nottinghamshire match at Trent Bridge; the home side won the toss and Richard Daft batted 3 hours and 10 minutes for his 81 out of 183 for the first wicket with Arthur Shrewsbury, who batted 20 minutes longer for his score of 118. Nottinghamshire then attempted to force the pace but were all out for 298 with Hill taking five for 84. David Eastwood then scored a somewhat fortuitous 56 to help Yorkshire to 208 all out. Yorkshire were compelled to follow on and seven wickets were down with Yorkshire only 26 ahead, but Clayton came in and hit 44 as the innings closed for 175. Shaw took seven for 51 in 69 overs. Nottinghamshire were set 100 to win in 86 minutes and in the time left scored 60 for four with Daft batting an hour for 12. Hill took three for 30 in 32 overs. While taking into consideration the state of the pitch, and Shaw's analysis which shows how difficult it must have been to score runs; one wonders whether a better effort should have been made by Nottinghamshire to score the runs needed. Today, with the introduction of the '20 overs in the last hour' rule, 28 or 29 overs would be bowled in 100 minutes (or 168–174 balls). In actual fact in those 100 minutes they bowled 63 four-ball overs (or 252 balls) in this match. That is the equivalent of 42 six-ball overs. Hill was a fast bowler with a short run and Lockwood a slow-medium bowler. The match was drawn. *Autres temps, autres moeurs* (as Mr Keighley would say).

Lancashire were Yorkshire's next visitors to Bramall Lane where Yorkshire won the toss and decided to bat. They always found runs difficult to come by and were dismissed for 129. At the end of the day Lancashire were 51 for one but next day wickets fell quickly and they were two behind at the end. When Yorkshire batted again Ulyett scored 20 but some fine fielding and bowling soon had Yorkshire back in the pavilion with only 86 to their credit. Needing 89 for victory, Lancashire began well with only three down and 62 on the board, but top scorer E. B. Rowley went for 18 and the last seven wickets fell for the addition of eight runs. Allen Hill finished with six for 28 and Emmett took four for 23.

Yorkshire's next match was with Gloucestershire at Bramall Lane with 20,000 watching on the first two days, with W. G. Grace the usual attraction. Winning the toss, W. G. Grace went very early to Lockwood who took three quick wickets as Gloucestershire slumped to 35 for three before F. Townsend (30) and G. F. Grace (42) added 57 for the fourth wicket. Gloucestershire reached 156. G. F. Grace then had a splendid spell of bowling to take eight for 43 in 45.1 overs with only Andrew Greenwood (39) in good form as Yorkshire were bowled out for 118. W.G. then found his real form as he scored 57 in 'capital style' but still Gloucester reached only 133 with Emmett taking four for 31. Yorkshire therefore needed 172 to win and Ulyett, opening the innings, played very steadily for 33 but apart from useful contributions from Eastwood and Clayton Yorkshire never really looked like winning and in the end went down by 17 runs. This time G. F. Grace took five for 68 and his brother four for 47. The third brother, E.M., took five catches in the match.

At Bramall Lane, Yorkshire won the toss against Middlesex and scored 208 with Tom Armitage scoring a fine 95, although the Middlesex bowling and fielding was below standard. Middlesex made 132, Armitage following up his huge innings by taking six for 70. Batting again Yorkshire lost Armitage and Ulyett with only three on the board before Lockwood (42) and Eastwood (36) added 57 and then newcomer Walter Robinson, 'hitting like a steam-engine' (*Bell's Life*) scored 68. Then a last-wicket stand between Allen Hill (49) and Pinder (18 not out) took Yorkshire to 262 all out. Middlesex were set 339 to win but they saved the match very comfortably with I. D. Walker (94) and W. H. Hadow (62) putting on 142 in a second-wicket stand. Middlesex finished with 234 for five. This match at Bramall Lane was the last in which the amateurs and professionals had separate dressing-rooms.

Walter Robinson, who scored so well on his debut against Middlesex, was a hard-hitting right-handed, powerful middle-order batsman who played twice for Yorkshire in 1876 and five times in 1877 but averaged only 11.51 and left to play for Lancashire from 1880 to 1888. He scored 111 not out against Yorkshire in 1887.

At Cheltenham, Gloucestershire won the toss and at the end of the first day had scored 353 for four with W. G. Grace (216 not out) and

45

W. O. Moberley (73 not out) having added 185 runs in an unbeaten fifth wicket stand. On the second day Gloucestershire went on to score 528, with W. G. Grace 318 not out after eight hours at the crease. W. O. Moberley scored 103 out of 261 put on for that wicket. Yorkshire scored 127 for seven when rain stopped play and the match was drawn.

A low-scoring match at The Oval saw Yorkshire win the toss and fail completely, being bowled out for 68. W. W. Read with 60 not out stood firm as Surrey replied with 118. When Yorkshire batted again Lockwood played a very fine and valuable innings of 78 out of the total of 151, and Surrey then collapsed in their turn with Emmett taking five for 45 and Hill four for 18. Yorkshire won by 24 runs.

On the Bramall Lane ground, George Ulyett with 34 was the only batsman to reach double figures for Yorkshire who chose to bat and were dismissed by Nottinghamshire for 87. Then Nottinghamshire were bowled out for 44, with Clayton taking six for 20 and Lockwood two for 4 in 14 overs. Ulyett again reached double figures with 11 when Yorkshire batted again, but they were all out for 32, Morley taking his match analysis to 13 for 45. Nottinghamshire knocked off the 74 needed for the loss of two wickets with Richard Daft 39 not out in 77 overs. The match had 240 runs in it for the loss of 32 wickets in 249.2 overs (157 maidens).

On the Castle Hill Ground at Scarborough, A. N. Hornby (50) and R. D. Walker (53) added 64 for the MCC's third wicket but they were eventually dismissed for 150 with Clayton taking six for 48. Yorkshire then gave a dismal display and were dismissed for just 46 with C. K. Francis taking seven for 12. When Yorkshire followed on Myers (31) and Hill opened with a stand of 26 yet nine wickets were down for 99 before Pinder hit out valiantly for 27 not out and Yorkshire reached 134. Alfred Shaw took eight for 37, at one stage bowling 15 successive maidens. Requiring only 31 to win, the MCC lost three wickets getting them. Yorkshire had won five matches; lost three and drawn the other four, a moderate performance.

Ephraim Lockwood headed the batting averages with 407 runs at 21.47 followed by M. Myers with 248 runs at 17.71 and Ulyett third with 360 at 17.23. Eastwood and Andrew Greenwood both scored over 200 runs.

With the ball Allen Hill's 62 wickets cost 11.48 each and he had an excellent season. Emmett's 30 wickets cost 17 runs each and Clayton's 24 wickets cost 16.08 each. The only other bowler of any significance was Tom Armitage, who took 46 wickets at 14.03. Lockwood took 16 wickets and Ulyett 11 at 21 each.

It was a far from representative side that Yorkshire turned out at Lord's for their first match of the 1877 season against Middlesex. Their contingent of players who had toured Australia had arrived back in England only on 2 June and the Middlesex match was to begin on 4 June. Yorkshire won the toss and batted and an opening stand between Myers (49) and H. Lockwood (45) put on 87 for the wicket. Geroge Pinder also scored 28 and Yorkshire finished with 182. Middlesex succeeded in passing this total by 21 runs. William Bates, making his debut, took four for 69. In their second innings Myers (25) and two newcomers Wright (22) and Beaumont (24) all did well but it was David Eastwood with 68 who turned the game Yorkshire's way with some fine strokes. All out for 230, Middlesex were set 210 to win and made a good effort to obtain them, but were bowled out for 174.

Of Yorkshire's newcomers, the 21-year-old William (his birth was registered as 'Willie') Bates – known as 'The Duke' or 'Silver Billy' (because of his smart appearance) – was to prove the best. A brilliant hard-hitting batsman and off-break bowler of skill, he was brought up at Lascelles Hall and when only 17 became professional to the Rochdale Club. In 1877 he took all ten wickets when playing for Yorkshire Colts against the Nottinghamshire Colts at a cost of 21 runs and immediately gained a regular place in the Yorkshire team. He played for Yorkshire for eleven seasons as an outstanding all-rounder and very fine close-in fielder. He averaged over 20 with the bat for Yorkshire and took 660 wickets at 16.70 each. He played in 15 Test matches, and toured Australia five times and also Canada in 1879. He performed a hat-trick for England v Australia in January 1883, when he took 14 wickets in the match. On his fifth tour to Australia in 1887/88 Bates was severely injured in the nets and lost his left eye. He never played first-class cricket again, but had professional engagements at Haslingden in 1891 and Leek in 1892. He went coaching in Johannesburg in 1892/93 and received £300. He caught a cold at John Thewlis's funeral after Christmas in 1899 and died from pneumonia aged 44. He was buried at Kirkheaton Cemetery next to John Thewlis's grave. No stone was erected to his memory.

At Bramall Lane, Hill was unable to play for Yorkshire owing to the death of one of his children and at the end of the first day Surrey were well on top. The visitors won the toss and were dismissed for 137. At the close of play Yorkshire had replied with 50 for seven. Emmett (47) and Blackburn (23) took the score to 137 – the same as Surrey's, with Southerton having the remarkable analysis: 46-29-28-6. H. Jupp (27) and R. Humphrey (25) then put on 51 for Surrey's first wicket and E. Barratt scored 30 as Surrey were bowled out for 151 with Armitage taking seven for 58. On the last day Yorkshire needed 152 to win, but only Armitage and Emmett offered any resistance as Yorkshire were dismissed for 85.

At Trent Bridge, Arthur Shrewsbury played a fine innings of 62 to lay the foundations of the home side's victory by 22 runs. Yorkshire, against an attack lacking Alfred Shaw, scored 140 to leave them 28 behind, but Emmett (six for 52) and E. Lockwood (four for 43) put Nottinghamshire out for 115, setting Yorkshire 144 to win. After losing seven wickets for 78 (Tom Armitage 30) a stand between skipper Lockwood (31 not out) and Walter Robinson (20) took the score to 111 without further loss before Yorkshire were all out for 121.

The next match at Bramall Lane saw Derbyshire play Yorkshire for the first time. The home team won the toss and batted. E. Lockwood with 45 and T. Emmett with 70 added 83 for Yorkshire's fifth wicket and Yorkshire scored 210. The visitors were dismissed for 108, Emmett taking five for 25. After following on, Derbyshire gave a much brighter batting display with W. Rigley cutting extremely well in scoring 57 while Hickton finished with 42 not out in a fine display of hitting. Derbyshire were all out for 189, leaving Yorkshire with 88 to win. After losing Robinson at 11, M. Myers (45 not out) and A. Greenwood (35 not out) took Yorkshire to an easy victory.

In the next match at Fartown, Yorkshire were dismissed for 122 with Ulyett (39) and E. Lockwood (28) alone doing anything of substance for the home side and at the close Lancashire were 78 for four with Barlow 24 not out. Next day Barlow went on to 37 and Alfred Appleby (69 not out) batted so well that he was presented with a prize bat from the St John's Club. Lancashire gained a first innings lead of 85. When they batted again, Yorkshire lost half their wickets for 52 before Ulyett and Andrew Greenwood (41) added 30 for the sixth wicket. Yorkshire went on to be all out for 113. Lancashire won the match with ease by nine wickets.

The Gloucestershire match at Bramall Lane was as popular as ever with 22,000 attending on the three days. Gloucestershire won the toss and were in trouble with four wickets down for 48 before E. M. Grace (29) was joined by G. F. Grace (51) and the pair added 43. Another 43 was added for the ninth wicket, taking Gloucestershire to 185. Andrew Greenwood then made 91, batting for over six hours. Yorkshire finally finished with 236, Gilbert, a cousin of the Graces, taking six for 34. In the second innings, W. G. Grace gave a fine display before being dismissed for 84, and Gloucestershire made 189 leaving Yorkshire with 139 to win. Only Willie Bates with 36 batted with any distinction for Yorkshire, and at the close they were 121 for nine and a splendid match finished as a draw.

The return match with Lancashire at Old Trafford was another exciting affair. Lancashire won the toss and A. N. Hornby (88) and Barlow (24) began well by putting on 92 for the first wicket and set Lancashire on the road to victory as their innings expired for 215. Clayton bowled very well to take eight for 66. Yorkshire were 96 for eight when Armitage (30) and Clayton (18 not out) came together to save the follow-on and take Yorkshire to 144. At the end of the second day Lancashire had taken their score to 38 for five and the match had swung towards the visitors. Lancashire were finally dismissed for 72 with Armitage taking six for 32 and Clayton four for 38. Yorkshire then lost three early wickets before Greenwood (25) and the skipper (19) came together to add 27 for the fourth wicket. Then came a collapse and Yorkshire were all out for 108 to lose by 35 runs.

At Bramall Lane, Middlesex won the toss and reached 175 before the third wicket fell. Hill with six for 40 was easily Yorkshire's best bowler as Middlesex totalled 254. Yorkshire replied with 251 with Ulyett scoring 76, Andrew Greenwood 49 and Ephraim Lockwood 46, with the first two named partaking in a stand of 106 for the third wicket. Middlesex were then dismissed for 125 with Tom Armitage taking five for 29, but rain prevented further play.

On the Clifton ground, Gloucestershire completely outplayed Yorkshire to win by nine wickets. Yorkshire on winning the toss batted very slowly to obtain 67 all out on a very slow-paced pitch. M. Myers scored 22 and E. Lockwood 23 as a total of 61 for two at one stage changed to their all-out total of 67 with five wickets falling at that total. W. G. Grace took five for 31 in 43 overs and R. F. Miles four for 10 in 19 overs. On the next day W. G. Grace (71) and Midwinter (68) put on 103 for the second wicket; Midwinter being presented with 15 guineas which was collected on the ground. He had batted for 4 hours. G. F. Grace also scored 31 as Gloucestershire were dismissed for 228, with Emmett taking eight for 46 and bowling with great accuracy and determination. Yorkshire's second-innings 260 meant Gloucestershire needed 100 to win. Once again the Graces made light of the task and 101 for one arrived in 77 minutes with E.M. scoring 53 not out and G. F. Grace 43 not out. The proceeds of this match went towards 'The Grace Testimonial Fund'.

At Derby, the home side managed to force a draw after being behind on the first innings by a margin of 204 runs. Yorkshire won the toss and started well with Ulyett (30) and H. Lockwood (24) putting 51 on for the opening stand. Andrew Greenwood (75) and David Eastwood (57) then took the score from 141 to 218 for six and Yorkshire were eventually out for 278. Derbyshire were then dismissed for 74; Clayton took seven for 35 and Emmett three for 31. Following on, Derbyshire were 185 for nine when the last man came to the crease and the match appeared to be won by Yorkshire. But the last pair took the score to 220 before succumbing at which point there were only ten minutes left and so the game was drawn.

Rain ruined the match against Surrey at The Oval, the home side probably being robbed of victory. Yorkshire had by far the worst of the first day's play being dismissed for 159 after winning the toss, Surrey scoring 101 for no wicket. They took their score to 206 before losing a wicket. Walter Read went on to score 140 as Surrey totalled 300. All the Yorkshire players bowled apart from Greenwood, Tom Armitage taking six for 43. Yorkshire were 69 for one with one day ahead of them but reached only 91 for one before rain washed out play for good.

Yorkshire *v* I Zingari was designated the first match of the 'Scarborough Cricket Week' at the Queen's Ground on 27 August. The weather was bad and the pitch difficult when I Zingari won the toss, batted, and were bowled out for 103. Yorkshire in their turn could total only 88. I. Zingari then replied with a nondescript 93 and then in just over an hour they bowled out the home side for 37. On the following day the second game of the week took place against the MCC but owing to the persistently poor weather did not commence until 3 pm when Yorkshire, on winning the toss, were dismissed for 71. The MCC were then dismissed for only 31 with Tom Emmett taking eight for 16. Yorkshire were then bowled out for 46 with Lockwood and Ulyett alone reaching double figures. On the last day, MCC with 49 for three on the board and batting in altogether better conditions won the match without further loss. This was the last match to be played on the old Castle Hill Ground. It was reported: 'that the Committee of the Scarborough Cricket Club have purchased the ground for about £3,000 and are spending £1,500 on improvements'. Whether this meant the new ground in North Marine Road which was used in the following year or the Castle Hill (or Queens Ground) is not clear.

The last match of the season was against Nottinghamshire at Bramall Lane and resulted in a draw. Nottinghamshire won the toss and were in dire straits at 59 for eight before reaching a total of 110. Armitage took five for 39 and Emmett four for 45. By the end of the day Yorkshire had gone one run ahead of their opponents and had lost only three wickets. Ulyett with 31, Emmett 35 and the Revd E. S. Carter with 32 all batted well but on the morrow the other wickets fell quickly and Yorkshire's lead was only 35 runs. Thanks to Richard Daft with a well-played 53, Nottinghamshire then scored 143 with Yorkshire fielding at their best as Armitage took five for 35 and Lockwood three for 13. At the close Yorkshire had reached 49 for one with Ulyett 33 not out. On the first day of the match the wet weather had prevented any play.

Yorkshire finished the season with two wins, seven defeats and five draws and was one of their poorest ever seasons. They had gone through the last ten matches without a victory.

Andrew Greenwood finished top of the batting averages but he

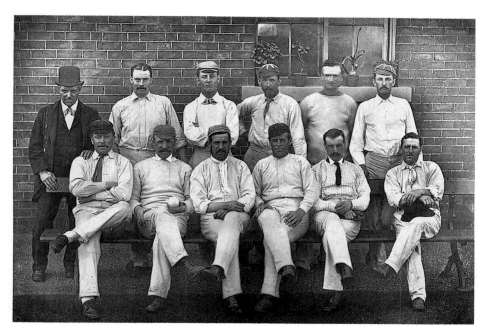

The Yorkshire team of 1877. Back row: G. Martin (umpire), G. Ulyett, E. T. Hirst, Allen Hill, G. Pinder, L. Wallgate. Front row: T. Armitage, T. Emmett, D. Eastwood, E. Lockwood, R. Clayton, A. Greenwood.

scored only 381 runs at an average of 25.06. Ulyett was next with 465 runs at 22.14 while Lockwood had 461 runs at 20 and, Emmett 426 runs at 20. Myers and Eastwood were both very disappointing and Clayton, Hill and Pinder rarely succeeded.

Emmett was the only bowler who could look back on the season with much relish; his 55 wickets cost 11.65 each, although Armitage did take 42 at 11.66. Most of the others were expensive with Clayton's 31 wickets costing 19.45 each while Hill, not as fit as he would have wished, took only 27 wickets at 17.16 each. Ulyett seemed to be under-bowled with 20 at 16 and the skipper took 18 at 16.05 each.

It was a disappointing season from all aspects and the Yorkshire County Cricket Club decided to make changes. A resolution was passed on the captaincy as follows: 'Resolved that T. Emmett be made captain in the absence of a Gentleman'.

That minute is not entirely clear in that it could have meant that if an amateur were picked in a forthcoming game then he would assume the captaincy; or it might have meant that Emmett had been appointed captain as there was no amateur (or gentleman) able or willing to take on the role of captaincy.

The new season of 1878 opened at Fenner's with a game against the University played in unpleasant conditions. Yorkshire won the toss and were dismissed for 105 with Greenwood top scorer with 38. Cambridge went on to obtain 174 with the Hon E. Lyttelton scoring 74. Emmett began the season well by taking five for 31. When Yorkshire batted again, E. Lockwood (31) and G. Ulyett (28) added 47 for the second wicket but the side were soon rattled out for 100 with A. G. Steel taking his match figures to 13 for 85. The University won very easily by ten wickets but it was one of the strongest Cambridge sides ever to take the field.

At Bramall Lane against Derbyshire, rain prevented play on the first day apart from two hours in which the visitors totalled 108 for nine. They added a single on the next day. Yorkshire found runs difficult to get but George Ulyett stood firm and hit two sixes out of the ground, and when Bates came in he hit 25 useful runs so that Yorkshire gained a 13-run lead on the first innings. When Derbyshire batted again they scored only 34, with Emmett taking six for 12 and Bates four for 21. Yorkshire lost five wickets in obtaining 22 to win.

The next match was at Fartown against the Australians, who won the toss and put Yorkshire in to bat. Ephraim Lockwood batted well to score 33 before being last out with 72 on the board. He had added 26 for the last wicket with George Pinder. The Australian innings closed for 118, with Emmett again in good form as he took five for 23. In the second innings Yorkshire made only 73. Spofforth, who had taken four for 30 in the first Yorkshire innings took five for 31 while Boyle followed up his five for 32 by taking two for 15. The Australians won by six wickets. Over 5,000 watched play on each of the first two days.

Yorkshire played their only match on the College Grove ground at Wakefield on 13, 14 and 15 June. The match did not start until 2.45 as a storm had broken over the town but Sussex batted after winning the toss and were all out by the close of play for 98. On the second day, T. S. Dury (29) helped Ulyett to take the score to 50 before E. Lockwood, with 62, added 100 for the third wicket with Ulyett (67). Yorkshire went on to score 204. Next morning Sussex were soon dismissed for 103, with Bates taking five for 38 and Emmett four for 48 for Yorkshire to win by an innings and three runs. The organisers of the game were reckoned to have lost £70.

Yorkshire gave one of their best performances for many a day when they defeated Nottinghamshire by an innings and 97 runs at Bramall Lane. Yorkshire won the toss and at the end of the first day had scored 314 for seven with George Ulyett scoring 94 and Tom Emmett 79. Next day Bates went on to score 102, adding 108 for the eighth wicket with Pinder (23) as they ran up a score of 419. At the end of the second day Nottinghamshire had scored 195 for eight, and on the last day

John Selby went on to score 107 and Nottinghamshire were out for 248. F. J. Whatmuff (also known as Whatmough), on his debut, took three for 58 and Nottinghamshire were forced to follow on 171 behind. In the second innings the side was dismissed for 74, with Bates taking five for 17 and Ulyett three for 9. A total of 17,000 attended the match on the first two days.

Yorkshire's second match against the Australians took place at Bramall Lane, where 23,000 watched the two days' play. The Australians won the toss but came badly unstuck against Bates (three for 30) and Ulyett (four for 14) Yorkshire were in trouble at 32 for five before Ephraim Lockwood, with 30, added 54 for the sixth wicket with Andrew Greenwood (31) and Tom Armitage (45) and Allen Hill (27 not out) took Yorkshire to a strong position with a stand of 59. Yorkshire's final total stood at 167. In the Australian's second innings of 104, Ulyett took four for 27 and Bates four for 42. Yorkshire went on to win easily enough by nine wickets.

The inconsistency shown by the Yorkshire team is proved by the match at Old Trafford, where the old enemy defeated Yorkshire by an innings and 26 runs. After rain had fallen, A. N. Hornby and Barlow opened with a remarkable stand of 87 for the first wicket in which Hornby hit Ulyett for four fours in one over and was 78 when Lockwood had him caught. Barlow (60) then had a partnership of 75 with Vernon Royle (42). Lancashire were finally all out for 267. Only Ulyett shone with the bat, scoring 46, while Bates made 21 not out, but the rest of the Yorkshire batsmen failed utterly against A. G. Steel (five for 49). When they followed on Steel took nine for 63 bowling very well, but as four were stumped by Pilling, then it can be assumed that there were some miscalculations on the batsmen's part. Yorkshire were all out by 7 pm on the second day for 118.

One illustrious newcomer to the Yorkshire side in this match was Joseph Hunter as wicket-keeper in place of the injured Pinder. Joseph Hunter was 22 years old when he first appeared and played in ten matches altogether in 1878 but did not reappear for Yorkshire until 1881. He was born at Scarborough in 1855 and was the eldest of five brothers, three of whom were wicket-keepers, and all learnt their cricket with Scarborough CC. From 1881–1887 he was the first choice Yorkshire wicket-keeper and he toured Australia in 1884–85, playing in five Test matches. He dropped out of the side in 1888 due to injury (possibly a hand injury) after which he returned to play for Scarborough. In 1889 his brother David gained a regular place in the Yorkshire side and though the latter did not play for England, he would certainly be considered the better-known of the two brothers and possibly the better wicket-keeper of the two. Yet Joseph Hunter in 1887, at the age of 30 and in his last full season of first-class cricket, had a better season with Yorkshire as far as victims per match are concerned than David ever achieved during his long and distinguished career. Joseph Hunter died in 1891 aged 35.

At Bramall Lane against Surrey, Yorkshire produced a good display to beat Surrey by an innings and 104 runs, a further instance of their inconsistency. Yorkshire won the toss and scored at a good rate against a moderate attack and poor fielding to total 309. After two wickets were down for four runs, Ulyett (67) and Andrew Greenwood (61) put on 122 for the third wicket and then Tom Armitage hit finely for 71 and Haggas (37) and Hill (32) enhanced the Yorkshire score. Before close of play Surrey lost four wickets for one run and finished at 16 for five. Next morning they went on to score 78, with Ulyett taking seven for 30 and the newcomer H. E. Pearson three for 37. In their second innings it was a similar story with Surrey being dismissed for 127.

At Lord's, Middlesex made a bad start after winning the toss, losing four wickets for 16 before they were finally dismissed for 196. George Freeman, back in the Yorkshire team as an amateur, took three for 35. Yorkshire lost two wickets without a run on the board and then Ulyett (30) and Emmett (37) added 43 and Armitage came in to score 26 not out as Yorkshire finished 53 behind on the first innings. The Middlesex second innings was completed, and at the end of the second day's play Yorkshire, needing 400 to win, were 25 without loss. T. S. Dury (40) and Armitage (26) put on 48 for the first wicket and then Ulyett combined with E. Roper, playing in his first match for Yorkshire, and they put on 103 for the third wicket which fell at 194. Ulyett scored 57, which included some powerful strokes. Roper went on to hit 68, and Allen Hill 35, but Yorkshire had to admit defeat when they were finally dismissed for 309.

Yorkshire gave a poor display at Trent Bridge with Nottinghamshire scoring 228 and Yorkshire all out for a paltry 69. Following on, Bates, who top-scored with 26 in the first innings, again made the top score of 24, but the Yorkshire batting was again very poor and they scored only 95 to lose heavily by an innings. Their only excuse was the fact that Andrew Greenwood did not bat at all owing to gout, and Ephraim Lockwood had to have a runner owing to rheumatism. Morley took 14 for 94 in 82.2 overs.

At The Oval rain delayed the start until 3.0 pm with Yorkshire bringing Louis Hall back into the side. He opened the innings and made 35, adding 52 for the second wicket with Ephraim Lockwood who also scored 35, but Yorkshire were dismissed for 170 — a very laborious innings. Surrey started well and were 103 for one at one stage before a collapse set in and they finished five runs behind Yorkshire. Both Bates and Emmett took three for 47. Yorkshire made 177 in the second innings, and Surrey, requiring 183 for victory, again made a good start, reaching 65 for one, but after that a collapse set in with off-spinner Bates taking five for 30 and Hill three for 16. From 99 for three Surrey became 107 all out to lose by 175 runs.

At home to Gloucestershire, Tom Emmett's benefit proved a resounding success with 10,000 attending the first day's play at Bramall Lane. Ulyett made 29 of the opening stand of 35 with Hall, who went on to make a patient 45 which took nearly three hours. Only I. H. Bottomley with 29 showed up well and the innings closed at 158. At the close, Gloucestershire had replied with 59 for four. Stands of 38 and 48 involving W. G. Grace and E. R. Moline (28) and E. M. Grace (16) followed and the great batsman went on to score 62 as A. Robinson (54 not out) in a useful last-wicket stand saw Gloucestershire's score up to 201. By the end of the day Yorkshire had more than redressed the balance. Ulyett and Hall started off with a stand of 80, and Ulyett enjoyed some fortune, took the score to 164 before being bowled by Midwinter for 109. He had hit 16 from one over of Miles, and at the end of the day Yorkshire were 221 for three, with Lockwood 73 not out. The latter's fine innings of 107, one of his best efforts, came to an end at 276 and Bates with 38 not out and help from the tail went on to take Yorkshire to 360. W. G. Grace, opening the innings, actually carried his bat to be last man out for 35 out of his side's 73, with only E. M. Grace giving him any support with 21 – the next highest score was G.F. with 6. Yorkshire's margin of victory was 244 runs as Bates took seven for 38 and Ulyett three for 32.

The inconsistency of this Yorkshire team was self-evident when they then went to Derby and were beaten by seven runs. Winning the toss, Derbyshire made 106 with all the bowlers taking wickets. At the close of play Yorkshire were 78 for seven and they were soon dismissed for 84. Derbyshire were bowled out for 57 with Hill, Emmett and Bates sharing the wickets. Yorkshire therefore needed 80 for victory, but Mycroft, a model of accuracy, followed his first-innings five for 29 with six for 16 for Derbyshire to win by seven runs.

There was a remarkable turnabout in fortunes at Fartown where Yorkshire, after winning the toss, were dismissed by Lancashire for only 47 in 54.1 overs, with Barlow taking eight for 22. At the end of the day's play Barlow was still batting with Lancashire on 66 without loss. If the first day had gone Lancashire's way, the second day was undoubtedly Yorkshire's. Barlow went straight away and rampant Bates bowled out Lancashire for 123. Bates took eight for 45 and Yorkshire spent the rest of the day compiling 151 for four to be in a strong position. At the close of play Ulyett was 91 not out after a magnificent display of attacking batmanship. Unfortunately rain interfered to ruin the prospects of a fine finish.

At Hove, Yorkshire proved far too strong for Sussex who were dismissed for 35 and 24 with Bates having match figures of nine for 34 and Emmett bettering that with ten for 21. For Yorkshire, who won the toss and batted, Louis Hall carried his bat through the innings for 31 not out of his side's 94, with Emmett aiding him in a stand of 33 for the fourth wicket, Emmett's share being 30. Yorkshire scored 191 in their second innings. Louis Hall this time scored 51 and Andrew Greenwood 47 both batting patiently on a dead wicket. Yorkshire went on to win by 226 runs.

Yorkshire, lacking Greenwood with a recurrence of gout, lost by an innings and 94 runs to Middlesex at Bramall Lane in another display that was eminently forgettable. They won the toss and were dismissed for 94, and at the close of play Middlesex were 171 for one. They reached 294. Hill had the remarkable analysis of five for 17 in 20.3 overs, and when one considers that Bates took one for 80 one wonders if the worthy Emmett had switched his bowlers as the game required. Allen Hill also made the top score of 24 when Yorkshire batted again to be bowled out for 110.

At Cheltenham rain spoilt the Gloucestershire match after Yorkshire had gained a lead of 39 on the first innings, with Louis Hall playing a remarkable innings of 82 not out which took him almost the whole of one day. Allen Hill helped him in a stand of 56 by making 36; and Armitage in a stand of 64 with 29.

At Scarborough, on the new North Marine Ground, A. J. Webbe scored a splendid 100 for the I Zingari out of his side's total of 175 and Yorkshire, giving a consistent display of batsmanship, replied with 296 with Lockwood making top score of 61. In their second innings I Zingari made 155 and Yorkshire went on to win comfortably by nine wickets. In the other match at Scarborough, after the MCC and Yorkshire had each scored 181 in their first innings, Yorkshire, requiring 115 to win, made 88 for seven in 92 overs as the game was drawn with honours even. For Yorkshire, Ulyett was seen to advantage with 72 and 40, and Bates took seven for 46 in the second innings.

There was one other match played by Yorkshire – on 23 and 24 May against the Gentlemen of Scotland at Raeburn Place. The Association of Cricket Statisticians have failed to recognise this game as first-class partly because at the same time an England Eleven was playing at the Merchiston Castle Ground also in Edinburgh. Yorkshire have always included the former match in their records as indeed had *Wisden* and *Lillywhites*, and saw no cause to change this. While Yorkshire's opponents were mainly from Edinburgh, there were two or three outstanding names in the side and the match was arranged and played in a proper manner. The team that faced an England Eleven comprised a motley crew of professionals and one or two leading amateurs and was played for the benefit of a professional called Wright. It was also played on a new ground – a school ground which might preclude it from being considered as important as the other game. For the sake of uniformity with the Yorkshire records it is included. (The scorecard may be found in *Scores and Biographies* Vol 14, page 506). George Ulyett was in fine form at Raeburn Place scoring 107 out of his side's total of 195, Ephraim Lockwood helping him with a score of 31. The Gentlemen of Scotland replied with 44 and following on made 83. E. Lockwood had match figures of six for 38, T. Emmett eight for 24 and A. Hill five for 41.

Yorkshire's final record in 1878 was ten victories, seven defeats and three draws, from the longest fixture-list they had ever embarked on. A little more consistency and Yorkshire had the makings of a 'champion county'.

George Ulyett finished on top of the batting averages with 1,074 runs at an average of 34.32, an excellent record. E. Lockwood was second with 681 runs at 34.05, and Hall third with 351 runs at 27.00. Bates, Andrew Greenwood, Armitage, Emmett and Hill all scored over 300 runs. The only colts to make much progress were Haggas and T. S. Dury.

Bates headed the bowling averages with 94 wickets at 11.13, with Emmett a good second with 84 at 11.32. Hill took 48 wickets at 13.35 and Ulyett 44 at 13.36. Armitage and Lockwood also took a few wickets. The shortage of a regular wicket-keeper following Pinder's injury did not help the side to perform at its best and there seemed a doubt about Emmett's abilities as a captain, although he was willing and keen at all times.

There were few changes in the Yorkshire side that would take the field in 1879; the captaincy would remain in the hands of Tom Emmett but Tom Armitage had played his last match for the county although he was only 31, and Andrew Greenwood at the same age would play only one more game for Yorkshire.

Yorkshire began at Lord's with a nine-wicket defeat at the hands of the MCC, only the technically correct Lockwood batting well with 31 not out which he followed up with top score in the second innings of 26 as Yorkshire totalled 94 and 59.

Yorkshire's next match was also at Lord's where they overcame Middlesex by eight wickets after winning the toss and scoring 183. T. S. Dury (23) helped Ulyett (52) to put on 47 for Yorkshire's second wicket before Bates (49) joined H. Wood in a stand of 61 for the eighth wicket. Wood on his debut batted well for his 35. Yorkshire, helped by two run outs, bowled out Middlesex for 95. Middlesex certainly batted better in the second innings with Hon Alfred Lyttleton scoring 62 in brilliant style, but Bates with five for 51 bowled out the southerners for 179. Requiring 92 to win, Yorkshire had Ulyett again in good form with 50 not out as Lockwood (27 not out) helped him add 64 in an unfinished stand to win the game.

The Nottinghamshire game at Trent Bridge was drawn after the home side had scored 170 and then dismissed the Yorkshire side for 46. Rain had interrupted play for most of the first day and for most of the third, when Yorkshire had followed on and were 2 for no wicket. Hill took six for 49 for Yorkshire.

Edmund Peate on his debut for Yorkshire in this match took two for 31 in 39 overs. A left-handed batsman of little merit and left-arm slow bowler who was considered by some to be the greatest of the line of famous left-arm slows produced by the County, he received his early training as a cricketer at Yeadon and actually began his career as a fast bowler. He then went to Batley as a fast bowler and to Carlisle where his bowling met with much success before he became a professional to the Manningham Club in 1878–79 where he changed to slow bowling. In 1879 he took 17 wickets for the Yorkshire Colts and was immediately drafted into the Yorkshire side, where he remained until dropped by Lord Hawke during the 1887 season when he was only 32 years old. His dropping may have been because the discipline in the side was lax and he had put on weight. Not much good as a batsman and unreliable in the field, he was known to drink a little too, but the fact that Peel was able to take over his position may have been the real reason. One thing is certain – his bowling had never deteriorated. He took 794 wickets for Yorkshire at 12.57 each or at a cheaper rate than any other bowler in the County's history. He never raised his arm above his shoulder. 'Ted' Peate was registered as Peat at birth, not Peate.

Yorkshire played their first and only match at the Argyle Street ground in Hull on 12, 13 and 14 June (although there was no play on the 12th because of rain) when Surrey were dismissed by Yorkshire for 50, J. Shuter making 25 of those. Allen Hill had the remarkable analysis of 29-20-14-7 while Bates took three for 18. At the close of play Yorkshire had scored 55 for one, with Ulyett, who made top score in the match, out for 29. Billy Bates then came in and scored 27 as Yorkshire were dismissed for 118, with former Yorkshire bowler Blamires taking five for 51. In their second innings Surrey were dismissed for 58 with Bates taking six for 26 and Emmett four for 9. Yorkshire won by an innings and ten runs.

Straight afterwards at Bramall Lane, Yorkshire accounted for Kent by 61 runs. Yorkshire won the toss and when rain stopped play for the day they were 55 for two with Ulyett run out for 25 – the top score of the innings. Yorkshire were dismissed for 114. Kent ended 17 in arrears as Peate bowled well once again to take six for 39. Yorkshire then scored 124 with their chief run-getters again being Lockwood (30) and Ulyett (24). At no time did Kent look capable of reaching their target of 142 to win with only C. Absolom (29) holding up Peate as he took six for 38 in Kent's score of 80.

The wet season continued and at Bramall Lane against Nottinghamshire, the wickets were described as 'unfit for cricket'. After a late start, Nottinghamshire, winning the toss, were bowled out for 117 with Hill taking five for 47. By the close of play Yorkshire were 115 for three with Ulyett 74 not out. He went on to score 81 'in one of the finest pieces of cricket seen in Sheffield' and Yorkshire finished with 180. In the second innings Nottinghamshire were dismissed for only 79; Peate took five for 38 and Bates four for 33 as Yorkshire went on to win by nine wickets.

At Old Trafford, Lancashire soon dismissed Yorkshire for 79 with Ephraim Lockwood top scorer with 28 as A. G. Steel, a scourge of Yorkshire batsmen, took seven for 34. Lancashire replied with 180 and in their second innings Yorkshire were dismissed for 69. Lancashire won by an innings and 32 runs.

Derbyshire won the toss at Bramall Lane and proceeded to score 129 with T. Foster scoring 68, a very fine innings on a swamp of a wicket. Hill took five for 16 and in reply Derbyshire dismissed Yorkshire for only 80 with Willie Bates scoring 52 not out. Derbyshire then gave a feeble batting display to be all out for 45 with Peate taking six for 36 and Hill four for 49 in 23 overs and 17 maidens. Yorkshire needed 95 to win but lost six for 26 before recovering to 67, but Derbyshire were the victors by 27 runs. Mycroft took 13 for 65 in the match.

The Kent match at Mote Park proved to be a thrilling affair and although there had been a considerable amount of rain, *Wisden* stated 'that there was little to complain about the wickets'. Kent were dismissed for 106 but in reply Yorkshire could score only 90. In the second innings Kent scored 105 with Emmett taking five for 22 in 33 overs and Peate two for 13 in 23 overs. Kent's second innings took 112 overs in all as Yorkshire were set 122 to win. George Ulyett made a valiant effort to win the game for his side, being the sixth out of 76. Tom Emmett with 16 not out and Champion took the score to 107 before the eighth wicket fell but Yorkshire were all out for 114, with Kent winning narrowly by seven runs. There was another exciting game at Bramall Lane against Gloucestershire who won the toss and scored 253, after having five wickets down for 57. Peate bowled very well taking five for 71 in 60 overs. Yorkshire were bowled out for 130 and could not avoid the follow-on. At the end of the day Ulyett, with 69 not out had taken Yorkshire to 135 for six, or ten runs in front. Ulyett's brilliant innings came to an end when he had made 98 and he was last out at 195, which meant that Gloucestershire needed 71 to win. Gloucestershire seemed well on the road to victory as they reached 37 before the second wicket fell, but Bates bowled W.G. for a duck and a collapse occurred which resulted in Yorkshire winning in a tight finish by seven runs. Peate took six for 40 and Bates four for 12 in an inspired display, with Emmett taking a brilliant catch.

Still without Hill, Yorkshire met Derbyshire on the Racecourse ground and once again proved that their inconsistency was becoming a byword. Defeat by Derbyshire was by an innings and two runs; it was their second defeat at the hands of Derbyshire, who did not win another game during the season. Winning the toss, Yorkshire were dismissed for 81 with Ulyett scoring 22 and Pinder hitting 31. Derbyshire then scored consistently well to total 146. Another deplorable batting display saw Yorkshire dismissed for 63 with once again Pinder making the highest score with 16. Hay and Mycroft each took ten wickets.

The wet weather provided a bowler's wicket at Fartown, where Middlesex could only make 96 with Peate providing figures of 27-19-14-6. In reply Ulyett and Hall both scored 18 but Yorkshire trailed by six runs on the first innings. The visitors were then bowled out for 45. Bates took six for 11 and Peate three for 34, and Yorkshire required 52 to win. George Ulyett gave them a good start with 22 and the target was achieved for the loss of five wickets.

At Bramall Lane against Lancashire (who lacked A. G. Steel) Yorkshire maintained their improved form by defeating their chief rivals by an innings and 80 runs. George Ulyett had a field day as Lancashire won the toss and batted. Ulyett took seven for 32 – all bowled – and then scored 55, adding 70 for the second wicket with Ephraim Lockwood (39). At the close of play Yorkshire were 200 for six with Bates 53 not out, which he improved to a chanceless 118 on the next day as Yorkshire reached 353. When Lancashire batted again, they made a much better start, Hornby (55) and Barlow (35) putting on 72 for the first wicket while Vernon Royle made 47, but they could not sustain this improvement and were bowled out for 186 with Emmett taking five for 38 and Peate four for 54.

At Cheltenham rain ruined the match against Gloucestershire, who bowled the visitors out for 135 with Emmett making 44. Gloucestershire then lost four wickets for 57 but recovered and with more rain turning the pitch into a mud-heap, Yorkshire's bowlers found difficulty in gaining a foothold as Gloucestershire went on to score 269. Yorkshire were 63 for one at the close with Lockwood 33 not out. At The Oval further rain ruined the Surrey match with Yorkshire 92 all out and in reply the home side only 59, with Bates taking eight for 21 in 34.3 overs and 20 maidens. Rain washed out the second and third days' play.

Hall and Peate were the only professionals who played against the I Zingari at Scarborough with G. A. B. Leatham keeping wicket and stumping four batsmen off Peate. Yorkshire scored 298 and when I Zingari batted Peate took five for 61 and newcomer A. Motley four for 48 as the visitors were dismissed for 127. When I Zingari followed-on they batted much better to made 311. The game was drawn.

Yorkshire's season finished with another drawn game at Scarborough with MCC.

So ended what *Lillywhite's Companion* described as 'the worst season ever known . . . from early May to late August . . . we doubt . . . whether there were three consecutive days of real summery weather . . .' Yorkshire finished the season with seven victories; five defeats and five draws – an unsatisfactory record, because at their best they were capable of beating any side. They suffered too many defeats against indifferent opposition.

Ulyett again headed the Yorkshire batting averages with 637 runs, average 25.48, and he was far ahead of Lockwood who scored 336 runs at 18.66, with Bates third with 387 runs at 17.59. Hall scored 294 runs with an average of 12.34. Emmett, Pinder and Haggas are barely worth a mention.

On the bowling side, Hill, injured for most of the season, took 29 wickets at 6.82 each, followed by Bates who took 65 wickets at 11.09 apiece, slightly ahead of Emmett with 41 wickets at 11.51 each. Peate took the most wickets, with 75 at 12.00 each. Ulyett took 15 wickets and H. Wood 10.

For the 1880 season the captaincy remained in the hands of Tom Emmett. The new season began at Fenner's with the formidable Cambridge University side defeating Yorkshire by ten wickets with the Hon Ivo Bligh scoring 70 and 57 not out. Cambridge batted well into the second day to total 272, with Emmett taking five for 49. J. Taylor, making his debut, scored 44 and Ulyett 64 as they added 105 for the fourth wicket but Yorkshire were soon out for 161. Following on, Lockwood (45) and Grimshaw (26), another new player, opened with a stand of 51 and Ulyett made 30 with Bates and M. Riley also seen to advantage. Yorkshire finally scored 184 with A. G. Steel taking seven for 64 (11 in the match). Cambridge won by scoring 75 without loss in an hour.

A poor exhibition followed at Lord's against the MCC where Yorkshire's batting failed twice for 84 and 44. The match bowling analyses make interesting reading: A. Shaw 71-50-50-11; A. Rylott 64.1-39-61-9. Peate took six for 35 and MCC went on to win by ten wickets. The match was over before 12.30 on the second day.

Yorkshire then met Middlesex at Lord's, the home side consisting of 11 amateurs. Yorkshire won the toss and were dismissed for 153.

When Middlesex batted I. D. Walker (63) and A. J. Webbe (32) put on 65 for the first wicket in just over 40 minutes. Middlesex went on to score 197, with Bates taking five for 47. Yorkshire reached 307 with Hall (66) and Lockwood (60) being highest scorers. Before the end of the second day's play Middlesex had lost three wickets for 80 and finally went on to score 175 as Yorkshire won by 88 runs. Emmett was the best Yorkshire bowler with four for 27.

Yorkshire did not play any matches at Bradford in 1880, the ground having been declared unfit for county cricket by the Yorkshire committee, who also refused to use Hull or Holbeck for the same reason. The Hull and Bradford grounds were not the present grounds which have been used for cricket in the post-war period. The committee decided to play more cricket at Fartown, Huddersfield. A letter was received from the Mayor of Bradford asking for the Lancashire match to be played there, but the committee declined as all matches had been arranged.

Yorkshire's next home match was with Kent at Fartown, where Yorkshire made 245 with Lockwood scoring 47 and Bates 43. Kent who were 4 without loss at the close, but with rain stopping play, they had only advanced to 28 for four when the third day commenced. Peate took six for 32 in 46 overs and Bates four for 40 as Kent were bowled out for 73, and when rain came along again to finish the match they were 59 for two in the second innings.

Yorkshire were without Ulyett, playing at Lord's, when the Australians made their first visit to Yorkshire to face the County at Dewsbury. W. Bates made 23 out of his side's 55 all out as G. E. Palmer took five for 22 and F. R. Spofforth five for 31. The Australians barely improved on that being dismissed for 65, with Bates taking six for 41 and Peate four for 20. Yorkshire then opened with a stand of 43, Hall going on to score 39 as Spofforth, with six for 45 and Palmer, four for 36, Dismissed them for exactly 100. The Australians went on to win by five wickets.

Yorkshire batted first against Surrey at Bramall Lane and recovered from 43 for five to score 169, Tom Emmett scoring 68 and Bates 40. By the end of the first day Surrey had replied with 109 for four. When rain ended play early next day, Surrey had taken their score on to 233 for seven. When play restarted at 2.30 on the last day, Surrey finished their innings at 284, with Jupp having carried his bat for 117 not out. At the close Yorkshire had easily saved the match with their score on 214 for four, Ulyett finishing with 92 not out.

At Trent Bridge, Yorkshire won the toss and Ulyett and Hall opened with a stand of 33 in which Ulyett scored 28. Hall batted for 2 hours for his score of 17 and Yorkshire's all out score of 66 took up 97.1 overs. At the close of play Nottinghamshire were 95 for nine, the main difference between the two sides being the partnership of 41 between A. Shrewsbury (21) and R. Daft (25). When Nottingham-shire were out for 98 Bates had taken six for 34 in 55 overs. When Yorkshire batted again the best batting came from Lockwood who went in at 5 for two and was there at the end with 43 not out as Yorkshire were all out for 84. Morley had 13 for 83 in the match. In spite of the slow scoring, the cricket was absorbing and continued to be so as Nottinghamshire struggled towards their ultimate target of 53 to win. Losing four wickets for 14, and then seven for 40, Nottinghamshire finally won through by two wickets. Bates took five for 33. A dropped catch behind the wicket at a crucial part of the last innings probably cost Yorkshire the match.

The Lancashire match at Bramall Lane turned out yet another damp squib after an absorbing first day as no play was possible after lunch on the second. Lancashire won the toss and made 125, to which Yorkshire replied with 154 (Emmett 51), but there was little more play.

At Mote Park, Maidstone, Kent won the toss to score 174 against the strong Yorkshire attack of which Peate took five for 47 in 48 overs. Yorkshire finished two runs behind. In their second innings Kent reached 190 (Peate seven for 61) which meant that Yorkshire needed 193 to win. They began badly and totalled 128 to lose the match by 64 runs.

The return match with the Australians at Fartown was drawn, there being no play on the last day and only a limited amount on the second. Yorkshire won the toss and were dismissed for 78 as Palmer took five for 31 and Spofforth five for 45. At the end of the match the Australians had replied with 229 for six.

The Gloucestershire match at Sheffield was put aside for George Pinder's benefit, but there was very little play; the first day was washed out and the second and third days were both curtailed because of bad weather. Pinder made nothing out of the game and a substitute game was played at the end of the season. Yorkshire were dismissed for 95 after a good start and Gloucestershire reached 190. That was the end of the match.

John Thomas Rawlin (nicknamed 'Tubby' and 'Turkey-Cock'), who played in this match, and made two appearances for the County in 1880, going on to take a regular place in the team in the following season and returning to the side for nine more games in 1884 and 1885. He then joined the Lincoln Lindum Club before moving to Middlesex and playing for them from 1889 to 1899 with great success. He joined the MCC staff in 1887 staying there until 1911 and last appearing in first-class cricket in 1909. He was a right-hand bat and medium-fast bowler with a 'curl', and could turn the ball too. As a batsman he was reliable and could hit hard. In 1886 and 1887 he took over 100 wickets in each season for Lincoln Lindum and he appeared for the Players *v* Gentlemen in 1887 and 1888, also touring Australia with G. F. Vernon's team in 1887/88.

At Derby, Yorkshire took advantage of the toss to score 109 at Derby against the Derbyshire side, and when Derbyshire batted they dismissed them in 26.3 overs for 26. Peate taking five for 11 and Bates five for 15. Following on, Derbyshire made 103, Peate taking six for 52 as Yorkshire went on to win by seven wickets.

The return match with Lancashire at Old Trafford also ended in a draw, heavily in Yorkshire's favour. After a delayed start Lancashire put on 45 in an opening stand but were out for 132 with Peate taking six for 56 and Bosomworth – playing his first match for five years, two for 15. Yorkshire were all out for 125. Lancashire collapsed in their turn with Barlow carrying his bat through the innings for 10 not out in a total of 47. Peate had the astonishing analysis of 38-20-24-8. Unfortunately when Yorkshire had scored 4 without loss further rain fell, with most of the last day's play washed out.

At Bramall Lane, Yorkshire gained revenge for their defeat at Trent Bridge, by beating Nottinghamshire by five wickets. Nottinghamshire won the toss in fine weather and lost two early wickets, finally being dismissed for 102. When Yorkshire batted two wickets fell without a run. Lockwood (32) fought back but the innings closed at 77. Nottinghamshire then gave a wretched batting display to be all out for 92, with Bates taking six for 29. Yorkshire lost four wickets for 56 but Hall (31 not out) stayed and on the last day Yorkshire soon obtained the last ten runs needed. About 15,000 spectators watched the first two days' play.

The visit to The Oval saw Yorkshire occupy the wickets for the whole of the first day to score 332 for six with George Ulyett at his best, scoring 141 in $3\frac{1}{2}$ hours. Newcomer C. J. Gifkins with 23 helped him in a first-wicket stand of 71 while Emmett (29) helped him to add 91 for the third wicket before Bates came in to score an aggressive 57. On the next day, Grimshaw 45 and Sowden helped to take Yorkshire to 398. This match was played for James Street's benefit. When Surrey batted they were dismissed for 176. Peate bowled very well to take five for 78. Pooley had opened the innings for Surrey in their second innings and he obtained a dashing 53 but he received little help as Surrey were bowled out for 99 with Allen Hill taking six for 26 and completing a hat-trick with the last three balls of the innings. Yorkshire won by an innings and 123 runs.

At Bramall Lane, Middlesex won the toss and batted against a Yorkshire side without Bates, who was ill. They made 189, Allen Hill taking five for 69. Yorkshire then completed their innings by the end of the day, being dismissed for 104. Lockwood was at his best as he scored 57 but only Hill with 18 offered him much assistance. On the following day, after following on, Yorkshire were dismissed for 155. Set 71 to win, Middlesex got home by six wickets.

At Huddersfield Yorkshire won the toss against Derbyshire and scored 226 with Ulyett scoring 56 and Emmett 54, while Grimshaw (27) and Peate (27 not out) put on 53 for the last wicket. Derbyshire were bowled out for 127. Peate took five for 50 and when they followed on took five for 31, with support from Hill who took five for 24. In their second innings Derbyshire scored 62.

At Clifton, Gloucestershire, held up by rain finished the day with a score of 231 for six to which W. G. Grace had contributed 89, G. F. Grace 36 and cousin W. R. Gilbert 39; next day they took their score to 302. By the close Yorkshire were dismissed for 195. In the second innings Lockwood batted well to obtain 45 but eight wickets were down for 105 before Pinder came in to hit 57 in 45 minutes and take Yorkshire to a more respectable 190. W. G. Grace proceeded to score 57 not out as Gloucestershire attempted 84 in 90 minutes. They got them with 15 minutes to spare.

The first match of the Scarborough Week, promoted by Sir Harcourt Johnstone, was against the MCC and Yorkshire batted first scoring 128 with George Ulyett top scorer with 40. Yorkshire bowled MCC out for 74 with Peate taking seven for 35 and Bates four for 36 (it was a 12-a-side match). Yorkshire did little better than this in the second innings as they were dismissed for 79. Requiring 134 to win, the MCC were never in contention as they were bowled out for 100. Pinder had six victims behind the stumps; four being stumpings.

Yorkshire's last match of the season was against the I Zingari, who won an exciting match by three wickets. Yorkshire reached a total of 168 with Lockwood making the top score of 69; A. G. Steel took six for 52. I Zingari replied with 127, Peate taking five for 65 and Hill four for 11. In their second innings Yorkshire were bowled out for 79, with Lockwood scoring 20 and C. T. Studd taking five for 31 and Steel four for 45. I Zingari obtained their target of 118 mainly through Ivo Bligh, who scored 70 not out, G. B. Studd (27) helping him in a stand of 55 for the fifth wicket.

Yorkshire finished a disappointing season with six wins, eight defeats and six draws, yet at their best they looked a very capable side indeed. There may well have been a lack of discipline in the side that could have accounted for their inconsistency.

The batting averages were headed by Ulyett who scored 785 runs at 29.07, with Lockwood a worthy second with 790 runs at 25.48. Emmett came next with 559 runs at 19.27, while Hall scored 354 runs at 16.09 – a disappointing season for the stonewaller. Grimshaw scored 354 runs at 14.75; and Bates 417 at 13.90, a poor record for one of such talents.

If the batting was disappointing, it should be remembered that 1880, like the previous year, was an extremely wet one, favouring the ball throughout the season with only one or two pitches really suitable for batsmen.

Edmund Peate headed the bowling averages with 131 wickets at 11.55 – an excellent season's work. Bates also did well with 74 wickets at 14.82 as did Hill with 43 wickets at 14.95. He was unfit for some of the season and only came into his own at the end. Emmett was disappointing with 32 wickets at 16.81. Pinder's wicket-keeping was not as good as usual and he was dropped from the side at one time. In fact it was Pinder's last season with the county; he was now 39 years of age.

Tom Emmett was re-appointed captain for the new season and there was one new resolution passed concerning the professionals in the Yorkshire side. The resolution was as follows: 'That the players be engaged subject to their not accepting any engagement to play in any match styled Yorkshire versus any other county . . .'

This would presumably put an end to such matches as Yorkshire v Australians which was played in the 1880 season and yet was not under the jurisdiciton of the Yorkshire committee. To escape such a clause sides would style themselves 'Tom Emmett's XI' in the future if such matches were to be arranged. They were played but the games were never included in the Yorkshire records or averages, although they were first-class matches.

The 1881 season opened at Fenner's with Yorkshire beating Cambridge University by eight wickets. In spite of the three Studds and A. G. Steel playing for the home side, the opposition was not up to the standard of past years. At the end of the first day's play, Yorkshire were 180 for one, with Ulyett out for 66 (as he put on 103 with Louis Hall). Hall and Bates added 90 for the second wicket with Hall scoring 77 and Bates 45, but Yorkshire collapsed to 248 all out. The Cambridge batting was very sketchy as they were dismissed for 88, with Peate taking six for 33. Following on, G. B. Studd (68) and A. G. Steel (71) put on 104 for the second wicket but wickets then fell regularly as Cambridge were dismissed for 223, and Yorkshire went on to win comfortably.

At Lord's, Yorkshire won the toss against Middlesex and compiled 198, with Tom Emmett scoring 89 not out in $2\frac{3}{4}$ hours of hard and brilliant driving. Middlesex, hardly at full strength, were 32 for seven at the close of play but next morning improved to 91 all out. In their second knock Middlesex scored only 98 and Yorkshire won by an innings and nine runs. Joseph Hunter took five victims as the Yorkshire wicket-keeper and was to establish his place in the side.

Remaining in London, Yorkshire next met a strong MCC side, who triumphed over them by eight wickets after putting them in to bat and dismissing them for 68 and a second time for 105. The match figures of the destroyers were: Shaw 100.2-54-75-9; Mycroft 92.1-58-78-11. Allen Hill took six for 18 in MCC's first-innings 100.

At Fartown, Yorkshire batted all day against Surrey for the tremendous total of 388, with Ulyett scoring 112 and E. Lockwood 109. With Hall (47) Ulyett added 134 for the second wicket and Bates (55) helped Lockwood in a stand of 130 for the fourth wicket, while Emmett scored 41. For Surrey only A. P. Lucas with 62 could make anything of the bowling of Peate, who had match figures of 14 for 77, and Hill, who had six for 85, the two bowling unchanged as Surrey scored 110 and 61. Yorkshire won the match by an innings and 217 runs.

On 13 and 14 June Yorkshire played their first match on the new Horton Park Avenue ground at Bradford against Kent. They began in style by putting on 100 for the first wicket before Hall was dismissed for 26. Ulyett scored 79 and J. T. Rawlin batted well for 31 as Yorkshire totalled 213. Kent were then dismissed for scores of 62 and 64. Yorkshire were at their best with the ball and in the field, Peate taking five for 32 and four for 25 while Hill took five for 25 in the first innings and W. Bates six for 23 in the second innings.

After such a good start to the season, it would have been typical to fall by the wayside in their next match at Bramall Lane, against Sussex. The visitors won the toss, batted and opened with a stand of 113 for the first wicket but the rest of the batting plummeted to an all-out score of 187, with Peate taking five for 79. Yorkshire went on to score 239 with Ulyett (73) and Lockwood (58) adding 80 for the second wicket. Only an eighth-wicket stand of 42 held up Yorkshire as Sussex were dismissed for 87. Bates took six for 25 as Yorkshire went on to win by nine wickets.

Yorkshire's success continued at Trent Bridge with victory by an innings and seven runs. Nottinghamshire were having problems with their players during this season and the Nottinghamshire team was far from representative. Nottinghamshire were dismissed for 71 as Bates took five for 30. For Yorkshire Ulyett with 35 and E. Lockwood 29 along with the skipper Emmett with 19 took Yorkshire to 103 for four, but the side was all out for 113. In their second innings Nottinghamshire were dismissed for 35, as Bates took six for 17. A crowd of 12–14,000 watched the first day's play against Lancashire at Bramall Lane. Lancashire won the toss and collapsed from 152 for four to 162 all out. At the end of the first day, Yorkshire were 155 for seven with Ephraim Lockwood batting brilliantly for 73. Yorkshire's lead proved to be exactly one run. Lancashire built a lead with Barlow batting well for 69, and finally obtained 196. At the end of the second day Yorkshire were going well at 76 for two but a heavy thunderstorm overnight put a different complexion on the game. Yorkshire soon lost further wickets and were dismissed for 145, Lancashire winning by 50 runs.

At Mote Park, Maidstone, Yorkshire won the toss and batted, with Irwin Grimshaw top scorer with 36 out of the side's total of 182. Kent were dismissed for 117, with H. Mosley taking three for 12 on his debut for Yorkshire. In their second innings Bates reached his century before lunch, making his 108 out of 148. Henry Lockwood then came in to score 54, putting on 71 for the seventh wicket with Joe Hunter who made 31 not out as Yorkshire reached 260, a good performance in view of the fact that Ulyett strained his side in Kent's first innings and could not play for over a fortnight. Kent collapsed for 74, leaving Yorkshire winners by 281 runs. Peate took six for 33 in Kent's second innings.

Gloucestershire's visit to Bramall Lane saw the Yorkshire side lacking both Ulyett and Hill and they gave a patchy batting performance on a dead wicket. Hall with 24 and E. Lockwood 30 added 45 for Yorkshire's second wicket, and then newcomer Clegg was run out for 16. Yorkshire were finally all out for 116. Gloucestershire soon lost the 'Champion', but at the end of the day were 142 for eight. They were all out for 150 on a day shortened by rain, Peate taking five for 56, and Emmett three for 29. At the end of the curtailed second day Yorkshire were 48 for three. On the Friday Yorkshire reached an all out score of 121. Gloucestershire needed 88 to win, and got home by five wickets.

At Old Trafford, Yorkshire won the toss and batted. Only the Lockwoods, Henry (32) and Ephraim (15), along with Emmett (20) succeeded in reaching double figures and the side was bowled out for 96 by Lancashire. A. G. Steel took seven for 59, Yorkshire taking 107 overs to score 96 runs. Lancashire were dismissed for 212, with Emmett taking five for 42. At the end of the second day Yorkshire had scored 96 for seven and were in real trouble. The one real stand of the innings was between Tom Emmett, who scored a fine attacking 75, in conjunction with Peate who finished with 28 not out as the pair added 70 valuable runs. A. G. Steel took six for 87. Lancashire lost two wickets in obtaining the 70 needed to win.

At Derby, the home side did well to score 174 against the keen Yorkshire attack and this was almost entirely due to the batting of R. P. Smith (41) and L. C. Docker (68). Peate took seven for 59 and at the close of play Yorkshire had replied with 101 for two. Hall and

Emmett took their partnership to 93 before Hall was out for 40, but Emmett went on to score 76 as Yorkshire took a ten-run lead on the first innings. Derbyshire were soon dismissed in their second innings for 80 as Bates took six for 37, leaving Yorkshire with 69 to win. Ephraim Lockwood was in fine form as he guided Yorkshire to a seven-wicket win with 46 not out.

Surrey batted first at The Oval, and took their total to 224, with Bates and Peate each taking four wickets. At the close of play Yorkshire were 93 for one; this was followed by a wet day. Yorkshire took their second-wicket partnership to 104 before Emmett went for 61. Bates (44) then helped E. Lockwood (50) to take the score to 137 and later Grimshaw (32 not out) and Peate (22) put on 49 for the ninth wicket to put Yorkshire in front on the sodden turf by 32. At 3.45 Surrey commenced their second innings on a pitch quickly drying out and they were in a sad plight after reaching 54 for two. Emmett with eight for 22 was quite unplayable as Surrey were bowled out for 66 and Yorkshire gained a nine-wicket victory.

Yorkshire won the toss at Cheltenham and batted for the whole of a first day somewhat curtailed by the weather to score 212 for nine with Ephraim Lockwood batting very well for 79 and his brother 63 not out at the close of play. On the next day the last wicket stand was extended to 74 runs with Peate batting well for 27 and helping Yorkshire to a total of 267, with Henry Lockwood finishing with a very sound 90 not out. Gloucestershire were only 13 in arrears at the end of the first innings, and in the limited time remaining, Yorkshire finished with 194 for three.

At Huddersfield against Middlesex, Yorkshire brought back E. T. Hirst into the side for the first time for three years and also played his younger brother E. W. Hirst in the team. On a dead wicket, Yorkshire found runs hard to score but Ulyett (32) and E. W. Hirst (28) both batted well against a strong Middlesex bowling side and Yorkshire reached a respectable 150. Middlesex took their score to 102 before the third wicket fell, and the visitors gained a lead of 33 on the first innings. In the second innings Hall (20) and Grimshaw (35) opened with a stand of 45 and then wickets fell steadily with only Ephraim Lockwood (36) and Emmett (30) holding up the Middlesex attack as Yorkshire finished at 153. Requiring 121 to win, Middlesex lost four wickets for 23 and never recovered from such a bad start with their only hope of victory coming in a last-wicket stand of 20, which ended with a run-out 15 runs short of victory. For Yorkshire, Bates took six for 56.

At Bradford on a very poor wicket that was changed at the end of the Derbyshire innings, Derbyshire added 37 for the second wicket before the side were all out for 76. Emmett took six for 19. In reply

Yorkshire reached 141 for nine by the close of play with Ulyett scoring 48. No further play was possible owing to rain.

Another draw followed at Bramall Lane where Nottinghamshire scored 173. Bates took four for 59 in 60 overs and followed that up with 34 as he added 41 for the fifth wicket with Grimshaw (41). That ended the match as there had been no play on the second day and not much on the first.

The Scarborough Week followed with the team against MCC match not selected by the Yorkshire committee but it was always considered to be the Yorkshire team. Yorkshire on a sodden wicket and in miserable conditions scored 100, with Emmett 30 and Ephraim Lockwood 27 contributing most of those. In reply the MCC slumped to 60 for seven before A. G. Steel came to the crease to play a magnificent innings of 106 not out in 80 minutes to help MCC reach 188. Peate took five for 35. Apart from Ulyett (19) and Bates (15), Yorkshire offered very little in their second innings as the County were bowled out for 53 and the MCC won with an innings and 35 runs to spare.

The Hon M. B. Hawke made his first appearance for Yorkshire in this match and also played in the second match at Scarborough with more success.

I Zingari also inflicted defeat on Yorkshire by 159 runs, outplaying the County from the start of the second innings. The visitors went in first and were dismissed for 124 with Peate finishing with six for 63. Only Lockwood with 28 and E. S. Carter 21 contributed much for Yorkshire, who were dismissed for 121. In the second innings Emmett was Yorkshire's best bowler with seven for 68 as I Zingari compiled 236. Yorkshire's second innings was a procession with six down for 35 until the Hon M. B. Hawke came in and scored 32 in plucky style and Yorkshire reached 80.

For their last match of the season at Hove, on 8 September, the bowlers had a wet ball to contend with throughout the match. Sussex won the toss and scored 149. Peate finished with six for 61 in 62 overs. When Yorkshire batted they lost Hall for o but Ulyett (69) and Ephraim Lockwood (43) put on 84 for the second wicket, which Emmett (52) and Bates (48) augmented with 85 for the fourth wicket. They were all out for 247. Sussex made 169 in fits and starts, with Peate taking eight for 69 to complete match figures of 116-55-130-14. Yorkshire needed 72 to win and got them for the loss of four wickets.

Yorkshire finished a much better season in second place behind Lancashire in the 'unofficial' County Championship. They had played some good cricket and looked a strong all-round team, although they had been comprehensively beaten by the Champions.

Ulyett with 817 runs at an average of 31.42 headed the batting averages with Ephraim Lockwood only just behind him with 896 runs at 30.89, while skipper Emmett showed his value as an all-rounder with 720 runs at 24.82. Bates had a much better season with the bat, scoring 631 at 20.67. Henry Lockwood scored 258 runs at 19.84; Grimshaw 370 at 18.50 and Hall, who was disappointing, 475 at 17.59. They were a fairly consistent side, and even the tail-enders such as Peate were capable of rising to the occasion.

Allen Hill headed the bowling averages with 36 wickets at 9.44 each and had the misfortune to break his collar-bone, missing more than half the season. Emmett took 57 wickets at 11.31 and perhaps he could have used himself more than he did. Peate was the main bowler and 133 at 12.26 shows just what a good bowler he was. Bates, with 80 wickets at 176.15 was not quite as reliable as before, but he was a most valuable member of the team. Ulyett, rarely used, took eight wickets at just over 15 runs each. Joseph Hunter established himself as the wicket-keeper and looked to have a good career in front of him; his batting showed signs of improving.

The committee minutes never mention the captaincy for the forthcoming season and in view of the success of the side and of Emmett's performances as a player it can be assumed that he retained the captaincy, because there was no adverse criticism of him. There was one interesting point that was under discussion by the Yorkshire committee. A deputation from a meeting in Leeds asked for representation from five districts of Yorkshire; this was agreed by the committee and would be implemented in due course.

The new season of 1882 opened at Trent Bridge with Nottinghamshire winning the toss and scoring 104, Bates taking six for 14. Yorkshire replied well with Ulyett in fine form before being second out for 46 with the score at 67. W. Bates (38) and E. Lockwood (34) with help from Grimshaw (44) took the score to 190 before the sixth wicket fell but they were all out with only one more run scored. Nottinghamshire, with several of the players who had been on strike restored to the side, were watched by 10,000 paying attendance during the match. In their second innings, with Yorkshire's fielding below its best standard, Nottinghamshire took their score to 241. Set 155 to win, Yorkshire batted badly and were all out for 64. Morley took 12 for 104 in the match.

Against the MCC at Lord's Yorkshire's batting again let them down after Ulyett (30) and J. Padgett (22) had given them a good start with an opening stand of 55. They were bowled out for 92. MCC collapsed to 161 all out, Peate taking five for 46. Next morning only Louis Hall stayed for long as Yorkshire were dismissed for 74. MCC went on to win by eight wickets.

At Fartown, Derbyshire recovered from 10 for four to obtain 158 against Yorkshire. Ulyett (26) and Hall (34) opened with a stand of 52 and at the close of play, Yorkshire were in a strong position at 131 for two. Bates (54) and Ephraim Lockwood (26) soon went on the next morning as Yorkshire were all out for 207. An abject batting display from Derbyshire followed as they were dismissed for 64, with Bates taking six for 31 and Yorkshire went on to an eight-wicket win.

The first day of the Australians' visit to Bradford was washed out but the Australians could score only 128 in their innings, and at the end of the day Yorkshire were well-placed at 100 for four. Ephraim Lockwood went on to score a fine and chanceless 66 as Yorkshire were dismissed for 146. In their second innings the Australians recovered from 53 for five to total 135, with Bonnor hitting Peate for three sixes in his score of 35, Peate finishing with five for 75. Yorkshire, needing 118 in 45 minutes, scored 30 for three in an honours-even draw.

Robert Sidgwick, a very useful right-hand opening batsman and one of the finest cover-points of his day, played in nine matches for Yorkshire during the 1882 season. He once scored 203 not out for Skipton against Keighley Albion in 1884. In 1892 he became a coffee planter in Jamaica and played for Jamaica in 1894–95 and is believed to have died there in 1934. An interesting note in the Club minutes of 20 June 1882 stated: 'That a presentation bat be given to Mr. Sidgwick for his kindness in playing for the Yorkshire County CC'.

At Lord's against Middlesex, Yorkshire gave a disappointing display to be dismissed for 151. Middlesex replied with 182. Interruptions for rain meant that Yorkshire had only advanced to 40 for one at the end of the second day, when the game was still evenly poised. On the last day, run-getting became more difficult and the Yorkshire batting fell apart, and they were all out for 72. Needing only 42 to win, Middlesex made heavy weather of their task as Peate took four for 26 and Bates three for 16 but they eventually won through by three wickets.

Kent were no match for Yorkshire at Bramall Lane. At lunch Kent were 91 for one, but a rainstorm changed the condition of the pitch and eight wickets fell for seven runs, with Peate taking seven for 31 in 47.3 overs. Yorkshire were 77 for one at the close of play with Ulyett having scored his first 50 in half-an-hour out for 63. On the next day Hall went on to bat for $3\frac{1}{2}$ hours for his 29 as Yorkshire were dismissed for 172. Peate went on to perform the hat-trick including two Lords among his victims as Kent were bowled out for 39. Bates had the analysis: 18.3-12-12-6. Peate had to be satisfied with his hat-trick victims. Yorkshire won by an innings and 20 runs.

At Dewsbury, Sussex cut poor figures as they were dismissed for 104, with Peate taking five for 41, and by the close of play Yorkshire had the match well in hand with 149 for seven on the board. Ulyett had scored 33 and Bates 56, having been dropped twice. Yorkshire were all out for 184. With Peate taking six for 38 and Bates four for 36, in the second innings, Yorkshire finished the match by scoring 23 needed without loss in ten minutes.

It was reckoned that 32,000 people watched the first two days of the visit of the Australians to Sheffield where the visitors gained the victory by six wickets. Only Ulyett 38 and Ephraim Lockwood with 20 not out performed with much aptitude as Yorkshire were dismissed for 92, with the Aussies two runs in front at the close of play with only four wickets down. Next day W. L. Murdoch took his score to 54 as the visitors were all out for 148, Peate taking seven for 51 in 59 overs. Ulyett and Bates each scored 30 when Yorkshire batted again and they were at one stage 96 for three, after which Emmett scored 25, but the innings closed at 153, leaving the Australians needing 98 to win. Alec Bannerman (36) and H. H. Massie (32) took them to 91 before the second wicket fell and they eventually won by six wickets.

Frederick Lee made his first appearance for Yorkshire against the Australians at Bramall Lane, and his second in the next match with Nottinghamshire. He did not play again for Yorkshire until 1884, when he gained a regular place in the side until 1890. He scored 4,992 runs at an average of 23.65. A free stylish, enterprising right-hand batsman when at his best, he could also keep wicket. He was only 33 when he lost his place in the Yorkshire side and had assisted Players *v* Gentlemen. Probably Lord Hawke had a hand in his leaving the Club. He died from pneumonia and pleurisy in 1896 aged 39.

At Bramall Lane, Nottinghamshire won the toss and put Yorkshire in to bat. Ulyett (56) and Hall (26) opened with a partnership of 77, during which Morley had to go off injured. Bates (39) and Ephraim Lockwood (74) then put on 74 for Yorkshire's third wicket. Next morning the innings closed at 264 and in reply Nottinghamshire made 143, with Bates taking six for 58 and Peate four for 46. When Nottinghamshire followed on they made 148 with Peate taking seven for 68, and Yorkshire went on to win by eight wickets.

The Hon M. B. Hawke returned to open the innings for Yorkshire against Surrey at Bramall Lane and he opened with Ulyett in a stand of 36, of which Hawke scored 20. Hall then helped Ulyett to take the score to 101 before Hall left for 23 and then Ephraim Lockwood (64) added a further 112 with Ulyett before George was dismissed for 120. Yorkshire took their score to 277. Surrey were all out on the following day for 123. Peel on his debut took four for 46. Surrey made a better show on following on and reached 197. Peel took five for 83. Yorkshire were set to score 44 in half an hour. They obtained only 35 for no wicket with Ulyett 25 not out and the match was drawn. There had been several interruptions due to rain, especially on the last day.

Peate was unable to play owing to injury and Bates was also injured during the first day's play.

Robert Peel, a left-handed batsman and left-arm slow bowler was born at Morley in 1857 and played his early cricket with Churwell from about 1872. After the Surrey match he soon gained a regular place in the Yorkshire side, although he was second fiddle to Peate until Peate retired in 1887. Peel continued to play for Yorkshire until 1897 when he was sent off the field by his captain, Lord Hawke, and was suspended for the rest of the season. It is believed he may have been the worse for wear after a drinking session; a state that he had been warned about on a previous occasion. When bowling, Peel brought his arm behind his back with a peculiar flourish-like action and then 'whipped the ball down'. Dangerous to a degree on a helpful wicket, he would speed up his action on a slower wicket. He also spun the ball with a late swing. Also a great cover-point and a good batsman when needed, he was hard to hit on a good wicket, as he bowled quicker than Briggs, his great rival. MacLaren considered him the greatest of all left-arm slow bowlers. He played in 20 Test matches, taking over 100 wickets, and he toured Australia on four occasions, the first being in 1884/85.

Rain also ruined the match with the Australians at Dewsbury, where Ulyett scored 61 out of his side's 129. Alec Bannerman (34) and W. L. Murdoch (30) took the Australians to 141, with Peel taking six for 41. In their second innings, Yorkshire scored 64 for one with Ulyett scoring 34 and Hon M. B. Hawke 26 not out. The match was drawn. Yorkshire's next match was also against the Australians at Bradford; the tourists batted first and made a useful total of 132, with Emmett taking five for 10. The heavy rain had rendered the pitch very difficult to score on and the Australians had taken over 122 overs to obtain their score. When Yorkshire batted they scored only 68 runs in 81.1 overs with Hall finishing on 19 not out from 57 made while he was at the crease. On going in again the tourists scored 67, with Emmett taking six for 22. Yorkshire had little hope of attaining 132 for victory but Hon M. B. Hawke did reach 27 before being badly-run out as Yorkshire were bowled out for 84 to give the Australians victory by 47 runs.

The Australians made another visit to Yorkshire, to the Linthorpe Road Ground at Middlesbrough, and gained a more comprehensive victory at Yorkshire's expense. They made 222, with Ulyett taking five for 42. Irwin Grimshaw (30 not out) made the top score when Yorkshire batted. They scored 129, with Garrett taking seven for 49. Following on Yorkshire improved a little to total 140 with Grimshaw again making the top score with 37. The tourists went on to win comfortably by seven wickets.

The Roses match at Bramall Lane was played for the benefit of Ephraim Lockwood but the weather was wet and eventually the game was drawn very much in Lancashire's favour. The visitors won the toss and made 152, with Barlow scoring 32. In reply Yorkshire made a remarkable start, hoisting 60 for the first wicket before Hall left for six and Ulyett shortly afterwards for a hard-hit 53. No one else could do anything. When Lancashire batted again they were indebted to a fine innings of 27 by former Yorkshire batsman E. Roper for a total of 75, as Emmett took six for 34 and Peate four for 29. At the close Yorkshire had scored 67 for four.

At The Oval, Yorkshire won the toss and scored 203 with Ulyett scoring 46. Surrey were dismissed for 105, with Peate taking three for 31 and Peel two for 12. In the second innings Surrey batted much better for a time, but they collapsed for 160, with Peate taking five for 43 and Emmett three for 11.

Lord Hawke made his first appearance in the Club minutes book dated 24 July 1882: 'Resolved that the Hon Mr Hawke . . . be invited to play on Thursday at The Oval against Surrey and on the 31st against Gloucestershire at Sheffield'.

On 31 July the match against Gloucestershire at Bramall Lane commenced with Yorkshire batting first and Ulyett scoring a brilliant 45 out of 60, the only worthwhile batting of the innings. They were all out for 112. Gloucestershire, with the two older Graces and cousin Gilbert out for a mere single between them, struggled to 120, with Peel taking four for 22 and Peate four for 66. When Yorkshire batted again the Hon M. B. Hawke with 66 played with any confidence in an innings noted for its on-driving and leg-hits as Yorkshire were dismissed for 146. For Gloucestershire, W. G. Grace batted well in scoring 56 but apart from Woof (15), no other batsman performed well and Yorkshire gained a well-merited victory by 29 runs, with Emmett taking four for 30.

Between meetings of the committee on 11 August and 27 September, the Club's printed rules had been pasted into the minutes book and Rule II (two) reads as follows:

> The affairs of the Yorkshire County Cricket Club shall be under the management of a President, Vice-President, Treasurer, and twelve other members *to be elected at a General Annual Meeting to be held at Sheffield* (seven of whom shall be the Ground Committee of the Sheffield United Cricket Club) and on one representative from each of the following districts, viz.:

That part of the rules in italics had been added in ink, while under the final word 'viz' was a blank space that had not been filled in, but at the end of the printed list of Rules had been added the following in pencil: 'That the blank in Rule 2 be filled up at the discretion of the Committee'.

Yorkshire's next match was at Old Trafford where an excellent match took place with Lancashire putting on 65 for the first wicket and Barlow (68) anchoring the innings which ended at 218. Peel took five for 41. Yorkshire batted steadily on the following day but only Peate with 38 stayed for very long as Yorkshire were dismissed for 158. A. G. Steel took five for 81. When Lancashire batted again only Barlow and Royle held up Peate and Ulyett for long as the home side were dismissed for 97. Peate, back to his best form, took five for 25. Yorkshire required 158 to win. Peate (21) opened the innings with Emmett (38) and the pair put on 35 for the first wicket before Peate was out. Six wickets were down for 86 before a timely 16 from Haggas and 15 from Grimshaw took the score to 124 before the eighth wicket fell. The last fell with Lancashire winners by 16 runs. Both sides claimed that its opponents' umpire favoured his own side.

At Derby, the home side lost two wickets for three runs before T. Foster came in. Eventually Foster was out for 101 made out of 147 in $2\frac{1}{2}$ hours. W. Cropper also batted well for 33 and Derbyshire's total was 217. Next day Yorkshire took their score to 181, with Grimshaw making the top score of 48, adding 76 for the ninth wicket with R. Peel (35 not out). When the second day ended the home side were 56 for eight so Yorkshire had recovered well. J. Richardson (who had taken seven for 76) was top scorer for Derbyshire with 15 as they were all out for 68. Peate took six for 12 in 27 overs. Yorkshire then lost three wickets for 44, but Ulyett (59 not out) and Emmett (24 not out) took Yorkshire to a score of 105 for three to win the game by seven wickets.

Moving down to Hove, Yorkshire won the toss and made 208. A last-wicket stand saved Sussex from having to follow on. Juniper, with 23 not out, helped by Tester, took the score from 104 for nine to 134 all out. In their second innings Yorkshire, with Flaxington, in his first match, making 57 and Ephraim Lockwood 50, advanced to 285. Requiring 355 to win, Sussex collapsed to 153 all out, with George Ulyett taking five for 20.

At Cheltenham, Gloucestershire won the toss and W.G. (38) and E. M. Grace (37) put on 73 for their first wicket and then W. O. Moberley scored 40 before W. W. F. Pullen (aged 16) played a perfect innings of 71, as Gloucestershire were dismissed for 256. Overnight rain then made the pitch difficult. Ulyett with 29 and Hall 37 both batted well in Yorkshire's first innings of 115, but on following on, Yorkshire's batting, apart from 35 from Emmett, failed to rise to the occasion as they were dismissed for 96. Gloucestershire won by an innings and 45 runs.

At Bramall Lane, Yorkshire reached 114 with S. Flaxington scoring 26 and T. Emmett 25 as they helped Yorkshire to recover from 60 for six. At the close of play Middlesex were 105 for two. On the next day Middlesex collapsed to 135 all out with Bates taking six for 33 and Peate four for 63. Bates then made a beligerent 50 for Yorkshire as he opened the innings but the only other stand of any moment was for the last wicket when I. Grimshaw (35 not out) and Hunter (13) added 27 to take Yorkshire to 159 all out. At the close of play Middlesex were 10 for none on their way to score 139 for victory. Unfortunately for them overnight rain rendered the Sheffield pitch suited for Peate's bowling, and Middlesex were all out for 118. Yorkshire won by 20 runs with Peate taking eight for 32 in 36 overs. A. J. Webbe carried his bat through the innings for 62 not out – a magnificent innings in such adverse conditions.

Kent outplayed Yorkshire at the Bat and Ball ground at Gravesend where Lord Harris (51) and W. H. Patterson began well with an opening stand of 90 but the rest took Kent only to 174, with Peate taking five for 35. Ulyett scored 41 but Yorkshire were bowled out for 106. Lord Harris was again in good form with 54 as Kent batted again and reached 185 all out. Needing 254 to win, Yorkshire never looked like achieving the task with five wickets going down for 39. They were bowled out for 152, and defeated by 101 runs. W. Foord-Kelcey took eight for 53 in a remarkable spell of bowling.

Yorkshire's two remaining matches took place during the Scarborough Week and innings victories were recorded over both MCC and I Zingari. Rain seriously affected the MCC match with the visitors winning the toss and putting Yorkshire in to bat; the home side duly completed their innings for 265 on the third day. There seemed only a remote chance of a finish when the MCC reached 59 before the second wicket fell, but then the visitors collapsed for 115 and 80. Peate took two for 19 and five for 47 and Emmett took eight for 52 and five for 31 in a hollow victory for the home side. In the other game Yorkshire finished the first day with their score at 299 for five with Bates scoring 76, and on the second day went on to score 407 with Ephraim Lockwood (104 not out) and H. E. Rhodes (63) taking their sixth-wicket partnership to 119. In reply G. B. Studd (43) and his brother C.T. (30) alone played Peate with confidence as the spin bowler took five for 46 and when the I Zingari batted again the Hon Alfred Lyttelton (40) and his brother Edward (56) gave I Zingari a good start before they again collapsed for 190. Emmett took five for 58 and Peate five for 75.

Yorkshire's record of 11 wins, nine defeats and four draws – their biggest programme ever to date – meant that they were well behind Lancashire and Nottinghamshire in any comparative list of results of the first-class counties, but in fact they were theoretically as good as the other two sides when at their best. Ulyett headed the batting averages with 1,158 runs at 28.95 with Ephraim Lockwood in second place with 742 runs at 23.18. Bates was next with 731 at 17.82 while Emmett scored 569 at 16.72. Hall was again disappointing with 526 runs at 14.62. Grimshaw scored 462 runs at 14.00 and Peate scored 332 runs at 10.70. The only other batsman to come forward was the Hon M. B. Hawke, who scored 343 runs at 14.91, showing good form on several occasions.

The bowling was in the hands of six bowlers in all, with Hill missing several matches. Emmett headed the bowling averages with 79 wickets at 10.65 each, followed by Peate with 165 wickets at 11.13, which made him the outstanding bowler in the country. R. Peel took 29 wickets at 12.75, Ulyett 47 at 14.38, a greatly improved record, W. Bates 70 at 18.02 and A. Hill 30 at 18.66 each.

HIS LORDSHIP IS GIVEN THE REINS

BETWEEN 11 OCTOBER AND 15 NOVEMBER 1882, the Rules of the Yorkshire CCC were again pasted into the minutes book and after the phrase in Rule II (two): '. . . and of one representative from each of the following districts, viz . . .' had been added in pencil the following: '. . . Bradford, Huddersfield, Halifax, Hull, Dewsbury, Leeds and York.'

The minutes of 15 November state that the seven representatives of the towns mentioned above attended their first meeting of the committee, except that the member for York appeared to be absent.

There was a committee meeting held in April 1883 in which one resolution read: 'That T. Emmett be re-appointed Captain until the Hon M. B. Hawke plays.' That was the first intimation of the Hon M. B. Hawke taking over the captaincy, although newspapers in their reports of matches referred to Hawke as being captain even when Emmett was in the team, particularly in the last two matches at Scarborough in 1882. The Association of Cricket Statisticians, in *First Class Cricket Matches 1882*, placed an asterisk against Hawke's name in both those matches to signify that he was the captain. After abortive research in *Cricket, Wisden* and both *Lillywhite* annuals, the problem was referred to Lord Hawke's 'Recollections and Reminiscences', where he stated that Emmett offered him (Hawke) the captaincy during the 1882 season but that he replied: 'No, no, I prefer to play under you for the season and to pick up a few wrinkles'. He went on to state that seven amateurs played for Yorkshire in that season but always Tom was captain. In the absence of anything different in the Yorkshire committee minutes then this explanation of that little problem must be considered the correct one.*

In 1883 Yorkshire started off their programme with a match at Lord's on 21 May in which the home side suffered defeat by ten wickets. MCC made 125 all out, but Yorkshire were dismissed for only 121. In the second innings, MCC were bowled out for 113. Yorkshire then sent Ulyett in with the captain, and the former in a brilliant display scored 79 not out as he and Emmett (35 not out) knocked off the runs without loss in about two hours.

Frank Howe Sugg, a brother of Walter Sugg, took part in this match and seven others for Yorkshire in 1883, averaging ten with the bat. A right-hand batsman, very strong on the leg-side, he appeared

*Rob Brooke, a founder of ACS and one of the compilers of the aforementioned book, agrees with this interpretation.

for Derbyshire in 1884–86 and for Lancashire in 1887–99, scoring 16 first-class centuries during his career and 11,859 runs, at an average of 24.45. He also assisted Players *v* Gentlemen and England *v* Australia. He was also captain of Sheffield Wednesday, Derby County and Burnley, and shone too at swimming, billiards, rifle shooting, bowls, weightlifting, putting the shot and throwing the cricket ball (115 yards). He also excelled at long-distance running and was one of the finest all-round sportsmen ever. He was a first-class umpire in 1926–27. He was the fifteenth non-Yorkshireman to play for the County.

At Fenner's, Cambridge University won the toss and batted and made 105. Yorkshire finished with 176. In their second innings Cambridge did a little better with M. B. Hawke making 37 as they were dismissed for 155. At the close of play Yorkshire were 7–0 but with rain washing out the last day, the match was abandoned as a draw.

At Dewsbury, Yorkshire compiled a formidable 275 against Kent, with Bates (79) and Ephraim Lockwood (59) putting on 97 for the fourth wicket. At the end of the day, Kent were 33 for six and were well on their way to defeat. Kent eventually reached 65 and following on were bowled out again for 79. Harrison and Peate bowled unchanged as Yorkshire won by an innings and 131 runs. Harrison took six for 27 and five for 49 and Peate four for 30 and four for 29.

After such a hollow victory it was perhaps typical of Yorkshire cricket of the 1880s that they should lose to Sussex at Bramall Lane by three runs. Sussex won the toss and after losing early wickets, managed to reach 182. Yorkshire finished the day with 95 for nine, but on the next morning, Peate (29 not out) took Yorkshire to 126. For Sussex, a fourth wicket partnership of 62 enabled them to score 128, and a fifth-wicket stand of 52 between E. Lockwood (44) and Hall (42 not out) gave Yorkshire ideas of victory with the score at 123 for five. While Hall stood firm the score steadily rose until at 177 for seven, needing only eight for victory, they suddenly collapsed to 181 all out, and Sussex ran out victors by three runs.

Middlesex won the toss in a well-fought match at Lord's and scored 160, to which Yorkshire replied with 161, with Ulyett playing an attacking innings of 62. Middlesex were all out for 162, and after Yorkshire had lost two wickets for 27 Ulyett (69), in another fine display, was joined by Hall and they added 89 for the third wicket. Hall (63 not out) stood firm as Yorkshire won the game by five wickets.

Rain spoilt the Nottinghamshire match at Bramall Lane where the bowlers were always on top. Yorkshire were dismissed for 90 and Nottinghamshire were 27 for six when William Gunn came to the crease at the close of play. A crowd of 10,000 had watched the day's play, which continued on the next day between showers; Gunn drove cleanly and with vigour and was 42 not out when Nottinghamshire were out for 87. In Yorkshire's second innings Ulyett made 40 in his usual style as Yorkshire were finally out for 95 on the third morning. Needing 99 to win Nottinghamshire had scored 45 for six when more rain finished the match at 3.30. Peate took five for 17.

On 2 July 1883, the Hon Martin Bladen Hawke made his first appearance as captain of the Yorkshire side at Trent Bridge against Nottinghamshire, having finished his term at Cambridge University. M. B. Hawke had played two matches for Yorkshire in 1881 and had played regularly in 1882, when he came down from Cambridge. A right-hand batsman and occasional bowler, he was born at Willingham Rectory (Lincs) in 1860 and was a member of an old Yorkshire family. He was the 14th cricketer to play for Yorkshire who had been born outside the county boundaries. His father was Rector of Willingham but moved to Wighill Park on inheriting the title in 1874 and M. B. Hawke lived there from 1874 to 1924. He was educated at Eton where he was in the eleven in 1878–79 and was in the Cambridge University eleven in 1882, 1883 and 1885, when he captained the side. He succeeded his father as 6th Baron in 1887. He was the captain of Yorkshire from 1883 to 1910 and has been credited with doing more for professional cricketers than any other person as well as with transforming the Yorkshire team from a side of undisciplined but talented players into a team of professionals who earned and deserved a respect that they had never received before. As a cricketer, he was a hard-hitting batsman, tall and strong, who could defend when the situation demanded. He was not in the top class, but he did score 16,794 runs in first-class cricket at an average of 20.15, including 13 centuries. He was a very safe catch and dependable fielder who made every effort to improve in that department, as, indeed, he attempted to improve the fielding of Yorkshire sides. He took part in five Test matches and toured Australia, India, North America, South Africa, West Indies and Argentine. He was President of Yorkshire CCC from 1898 until his death in 1938. He is credited with introducing winter pay for cricketers and the Yorkshire badge and the Club colours. He was a president of the MCC, and served on the cricket committee and as treasurer. He was also a good soccer player, playing for the Remnants with C. W. Alcock. He used to invite the Yorkshire team to his home at Wighill Park for many years.

Nottinghamshire won the toss in Hawke's first match as skipper, and recovered from 19 for three to 151. Yorkshire, in reply made a wretched start and were 52 for eight at the close of play. The innings closed for 61, but following on, Hall (16) and Ulyett (61), put on 61 for

81

Yorkshire's first wicket. However, Yorkshire were dismissed for 114, and Nottinghamshire went on to win by nine wickets. It was hardly an auspicious start for the new captain, who scored two and three.

Hon M. B. Hawke was missing from the Yorkshire side when they visited Old Trafford, and Lancashire, winning the toss, made a score of 79 with Teddy Roper making the top score of 23. Harrison took seven for 43, bowling five of the Lancashire batsmen. Early next day Yorkshire were all out for 143 and Lancashire could muster only 120 as Ulyett took four for 25 and Emmett three for 13. Hall and Lockwood with an unfinished stand of 38 for the third wicket took Yorkshire to an eight-wicket win.

On the Spa Ground at Gloucester, the Doctors Grace started with an opening stand of 62 towards the home side's 143 and at the close of play Yorkshire were 106 for one. By lunchtime next day Yorkshire had been dismissed for 196, with Ulyett's 80 containing three sixes. After Gloucestershire had scored 7 for one, there was no further play and the match was abandoned.

In a game that lasted for only two days but attracted 19,000 spectators to Bramall Lane, Lancashire won the toss and were soon dismissed for 83. Ulyett completed the hat-trick in his five for 16 and Harrison took five for 25 as nine of ten batsmen were bowled. Yorkshire took much longer to score 93, with Bates top-scoring with 19. Lancashire were then 68 for seven before Barlow (33) and the Rev Vernon Royle (38) added 31 for the eighth wicket and Lancashire were finally all out for 127. Yorkshire set about their task of scoring 118 to win with Ulyett scoring 61 out of 94 in a brilliant innings, and Hall went on to score 30 as Yorkshire won easily by eight wickets.

Yorkshire spent the whole of the first day at Derby in scoring 299. Hall played an excellent innings of 74, and after eight wickets had fallen for 195, Emmett (49) and J. Hunter (51 not out) put on 98 in fine style. At the end of the second day with rain interrupting, Derbyshire had taken their score to only 79 for two. On the final day Derbyshire were dismissed for 220 and Yorkshire were 20 for no wicket at the close.

At Holbeck, Yorkshire won the toss and an opening stand of 35 between Ulyett (21) and Hall (22) gave them a good start which Bates improved upon with an excellent 55 as Yorkshire finished with 116. In reply, Surrey were all out in 32 overs for 31, as Peate took eight for 5 and Bates two for 21. Following on, Surrey were dismissed for 82, with Harrison taking five for 23 and Peate three for 25.

The return match at The Oval saw Louis Hall score 35 out of 70 for five as Yorkshire won the toss and batted. The Hon M. B. Hawke (60), helped by E. Lumb and Peel, hoisted the total to 181. Surrey replied with 166. On the last day E. Lumb scored 60 not out in a very careful display of batting, and with Emmett (50) added 81 for the eighth wicket. When Yorkshire were dismissed for 251 Surrey needed 267 to win but hardly had the time to get them. Surrey recovered from 114 for seven to 226 for eight at the close, with J. M. Read not out. Owing to Hunter injuring his hand in the first Surrey innings, Lockwood kept wicket and missed many chances which undoubtedly cost Yorkshire victory.

At Park Avenue, the Graces opened with a partnership of 53 runs, and J. Cranston came in and carried his bat through the innings for 67 not out but no one was able to stay with him for long and Gloucestershire were dismissed for 177. At the close of play Yorkshire were 118 for five, but Bates (57) and Emmett (44) added 73, and when Peel and Peate came together they took the score from 189 for seven to 315 for eight with Peel scoring 74 and Peate 61. Yorkshire were all out for 328. Once again the Graces gave Gloucestershire a good start, putting on 94, but they were all out for 213. Emmett and Harrison each had eight wickets in the match. Yorkshire scored 64 for two in winning the game which 13,000 attended on the first two days.

Ulyett (36) and Hall (20) put on 50 for Yorkshire's first wicket at Bramall Lane against Derbyshire and later Emmett scored 37 as Yorkshire reached 173. When Derbyshire batted, only a last-wicket stand of 23 advanced them to 70 all out as Peate took five for 36 and Harrison four for 26. In their second innings, Harrison took four for 7 and Peel four for 29 as Derbyshire were completely outplayed. It was a very feeble batting display by the visitors.

At Gravesend, Yorkshire batted the whole of the first day to score 349 for seven with Ephraim Lockwood scoring 208 out of 297 in $4\frac{1}{4}$ hours batting. It was the first double century ever to be made for Yorkshire, who were eventually dismissed for 392. When Kent batted Lord Harris gave two magnificent batting displays with 80 not out when he carried his bat through the Kent first innings of 148 and then 79 in 65 minutes in the second innings as Kent collapsed again for 150. Peate took five for 40 in Kent's first innings and Ulyett five for 69. In the follow-on Emmett took four for 34 and Harrison four for 35.

Moving to Hove, Sussex, batting first, scored 174, with Bates taking five for 55. Hall then carried his bat through the Yorkshire innings and in six hours' batting, made 124 not out, out of 331. Sussex's second-innings score was 105 as they lost by an innings and 52 runs, with Bates taking six for 57. The match was played for Charlwood's benefit.

The next match was at Fartown against Middlesex, who won the toss and scored a formidable 305. E. Lumb with a patient 70 not out in $4\frac{1}{2}$ hours and Ulyett (65) helped Yorkshire reach 236. Middlesex made

242 in the second innings with Peate taking five for 61 and Peel four for 53. In the 190 minutes left to obtain 312 to win, Yorkshire scored 198 for four with Hall making 87 not out and Ulyett 32.

Yorkshire finished their season at Scarborough against the MCC and scored 228 after batting all day after a late start. Bates made 75 and Peate 60. The MCC soon lost six for 72 but recovered to 222, with Emmett taking five for 81 and Peate four for 40. On the last day Ulyett scored 84 and then Lockwood hit 79 in fine style as Yorkshire scored 262. When stumps were drawn the MCC had scored 63 for two.

In all matches in 1883 Yorkshire won ten, lost two and drew seven. It was the best season that Yorkshire had enjoyed since 1870 and the new captain undoubtedly had an influence on the team's performance. Nottinghamshire were generally recognised as the Champion County, although some credited Yorkshire with the top place.

Hall topped the batting averages with 821 runs at 41.05 – easily his best season – and Ulyett was second with 956 runs at 32.96. Lockwood scored 671 runs at 27.79 and then came E. Lumb with 277 runs at 25.17 and Bates with 571 at 21.14. Hunter, Emmett, Hawke, Peel and Peate all had their good days with the bat but Emmett was generally disappointing, while Grimshaw had a very poor season.

Harrison in his first season topped the bowling averages with the excellent record of 88 wickets at 11.82, with Peate next with 70 at 12.65, followed by Emmett 39 at 13.75, Bates 51 at 16.05, Peel 39 at 16.69, and Ulyett 31 at 17.12. Possessing a good all-round attack with three quick bowlers and three slow, Yorkshire had as strong an attack as any other county, even if Allen Hill, plagued with injury, had dropped out of the side. Harrison, a genuinely fast bowler, had filled his place with rather more success than anyone expected. Behind the stumps, Hunter was considered as sound a keeper as any in the game but did miss matches through niggling injuries. The future nevertheless looked bright, although the coming season would see the last of Ephraim Lockwood after a fine career in which he could fairly claim to be the outstanding batsman for a decade and more.

On 8 April 1884, at a committee meeting, it was resolved that '. . . the Hon M. B. Hawke be Captain . . . and that L. Hall be Captain in the absence of Mr Hawke'. When the team was picked for the opening matches Emmett was considered to be only a reserve but came into the side in view of the absence of E. Lumb, who had been chosen to play for the whole season but in fact was unable to play at all. Frank Sugg was another who was expected to play in the early matches but in fact turned out for his native county. Grimshaw was another who was not considered yet appeared in the opening games.

In the first match at Moreton-in-March against Gloucestershire Peate performed the hat-trick and finished with 18-10-13-6.

After being defeated by MCC at Lord's, Yorkshire went to Fenner's where a weak University side was no match for the county. Cambridge won the toss and were bowled out for 114 with 26 extras as the highest score. Emmett had the remarkable analysis of 53-39-34-6. At the close of play, Hall was 49 not out and Bates 80 not out and the score was 163 for two. On the next day the pair took their third wicket stand to 219 when Bates was out for 133 after 3 hours and 25 minutes at the crease. Then Grimshaw came in and after they had added a further 105 Hall was dismissed for 116 at 347 after $4\frac{1}{4}$ hours' batting. Peel then scored 57 in an hour as he and Grimshaw added 96. Grimshaw went on to a chanceless 115 as he became the third centurion of the innings. This was the first occasion in first-class cricket that three batsmen had each scored a century in the same innings, the total being 539. When the 'varsity batted again they were more successful with H. W. Bainbridge (29) and J. A. Turner (63 not out) helping Cambridge from 100 for eight to an all out score of 222, F. Marchant scoring 27 and H. E. Knatchbull-Huggesen making 21. Ulyett took three for 22.

Thomas Arthur Wardall made his debut for Yorkshire in the above game and he failed to score in his only innings and took two catches. A good, sound, and rather over-cautious right-hand batsman he also bowled slow, very slow donkey-drops which were very useful at times. He also played in a couple of games in 1887 but played regularly in the side from 1891 to 1893 and four further games in 1894. For 30 years he was coach at Rossall School.

At Bramall Lane, Yorkshire lost the toss to Kent who batted and were at one time 140 for three before collapsing to 151 all out. Frank Hearne (61), Lord Harris (26) and A. J. Thornton made 31 before Ulyett finished with seven for 33 including a spell when his last five wickets cost one run. Yorkshire made a good start before losing Ulyett for 30 out of 50 but Hall added 46 with Bates who reached 36 and at the close of play Hall was 61 not out out of 153 for four. Peate then scored 26 to help Hall to obtain his 100 at which score he was run out and Yorkshire were soon all out for 250 as Herbert Hearne took five for 84. Kent had very little to offer in their second innings as they were bowled out for 129 with Frank Hearne scoring 32 and Lord Harris 38. Peel took three for 25 and Bates two for 7 as Yorkshire went on to win by eight wickets.

George Robert Baker played his first of seven matches for Yorkshire in 1884 in the above match but he did little of note. He played for Lancashire from 1887–99.

Another debutant in the Kent match was Peter Pullan who scored 14 and took one catch and never played again for his county.

At Lord's there was only time for Middlesex to score 62 for two after being put in to bat with I. D. Walker 40 not out. Rain ended the game at that point. Against the Australians at Park Avenue on what can only be described as a treacherous and sodden pitch, only Bates with 24 out of 55 could play Spofforth or Palmer, and Midwinter with 18 was top scorer for the visitors who replied with 60, Emmett taking six for 27 and Peate four for 29. Yorkshire were dismissed again for 72 in their second innings (Emmett 16); this time Palmer took six for 29 and Spofforth four for 32. A second wicket stand between Alec Bannerman and Midwinter virtually won the match for the Australians.

A somewhat weakened Sussex were far from a match for Yorkshire at Bramall Lane, where Sussex made a good start with Tester (46) and E. J. McCormick putting on 59 for their second wicket. Only G. N. Wyatt (17) prospered after that as Sussex were all out for 133 with Emmett taking eight for 32. Yorkshire soon lost four for 42 in reply but were 160 for five at the close. On the next day Yorkshire finished with 285, Hall carrying his bat through the innings for 128 not out in slightly over four hours. Sussex then collapsed to Bates giving Yorkshire an easy victory.

At the same ground three days later, Yorkshire won the toss against Nottinghamshire and soon lost six wickets for 34 but some resistance took their score to 129. Nottinghamshire, however, collapsed to 117 all out, Emmett taking four for 18 in 43 overs and 33 maidens. In their second innings Yorkshire were completely routed by Shaw (six for 16) and it was stated that 'the crowd laughed with irritating frequency' during Yorkshire's second innings batting which closed at 40 all out. Set 53 to win Shrewsbury and Scotton put on 20 without loss but they soon lost six wickets for 32 before Attewell and Wright took the score to 49 for seven. Then Wright played a ball to point and Lockwood appealed for a brilliant catch but neither umpire saw the catch and Wright was given not out with the result that the crowd hooted the umpires as Nottinghamshire went on to win a narrow victory by three wickets.

The Hon M. B. Hawke had appeared for Cambridge University against Surrey – his only appearance for the University in 1884 – and in the next match appeared for MCC against them when Yorkshire were playing at Derby. It seemed rather a strange state of affairs.

Derbyshire won the toss and scored 98, Peate taking five for 30. Ulyett soon reached 43 in Yorkshire's reply and then Fred Lee with 34 and Peel ensured that Yorkshire obtained a lead of 50. Derbyshire lost seven wickets for 28 in their second innings before G. G. Walker made a determined 29 not out, the all-out total being 57. Emmett took seven for 20, Yorkshire going on to a comfortable ten wicket win.

The Hon M. B. Hawke returned to the team for the next match at

Old Trafford against Lancashire who won the toss and gave a dreadful batting display until E. E. Steel came in and hit 51 out of 73. They were finally dismissed for 123, Ulyett taking five for 38. Yorkshire replied with 181. Lancashire slipped to 26 for four in their second innings but H. B. Steel (48) and his brother E.E. with 30 not out helped Lancashire to a total of 154 with Peate taking four for 42 and Peel two for 10. Yorkshire soon lost two wickets for 7 before Lee (19) was out at 41 for 3 and Ulyett (32) went on with Hawke (22) to take the score to 69 for six. Ulyett took Yorkshire to 92 for seven before he was out. Yorkshire won narrowly by three wickets.

The return match with Lancashire took place at Bramall Lane where Yorkshire won the toss and were dismissed for 128, Bates returning figures of seven for 38. At the close of play Lancashire had scored 107 for four with A. G. Steel out for 37 and J. Briggs 34 not out. Next morning Briggs went on batting well to take his score to an unbeaten 75 at which stage Lancashire were all out for 170 with Peate taking seven for 46. In the second innings Yorkshire lost half their wickets for 15 but staggered to 72 all out. Needing only 31 to win Lancashire lost four wickets before reaching the target. The match was played for the benefit of Allen Hill and 6000 watched the first day's play.

Harry Haley made his first appearance for Yorkshire in the above match and he continued to play in odd matches for the county until 1898. From 1891–1902 he was professional at Leeds scoring 10,440 runs for them and taking 876 wickets and later played for Wakefield before returning to Headingley. Also a cricket-bat maker in Leeds and Bradford, he was founder of H. Hayley Ltd, Sports Outfitters, of Corn Exchange, Wakefield which was still in existence in 1951. A short, powerful figure and a typical Yorkshireman, he died in St John's Nursing Home, Wakefield aged 62.

Another defeat followed at Trent Bridge where Yorkshire won the toss but were dismissed for 95 in 108.3 overs. William Attewell took five for 44 and Flowers five for 23. At the close of play Nottinghamshire were 46 for four and they went on to be all out for 114. When Yorkshire batted again the innings was completely dominated by William Bates who scored 116 out of 137 in 2 hours and 35 minutes, a brilliant innings which he had never bettered during his career. Rawlin (14) helped him to add 91 for the fourth wicket in a very sound defensive display and at the close of play Yorkshire had been dismissed for 199. Nottinghamshire then opened with a stand of 90 between Shrewsbury (61) and Scotton (33) and the result was a splendid Nottinghamshire victory by seven wickets. This match was played for J. C. Shaw's Benefit and proved an outstanding success financially.

At Dewsbury, Surrey were the visitors, but rain ruined the match which was drawn.

Yorkshire returned to something like form in their match at Bradford against Gloucestershire. Gloucestershire won the toss and batted. The Graces were absent owing to the death of their mother. Only F. Townsend with 44 batted well for the visitors who were dismissed for 117 with Peel taking six for 40. In their innings Yorkshire totalled 301. In their second innings, which for a time was played in thick fog, Gloucestershire were dismissed for 127 with Peel taking five for 47. Yorkshire won with an innings and 57 runs to spare.

Mr William Henry Woodhouse, a talented right-handed batsman, played in nine matches for Yorkshire in 1884 and 85. He was a member of the Manningham Cricket Club, living in Bradford where he died in 1938.

Yorkshire were not at full strength when they went down to Gravesend for the Kent match. MacKinnon hit brilliantly for 102 out of 185 for six in just over 3 hours but Kent were all out for 205 with Peate bowling very well to take eight for 63. In an hour before the close, Yorkshire scored 99 without loss, Ulyett (35) and Bates (53) both driving well. Next day Ulyett left at 105 but Grimshaw (35) helped Bates to take the score to 176 for two. A. Sowden, Peel, Rawlin and W. Harris, a newcomer who scored 25, all made useful scores as Yorkshire were all out for 338. When Kent batted again Lord Harris and MacKinnon each scored 30 but they were all out for 137. Yorkshire went on to win by ten wickets.

William Harris made two appearances for Yorkshire in 1884 and two in 1887 but his 25 in the above match was his only successful score.

Middlesex won the toss at Bramall Lane and sent in Yorkshire who soon lost four wickets for 40 after which Burton fell ill and was unable to bowl again in the innings. Hall and Grimshaw then came together to add 98 for the fifth wicket before Grimshaw left for 42 but Hall batting with more freedom than usual went on to score 96 in 2 hours and 25 minutes as Yorkshire amassed 212. Middlesex replied with 202 and at the end of the second day, Yorkshire were 32 for one having lost Bates but there had been rain which prevented a start until after lunch. On the last morning Hall and Ulyett came together at 50 for two and added 173 when Ulyett was out after a brilliant innings of 107. Hall went on to add 95 for the sixth wicket with Peel before he himself was out for 135 – his fourth century of the season made in $4\frac{3}{4}$ hours – with the score at 342. Peel went on to score 50 and at the close Yorkshire were all out for 390, the match being drawn.

On the Hove ground, Sussex gained one of the most spectacular victories in their history when they defeated Yorkshire by an innings and 19 runs. The home side won the toss and after losing Tester at 31,

H. Whitfield (80) and W. Newham (100) took the score to 190 before they lost their second wicket, Newham having batted for $3\frac{1}{4}$ hours for his century in which he gave a chanceless display. Whitfeld was then joined by Walter Humphreys (65) and after adding 51 Whitfeld's fine display of defensive cricket came to an end after $5\frac{1}{2}$ hours at the crease. Humphreys was sixth man out at 279 and W. Blackman hit hard for his 53 and the innings was over at 359, 292 overs having been bowled by Yorkshire. Yorkshire then went in and were dismissed for 164 with Humphreys bowling well to take seven for 57. Following on Yorkshire were bowled out for 176, giving Sussex a brilliant victory.

At Bradford, Yorkshire beat Derbyshire by ten wickets. The county then went on to a rain-ruined draw at The Oval where W. W. Read scored 42 out of Surrey's 110 as Emmett took six for 30 and Yorkshire replied on the only day that cricket took place with 134, Ulyett scoring 36. Surrey were 11 for no wicket when the game finished. At Scarborough for the MCC match the Hon M. B. Hawke returned to the side but the first day of the match went very much the visitors' way with Yorkshire bowled out for 96, Ulyett scoring 21 and newcomer, H. Leadbeater, making 18 not out. MCC were dismissed for 186 with Emmett taking four for 61. Hawke opened for Yorkshire in the second innings and was dismissed for 18 out of 19; Hall was then joined by Ulyett who was straight into his stride although he lost Hall (20) at 89 and when rain stopped play just before the close of the second day, Ulyett was 99 not out and Grimshaw 29 not out out of 169 for two. On the last day Ulyett and Grimshaw took their stand to 109. Ulyett, who hit three sixes in all, went on to score 146 not out as Yorkshire were dismissed for 248. On a pitch now helping the bowlers, the MCC were soon in trouble although Barnes, Gunn and Flowers all got into the twenties. They were bowled out for 116 to give Yorkshire victory by 42 runs. Emmett bowled extremely well to take six for 31.

Mr Harry Leadbeater, a free-scoring left-hand batsman, was a native of Scarborough. A Scarborough player all his life, in 1888 he scored 178 when Scarborough scored 613. He also toured Holland with Yorkshire Wanderers in 1893 and played in many important matches in the North and East Ridings.

Yorkshire finished the season with 10 wins, 6 defeats and 4 draws which was most disappointing in comparison with the previous season. Unlike 1883; there was no doubt about the destination of the title 'champion county' – that honour went to Nottinghamshire.

Louis Hall had a splendid season with the bat – his best ever for Yorkshire – notching four centuries and leading the side for most of the season in the absence of Hon M. B. Hawke. He scored 941 runs at an average of 31.36. Ulyett also performed very well and scored a couple of centuries; his aggregate being 803 runs at 27.68. Bates scored 700 runs at 23.33 and Grimshaw 627 at 20.90. Fred Lee did well towards the end of the season as he scored 334 runs at 20.87.

Tom Emmett finished top of the bowling averages with the excellent record of 87 wickets at 10.98 closely followed by Peate with 81 at 12.37. George Ulyett took 42 at 14.19 and Peel, with limited opportunities, took 39 at 15 runs each.

Hunter had another excellent season and thoroughly earned his selection as keeper to Shaw's team in Australia. The Hon M. B. Hawke only took part in six games and his captaincy could have had little influence on the team's progress. Perhaps the team was a top-class bowler short and a batsman was needed to replace Lockwood who lost his place in the side.

Yorkshire began their new season of 1885 by scoring 233 for five against Sussex on the first day. Ulyett (53) and Bates (50) added 93 for the third wicket and then W. H. Woodhouse (63) and F. Lee (60) put on 122 for the fifth wicket before Peel (44), Emmett (53) and Peate (31) took Yorkshire to a formidable 377. When the weather finally finished the match Sussex had been dismissed for 105 with Peel taking four for 29.

The Hon M. B. Hawke was still at Cambridge University in 1885 thus missing Yorkshire's early matches though on 25 May he represented the North v South at Lord's – the only Yorkshireman to do so. On the same dates Yorkshire met Kent and were bowled out very cheaply for 86 with Alec Hearne taking five for 13 as Grimshaw was the only batsman to make as many as 21. Kent scored very slowly in reply but Frank Hearne (37) and W. H. Patterson (29) added 64 for the third wicket but they then struggled to obtain a lead of 19 with Peel taking seven for 51. On the following day Yorkshire commenced their second innings and once again it was a procession although Hall stood firm to carry his bat throughout the innings for 32 out of 81. Kent only needed 63 to win and they obtained these for the loss of two wickets.

At Fenner's the Hon M. B. Hawke beat Hall at tossing and chose to bat first. At the end of the first day Yorkshire were 65 without loss in reply to Cambridge's total of 138. Next morning Hall (38) and Ulyett took their stand to 77 before the latter left for 48 after which Fred Lee (20) and Grimshaw (23) added 45 for the sixth wicket and Yorkshire gained a lead of 30 with C. Toppin taking four for 31. In their second innings, in spite of C. W. Rock batting $1\frac{3}{4}$ hours for 18, Cambridge were all out for 44 with Peate taking five for 12 in 39 overs and Ulyett three for 10. Yorkshire won by nine wickets.

Mr Albert George Day of the Dewsbury Savile Club made his debut in the above match, but only played in five other games for the county.

The Yorkshire fixture at Lord's was arranged for two days only as Derby Day was the third day of the match. J. S. Russel with 33 and S. C. Newton (26) helped the MCC to a total of 148 but in reply Yorkshire could only score 69. After such a drab display MCC found runs coming easily in the second innings, hitting 449 for four with William Gunn (203) and William Barnes 140 not out adding 330 for the fourth wicket in 280 minutes. Barnes batted for $5\frac{1}{2}$ hours for his score and Gunn for 4 hours and 50 minutes.

Joseph Merritt Preston, a pretty and stylish right-handed batsman with a good defence and a very capable medium pace off-break bowler, played for Yorkshire for the first time in this match. He had four seasons with the county before dropping out during 1889. He had toured Australia and New Zealand with Shaw's and Shrewsbury's team in 1887–88 but he never realised the great hopes expected of him. A victim of his own weaknesses, he was a smart, well-dressed man and after leaving Yorkshire he was believed to have been engaged at Swinton and Farnworth. He died at his father's house, the Blue Bell Inn, at Windhill, from lung congestion following a chill in 1890 aged 26. In 1883 he had killed A. Luty (who had been married for only seven days) when bowling to him and he was buried in Yeadon Cemetery close to Luty along with Charlie Dawson who was keeping wicket in the same game. He was only 24 when he played his last game for Yorkshire.

The day after the Derby, Yorkshire returned to Lord's to meet Middlesex who won the toss and scored 231 with A. J. Webbe (38) and J. E. West (42) opening with a stand of 80; wickets fell fairly frequently until C. E. Cottrell came in to make the top score of the innings (46) with some good drives in a total of 231. By the close, after Ulyett (71) and Hall (32) had opened with a stand of 107, Yorkshire had collapsed to 158 for seven. They finally reached 222. In the final innings Yorkshire required 123. Hall lost Ulyett with 18 on the board but Bates (37) helped him to add 57 for the second wicket and then Grimshaw (23) helped Hall to take the score to 106 before the fourth wicket fell. At the end Hall was 39 not out as Yorkshire won by four wickets.

Alfred Wormald who kept wicket in seven matches for Yorkshire from 1885 to 1891 commencing with the above match was a right-hand batsman and very capable wicket-keeper, who understudied Joseph Hunter on occasions and was in contention for a regular place in the Yorkshire team in 1888 when Hunter had to retire. His local cricket was for Gomersal. Around 1924 he was a publican in Bradford and died at Gomersal in 1940.

After losing the first day because of rain at Huddersfield, Derbyshire after winning the toss were bowled out for 103. Lacking Ulyett, whose father had died, Yorkshire lost Hall for 1 but Bates (55) and

Grimshaw (27), batting in a restrained manner, took the score to 76 for two but the side slumped to 122 for nine when Peate with 29 not out and Hunter (10) added 40 for the last wicket. Derbyshire then gave a wretched batting display being dismissed for 53, Yorkshire winning by an innings and six runs.

A return with Cambridge University took place at Bramall Lane where rain and high scoring created a draw.

At Old Trafford for the Roses match, only a stand of 90 between F. Taylor (39) and A. N. Hornby (61) stopped Yorkshire's bowlers as Lancashire were dismissed for 168. Harrison, back in the side after a long absence, took four for 64 and Peel four for 24 and at the end of the first day, Yorkshire were 117 for two with Hall and Grimshaw scoring most of the runs, but the rest of the team collapsed to 158 all out. Lancashire found runs difficult to obtain but W. E. Leach batted soundly for $2\frac{1}{4}$ hours for 39 out of 112 for eight and Lancashire reached 138. Emmett bowled very well to take seven for 50. In a curtailed last day, Yorkshire batted 85 overs to score 75 for six with Hall scoring 31, as rain returned soon after tea allowing Yorkshire to get away with a draw.

On a very slow wicket at Bramall Lane, Yorkshire lost the toss and took 129 overs to bowl Nottinghamshire out for 122. After 90 minutes Yorkshire were 59 for two at the close of play with Bates out for 23. Hall went on to score 39 after batting for 25 overs without scoring a run and went on to bat for $3\frac{1}{4}$ hours. When Preston was the sixth to be out at 127, F. Lee (66 not out) and Emmett added 110 for the seventh wicket as Yorkshire reached 269 with Lee making his highest score for the County and Emmett driving and hitting to leg in brilliant fashion. Nottinghamshire batted out the rest of the match with little difficulty.

The return match with Nottinghamshire took place at Trent Bridge where Yorkshire batted all day to score 304 for five with Grimshaw batting $4\frac{1}{2}$ hours for 114 and putting on 106 for the third wicket with Bates (72). The Nottinghamshire fielding was very poor and next day Yorkshire took their total to 424 with Fred Lee scoring 101. Nottinghamshire replied with 187, and followed on. They made 209 in their second innings, giving Yorkshire a substantial win.

Ulyett and Hall gave Yorkshire a good start at the Spa Ground, Gloucester with an opening stand of 98 in two hours with Hall scoring 34 and Ulyett going to make 73. Grimshaw (44) and Bates (70) in 75 minutes put on 89 for the third wicket, after which Fred Lee came in to score a fine 68. Yorkshire were all out for 378 early on the second day. Gloucestershire made only 153 in reply. Following on W. G. Grace and Gilbert put on 80 for the first wicket. Gilbert, who went on to spend four hours over 102, received little support,

Gloucestershire being 222 all out and Yorkshire winning by an innings and 4 runs.

Against Surrey at Bramall Lane, Yorkshire won the toss and lost five wickets for 51 before F. Lee (39) and J. M. Preston (36) added 65 for the sixth wicket. They were all out for 154. J. Shuter scored 27 in reply but Surrey were 70 for five at the close of play and finally reached 104. In their second innings Ulyett scored 43 out of 58 put on for the first wicket after which some steady batting and quite dreadful catching from the Surrey side took Yorkshire to 240 for eight by the close of play. On the next morning they reached 275 with Louis Hall carrying his bat through the innings for 79 not out. Surrey were set 336 to win but were all out for 147 with Bates taking seven for 43.

At Fartown, William Bates was again in good form taking six for 85 as Lancashire were dismissed for 232. Yorkshire lost Ulyett for 40 before Bates came in and in $2\frac{1}{2}$ hours of brilliant batting scored 98 in spite of being dropped when 6. J. M. Preston and Emmett then added 90 for the seventh wicket as Yorkshire gained a 69 run lead. Briggs took four for 96 and then Lancashire lost two for 35 and though G. M. Kemp in an innings lasting 3 hours scored 109 out of 156, they were all out for 214. Left 146 to win in 170 minutes, Yorkshire lost two wickets for 19 but Bates hit 82 not out in 85 minutes to win the game by eight wickets.

On a fine batting surface at Bradford, Yorkshire won the toss against Gloucestershire and scored 236 after Ulyett was out for 30 of the first wicket partnership of 46. Hall (40) and Grimshaw (62) took the score to 118 for two but the rest of the side could only just double the score to 236. Dr W. G. Grace was at his best scoring 132 in $3\frac{1}{4}$ hours as Gloucestershire were finally dismissed for 287. W.G. was run out and protested strongly at the decision. Yorkshire were soon in trouble at 66 for four but Bates (84) and J. M. Preston carried the score to 153 for five by the close of the second day when J. M. Preston, after a very fine innings, went for 36; Bates was then 75 not out. Bates soon left next morning for 84 and the odds favoured Gloucestershire but Peel and Emmett (27) took the score to 211 for seven after which Peel's 62 in partnership with Joseph Hunter took the score to 275 before the eighth wicket fell. In the end Hunter was not out 62 as Yorkshire's innings closed for 325 and Gloucestershire were set 275 to win; an impossible task that they never attempted after Peate had bowled W. G. Grace for 1.

Yorkshire had very much the worse of a draw at Canterbury against Kent, rain interrupting the match.

At Derby, Yorkshire won the toss and were dismissed by Shacklock for 96. W. S. Eadie with 23 helped to put Derbyshire on top by the close of play as they reached 68 for four. On the next day,

93

W. Chatterton batted very well to score 62, adding 63 with F. H. Sugg (34) and 53 with E. A. J. Maynard (37) as they gained a lead of 127 runs on the first innings. Yorkshire batted much better in their second innings with Hall and Ulyett putting on 60 for the first wicket before Ulyett left for a dashing 48. Irwin Grimshaw scored 57 and he and Hall took the score to 86 before Hall went for 18 and then Fred Lee (35) helped Grimshaw to take the score to 155 for four in a stand of 69. Rain had stopped play on the third day and when Yorkshire were all out for 196, Shacklock had taken his match figures to 13 for 142. When play was resumed the home side were set to score 70 in 75 minutes but after losing two wickets without a run they struggled to 54 for five at the close.

Yorkshire met M. B. Hawke's eleven in a Charity match at Horsforth Hall Park ground on 13, 14 and 15 August in the only first-class match ever to take place on the ground. It was not considered to be one of the Yorkshire CCC fixtures, the ground being considered to be too small for county cricket. Ulyett and Hall gave Yorkshire a good start with a stand of 125 when Ulyett was bowled by Bainbridge for 73. Hall went on to score 44 out of 133 for three before being dismissed for 215. Hawke's eleven then lost seven wickets for 48 before recovering to score 150 with Hawke batting brilliantly for 42 not out. At the close of play on the second day, Yorkshire had scored 73 for three with Hall and Lee being not out. Hall went immediately next morning without addition and Lee only added two before R. Peel with 32 helped Yorkshire to a total of 136 with C. W. Rock taking eight for 36 in 43 overs; seven of his victims being bowled. Hawke's Eleven were set 202 to win in about three hours and won with three wickets to spare.

Yorkshire's next match was at Bramall Lane against Middlesex who won the toss and were dismissed for 169. J. M. Preston bowled better than ever before to take six for 37. Yorkshire then lost four wickets for 11 but Lee and Peel took the score to 74 by the close of play. Next morning the pair proceeded to put on 136 for the fifth wicket before Lee was dismissed for a faultless 72; Peel went on to score 71 as the home side was dismissed for 201. Middlesex were dismissed for 226 with Peate and Preston taking four wickets each. Yorkshire needed 195 to win. They soon lost four wickets for 39 and though Grimshaw (37) and Peel (17) took the score to 71 Yorkshire were dismissed for 145, Middlesex winning by 49 runs.

A heavy scoring draw at Hove followed in which there was never any likelihood of an outright result.

At The Oval, R. Abel (52) and J. Shuter (72) gave Surrey a good start by putting on 125 for the first wicket but Surrey collapsed to 187 all out. At the close Yorkshire were 14 without loss with rain early on

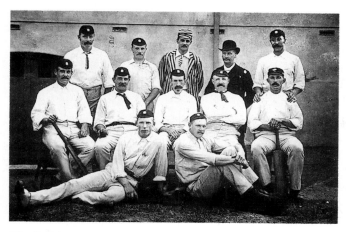

The Yorkshire team in 1885. Back row: G. Ulyett, R. Peel, W. H. Woodhouse, Mr. Turner (scorer), J. Hunter. Seated: W. Bates, E. Peate, L. Hall (captain), T. Emmett, F. Lee. Front: J. M. Preston, T. Grimshaw.

having prevented a prompt start. Fred Lee (47) and Ulyett (37) added 53 for Yorkshire's second wicket and then Bates (60) and Grimshaw (48) combined with the tail to take Yorkshire to 268. On the last day W. W. Read scored 28 and E. J. Diver made 53 out of 74 as Surrey made 202. Fred Lee held Yorkshire's innings together, making 48, and victory was achieved by three wickets.

The last match of Yorkshire's season took place at Scarborough against the MCC with each side fielding twelve men. Ulyett and Hall put on 67 for the first wicket before Hall was out for 27. Fred Lee (23) and Ulyett then took the score to 110. Ulyett left at 122 and then Grimshaw (29) helped H. Leadbeater to take the score to 187 and the latter was not dismissed until he had scored 65. The Hon M. B. Hawke also scored 38 as Yorkshire totalled 322. Interruptions from rain meant that at the end of the second day, the MCC had scored 102 for seven with C. I. Thornton making 63 out of 92, some big hitting being as usual a feature of his batting. All out for 165, William Bates took four for 23 and Emmett four for 45 and when the MCC batted again they finished at 156 for five. The match was drawn.

Yorkshire finished the season with 8 wins, 3 defeats and 11 draws. A satisfactory season's work although Nottinghamshire were the Champion County.

The leading batsman for Yorkshire was George Ulyett with 1035 runs at 34.37, just ahead of Fred Lee, who had a good season with 875 runs at 31.25. Grimshaw had his best season too with 888 runs, average 27.83, followed by Hall 797 runs, average 27.75. Bates could also boast a good season with 797 runs at 27.75. J. M. Preston did very well for a youngster scoring 452 runs at 19.65.

Pride of place in the bowling must go to Peate with 80 wickets at 15.96 with Emmett next with 67 at 17.71 (an excellent season for a 44 year old); Harrison did much better with 38 wickets at 18.62 while Bates's 66 wickets cost 20.21.

The Hon M. B. Hawke had played one match for Yorkshire during the 1885 season. What influence his presence or absence had on the team or its performances is very difficult to ascertain. During the coming winter months the captaincy is never mentioned at all in the Yorkshire CCC minutes but one resolution read as follows: '. . . The President to invite the Hon M. B. Hawke to play in all Matches.'

The 1886 season opened at The Oval on 25 May with Louis Hall leading the Yorkshire side on to the field after Surrey had won the toss. Emmett (six for 28) did very well to bowl out Surrey for a mere 56 runs. Yorkshire started well in reply and had 48 on the board before losing their third wicket but the total only reached 71. Surrey were 57 for three at the end of the second day with the first having been washed out by rain. In the final innings Yorkshire were set 91 to win. They made a poor start with five wickets down for 19. Hall (19) and Preston came together to take the score to 54 before the sixth wicket fell and then the last four fell for 9 runs, Surrey winning by 27 runs. Yorkshire were unfortunate in the way some of their batsmen were dismissed but Surrey fought hard for their first victory over the northerners since 1877.

At Fartown the first day's cricket was again a blank one and scoring remained low, Sussex dismissing Yorkshire for 93. Sussex, eight for 3 at the close of play, were soon out next day for 46 with Peate taking six for 16. Yorkshire lost Ulyett run out for 2 but Hall and Bates (63) added 89 before Bates left after a brilliant dashing innings. Wickets then fell regularly until Peate came in at 134 for eight and hit out for 30. Yorkshire were all out for 173, the obstinate Hall having carried his bat through the innings for 50 not out in 4 hours. Sussex then batted out time.

At Fenner's a weak-looking Cambridge side defeated Yorkshire by 26 runs.

After such a disappointing start to the season, Yorkshire welcomed back M. B. Hawke at Lord's for the Middlesex match. Yorkshire batted first and Hawke came in with two wickets down for 4. He added 102 for the third wicket with Hall (32) and went on to score 63. Peel (43) then joined with newcomer J. Ambler (25) to add 45 for the sixth wicket and Yorkshire's total reached 237. G. Spillman then played a brilliant innings to reach his 50 in 50 minutes and was 71 not out at the close of play out of 111 for four. Spillman went on to score

86 as Middlesex were all out for 192 with Bates taking four for 31. When Yorkshire batted they gave a greatly improved display. Ulyett in his usual dashing style scored 75 out of 106 for one in 90 minutes and Hawke (29), Fred Lee (32) and Peel (75) helped Hall, who batted for nearly $4\frac{3}{4}$ hours for 91, as Yorkshire compiled 409 on an excellent pitch. With only four hours left Middlesex batted until the close making 255 for four.

Joseph Ambler, known as 'Big Boam', made his first of only four appearances for Yorkshire in 1886 in the above match without doing anything of note. He had also played for Somerset from 1883. He was born at Lascelles Hall in 1860 and was professional at Yatton, nr Bridgwater when he played for Somerset. A tall and lanky person, he shone in the slips and was often mixed up with John Ambler.

Yorkshire won the toss against Kent at Bramall Lane and were dismissed for 218 with the Hon M. B. Hawke (76) and Hall (54) putting on 122 for the third wicket. Kent began well with W. H. Patterson (69) and Frank Hearne (56) opening with 106 for the first wicket in 80 minutes and at the end of the 2nd day, Kent were 186 for five. Next day, the Rev R. T. Thornton (31) and J. N. Tonge (40) added 71 for the seventh wicket and Kent went on to score 255. Irwin Grimshaw, who had had a bad season so far, went in first and stood firm while six wickets fell for 67. He went on to add 37 for the seventh wicket with Hon M. B. Hawke and the pair saved the game for Yorkshire with the captain scoring an unbeaten 56 as Yorkshire were dismissed for 156. Kent were left 80 minutes to score 122 to win but losing five wickets for 28 they were content with a draw.

The captain was again missing from the match at Derby, appearing instead for the Gentlemen of England against the Australians. Derbyshire won the toss and in poor conditions and bad light Derbyshire scored 92 in 108 overs. Yorkshire were 47 for four at the end of the day and eventually fell five runs short of their opponents; three run outs helping the home side. When Derbyshire batted again, Frank Sugg batted for three hours to score 62 as Derbyshire in improved conditions scored 156. Needing 162 for victory, Yorkshire were 12 for one at the close of the second day. Hall, batting at number 3, kept his end up but five wickets were down for 61. Fred Lee (14) helped him to put on 40 for the sixth wicket, and Grimshaw (18) 31 for the seventh, and then Preston stayed with Hall (51 not out) until the game was won. Hall batted for $3\frac{1}{2}$ hours for his match-winning innings.

At Bramall Lane, Yorkshire gained revenge over Cambridge following their defeat at Fenner's. Saul Wade made his first appearance for Yorkshire in this game scoring 28 and adding 77 for the second wicket with Peel. He played regularly for Yorkshire for four seasons before dropping out of the team in 1890. He gave good service with both bat and ball. Born at Farsley in 1858 he was a right-hand opening batsman and a very slow off-break bowler with a large amount of turn. He played his early cricket at Farsley but was discovered by Yorkshire when opening the innings for Saddleworth in 1880, averaging 49, and his first important match was for L. Hall's XI in 1885. He was said to have been his own worst enemy when with Yorkshire, otherwise his career might have been a longer one. He became a first-class umpire in 1904 and he died at Oldham in 1931.

A fine start by Surrey saw R. Abel (36) and J. Shuter (70) open with a stand of 109 before each left at that score. After Diver and W. W. Read had taken Surrey to 144 for three, J. M. Read came in and hit 56 with power and freedom and with three of the tail obtaining double figures Surrey reached a presentable 260. Yorkshire took their overnight score of 15 without loss to 26 before losing Wade. Hall went on to score 28 before Ulyett (33) added 45 for the fourth wicket with Preston. The latter went on to make a fine 62 but Lohmann and Bowley ensured that Yorkshire followed on. Ulyett opened the second innings and proceeded to score 78 in less than two hours in his old familiar style. Only Preston, however, stayed for any length of time and Surrey went on to win comfortably by seven wickets.

Yorkshire's misfortunes continued at Trent Bridge where they lost narrowly by 8 runs on a pitch that was by no means as bad as the scores suggested. Nottinghamshire won the toss and were bowled out for 120 with Peate taking five for 51. Yorkshire did even worse, carrying their overnight score of 96 for six to 100 all out. Then Wade's puzzling off-spinners took advantage of a crumbling pitch, Nottinghamshire being all out for 149. After a thunderstorm held up cricket Yorkshire were 22 for no wicket at the end of the second day and Hall (32) and Ulyett took their first wicket partnership to 66 but five wickets were down for 91. Preston with 28 and Peate (22) made a big effort for Yorkshire before being run out at 159 and Hunter was last man out at 161.

Another defeat followed at Old Trafford – this time by four wickets. Yorkshire were all out for 133 with Barlow taking six for 58. Lancashire were in their turn completely demoralised by Emmett's fine bowling as he finished with seven for 33. Lancashire began none too well when needing 178 for victory and they lost five wickets for 93. A. G. Steel made a splendid 80 not out as Lancashire gained a fine victory by four wickets.

The Australians were Yorkshire's next opponents at Bramall Lane and it was no surprise to see them finish up victorious by six wickets after a well-fought match.

Yorkshire met the Australians immediately afterwards at Fartown on a good wicket but there was very little play on the first day due to rain. Yorkshire, having been 30 without loss on the first day went on to 258 all out. George Giffen took six for 88. The Australians had the worst of a drying wicket and were soon reduced to 78 for seven before J. McIlwraith (41) and T. W. Garrett (38) came together and added 68 for the eighth wicket. All out for 169, Australia followed on and were 24 for one when the game ended in a draw.

The Lancashire match at Savile Town was ruined by the rain but on the first day Yorkshire did score 97 for seven and after a blank second day went on to 112. Briggs took five for 57. In reply John Briggs scored 20 out of his side's total of 53 with Bates taking six for 19. At the close of play Yorkshire were 107 for seven with Ulyett scoring 32 and Bates 30.

Kent certainly shocked Yorkshire at Canterbury batting the whole of the first day for 273 for the loss of two batsmen. Frank Hearne had scored 41 then C. Wilson joined G. G. Hearne, the pair adding 215 runs for the third wicket with Hearne scoring 117 in $5\frac{1}{2}$ hours and Wilson 127 in $4\frac{1}{4}$ hours. After that Emmett cut loose to take six for 62 in 59 overs as Kent were dismissed for 335. When Yorkshire batted they gave a poor display on the hard wicket but with Hall still at the crease with the score at 81 for eight Emmett played a fine attacking innings of 48 and helped Hall to add 91 for the ninth wicket. Hall finished with 74 not out as Yorkshire were dismissed for 172. Following on, Bates scored 34 out of 55 for three but Hall who had come in at number four added 50 for the sixth wicket with J. M. Preston. Yorkshire were dismissed for 226 with Louis Hall again Yorkshire's hero with 75 not out. Kent went on to win easily by six wickets.

On a very slow Bramall Lane pitch and in very poor conditions, Nottinghamshire scored 100 in three hours for the loss of three wickets, but the remaining batsmen gave little trouble and the all out total was 156. When Yorkshire batted after a blank second day, they took 155 minutes and 95 overs to score 58, with R. Peel top scoring with 19 not out. Flowers took seven for 33. Following on Yorkshire were 75 for five at the close.

Middlesex made a good start after winning the toss at Park Avenue putting on 55 for the first wicket, with A. J. Webbe scoring 39 and A. E. Stoddart 20, yet they collapsed before the slow spin of Saul Wade (six for 26). In reply Yorkshire were 74 for two at the end of the second day with Bates out for 25. Louis Hall (56) added 57 for Yorkshire's fourth wicket with J. M. Preston who went on to score 76. Grimshaw scored 38, Emmett 35, while Wade made 74 not out. Yorkshire finally scored 401. Emmett (seven for 46) then bowled out Middlesex for 82 and Yorkshire won by an innings and 196 runs.

Albert Ward, a right-hand batsman with a powerful defence who could hit the ball very hard but perhaps over-emphasised his defensive qualities, made his debut in the above match. He first played with the Hunslet CC, walking 5 miles to the club for coaching from John Tye of Nottinghamshire and others. He was then an assistant schoolmaster at St Simon's, Leeds and was tried for Yorkshire in 1886 in four matches but did not meet with much success. In 1886 he was poached by John Stanning of Leyland (Lancs) and qualified for Lancashire for whom he played from 1889 to 1904 and during his career scored 17,809 runs at an average of 30. He played in seven Test matches with some success and was at one time a sports outfitter in Bolton. He died at his home in Bolton in 1939.

At Cheltenham, Yorkshire proved too strong for Gloucestershire, winning a low-scoring match by five wickets.

Yorkshire's visit to Hove produced some remarkable cricket but the result was a draw with Yorkshire well on top. Winning the toss Yorkshire lost two wickets for 34 when M. B. Hawke joined Ulyett (52) and they added 90 for the third wicket; Preston then scored 33 out of 88 added for the fourth wicket and when Hawke was dismissed for 144 at 283 for seven, he had been batting for $3\frac{1}{4}$ hours for his then highest score in first-class cricket. Jesse Hide and Humphreys each took four wickets and Sussex took their score from 76 for two at the end of the first day to 223. Emmett took six for 94. At the end of the second day, Yorkshire had reached 182 without loss and when Bates was out at 186 for 136 he had been batting for $2\frac{1}{2}$ hours. Hall went on to score 92 in $4\frac{1}{2}$ hours, being the sixth man out at 271, and Yorkshire made 343 leaving Sussex to bat for only $2\frac{1}{4}$ hours. *Wisden* was critical of the time that was wasted on the last day and stated that lunch lasted for 'an hour and 8 minutes'. On a perfect pitch Sussex finished the match with 173 for five. The inevitable draw on a good pitch was not uncommon in those days with neither side making much effort to force a victory.

The Holbeck ground provided a good game against Derbyshire with Yorkshire's Bates once again in great form, hitting 106 out of 148 for five. It was not a chanceless innings but he produced some fine attacking strokes with only the captain (18) giving him any support whatsoever. Derbyshire managed to pass Yorkshire's total of 161 by 21 runs, thanks mainly to W. Chatterton and L. C. Docker. Only Ulyett did much with 34 when Yorkshire batted again and the home side were soon 99 for six. At this point the game changed with Grimshaw and Peel taking Yorkshire's overnight score of 193 for six to 265 for seven. A stand of 166 for the seventh wicket had swung the game in Yorkshire's favour as Peel made 55 and Grimshaw 122 not out in a chanceless display. Derbyshire needed 266 to win in $3\frac{1}{2}$ hours and a good start gave them a little hope but Bates again bowled well ensuring Derbyshire's dismissal for 144 and defeat by 121 runs.

A strong MCC side dispensed defeat to Yorkshire by 133 runs in the last match of the season at Scarborough. C. I. Thornton (33) and W. Barnes (30) helped MCC to recover from a bad start and then J. G. Walker scored a fine 55 before the innings closed at 191. In reply Yorkshire were 34 for one at the end of the first day and Bates was the next wicket to go at 61, having made 36. Six wickets were down for 118 with Hall out for 52 before Grimshaw with 61 and Peel (30) added 52 for the seventh wicket and Yorkshire gained a lead of 20 runs. The MCC did not begin very well in their second innings but their final total was a respectable 265. Yorkshire, with no time to attempt a victory, lost five wickets for 32 before Ulyett hit 42, but apart from Peel with 24 not out there was little resistance to the bowling of Barnes, who took five for 28, while W. G. Grace, buying his wickets, finished with five for 83 in a thoroughly poor batting display.

Lewis Franklin Wrathmell played one match for Yorkshire in 1886 against Cambridge University at Fenner's when he scored 17 and 1 and never played for the County again. A useful right-handed batsman, he was born at Kirkheaton in 1855 and had several professional engagements including Almondbury Grammar School, Blackburn, Golcar (1882–83) and Mirfield. He died at Upper Hopton in 1928 and was interred there.

Taken at face value, 5 victories, 8 defeats and 8 draws could not constitute anything other than a thoroughly bad season for Yorkshire. The fielding and catching was very poor indeed and even Joseph Hunter lost form and had to be dropped from the side. The Hon M. B. Hawke played in most of the matches so he must have been able to see for himself exactly what was wrong with the side.

In first-class county matches, Louis Hall was as dependable as ever and scored 811 runs at 30.03 and he continued to lead the side in the absence of M. B. Hawke who also did very well with the bat scoring 615 runs at 25.62. Bates too did well with 747 runs at 24.09 often batting brilliantly. Grimshaw was dropped from the side for a time but came back to do reasonably well with 308 runs at 22.00.

Saul Wade finished on top of the bowling averages with 32 wickets at 9.34 – his big slow off-breaks puzzling even the best of batsmen. The question was whether he would be so effective after batsmen had become accustomed to his style. Emmett took 96 wickets at 11.13 each; wonderful figures for a man of 45 years. He bowled more overs and maidens than any other bowler in the side. Peate had a poor season, only taking 39 wickets at 14.26, and Bates was also disappointing with 42 wickets at 15.37.

Yorkshire's problems, apart from poor out-cricket, were that the younger players had not made the advance that was hoped and that two or three of the best players were reaching the veteran stage.

The new season of 1887 began at Lord's with the MCC winning the toss and putting together a formidable total of 248. J. M. Preston scored 45 when Yorkshire batted but he was not quite at his best. Hall scored 28 and the skipper 23 but could not prevent Yorkshire following on. They fared even worse in their second innings and MCC had no difficulty in scoring 54 for victory to win by nine wickets.

Kent won the toss at Bramall Lane and were fortunate to bat first on a wet wicket that was soon to become difficult and remain so for the duration of the match. Frank Hearne made 38 – the highest score of the match – as Kent were bowled out for 92. Peel took five for 14 in 27.1 overs, Yorkshire replied with 77, only a stand of 42 between Peel (24) and Preston (20) holding up the Kent bowlers. At the close Kent were 4 for one in their second innings but Emmett had them all out for 89 on the following morning. A crowd of nearly 6,000 watched this second day's play, with Yorkshire requiring 105 to win. Five wickets were down for 42 with Ulyett run out for 21, before the Hon M. B. Hawke went on to score 36 not out, hitting the winning runs with a six as Yorkshire won by four wickets.

At Fenner's, only the poor weather saved Yorkshire from a heavy defeat against Cambridge University.

Yorkshire paid their second visit of the season to Lord's for the Middlesex match where, put in to bat on a sticky dog, the visitors were dismissed before lunch for 55. A. J. Webbe (34) and J. G. Walker (29) both batted well and Middlesex were 82 for four at one stage before collapsing to 99 all out. Yorkshire took advantage of an easier wicket and some dropped catches, but Middlesex only needed 116 for victory, a task they achieved with six wickets in hand.

Mr Edward Robinson made his only appearance for Yorkshire in the above game as a middle order right-hand batsman but soon afterwards left to live in Bristol where he settled to become well-known in Gloucestershire sporting circles.

Joseph Denton, an elder brother of David Denton, was given an extended trial this season. A good right-hand batsman, he did not quite measure up to his early promise but afterwards was a leading light with Hodgson's and Simpson's CC, where he played for many years, as did many other members of the Denton family. He was the father of several Featherstone cricketers, one of whom played for Featherstone Rovers and Yorkshire at Rugby League football.

The Nottinghamshire match at Trent Bridge turned out one of those games which if played in our present County Championship would have undoubtedly sounded the death-knell of three-day cricket in our present-day tabloids. By any standards its dirge-like moments had little to commend them. The game was played for the benefit of

John Selby, and unfortunately for him, only 2,000 per day came to see the game. Yorkshire batted the whole of the first day for 222 in 200.2 overs. Shrewsbury and Scotton then spent 185 minutes in putting on 97 for Nottinghamshire's first wicket, with Shrewsbury going on to score 81 in 4 hours and 20 minutes. At the end of the second day Nottinghamshire had taken their score to 216 for eight and finally reached 253. Emmett returned the following remarkable figures: 65-44-46-0. Yorkshire spent the rest of the match scoring 227 for six with M. B. Hawke making 78 not out. *Wisden* remarked 'During the 3 days only 702 runs were made for the loss of 26 wickets – an instance of slow scoring which, as was remarked at the time, would have scarcely been possible on any other ground in England than the Trent Bridge at Nottingham.' (No doubt our present umpires would have awarded the pitch full marks and described it as an excellent wicket.)

As might be expected, the first day at Bradford against Sussex produced almost twice as many runs as the first day of the previous match, the visitors making 254 and Yorkshire 142 for five. On the following day, J. Denton (59) and R. Peel (91) put on 86 for Yorkshire's sixth wicket and Yorkshire went on to score 304. At the end of the second day, which was Jubilee Day and a public holiday attracting a huge crowd, Sussex had been dismissed for 188. Requiring 139 to win on the last day, Ulyett scored 111 in 140 minutes as he and Hall knocked them off without loss. Ulyett's was a brilliant innings although he was dropped when only 16.

At Aigburth against Liverpool & District, Yorkshire met with defeat by 38 runs. A. G. Steel with 44 and 68 and four for 61 in the first Yorkshire innings along with the Nottinghamshire professional Henry Richardson, who scored 5 and 55 and took nine for 98, dominated the game.

Yorkshire spent the first day at Derby scoring 360 for eight, finally being all out for 371. Bates scored 103 in a brilliant innings lasting 2 hours. Derbyshire replied with 163 and following on they soon lost four wickets for 19 before Cropper with 32 and George Davidson took the score to 69. Davidson went on to score 75 in $2\frac{1}{2}$ hours, but Yorkshire still won by an innings.

At the Spa Ground, Gloucester, the bat beat the ball to a huge extent and the game was drawn without either side ever being in a position to win. Dr W. G. Grace had a remarkable match scoring 92 and 183 not out. For Yorkshire, Hall made 70 and Ulyett 104.

George Ulyett's benefit match took place at Bramall Lane on 4 July against Surrey and crowds of almost 20,000 paid for admission on the first two days. Surrey won the toss and batted the whole of the first day for 301 with J. Shuter and W. W. Read dominating, putting on 111 for the third wicket. Ulyett, appropriately enough, was Yorkshire's best bowler with five for 56. Rain overnight and poor light made the conditions far different on the second day, but Yorkshire gave a poor batting display and were bowled out by Lohmann for 111. Following on, Yorkshire did little better and they were soon dismissed for 175, presenting Surrey with an innings' victory.

Yorkshire remained at Bramall Lane for the match against Derbyshire, who went in first and were soon bowled out for 129. By the close of play Ulyett had reached 102 out of 188 for five and he and J. M. Preston (93) put on 150 for the sixth wicket in 2 hours and five minutes. Yorkshire were all out for 399, George Ulyett carrying his bat through the innings for 199 in 5 hours and 50 minutes. It was to remain Ulyett's highest score of his career. Derbyshire were then dismissed for 107 as Yorkshire won by an innings and 163 runs.

At Dewsbury a remarkable game was played against Gloucestershire. Yorkshire won the toss and batted first with Ulyett scoring 98 in 95 minutes out of 127 put on for the first wicket. He batted at his most brilliant and only got himself out rashly in going for his century. Hall carried his bat through the innings scoring 119 not out out of 334 in 265 minutes. Gloucestershire were 55 for one at stumps and on the following day W. G. Grace (97) and J. H. Brain (74) put on 149 for the second wicket before W.G. was out after batting for $3\frac{1}{4}$ hours. Later W. W. F. Pullen scored 78 out of 113 and Gloucestershire gained a lead of 29 runs on the first innings. Yorkshire were 65 for one overnight but rain during the night prevented a prompt start and altered the state of the pitch. Lee (29) put on 68 for the second wicket with Hall, who went on to make 49, and M. B. Hawke made 37 before Yorkshire were out for 184. Roberts took seven for 70. When Gloucestershire went in again, Wade proved to be unplayable, taking six for 18, and Yorkshire won by 70 runs.

Canterbury saw a brilliant batting exhibition from Yorkshire. At close on the first day Yorkshire were 305 for the loss of Ulyett (124) with Hall 89 and Lee 82 not out. Both overnight batsmen reached three figures and Yorkshire made 559 in 610 minutes. A tired Kent side were 51 for four at the close of the second day and next morning were soon out for 129. Following on W. H. Patterson (39) and Frank Hearne opened with a stand of 96 before Kent slumped to 102 for four but Hearne, in pain for most of his innings, went on to score 144 and Kent managed to draw with a score of 277 for six. Hearne was badly missed by Preston when 68, which obviously could have cost Yorkshire victory.

Yorkshire's batting continued in even more remarkable fashion in the Roses match at Bradford. Ulyett began well with 67 out of 89 in 56 minutes and then Lee joined Hall to add 280 for the second wicket in $3\frac{1}{2}$ hours when Fred Lee was dismissed for 165. He produced the best batting of his career with strokes all round the wicket. At the close of play Hall and Hawke had added a further 65 runs and the score was 434 for two. Next day Hawke went for 58 out of 74. Bates then scored 38 and when Hall was dismissed at 529 for five, he had been batting for 6 hours and 40 minutes for 160, showing his usual defensive qualities and excellent leg-hitting. After lunch the innings closed for 590. A. N. Hornby (69) and Barlow (37) put on 84 for Lancashire's first wicket but five wickets were down for 106 when Robinson joined Barlow to take the score to 167 for six before Barlow was out. Robinson was not out at the close of play and on the last day took his score to an unbeaten 111. Following on, A. N. Hornby with 92 and 57 from J. Eccles helped to ensure a draw.

Moving on to Fartown, Middlesex won the toss and were dismissed for 130. Bright batting by Yorkshire gained the county a lead of 51, and at the close of an interesting day, Middlesex were 46 for two. Next day A. J. Webbe took his score to 243 not out, carrying his bat through the innings lasting 6 hours and 10 minutes. Yorkshire reached 13 for two but rain prevented any play on the last day.

Walter Quaife was top scorer with 34 when Sussex batted first at Hove and at 110 for three seemed to be on their way to a bigger score than the 172 they obtained. At close of play Yorkshire had replied with 55 for two with Hall 23. At 125 for six Yorkshire were by no means in command but Hall was then joined by R. Peel who scored 46 out of 62 added for the seventh wicket and a last wicket stand of 28 with Emmett took Yorkshire to 218. Hall carried his bat through the innings for 82 in four hours. Sussex batted much better in their second innings with Quaife (46) and W. Newham (58) putting on 89 for the Sussex second wicket before Newham was dismissed and at the close on the second day, Sussex were healthily placed at 140 for two. More steady batting followed with W. A. Humphreys scoring 37 as Sussex totalled 252 with Peel taking seven for 72. Left with 165 minutes to score 207 Yorkshire soon lost six wickets for 53 but Hall (31) stayed until the last over and with Peel scoring 17 they finished with 82 for seven to achieve a draw. Joseph Hunter was rested from this match and his place was taken by Pride who distinguished himself by capturing seven victims.

Thomas Pride was only 23 when he played in the above match – his only game for the county – giving a good impression to all. He learnt the game in York and lived most of his life there and in club cricket was a good right-hand batsman. It was thought that his hands would not stand up to the rigours of three-day cricket but around 1887 he went to Edinburgh Presbyterian College to qualify as a schoolmaster and he eventually became headmaster of Canonbie School in Scotland where he died in 1919.

William Lord Dyson a useful right-hand batsman who was a professional with Brighouse, played his first match for Yorkshire *v* Sussex at Hove and in one other match for Yorkshire in the same season, 1887, without success.

At The Oval, Surrey defeated Yorkshire inside two days on a rain-affected pitch by an innings and 10 runs. Over 10,000 people paid for admission to the match which was played for Edward Barratt's benefit.

For two days at Bramall Lane, the return with Nottinghamshire followed the trend of the earlier wretched game at Trent Bridge. Nottinghamshire won the toss and had two wickets down for one run before Shrewsbury and Barnes (27) added 54 for the third wicket. H. B. Daft with 35 then helped Shrewsbury to put on 71 for the fourth wicket but at 165 Shrewsbury was dismissed for a fine innings of 75 against a keen attack and good fielding. Wilf Flowers came in and scored 45 as the Nottinghamshire innings finished at 245 at the end of the day. When Yorkshire batted Ulyett scored 39 out of the first 56. Peel batted well for 41 and Wade went on to make 66 but Hall had spent 4 hours and 25 minutes in amassing 40 and at the end of the second day Yorkshire were 214 with the last pair at the crease. On the last morning Wade and Joseph Hunter added 64 for Yorkshire's tenth wicket. Nottinghamshire were dismissed in their second innings for 135 leaving Yorkshire 119 to win in 95 minutes. Bates made a fine effort and scored 63 out of 91 for four in 57 minutes and only a run a minute was required after that. More wickets fell however and in the end Yorkshire needed 3 runs to win with two wickets left. A sporting contest was finished with honours even although the Sheffield crowd accused Nottinghamshire of time-wasting which was hotly denied by the Yorkshire players.

Mr John Wilson, a useful right-hand batsman and slow lob bowler, made his debut in the Nottinghamshire game at Bramall Lane, when he took three for 43 and two for 16 and also took two wickets in his next game at Old Trafford. He played in two games for Yorkshire in 1888 with some success as a bowler. In the Trent College Eleven, he first played in the Elsecar team that won the Wake Challenge Cup in 1883 and later played for Pitsmoor, Sheffield Wednesday, Barnsley (as captain) and Millhouses and became President of the Sheffield Cricket Association.

At Old Trafford, Yorkshire gained an immediate ascendancy which they never relaxed and ran out easy winners by an innings and 39 runs. Only Briggs with 25 offered much resistance as Lancashire were dismissed for 129. Bates soon scored 33 out of 37 for Yorkshire's first wicket and then Lee (57) helped Hall (62) in a stand of 119 for the second wicket and at the close of play Yorkshire were 162 for two.

Next morning Hall left after three hours at the crease and then Hawke partnered Ulyett (44) in a stand of 78 although both were dropped in single figures; then Peel (66) and Hawke added 138 for the fifth wicket. M. B. Hawke went on to score 125 in 3 hours and 50 minutes as Yorkshire reached 414. Lancashire going in again soon lost six wickets for only 64 with F. H. Sugg scoring 34 but Walter Robinson came in to score 92 in 2½ hours against his native county and a ninth wicket partnership of 68 with Alex Watson took Lancashire to a total of 246.

Yorkshire's final match at Scarborough was drawn with Peel (71), Ulyett (64) and Fred Lee (55) helping Yorkshire to a total of 291 on the first day. Rain interferred with play on both the second and third days as MCC replied with 286. In their second innings Yorkshire were dismissed for 94 with A. E. Stoddart taking six for 33. (He had failed to take a wicket in the Championship for Middlesex.) At the close of play Middlesex had scored 46 for one.

Yorkshire had finished the season with 6 wins, 5 defeats and 9 draws to complete an unsatisfactory season in many ways and yet there had been some excellent performances.

In what was a very dry cricket season, George Ulyett headed the first-class county averages with 1122 runs at 48.78 with Hall a very close second with 997 runs at 47.47. Fred Lee recaptured a regular place in the side scoring 498 runs at 29.29 and then came the Hon M. B. Hawke with 636 runs at 28.90. R. Peel also batted well with 526 runs at 25.04, as did Bates with 594 runs at 24.75. Saul Wade did not advance much as a batsman but scored 423 runs at 21.15. J. M. Preston fell right away with only 258 runs at 13.84. Emmett and Hunter's batting was of very little account while Grimshaw failed completely.

With the ball R. Peel took 59 wickets at 17.94 with J. M. Preston second with 43 wickets at 18.13. Tom Emmett's 53 wickets cost him 19.60. S. Wade took 34 wickets at 22.58 each which was rather disappointing, but Ulyett did much better with 37 at 23.08. Bates fell away in a season that did not suit him but he took 29 wickets at 32.89.

Joseph Hunter showed much better form than in the previous season but his hands caused problems. The fielding too was not consistent and many catches were dropped that should have been taken. Peate too had dropped out of the side and this resulted in Peel showing better form with more opportunities.

During the winter William Bates received a very bad injury to his eye while practising during his tour of Australia – it ended his County career. Grimshaw and Peate were two others who did not appear again for the County.

One rather strange entry in the YCCC minutes was a letter from the Heavy Woollen District Challenge Cup Committee requesting the admission of a member to the Committee. It was resolved not to increase the number of the Committee at present.

In November there was a resolution about Tom Emmett, who had evidently announced his retirement from the team, thanking him for his services and the way 'he had conducted himself during his 21 years' connection with the county eleven'. In fact Emmett was to play in two matches in the forthcoming season.

It was a very strange team that took the field on 7 and 8 May 1888 for Yorkshire's first match against the MCC at Lord's. Lord Hawke was not available and Ulyett and Preston had not returned from their tour to Australia. A weak county side was beaten by 103 runs.

Mr Henry Hill scored 29 and 27 in this his first match for Yorkshire. A right-hand opening batsman he was born at Thornhill, Dewsbury in 1858 and captained the Dewsbury & Savile Club for many years and also served the Dewsbury district on the Committee up to his death in 1935. A hard worker for Dewsbury cricket he continued to play in local cricket until he was 70 and he was famed for his good sportsmanship.

Herbert Thewlis, a good right-hand batsman but poor fielder, played twice for Yorkshire in 1888. He played for the Holbeck Club, and Eagley in the Bolton League.

Edward Wainwright was a third player to make his debut in this MCC match at Lord's. He soon gained a regular place in the Yorkshire side and kept it until 1901. A right-hand batsman, who invariably got runs when they were wanted, he possessed a sound defence, could drive hard, and score quickly as a reliable middle-order batsman. As an off-spin bowler, he was deadly on a bad wicket and always bowled well on wet wickets although by no means as successful in dry weather. As a fielder he was outstanding as a slip fielder and he performed the double for Yorkshire in 1897. He assisted the Tinsley club in his youth and generally lived in the village. After his playing career with Yorkshire he had various engagements in the Bassetlaw League with Wiseton Park and with Worksop for several years and for many seasons was coach at Shrewsbury School, where at one time he had Neville Cardus as an assistant. Wainwright was a true Yorkshire character, with a wry sense of humour. He died in 1919 at his home in Sheffield, being buried in City Road Cemetery.

Mr Herbert ('Herbie') William Hart, a left-handed batsman and fine left-arm fast bowler played only once for Yorkshire against the MCC at Lord's in 1888 when he took none for 13 and two for 19, bowling out C. W. Wright for 14 and W. Flowers for 0, and scoring 0 and 6 with the bat. He was born at Hull in 1859 and played with success for the Hull Town Club from 1879 when he took 50 wickets at

7.1 each and continued to play for them until his death from typhoid in 1895 at his home in Hull aged only 36. He was a member of the firm, Hart Bros, of Hull.

John Usher was the fifth newcomer to the Yorkshire side that played against the MCC in 1888 and like H. W. Hart never played in another first-class match. A left-handed batsman and left-arm slow bowler he was at varying times a professional at Bacup in 1892–93; Rishton in 1894; Whalley in 1898 and at Haslingden from 1900–02 and also had engagements with Holbeck, Holmfirth, and possibly Wortley.

On a good pitch at Bramall Lane *v* the Australians, Yorkshire won the toss before a paying attendance of 13,103 and were dismissed for 125. The visitors then lost three wickets for 61 before G. J. Bonnor hit hard for 94. By the close of play the Australians were in a strong position at 259 for seven, finally being dismissed for 292. Ulyett (24) and Hall (33) began Yorkshire's second innings by putting on 40 for the first wicket but only Wade with 12 not out made any other progress against Turner and Ferris. Yorkshire, all out for 103, were defeated by an innings and 64 runs. After the match George Ulyett was presented with a cheque for £1,000 for his benefit from the previous season. The Australians contributed £20.

Yorkshire returned to Lord's for their first Championship match against Middlesex with two new players in their line-up. Yorkshire, winning the toss, scored only 137 on what was considered to be a good wicket. Middlesex fared even worse with four down for 19 before J. G. Walker (27) and T. C. O'Brien (44) added 35, and then last man J. Robertson with 15 not out helped his side towards a total of 122. Creighton on his debut made top score when Yorkshire were bowled out for 43 in 75 minutes, George Burton taking seven for 18 and Middlesex went on to win by nine wickets.

Ernest Creighton played in only three other matches for Yorkshire taking ten wickets at 18.80 each. A left-arm slow bowler, who was a builder by trade, he was professional at Ramsbottom in 1879. He was later at Todmorden in 1888, in 1894 and in 1900–01 and latterly lived at Doncaster.

William Hendy Harrison also made his debut for Yorkshire at Lord's in the above match and played in two other games in 1888 without achieving anything of note.

During the Middlesex match, Joseph Hunter received a bad injury in an accident which prevented his ever playing for Yorkshire again. In the next match at Fenner's James Yeadon took his place and Yorkshire batted first after winning the toss. Moorhouse making his first appearance took the eye with 42 as Yorkshire scored 172. In reply

Cambridge had scored 108 for seven at the end of the day. In the end Cambridge required 172 to win, and hit off the runs with four wickets in hand.

James Yeadon was born at Yeadon in 1861 and was a right-hand batsman and wicket-keeper who played in three matches for Yorkshire in 1888; his career in top class cricket however ended shortly afterwards due to a serious leg injury. He umpired in first-class matches for three or four seasons at the turn of the century.

Robert Moorhouse, elder brother of Fred Moorhouse of Warwickshire, was a short man and one of the greatest cover-points of all -time. He was a very brave batsman who received many bruises and injuries during his career while insisting on standing up to fast bowlers on dangerous pitches. A right-handed batsman, he had by no means a perfect technique but often got runs when they were badly needed, and he was also a useful off-break bowler. He was born at Berry Brow in 1866 and was a product of the Armitage Bridge CC. He became a regular in the Yorkshire side almost from the start although he was only on the fringe of the side when he last appeared for Yorkshire in 1899. He scored over 5,000 runs for Yorkshire at an average of 19. He was subsequently coach at Sedbergh School.

At Bramall Lane, Sussex won the toss, put Yorkshire in to bat and dismissed the home side for 178. Sussex were quickly in trouble with eight wickets down for 51 before G. Brann (32) was joined by Arthur Hide (22) doubling the total. Ulyett (33) and Fred Lee (26) put on 54 for Yorkshire's second wicket and Peel again batted well to score 50 as Yorkshire scored 148. After Walter Quaife (20) and Tester (28) had opened with a stand of 41, Sussex collapsed to 105 all out to give Yorkshire victory by a substantial margin.

Yorkshire were soon in trouble at The Oval after winning the toss, only a stand of 30 between Hall and H. Hill (23) holding up the Surrey attack as Hall carried his bat through the innings for 34 not out in a stay of $2\frac{1}{2}$ hours. J. Beaumont took eight for 49. At the end of the first day Surrey were 229 for three, which they carried on to 356 all out with W. W. Read batting 3 hours for 103. When Yorkshire batted again, H. Hill (24) and Wainwright (37) put on 63 for the fifth wicket but they were dismissed for 135 giving Surrey victory by an innings.

A return match at Park Avenue against the Australians took place on a perfect pitch and the visitors on winning the toss batted most of the day for 367. Yorkshire, 8 without loss overnight, were all out for 228 with Harry Trott taking five for 74. In the follow-on, Wainwright opened the innings and went on to score 105, adding 124 for the second wicket with Hall (42). At the close Yorkshire had forced a draw at 344 for seven.

Willie (registered as such) Middlebrook was born at Morley in 1858 and was a moderate right-hand batsman and medium-fast bowler who took 50 wickets for Yorkshire in 1888–89 at 17.90 each and proved himself to be a talented bowler. Unfortunately he was 30 years old before he was given a chance for his county. A cloth presser by trade, he appears to have always lived in Morley and he had various professional engagements with Preston, Morley, Bradford and Leeds Buckingham.

Also playing against the Australians – he also played one other match for Yorkshire in this season – was Mr William Coverdale, a useful amateur batsman and wicket-keeper who played for both Bridlington and Rotherham Town.

When rain allowed play to start at Fartown, Yorkshire made a good start, but were all out for 195. Kent, 15 for three overnight, went on to lose four more cheap wickets before struggling to 107. Following on, they were 153 for three at one stage and eventually Yorkshire required 113 to win in an hour. Stumps were drawn with the score 31 for two. Another draw followed at Bramall Lane in the Roses match where rain prevented any play until the last day.

There were two new players in the ranks of the Yorkshire side against Lancashire.

One was Mr Frank Edmund Baines who played in just this match and never played again. He was born at Ecclesall, Sheffield in 1864 and was a right-arm medium-fast bowler. He died at Worksop in 1948.

John Ernest Ellis, a right-hand batsman and capable wicket-keeper, was born at Sheffield in 1864 and was living at High Wincobank in Sheffield when he first came into the Yorkshire side 1888, and was one of the favourites to take over Joe Hunter's position as wicket-keeper after the latter's accident. Ellis played in eight matches for Yorkshire in 1888 and three more in 1892. He lived at Shiregreen and was connected with the Shiregreen Cricket Club and was founder of Shiregreen Reading Rooms and supporter of the local chapel. He was playing for Sheffield United in 1907–08, and died at Sheffield in 1927.

Another draw followed at Trent Bridge where the first day was washed out by rain. Apart from W. Barnes (63) and W. Gunn (30), Nottinghamshire gave a poor batting display to be out for 143. Then Yorkshire gave a very slow exhibition of cricket to finish the day at 88 for four in 3 hours and 5 minutes, with opener Hall still there with 14. Hall was eventually out for 22 and Wainwright scored 33 as Yorkshire gained a lead of nine but they had taken 210 overs and 3 balls to make 152. When Nottinghamshire batted again they scored 114 at the rate of 1 run per over with Scotton scoring 26 while Wainwright bowled very well in conditions that suited him to take five for 20. Yorkshire needed 106 in 55 minutes to win but only reached 21 for two.

On a bowler's pitch from the start, Lancashire batted first to make

79 with only Frank Sugg with 27 batting with much conviction. Peel took five for 32 and Wainwright three for 8, Yorkshire replied with 51 with L. Hall batting 45 minutes without scoring while Ulyett scored 18 and H. Hill 13 as J. Briggs took six for 24 and Watson three for 9. Lancashire were 13 for five in their second innings at the end of the first day. On the following morning Peel continued the rout, taking seven for 30 and Lancashire were all out for 82. Yorkshire were set 111 to win and they made an interesting start with Ulyett scoring 30 out of 40 for four. Peel with 20 took the score to 90 for five and Yorkshire reached their target with two wickets to spare.

Mr Ernest Smith made his debut for Yorkshire in this match without scoring a run, taking a wicket or making a catch. He continued to play for Yorkshire until 1907 and was a thoroughly useful member of the team in nearly every season although he never played regularly. He averaged 20 with the bat for Yorkshire and took 248 wickets at 25.31 each. A good right-hand batsman who liked to attack the bowling, he could defend dourly when required. He was in the Clifton XI in 1886–87 and played in the University matches of 1890 and 1891 on the side of the Dark Blues. His highest score was 164 not out for Leveson-Gower's XI v Cambridge University in 1912 and at the age of 53 he scored 160 for Eastbourne against Uppingham Rovers. Also a good golfer and rugby player, he was headmaster of a prep school at Eastbourne for many years and made many runs there in club cricket. He died at Eastbourne aged 75; his death being caused by blood poisoning, which spread from one leg to the other; amputation of both legs did not save his life.

Rain affected the pitch and the game at Bramall Lane against Nottinghamshire who won the toss and were bowled out for 24 with Peel taking eight for 12. R. Peel also made top score for Yorkshire with 13 as his side was dismissed for 46. Nottinghamshire spent 74.3 overs in scoring 58 with Scotton carrying his bat through the innings for 17. Peel took six for 21. That finished the first day's play and when further rain fell it rendered the pitch much easier so that when Yorkshire batted again it was 3 p.m. and Yorkshire knocked off the 37 needed for victory in 40 minutes with Ulyett unbeaten with 26.

At Fartown rain restricted the cricket to just one day's play against the Australians. Yorkshire won the toss and made a good start with Ulyett 48 and Hall 11 putting on 53 for the first wicket. Fred Lee then came in and scored 25 before Yorkshire were bowled out for 107. The Australians then struggled to obtain 48 with G. H. S. Trott scoring 28 as Peel took six for 19. At the close, Yorkshire had just one second innings wicket left and only 49 on the board, thus leaving the match in an intriguing state.

On a cold and windy morning at Thrum Hall, the first important match on the new Halifax ground began against Gloucestershire on 30 July. The prepared pitch was saturated and another one was laid out and Gloucestershire decided to bat first. W. G. Grace took his brother out with him but was soon dismissed by Peel for two and the side were all back in the pavilion for 89 with only H. V. Page – run out for 31 – doing anything of note. Peel finished with seven for 39. Yorkshire took a lead of 33 on the first innings. The next day went very much the same way with W. W. F. Pullen batting well for 43 but Gloucestershire could only score 102 with the lethal Peel this time taking six for 45. Requiring 70 to win, Yorkshire scored 21 in 20 minutes before lunch for the loss of Hall with Ulyett going on to score 23 out of 36 before becoming Woof's second victim. Yorkshire struggled and only won by three wickets in the end.

The next match at Bramall Lane saw Yorkshire win the toss and Ulyett dominate the first Yorkshire innings with 40 out of 113 all out as George Burton took eight for 48. When rain stopped play at 5 pm Middlesex were well placed at 61 for four with T. C. O'Brien not out 27. Next morning he was out without addition to his score and only G. F. Vernon with 30 offered much resistance to the Yorkshire attack, the innings ending at 98. In the second innings Hall was out straight away stumped for 0! Lee (58) did most of the scoring as Yorkshire were all out for 122. Middlesex wanted 138 to win and soon had three wickets down for 42 but O'Brien and Hadow had doubled the score by the end of the second day. E. M. Hadow was dismissed next morning for 34 then O'Brien, hitting with freedom, took Middlesex to victory with a fine score of 79 not out as they won by six wickets.

Yorkshire's next match was at Clifton where Gloucestershire won the toss. Dr W. G. Grace hit 148 in $3\frac{1}{2}$ hours as Gloucestershire were bowled out for 248. Preston, in fine form, took seven for 82. At the close of play on the first day, Yorkshire were 35 for two and they carried on batting for the whole of the second day when they had scored 427 for eight. Night-watchman Wormald made 80, Wade 68 and Moorhouse 70. The following day Yorkshire were all out for 468 with Hall scoring 129 not out in over seven hours. In the second innings for Gloucestershire W.G. again dominated the proceedings by scoring 153 in 3 hours and 10 minutes out of 268 for seven. The match was drawn with Yorkshire 29 for none in their second innings. Owing to the death of his mother Yorkshire were without the services of Peel after Gloucestershire's first innings.

John Parratt, who appeared in two matches for Yorkshire, the one above and the other in 1890 doing little of note, was a useful all-rounder, who was professional with Selkirk in 1885 and Werneth in 1887–88 later playing for Morley in 1900–01. He died at the 'Royal Oak', Morley, where he had been the landlord in 1905.

At Park Avenue, Surrey were 326 for five at the end of the first day with Maurice Read having scored 109 in 3 hours, the fielding becoming loose as the day wore on. Rain had prevented a prompt start on the second day and bad light also caused the conditions to deteriorate. When Yorkshire batted they were dismissed for totals of 101 and 126 with George Lohmann taking thirteen cheap wickets, giving Surrey an innings victory.

Yorkshire batted almost the whole of the first day at Maidstone against Kent, making a moderate total of 192, Hall spent three hours over 49. In 20 minutes' batting, Kent were 7 for the loss of four wickets at the end of the day. W. H. Patterson then spent $2\frac{1}{2}$ hours over an admirable 58 but received only minimal support as Kent were all out for 120. Peel's 25 was the only resistance when Kent bowled out the visitors a second time for 75, thus setting Kent 148 to win. By the end of the second day Kent were 53 for four notwithstanding another fine 32 from Patterson; heavy overnight rain did not improve Kent's chances as they were dismissed for 96.

Yorkshire's final county match was at Hove where Sussex gave a poor batting display after winning the toss. Yorkshire did little better, being bowled out for 115. Overnight rain only gave time for Sussex to be dismissed for 66 as Preston, bowling in lively fashion, took eight for 27. Yorkshire were 13 without loss before more rain came making the pitch even more difficult. Only 34 runs were needed when Hawke and Hall resumed batting, but the two Hides bowled well and Yorkshire had to struggle to obtain the runs. They eventually won by three wickets.

The season was wound up at Scarborough, MCC being the visitors, with the pitch so wet after several hours of rain that the match did not start until 1.30. Yorkshire won the toss and at the end of the first day had scored 179 for seven, going on to 207 with Hall batting with more freedom than usual in compiling 45 and Lee batting well until a run out ended his innings at 38. By arrangement a fresh pitch was prepared for the MCC second innings but a total of 53 for seven saw them in a poor light until William Gunn (20)) and H. W. Forster (23) came together to take the score to 98. Thornton came in later on to hit 48 and prevent the follow-on. Yorkshire, 9 for one at the end of the second day, were dismissed for 100. At the end MCC were left with 153 to win but after Thornton was second man out for 24 out of 38, the MCC collapsed against Preston, who took nine for 28 in an excellent spell of bowling which dismissed the visitors for 92.

After trying several wicket-keepers in place of Joseph Hunter, including A. Wormald, J. E. Ellis, W. Coverdale and J. Yeadon, Yorkshire brought in David Hunter for this last fixture and he retained his place until the end of the 1909 season when he retired. An unobtrusive wicket-keeper, reliable both on and off the field, how he compared with his brother, or with later Yorkshire wicket-keepers, it is impossible to say. He never appeared in Test cricket and his batting was never more than useful, so it can be assumed that he was never quite good enough to command a place in a respresentative side by his 'keeping alone (unlike Strudwick, or Duckworth) but Yorkshire considered him highly and his advice as to the condition of pitches was often sought by Lord Hawke. Known as 'Old Ironsides', David Hunter had one advantage over his elder brother Joe insomuch that he kept fitter than Joe and damaged hands did not keep him out of the side quite so often. Born at Scarborough in 1860, he was the youngest of five brothers, their father being a builder, and four of the five took an interest in cricket with three keeping wicket; David followed Joseph as the Scarborough wicket-keeper as well as Yorkshire's. For years he lived near the Scarborough ground and he liked clog-dancing, kept canaries and pigeons; was interested in weightlifting and boxing as well as hand-bell ringing. He was somewhat deaf in later years but was a well-known coach at Scarborough and was respected in many ways, particularly for his tolerance with young cricketers. He died at Scarborough in 1927.

Thus ended a somewhat unfortunate season for Yorkshire who won 7, lost 7 and drew 6 of their first-class matches. In the County Championship they could be bracketed second with Kent, which does not indicate anything other than a satisfactory season in view of their wicket-keeping problem and the fact that Emmett, Bates and Joe Hunter had retired. Compared with the County Champions, Surrey, all the other counties seemed to suffer by comparison, so big was the gulf between them and the other counties in 1888.

During the 1888 season it was resolved by the YCC Committee that Barnsley should have a representative on the County Committee.

In what was a dreadfully wet season in 1888, Hall finished on top of the first-class county averages with 473 runs at 20.52, with Ulyett closely behind him with 509 runs at 20.36. Peel scored 351 runs at 15.95 and Fred Lee scored 346 runs at 15.72.

The bowling figures make much better reading with Peel leading the way with 86 wickets at 11.37. Wainwright took 34 at 14.02 and J. M. Preston 49 at 14.61.

Before the new season began, the only apparent change in the team's format was 'that G. Ulyett be deputy Captain during the ensuing season.'

The new season of 1889 was to begin on 13 May but due to the state of the ground the first match was abandoned without a ball being bowled. Yorkshire met Liverpool & District on 30 May in a match which had been accorded first-class status by the Association of

Cricket Statisticians but was not given recognition by the Yorkshire CCC. *Wisden* ranked the same fixture in 1887 and in 1890 as first-class, but for some unspecified reason demoted this 1889 game. Yorkshire won by an innings and 41 runs.

After victory by eleven runs against Cambridge, Yorkshire went to Lord's where a remarkable match took place with Middlesex which resulted in the southern county gaining victory by four wickets in a match containing 1295 runs. In glorious sunshine on a hard fast wicket, Yorkshire won the toss and were all out for 259 in 4 hours and 5 minutes, Louis Hall carrying his bat through the innings for 85 not out. Stoddart began well for Middlesex with 46 out of 68 and at the end of the first day they had scored 116 for two. Next morning Middlesex managed to reach 368. Yorkshire soon lost two wickets for only 8 but Hall and Peel by the end of the day took the score to 222 for two. Their partnership reached 229 before Peel was dismissed for 158, an innings lasting 4 hours and 50 minutes. Hall left for 86 at 313 for five, having been batting for 5 hours and 50 minutes and Yorkshire were finally dismissed for 388. Middlesex needed 280 in 215 minutes and at 129 for four with Scott having made 36, the match seemed to be heading for a draw; then O'Brien came in and in 80 minutes hit a thrilling 100 to win the game for Middlesex with 10 minutes to spare. It was suggested that the large number of runs scored was partly due to the number of balls in an over being increased from four to five.

Lees Whitehead made his debut in this match and became a regular member of the Yorkshire side in his first season. He continued to play until 1904 and had the reputation of being a dependable 12th man and was given a grant of £250 by the County in 1905. He was born at Birchen Bank, Friarmere in 1864 and was a right-hand batsman with a sound defence whose best innings for his county were played when runs were badly needed. He used to play for Friarmere in the 1880s and he was on the ground-staff at Lord's when he first represented Yorkshire. Also a right-arm medium-fast bowler he had several remarkable performances and was also a fine fielder. He went to live in West Hartlepool where he played as professional from 1899 to 1904, settled in business there and coached in the local League. He died in 1913 after catching a chill at a football match at West Hartlepool.

At Bradford, Sussex shocked Yorkshire by defeating them by four wickets. The visitors won the toss and batted with W. Newham batting brilliantly for 110 out of 143 in 2 hours and 5 minutes. Jesse Hide scored 36 and W. A. Humphreys 45 but poor fielding and catching did not help Yorkshire's cause. Sussex totalled 273. Next day Yorkshire were dismissed for 150 with most of the Sussex bowlers taking wickets. Following on Yorkshire batted better in their second innings but there were six wickets down for 129 before R. Moorhouse

(54) and E. Wainwright (53) put on 93 for the eighth wicket as Yorkshire were dismissed for 242. On the last day, Sussex, though losing wickets, made the 120 required for victory without too much difficulty.

At the Spa Ground at Gloucester, the home side won the toss with the Graces opening with a stand of 91. W.G. made 50 and E.M. 37, but wickets then fell regularly and the side were out for 231. At the close of play on the first day Yorkshire were only 119 for six and on the second Gloucestershire gained a lead of 71. By the time Gloucestershire had been dismissed a second time the lead had grown to 325. Yorkshire never appeared likely to reach this figure and lost by 93 runs. Yorkshire's bad run continued at Bramall Lane, with Surrey proving comfortable winners by nine wickets. Surrey began well with J. Shuter scoring 56 and J. M. Read 90 as they put on 95 for the second wicket, then W. W. Read (50) helped his namesake in a stand of 93 and Surrey were 218 for three, but collapsed to be all out for 257. Yorkshire, 8 for one overnight, were bowled out for 141, Lohmann taking six for 60. In their second innings, Hall and Ulyett (34) opened with a stand of 53 and then Hill (33) and S. Wade (36) made useful scores but Hall made 48 out of 138 for four before they were all out at the end of the day for 187 with Lohmann picking up another six wickets. On the next morning Surrey knocked off the 75 needed losing only Shuter in the process.

Worse was to come with Kent at Mote Park defeating Yorkshire by an innings and 106 runs. Yorkshire won the toss and put Kent in to bat; a decision that turned out to be a sad failure with G. G. Hearne (64) helping his side to a formidable 239. The Yorkshire bowling and fielding was well below its best form. Other than Lord Hawke with 22, Yorkshire batted poorly and were dismissed for 71. They followed on and in their second innings were 32 for three at the end of the second day. It was all over before lunch on the last day – Yorkshire bowled out for 62.

Yorkshire met Lancashire at Huddersfield and won the toss on a pitch that gave bowlers help throughout the game. Lancashire were bowled out for 81 with Ulyett taking seven for 50. Yorkshire did much better when they batted with Fred Lee scoring 42 in an hour and Lord Hawke scoring an aggressive 52 not out although he was dropped when only 4. Yorkshire gained a first innings lead of 79. At the close of play Lancashire were 22 for four in their second innings with all four wickets taken by Ulyett. On the next day, the fifth wicket fell at 27 before Briggs joined F. Ward and they took the score to 78 for six before Ward left for 22. Briggs went on to score 41 and with Baker making a fighting 29, Lancashire reached 153. Needing only 75 to win Yorkshire lost four wickets for nine runs and then had seven down for 38. Nine wickets were down for 71 when Hunter was joined by Middlebrook who was immediately caught off Mold for 0. Lancashire thus gained a sensational victory by three runs.

Yorkshire's misfortunes continued at Bramall Lane, where Nottinghamshire won the toss and batted first making 225 – a score that would have been much less but for indifferent catching. At the close of play Yorkshire were 83 for three with Fred Lee run out for 41. Peel with 60 and Ulyett (28) added 73 for Yorkshire's fourth wicket before Ulyett was out at 143 for four but the County collapsed to 201 all out. An hour's rain held up play as Nottinghamshire finished the second day with 131 for six. On the next day Nottinghamshire were bowled out for 134. When Yorkshire batted again they soon lost five wickets for 24 but Hall (24) and Wainwright (50) took Yorkshire to 68 after 2 hours at the crease. Wainwright was eventually eighth out at 121 and Nottinghamshire went on to win by 36 runs.

John Wesley Parton was born at Wellington (Shropshire) and played in one match for Yorkshire v Nottinghamshire at Bramall Lane in 1889 when he scored 2 and 14 and took one for 4 in 10 overs and 7 maidens. At the time he was engaged by the Worksop club and afterwards was professional with Werneth for many years. He was Yorkshire's 16th non-native to represent the County.

At last Yorkshire met with success at Bradford against Gloucestershire who won the toss and were soon in trouble with three down for 39 including both the Graces. J. H. Brain with 50 was joined by J. Cranston who batted for two hours and 20 minutes for his 51 and with A. C. M. Croome scoring 29, Gloucestershire were all out for 200. Yorkshire, due to 63 from Peel, obtained a lead of 13. Apart from an opening stand of 48 between W. G. Grace who went on to make 52, and O. G. Radcliffe (22) Gloucestershire had little to offer in their second innings and were dismissed for 138 leaving Yorkshire with 126 to win. They had obtained 18 for one by the close of the second day and on a pitch that was getting better, Yorkshire, thanks to Hall who made 42 not out, went on to win by five wickets.

Jeremiah Driver, a good right-hand batsman who appeared twice for Yorkshire as a wicket-keeper in 1889 commencing with the above match, was born at Keighley in 1861 and when 17 appeared at Lawkholme against the Australians. He scored 2504 runs for Keighley from 1878–83 and appeared for the Yorkshire Colts in 1885 and was also professional at Bradford and at Nelson where he was captain and groundsman for many years. He died at hospital in Keighley in 1946, his funeral being at Keighley Cemetery.

John Thomas Brown sen. (of Driffield), always known as such to distinguish him from his namesake John Thomas Brown jun. (of Darfield), made his debut for Yorkshire against Gloucestershire at

Bradford and remained in the side until forced to retire owing to ill-health early in 1904. He was born at Driffield in 1869 and was therefore only 19 when he first played for the county as a forcing right-hand batsman and occasional leg-break bowler. A short, stocky man and a brilliant out-fielder, he specialised in the late cut and hook but could play every stroke in the book and he still holds the record for the quickest Test match 50 against Australia in 1895 at Melbourne which took 28 minutes. He was believed to have been only eleven years old when he first played for Driffield Town. It was at Perth that his fatal illness was first caused by neglect of himself against the mists and chills of Scotland on summer evenings. (He was engaged at Perth in 1888 and 1889.) In 1891 and 1892 he seldom played owing to an attack of 'flu in the first year and he was not fully fit for a couple of years. In 1892 he acted as professional at Brighouse and went to live at Halifax in 1893 or 1894 where he was professional from 1893–95 and once scored 140 against Elland. At Halifax he had a sports outfitting business before moving back to Leeds where he had a tobacconists' shop and lived during his later years. He died in London from congestion of the brain and heart failure and asthma having been sent there by Yorkshire CCC in an effort to improve his failing health. He was only 35 years old; his funeral being at Lawnswood Cemetery, Leeds. In Test cricket he had an average of 36 and for Yorkshire he scored 16,380 runs at an average of 29.30 which would have been much improved had he had normal health during his last two or three years. In 1969 a match was played to commemorate the centenary of his birth at Driffield.

Yorkshire won the toss at Old Trafford and elected to bat against Lancashire who quite outplayed their opponents on the first day. A poor batting performance saw Yorkshire dismissed for 117 in a little less than 3 hours. Lancashire were 151 for two at the close of play with F. H. Sugg out for 32 and A. N. Hornby 78 not out. On the following day Hornby left without addition and Lancashire were bowled out for 215. In 175 minutes batting, Yorkshire made 139 at their second attempt, Hall being the last man out for 48, and Lancashire cruised to a ten wicket victory.

Yorkshire's next match was at Bramall Lane against Kent who had the advantage of batting first after winning the toss on a typical Bramall Lane wicket of this period. After losing six wickets for 32, C. J. M. Fox (40) and A. Hearne (42) came together to add 67 valuable runs as Kent were finally dismissed for 121. Yorkshire were soon out next morning for 47 without any batsman reaching double figures, Martin took six for 21. When Kent batted again, they struggled to 102. Peel took six for 50. Wright took six cheap wickets in Yorkshire's second innings to bring Kent victory by 82 runs.

Rain spoilt Yorkshire's chances of defeating Middlesex at Halifax with a blank third day which left Yorkshire firmly anchored at the bottom of the Championship table. Yorkshire won the toss and scored 151. Middlesex began rather well in reply with 57 on the board for the loss of only two wickets but A. J. Webbe then left for 29 and Middlesex could only reach 108 as Peel took five for 36. In their second innings Yorkshire were dismissed for 90. Middlesex were 22 for one when the match had to be abandoned. Another draw followed at Trent Bridge with rain interrupting each day at some time or other.

Yorkshire's next match was at Hove and on it depended the destination of the wooden spoon in the County Championship, each side having won only a single game. Yorkshire were dismissed for 158 and with rain occasionally intervening, Sussex were 42 for two at the close of play. Peel took seven for 43 as Sussex were dismissed for 95. Yorkshire also struggled, their score being 72 for seven before Wade (19) and Moorhouse (44) added 45 for the eighth wicket, Yorkshire finally reaching 150. At the end of the second day Sussex were 61 for four, and with Peel in good form they were all out for 145, giving Yorkshire victory by 68 runs and Sussex the wooden spoon.

Yorkshire had first choice of a very wet and sluggish pitch at The Oval but after Ulyett and Hall had opened with 34, wickets fell regularly until seven were down for 71 at which score Wade (23) and Moorhouse (47) added 59 for the eighth wicket. Yorkshire were all out for 138. Surrey, however, finished 24 in arrears with Peel taking five for 50. Lee with 32 and Hall (33) took Yorkshire's score to 73 before the third wicket fell but Yorkshire were bowled out for 141 in their second innings. Surrey therefore required 166 in $3\frac{1}{4}$ hours if the game was to finish inside two days. Surrey found runs difficult to get with K. J. Key run out for 33 as their score stood at 105 for seven. R. Henderson stood firm and J. W. Sharpe with 14 batted well and put on 31 before being eighth out at 136. When time for stumps to be drawn had been reached Surrey still required 26 for victory, and the captains agreed that an extra half hour should be played. Fourteen were still needed when the extra half-hour had been used and it took a further 20 minutes in fading light before Surrey finally won by two wickets, with Henderson batting for $2\frac{3}{4}$ hours for his chanceless 59. The gas-lights had been on for 20 minutes when the match finished and the game since then has always been known as the 'Gas Lamps Match'.

Yorkshire's final match took place on 2 September against the Gentlemen of the MCC, who had assembled a very strong team. The MCC won the toss and W. G. Grace made 27 out of 38; later G. F. Vernon also scored 27 but the highest stand of the innings was for 33 runs between S. M. J. Woods (15) and H. Philipson (19) as they took the total to 175. Yorkshire soon lost three wickets for 15 before Hall (24) was joined by Peel (31) as they added 45 for the fourth wicket. Yorkshire went on to be dismissed for 128 with Sammy Woods taking six for 40. On a pitch that was improving, the MCC lost three wickets for 48 but recovered to all out 215 by the end of the second day. Yorkshire were set to score 263 on the last day but three wickets fell for 56 before R. W. Frank, making his debut in a first-class match for Yorkshire, scored 46. However only Peel gave him much help and the MCC won by 35 runs.

Mr Robert Wilson Frank, a cousin of Joseph Frank, was a right-hand batsman and slow bowler whose chief claim to cricketing fame was for his dedicated service as captain of the Yorkshire 2nd XI in 1900–14. He was born at Pickering in 1864 and was educated at Elmfield School, York and played for Yorkshire from 1889 to 1903 but only in 18 matches. He was a powerful hitter and once scored 309 out of 382 in $3\frac{1}{2}$ hours for Middlesbrough v Scarborough at the North Marine Ground in 1893. He served on the Committee of the Yorkshire CCC and became a Vice-President and attended the Scarborough Festival for 64 years up to 1949.

Mr Edward Thornhill Beckett Simpson played for Yorkshire against the Gentlemen of the MCC in 1889 scoring 1 and 0, having also played against Liverpool & District earlier in the season. He was born at Crofton near Wakefield in 1867 and was a right-hand batsman of some ability, who was educated at Harrow but did not get into the eleven, though he gained his Blue at Oxford in 1888. He was a member of the firm of Hodgson's and Simpson's which ran a successful cricket team in the Wakefield area for many years and he played for that team from 1898–1905. A Governor of Wakefield Grammar School and a member of Walton Parish Council, he lived at Walton Hall at one time (it became a famous bird sanctuary) and he died at his home in Walton, Wakefield in 1944.

The 1889 season was remembered as one of the worst for cricket followers in Yorkshire. The side itself was weaker than in previous seasons with several players having retired or been sacked, but that hardly accounts for the deterioration in fielding, which had never been worse. Emmett had left the side through old age; Bates had left because of an unfortunate injury. Peate and Preston were top class players who left the Club for other reasons than lack of form. There were other players such as Grimshaw, Wade and Fred Lee, who for one reason or another had failed to live up to expectations. In their first-class programme (excluding Liverpool & District) Yorkshire won 3, lost 11 and drew 2 matches.

The first-class county batting averages were headed by Hall who scored 664 runs at an average of 26.56. R. Peel was second with 640 runs at 23.70, and then came Lord Hawke with 351 runs at 19.55. Wainwright showed consistency with 448 runs at 19.48.

The bowling averages were better than the batting with Peel

leading the way with 80 wickets at 15.75, an excellent performance especially if one takes into account his batting skills. George Ulyett had a much better season with the ball, taking 34 wickets at 15.91 — a fine performance for a medium-fast bowler at the age of almost 38. William Middlebrook played in half the matches and took 23 wickets at 18.26 each, just above Lees Whitehead, who in his first season took 29 wickets at 19.03. Wainwright proved rather frustrating as the leading off-spinner with 33 wickets at 22.30. Perhaps the pitches needed to be wetter for his type of bowling.

On 5 August 1889 appeared the following paragraph in the YCCC Minute Book which had some significance for the future of Yorkshire cricket '. . . that G. Herbert Hirst of Kirkheaton be engaged for the Lancs. Match.' (Presumably he acted as twelfth man.)

The 1890 season began at Bristol. The home side decided to bat first and though Cranston made 101, the team total was only 194. Whitwell on his debut dismissed E. M. Grace for 0. At the close of play Yorkshire were 75 for one. The following day saw Ulyett (107) and Lee (67) put on 135 for the second wicket in 105 minutes before Lee left. Ulyett went on to bat for three hours and 20 minutes for an excellent knock. Peel, Wainwright, Brown and Lees Whitehead all did well as Yorkshire scored 330. In their second innings only Radcliffe with 61 and to a lesser extent J. R. Painter (29) played any innings of substance as they were dismissed for 178. Yorkshire went on to win by eight wickets.

Mr William Fry Whitwell was a well-built hard-hitting right-hand batsman and right-arm medium-fast bowler who was in the Uppingham XI from 1883–1886 being captain in his last years. He was born at Stockton-on-Tees in 1867 and played in 10 matches for Yorkshire in 1890 with some success with the ball but never played again for the county. In 1887 when 19 he scored 181 for Redcar against Middlesbrough in the Cleveland Cup final and also assisted the Gentlemen *v* Players at Scarborough in 1900 as well as touring America and Canada under Lord Hawke in 1894. He was one of Saltburn's early players who along with his brother J. F. Whitwell did much to ensure that the club survived along with its ground in Marske Mill Lane. He captained Durham CCC from 1893–1896 and played for Norton-on-Tees as well as Saltburn in the NY & SD League. He died in 1942 aged 74 at Newcastle-upon-Tyne.

At Aigburth, Yorkshire played a friendly first-class game against Liverpool and District and beat the local combination fairly easily, Peel taking ten wickets in the match for only 70 runs.

In their next match Yorkshire accomplished a fine feat when they defeated the touring Australians at Bramall Lane by seven wickets, over 24,000 paying to watch the two days' play. Batting first the visitors batted poorly for 87, Peel taking six for 34. Yorkshire replied with 161 with R. Peel batting well for 39 and Lord Hawke scoring 28. Peel took six more wickets in the second innings and Yorkshire had no difficulty in scoring the 52 required in the final innings.

Yorkshire's journey to Fenner's and their defeat by nine wickets produced some good cricket with Yorkshire's main satisfaction perhaps coming from the bowling of F. S. Jackson who took five for 61 when Yorkshire were bowled out for 193. When Cambridge batted, C. P. Foley (34) and R. N. Douglas (72) opened with a stand of 98 but only D. L. A. Jephson with 37 did much until nine wickets were down for 228 when A. J. L. Hill (49) and E. C. Streatfield (57) put on 101 for the last wicket in 75 minutes. In Yorkshire's second innings only Fred Lee with 59 batted well as the visitors were bowled out for 146. F. S. Jackson this time took seven for 53.

At Park Avenue, Sussex spent the whole of the first day scoring 285. Yorkshire in reply reached a formidable 388 on this fine run-getting wicket. At the close of the second day Sussex were 105 for three having lost Walter Quaife for 37 and W. Newham for 49. On the last day George Bean went on to score 45 and F. C. New 43 and Sussex were going very well at 196 for four before Brown's rarely used leg-breaks broke through and Sussex were bowled out for 260. Yorkshire made light work of winning the match by six wickets, Lord Hawke scoring 48 and Hall anchoring the innings down with 35 not out.

Yorkshire's first and last game at Bootham Crescent, York, home of Yorkshire Gentlemen's CC but now the home of York City AFC, took place on 9, 10 June. Kent won the toss and in atrocious light were bowled out for 46 although three batsmen could not take their innings as they failed to turn up in time. Yorkshire scored 114, but even this total gave them a lead of 68. Kent did much better at their second attempt with G. G. Hearne (22) opening with 41 with his brother Alec who went on to score 39. L. Wilson made 20 and W. H. Spottiswoode 37 as Kent were finally dismissed for 167. Peel took five for 27. Yorkshire were set 100 to win and with Hall in his usual unyielding mood, Yorkshire duly recorded victory with eight wickets to spare.

Yorkshire's fine form continued down at Lord's where Yorkshire scored 165 due mainly to Ted Wainwright who scored 59. In reply Middlesex began well with 63 for one on the board but after A. J. Webbe had left for 32 and S. W. Scott for 29, wickets fell quickly and they were dismissed for 113 with Peel taking five for 40. Yorkshire left Middlesex with 206 to win on a pitch that was getting progressively more difficult. Only T. C. O'Brien who hit 25 made any impression on the Yorkshire spin attack as the home side were summarily dismissed for 49. Peel and Wainwright each took five wickets. At this stage of the season Yorkshire were unbeaten at the top of the Championship table.

At Bramall Lane, Nottinghamshire won the toss and managed to score 138 mainly because of 47 from Arthur Shrewsbury, who stayed in for 2½ hours. Wainwright bowled very well to take six for 47. At the end of the day, with 14,000 watching the play, Yorkshire were handily placed at 61 for three with Hall still there on 14. Next day, Hall left at 66, and only Peel with 25 reached double figures as Yorkshire were tumbled out for 96. William Attewell took five for 26. Shrewsbury (38) and William Gunn (26) put Nottinghamshire on top after J. A. Dixon had been dismissed for 31, but the visitors were all out for 225, leaving Yorkshire 268 to win. Accurate bowling by Attewell caused the batsmen all sorts of problems and Yorkshire were skittled out for just 69, leaving Nottinghamshire winners by 198 runs.

The return match with the Australians at Park Avenue was keenly anticipated following the defeat of the visitors in the previous game. The Australians won the toss and lost six wickets for 36, but the lower order resisted stoutly and with Barrett hitting 61 in 195 minutes the total reached 177. At the close of play Yorkshire were 63 for three. Next day, Hall and Peel added 119 for the fourth wicket before Peel was run out for 73; Hall went on to score 64 in 3 hours and 10 minutes, Yorkshire being dismissed for 171. In their second innings the Australians lost seven wickets for only 20 runs before Dr Barrett again came to the rescue with a well-judged 48. This left Yorkshire needing 148. Fred Lee and Lord Hawke took Yorkshire to an eight wicket victory.

At Bramall Lane, Yorkshire's match with Surrey was unfortunately ruined by bad weather which was very upsetting for the beneficiary, Louis Hall. Yorkshire were all out for 110. Surrey then replied with 129, Peel taking eight for 60, and the match finished with Yorkshire 71 for four.

Joseph Redfearn played in one match for Yorkshire in 1890 against Surrey at Bramall Lane scoring 5 in his only innings. He was a son of Tom Redfearn, the old Lascelles Hall player, and was a left-handed batsman who was born at Lascelles Hall in 1862. He died in his native village in 1931.

At Old Trafford, Lancashire totalled 161 with J. Briggs making top score before being run out for 52 in 2 hours 20 minutes. When Briggs was called for a run by A. N. Hornby, the former was injured so badly that he had a runner in the second innings and was unable to bowl. When Yorkshire batted Mold was in deadly form and took eight for 38, only Ernest Smith offering much resistance with 23. In the second innings, Lancashire soon lost three wickets before Briggs with a runner scored 54 in $1\frac{1}{4}$ hours. Lancashire were finally all out for 187. At the end of the day Yorkshire were 2 for two and fortunately for them rain prevented any play on the last day and so the visitors got away with a draw.

Henry James Tinsley made his debut for Yorkshire in the above match and altogether played in nine matches for Yorkshire in 1890 and the following year with very little success. He was born at Welham Grange, Malton in 1865 and was a right-hand bat and medium-fast bowler. He later appeared in the ranks of Lancashire for three seasons, his brother also playing for that county. He died in 1938 at Heworth, York.

Yorkshire's return match with Lancashire at Fartown proved a disaster for the home team after rain had washed out the first day's play. Yorkshire won the toss and were bowled out for 90 in less than $2\frac{1}{2}$ hours with Ulyett alone withstanding the fast, lively bowling of Arthur Mold on a pitch that was ready made for him. Mold took nine for 41. Lancashire finished with a lead of 85 on the first innings with Peel taking six for 43. When Yorkshire batted again Ulyett made 13 and Hall 21 but Yorkshire were dismissed for 57 to lose by an innings and 28 runs. F. S. Jackson made his debut in this match.

Rt Hon Sir Frank Stanley Jackson, GCSI, GCIE, a son of Rt Hon W. L. Jackson (1st Lord Allerton) who was a Cabinet Minister in Lord Salisbury's Government, was born at Chapel Allerton, Leeds in 1870 and was a sound, orthodox right-hand batsman who liked to attack the bowling when set and could bat anywhere in the order. He was also a right-arm fast medium bowler with a fluent action who also bowled medium-paced off-breaks and was a brilliant fielder usually in the covers. His chief claim to cricketing fame was to lead England in 1905 against Australia when he not only retained the Ashes but headed both the batting and bowling averages. Jackson was educated at Harrow, where he was in the eleven from 1887 to 1889, captaining the side in his last year, and had Winston Churchill as his 'fag'. He went up to Cambridge University where he was in the eleven for four years and was captain in his last two. In 1892/93 he toured India under Lord Hawke and first played for England in 1893, but he never toured abroad again and was restricted in his cricket by business and parliamentary affairs. Sir Stanley Jackson first played for Yorkshire in 1890 and played over 200 matches for the County until his final retirement in 1907. In two seasons 1900 and 1901 he did not turn out at all and in only two seasons – 1897 and 1898 – did he play regularly for the team. Yet he succeeded in taking over 500 wickets and scored over 10,000 runs for Yorkshire and in 1898 completed the 'double' in all first-class matches. He was never appointed captain of Yorkshire but often led them in the absence of the official captain and he had the knack of coming into the side at any time and reproducing his best form without any practice. He became President of the MCC in 1921 and followed Lord Hawke as President of Yorkshire CCC, also acting as Chairman of the Test Selectors. MP for North Leeds in the Conservative interests, he became MP for Howdenshire from 1915 to 1926 and was Governor of Bengal from 1927 to 1932, where an attempt was made to assassinate him. He was chairman of the Conservative Party from 1923. In 1946 he was knocked down by a taxi and badly injured. He died in 1947 in Knightsbridge, London aged 76. He was buried in Welton Cemetery.

Yorkshire's next match was at Lord's against the MCC with Yorkshire making a bad start by losing five wickets for 28 before F. S. Jackson (68) and Moorhouse added 134 for the sixth wicket in 90 minutes. Moorhouse went on to score 105 in 105 minutes to record his first first-class century. Compared with Yorkshire's 217, the MCC could only score 86 and 60, thus providing the County with victory by a large margin.

Mr Arthur Sellers, the father of A. Brian and G. J. Sellers, played in the above match and one other, also in 1890, then in 1892 and 1893. He scored over 1000 runs in 1893. He was born at Keighley in 1870 and was an aggressive free scoring right-hand batsman not unlike his son Brian in style and a brilliant close-in fielder. An engineer by profession, he was prevented by his business commitments from playing regularly in first-class cricket but served on the Yorkshire CCC Selection Committee for many years, later being a Vice-President of the Club.

Gloucestershire came to Dewsbury and, winning the toss, were dismissed for only 72, Peel being unplayable. Yorkshire took the lead with only two wickets down as Peel made 51 in 55 minutes, putting on 65 for the third wicket with Louis Hall going on to bat for 2 hours for his 49. Yorkshire finished the day all out for 209. Gloucestershire then lost three wickets, all to debutant Bolton, with only 19 on the board but W.G. with 98 added 188 for the fourth wicket with J. Cranston in 140 minutes. Grace had batted for 2 hours and 40 minutes but Cranston went on to score 152 in $3\frac{1}{2}$ hours in a total of 341. B. C. Bolton finished with four for 63 and Ernest Smith took four for 66. Requiring 251 to win, Yorkshire collapsed to 120 all out and were defeated by 84 runs.

Mr Benjamin Charles Bolton, a right-hand batsman and right-arm fast-medium bowler, played in just four matches for Yorkshire in 1890 and 1891. He was born at Cottingham near Hull in 1862 and played for Hull Town for many years. He died after falling from an express train near Brough in 1910 and was buried in Hornsea Cemetery.

Nottinghamshire spent all day scoring 245 against Yorkshire at

Trent Bridge with Arthur Shrewsbury spending 3 hours 20 minutes in scoring 69. Yorkshire then proceeded to bat very poorly and the score was 119 for eight when Peel was joined by J. T. Brown. The pair added 55 for the ninth wicket with Peel scoring 83. After Shrewsbury (31) and J. A. Dixon (37) had put on 69 for the first wicket, Nottinghamshire were 140 for four at the end of the second day. With an hour lost to rain before the start of the last day, Nottinghamshire set Yorkshire 249 to win in 215 minutes but the visitors decided to concentrate on the draw, finishing the game at 139 for eight.

Mr Joseph Fry Whitwell, brother of W. F. and A. P. Whitwell, made his only appearance for Yorkshire in the above match, taking the wicket of Scotton at the cost of 11 runs. A powerfully built man, who stonewalled as a right-hand batsman but was a very capable medium paced bowler, he was in the Uppingham XI from 1883 to 1887, captaining the side in his last year and went on to captain Durham from 1899 to 1902 leading them to the 2nd Class Counties Championship in 1901. An Ironmaster in business, he played with Norton and Saltburn and died in 1932 at Langbaurgh Hall, Great Ayton.

Bad weather prevented Yorkshire beating Middlesex at Bradford where there was no play at all on the first or last days.

Surrey won the toss at The Oval and continued batting into the second day to obtain 293, W. H. Lockwood making 102 in $2\frac{1}{2}$ hours. Yorkshire had recalled G. P. Harrison for this match and he bowled extremely well to take five for 72. After Ulyett (19) and Hall had put on 38 for the first wicket, Hall went on to score 56 in $2\frac{1}{2}$ hours. Moorhouse scored 20 as Yorkshire were all out for 137. In their second innings on a much-improved pitch, Ulyett batted very well to score 90 in $2\frac{1}{4}$ hours with Brown, Lord Hawke (36), Moorhouse and David Hunter all making useful contributions as Yorkshire took their score to 247, leaving Surrey with only 92 to win. On the last day, after very heavy rain, Surrey went in on a very difficult wicket and were shot out for 76, Harrison taking five for 22. Yorkshire won by 15 runs. For Harrison, bowling at a much slower pace than previously, the match was quite a triumph.

The Kent match at Maidstone was another draw with only 2 hours possible on the second day and little more on the last day. Moving on to Hove, Sussex chose to bat first on a slow wicket and in a little less than two hours were bowled out for 48 with Peel taking seven for 25 and the revived Harrison three for 21. Hall and Ulyett gave Yorkshire a good start by hoisting 42 for the first wicket before Brown (41) and Lord Hawke (65) added 67 for the third wicket in good style. On the second day Yorkshire were soon all out for 208 with that great London Club cricketer, the Rev C. J. M. Godfrey making one of his all too rare first-class appearances by taking five for 22. In their second innings, Sussex were dismissed for only 82, leaving Yorkshire the winners by an innings and 78 runs.

Yorkshire's last match was a 12-a-side game with the MCC at Scarborough which was drawn after various stoppages for rain.

Yorkshire finished the season in third place equal with Kent which was certainly satisfactory in comparison with the previous season. Lord Hawke finished on top of the batting averages in first-class county matches (he missed four games) with 444 runs, average 26.11, just ahead of Ulyett who scored 623 runs at 25.95 and recovered his form which had deteriorated so much in 1889. Peel scored 407 runs with an average of 20.35 just ahead of Hall with 447 runs at 20.31. (The last two had very modest records indeed even in a season that was no help to batsmen).

Harrison headed the bowling averages with 21 wickets at 10.19 coming with quite a bang in the closing weeks to also head the first-class bowling averages. Peel was second with 91 wickets at 12.80 – an excellent performance well ahead of Wainwright whose 37 wickets cost 14.89. B. C. Bolton with 12 wickets; Ernest Smith with 14 and W. F. Whitwell with 23 at 20 apiece all showed promise but none was thought likely to be available for long.

Yorkshire should have started the new season of 1891 on 25 May at Lord's but regrettably the game had to be abandoned without a ball being bowled. H. Walton who only played in one match against Liverpool & District in 1893 in a match excluded from the Yorkshire records and J. Bretherton who was never chosen again were both included in the eleven. Their first match was therefore at Fenner's where the University went on to win an exciting match by four wickets.

Sussex brought Yorkshire down to earth in the first County Championship match of 1891 at Dewsbury, where they decided to bat first and accumulated 187. Walter Quaife scored 47 in 2¼ hours and then C. A. Smith (19) joined W. A. Humphreys (49) to add 54 for the sixth wicket as Sussex reached a very respectable total of 187. Sussex were aided by some poor Yorkshire catching, though Harrison bowled well to take six for 43. Yorkshire were 45 for three at the close of play with Hall 13. Heavy rain on the following morning made the wicket more spiteful and in spite of Hall going on to make 31, Yorkshire were soon all out for 95. In their second innings Hall was 50 minutes ove 13 and Wainwright scored a plucky 20 but the side was soon dismissed for 61, for Sussex to win by an innings and 31 runs. George Bean bowled magnificently to take eight for 31.

Yorkshire kept faith with their players as they visited Lord's and completely outplayed the home side on another bowler's wicket.

A. J. Webbe put Yorkshire in to bat and after Brown (29) and A. Sellers (22) had helped Hall (32) in useful stands with the third wicket not falling until 67, Yorkshire collapsed to 109 all out with J. T. Hearne taking seven for 37. When Middlesex batted they were in trouble from the start and were skittled out for 63 with Harrison taking five for 14. There was still time for Yorkshire to get out before the close, only Wainwright with 28 batting well as the visitors were dismissed for 77. Hearne again bowled splendidly to take seven for 28. Further overnight rain did Middlesex no favours. Although a stand of 25 between E. A. Nepean (13) and S. W. Scott (20) gave rise for hopes, they soon collapsed to 54 all out, Yorkshire winning by 69 runs.

An undistinguished performance against Nottinghamshire at Trent Bridge followed. Yorkshire won the toss and Ulyett and Hall (11) put on 34 for the first wicket but although Ulyett went on to score 40, Yorkshire had lost five wickets for 77. John Tunnicliffe in his first match scored a promising 33 but Yorkshire were dismissed for 148. Nottinghamshire were 61 for two after 100 minutes' batting at the end of the first day. William Gunn (58) and Barnes took the score to 107 for three, having added 70, with Barnes carrying on to score 104 in 4 hours and 45 minutes at the crease. The tail batted well with H. B. Daft scoring 37 and Attewell 33 and Nottinghamshire totalled 336. Yorkshire gave a poor batting display on the last day with only Hall (39) and Peel (36) putting up much resistance in a stand of 60 for the third wicket. Nottinghamshire won by an innings and 25 runs.

John Tunnicliffe made his debut for Yorkshire in the above match and he showed steady improvement during this and the following season before gaining a regular place in the side in 1893, which he kept until his retirement in 1907. A tall right-hand batsman who could attack if it was required, he was usually the sheet-anchor of the team, in contrast to the quick-scoring robust cutter and hooker, Brown, and the dapper, quick-footed Denton. Although he was a fair slow bowler and useful wicket-keeper, perhaps his chief claim to fame was in his slip-fielding, which could only be compared with other great slip-fielders such as Woolley, Hammond, Simpson and Sharpe. Tunnicliffe was born at Lowtown, Pudsey in 1866 and joined Pudsey Britannia when aged 16 and scored his first century on his 18th birthday for that club against Armley. He was a hard-hitting batsman in those days, as indeed he was when he first came into the Yorkshire side, but he soon settled in a more defensive role. Regarded as Lord Hawke's right-hand man, he was highly respected and a devoted churchman. His sister married William Muff of Pudsey, composer of the Pudsey Anthem. After his playing days he became coach at Clifton College and eventually became a member of the Gloucestershire Committee; his son W. G. Tunnicliffe acting as Secretary of the

John Tunnicliffe, opening batsman, brilliant slip fielder and the senior professional greatly respected by Lord Hawke.

County Club from 1921 to 1935. He died at Westbury Park, Bristol in 1948.

Lancashire were the next visitors to Park Avenue and they were fortunate to win the toss and bat first. A. N. Hornby was run out without a run on the board and five wickets fell for 67, including Frank Sugg who was bowled by Peel for 37. S. M. Crosfield then added 57 for the sixth wicket with Briggs and 91 for the seventh wicket with G. Yates, who departed at 215 for seven. Crosfield went on to score 82 not out. Mold assisted in a last-wicket stand of 55 before Lancashire were all out for 278. Peel finished with seven for 90 and at the close of play on the first day Yorkshire were 51 without loss. On the second day they batted badly with Hall going early for 13. Ulyett went on to score 55 and T. Wardall, recalled to the side after an interval of four years, made a steady 29 not out but nothing could stop Yorkshire from following on 97 behind. Briggs took six for 80. In their second innings Hall spent 2½ hours in compiling 48, after he had lost Wardall for a well played innings of 51 out of 75 for the first wicket. After that Yorkshire fell apart and Lancashire won by eight wickets.

John Richard Leopold Bulmer was a quick scoring right-hand batsman and medium-fast bowler who made his single appearance for Yorkshire in this match. He was born at Guisborough in 1867 and was engaged at Lancaster in 1891–94 before becoming a member of the Liverpool CC groundstaff. He joined the Royton Club in 1896 being professional there from 1897 to 1899 before joining Werneth as an amateur in 1900. He returned to Royton in the following year. He died at Werneth in 1917.

Yorkshire met Liverpool and District at Aigburth in a match which again was excluded from the Yorkshire records although the ACS include it as a first-class match. A. G. Steel scored 100 for Liverpool, out of a total of 269, to which Yorkshire replied with 271 with Ulyett making 54 and Cartman 49. Liverpool then scored 217 with Peel taking four for 55 and leaving Yorkshire with 216 to win. Thanks to Edwin Smith, with seven for 59, Yorkshire were bowled out for 161, Liverpool and District winning by 54 runs.

The Surrey match at Bramall Lane was played for the benefit of Louis Hall, whose benefit in the previous season had been ruined by bad weather. Surrey won the toss and due to some determined batting by Maurice Read (135) reached 296. Yorkshire, in contrast, were dismissed for 180 and went in again on a wicket that had turned quite treacherous. Ulyett, with 18 out of 31 in half-an-hour, gave Yorkshire a bright start but they were soon all out for 89, Sharpe taking six for 39. Surrey won by an innings and 27 runs.

Joseph Thomas Mounsey made his first appearance for Yorkshire in the above match when he scored 3 and 6 and failed to take a wicket. He was born at Heeley, Sheffield in 1871 and was a sound, reliable right-hand batsman who could hit hard when set although he perhaps lacked the best of techniques. He was also an off-break bowler and roundarm medium-paced bowler – a very accurate and hard-working cricketer with a benevolent nature. He played for Sheffield Heeley when he first played for Yorkshire and also played for Sheffield United. He played one regular season for Yorkshire in 1894 and altogether played in 93 matches for his County from 1891 to 1897, averaging 15.57. He became coach at Charterhouse School at Godalming in 1899 where he remained until 1927 after which he acted as groundsman until the end of the 1938 season. He was later umpire to the Grasshoppers and the Charterhouse Friars after his retirement from the School until his health gave way in 1947. He died in 1949 at Godalming.

After heavy rain at Bristol, Gloucestershire won the toss and batted when the match was allowed to start at 3.30 pm. W. G. Grace, with 31, made the top score, but at 107 for six came further rain and the match was interrupted until the second day, when Gloucestershire were dismissed for 137. With the bowlers handicapped by a wet ball, Yorkshire's batsmen hit 225 for eight, at which point Hawke declared. When Gloucestershire batted again the wicket was at its worst and they were soon bowled out for 48, Yorkshire winning by an innings and 40 runs. Peel took six for 21 and Harrison had the remarkable analysis of 13-12-1-2.

Joshua Hudson Penny made his one and only appearance for Yorkshire against Gloucestershire in the above match. Born at Yeadon in 1856 he was a left-handed batsman and left-arm slow bowler who was engaged at Undercliffe in 1881, Guiseley in 1882–83, Ramsbottom 1884–85, Dewsbury and Savile 1886–88, Preston in 1894, Little Lever in 1895 (taking 134 wickets at 8.6), Ramsbottom 1897 and Dewsbury again from 1898. He died in 1902 in Savile Town, Dewsbury.

At Bramall Lane on 13 July Yorkshire won the toss against Nottinghamshire, who bowled out the home side for 110. Nottinghamshire replied with 292. Yorkshire failed a second time and Nottinghamshire achieved victory with an innings to spare.

Wiliam Henry ('Graff') Cartman, a free scoring right-hand bat in club cricket who played in three matches for Yorkshire in 1891, was born at Skipton in 1861 and lived most of his life there. He was for seven years professional for his local club.

At The Oval, Surrey defeated Yorkshire by ten wickets inside two days, Lohmann with twelve wickets being mainly responsible for this second successive reverse.

The Somerset match at Taunton which followed on 23 July saw the debut for Yorkshire of George Herbert Hirst. Yorkshire won the toss and without F. S. Jackson and Peel, Lord Hawke opened the innings and in three hours scored a brilliant 136 out of 233 for five in three hours with Ernest Smith also scoring 50. Somerset were 111 for two at the close of the first day with H. T. Hewett out for 39 and L. C. H. Palairet 45 not out. After rain overnight, the pitch was more helpful to the bowlers and after Palairet had been dismissed for 76, the home side were soon all out for 220, Wainwright taking six for 66. When Yorkshire batted again Lord Hawke was again in form as he scored 42 out of 64 for two but Ulyett went on to score 118 in 2 hours and 35 minutes with Tunnicliffe scoring 34 and Wainwright 54 in about 50 minutes. When Somerset batted again, V. T. Hill scored 30 and S. M. J. Woods 25 as Somerset were dismissed for 124 giving Yorkshire victory by 232 runs.

George Herbert Hirst (affectionately referred to by all as 'George Herbert') was born at Kirkheaton in 1871 and left school at 10 to become a wirer for a handloom weaver. He later worked as a postboy at a local Dalton dyeworks. He took part in his first match for Kirkheaton 2nd XI v Rastrick 2nd XI at Rastrick, appearing for Kirkheaton from 1885–89 and then went as professional to Elland in 1890, Mirfield in 1891 and Huddersfield in 1892, after which Yorkshire stopped county players from taking club engagements. A forcing right-hand batsman with the pull and drive among his favourite strokes, he was at his best in a crisis and rarely failed in situations where his side needed a rescue act. A left-arm medium-fast bowler, he was a shortish, stockily built figure with a huge capacity for hard work. His natural swerve made him one of the most difficult bowlers to face in conditions that suited him. He possessed that gift of getting life out of a pitch that all top-class bowlers have and, if he did have off-days, they appeared to be at times when other players could handle matters without 'George Herbert'. He was a generous hearted man in the Roy Kilner/Maurice Leyland mould and there was never a more popular cricketer anywhere in the world. Figures meant little to him yet he performed the unique double of 2,000 runs and 200 wickets in a season. He made the highest score ever made for Yorkshire of 341; and he completed the 'double' on more occasions – 14 – than any other cricketer apart from Wilfred Rhodes. It is remarkable that these two cricketers should both have been right-hand batsmen; both have been left-handed bowlers; and both come from the village of Kirkheaton. Which was the greater all-rounder it is impossible to say. Rhodes was undoubtedly a better bowler than a batsman at one part of his career and a better batsman than bowler at another; when required again to develop his bowling, he did so and his batting took second place. On the other hand once Hirst had climbed up the batting order and became recognised as a batsman, it could never be said that either bat or ball was predominant. His capacity as batsman or bowler always appeared to be equal. That cannot be said of any other player in the game. Hirst continued to play for Yorkshire until 1921 (he played once in 1930 too) and then became coach at Eton from 1920 to 1938 and was also involved in coaching Yorkshire's young cricketers almost up to his death. He was worshipped by players, spectators and all who came into contact with him. In 1950 he and Wilfred Rhodes laid a foundation stone for a pavilion to be built as a memorial to themselves in the Kirkheaton cricket ground. He died at Greenlea Hospital, Lindley, Huddersfield in 1954, aged 82, and was cremated at Lawnswood Cemetery, Leeds.

Moving on to Bramall Lane, Yorkshire won the toss against Gloucestershire and scored 283 with Lord Hawke (36) putting on 63 with Hall for the first wicket. Hall went on to score 60 and Ernest Smith 34 before Wainwright came in and hit 68 in about an hour. At the close of play Gloucestershire had replied with 81 for seven which next day became 91 all out. Wainwright took seven for 47. When they followed on E. M. Grace (26) and O. G. Radcliffe (50) put on 75 before a wicket fell. At 81 for four Gloucestershire seemed to be heading for a quick defeat but E. Sainsbury (36) and W. W. F. Pullen came together to add 123 for the fifth wicket in only 75 minutes, and in the end Gloucestershire scored 222. Yorkshire hit off the 31 runs required for victory without losing a wicket.

At Old Trafford, Lancashire made a good start by obtaining 288. Albert Ward (70) and Frank Sugg (77), both former Yorkshire players, put on 118 for the second wicket in 105 minutes with Ward batting for $2\frac{1}{2}$ hours. The pitch was deteriorating when Yorkshire batted and five wickets went down for 55. Peel, with 69 not out, added 50 for the sixth wicket with Wainwright (26) and lifted the overnight score of 97 for five to 150 all out. When they followed on the innings collapsed to 89 all out leaving Lancashire winners by an innings and 49 runs. Briggs took eight for 46.

Mr Samuel Robinson Jackson made his only appearance for Yorkshire in the above match. He replaced Arthur Sellers in the Yorkshire side after lunch-time on the first day, Sellers having been taken ill and Lancashire allowed the substitute to bat. He scored 9 and 0 being caught off Briggs in each innings. He was for many years captain of the Leeds CC. He served as the Leeds district member on the Yorkshire Committee and later became a Vice-President. His son Edmund H. Jackson was also a Leeds player and served on the Yorkshire Committee. S. R. Jackson used to live at Clifford House, Shadwell and ran the Clifford House CC on one of the prettiest grounds in the area. He belonged to the family business of Jackson's Ltd (Hatters).

At Bradford, Yorkshire won the toss and were immediately in trouble against Sammy Woods. They lost two wickets for 8 and then R. W. Frank broke a bone in his hand when facing Woods and this put him out of the match, Wardall helped Peel to take the score to 50 before he was run out and then Ernest Smith (41) joined Peel and they added 88 in 45 minutes. Peel went on to score 70 in 90 minutes as Yorkshire were all out for 175. Somerset were in even worse trouble against Wainwright and lost five wickets for 18 before L. C. H.

Palairet was joined by Woods, and they added 74 in only forty minutes before the fast bowler was dismissed for 50. Somerset went on to gain a lead of 26 on the first innings. Wainwright finished with seven for 73. In their second innings, Hall (37) and T. A. Wardall (43) put on 77 for Yorkshire's second wicket after the early loss of Ulyett but Woods then went through the rest of the Yorkshire side to finish with six for 64. Somerset knocked off the 91 runs needed for victory for the loss of four wickets.

Widespread rain at Bramall Lane prevented any play on the first day of the match with Middlesex at Bramall Lane. On a very soft wicket Middlesex won the toss and decided to bat. T. C. O'Brien opened the innings for the visitors and scored 72 in just over two hours, batting with great judgement and picking the right balls to hit, but so meagre was the support he received that they were all out for 155. Yorkshire fared even worse against some tight bowling by J. T. Hearne and Rawlin and were 38 in arrears at the end of the first innings. On the last day, Wainwright ran through the Middlesex side taking eight for 49. Yorkshire needed 147 for victory but with the pitch still favouring the bowlers, were bowled out for 79 and lost by 47 runs.

Yet another defeat followed at Mote Park, Maidstone with the home side winning the toss on a soft wicket which got worse as the match progressed. One hundred behind on first innings, Yorkshire followed on and disintegrated a second time, providing Kent with victory by nine wickets.

The match with Sussex at Hove brought back memories of 1889 when Yorkshire defeated Sussex at Hove to avoid the bottom place in the Championship. This time Gloucestershire were below both Yorkshire and Sussex, but, with matches in hand, the Western county could overhaul its rivals. Sussex won the toss and were bowled out for 139. At the close of play, in spite of losing two wickets for 29 runs, Yorkshire were 173 for two, Ulyett and Peel having added the last 73 in 35 minutes. Ulyett's fine display finished when he had scored 109 out of 209 for three in two hours and 40 minutes, and then F. S. Jackson (40) helped Peel to add 54 for the fourth wicket. Peel went on to score 128 out of 338 for eight made in 4 hours and 20 minutes. Ernest Smith and Wainwright ran through the Sussex batting in the second innings, providing Yorkshire with a most welcome victory.

Dr George Thornton was a left-handed batsman and left-arm medium-slow bowler who made his debut against Sussex. Recommended by A. E. Stoddart, Thornton had been playing for Hampstead CC in London club cricket for some years. His appearances for his native county were restricted to 1891 and later he played for Middlesex. He played for South Africa *v* Australia in 1902–03 living in Transvaal for several years and also represented Ceylon, touring

Madras in 1909–10 and became President of Colombo CC. His son P. A. Thornton appeared for Ireland in 1928 and Border in 1933–34. Dr Thornton, who played in spectacles, was a brisk attacking batsman.

Rain ruined Yorkshire's return match with Kent at Headingley with Yorkshire making 148 and 78 for five, and Kent 126. The first match of the Scarborough Cricket Festival against the MCC was abandoned without a ball being bowled and so Yorkshire's dreadful season of 1891 was over with the club finishing second from the bottom of the County Championship and with a record of 5 wins, 11 losses and 1 draw.

Peel finished top of the Yorkshire batting averages in first-class county matches with 588 runs, average 24.50. Ulyett scored 645 runs at 23.03 and Hall 620 runs at 22.14. Jackson did not play many matches and averaged only 16, with Lord Hawke also missing half the matches with the same average.

With the ball, Wainwright had the best record with 67 wickets at 15.64, with Peel second with 66 wickets at 17.17. Harrison took 38 wickets at 17.78. Ernest Smith took 15 wickets at 18.00 and F. S. Jackson 12 at 20.41.

The season which was such a poor one for the Yorkshire team and its followers gave vent to much discussion in the press. Even *Wisden* itself suggested that the inadequate representation of areas outside Sheffield may be most undesirable and suggested that the way to remedy '. . . such a state of things is not by abuse of authorities and of players such as disgraced Yorkshire last summer, but rather by encouraging both to further effort.'

It was not the missing of colts that was the problem – it was getting rid of the old players who had proved themselves to be inadequate. This 1889–1892 period was the most important in Yorkshire cricket; the constitution of the Committee was improved to give more adequate representation throughout Yorkshire and the team changed completely, with a different type of player selected – more like the modern Yorkshire professional. The sacking of Peel – while unfortunate and regrettable – was probably a good example of the correctness of Lord Hawke's policy of getting what he considered to be the right type of player into the Yorkshire team. The fact that Peel might have had a drink or two was sad if it affected him in any way. No doubt other Yorkshire cricketers have taken a drink or two too many, but for a Yorkshire player to have had too much in the presence of other players and members was something that would not be tolerated in a Yorkshire team. Peel may have been replaced by a better batsman and perhaps a better bowler in Wilfred Rhodes. Where Lord Hawke was right in picking Rhodes was not the fact that he could rely on Rhodes to bowl as well as Peel or better than him but that he would grow into the type of cricketer that Lord Hawke – and Yorkshire – needed. History would show that he did.

During the winter of 1891–92, the Committee spent a great deal of time in reconstituting the Yorkshire CCC and there were many resolutions put forward with regard to a new set of rules. There were deputations from various towns and areas throughout the county in their efforts to better matters for their particular district and to rally the cause for the County Club which had fallen on such bad times. It was suggested that each district should be able to obtain 50 members to subscribe to the Club. One gentleman from Dewsbury claimed to be representing 140 club secretaries who had met in the previous summer to discuss the problems. Another from Thirsk asked that his area would not ask for matches to be played in the area but that the Committee should see some of the young players from his area as potential players for the County.

Also in the Minutes of 23 December 1891 was a request: 'The President asked that members of the Commitee would not be interviewed by newspaper Reporters.'

The new season of 1892 got under way with a match against the MCC on 16 and 17 May. Yorkshire won the toss and Ulyett (25) and A. Sellers (20) put on 25 for the third wicket and at 110 for 9, W. Fletcher, a newcomer, came in and scored 31, helping Hirst to add 42 for the last wicket. MCC lost Foley at 0 before Hearne (26) and Barnes (61) added 87 for the second wicket. But MCC collapsed to 144 all out, Fletcher achieving a hat-trick. When Yorkshire batted again the game took a similar course to the first innings with A. Sellers (45) batting well then, at the end, Fletcher with 27 and Hirst (43 not out) took the all out score to 188. Hearne with 34 defended well and was third out at 146 having added 71 out of 98 for two and A. E. Gibson with 34 and D. R. Napier took MCC close to their target as they went on to win by four wickets.

William Fletcher's first match for Yorkshire was a distinct success but he met with only limited success on his other four games for Yorkshire. He was a right-handed batsman capable of getting runs in any company and a medium-fast bowler who had engagements at Low Moor, Leeds, Colne, Rishton and Meanwood. From 1924–34 he was a 2nd Class Umpire. He died at Knaresborough in 1935.

At Bramall Lane, Sussex were the visitors for Yorkshire's first Championship match and when they won the toss and batted first, they were soon in a good position with the score at 136 for three, but after Marlow was dismissed wickets fell quickly and they were all out for 171. There were complaints about the state of the Bramall Lane turf, which seemed justified when Yorkshire scored only 81. Following on, a magnificent 104 in two hours by Wainwright set

Sussex needing 137. In ninety minutes Hirst (six for 16) bowled out the Southerners for 96.

In a low scoring match at Cambridge, Yorkshire beat the University by seven wickets. The County then returned to Bramall Lane for the Roses match. Lancashire won the toss and proceeded to bat. A. Ward (23) and A. C. MacLaren (21) put on 40 for the second wicket and F. H. Sugg batted well for $1\frac{1}{4}$ hours for 39, but the side then fell to Peel who took six for 43. Yorkshire batted little better, but did achieve a lead of 31. On the second day, the bowlers remained on top, although G. M. Kemp batted well for 21, and Lancashire were soon dismissed for 101. Yorkshire then lost six wickets for 33 before Wainwright and Tunnicliffe overcame the crisis to take Yorkshire to victory.

Yorkshire's good start to the season was maintained at home to Kent, the home side getting away to a good start by scoring 200 with R. Peel the top scorer with 50 in $2\frac{1}{2}$ hours, putting on 50 for the fourth wicket with A. Sellers (29). Hirst later hit out well to score 23. Alec Hearne and F. Marchant (25) then put on 38 for Kent's second wicket and the former went on to score 61 in a little over two hours – a fine defensive knock but he received little support and Kent were 50 in arrears on the first innings. Yorkshire then lost four cheap wickets before A. Sellers was joined by R. Moorhouse (32) and the pair added 73 runs in an hour. Later Sellers and Wainwright came together and added 114 in 75 minutes to finish the second day at 243 for five. A. Sellers was out for 92 in 3 hours and 10 minutes and Wainwright batted just over 2 hours for 81, the total reaching 305. Kent began well with a stand of 64 between H. M. Braybrooke (52) and A. Hearne (40) and Martin made 29 not out but Kent were never likely to win and they went down by 136 runs.

At Lord's, at the end of the rain-restricted first day, Middlesex were well on top with their score reading 278 for six. Next day, Scott went for 80 and Middlesex only scored 14 more runs on a pitch now visibly helping the bowlers. After losing four wickets for 54 Yorkshire found the pitch easing. Peel batted well to score 54 and Wainwright an aggressive 73. S. W. Scott again batted well for Middlesex with 54 out of 184 and timely contributions came from Rawlin, Hearne and R. S. Lucas. Requiring 249 to win, Yorkshire were aided by some shoddy Middlesex fielding but Ulyett played very well for his 111 in 3 hours. Batting with both confidence and judgement, he added 70 for the second wicket with Ernest Smith (39) and 78 with A. Sellers (22) for the fourth wicket. Then Wainwright came in to win the match for Yorkshire with a well-played 37.

Yorkshire's triumphant start to the season came to a stop at Headingley where Surrey, the reigning Champions, were their opponents. There was no play on the first day because of rain but on the second Surrey won the toss and decided to bat on a pitch that gave help to the bowlers. They quickly lost five wickets before J. M. Read (45) and later K. J. Key (30) helped Surrey to a total of 151; Peel bowled splendidly to take seven for 43. The pitch became worse when Yorkshire batted and they were dismissed for only 87, only Moorhouse (26) and Hayley (17) preventing a follow-on. Lohmann took six for 37. When Surrey batted they were 20 for three at the close of play and it was only a score of 21 from R. Henderson and 27 from J. Shuter that enabled them to declare at 81 for seven and allow Yorkshire to have 2 hours and 5 minutes' batting. The home side made a bold move for victory, after losing four for 21. Wainwright scored 44 in about 50 minutes and with Tunnicliffe (23) and Hayley (24) both batting well, Yorkshire were always in with a chance but George Lohmann was at his best and took eight for 70 to gain his side victory by 17 runs with 3 minutes to spare.

At Bramall Lane, Yorkshire took 215 minutes to score 136 off the Nottinghamshire attack, with Louis Hall, the highest scorer, making 26 in a tame day's play that was interrupted by rain. Play did not start until 1.00 on the second day and there was no play at all on the third day. Nottinghamshire replied with 146, with William Gunn scoring 42 and J. A. Dixon 28, while Peel took six for 54. Yorkshire then scored 62 for the loss of four wickets before the game was abandoned.

According to Richards, the well-known Nottinghamshire scribe: 'The conduct of the spectators towards the Nottinghamshire players was very unsportsmanlike and called forth the severe criticisms of the press'.

On 11 July Liverpool & District defeated Yorkshire by six wickets in a match that the Yorkshire CCC does not consider first-class but which is considered such by the ACS. Liverpool scored 230 with the Rev T. R. Hubback scoring 67 as Hall took four for 51, and 197 for four with A. C. MacLaren scoring 84 and T. Ainscough 61 not out, while Yorkshire scored 69 and 354, T. A. Wardall making 112 and L. Hall 101.

The return with Nottinghamshire at Trent Bridge was also drawn. On the first day George Ulyett scored 35 out of Yorkshire's total of 107, with Attewell taking five for 36, and at the close of play on the first day Nottinghamshire were handily placed at 104 for five with Shrewsbury 48 not out. Shrewsbury went on to score 116 in $4\frac{3}{4}$ hours as he added 120 for the seven wicket with J. S. Robinson (71). Attewell, H. B. Daft and Sherwin all contributed to the humiliation of Yorkshire as Nottinghamshire scored no less than 369. When the match was completed at the close of play on the second day – the third day was washed out completely – Yorkshire were 33 for four wickets.

Yorkshire's sad fall from the top continued at Headingley where Middlesex gained a very comfortable nine wicket victory. Winning the toss they were dismissed for 100 with Lord Hawke making the top score of 22 as Yorkshireman J. T. Rawlin took eight for 52. On a dreadful pitch A. E. Stoddart hit out to score 46 out of 63 for the first wicket before the effects of the roller had worn off, but apart from A. J. Webbe (18) and S. W. Scott (24) the rest of the batting was no more successful than Yorkshire's. Middlesex managed a lead of 22. The second day was a blank owing to rain but when play was resumed at 12.30 on the last day, Yorkshire found the conditions so bad that they were dismissed for 46 with F. S. Jackson compiling exactly half of those, during which time he was dropped twice. J. T. Hearne took six for 33 and Rawlin four for 13 as Middlesex went on to an easy win.

At The Oval Surrey completed the double at Yorkshire's expense with 72 runs to spare in a match which was really won in the first partnership of the game, R. Abel (50) and W. W. Read (75) putting on 109.

Lockwood took advantage of the poor light when Yorkshire went in and provided Surrey with a lead on first innings of 78. The home side raised this lead to 267 in their second innings and it was a total Yorkshire looked like achieving when the score rose to 129 for two, but Lohmann came on to take seven for 50 and the batting collapsed.

O. G. Radcliffe batted well for 32 when Gloucestershire won the toss at Bradford and decided to bat first on a good wicket. He was second out at 42, when R. W. Rice (51) was joined by J. J. Ferris (46) and the pair proceeded to add 84 runs for the third wicket in a steady partnership. W. G. Grace then showed his old form in scoring 53 and S. A. P. Kitcat took Gloucestershire to 276 after an innings of 55 lasting 2 hours. When Yorkshire batted Lord Hawke was dismissed for 2 before Wardall and Peel put on 108 for the second wicket. Wardall went on to score 105 in $3\frac{3}{4}$ hours while Ulyett scored 60 not out in an innings lasting 100 minutes. Yorkshire scored 295. At the end of the second day, Gloucestershire were 13 without loss but on the last day they slipped to 126 for six with Radcliffe having scored 41 of those and F. G. Roberts, who opened and put on 65 for Gloucestershire's second wicket, making 38 before getting out at 88 for two. W. G. Grace with 32 then helped in a stand of 40 for the seventh wicket and the side set Yorkshire 200 in 105 minutes. At the close the Yorkshire score was 146 for three.

The Roses match at Old Trafford proved to be the biggest hiding yet suffered by the White Rose County. Lancashire lost Sugg with 24 on the board and then Albert Ward and A. P. Smith put on 189 for the second wicket before Smith left with 80; Briggs joined Ward in a stand of 113 for the fourth wicket before Albert Ward's epic innings of 180 in a stay of $4\frac{1}{4}$ hours came to an end. Briggs scored 115 in $2\frac{1}{2}$ hours and G. R. Baker scored 49 as Lancashire reached 471 at almost 70 runs per hour. There had been early rainfall on the second day which affected the wicket and Yorkshire's batsmen were soon in trouble except for Ernest Smith who made a fighting 57 with Tunnicliffe also showing his fighting abilities with 31 not out. Briggs took eight for 113 as Yorkshire were all out for 209. At the end of the second day Yorkshire were 74 for one in their second innings with Lord Hawke out for 35. After Tunnicliffe had completed a fighting 50 the rest of the side were soon out for 179 leaving Lancashire victors by an innings and 83 runs. Watson and Briggs took five wickets each. About 20,000 attended the first day's play and 10,000 watched on the second.

At Hove, Sussex won the toss and batted and with George Bean (44) and W. G. Heasman (25) together Sussex were going very well, but 89 for one turned quickly to 127 for six, Peel taking six wickets. By the close of play on the first day, Yorkshire had taken the lead with only five wickets down. Sussex began their second innings without much hope of saving the game, but W. Newham with a well-played 40 managed to stave off an innings defeat, adding 30 with W. G. Heasman (17) before they were all out for 99. Yorkshire went on to win by nine wickets.

The visit of Somerset to Bramall Lane proved another sad match for Yorkshire, yet Somerset, winning the toss, were summarily dismissed for 74, Jackson taking five for 20. Yorkshire began almost as badly on a pitch where the ball got up dangerously but they managed a lead of 36, thanks to Jackson. At the close of play Somerset had redressed the balance by scoring 84 for one. Next morning L. C. H. Palairet went for 32 and J. B. Challen 39, four wickets being down for 126, but then Woods hit out boldly to score 76 out of 117 in less than 90 minutes and Somerset took their score to 248, setting Yorkshire 213 to win. With the ball still rearing dangerously Yorkshire were dismissed for 125 to give Somerset a comfortable win.

In what was turning out to be a very wet season, the match at Mote Park with Kent was abandoned as a draw after Ernest Smith with 88 had made the majority of the runs in Yorkshire's total of 188. When the game ended Kent had just completed their first innings. Going to the West Country, Yorkshire ended their inter-county programme with two rain-ruined draws against Gloucestershire and Somerset.

There was also a draw at Scarborough to finish off the season. Yorkshire scored 208 with J. T. Brown scoring 65 not out in confident style in 90 minutes. The MCC scored 126 with C. I. Thornton top scorer with 27 as Peel took seven for 60 and, following on, reached a total of 224. J. Burns made 79 and G. F. Vernon 38 with Wainwright and Peel each taking three wickets. When the match was drawn Yorkshire were 56 for two.

Yorkshire ended with a record of 6 wins, 6 defeats and 9 draws which was far from satisfactory after making such a good start to the season. They finished in sixth place in the County Championship, which was probably a fair reflection of their form but bitterly disappointing after leading the table up to the middle of June.

In the County Championship matches, the batting averages were headed by Ernest Smith, who scored 368 runs at an average of 28.30. Wainwright scored 644 runs at 27.86. F. S. Jackson only played in a few games but scored 267 runs at 24.27. Young Tunnicliffe scored 379 runs at 23.68 and showed great promise. Hall fell away badly and was dropped from the side.

As might be anticipated in such a season, Wainwright headed the bowling averages with 77 wickets at 16.22, only just ahead of Peel whose 88 wickets cost 16.39 each. Hirst was third with 17 wickets at 20.35 but his services were rarely needed in such a summer. F. S. Jackson took 18 at 28.38 and E. Smith 18 at 32.16.

Looking on the bright side, Brown came in at the end of the season and showed that he had some class in his batting. The younger element in the side undoubtedly improved the fielding of the side. Both Harrison and Hall had ended their county careers – though the latter did make one more appearance.

A review of the 1892 season was recorded as the First Annual Meeting of the Yorkshire CCC. Extracts from it read as follows:

'In presenting this the first Report under the new constitution of the YCCC of the cricket season of 1892 . . . did not fulfil the promise held out by its commencement, and that the accession of the full strength of the County Team did not realise the expectations which had been hoped for from it. Some considerable addition to the bowling strength of the team is urgently needed, but so far this fails to present itself . . . In accordance with Rules 4 and 5 the Committee for the year 1893–94 and 95 has been elected . . .'

The areas that elected members to the committee were as follows: Barnsley, Bradford (3 members), Craven, Dewsbury, Halifax, Huddersfield, Hull, Leeds (3 members), Scarborough, Sheffield (7 members) and Wakefield. Elections were reported in the minutes and some were conducted with a certain amount of acrimony. A member was elected for the York area in 1895, for the Harrogate area in 1899 and for the North & East Riding in 1900.

Before the 1893 season started numerous matches between teams of Colts took place and the new style committee appeared to be combing the County in the search for new players. A new dawn appeared to be on the horizon.

DAYS OF SUCCESS

ALTHOUGH LACKING LORD HAWKE, Peel, F. S. Jackson and Ernest Smith, Yorkshire won their opening match of 1893, beating MCC at Lord's by 17 runs.

Luther Whitehead made his first appearance for Yorkshire in this match; also playing in one other game in the same season without success. A useful right-hand batsman, he was born at Hull in 1869 and was educated at East Riding College and Hull Grammar School and played with Leeds Leamington at one time. From 1907 until about 1913 he played for Ossett, acting as professional for a time. Latterly he lived at Huby near Leeds and was head of the Leeds Meter Co., Tower Works, Armley and he died in 1931 while on business in Buenos Aires.

Dick Squire made his single outing for the county in the above match. A right-hand batsman and left-arm slow bowler, he failed to take a wicket and scored 0 and 0. Born at Cleckheaton in 1864, he was chiefly connected with Brighouse and Scholes cricket clubs.

At the Spa Ground at Gloucester, the home side lost two wickets for four runs before W. G. Grace (54) was joined by Painter (81) to add 124 for the third wicket in only 65 minutes. Gloucestershire went on to score 235. Yorkshire made a good reply with Tunnicliffe (54) and Wardall putting on 92 for the first wicket and at the close of play Yorkshire were 161 for two. Wardall went on to score his second century (106) against Gloucestershire in 2 hours 35 minutes and then Ulyett scored 54 before a last wicket stand between Hirst (31 not out) and Hunter (32) added 52 taking Yorkshire to 385. Gloucestershire collapsed to 152 all out with Wainwright taking six for 56 and Yorkshire won very easily.

At Fenner's the University won a good contest by 27 runs on a pitch always favouring the bowlers.

Frank Ellis Woodhead, a fine right-hand batsman, who never did himself justice in the first-class game, appeared for Yorkshire in this match. He was educated at Loretto where he was in the eleven and Cambridge University for whom he played once in 1889, 1893 and two in 1894 but accomplished little of note. He toured Canada and Holland and was also an excellent Rugby wing-threequarter. A fine golfer, he won the Yorkshire Amateur title in its first year, 1894.

Yorkshire had the satisfaction of outplaying the Australians at Bramall Lane, defeating them by 64 runs. J. T. Brown (38 not out) batted splendidly when Yorkshire won the toss and Tunnicliffe too was shown to advantage with 32 as Yorkshire scored 137 with Hugh Trumble taking seven for 50. Only W. Bruce with 30 did much for the visitors, who were bowled out for 86 with Ted Wainwright taking five for 36. Yorkshire finished the day at 11 without loss but next day were bowled out for 71 with Trumble this time taking five for 31. On this pitch, the Australians had no chance and were dismissed by Peel and Wainwright for 60, the home side winning by 64 runs. The Australian fielding was very poor and *The Field* remarked, '. . . Seldom has a worse wicket been played upon by first-class teams.'

Sussex won the toss at Headingley and after George Bean (58) and G. L. Wilson (20) had put on 41 for the first wicket, Sussex collapsed to 125 all out, Peel taking seven for 55. Yorkshire did even worse and had nine wickets down for 61 when Hirst was joined by David Hunter and the pair took the score to 111, with A. W. Hilton producing his best-ever performance in taking seven for 47. Sussex's second innings was of short duration, but Yorkshire still lost six wickets making the 76 runs needed for victory.

Middlesex won the toss on a good Lord's wicket and disappointingly were bowled out for 169, Smith taking four for 53. At the close of play, Yorkshire had replied with 159 for four with A. Sellers 90 not out. He went on to score 105 in 2 hours 55 minutes and Yorkshire totalled 304. In their second innings, A. E. Stoddart (88) and S. W. Scott (62) put on 87 for Middlesex's second wicket and C. P. Foley came in to score 60 not out. Middlesex were finally dismissed for 279. Yorkshire only had 145 to win but they soon lost three wickets before Tunnicliffe and Brown came together to add 43 and then Peel helped the latter to take the score to 103 for five. Two more wickets then fell for one run which meant that 41 were required with three wickets left. Ulyett was missed straight away but he finished with 27 not out while E. Smith was 18 not out as Yorkshire won by three wickets.

The Australians had all the best of the game at Park Avenue but had to be satisfied with a draw after Yorkshire had followed on. At the end of the first day, the visitors had scored 336 for five with George Giffen scoring 171 in 4 hours and 10 minutes. W. Bruce scored 47 and H. Graham went on to score 67 and it was after three o'clock on the second day before the innings finished at 470. When Yorkshire batted the light was never good after A. Sellers had made 53 and seven wickets were down for 129 as Yorkshire lost five wickets in the 120s. Then Ulyett with 41, with help from Mounsey (19) and Hirst (22 not out), took Yorkshire to 220 with Giffen taking five for 89 and G. H. S. Trott three for 46. Yorkshire, following on, soon lost five wickets for 73 before Wainwright (62) and Moorhouse (57 not out) added 103 for the sixth wicket and at the close Yorkshire were 196 for six.

Wilson Earnshaw, a useful right-hand batsman and wicket-keeper, played in six games for Yorkshire between 1893 and 1896, and was born in Morley in 1867. The son of a woollen manufacturer, he played for Dewsbury & Savile, Chickenley, Ossett and Barnoldswick and was a licensee at various public houses in the area. He died at Lowtown, Pudsey in 1941 and his funeral was at Dewsbury Cemetery.

On what was yet another dreadful pitch at Bramall Lane, the ball taking pieces of turf away from the start, Yorkshire beat Surrey by 58 runs with very few innings of note in the match. Yorkshire decided to bat, but lost seven wickets for 23. A very plucky innings of 39 by Moorhouse, who suffered greatly from blows from the Surrey pair of fast bowlers Richardson and Lockwood, took the total to 98. Richardson was in deadly form as he finished with nine for 47. Surrey were then dismissed for 72. When Yorkshire batted again they succumbed very quickly for 91 with Bobby Moorhouse this time scoring a brave 38 not out as Lockwood took eight for 39. A 31st wicket fell on the opening day as Surrey finished at 19 for one and in 70 minutes more play the match was over with Surrey dismissed for 59, Wardall and Hirst sharing the wickets.

Taunton was the scene of Yorkshire's next match; the home side compiling 227 on a pitch somewhat different from the Bramall Lane dust-bowl. G. B. Nichols was top scorer with 45 and Wainwright took four for 49. A. Sellers (50) and Tunnicliffe (65) put on 103 for the second Yorkshire wicket which was followed by Brown (84) and Peel (69) adding 148 in 105 minutes for the fourth wicket. Ulyett came in at 282 for six and he and Wainwright (78) added 147 for the seventh wicket with Ulyett scoring 73 as Yorkshire were all out for 469. Brown's leg-breaks were too much for Somerset in the final innings and it was not necessary for Yorkshire to bat a second time. David Hunter took seven victims behind the stumps and kept brilliantly.

At Headingley, Yorkshire met with their first reverse, Lancashire winning by an innings and 9 runs. On a pitch always giving the bowlers help Yorkshire collapsed from 80 for 1 to 107 all out, Mold taking six for 40. A. C. MacLaren played an admirable innings of 54 in $2\frac{3}{4}$ hours to put Lancashire on top with G. R. Baker also batting well before being run out for 37. They added 60 for the fifth wicket as Lancashire finally made 169 with Peel taking five for 28. When Yorkshire batted again only Wardall who was run out for 25 faced Briggs with any confidence at all and magnificently though he bowled, the wicket suiting him admirably, the Yorkshire batting was feeble in the extreme. He took eight for 19 in their total of 53.

At The Oval, Yorkshire suffered a second defeat. Surrey won the toss, Abel and Shuter giving the Champions a good start with a stand of 62, yet four wickets were down for 121. Key then played a magnificent innings scoring his 100 out of 152 in two hours and with

Lockwood scoring 61 in 75 minutes, Surrey finished with 356. At the close of play Lockwood and Sharpe had reduced Yorkshire to 9 for three. Next morning the rout continued and Yorkshire finished 231 behind. Wardall completed a 'king' pair when Yorkshire followed on; Brown made 64 out of 127 for four. Yorkshire just avoided an innings defeat, but two defeats meant that Yorkshire had slipped from Championship leaders to second place behind Middlesex.

Lord Hawke returned to Yorkshire for the Nottinghamshire match at Park Avenue. Winning the toss Yorkshire soon lost their opening pair before Tunnicliffe (54) and Brown (48) added 93 for the fourth wicket. Peel then hit 65 in $2\frac{1}{2}$ hours as Yorkshire scored 220 with Shacklock taking five for 98. Rain had interfered with play on the opening day and by the end of the second, Nottinghamshire were 125 for one. Barnes left early next morning for 61 but Gunn went on to bat for $5\frac{1}{2}$ hours for his 150 with Nottinghamshire making little effort to force the pace and when they declared at 321 for eight, with only two hours left, the match petered out.

At Bramall Lane against a weak Somerset side, Yorkshire gained an easy innings win with 13 runs to spare. F. J. Poynton, with 51, alone troubled the Yorkshire attack, who dismissed Somerset for 161. At the end of that day Yorkshire had taken the lead with 175 for three of which Tunnicliffe had made 77, putting on 162 with Sellers in 100 minutes. Sellers went on to score a very fine 105, Yorkshire gaining a lead of 139 on the first innings. Wainwright then dismissed Somerset for 126, providing Yorkshire with a substantial win. Yorkshire were now back on the top of the table. George Waller made the first of three appearances for Yorkshire in this match and gained a place in the record books by capturing a wicket with the first ball he bowled. He was much better known in soccer circles playing for Sheffield United as well as Sheffield Wednesday for whom he appeared in the 1890 Cup final when they lost 6-1 to Blackburn Rovers. He also assisted Middlesborough and was with Sheffield United AFC for 40 years as player and trainer before retiring in 1930.

Heavy rain made the Headingley pitch all in favour of the ball when the Australians won the toss and the tourists were dismissed for 142, mainly due to dropped catches. Yorkshire only managed 95, C. T. B. Turner capturing six for 36 – all his victims being bowled. In their second innings, the Australians lost six wickets for 47 before Trumble and W. F. Giffen helped Turner (41 not out) to take the Australians to 146 with Peel taking five for 47. In their second innings Yorkshire lost eight wickets for 11 runs but recovered somewhat to total 48 – defeated by 145 runs.

At Trent Bridge, Nottinghamshire had little to offer apart from a fine 50 from W. Barnes as they were bowled out for 124, Jackson and

Wainwright each taking five wickets. Yorkshire then lost two wickets for 12 but Jackson scored 59 out of 77 in a splendid innings on a none too easy pitch to give Yorkshire a lead of 58 on the first innings. Nottinghamshire gave a dismal display in their second innings with only last man Sherwin reaching double figures and Yorkshire won by an innings and 20 runs.

On a soft pitch at Fartown that became increasingly treacherous, Yorkshire were fortunate to win the toss but they lost six wickets for 71 before Brown batted well to score 37 in 85 minutes and then after Moorhouse had made 27, Hirst played an innings typical of him reaching 35 not out in only 40 minutes to put Yorkshire well on top with a score of 162. Gloucestershire were bowled out for 74 in 90 minutes with Peel taking six for 27. In their second innings, W. G. Grace scored 31 and R. W. Rice 27 but after they left Gloucestershire slumped to 91 all out. Yorkshire went on to win by ten wickets.

A large attendance watched the two days of cricket at Blackheath, where a full-strength Kent side won the toss but never got on top of the keen Yorkshire spin attack of Peel, whose 22 overs cost only 6 runs, or Ted Wainwright, who finished with five for 32 as Kent were dismissed for 77. Yorkshire then lost their three amateur batsmen for only 8 runs, but by the close of play they had recovered to 112 for five, with Tunnicliffe out for 29 and J. T. Brown unbeaten on 56. Brown went on to score 81 in an accomplished knock lasting $2\frac{1}{4}$ hours on a treacherous wicket. Yorkshire scored 220. In their second innings, Kent were soon 40 for eight before G. G. Hearne played a splendid innings of 65 not out in a total of 132. Yorkshire won comfortably by an innings and 11 runs.

Over 32,000 (a record paying attendance) watched the first two days of the Lancashire *v* Yorkshire match at Old Trafford where the Red Rose county had the satisfaction of completing the double over their great rivals. Lancashire had the better of a difficult slow pitch but batted very poorly with the two Yorkshiremen Ward (19 in 115 minutes) and Baker (21) making over half the total. Briggs (six for 35) then dismissed Yorkshire for 58, giving his side a lead of six. Lancashire replied with 7 for no wicket but next morning their opening pair of A. C. MacLaren (16) and A. Ward (12) were the only players to reach double figures as they were bowled out for 50, with Peel taking six for 24. Requiring 57 only to win, Yorkshire were 42 for six by lunchtime. Twenty-five minutes after the interval it was all over, Lancashire winning by five runs, Briggs was the architect of victory with five for 25. Yorkshire were still narrowly ahead of Lancashire in the Championship table.

At Park Avenue, Middlesex lacked Stoddart and MacGregor, who were playing for England, while Jackson was missing from the Yorkshire side. After the first innings Yorkshire had a lead of 43. This was increased by 184, to set Middlesex the difficult task of obtaining 228 in the fourth innings on a wearing pitch. Hirst was almost unplayable and Yorkshire won by 145 runs.

Yorkshire beat Kent by eight wickets at Bramall Lane with Kent scoring 161 only because F. Martin scored 41 not out at number 10 after the visitors had lost eight for 100; Peel taking seven for 60. Yorkshire were 86 for three at the end of the first day with A. Sellers out for 50. Next day Tunnicliffe made 33, but Yorkshire were only 148 for eight when Hirst came in and in a sensible display of batsmanship scored 43 in 50 minutes, while Moorhouse made 35 to give Yorkshire a comfortable lead of 50. Kent could only acquire 127 in their second innings and Yorkshire had no problem in obtaining a second successive victory. This win secured the Championship title for Yorkshire, since with one match to play they had a lead of three points over Lancashire in second place – even if Yorkshire lost their last match and Lancashire won theirs Yorkshire would remain one point ahead. As it was Yorkshire beat Sussex whilst Lancashire lost to Nottinghamshire, thus Yorkshire closed a triumphant Championship season well ahead in the league table.

At Scarborough, Yorkshire gained a seven wicket win over the MCC with E. Smith earning the bowling honours with ten wickets in the match.

Yorkshire's final match was again at Scarborough against the South of England, who were in a strong position at the end of the first day at 90 without loss in reply to Yorkshire's 226. The South only managed in the end to gain a first innings lead of five, then on a bumpy pitch Yorkshire totalled 167 in their second innings. With rain having spoilt most of the second day's play, the South batted out the final fifty-five minutes of playing time.

In the Championship Yorkshire won 12 matches, lost 3 and drew 1. Lord Hawke played in only six of those matches, George Ulyett leading the side for most of the season. Curiously neither Lord Hawke in his *Recollections & Reminiscences* nor Holmes's *History of Yorkshire County Cricket 1833–1903* make any reference to Ulyett in connection with the 1893 season.

J. T. Brown finished top of the Championship averages with 712 runs at 28.48 with Tunnicliffe next to him with 653 runs at 28.39. Strangely this great opening pair never opened the innings together and each had just one match in which they opened the innings in the first innings of a match. Arthur Sellers scored 653 runs at 27; Hirst was the only other player to average over twenty.

With the ball F. S. Jackson took 13 wickets at 12.30 but it was Wainwright who had the best record with 90 wickets at 12.55, just ahead of Peel, who took 65 wickets at 14.18. Perhaps the most significant reason for Yorkshire's success was the fielding and catching of the younger players which appeared to be of a higher standard than anything in the past. Brown, Tunnicliffe and Wainwright, to say nothing of Hirst and the remarkable Moorhouse, were all young, active and quite outstanding.

On 25 April 1894 it was resolved that '. . . Lord Hawke be captain; Mr F. S. Jackson, Vice . . .' No mention was made of George Ulyett who had retired and had played his last match for the County.

In the previous year a new innovation was the fact that several clubs in the West Riding or other leagues were to be subsidised at the rate of 15/- per week by the County Club for having certain young professionals in their teams. Specified clubs mentioned are: Sheffield, Dewsbury and Leeds. The players mentioned as becoming registered with those clubs are also named as follows: Ringrose, Foster, Fletcher and Mitchell.

Yorkshire's success in 1893 was soon reflected in the number of members who joined the club. Previous to the Championship victory new members and their addresses are entered in the minute book at the rate of one or two or three – at the most six – along with their addresses. On 4 June 1894 there is a list of new members amounting to the remarkable total of 112 names.

Lord Hawke led the Yorkshire team on to the field in 1894 for their first match against Lancashire at Old Trafford. The pitch had been covered prior to the match but Hawke objected and a fresh one was prepared. The game was played for the benefit of Johnny Briggs and over 20,000 paid for admission on the two days. Lancashire won the toss and lost their first four wickets without a run having been scored. 17 for seven was hardly a recovery but G. R. Baker and A. T. Kemble did add 28 and Lancashire managed to reach 50, with Hirst taking seven for 25. Yorkshire passed that score with only three wickets down but Briggs was in good form and Yorkshire were in trouble at 76 for seven. Some effective batting by the tail then all but doubled the total. Lancashire were dismissed before lunch for 98, Peel and Wainwright taking the wickets, so Yorkshire won a low scoring game by an innings.

Yorkshire then fielded a weak side in a friendly meeting with Leicestershire and paid the price, losing by 47 runs.

Thomas William ('Tommy') Foster was a right-hand bat and medium-fast bowler who made his debut in this fixture. He played his early cricket with Dewsbury before moving to Rawtenstall as professional in 1897. Later he took engagements at Dewsbury and in West Riding League. He later became a very keen bowls player and died at Dewsbury in 1947.

While the Leicestershire match was in progress, Lord Hawke was scoring 157 for A. J. Webbe's XI *v* Cambridge University at Fenner's. Yorkshire were due at Fenner's for the next match but his Lordship had moved down to Lord's where he appeared for the MCC against Kent. It all seemed rather strange. At Fenner's, Cambridge University were dismissed for 155 with Frank Mitchell, who was to play for Yorkshire later in the season, scoring 75 in 2 hours and 50 minutes. Yorkshire were bowled out for 147 by the close of play. In their second innings, Cambridge batted well with Mitchell scoring 92 in 2 hours and W. G. Druce 66 not out as Cambridge scored 340 for seven declared. Wardall (36) and Tunnicliffe (47) then gave Yorkshire a good start with 81 for the first wicket but only Mounsey (54) did much after that as Yorkshire were dismissed for 229, leaving the home side victors by 119 runs.

Lord Hawke returned for the Sussex match at Hove, opening the innings and scoring 31 out of 80 after Sussex had been bowled out for 114. F. S. Jackson went on to score 131, putting on 141 with Tunnicliffe (78) and then Brown came in to score 39. Jackson's innings only lasted for 140 minutes. Sussex started their second innings with both Marlow and Bean out of the match with injuries so with four down for 75 their position seemed hopeless and so it proved, Yorkshire winning by an innings.

Yorkshire began well at Trent Bridge by bowling out the home side for 109 and at the end of the day they had replied with 63 for one. F. S. Jackson soon went next morning for 42 as did his partner, newcomer F. Mitchell who made 20 as Yorkshire collapsed to 94 all out. R. G. Hardstaff took seven for 44 and when Nottinghamshire batted again only William Gunn with 45 and A. Pike (24 not out) offered much resistance on a bowler's wicket. Yorkshire slumped to 44 for four by the end of the second day and on the following morning a shower of rain rendered the ball wet and eased Yorkshire's task. Brown (36) and Peel (24) took the score to 98 before the sixth wicket fell and after that Wainwright and Mounsey took Yorkshire to victory by three wickets.

Frank Mitchell, who made his debut for Yorkshire in 1894, had only two full seasons for Yorkshire, in 1899 and in 1901, but played occasionally until 1904. A very sound and at times brilliant right-hand batsman, he specialised in the drive although no stylist. He was in the St Peters' School XI at York and the Cambridge University eleven from 1894 to 1897, and then went to Brighton as a school master scoring many runs in club cricket. He served in the Boer War and afterwards returned to act as secretary to Sir Abe Bailey and played for Transvaal, going on to captain South Africa in Test cricket. He led the sides to England in 1904 and 1912. He was also a good Rugby Union player, captaining Cambridge U, and playing for Blackheath and was an England International on six occasions. The father of T. F. Mitchell, who played for Kent from 1928, he died at his home at Blackheath in 1935 being buried in Charlton Cemetery.

Rain interfered with the first day at Lord's where Middlesex, winning the toss, were bowled out for 92 on a pitch that helped both Wainwright and Peel; at the end of the day Yorkshire were 22 for one. Next day they slumped to 38 for seven, with Peel having batted for 90 minutes for 14 in what was a very brave innings. Mounsey and he added 42 for the eighth wicket and when Yorkshire were all out for 81 Mounsey was unbeaten at 33. Middlesex in their second innings were quickly reduced to 32 for nine but it was a last wicket stand between G. McGregor and J. T. Hearne which took Middlesex to 63, leaving Yorkshire with 75 for victory. Tunnicliffe with 28 held the Yorkshire batting together as they collapsed to 48 for seven before Mounsey and Wainwright knocked off the remaining runs. The next match at Bradford against Kent was abandoned without a ball being bowled.

There was more rain before the Sussex match at Dewsbury rendering the ground very difficult. Yorkshire won the toss but the score slumped to 77 for eight. R. Moorhouse and Hirst then added 39 and Yorkshire finally reached 133. When Sussex batted George Bean with 14 and 19 was the only batsman to reach double figures as Sussex were dismissed for 55. Yorkshire made 139 in their second innings with A. Sellers scoring 41 and J. T. Brown 23 as they added 42 together. In the final innings of the match Wainwright performed the hat-trick in one over and took two wickets with the first two balls of his next over to take five wickets in seven balls. He finished with seven for 20 as Yorkshire won by 166 runs.

Surrey were lucky to win the toss on a pitch that was poor to start with and got progressively worse and Lockwood, opening the innings, scored 31 after putting on 30 for the first wicket with Abel. W. W. Read made 38 and K. J. Key 24 as they put on 46 for the sixth wicket as Surrey advanced to 143. Yorkshire could only manage 64, Lockwood taking six for 32; Surrey fared little better and Yorkshire required 168 to win. Jackson and Mounsey took Yorkshire to 70 for four, but they were dismissed for 79 with Richardson taking six for 42. With both teams as yet unbeaten in county matches, the interest had been tremendous for this match with 18,000 watching the first day's play. Surrey won by 88 runs. The County were, however, defeated in a friendly first-class game against MCC at Lord's and then played a draw in a non-Championship match at Edgbaston. The next match saw Yorkshire beat Liverpool & District by ten wickets at Aigburth. Foster was in form for Yorkshire with match figures of eleven for 93. With nine wickets down for 185 against Liverpool's 153, J. T. Brown (141) and D. Hunter (25 not out) added 121 for the last wicket. Brown's excellent score came in 135 minutes. A. G. Steel took four for 70 as Yorkshire won by ten wickets.

Frank William Milligan, an exciting right-hand batsman and fast bowler if somewhat erratic, made his debut for Yorkshire in the above match without having much success. He continued to play for the County with some regularity up to the end of the 1898 season after which he toured South Africa under Lord Hawke playing in two Tests and was killed in the Boer War while serving under Colonel Plumer in a bid to relieve Mafeking. He used to work at the Low Moor Iron Works but left when his ideas were turned down and a Memorial was erected to him in Harold Park, Low Moor which was renovated in 1988. In 1901 members of the Yorkshire team attended St. Mark's Church, Low Moor where Lord Hawke unveiled a monumental tablet to his memory. Milligan assisted the Gentlemen v Players in 1897 and 1898 and also toured North America in 1895 and he appeared also for Staffordshire.

Nearly 27,000 watched the two days of the Surrey match at The Oval where Surrey scored 401, Brockwell and Walter Read both hitting centuries. Lockwood then dismissed Yorkshire for 142 and though, when they followed on, Yorkshire's batting improved considerably, Surrey still won by ten wickets with a day to spare.

At Leyton, Essex, winning the toss, were bowled out for 192. Yorkshire had gained the lead by the close of play and next day finished at 243. Essex were facing defeat in two days with six second innings wickets down for 66, but R. J. Burrell scored 40 and some bad lapses in the field allowed Kortright to hit 86 in 105 minutes. Yorkshire required 216 to win and by lunch time on the third day they had achieved their object with six wickets in hand.

At Headingley Yorkshire continued in their winning vein, beating Nottinghamshire by 201 runs, due to some splendid all round cricket from Jackson who hit 145 and took five for 37 in the first innings of the match. Both sides were weakened at Derby for the friendly match with Derbyshire which brought Yorkshire another victory, this time by three wickets.

Albert Percy Charlesworth, a right-hand opening batsman, made his first appearance for Yorkshire at Derby in the above match, when he was dismissed for 0 in each innings by J. J. Hulme. He played in six other matches for the County in 1894 and 1895. A professional at Harrogate, Rawtenstall and Morley, he died in Hull in 1926.

Few people turned out to see the friendly match against Essex at

Thrum Hall where Yorkshire had few problems in beating the visitors by seven wickets. In a rain-ruined game at Bramall Lane, Warwickshire just managed to avoid defeat.

David Denton made his debut in this Warwickshire match and played in three other games in 1894 claiming a regular place in the Yorkshire side from 1895 which he maintained until the end of the 1920 season. He was a small, slightly built figure, quick on his feet and had a penchant for attacking the bowling at all times unless the situation demanded something different. Nicknamed 'Lucky' Denton because he tended to give chances and get away with them, he had the misfortune to be a contemporary of John Thomas Tyldesley, considered the best professional batsman during the golden age of amateur batting supremacy. Denton did play in eleven Tests for England with some success but he will be best remembered as a

D. DENTON.

David Denton, a batsman who played 676 matches for Yorkshire and who was a brilliant fielder. (NCCC)

153

middle-order batsman for Yorkshire and as a brilliant outfielder who had a reputation of never dropping a catch. A right-handed batsman, he possessed all the strokes with cutting his speciality. He played his early cricket with Hodgson's and Simpson's, soapmakers in Thornes, and he scored his first century for them in 1892 against Pudsey Britannia. He moved to Castleford in 1894, also working in the soap factory when young. When he retired in 1920, he declined a seven year contract as coach at Haileybury owing to a spinal ailment but he was a first-class umpire from 1925–30 and acted as Yorkshire's scorer for a time. During one of the proudest periods of Yorkshire cricket, Denton was an example of the new type of cricket professional that Lord Hawke's reforms had produced. A sober-minded cricketer, a keen methodist and a man who brought up his family in a strictly Christian code, he was proud of his ability as a cricketer and there was no doubt that the way he played his cricket appealed to the spectators who flocked to watch him and his colleagues. Denton earned a good benefit and he died comfortably off by any standards at his home opposite the park in Denby Dale Road, Wakefield in 1950. Unusual amongst cricketers of any period, he had a large collection of cricketing mementoes, pictures and paraphernalia which filled every room in his house including that smallest room. His elder brother Joseph Denton also played for Yorkshire; and several of Denton's nephews and great-nephews played rugby league either locally or for Featherstone Rovers.

Returning at last to Championship cricket, Yorkshire dismissed Somerset twice in one day and won the match by an innings and 5 runs. Somerset scored 74 and 94. Yorkshire's fielding was stated by *Wisden* as never having been surpassed, while with the ball Wainwright took eight for 85 in the match. This victory put Yorkshire level with Surrey at the head of the table.

At Headingley on 23 July, Yorkshire defeated Gloucestershire by 26 runs. Winning the toss Yorkshire struggled to obtain 140 with Peel making 28 – the top score – in 90 minutes. W. G. Grace (41) and J. J. Ferris put on 65 for the first wicket after which all the other wickets fell for 43 runs. When Yorkshire batted again they had a dreadful time with nine wickets down for 19 before Hirst and David Hunter added 42 for the last wicket. Requiring 94 to win Gloucestershire were not expected to succeed on this tricky wicket, and they were dismissed for 67, Ted Wainwright taking seven for 34.

A friendly match at Bramall Lane against Derbyshire saw the home side well-beaten by nine wickets, but Yorkshire only fielded a moderate team. Yorkshire returned to full strength for their Bank Holiday game at Old Trafford, but Lancashire seemed to be well on top with 102 for two on the board in reply to Yorkshire's 183. On the second day Lancashire collapsed to be all out for 181. Yorkshire soon lost two wickets for 9 runs but F. S. Jackson and Brown added 72 for the third wicket. Mounsey and Ernest Smith put on 61 for the sixth wicket as Yorkshire totalled 217. Lancashire had the whole of the last day to score 220 but overnight rain gave the bowlers some help and the Lancashire batting was moderate at best. Yorkshire-born Baker made top score of 39 as Lancashire were bowled out for 102.

Yorkshire's next match was at Canterbury with 10,000 watching the first day's play when Kent were dismissed for 123. Yorkshire then took their overnight score of 75 for five to 213 all out thanks almost entirely to a brilliant innings of 95 not out by J. T. Brown in 3 hours. Kent made a good start to their second innings on the last day, J. R. Mason (42) and the Rev Rashleigh (44) opening with 68 but Wainwright, six for 37, bowled out Kent for 115 in conditions that suited the spinners and Yorkshire went on to win easily by ten wickets. The Yorkshire fielding was considered to be as brilliant as anything ever seen on the St Lawrence Ground. As Surrey also continued to win, they remained tied with Yorkshire at the top of the Championship.

Yorkshire's next match was at Bramall Lane against Middlesex, who were completely outplayed on the first day, Yorkshire bowling them out for 98. Yorkshire gained a first innings lead of nearly a hundred and with Wainwright unplayable in the second innings, Middlesex were beaten by four wickets. A friendly with Leicestershire at Harrogate followed which Yorkshire won comfortably by 74 runs in a low-scoring match. It was the first first-class match staged on the St. George's ground.

As anticipated the weak Gloucestershire side were no match for Yorkshire at Bristol where the home side were dismissed for 114 and 151, Wainwright taking nine wickets in the match. Hirst hit 115 not out in 110 minutes, giving Yorkshire an innings victory. Both Surrey and Yorkshire had won 12 and lost two matches and both counties had one game to play.

Surrey won their match with Sussex at Hove by an innings and 15 runs, despite the loss of the first day through rain. Yorkshire, playing at Taunton against Somerset, lost both the first and third days to the weather and therefore had to concede the title to the Southern county.

As Yorkshire also had their match with Kent abandoned without a ball being bowled, it might be said that the rain deprived Yorkshire of the title. On the other hand Surrey had beaten Yorkshire twice during the season and as far as these two games were concerned had proved themselves the better side. At Scarborough, Yorkshire managed to defeat the MCC by an innings and 11 runs after scoring a modest 219. MCC were dismissed for 59 and 149, Wainwright finishing with match figures of ten for 60.

The Rev Edgar Beckwith Firth made his only appearance for Yorkshire in the above match when he scored a single before George Davidson bowled him out. He was born at Malton (where his father was Vicar) in 1863 and played for Yorkshire Gentlemen, topping their batting averages in 1895. About the turn of the century he emigrated to South Africa and it is believed died there before the First World War.

Yorkshire's last match in 1894, against Lancashire, took place at Scarborough, being the final match of the Festival. Strictly speaking it had nothing to do with the Yorkshire CCC Committee but has since been incorporated into the Yorkshire records as a Yorkshire match, the teams having been got up by Lord Hawke and S. M. Crosfield of Lancashire. The match was unfortunately spoilt by the rain. Lancashire won the toss, batted and were all out for 181, the three leading scorers, F. H. Sugg, A. Tinsley and G. R. Baker, all having Yorkshire connections. Yorkshire replied with 152 with Jack Brown scoring a fine 53 as W. Oakley took six for 50. Lancashire were 103 for three when stumps were drawn.

In the County Championship, F. S. Jackson finished top of the batting averages with 659 runs at 28.65 – a good record in a season that had very few pitches favouring the batsman. E. Smith, who only played in six matches, scored 275 runs at 27.50. J. T. Brown was in third place. After a poor start he batted in his old manner towards the end of the season to reach 548 runs at 24.90.

E. Wainwright had a magnificent season with the ball in conditions made for him. He took 97 wickets at 10.17 while R. Peel was very close behind him with 79 wickets at 11.13. Hirst also bowled well with 56 wickets at 13.05.

A glance at the first-class bowling averages shows that Yorkshire had two players in the top ten with Wainwright taking 166 wickets at 12.63 while Peel had 145 wickets at 13.44 each.

For the 1895 season 14 counties took part in the County Championship, Yorkshire having arranged to meet the other thirteen sides twice each; home and away.

The season started off well at Lord's with the MCC going down by nine wickets after being skittled out for 105 before lunch on the first day. Yorkshire's Championship programme opened at Bradford where Warwickshire won the toss and were dismissed for 198 and at the close of play Yorkshire were 98 for two with Brown and A. P. Charlesworth in good form. Brown went on to 44 and Charlesworth 48 as they added 79 for the third wicket after which Moorhouse (74 in

90 minutes), and Lord Hawke (79) came together to add 85 for the seventh wicket, before Hirst hit out well in making 64 in 75 minutes, Yorkshire gaining a lead of 165. Warwickshire improved greatly on their second attempt with Walter Quaife (74) and A. Law (42) adding 87 for the second wicket before the former was run out. Lilley then came in to score 50, but Warwickshire were dismissed for 271 with Brown's leg-spin accounting for three for 44. Set 107 to win in less than an hour, Yorkshire's hero was again Brown, who in a dashing and brilliant innings scored 65 out of 92 for two to bring an eight wicket win for his side.

At Trent Bridge, Yorkshire were always struggling after F. S. Jackson was run out for 0. Five wickets were lost for 55 before Wainwright (63) and Moorhouse (67) saved Yorkshire with a stand of 73, and with help from the tail Yorkshire reached 237. Nottinghamshire also lost early wickets but had recovered to 112 for four by the close of play. William Gunn and Dick Attewell both hit fifties, but Nottinghamshire were all out for 209. Yorkshire gave a much better batting performance in their second innings to take the score to 253 for six at the end of the day. A. P. Charlesworth (63) and Wainwright (81) added 97 for the fifth wicket and on the last day Yorkshire were able to declare at 312 for eight, setting Nottinghamshire 341 to win in 290 minutes. Nottinghamshire replied with a score of 279 for four which *Wisden* claimed 'earned them more credit than either of their victories over Sussex or their win against Leicestershire'. (There was no suggestion that they might have quickened up and perhaps won the game.) W. Flowers scored 119 in 3 hours and 20 minutes, putting on 155 for the fourth wicket with J. A. Dixon (55). A. O. Jones had earlier scored 67.

Yorkshire's next match was at Oxford on the Christ Church ground where the University batted first and scored 256 with G. J. Mordaunt, H. D. G. Leveson-Gower and F. A. Phillips all passing the half-century. Yorkshire – 40 for one overnight – scored at a good rate to total 293, with Peel and Lord Hawke each scoring 48 and Hirst 42. At the end of the second day Oxford were 236 for seven with P. F. Warner having scored 52 and Leveson-Gower 61 not out. The latter went on to score 95 as Oxford were dismissed for 288. Yorkshire needed 252 for victory. In spite of Milligan's 46, Yorkshire had seven wickets down for 114 and with Arkwright taking six for 87, the university won by 54 runs.

A trip to Fenner's saw half the match washed out by bad weather. In the time available, Yorkshire scored 334 and Cambridge replied with 220 for eight.

Nearly 20,000 people witnessed the first day of the Roses match at Sheffield. Lancashire won the toss and never found run-making easy.

With three Yorkshire born players making the three highest scores – all in the twenties – the visitors were all out for 166 with Peel taking four for 41 in 39 accurate overs on the very soft turf. Yorkshire then lost six wickets for 43 before Wainwright with 35 pulled them round along with Denton and they finished the day at 111 for seven. Next morning Denton went on to score 44 not out and Lord Hawke made 34, Yorkshire finishing five runs behind their rivals. After MacLaren was run out, Albert Ward (68) and A. G. Paul (87) added 144 for the second wicket and with Sugg scoring 58 and Baker 38 not out Lancashire did well to score 304 on a pitch that gave some help to the bowlers. Yorkshire could make nothing of Mold, who finished with seven for 68, and the match was lost by 145 runs. At Leicester, the home side gave Yorkshire a good run for their money before Yorkshire won by 87 runs. Hirst took eleven wickets, including performing the hat-trick in the second innings. At Lord's Middlesex gave as good as they got up to the half way stage before Yorkshire triumphed by 298 runs. Yorkshire, on winning the toss, made a good start with F. S. Jackson (30) and Brown (62) opening with a stand of 93 in 70 minutes, as Yorkshire went on to total 258. Middlesex soon lost four wickets for 55 but Rawlin and Sir T. C. O'Brien took them to 98 without further loss at the close of play. Next morning Rawlin left at 107, Vernon then added 49 in a seventh wicket stand and O'Brien went on to score 76 with H. B. Hayman's 53 allowing Middlesex to come within two of Yorkshire's total. In Yorkshire's second innings Brown (47) and Tunnicliffe (101) put on 95 for Yorkshire's second wicket. The latter then added 86 in 50 minutes with Denton (57). Yorkshire finally declared at 411 for seven after an unfinished stand of 104 between Moorhouse (65) and Lord Hawke (52). On a wearing pitch Middlesex collapsed to 115 all out with O'Brien again making top score.

On 13 June Hampshire met Yorkshire in the first match ever to be played between the counties, the venue being Southampton. Winning the toss Hampshire made a good start with V. A. Barton (49) and H. F. Ward (42) putting on 60 for the third wicket and Hampshire were 113 for three. A collapse then occurred and Hampshire were dismissed for 160 with Peel taking five for 59. At the end of the first day, which was curtailed by rain, Yorkshire had scored two for one. In the evening a banquet was held by the Hampshire Club in honour of the Yorkshire team in appreciation of the help that Yorkshire had given to Hampshire when the county applied for first-class status. On the next day Yorkshire lost six wickets for 85, but F. S. Jackson (55) was joined by Lord Hawke and they took the score to 124 before Jackson was out. Hawke went on to score 60 in 65 minutes as Yorkshire were all out for 198. Hampshire then carried their overnight score of 59 for four to 116 all out, Yorkshire lost five wickets in making the eighty required for victory.

Back at Bradford, Yorkshire won the toss against Surrey and after losing Brown at 17, Jackson with 50 added 106 for the second wicket with Tunnicliffe (64) but only Wainwright with 36 was subsequently able to play Richardson with any confidence as Yorkshire were dismissed for 205. Surrey, aided by a century from Hayward, gained a first innings lead of a hundred. By the close of play Yorkshire had all but levelled the scores with six wickets in hand. The rest of the Yorkshire batsmen found Richardson too much for them and Surrey won the game – with ease – Richardson took thirteen wickets in the match.

Derbyshire were visitors to Headingley and on winning the toss scored 257. In reply Yorkshire lost three wickets for 102 with Tunnicliffe run out for 37 and Denton scoring 47. Lord Hawke hit a brilliant 54 out of 222 all out. G. G. Walker took four for 89 for the visitors who then replied with 192.

Yorkshire required 228 to win but when Tunnicliffe was run out for a second time in the match for 1, Yorkshire seemed to lose heart and were quickly dismissed, leaving Derbyshire victors by 107 runs.

Yorkshire regained some of their self-respect at Bramall Lane against Nottinghamshire, who won the toss and soon had three wickets down for 5. But C. W. Wright with 63 in 2 hours and J. A. Dixon, also with 63 in 2 hours and 5 minutes, eventually took Nottinghamshire to a respectable 214. Yorkshire passed that score by 20 runs thanks to an innings of 104 from Tunnicliffe. Lord Hawke also scored 27 in $1\frac{1}{4}$ hours on a crumbling wicket. Only William Gunn with 31 stayed for long in the Nottinghamshire second innings which amounted to 72 runs in 79.2 overs. Peel took six wickets and Hirst the remaining four. Yorkshire knocked off the runs, losing only one wicket in the process.

William Whiteley Lancaster, a brother of the Lancashire batsman Thomas Lancaster, and son of Joe Lancaster, a well-known local cricketer in the Huddersfield area, was a capable right-hand middle-order batsman and round-arm medium-fast bowler who turned professional in 1895 when he played in seven matches for Yorkshire with some success, the above being his first. He was born at Scholes near Huddersfield in 1873 and started his cricket at Thongsbridge and acted as professional at Burnley in 1896. He died at Marsh, Huddersfield in 1938.

At Edgbaston, Warwickshire won the toss and put Yorkshire in to bat and though Wainwright batted well for 61 in 75 minutes and Hirst hit up 30, they were dismissed for 163. Warwickshire opened with a stand of 114 by Walter Quaife and Bainbridge. Bainbridge went on to score 97 but was dropped four times. The remaining Warwickshire batsmen could only take their score to 253. Batting again on a now perfect pitch, Yorkshire lost three wickets for 56 before Denton (45) and Peel (78) took the score to 122 – after which Moorhouse added 96 for the sixth wicket with Peel. Moorhouse went on to bat for 3 hours and 20 minutes making 102 not out before Yorkshire declared at 378 for eight. Warwickshire were set 289 to win in 165 minutes but a shower of rain caused the match to be drawn.

At Leyton, the home side batted first after winning the toss and after H. G. Owen was run out for 35 Essex collapsed to 125, Peel taking five for 30. Yorkshire replied with 90 for one at the end of a day which had started late owing to rain. Next morning Tunnicliffe (41) and Denton (36) had a partnership of 64 but only a useful stand between Moorhouse (28) and Lord Hawke (also 28) enabled Yorkshire to reach 216. Essex were soon in trouble in their second innings and were bowled out for 105 having once again had the worst of the pitch. Peel took five for 41 and Yorkshire went on to win by seven wickets.

Moving to Hastings for the first Championship match on that ground since 1880, Sussex were in trouble with two wickets down for 21 before Ranjitsinhji (59) and W. L. Murdoch (38) put on 76 for the third wicket. The home side eventually reached 189 after the last pair had put on 47. F. S. Jackson with 38 and Tunnicliffe (45) and some consistent batting from most of the others took Yorkshire into a 68 runs lead. Sussex then knocked off the deficit for the loss of Marlow's wicket. G. L. Wilson (29) and Ranjitsinhji added 52 for the second wicket and Ranji went on to score a brilliant 74 without receiving much help from his colleagues. Yorkshire deservedly gained a nine-wicket victory with Tunnicliffe and F. S. Jackson adding 94 together in less than an hour.

A good pitch at Derby provided a fine game of cricket and over 1,100 runs in the three days. Yorkshire won the toss and Denton (65) batted very well, adding 72 for the second wicket with Frank Mitchell. Later W. W. Lancaster made his best score for the County with 51 and with Lord Hawke (41) added 65 for the sixth wicket before F. W. Milligan (38) and Haigh – on his debut – added 50 for the ninth wicket before Haigh went for 25. Yorkshire made 322 (J. W. Bennett four for 38) and at the end of the day Derbyshire had lost three wickets for 49. Thanks to the efforts of Harry Bagshaw, who scored 127 not out in $3\frac{1}{4}$ hours, and S. H. Evershed, who batted for two hours for his 112 (the pair added 190 for the fourth wicket) Derbyshire managed to reach 312 – only 10 runs in arrears. When Yorkshire batted again Frank Mitchell made 63 but was sixth man out with the total at 129 before Lord Hawke and Hirst came together. They took the score to 173 for six by the close of play and on the last day took their partnership to 80 before Hirst left for 41. His lordship went on to score 65 and Yorkshire fnished with 315, Bennett again being the best bowler. Derbyshire needed 326 to win and at 115 for two were in a strong position but they had not reckoned on Milligan's fiery fast bowling, which accounted for six for 26. Derbyshire, all out for 154, were beaten by 171 runs.

Schofield Haigh made a remarkable debut with both bat and ball in the above game. He gained a place in the Yorkshire side in 1896 and went on to play for the County until 1913, when he retired. Born at Berry Brow in 1871, he learnt his cricket with Berry Brow Salem CC whom he joined at 14. Two seasons later he joined Armitage Bridge where he played for three years and was coached by Louis Hall who advised him to go to Aberdeen, where he was professional from 1891 to 1893, moving on to Perth for the two following years. In 1895 he took seven for 12 for Scotland *v* Yorkshire and was induced to return to Yorkshire. He was a very popular cricketer but, working in the shadow of Hirst and Rhodes, rarely took the headlines. A cheery countenance greeted his fellow-players and spectators alike and much better use could have been made of his batting if it was required. A hard-hitting batsman, he could defend if necessary but preferred a swashbuckling role. As a bowler he was fast-medium with a break-back, and bowled with an extended long stride which possibly affected his health in later years. After some seasons he tended to bowl much slower, bowling as a medium-paced off-spinner, who was deadly on pitches that offered him any help. He was said to worship George Herbert Hirst and they were always the best of friends. One of the best types of professional cricketer imaginable, he had many eccentricities, and during the winter was devoted to billiards, captaining a local team. He was one of six players to score over 10,000 runs for Yorkshire and take over 1,000 wickets. Only Hirst and Rhodes took more wickets than Haigh and he took his wickets at a lower cost than either of the other two. He played in eleven Tests altogether. After his playing days were over, he moved to Winchester as coach with a ten year contract and he stayed there until his death from heart trouble in 1921. His son, Reg Haigh, became President of the Huddersfield League in 1961 and served on the Yorkshire CCC Committee. Haigh also used to umpire during the Scarborough Cricket Festival and during the Great War also turned out for Keighley CC in the Bradford League.

Against Kent at Dewsbury, Jackson was in fine bowling form as he took five for 32 with Marchant making top score (41) as Kent struggled to a total of 204. Showery conditions affected the play from time to time and at the end of the day Yorkshire were 25 for two. Denton (55) and Brown (61) then added 106 for the third wicket but the other batsmen made little progress and Walter Wright took five for 57 as Yorkshire were all out for 211. J. R. Mason was in fine form when Kent declared with 253 for eight, giving Yorkshire three hours in which to score 247. Jackson scored 81 for Yorkshire and Denton 44 not out but the match was drawn with 188 for three on the board. (*Wisden* described Jackson's innings as 'brilliant' but one wonders what the press would say today about the same situation?)

At Bramall Lane, Yorkshire had a much easier time defeating Leicestershire by an innings and 256 runs.

Henry ('Harry') Riley, who made his debut *v* Leicestershire, was a left-arm medium-fast bowler who lived at Idle from 1895 to 1900 and may have been with Sheffield United at one time. He later played in the Bradford League for Windhill in 1911 and he also assisted Ossett in the Heavy Woollen Cup. He died at Bradford in 1922 aged 47. He played in one match for Yorkshire against Leicestershire in 1895 and three matches in 1900 but his single wicket cost 54 runs.

Yorkshire's next match at Fartown against Sussex was washed out, there being no play on the second or third days.

George William Wood appeared in two matches for Yorkshire in 1895 as a substitute for David Hunter including the above match. He was born at Huddersfield in 1862 and died at Moldgreen, Huddersfield in 1948.

At Headingley, there had been three days of rain before the match, so the pitch therefore helped the bowlers from the start. Yorkshire won the toss and only Tunnicliffe could do anything when facing W. C. Hedley, whose fast bowling accounted for eight victims for 18 runs. In facing Peel's bowling Somerset did even worse, being out for 69 as Peel took nine for 22. On the next day, F. Mitchell (26) and Denton took the score to 58 for two and Denton went on to score 60, batting splendidly with mature judgement. Yorkshire were all out for 163, Hedley taking his wicket total to fourteen. In their second innings V. T. Hill and G. Fowler were the only players to reach double figures. Somerset lost by 103 runs. Yorkshire were now standing second to Surrey in the table.

On a treacherous pitch at Park Avenue, Gloucestershire were the visitors and winning the toss made scores of 71 and 51, Peel taking ten wickets and Wainwright nine. Yorkshire won the match by 1 o'clock on the second day.

At Bramall Lane, Hampshire succeeded in bowling Yorkshire out for 110 with only Brown (25) and Lord Hawke (23) meeting with any success against Buckland and Baldwin. For Hampshire, A. J. L. Hill played a fine innings of 46 providing his side with a lead of 17 runs. Brown scored 22 and Denton 32 when Yorkshire batted again but they were all out for 111 and Hampshire needed 95 for victory. After they lost three for 19, a shower interrupted play, and Captain F. W. D. Quinton batted half-an-hour without scoring, but went on to make 16, adding 55 for the fourth wicket with Hill, who again batted remarkably well in scoring 49. Hampshire, however, slipped to 88 for eight but Russell Bencraft and Baldwin took the score to 96 and victory by two wickets. Yorkshire had now dropped into third place.

At Old Trafford, a record crowd attended the first day's play in the Roses match, 25,331 paying for admission. Lancashire batted first and gave a poor batting performance on a very slow wicket, taking nearly three hours to score 103 all out against some fine bowling by Peel. F. S. Jackson (76 in 130 minutes) and F. Mitchell (38) put on 96 in 80 minutes and, at the end of the first day, Yorkshire were 146 for five. There was no play on the Tuesday, but on the third day R. Moorhouse (50) and Lord Hawke (61 not out) came together at 150 for six and took the score to 270 before the seventh wicket fell, at which point Lord Hawke declared. When Lancashire batted again, A. Ward (38) and A. C. MacLaren (46) opened with a stand of 76 and from then on the home side were never in danger of defeat.

Yorkshire returned to the victory trail at Canterbury with 12,329 watching on Ladies' Day – a record for the ground. Kent won the toss but, apart from a stand of 60 between Alec Hearne (46) and G. J. Mordaunt (27) for the fourth wicket, made little headway against the accurate Yorkshire attack and were all out for 135. Yorkshire gained a lead of 89 and Kent did not improve much in their second innings, Jackson having twelve wickets in the match. Yorkshire won with ease by seven wickets.

Moving along to The Oval for the Surrey match, it was a feather in Yorkshire's cap that they should defeat the Champions and leaders by an innings and 30 runs in a match set aside for Robert Abel's benefit. 15,301 paid to watch the first day's play and saw Surrey bowled out for only 136, with Peel taking five for 39 in 41.2 overs and Hirst five for 46. At the end of the day, Yorkshire were in a strong position at 142 for four. Rain ruined the chances of play on the second day and, on a wet wicket, Yorkshire took their final score to 244. Lohmann had taken six for 82. When Surrey batted a second time the pitch was drying and had become sticky; Hirst and Wainwright did what they liked and Surrey could only score 78.

The visit of Essex to Harrogate provided another bad wicket for batting. Twenty-three wickets fell in a day that did not commence until 1 o'clock. Essex batted first and were soon back in the pavilion for 87. George Hirst had the remarkable analysis of seven for 16. When Yorkshire batted, F. Mitchell (33) and Denton (45) both showed good form but a rot set in and Yorkshire's lead was only 30 runs. Walter Mead took seven for 56. At the close of play Essex were 38 for three.

Next morning F. G. Bull and A. S. Johnston added 62 for Essex's fourth wicket, and Johnston went on to score 63 in 85 minutes. After his dismissal McGahey continued alone to defy the Yorkshire attack to finish with 55 not out as Essex were dismissed for 165. Set 136 to win, Yorkshire at one time were 86 for two, but after Brown had gone for 28 and Denton for 23, they collapsed to 119 all out leaving Essex winners by 16 runs.

Thomas Burgess, a right-hand batsman and medium fast bowler made his only appearance for Yorkshire in this match. Most of his cricket was for the Harrogate Club, he being a native of that town.

At Headingley, Yorkshire won the toss against Middlesex and gave a poor batting display, the score being 89 for nine before Hirst joined Hunter in a last wicket stand worth 39. Good bowling by Hirst brought Yorkshire back into the match and a slender first innings lead was secured. A partnership of 130 for the third wicket won the match for the home side as Jackson, with 76 in $2\frac{1}{2}$ hours, and Tunnicliffe, with 58, came together, and with Denton staying an hour for 27, Yorkshire eventually reached 237. An unaccountable collapse by Middlesex to 57 all out saw Yorkshire gain an overwhelming victory by 205 runs, Hirst claiming twelve wickets in the match.

At Cheltenham, Yorkshire were dismissed for 221 and 143 with the young leg-break bowler Charles L. Townsend, aged only 18, taking fifteen wickets and dominating the Yorkshire batsmen throughout. Rain interrupted play on the second day and caused the wicket to slow down for the third day's play, when Townsend proved to be unplayable after Brown (35) and Tunnicliffe (52) had opened with a stand of 66. Needing 146 to win, Gloucestershire achieved victory with seven wickets to spare.

The Western tour continued disastrously for Yorkshire at Taunton where the home side succeeded in defeating Yorkshire by 25 runs in a match full of interest from beginning to end. Somerset won the toss and Nichols finished with the top score of 42 with R. B. Porch (34) and W. N. Roe (28) also getting amongst the runs. Peel took five for 52 for Yorkshire, who were 124 for four at the end of the first day's play, with F. S. Jackson scoring 46. Next day Denton left for 30 and Peel 34 but Mounsey came in to score a valuable 58 not out as he added 63 for the last wicket with Hunter (15). Yorkshire were all out for 245 with Tyler taking seven for 133. L. C. H. Palairet then played a masterly innings of 165 in 4 hours, adding 94 for the third wicket with W. N. Roe (44) and 95 with S. M. J. Woods (65) for the sixth wicket. Woods batted for 75 minutes as the Somerset innings closed for 353, leaving Yorkshire with 295 to win in 275 minutes. Wainwright (82) and Tunnicliffe (82) put on 140 for Yorkshire's second wicket in

105 minutes but then Tyler performed the hat-trick and Yorkshire were dismissed for 265, with Tyler taking seven for 114. This match ended the Championship fixtures, Yorkshire finishing third in the table. In the two games of the Scarborough festival, Yorkshire were beaten by MCC and then by an England Eleven. In the latter game, H. T. Hewett, the captain of the visitors, was barracked on the first morning, and, taking offence, he packed his bags and left the ground. The incident caused much press comment at the time.

In the County Championship, R. Moorhouse headed the batting averages with 928 runs at 35.69. He had batted well most of the season and had done better than ever before. F. S. Jackson was second with 853 runs at 30.46, with Tunnicliffe third with 1127 runs at 27.13, and Brown scoring 1118 runs at 26.00. Lord Hawke and Denton both scored over 800 runs. Hirst did very well and deserved a higher place in the order scoring 546 runs at 19.50. One could hardly fault the batting but there were times when the leading batsmen failed and it was left to a lower order batsman to bring them back into the game.

R. Peel topped the bowling averages with the splendid record of 136 wickets at 14.06 and then came F. W. Milligan with 18 wickets at 14.50 followed by F. S. Jackson who took 52 wickets at 14.92. George Herbert Hirst took 130 wickets at 16.93 and Wainwright 69 wickets at 19.34. S. Haigh showed promise when he played and the catching of Tunnicliffe and Wainwright was first-rate while David Hunter kept wicket in his usual reliable manner.

The financial position of the County was better than ever and the Club arranged a larger fixture list than usual for the 1896 season.

Yorkshire's first match was at Old Trafford against the old enemy on 4 May and Lancashire had the satisfaction of winning the toss. F. H. Sugg, by scoring 74 out of 87 in 75 minutes, saved his side from complete humiliation, but they were still bowled out for 150 by Peel and Hirst. Briggs and Hallam were quick to wrest the initiative from the visitors and despite 43 from Moorhouse, Lancashire gained a lead of 27, Briggs picking up five cheap wickets and Hallam three. On the following day A. G. Paul batted for over three hours for 52 as Lancashire struggled to 139, with F. W. Milligan taking four for 28 and F. S. Jackson four for 30 in 25 overs. Yorkshire needed 167 to win and they made good progress after tea on the second day. F. S. Jackson scored 41 and Denton 25, but at the close of play Yorkshire still needed 18 runs to win with two wickets to fall. Mounsey and Hirst rose to the occasion and knocked off the runs. The reason for playing the match so early in May was due to Yorkshire wishing to play the Australians over the Whitsun holiday; whether another date could have been found seems rather doubtful but the members and supporters both counties were not pleased with the decision and it was some time before the traditional dates were tampered with again.

At Edgbaston the remarkable match was played in which Yorkshire scored 887 – still a record for the County Championship. R. Peel scored 210 and Wainwright, F. S. Jackson and Lord Hawke all made centuries. Hirst also scored 85 and followed that up with eight for 59 as Warwickshire were dismissed for 203. In the second innings Warwickshire were 48 for one at the close as the match was drawn.

The match at Taunton, as in the previous year, proved an excellent advertisement for the game, with Lionel Palairet again scoring a century. He put on 95 for Somerset's second wicket with Fowler (47) and 100 with Robson (43) for the third, while Woods scored an aggressive 76. Palairet went on to score 113 as Somerset were dismissed for 323. When Yorkshire batted Moorhouse scored 113 and Yorkshire reached 400; Tyler taking eight for 196. Penetrative bowling from Wainwright who took six wickets resulted in Somerset being dismissed for 208 in their second innings and Yorkshire needed only 132 to win. They lost five for 96 before Peel and Hirst guided them to victory.

At Bristol, Yorkshire defeated the home side by nine wickets, only W. G. Grace with 30 and 70 making much headway against Milligan, Wainwright and Jackson.

Sussex were visitors to Park Avenue and once again an excellent batting pitch had been prepared with Yorkshire occupying the crease for the whole of the first day the score ending at 389 for five, Wainwright and Peel both completing hundreds. On the second day Hirst hit 90 and Yorkshire's final total was 543. Sussex were bowled out for 265 and though Ranjitsinhji batted brilliantly for 138 in the follow on, Yorkshire won by ten wickets.

A most eventful game took place at Lord's where Middlesex began by hoisting 218 for the first wicket, with A. E. Stoddart making 100 and H. B. Hayman carrying on to obtain 152. Gregor McGregor also scored 50 as Middlesex scored 384. Tunnicliffe and Brown retaliated with an opening stand of 139, Brown going on to score 203. Overnight rain altered the pitch when Middlesex began their second innings and only Sir T. C. O'Brien with 57 and R. S. Lucas (30) stayed for long as Peel bowled Middlesex out for 142. As the pitch had dried out before Yorkshire batted, they had little difficulty in hitting off the 147 needed for victory.

At Bramall Lane, 42,787 people paid to watch the match with the Australians, but the wicket proved so bad that Lord Hawke insisted that the next home match, also arranged for Sheffield, should be switched to Bradford. Despite the fiery wicket, the visitors scored 262 with Joe Darling making 57. When Yorkshire batted they found

Giffen's off-spin very difficult to play and collapsed to 118 all out. In the second innings Jones's pace proved the County's undoing and the tourists won by an innings.

A heavy scoring match at Trent Bridge resulted in a draw but some good cricket was played. Brown (107), Peel (87) and Hirst (67 not out) all enjoyed themselves as Yorkshire reached 450. Nottinghamshire were dismissed for 279, but in the follow-on Attewell and Wright saved their side from defeat by adding 131 for the seventh wicket.

At Fenner's, Yorkshire, lacking Hirst and Peel, were defeated by an innings and 35 runs. The County, on a rain-affected wicket, could only score 85 and 189 in reply to the students' total of 309.

James Shaw who made a promising debut in this match was a left-arm slow bowler who was born at Linthwaite in 1865. A woollen cloth manufacturer by trade, he was living at Linthwaite when he appeared for Yorkshire in three matches in 1896 and 1897; he was at one time a professional at Wakefield and later Scarborough.

Rain ruined the match with Surrey switched to Bradford from Sheffield. George Lohmann was in fine form when Yorkshire won the toss and batted and took seven for 61 in the home side's total of 135. At the end of the second day – the first had been a blank – Surrey were doing very well at 80 for three. On the last day Surrey were quickly dismissed for 147. Yorkshire hit out in their second innings and a declaration set Surrey 123 to win in two hours, but four wickets fell for 58 and Surrey were content to bat out for the draw.

The Essex match was also at Bradford on a rain affected pitch. Essex could only muster 109, but Yorkshire fared even worse against F. G. Bull (eight for 44) and were all out for 80. Wainwright then destroyed Essex and some excellent batting by Tunnicliffe, undefeated with 55, brought Yorkshire victory by seven wickets.

This was Sam Kilburn's only match for Yorkshire. A right-hand batsman, he played at various times for Kirkheaton, Church, and in the Huddersfield League.

At Leeds rain ruined the second match with the Australians who batted first and scored 144 with S. E. Gregory scoring 59 in $1\frac{1}{2}$ hours. Yorkshire were 97 for seven at the end of the first day and rain prevented any play until after tea on the second day with Yorkshire being dismissed for 108. The fearsome Ernest Jones took seven wickets for 36. The Australians were 31 for one at the end of the second day but further rain prevented any further play.

Yorkshire did very well at Leicester on winning the toss and at the end of the first day had scored 397 for five. After batting for 8 hours they reached 660 with every member of the side reaching double figures, only Moorhouse failing to reach 20. It was the highest score ever recorded at Leicester. Brown (131 in $3\frac{3}{4}$ hours) and Tunnicliffe

(79) put on 139 for the first wicket before Tunnicliffe was out for what was regarded as the best innings of the game. Jackson with 77 helped Brown to add 150 for the second wicket while Denton also scored 73. Hirst with 107 in 2 hours and F. W. Milligan put on 117 for the sixth wicket. Dispirited Leicestershire were dismissed for 165 and 193 to lose by an innings and 302 runs.

The remarkably consistent batting continued at Derby where the Yorkshire total was 403 for seven by the end of the first day. Hirst was top scorer with 68 but six other players scored 42 or more. Derbyshire scored 281 but on a still beautiful batting pitch, they proceeded to save the game by compiling 450 before declaring with about an hour's play left.

For their third match against Yorkshire the Australians won the toss for the third time at Bradford and scored 224, thanks to Harry Graham (67) and Joe Darling with 48. F. S. Jackson scored 45 when Yorkshire went in to bat but they were all out for 145 with McKibbin taking seven for 23. J. Darling (40) and H. Graham (29) then opened with a stand of 72 before the visitors lost four wickets for 121. F. A. Iredale came in to play a splendid innings of 114 as the Australians were out early on the third day for 251. Schofield Haigh bowled extremely well to take eight for 78. When Yorkshire batted again they made a good start and were 116 for two at one stage but with Tunnicliffe run out for 59, Jones again caused havoc and the home side were bowled out for 190 with E. Jones taking four for 40.

The return match with Derbyshire at Sheffield saw Yorkshire win the toss and Brown obtain 64 out of 89 for three. Denton then came in and added 55 for the fourth wicket with R. Moorhouse and then Mounsey helped Denton in a stand of 52 for the eighth wicket before Denton was bowled by Purdy for 113, Yorkshire totalling 298. Derbyshire took their overnight score of 33 for one to 151 all out. Haigh and Peel shared the wickets. Following on, Derbyshire were 58 for five, but W. Storer almost saved the game with yet another century. Yorkshire won by nine wickets.

Warwickshire won the toss in the next match at Headingley but only A. Law with 65 stayed for long in their innings of 165 and at the close of play, Yorkshire were 121 for four. Brown, not out overnight, went on to score 90, overcoming a difficult pitch with both skill and luck, and later Wainwright with 40 helped Peel to add 79 for the fifth wicket, with Peel going on to play an exceedingly fine knock of 72 not out. Hunter with 27 helped Peel to add 56 for the last wicket as Yorkshire were dismissed for 329. Warwickshire gave a sorry performance in their second innings and they were bowled out for 148 with Schofield Haigh maintaining his first-rate bowling form with seven for 49. Yorkshire won by an innings and 14 runs.

Yorkshire's first Championship defeat occurred in the next match at

Fartown against Nottinghamshire when the home club were caught on a treacherous wicket and were dismissed for 90 and 193 leaving Nottinghamshire with only 58 for victory. This they achieved for the loss of six wickets with Haigh bowling at his best to take three for 8.

In their return match with Essex at Leyton, Yorkshire lacked F. S. Jackson and Brown who were playing in the Gentlemen v Players match at Lord's. Winning the toss Yorkshire were dismissed for 203, F. G. Bull taking seven for 73. Essex continued to keep their grip on the game and went on to win by four wickets.

These two defeats opened up the Championship race, for up until then Yorkshire were well clear of the field. Now they had won only one more match than their nearest rivals Lancashire.

The Revd Clarence Eustace Macro Wilson (brother of E. R., C. R., Canon A. R. Wilson and father of D. C. Wilson) was a very sound defensive right-hand batsman who rarely hit the ball in the air and was very difficult to dismiss. He was also a right-arm medium-fast bowler who once resorted to bowling left-arm slows against Surrey for Cambridge University. He did not possess a strong constitution but was in the Uppingham XI from 1891 until 1893 when he captained the side and was also in the Cambridge University XI from 1894 to 1897, captaining the side in his last year. He played in only eight games for Yorkshire from 1896 to 1899 but succeeded in averaging 25 with the bat as well as taking twelve wickets at 21.41. He had a comparatively short career in first-class cricket giving up the game at first-class level on entering the church. He was a member of the Free Foresters in the 1890s and became a member of the Yorkshire Gentlemen's Club in the 1920s. In 1898 he scored 115 for Cambridge v Oxford University and he toured South Africa under Lord Hawke in 1898/99 taking part in two Test Matches. He was a very accurate bowler and possessed a notable collection of cricket books and cricketana and devoted himself to the knowledge of the history and theory of games. At one time he was vicar of Sand Hutton for many years and was appointed Rector of Eccleston (Cheshire) in 1911 and from 1940 until his death was prebendary of Bishopshull in Lichfield Cathedral. He died at Calverhall (Shropshire) in 1944.

Yorkshire's bad spell continued at Southampton where Hampshire were 350 for three at the end of the first day with E. G. Wynyard 211 not out. He had put on 100 with E. F. Ward (53) for Hampshire's second wicket and then added 184 for the third with F. W. D. Quinton. On the second day, Wynyard's innings came to an end at 268, he having been at the crease for just over six hours. His first 50 took 90 minutes but he later collared all the bowlers and with T. Soar making 39 the final total was 515. Yorkshire scored 307 and though the follow-on was enforced there was insufficient time for Hampshire to win.

Yorkshire returned to full strength for the important clash with Lancashire at Headingley, and had 130 on the board for the loss of two wickets, but Mold and Briggs then took command and the whole side were back in the pavilion for 190. Lancashire also found batting difficult and had a deficit of 21 on the first innings. Consistent batting enabled Yorkshire to obtain 209 in their second innings, Mold taking six wickets. Lancashire needed 231 in the final innings, but after a stand by Rowley and Paul had been broken, Peel had matters all his own way and Yorkshire won by 123 runs.

Somerset's visit to Dewsbury saw the home side give another even batting display after winning the toss, 251 being scored. Peel took ten for 80 and the Western county collapsed twice to give Yorkshire an overwhelming win.

Heavy rain had rendered Bramall Lane very soft and treacherous and Gloucestershire's spinners dismissed Yorkshire for 141. Gloucestershire in reply could only reach 79, Peel taking another six wickets, a tally he increased to ten when the visitors fell apart a second time, Yorkshire winning by over 200 runs.

At The Oval, 33,000 people paid to watch the three days play for the visit of Yorkshire, the match proceeds being awarded to George Lohmann for his benefit. Surrey won the toss and at the end of the first day were 350 for four, with Tom Hayward (164) having batted for 4 hours and 20 minutes. He had a little luck early on but with Baldwin added 221 for the third wicket. The pitch was by no means perfect and the Yorkshire bowlers were somewhat unlucky not to dismiss Baldwin who made 84. Rain overnight made the pitch much more lively on the second day and Surrey were dismissed for 439. Yorkshire started badly with three down for 29 before Tunnicliffe (47) and Peel (74) took the score to 93 before the fourth wicket fell. However, Yorkshire had to follow on 267 in arrears. The last day opened with Yorkshire losing three for 19 and only Denton with 35 did much until Ernest Smith came in and hit 55 out of 72 in about 40 minutes. This was nonetheless insufficient to avoid defeat by an innings. Despite the reverse, Yorkshire were still on top of the Championship.

At Harrogate, after heavy rain, Hampshire decided to bat, but collapsed to be out for 176 with F. E. Lacey's 44 being the top score. Wainwright finished with seven for 55 and then Yorkshire's Brown completed 120 in brilliant style, his first 73 coming in 100 minutes. A devastating spell from Haigh (eight for 35) demoralised Hampshire's second innings and Yorkshire went on to win by ten wickets.

Yorkshire won the toss at Scarborough against Leicestershire on 13 August, this being the first game to be played in the town outside the ordinary festival matches. Ernest Smith (35) and D. Denton with 46 took Yorkshire towards a reasonable total of 184. Bad light and rain did not help the progress of the match but intermittent sunshine ensured that the pitch remained difficult, Leicestershire being bowled out for 93. By the end of the second day Yorkshire increased their lead to 171 for the loss of five wickets, and on the last day they advanced to 130 for eight before declaring. In $1\frac{1}{4}$ hours, Leicestershire were dismissed for 59, with Peel taking six for 19 and Wainwright four for 38. Yorkshire won by 162 runs.

Middlesex came up to Bradford on 17 August and batting first on an easy wicket took their total to 178 without loss, but Wainwright then had Stoddart caught for 94 and less than a hundred runs later the entire Middlesex side was out. A stylish century from Jackson gave Yorkshire a substantial first innings lead, but the home bowlers were defied by O'Brien in the second innings, and by the time the Irish baronet had been removed there was insufficient time for Yorkshire to clinch the game.

The previous year a new method of deciding the Championship based on percentages had been created and clearly confounded most followers of the game. Following Yorkshire's draw with Middlesex the magazine *Cricket* contained the following paragraph:

'Although it is very improbable that Surrey can be at the head of the Championship Table, according to the recognised method of scoring, it is not impossible. Yorkshire has to play two more matches and Surrey four. At present Yorkshire has played in 19 finished games, of which three were lost; Surrey has played in 21 finished games of which five were lost; Readers with a mathematical turn of mind may like to amuse themselves for a few hours by trying to find out what Surrey must do to win, and what Yorkshire must do to lose.'

The next set of matches, commencing 20 August, in fact settled the matter, for whilst Yorkshire were drawing at Hove, Lancashire beat Surrey at The Oval, which result moved Lancashire into second place. Yorkshire drew further ahead by beating Kent at Tonbridge in a very low scoring game on a rain damaged pitch – Kent were dismissed for 98 and 103, Ernest Smith returning figures of seven for 47. The rain was even worse at Clifton College, where Surrey and Gloucestershire scarcely managed to complete the first two innings of their game.

Surrey suffered further setbacks when they lost to Somerset at Taunton, whilst Middlesex defeated Kent, and this meant that the final order in the 1896 Championship table read: 1. Yorkshire, 2. Lancashire, 3. Middlesex and 4. Surrey.

Arthur Bairstow appeared in the first of his 24 games for Yorkshire in the Sussex match. A useful wicketkeeper, he acted as David

Hunter's understudy until 1900. His local cricket was for Windhill and later for South Kirkby and his final first-class match was for an England Eleven *v* the Australians in 1902.

Yorkshire completed their 1896 first-class programme with two matches in the Scarborough Festival. The first was against a South of England Eleven and despite the first day being washed out by rain, the County proved victorious by five wickets. Peel, quite unplayable, took eight for 27 in the South's second innings, which amounted to only 76.

The fixture with MCC was even more badly affected by the weather, there being no play at all on the first and third days. The only performance of note were Jackson's innings of 70 and an analysis of eight for 74 by the old Australian fast bowler, Spofforth, now resident in England.

A remarkable season for batsmen proved to everyone that Yorkshire was the equal of any other side on hard dry wickets and were superior to the others on wet ones. J. T. Brown finished on top of the batting averages in County Championship matches with 1,556 runs at 45.75. He was not a model of consistency but scored runs quickly and attractively. F. S. Jackson scored 1030 runs at 42.92, and Peel was third with 1,135 runs at 35.43 – he often came to the side's rescue with a middle-of-the-order innings. Hirst made a big advance as a batsman, scoring 1018 runs at 32.83, while J. Tunnicliffe acted as the fulcrum of the batting line-up. Moorhouse did not do as well as the previous year but scored 675 runs at 28.12, while Lord Hawke scored 577 at 27.66. Wainwright and Denton each scored over 800 runs while Milligan, Mounsey and Ernest Smith each averaged over 21. Hunter and Haigh were useful tail-enders.

With the ball, Schofield Haigh, in his first full season, took 71 wickets at 15.28 each and for several weeks was unplayable. Ernest Smith took 22 at 17.05, and Ted Wainwright did very well with 90 wickets at 18.72. Peel had another good season with 97 at 19.07, while F. S. Jackson had several good days and took 37 at 21.02. F. W. Milligan did very well for a time with 33 wickets at 22.57, and the other mainline bowler, Hirst, took 80 wickets at 23.73. Leg-spinner Brown took 15 at 31.60.

Yorkshire's 1897 began with the match against MCC at Lord's. Tunnicliffe and Brown each scored 54 and they opened with a stand of 86 before Moorhouse came in and added 54 with Tunnicliffe, who batted for $2\frac{1}{2}$ hours for his 54. Moorhouse went on to score 78 as Yorkshire finally reached 274, MCC replied with 266. When Yorkshire batted again, Lord Hawke was the top scorer with 63 not out in brilliant style and Tunnicliffe made 34 as Yorkshire were all out for 217. P. F. Warner (108 not out) and Albert Trott (62) put on 145 for their second wicket as the MCC gained a comfortable win by seven wickets.

Yorkshire embarked on their Western tour and a visit to Bristol proved lucrative for the Champions. Only W.G. himself with 55 and W. H. Hale, 47 not out, made any headway against the keen Yorkshire atack as they bowled out Gloucestershire for 155, and by the end of the day F. S. Jackson and Brown had put Yorkshire in front for the loss of Tunnicliffe. On the next day Jackson (68) and Brown (72) left when they had put on 137 for Yorkshire's second wicket but Denton came in and scored 41 before Hirst joined Wainwright. These two added 185 for the seventh wicket with Wainwright scoring 100 and Hirst 134 as Yorkshire were all out for 494. C. L. Townsend had the remarkable bowling figures of seven for 207. Gloucestershire were so far behind that even a second innings total of 354 could not prevent defeat by ten wickets.

At Taunton after the early loss of Tunnicliffe and Brown, Hon F. S. Jackson with 124 in $2\frac{3}{4}$ hours and Denton with 112 in 2 hours put on 205 for the third wicket. Wainwright with 47 and Hirst (30) helped Yorkshire to a score of 385. At the close of play Somerset had slumped to 33 for five, but on the following day H. T. Stanley with 51 and G. Fowler (70) helped them to 223. By the end of the second day Somerset, after following on, were 200 for four and had lost the two Palairets for 79 and 41. Robson made 80 but the Somerset side were soon dismissed for 276 and Yorkshire required 115 to win. Tunnicliffe (30) and Brown (47) put on 62 for the first wicket as Yorkshire went on to win by five wickets.

Yorkshire won the toss against Essex at Leyton. The deadly Kortright soon reduced Yorkshire to a score of 26 for five. Moorhouse with 35 and F. W. Milligan 31 not out, with assistance from Hirst and Wainwright, rallied Yorkshire round to a score of 154. Kortright finished with five for 76 besides taking three catches. Essex were bowled out for 199 but Yorkshire again lost quick wickets with only F. S. Jackson (57) and Peel (45) offering any real resistance to the bowling of Bull who went on to take five for 95. Essex were then reduced to 93 for seven before C. J. Kortright joined Mead to take the home side to victory without further loss.

At Headingley, Yorkshire defeated Leicestershire by an innings and 129 runs after the home side had scored 399 for seven on the first day. Leicestershire could only manage 124 and 182 in reply, thus providing Yorkshire with a comfortable victory.

On a pitch greatly affected by heavy rain, Cambridge put Yorkshire in at Fenner's with Jackson and Tunnicliffe (24) attacking the bowling to score 54 for the first wicket. F. S. Jackson went on to score 61, which was more than half of Yorkshire's final total of 100 all out, in which G. L. Jessop took five for 19 and H. W. De Zoete five for 63. N. F. Druce with 31 and E. H. Bray helped Cambridge to take a lead of 38. Brown (30) and Wainwright (27) supported F. S. Jackson (59 not out) but Yorkshire were all out for 162, leaving the University to score 125 for victory. At 99 for six it was anybody's game but Wilson stood firm and G. L. Jessop hit out to take Cambridge to victory.

At Bradford, Yorkshire won the toss against Hampshire and scored 279 with F. S. Jackson scoring 57 in an hour out of 70 posted for the first wicket with Tunnicliffe. With three wickets down for 93, Denton added 110 for the fourth wicket with R. Moorhouse (32). Denton went on to score 90 in $2\frac{1}{2}$ hours. Hampshire were unfortunate that heavy rain spoilt their chances and on a tricky wicket they stumbled to 94 all out. At the end of the second day Hampshire were 41 for four but they finally reached 201 thanks to D. A. Steele who hit brilliantly for 67. Yorkshire went on to win by ten wickets.

Against Warwickshire at Sheffield, Yorkshire opened with a stand of 175 with F. S. Jackson making 81 and Tunnicliffe 96 before Brown scored 89 and at the close Yorkshire were 337 for five. That finished the match with rain stopping any further hopes of play. At Halifax, Yorkshire compiled 279 against Kent with Tunnicliffe scoring 92 and Hirst 68. In reply, on a wicket that gave increasing help to the bowlers, Kent were dismissed for 102 and 74, Peel captured eleven cheap wickets.

One of the most exciting games of the season took place at Derby, who were in trouble at 30 for three against the bowling of Hirst before Chatterton was joined by Davidson and they put on 111 for the fourth wicket. Davidson carried out his bat for 90 as the innings closed at 234. Yorkshire lost Jackson before the close of play, when the visitors were 42 for one. Next morning Tunnicliffe (34) and Brown (53) took the score past the hundred mark but with six wickets down for 127 it was thanks to the efforts of Wainwright, Peel, Mounsey and Haigh that Yorkshire reached 265. Derbyshire made another wretched start, losing four for 34, but Storer brought them back into the game by the close of the second day. On the last day he went on to score a splendid unbeaten 104 out of 184. Yorkshire needed 154 to win and started disastrously, losing Jackson at 0 and Brown at 2 before Tunnicliffe (19) and Denton took the score to 36 for three. Two more wickets fell at 58 before Denton was joined by the reliable Hirst. They added 69 before Denton went for a fighting 41 but there were 15 required when Yorkshire lost their ninth wicket. Hunter then came in and hit 16 not out in five hits, Yorkshire winning by one wicket.

At Lord's, Yorkshire batted for the whole of the first day to score 397 for eight. At one stage Yorkshire had lost six wickets for 134 with F. S. Jackson run out for 36 and Denton bowled by Hearne for 34. Then Wainwright was joined by Peel (46). They added 126 for the seventh wicket and then Lord Hawke came in and batted beautifully for 75 in his first county match of the season. Together they added 137 for their eighth wicket and when Wainwright was out for 171 on the next day, he had completed his highest score in first-class cricket in a stay of 4 hours. Yorkshire were all out for 439. When Middlesex batted the overnight rain was beginning to take its toll of the pitch and six wickets fell for 149. F. G. J. Ford had scored 79 but Dr Thornton and Webbe came together to take Middlesex to 235 for seven. The follow-on was almost avoided but they were finally dismissed for 311. With nothing but a draw to play for, Middlesex meandered to 211 for four by stumps. At this stage of the season Yorkshire were third in the table behind Nottinghamshire and Essex.

Heavy rain had turned Headingley into a bowler's paradise for the start of the Surrey match with over 20,000 people watching the first day's play. Yorkshire won the toss and apart from Denton's 22 were always struggling against Richardson who took seven for 55 as Yorkshire were bowled out for 90. When Surrey batted Haigh proved an even more difficult proposition for the batsmen. He took seven for 17 in a fine spell of bowling, Surrey being dismissed for 75. At the end of the day Yorkshire were 70 for one. Next morning, with 30,000 in the ground – the biggest crowd ever to watch cricket in Yorkshire – F. S. Jackson batted remarkably well to score 92 as he put on 96 with Denton who went on to make a splendid 77 before Yorkshire were dismissed for 256. Richardson again bowled well to take eight for 99. Surrey had little chance of obtaining 272 to win but W. S. Lees scored a lively 44 while W. W. Read scored 29 as Surrey lost by 100 runs.

The Nottinghamshire match at Trent Bridge turned out to be a draw on a pitch that was too good for the bowlers. Yorkshire batted for the whole of the first day to score 364. William Gunn and Shrewsbury replied by taking Nottinghamshire's total to 490 and Yorkshire were left with nothing to play for but a draw.

The Philadelphians came to Bramall Lane but the match was spoilt by the rain. The visitors batted first and scored 225 with A. N. Wood scoring 52, E. M. Cregar 50 and J. B. King 49. Yorkshire were 77 for four at the close of play. Little progress was made on the second day and the third was a complete wash-out.

John Thomas Brown junior (of Darfield) made his debut for Yorkshire in the above match dismissing J. A. Lester at the cost of 38 runs. He played in 12 games in 1899 and 11 in 1900 and continued to play in odd matches until 1903. Born at Darfield in 1874, he was a very hard-hitting right-hand batsman and a very fast bowler who took 97 wickets at 21.35 each during his mercurial career with Yorkshire. He was professional at Barnsley from 1898–1901 and also played for Darfield and Mitchell Main. Injuries to his knee and shoulder ruined his first-class career. For many years he lived at Duckmanton in

Derbyshire and he was the father of six sons and eight daughters. He was playing in the Chesterfield League in 1926 and died at his home in Duckmanton in 1950.

Yorkshire won the toss at The Oval and did well up to the time that the scoreboard read 155 for four. But when Denton left for 60 and Wainwright for 41, Yorkshire collapsed to 197 all out with Richardson again bowling at a tremendous pace and returning figures of eight for 108. Surrey lost Brockwell and Abel before the close of play when the score was 94 for two. Next day a last wicket stand by Jephson and Richardson enabled Surrey to reach 185. Yorkshire declared in their second innings at 309 for 9 setting Surrey 322 in 250 minutes, but they made a bad start. Abel was run out for 0 and Hayward left at 14. Brockwell with 69 and Baldwin (102) added 111 for the third wicket. Baldwin carried on to save the game for Surrey. Yorkshire remained in third place in the table, with Nottinghamshire and Lancashire above them.

A stand of 112 for the second wicket between Barton (125) and Wynyard seemed to bar the way to any further success for Yorkshire. When the latter was out Hampshire were 149 for two. It was a fine display of batting by the pair, but Jackson then took control and finished with six for 19 as the home side were dismissed for 251. Yorkshire gained a lead of 42 on the first innings and Hampshire were only 70 ahead with six wickets in hand. Brilliant bowling by Jackson meant that Yorkshire needed 138 for victory. Brown and Tunnicliffe knocked those off without any trouble for Yorkshire to record a ten-wicket victory.

At Sheffield, Yorkshire put on a superlative performance to beat their visitors by an innings and 307 runs. Sussex were without Ranjitsinhji, and only George Brann with 57 and young Joe Vine with 33 showed up well against F. W. Milligan and Haigh. For the home side Brown and Tunnicliffe created a new first wicket partnership record of 378. Tunnicliffe was out for 147, but the former went on to score 311 in six and a quarter hours. Yorkshire declared at 681 for five.

Yorkshire's next match at Dewsbury was a remarkable one against Nottinghamshire who at one stage looked certain winners but in the end had to struggle to avoid defeat. Batting first, the visitors made a workmanlike 260 with J. A. Dixon scoring 53 and Dench 42. Hirst took five for 80 and at the end of the day Yorkshire were 20 without loss. Next morning on what appeared to be still a good wicket, John Gunn made the ball 'kick' in a surprising manner and after getting rid of Denton for 44 proceeded to take six for 22 in 18.2 overs and Yorkshire were all out for 139. Following on John Gunn immediately got rid of Brown with only 9 on the board but the Hon F. S. Jackson played a brilliant innings of 77 as he and Tunnicliffe took part in a century stand. At the close Yorkshire were 146 for four with Tunnicliffe playing the anchor-role on 42. Next morning Tunnicliffe left for 58 but Wainwright played a fine innings of 103 in 2 hours and 40 minutes while F. W. Milligan hit well for 55 and Yorkshire were able to declare at 358 for nine. Nottinghamshire were set 238 to win and had to fight hard for a draw, finishing with 151 for eight. William Gunn made 86 – a masterly innings. Nottinghamshire were thus able to maintain their position at the top of the tale.

Poor Lancashire fielding at Bradford contributed greatly to Yorkshire's occupation of the crease for the whole of the first day's play. R. Moorhouse made top score of 61 and Denton 59, with Peel also making 48 and four other players scoring at least 28. They took their score to 345 all out. All Yorkshire batsmen were caught as were nine on the Lancashire side when they batted. After less than 2 hours of Lancashire batting, a downpour finished play for the rest of the second day in which time Lancashire were 167 for one. A. C. MacLaren in his first match of the season was undefeated on 110. Baker with 37 then helped MacLaren to add 67 for the fourth wicket and C. Smith made 45 as Lancashire reached 354. A. C. MacLaren's innings was one of his finest. When Yorkshire batted again the wicket had become quite treacherous and the first seven wickets fell for only 36 runs before Haigh improved the situation slightly, Yorkshire being bowled out for 66. There was no time for Lancashire to bat again.

The Essex match at Huddersfield provided one of the shocks of the season which at the time looked as if it would cost Yorkshire the Championship, but they were to lose three other games before the end of the season. This defeat was not of crucial significance. Yorkshire lacked Peel and Hunter as Essex won the toss and batted on a pitch that always offered some help to the faster bowlers. A. J. Turner batted well for Essex scoring a cultured 40 and helping F. L. Fane (24) to retrieve a desperate situation. Hirst bowled well to take six for 46 as Essex floundered to 139. Yorkshire then lost eight wickets for 62 before Hirst and Haigh added 43 for the ninth wicket in a characteristic rescue-act. In the end Yorkshire were only four runs behind their opponents. When they batted again, Essex soon lost five wickets for 51 mainly to the busy Hirst but A. J. Turner, in his first month of county cricket, batted splendidly adding 121 for the sixth wicket with F. L. Fane (47). A. J. Turner went on to score 111 and Kortright, with the long handle, hit a quick 39 to take Essex to a large total of 294, leaving Yorkshire with 299 to win. They began badly with four down for 23 before Moorhouse (68) and Wainwright (63) put on 115 for the fifth wicket. With those two out and the score at 169 for six, Hirst and Milligan came together and in 40 minutes they added 85 to the score before Milligan was bowled by Pickett for 64. Then Lord Hawke helped Yorkshire's cause by taking the score to 283 before Hirst was sadly run out for 54. Lord Hawke was still unbeaten when last man Bairstow was given out lbw to Mead for Essex to win by one run. The game was a credit to cricket with both sides playing on top form and Yorkshire fighting an uphill battle in the best possible spirit. Lancashire now led the Championship table with Essex in second place as Nottinghamshire had surprisingly been beaten by Gloucestershire.

At Headingley, Yorkshire gave a splendid exhibition of batsmanship against a rather weak Somerset side. F. S. Jackson began well with 44 in 50 minutes but J. T. Brown made the innings of the day by scoring 107 in just over 2 hours adding 142 for the third wicket with Denton (38). Hirst then came in and hit 52 in 50 minutes with Milligan doing rather better by scoring 51 in 35 minutes before the innings closed for 356. At the close of play Somerset were 88 for three with Woods 61. Woods went on to score 111 in less than two hours but received very little support as his side was bowled out for 188. In the second innings their total of 146 meant defeat by an innings and 22 runs.

Robert Whiteley Collinson made the first of just two appearances for Yorkshire in this match. He later moved to Norfolk and played with success in that county.

At Harrogate, Gloucestershire gave a good batting display to stay all day and score 370, of which G. L. Jessop made 101 out of 118 in only 40 minutes, hitting the ball to all parts of the ground 'inside and out' according to one report. C. L. Townsend then came in and hit 109. When Yorkshire batted, Brown scored 80 out of 166 for six, putting on 103 with Hirst who went on to score 55. At the completion of the innings Yorkshire were 94 in arrears. Gloucestershire gave an even batting display to take their score to 271 for nine before declaring. Set the huge total of 366 for victory, in $4\frac{1}{4}$ hours, Yorkshire lost two wickets for 38 before Brown (49) and Denton (55) took the score to 97. Hirst (35) then joined Denton and they added 31 for the sixth wicket when Denton fell and the match was heading for a draw until slow left-armer W. S. A. Brown was put on to bowl. Within the space of eight overs he had taken four for 14 and Yorkshire were all out for 225: defeated by 140 runs.

On 2 August Yorkshire visited Edgbaston and did well to dismiss Warwickshire for 172. When Yorkshire batted they soon got on top of the bowling, Denton playing a brilliant innings of 141 not out. A lead of 202 was gained and Yorkshire went on to win by nine wickets.

Yorkshire continued their good form at Canterbury where they made a total of 348 for eight by the end of the first day. They made a poor start before Denton (84) and Wainwright (46) put on 103 for the fourth wicket and then C. E. M. Wilson batted through to the end of the day for 84. Kent gave a wretched batting display until they had lost nine wickets for 74 when Walter Wright (37) was joined by last man W. M. Bradley and they took the score to 170 with Bradley hitting 67 in 45 minutes. Following on Kent did better than in their first innings without giving the impression that they would make a game of it. G. J. Mordaunt scored 45 as Kent reached 202, with Jackson taking his match figures to eleven for 126. Yorkshire went on to a ten wicket win.

Moving to Hove, Yorkshire lacked Peel and Brown when they batted first. Runs were difficult to come by and J. C. Hartley took six for 85 as the total reached 174. Sussex were 84 for four at the close of play, George Brann having scored 32 and Ranjitsinhji 33. W. Newham (96 not out) and George Bean (115) came together and added 163 for the seventh wicket in $2\frac{1}{4}$ hours; Wainwright took five for 68 as Sussex finished 327 all out. When Yorkshire batted again Denton made 44 out of 129 for five with Hirst 30 not out at the end of the second day. Hirst went on to score 88, adding 70 for the seventh wicket with Ernest Smith (45) and helping to take Yorkshire to 269 all out. J. C. Hartley took five for 96 this time. Sussex won the match comfortably by six wickets.

Yorkshire had another poor time of it at Old Trafford where they won the toss and decided to bat on a difficult wicket. They paid the penalty and were bowled out by Hallam for 160. Lancashire, 105 for three overnight, took their first innings lead to 126 with Frank Sugg, enjoying a little luck, playing a fine innings of 122 which lasted for four hours. W. R. Cuttell with 44 helped Sugg to add 73 for the eighth wicket. Heavy rain finished cricket early on the Friday with the result that Yorkshire were caught on a treacherous wicket on the last day and they were bowled out for 100, Cuttell and Briggs sharing the wickets. Lancashire won by an innings and 26 runs. Yorkshire were now down to fourth place in the Championship table without hope of improving that situation. Lancashire had wrested the lead from Essex, while the early front-runners, Nottinghamshire, had faded.

Yorkshire drew with Middlesex at Bramall Lane on a good pitch without any interference from the weather. Yorkshire won the toss and batted first, with Denton scoring 39 out of 52 in a second wicket partnership with Tunnicliffe, who scored 50 and also shared a stand of 98 for the third wicket with F. S. Jackson. Jackson went on to a fine 101, Ted Wainwright made 60 and Peel 40. The latter was playing his first match for a month: 'his first appearance after a long illness' according to *Cricket*. Yorkshire went on to total 366 with J. T. Hearne bowling well and taking six for 116. Middlesex started well, H. B. Hayman (56) and P. F. Warner (46) opening with a stand of 100 for the first wicket. Afterwards wickets fell regularly until R. S. Lucas defied the Yorkshire attack with an unbeaten 46 and Middlesex were 119 behind on the first innings with Peel taking five for 71. Yorkshire then attempted to score runs quickly but only Denton with 72 got on top of the bowling with Yorkshire declaring at 182 for six, setting Middlesex 302 to win in $3\frac{1}{4}$ hours. The match was drawn with Middlesex 219 for two.

Peel played his last match for Yorkshire in this game after apparently arriving at the ground the worse for drink. Whether it was the second day or the third day of the match in now immaterial. It seemed that it was not his first transgression and though his team-mates would do their utmost to keep him out of trouble, it seems that he went too far on this occasion and Lord Hawke and the Committee felt compelled to sack him for his misbehaviour. Reading the newspaper reports in the Sheffield press it is very doubtful whether Peel appeared on the field of play any the worse for wear but one can be sure that his dismissal from the team was a fair and correct decision. It has often been suggested that Peel urinated on the field during the match at which several thousand were present on each day but it is difficult to ascertain the truth behind this long-standing tale. It was a sad episode of Yorkshire's cricket history but it proved to many people that the change in the personnel of the Yorkshire team with the accent on self-discipline was probably completed with poor Peel's departure. Peel's suspension for the rest of the season was announced on the day after this match.

Derbyshire surprised Yorkshire by dominating the first half of this match, but having gained a lead of 45 on a bowler's wicket, they allowed Yorkshire to score 166 in the final innings and win by five wickets. At Leicester, Yorkshire occupied the first day scoring 325 for six with Hirst (88), Denton (51) and Wainwright (50), all in good form. There was no further play owing to the bad weather. Since neither county was in contention for the title, this wet end to the Championship season was not as serious as it might have been.

Yorkshire's last match at Scarborough resulted in a 69 runs win over MCC. Two innings had been completed by the end of the first day, the County having a lead of 21. F. S. Jackson (72) and Brown (46) put on 115 in 75 minutes for Yorkshire's second wicket – a stand that won the game for their side as Walter Mead came on and finished with seven for 64 out of Yorkshire's 205. W. Chatterton scored 35 for MCC and H. B. Chinnery and Davidson also made useful scores with Haigh the chief destroyer with four for 41.

And so ended a season with Yorkshire finishing in fourth position after looking likely Champions or runners-up for most of the season. The loss of Peel must have made some difference to the side and his successor was a matter for discussion. Among those about whom there must have been speculation was James Shaw of Linthwaite, who had taken 27 wickets for Yorkshire 2nds in 1897 but would be 33 years old when the 1898 season began. On 21 and 22 September at Bradford an Eleven of Yorkshire led by Lord Hawke met a team of 16 Colts of Yorkshire. Playing for Yorkshire was one A. Cordingley who captured eight for 33 in the first innings of the Colts. When the Yorkshire side batted again, another Cordingley took two for 41 dismissing both R. W. Collinson and F. W. Milligan. Playing for the 16 Colts was W. Rhodes who took just one wicket for 62 in 15 overs – his victim being R. W. Collinson 'c Tunnicliffe b Rhodes'. Robert Peel was conspicuous by his absence from the Yorkshire CCC Report of the season of 1897.

J. T. Brown headed the batting averages with 1431 runs at an average of 43.36 with Wainwright a very good second with 1372 runs at 39.20. Hirst had an excellent season with 1212 at 35.64, and Denton scored 1328 at 34.05. Next came F. S. Jackson with 1089. Lord Hawke, who was missing quite often, scored 436 runs at 31.14 and then came Peel with 514 at 28.55. Tunnicliffe also reached four figures but his average was only 28.34 which was a little below standard. Milligan played some very useful innings to average 22 and Moorhouse, too, averaged 20 yet he appeared to have slipped back somewhat. All-in-all Yorkshire's batting was probably as strong as any other county's and it had practically no tail whatsoever.

Peel was Yorkshire's best bowler with 56 wickets at 20.01, slightly ahead of Haigh who took 70 wickets at 20.17 with F. S. Jackson very close behind with 62 wickets at 20.48. The leading wicket-taker, Hirst, came next with 84 wickets at 22.85 each and then Wainwright who took 76 wickets as 24.43 each. F. W. Milligan had the worst record with 33 wickets at 24.66 but even he proved a match-winner in some games. Two quick bowlers, two spinners and two who could operate as speed men or spinners seemed the basis of a sound attack, especially as they were all good batsmen (or would be in the future in the case of Haigh). Yorkshire's main problem seemed to be to find another left-arm slow bowler.

A match took place at Bedale on 5 and 6 May when a full-strength Yorkshire side containing Rhodes played against 18 of Bedale & District who had A. Cordingley, a left-arm slow bowler, in the side. Rhodes took 6 for 40 in the match and for Bedale, Cordingley five for 75. Rhodes may have had the better figures but Cordingley did bowl Denton for 0 and J. T. Brown for 10.

On 9 and 10 May the Nottinghamshire Colts played the Yorkshire Colts at Nottingham and the Yorkshire side included both Rhodes and Cordingley. The former took one for 14 and the latter four for 37. Two days later, Yorkshire visited Lord's to play the MCC and batting

Wilfred Rhodes, one of cricket's greatest all-rounders, who is the only man to take over 4,000 first-class wickets. (NCCC)

at number 8 in the Yorkshire side was Rhodes, so clearly Wilfred had got the vote over Cordingley. Yorkshire won the toss and Brown set about the bowling to such an extent that he scored 46 out of 52 in 50 minutes before J. T. Hearne went through the Yorkshire side to take eight for 48, with only Hirst (20) offering much resistance on a bowler's wicket. The MCC had replied with 13 for three when a heavy downpour spoilt the rest of the day's play with W. G. Grace yet to open his account. On the next day Grace went for 18 and W. Storer made 36 with the Hon J. R. Tufton battling to 33 not out in 45 minutes as MCC took a lead of 17. Wainwright took four for 43 and Haigh three for 20 while Rhodes took two for 39 in his first match, Albert Trott being his first victim in first-class cricket. When Yorkshire batted again Wainwright played a fine innings of 63 in 80 minutes and Lord Hawke hit hard for 20, Yorkshire reaching 185.

Set 169 to win, the MCC were bowled out for 69 with F. S. Jackson (six for 45) and Rhodes (four for 24) taking advantage of a helpful pitch to bring victory to Yorkshire by 99 runs.

Wilfred Rhodes made his debut for Yorkshire at the age of 20 following the sacking of Bobby Peel during the previous season. He was born at Kirkheaton on 29 October 1877, and was a right-hand batsman with a sound defence who drove well and scored much quicker in his early days than he was given credit for, developing a pronounced two-eyed stance which was never very attractive to the onlooker. It was as a left-arm slow bowler that he took the world by storm in his early seasons, being soon recognised as one of the greatest slow bowlers of all time. He took more wickets in first-class cricket than any other bowler and performed the double of 1,000 runs and 100 wickets in a season on 16 occasions, twice more than his county colleague George Hirst. Rhodes developed from a useful batsman into an England opener with the great Jack Hobbs; for a time he allowed his bowling to be of secondary importance. After the First World War when Yorkshire's bowling strength was depleted, Rhodes redis-covered his ability with the ball, his 'flight' puzzling basmen just as it had done twenty years earlier. Deadly on a bad wicket, and never easy to hit on a perfect one, his main asset was being able to take advantage of any help that the pitch might offer. Rhodes was taught to bowl by his father who was captain of Kirkheaton 2nd XI and he practised by bowling at the wall of a barn at Kirkheaton. He worked at Mirfield Engine Sheds before going to Galashiels as professional in 1896, bowling with great success. He was turned down by Warwickshire after qualifying for a place on their groundstaff in 1897 and in 1898 was allocated to Sheffield United by Yorkshire who were then looking for a replacement for Peel. Rhodes began his Yorkshire career by playing against W. G. Grace in his first match and he finished his first-class career by bowling with success against the Australians, with Don Bradman in their side, in 1930. A dour, methodical and calculating cricketer, he was never worshipped by the public in the way that George Hirst was, but in later years, having lost his eyesight, he became a more relaxed, kindlier person. He died at Branksome Park, near Poole in Dorset in 1973 aged 95.

Yorkshire moved from London to start their West Country tour at Bath and were soon in a state of shock with the score standing at 65 for eight of which total Hirst had made 20. The captain, however, was in fine form with 50 as he added 83 for the ninth wicket with Haigh. In reply to Yorkshire's 163, L. C. H. Palairet, with 26, was the home side's top scorer as they were bowled out for 104 with Rhodes taking seven for 24 in his first Championship appearance. On the following day rain washed out nearly all the playing time and, when Lord Hawke declared on the last day with Yorkshire 174 for seven, Denton had also scored 39. Somerset were left 234 to win on a now treacherous pitch and they were summarily dismissed for 35, Rhodes again in irresistible form with six for 21.

At Bristol, in the time available, Yorkshire scored 263 for three with Tunnicliffe scoring 107 not out in three hours, while Jackson scored 67 and Wainwright 39 not out in depressing conditions that were bleak and cold and reminded elderly spectators of their Crimean experiences.

Fenner's followed and defeat for the home side by an innings and 22 runs. Haigh and Rhodes bowled Cambridge out for 67. Yorkshire led by 153 at the end of the first day with Tunnicliffe scoring 46 and Wainwright 45 as the visitors replied with 220. Only C. J. Burnup with 40 and T. L. Taylor with 35 batted well when Cambridge were dismissed a second time for 131, F. W. Milligan taking four for 33.

A trip to Southampton saw the match begun and finished in one day. It had been arranged for poor Harry Baldwin's benefit – the first ever to be granted by Hampshire CCC – and rain washed out the first day's play. Hampshire scored 42 and 36 with Haigh taking fourteen for 43 on a pitch that was tailor-made for him. Yorkshire managed to score 157 with Tunnicliffe batting very well for 58 while young Rhodes made 28.

Yorkshire's first home match was at Headingley against Warwickshire who scored 187 for nine on a very slow wicket on the opening day. Willie Quaife and Lilley put on 98 for the visitors' fourth wicket and with Devey making 30 Warwickshire went on to reach 218, Rhodes taking five for 69. On a dubious pitch, Yorkshire opened with a stand of 43 between Brown who was run out for 31 and Tunnicliffe (20) but they were all out for 112 with Sydney Santall taking five for 39. Rain continued to spoil the match and when Warwickshire were 50 for five in their second innings they declared, setting Yorkshire 157 to win in 110 minutes, a task they never attempted.

At Leyton, on another bowler's wicket, Essex batted first and were soon dismissed for 78; Jackson took five for 46 and Rhodes three for 9. Yorkshire then lost three wickets for as many runs before Denton (46) played a fine attacking innings and added 53 with Wainwright, Yorkshire gaining a lead of 40 runs. Essex batted better in their second innings with five players scoring 20 or more and at 149 for four looked to be well on top. Hirst and Wainwright changed matters by removing the last six batsmen for 19 runs and at the close of the second day Yorkshire were 3 for one having lost Brown and needing 129 to win. On the last day, with one end being treacherous for batsmen, Yorkshire struggled, but Essex dropped at least six catches and threw the game away. Yorkshire and Warwickshire were now joint leaders in the Championship.

At Bradford, a blank first day was followed by Surrey winning the toss and having the best of a pitch that was likely to become progresively worse. Despite an opening stand of 42, Surrey could only muster 139 all out, Wainwright and Rhodes taking five wickets apiece. Yorkshire were soon in trouble with eight wickets down for 105, but by the close Hirst and Haigh had taken them to 141. On the last day their partnership increased to 192, Hirst being undefeated with 130 and Haigh reaching 85. A declaration was made at 297 for nine. Then, in an inexplicable bad batting display, Surrey were bowled out for 37, Rhodes taking seven for 24.

At Huddersfield, Yorkshire began very well against Hampshire, 85 being on the board before Tunnicliffe fell for 50. Brown, who had been out of form for some weeks, went on to score 88. Of the later batsmen only Lord Hawke did much and Yorkshire were bowled out for 226. In reply a very dispirited Hampshire could only muster 45 and 83, Wainwright taking nine wickets and Rhodes seven. Yorkshire won by an innings and 98 runs.

Yorkshire's next match, against Kent at Sheffield, provided some more remarkable cricket. F. S. Jackson with 46 alone did well as Yorkshire slumped to 141 for nine but at that point Lord Hawke, who went on to score 107 not out, was joined by last man David Hunter (47) and together they put on 148 for the last wicket – a Yorkshire record which lasted 84 years. When Kent batted, J. R. Mason (65) and Alec Hearne (43) put on 82 for the first wicket and then B. D. Bannon scored 42 as Kent finished 71 in arrears. In Yorkshire's second innings Tunnicliffe batted very well for 108, before Hawke declared, leaving Kent to obtain 301 in four hours. Haigh immediately bowled Mason for 3 and Kent were bowled out for 171. Yorkshire's win took them to the top of the Championship table.

At Lord's, Yorkshire won the toss against Middlesex, and after they lost three wickets for 101, F. S. Jackson went on to score 133 in about three hours, adding 149 for the fourth wicket with Wainwright (76). At 291 for eight, Milligan (65) was joined by Rhodes (78) and the pair put on a further 97 in 50 minutes. Finally, Hunter and Rhodes added a further 57 to take Yorkshire to a formidable 445. F. G. J. Ford then made top score in each Middlesex innings – 35 and 127 – the latter taking only 110 minutes and containing some fine clean hitting all round the ground. Middlesex were all out for 118 with Haigh taking seven for 60. They followed on, 327 behind, H. B. Hayman (25) and P. F. Warner starting with a stand of 52. Ford and Warner put on a further 107 for the third wicket, taking the score to 182 for two at the end of the second day. Next morning Warner was bowled by Haigh for 70 and apart from G. MacGregor's 27, only Ford held up Yorkshire's progress. Middlesex were bowled out for 318 leaving Yorkshire winners by an innings and 9 runs.

Nottinghamshire had the better of a drawn match at Headingley but their first innings of 215 was undistinguished apart from a somewhat fortunate innings of 80 from William Attewell. In an hour before the close Yorkshire lost two for 57 with Brown not out 41. At 84 Brown was fourth out for 60, only Denton with 35 offering much resistance as Yorkshire were bowled out for 143. When cricket resumed on the last day, Nottinghamshire scored 105–5 before declaring and Yorkshire were set to score 178 in two hours. On a rain-affected pitch, they were happy to get away with a draw.

At Leicester, Yorkshire won the toss, and after Brown had gone at 31, Tunnicliffe (57 in 2$\frac{1}{2}$ hours) helped F. S. Jackson to put on 157 for the second wicket. When Jackson left after scoring 147, he had been batting for 2 hours and 40 minutes in a delightful innings. Denton went on to score 99 in a punishing knock and Yorkshire totalled 449. Heavy rain overnight ruined the pitch for batsmen and Leicester were all out in 1$\frac{1}{2}$ hours for 57 with Jackson and Rhodes each taking five wickets. Following on Leicester were dismissed for 126 with King making the top score of 30.

Another easy win was recorded over Essex at Bradford. Rain prevented play on the first day and when Essex batted first after winning the toss it was thought that the pitch would deteriorate later after recent heavy rain. The Essex innings was little more than a procession, however, Rhodes taking six cheap wickets in a total of 64. In Tunnicliffe's absence Lord Hawke opened with Brown and they put on 100 for the first wicket and made light of the conditions, passing the Essex score in less than an hour. Brown made 42 and Hawke 62. Yorkshire eventually reached 278. In Essex's second innings A. P. Lucas scored a fluent 49 out of 176 as Rhodes and Jackson bowled Yorkshire to an innings victory.

John Binns played only once for Yorkshire in 1898 when he stumped three Leicestershire batsmen at Leicester. A tall man, 6ft high, he was born at Woodhouse Carr, Leeds in 1870 and was a right-hand bat and medium-fast bowler as well as a wicket-keeper. A leather curer by trade, he was living in Leeds in 1898 and died at Leeds General Infirmary in 1934.

The return match with Leicestershire took place at Dewsbury with Yorkshire victorious once again by an innings and 24 runs. On a very soft wicket, Leicester were dismissed in two hours for only 56 by Wainwright and Rhodes and though C. J. B. Wood carried his bat through the visitors' second innings they again succumbed to the same two bowlers.

At Bradford, Sussex gave a good account of themselves until the final stages. After winning the toss they were quickly in trouble with three wickets down for 26 but C. B. Fry (67) and W. Newham (52) put on 111 for the fourth wicket with some excellent batting before Haigh came on again and went through the rest of the Sussex side to take five for 50 in their total of 189. Brown and Tunnicliffe replied with an opening stand of 62, with Tunnicliffe scoring 42 and then Denton (57) and Lord Hawke (52) took Yorkshire to a total of 282. Sussex did very well after losing C. B. Fry at 50, George Brann scoring 85 and with W. L. Murdoch adding 114 for the second wicket to bring the score to 164 for two, but the introduction of Brown into the attack caused consternation among the Sussex batsmen as his leg-breaks picked up six wickets for 52. Four of his victims were taken by reserve 'keeper Bairstow, who totalled seven victims in the match. Sussex were all out for 218, Yorkshire needing only 126 to win which they obtained for the loss of three wickets.

Ted Wainwright's benefit against Lancashire was greeted with glorious weather and a huge crowd of 25,000 on the first day. Yorkshire won the toss and surprisingly, after F. S. Jackson had made 38, they slumped from 92 for one to 134 for 6, when F. W. Milligan joined the opening bat J. T. Brown. Together they added 115 for the seventh wicket in 75 minutes before Milligan was out for 62. Rhodes (33) then joined Brown in a stand of 48 for the ninth wicket with Brown the last to go for 144 just before the close of play. Another large crowd assembled on the second day when Lancashire batted rather quicker than Yorkshire had done with Sugg scoring 70 and Cuttell playing well for 85 not out. At the close of play Yorkshire were 73 with nine second innings wickets in hand. On the last day they carried their score to 253 for two before declaring. Tunnicliffe and F. S. Jackson put on 206 for Yorkshire's second wicket. Lancashire were set to score 282 in three hours but after losing five wickets for 85 they settled for a draw.

At Maidstone, Yorkshire suffered their first defeat. Yorkshire won the toss but never found runs easy to obtain, being all out for 199. Kent equalled Yorkshire's total. In the final innings the home side needed 125 for victory and had made 25 without loss at the close of the second day. C. J. Burnup, after escaping early in his innings, went on to bat brilliantly to win the match for his side.

Somerset visited Scarborough and gave an even batting display to score 208 and by the close of play Yorkshire had scored 156 for three. On the second day F. S. Jackson went on to score 159 in three hours although he was dropped several times. Yorkshire made 397. S. M. J. Woods fought a lone battle in Somerset's second innings – 95 out of 242 – and Yorkshire won by four wickets.

Yorkshire's next match at Sheffield saw Jackson in great form once again: he batted for 3 hours and 40 minutes in scoring 160, a quite brilliant innings. When Gloucestershire batted F. H. B. Champain scored a stylish 57 and W. M. Hemingway 49, but the visitors were forced to follow on 139 behind. In their second innings C. O. H. Sewell played a sound but brilliant innings of 88, carrying his bat through the innings and receiving no support. Yorkshire won by an innings.

At Harrogate, Derbyshire held Yorkshire to a draw. They were set 336 in 190 minutes and after an opening stand of 66 between S. H. Evershed (44) and L. G. Wright (33), Bagshaw came in to make 100 not out in 95 minutes, Derbyshire were by this stage too far behind the clock and the last hour was academic.

At Edgbaston on 1 August, Warwickshire had first choice of a perfect batting pitch and spent the whole of the first day compiling 338 for seven. Yorkshire lost Brown for 0 and six wickets were down for 174 before Wainwright (92) was joined by Lord Hawke to add 91 in 70 minutes for the seventh wicket. Wainwright had batted for $2\frac{1}{4}$ hours for his runs with Lord Hawke carrying on to make a fine 134 in 3 hours and 10 minutes. Rhodes (36) helped him to add 97 for the eighth wicket and Haigh (41) 61 for the ninth, so that Yorkshire took a lead of 42 runs. Afterwards there was nothing to play for and Warwickshire having avoided an innings defeat indulged in some batting practice.

Surrey, at The Oval, won the toss and batted first with Abel (114) and Brockwell (93) putting on 143 for the first wicket. Then Abel was helped by Lockwood (51) to add 109 for the third wicket in 50 minutes. Hayward (46), D. L. A. Jephson (40), and K. J. Key (85), were also in fine form as Surrey, 438 for six overnight, continued to pile on the agony, eventually reaching 536. There was no excuse for what was to follow apart form the splendid bowling of Richardson and Lockwood, who took all 18 wickets to fall, with F. S. Jackson, unfortunately, absent hurt. Yorkshire were all out for 78 in the first innings. In their second innings, F. W. Milligan hit out to score a brave 63, but Yorkshire could not avoid an innings defeat. In spite of this, the County still led the Championship table.

At Nottingham, Yorkshire compiled 277 with Tunnicliffe scoring 66 in $3\frac{1}{2}$ hours and F. W. Milligan 74, the pair adding 125 for the fourth wicket after Yorkshire had three wickets down for 40. Rhodes went on to score 50 not out as John Gunn took eight for 108. Nottinghamshire made a good start with A. O. Jones (32) and Shrewsbury (25) putting on 40 for the first wicket but the wicket became more difficult and the home side collapsed to 90 all out with Rhodes taking six for 32. After following on, Nottinghamshire were

90 for one at the end of the second day, with Shrewsbury 50 not out and William Gunn 33 not out. Rain prevented any play on the third day.

Thomas Tait, a right-hand batsman who scored many runs in local cricket batted at number 10 against Nottinghamshire at Trent Bridge, scoring 3 in his only innings and in the following year, at number 3, scored 3 and 1 not out against Hampshire at Southampton. He was born at Langley Moor (Co. Durham) in 1872 and was living at South Kirkby when he appeared for Yorkshire. He was playing for Barnsley around 1902 and once scored 111 for them against Mitchell Main.

On a bowler's wicket, Lancashire seemed to have done well as they won the toss, batted first and then proceeded to have an opening partnership of 56 in less than an hour with A. C. MacLaren scoring 47. Ward went on to score 30 but the rest of Lancashire's batting collapsed to be out for 112 in 93 overs. Brown and Tunnicliffe hit up 48 in half an hour before the effects of the roller wore off. At the close of the first day Yorkshire had slumped to 98 for nine. Haigh went on to score 19 not out as Yorkshire gained a two run lead. The wicket had not improved when Lancashire went in a second time and although Ward batted for $1\frac{1}{2}$ hours for 19, they were bowled out for 64. Yorkshire hit off the 63 needed for victory in less than an hour to win comfortably by ten wickets.

At Leeds, Yorkshire seemed to be doing well as they obtained 142 which would have been much less if Middlesex had taken their catches. Middlesex were in a reasonable position at 108 for five at the close of play on the first day, A. E. Stoddart having scored 26 and P. F. Warner 24 but rain caused the pitch to become even more treacherous the following morning and the tail capitulated to Jackson who finished with seven for 42 to give Yorkshire a lead of 14 on the first innings. Tunnicliffe made 31 for Yorkshire before being run out but the rest could only take Yorkshire's score to 45 with Trott having the sensation at figures of 14.1-8-13-7. Middlesex won easily enough by eight wickets with F. G. J. Ford scoring 29 not out.

The Derbyshire match at Chesterfield provided a piece of history that was a sensation at the time when Yorkshire created the highest partnership for any wicket in first-class cricket. Brown and Tunnicliffe put on 554 for Yorkshire's first wicket with Tunnicliffe batting for 5 hours and 5 minutes for 243 and Brown five minutes longer for 300. The Yorkshire batsman threw their wickets away in the later part of the innings, with Denton scoring 45. When Derbyshire batted, George Davidson scored 36 out of his side's 118 and in their second innings they managed to score 157. Derbyshire lost, therefore, by an innings and 387 runs.

Yorkshire only needed to avoid defeat in their last Championship match of the season – against Sussex at Hove – to regain the title. This they ensured by hitting 355 for nine on the opening day, Brown making 150. C. B. Fry fought back with a brilliant 179 not out, and it appeared as if the game would be unfinished. Hawke declared the Yorkshire second innings closed at 166 for seven, leaving Sussex requiring a nominal 284 – in the event they completely disintegrated, being all out for 91, and so the new Champions ended their county programme on a triumphant note.

The two Yorkshire games in the Scarborough Festival – v MCC and C. I. Thornton's XI – were both affected by the weather and both ended in draws.

Yorkshire were certainly worthy Champions with Tunnicliffe topping the batting averages with 1538 runs at 46.60. He probably had his best season ever with the bat and was a model of consistency, combining the same obstinate attributes of Hall without being completely tied down to defence like his predecessor. In fact he played some fine attacking innings as well, and this, combined with his wonderful slip-fielding and his knowledge of the game, made him an indispensable member of the side. F. S. Jackson came next with 1326 runs at 45.72 and missed very few games. He always batted attractively wherever he batted in the order. Brown, who had such a poor start to the season and such a sensational end, scored 1389 runs at 36.55 and then came Lord Hawke himself who missed quite a lot of matches but managed 797 runs at 33.20. Hirst only averaged 15 and with the falling off in his bowling as well it was thought that his trip to Australia – as with Wainwright – had caused too much strain on the players and a rest was all that was required for them to recover form. Hunter batted well at times and his wicket-keeping was right up to his best form until a hand injury caused him to miss several games.

With the ball top spot went to Wilfred Rhodes who had a wonderful first season with 126 wickets at 13.83. Then came Wainwright with 56 at 14.32 followed by F. S. Jackson who took 80 wickets at 15.21 and was in splendid form. Haigh took 86 wickets at 18.38 which was another good season's work and Brown's leg-breaks accounted for 16 wickets at 20.12 each. Hirst we have already mentioned; his record was 26 wickets costing 27.69 each. Milligan's 14 wickets cost 29.35.

Yorkshire were a strong all-round side and if they were lucky to find a replacement for Peel so easily, they were equally fortunate to have two all-rounders in Wainwright and Jackson, so that Hirst's lack of success was not crucial to the side. It should be noted that three of Yorkshire's top bowlers were also in the top five in the first-class bowling averages.

The public clearly appreciated the County's success and the membership shot up from 1200 – it had been around 200 in 1893 – to

2433 in 1899. It was also reported that new stands had been built at Leeds, Bradford and Sheffield, and a new scoreboard provided at Headingley.

The new season of 1899 commenced without Milligan, who had gone to South Africa and was destined not to return. The season also saw the last appearances of Bobby Moorhouse and Arthur Sellers. The first match at Worcester saw Yorkshire captained by John Tunnicliffe in the absence of Lord Hawke and Jackson. Yorkshire made a poor start, being all out for 139 with only Frank Mitchell (32) and Wainwright (35) getting amongst the runs. In reply H. K. Foster (38) and Arnold (43) put on 50 for Worcester's second wicket, and then two more Fosters were run out with the score on 111 before Wheldon took Worcestershire into a lead of 72 on the first innings. Yorkshire then lost five wickets for 67 before Wainwright, who was lucky, scored 86 and, with Hirst, put on 115 for the sixth wicket before being dismissed for 205. Set 134 to win, Worcestershire were destroyed by Brown of Darfield, who took six for 19 and secured an unlikely victory by eleven runs.

There was another tight finish in the match at Lord's against MCC, when Yorkshire were set 197 in the final innings and still required twenty at the fall of the ninth wicket. Haigh and Jackson proved equal to the crisis and victory was achieved by a single wicket.

Back in the West Country at Bath, Yorkshire scored 429 for seven in 4 hours and 20 minutes against Somerset. Brown (42) opened with a 68 stand with Tunnicliffe (82), who then added 94 in 65 minutes with F. S. Jackson who was run out for 91 after batting for 2 hours. Denton then scored 67 in 70 minutes and Hirst 84 in an hour; the latter pair putting on 113 in 50 minutes. On the second day, Yorkshire's last three wickets took their score to 499 in a further 40 minutes. Somerset's E. Robson scored 71 out of his side's 125 and following on, the home team scored a mere 73, leaving Yorkshire the winners by an innings and 301 runs.

The next match at Bristol went very much the same way with Tunnicliffe (44) and Brown (52) putting on 85 for the first wicket and then Frank Mitchell, in 130 minutes, playing a very fine innings of 100 – his first century for Yorkshire, who were all out for 314. On a pitch that was giving more help to the bowlers, Gloucestershire were dismissed for 44 and 74 with Rhodes taking nine for 31.

Yorkshire's visit to Fenner's will be remembered for a remarkable innings by Gilbert Jessop: 171 not out in less than two hours. He came in with three wickets down for 40, joining A. M. Sullivan who had batted for 80 minutes for 3 runs, and he obtained his runs out of 206 as the University were dismissed for 246. That however was the sum total of the resistance and Yorkshire gained another innings victory.

At Leyton, Yorkshire won the toss and had first use of a pitch that gave increasing help to the bowlers. Mead enjoyed himself taking seven for 37 and Yorkshire were all out for 172. This modest total proved quite adequate, since Rhodes eclipsed Mead's effort with figures of nine for 28 (Essex 59 all out) and six for 28 (Essex 64 all out). Victory was won by 241 runs.

The Yorkshire bandwagon came to a shuddering halt at Lord's, however. Middlesex were also yet to meet defeat and were joint leaders in the Championship race. Batting first, the Northerners made 203. Middlesex, unlike Essex, were not overawed by the visiting attack and 164 from Albert Trott helped towards a first innings lead of 285. Tunnicliffe (85) and Brown (80) fought back with 152 for the first wicket before Brown was out, but afterwards only Hirst with 25 could do anything and Middlesex won by an innings and 2 runs. Middlesex therefore took the lead in the Championship race.

Yorkshire lacked Jackson, Hirst and Rhodes, all taking part in the first Test, when they visited Southampton to play Hampshire, who started well but could only take their all-out score to 184. Yorkshire lost five wickets for 83 before Wainwright (91) and Lord Hawke (127) added 225 in 145 minutes in a feast of batting and Yorkshire totalled 425. Though Robson and Barton realised 125 for the opening stand in Hampshire's second innings, Wainwright took care of the rest of the batting and Yorkshire won in fine style by nine wickets inside two days.

Back at Bramall Lane, Essex had their revenge. Turner hit 109 and Percy Perrin a tedious 144 to take the Essex total to 368. The wicket was still good when Yorkshire went in but the light was poor, and apart from a splendid 97 from F. S. Jackson there was little to commend the batting, Yorkshire being all out for 220. Following on, Yorkshire soon lost Brown to a catch behind, which the crowd disliked, and they never recovered. Essex went on to a crushing victory by nine wickets.

A weak Derbyshire side put up a better show than might have been anticipated at Dewsbury, where Yorkshire won the toss and Tunnicliffe (43) helped F. S. Jackson (82) put on 80 for the second wicket, after which Wainwright (46), joining Jackson, added a further 82 for the fourth wicket. Hirst hit well to score an unbeaten 63 as Yorkshire managed to score 343. William Storer held Derbyshire's innings together with a grafting 96, which proved to be almost half the total. Derbyshire fared even worse in their second innings and Rhodes ended with match figures of nine for 115. Yorkshire won by nine wickets.

Yorkshire's next match was the return game with the visiting Australians. They had already met briefly at Sheffield when in three days there was less than two hours' play. At Bradford, the visitors won the toss but their batting broke down against Hirst, who took eight for 48 on a good wicket. Tunnicliffe and Brown gave Yorkshire a good start, putting on 119 for the first wicket before Tunnicliffe left for 36. Brown senior left shortly afterwards, his superb innings lasting 105 minutes. Denton was run out for 30 and Yorkshire were dismissed for only 235, with M. A. Noble taking six for 83. In the second innings, Hirst immediately took two wickets but J. Worrall stayed to add 62 with Gregory and 98 with Noble, who went on to score 83. Worrall batted two hours for his 104 and then J. J. Kelly (59) and F. Laver (67 not out) thrashed the Yorkshire attack – the County rested Rhodes and Jackson – and their eventual score was 415. Needing 322, Yorkshire made a dreadful start, Noble dismissing Tunnicliffe and Denton without a run on the board, but Brown of Driffield and Frank Mitchell (31) added 57 for the third wicket and Brown and Wainwright 99 for the fourth before Wainwright was out for a stubborn 28. Brown, however, continued to bat magnificently and reached 167, saving Yorkshire from defeat.

There followed an easy win at Leicester, due to splendid all-round cricket by Ted Wainwright, who hit 153 and then took six for 44 in the final innings as Leicestershire's batting fell apart. It was, however, a different story when Surrey travelled up to Headingley. The Southern county proceeded to bat all day on a good wicket for 359 for six. Brockwell made 48 out of 67 for the first wicket. Abel continued to bat steadily and was in for $2\frac{1}{4}$ hours for 64, adding 85 for the second wicket with Hayes, who batted for an hour for 56. At 183 for four Hayward (75) and Lockwood (87) came together and they added 151 in 2 hours and then, after overnight rain, Surrey were all out for 393 with F. S. Jackson bowling well to take five for 98. On a soft wicket that gave some help to the bowlers, Yorkshire fought hard and batted consistently, but with insufficient runs on the board they were forced to follow on, and apart from Brown and F. S. Jackson who together made 61 for the second wicket there was no big stand. At 128 for five, Yorkshire were well on the way towards saving the game but when Mitchell was dismissed for 26 at 153, Yorkshire slumped to 170 for nine with half an hour left. Haigh and Hunter saved the day, the last pair batting out time.

Yorkshire's next match was at Scarborough where J. T. Brown scored a brilliant 62 and became the first player to complete a thousand runs in the country during 1899. The match did not start until 4 o'clock owing to the weather and run-getting was always difficult. Nine wickets fell for 134 before Rhodes, who was run out for 25, and Hunter added 50 for the last wicket. Haigh, with eight for 33 in 29 overs, was unplayable on the second day as Warwickshire were dismissed for 121. At the close of play on the second day, Yorkshire were 142 for two, with Brown out for 41, while Tunnicliffe went early on the third day for 71 as Yorkshire were dismissed for 212. Warwickshire wanted 276 to win, but they were all out for 108, Haigh and Rhodes each taking four cheap wickets.

The Roses match at Bramall Lane proved to be a triumph for MacLaren, who scored 126 in his own majestic manner in three hours on a pitch that gave the bowlers considerable help. No other batsman scored 20 as Lancashire were bowled out for 203. When Yorkshire batted, Brown was dropped twice off Mold before falling to Briggs, and only Tunnicliffe with 28 and F. Mitchell (31) stayed for long, Yorkshire finishing 88 in arrears. When Lancashire batted again, MacLaren batted well to score 30 out of 46 and later Briggs played well to score 40, so that the home side needed 245 in the final innings. Briggs took full advantage of a turning wicket and Yorkshire, despite an unbeaten fifty by Hirst, lost by 59 runs.

Brown and Tunnicliffe opened with a stand of 131 at Derby before Tunnicliffe was dismissed for 58 with his partner carrying on to score 192 in 4 hours and 20 minutes of splendid batting which was far ahead of anyone else in the match. Yorkshire went on to score 432. Derbyshire batted wretchedly, being bowled out for 78 and 194, and lost by an innings and 160 runs. Wainwright had a match analysis of ten for 109.

At Harrogate, Sussex put Yorkshire in after winning the toss and at 86 Denton was the sixth man out after scoring 54, Yorkshire being dismissed for 147. By the end of the first day Sussex had obtained a lead of just two runs on first innings. In their second innings Yorkshire did badly with six wickets down for 106, Denton making 32 of those, but Lord Hawke (51), Whitehead (60) and Rhodes (81 not out) all batted so well that Yorkshire were able to declare at 332 for nine. Sussex were set 331 to win in 3 hours and scored 262 for four by stumps.

Yorkshire's next match at Hull against Somerset was also drawn but this time because of bad weather, a thunderstorm ending play when Yorkshire required 23 to win with four wickets in hand.

Evelyn Rockley Wilson, a member of the well-known brotherhood, was born at Bolsterstone near Sheffield in 1879 and first played for Yorkshire in the above match. He played for Yorkshire in nine matches from 1899 to 1902 and then played on a regular basis during the school holidays from 1913 to 1923. A right-hand middle-order batsman with a sound technique who liked to score quickly, he was also a very accurate slow bowler who flighted the ball cleverly and was very difficult to score off. The youngest son of Canon W. R. Wilson, vicar of Bolsterstone, Rockley Wilson was educated at Bilton Grange before winning a scholarship to Rugby where he was in the eleven for three years and was coached by Tom Emmett. He was in the

Cambridge Eleven for four years and had great all-round success against Oxford. Becoming a schoolmaster at Winchester in 1903 he was in charge of cricket there from 1904 to 1928. He appeared for England in Test cricket in Australia, where he topped the bowling averages on the 1920/21 tour and he also made tours to USA in 1901, West Indies in 1902, Argentina in 1911–12 and South America. He possessed one of the largest and most comprehensive cricket libraries in existence and was an authority on the history of the game.

At Birmingham Yorkshire proved too strong for the home side, batting for the whole of the first day for 350 for six, with E. R. Wilson (79) and Hirst (85) putting on 128 for the fifth wicket. In reply Warwickshire soon crashed to 143 all out. Following on, Warwickshire did much better, Devey scoring 102 and Lilley 62. They finally scored 329.

The return with Leicestershire at Sheffield saw the visitors start very well, with C. E. de Trafford scoring 62 out of 107 put on for the first wicket. A. E. Knight went on to score 131 and Leicester's total was 337. On the second day, in spite of having a greatly weakened side out, Yorkshire piled on 452, Denton (110) and F. Mitchell (77) putting on 95 for the third wicket. T. L. Taylor, in his first match for Yorkshire, scored 42. Leicestershire gave a poor batting display after rain had affected the pitch and were bowled out for 112, leaving Yorkshire winners by an innings and 3 runs.

Tom Launcelot Taylor, a fine right-handed batsman who could attack in brilliant style or defend very soundly on a spinner's wicket, as well as being a top-class wicket-keeper, was in the Uppingham XI from 1894 to 1896, being captain in the last two years. He then represented Cambridge for three years, captaining the side in 1900. In 1902 he was 12th man for England v Australia at Lord's and played for Gentlemen v Players on four occasions. Although his career with Yorkshire spanned eight summers, he only appeared regularly in 1901 and 1902. He toured Australia and New Zealand in 1902/03 under Lord Hawke. He was President of Yorkshire CCC from 1956 until his death at Chapel Allerton, Leeds in 1960. At one time chairman of the Yorkshire Conservative Newspaper Co, as well as managing director of Taylor Bros, & Co Ltd, of Trafford Park, Manchester, he was President of the Yorkshire Lawn Tennis Association and with his brother established the North of England Lawn Tennis Championships at Scarborough.

At this stage of the season Yorkshire were well placed in the Championship table, being second behind Surrey. At Bradford, Middlesex scored 188 with F. G. J. Ford top scorer with 40 and Yorkshire were 216 for one at the end of the first day. They continued the next day with F. S. Jackson (155) and Denton (113) putting on 219 for the second wicket. Jackson's was a masterly innings and lasted for 4 hours while Denton, having some luck, batted for 2 hours and 40 minutes. F. Mitchell came in to score 121 in 4 hours and Wainwright and Hirst both obtained 50s as Yorkshire declared at 575 for seven. Rain saved Middlesex after they had obtained 87 for three, all to Rhodes for 24 runs.

Yorkshire's next match was at Leeds against Kent, who were outplayed and lost by an innings and 30 runs. At Fartown on a fast wicket, Gloucestershire batted evenly with Hale making the top score of 26 out of 173 all out. But only Wainwright, with 45, showed much application against the lively Jessop, who took seven for 61, Yorkshire being bowled out for 102. Gloucestershire crumpled to 28 for seven against the dangerous Brown but once again Hale saved Gloucestershire with 32 not out, with Board helping him to double the score. In the end Gloucestershire managed to obtain 91, Brown taking an excellent eight for 40. Then Jackson played a fine innings for 68 and Yorkshire gained an excellent victory by seven wickets. Yorkshire were now back at the top of the County Championship.

The end of July saw Yorkshire enter into a period of five draws in which the bat outshone the ball to an extent never seen before in Championship cricket. In those games over 700 runs were scored in one innings; over 500 in two others and over 400 in three other innings. Eleven centuries were scored in the five games and seven other individual scores of 80 or more.

George Pollitt was born at Chickenley in 1874 and played in one match for Yorkshire *v* Hampshire at Bradford in 1899 when he scored 51. He was living at Hitchin (Herts) in 1898 and 1899 where he was reported as being a successful professional – was still there in 1903. He played for Bedfordshire from their first match in 1900 also as a professional, and was still assisting them in 1908. He was playing for Chickenley from 1906 to 1908 and came to Ossett as professional in 1909, when he scored 459 runs at an average of 22.95.

On 17 August, in spite of the five successive draws, Yorkshire still retained the leadership but had only three matches to play, whereas Surrey had five. The percentage system still in vogue made calculations complex, but if Surrey won all five games the title would be theirs. At Trent Bridge, Yorkshire compiled 391 against Nottinghamshire, Hirst hitting 138 in $2\frac{1}{2}$ hours, his third century in successive matches. On a wicket which got progressively worse, Nottinghamshire found batting impossible and Rhodes had match figures of eleven for 122 as Yorkshire gained victory by an innings. In the meantime Surrey could only draw at Taunton, so the chances of Yorkshire claiming the title were greatly enhanced.

Yorkshire had only the southern tour to complete the season and

Kent at Tonbridge should not have presented many problems to the Champions. Winning the toss on a lively wicket, Yorkshire batted first with dire results as three wickets fell to Mason with only 18 on the board. Frank Mitchell with 55 and Hirst (60) both batted well by attacking the bowling but soon after lunch W. M. Bradley recorded a hat-trick by dismissing Hirst, Lord Hawke and Rhodes and Yorkshire were all out for 164, Bradley taking six for 84. When Kent batted, C. J. Burnup played a beautiful innings of 171 in $4\frac{1}{2}$ hours, receiving assistance in a stand of 118 with T. N. Perkins (47) in 95 minutes and with Rev W. Rashleigh (44) in a stand of 117 lasting 90 minutes. Kent were all out for 369. When they batted again, Yorkshire were soon in trouble at 57 for four, but they had pulled round to 208 for seven by the end of the second day with Wainwright and Lord Hawke holding the fort. On the last morning they took their stand to 138, with Wainwright scoring 100 and Lord Hawke 81 as the side was dismissed for 325. Kent needed 121 to win, and C. J. Burnup again batted brilliantly for 65 not out to gain victory by eight wickets. This unexpected reverse was even more serious because Surrey beat Gloucestershire. In their last match at Hove, Yorkshire's first wicket pair, F. S. Jackson (88) and Tunnicliffe (82), opened with a stand of 153 for the first wicket while the rest of the Yorkshire side scored consistently without anyone making a good score and Yorkshire were all out for 341, Bland taking five for 82. Sussex were 14 for one at the close of play and next day gave a moderate batting display, apart from Ranjitsinhji who scored 57. Following on, Sussex batted much better and were 140 for three when they entered the last day. After Ranji had gone for another fine innings of 70, Vine stayed for 3 hours and 25 minutes in compiling 73 while Killick gave him good support with 67 as Sussex brought off a draw with 339, there being insufficient time for Yorkshire to knock off the runs for victory. Surrey closed the gap in the table by beating Lancashire with an innings to spare and only had to avoid defeat to take the crown – in fact, the southern county won one and drew their last two matches.

Two Scarborough Festival matches closed the season for Yorkshire. Tunnicliffe, with 73 and Denton (43) helped Yorkshire to 237 against the MCC, who replied with 255 before rain ended the match.

In the other game, Yorkshire defeated C. I. Thornton's XI by 52 runs, with Yorkshire going in first and scoring 156, Tunnicliffe alone staying long for 48 as Albert Trott had a field day with eight for 64. Six of his victims were bowled. Thornton's XI then failed with only Warner and Trott able to do anything against Rhodes, who took seven for 56, Yorkshire gaining a first innings lead of 41. In their second innings they lost four wickets for 98 but F. S. Jackson was in fine form, scoring 101 in $2\frac{1}{4}$ hours, being well supported by Lord

Hawke in a defensive role. Along with Haigh they took Yorkshire to a good total of 302. Thornton's XI, needing 345, began well with 69 on the board for the first wicket as A. O. Jones went on to score 108 in only 75 minutes, putting on 112 with R. E. Foster for the fifth wicket. The others could not sustain that tempo and the visitors were bowled out for 292, Yorkshire winning by 52 runs.

And so ended a glorious season as far as the weather was concerned, and from Yorkshire's point of view, a very good season too with the cricket being first-rate and the Championship lost purely through the loss of one game. There is no doubt that the Yorkshire side was a very strong one, even when weakened by Test and other representative matches, and by the loss of Brown, who was in such prime form with the bat, but missed almost half the season through injury. There was no doubt that Yorkshire could look forward to the future with a greater confidence than ever before.

The County Championship batting averages were headed by F. S. Jackson who batted brilliantly throughout with 1149 runs at 45.96. Hirst was close behind and thoroughly recovered his old form with the bat to score 1,454 runs at 44.06, Frank Mitchell in his first full season proved himself to be as reliable as one could expect any batsman to be in the circumstances and his aggregate of 1,502 runs at 36.63 was an excellent performance. Denton, too, recovered his old run-getting abilities and scored 1,409 runs at 36.12. The fact that Brown was in fifth place is no criticism of his performances, but simply demonstrated the overall batting strength.

Rhodes again topped the bowling averages even if his record of 129 wickets at 15.66 did not compare with 1898 but taking into consideration the change in pitches, he had another first rate season. J. T. Brown junior was second and his fast bowling was a revelation until he had the misfortune to be injured; 54 wickets at 17.61 each was a good record. Haigh took 68 wickets at 21.42, and although he found the dry wickets a handicap, he put his heart into everything he did. The same applied to Wainwright who took 54 wickets at 22.27. Brown senior's wickets accounted for 18 at 23.94 and Ernest Smith had some very good days with 38 wickets at 27.57. Bairstow, the reserve wicket-keeper, performed adequately when required and the other professional, Lees Whitehead, had days of success and continued to fill his twelfth man role in the same uncomplaining manner which endeared him to all.

CHAPTER FIVE

THE GOLDEN DAYS

DURING 1899 A NEW SCORING BOARD had been provided at Leeds and in the following year one was erected at Park Avenue with the promise of another at Bramall Lane when the new pavilion was completed. New stands had been erected on the three main Yorkshire grounds in the previous year.

The 1900 season began with Yorkshire lacking five old hands – Moorhouse, Jackson, Mitchell, Arthur Sellers and C. E. M. Wilson. An all professional side apart from the captain were at home to Worcestershire at Bradford for their first match. On a bowler's pitch, Yorkshire bowled out the visitors for 42. After being 9 for five Yorkshire recovered to take the lead without further loss, with Wainwright (34) and Hirst (24) taking them to a total of 99. Yorkshire duly completed the match inside a day as Rhodes (seven for 20) bowled out Worcestershire again for 51. This was followed by a 131 run victory over Kent at Catford and prospects for the new season were looking bright indeed.

A drawn match with Derbyshire at Sheffield was mainly due to the poor weather. Yorkshire gained a lead of 84 on the first innings before declaring at 259 for eight with Brown senior (82) adding 137 for the second wicket with Denton (76) and then Washington scored a rapid 42. Storer had scored 73 for Derbyshire, Rhodes taking seven for 72. Derbyshire were only 9 for one when time ran out. For a time Leicestershire put up a good fight at Fartown and in their score of 262, Whitehead scored 67 and C. J. B. Wood 52, Yorkshire replied with 302 after Brown and Tunnicliffe had put on 90 for the first wicket, Brown went on to score 128. Only Pougher's 30 held up Rhodes in the second innings and Yorkshire, at 61 for none, won comfortably by ten wickets.

In the two early first-class friendlies, Yorkshire were comprehensively beaten by MCC at Lord's but at Fenner's they overcame the University with an innings to spare.

William Arthur Irving Washington (always known as 'Irving') was born at Wombwell in 1879 and was the son of Mr William Washington, general manager of Mitchell Main Colliery and chairman of Wombwell UDC. Educated at Doncaster Grammar School, he gained a place in the Mitchell Main XI in 1895 at the age of 15 and in the following year first played for Barnsley. He made his first appearance for the Yorkshire Colts when 17 and in 1898 was appointed captain of Mitchell Main. He first played for Yorkshire in 1900 when he did little of note apart from 86 against Hampshire at

Hull but did take part in 15 matches. In 1901 he averaged 47 for the Yorkshire 2nd XI but did not play in the first team, but in 1902 he played for the whole season, scoring over 1,000 runs and making a great impression as an attractive and stylish left-handed batsman. His batting was widely praised in *Wisden* and it was one of the tragedies of Yorkshire cricket that he never played for the County again. Soon after the end of the 1902 season he caught tuberculosis and was sent to Torquay and later to South Africa in order to recuperate. While in the Union, he appeared for Griquland West in 1904/05 and Transvaal in 1906/07 and was fit enough to play in league cricket when he returned to England. He served on Wombwell UDC for three years and had been Sanitary Inspector to the Council for 16 years, always living in his native town. In 1913 he scored 108 for Mitchell Main against Mexborough and was playing for Barnsley in 1911. He died in 1927 at his home in Wombwell aged 47. He was the uncle of Roy and Norman Kilner.

Warwickshire's visit to Leeds saw the visitors score 228 with Lilley (63) and Charlesworth (57) defying the Yorkshire attack. Yorkshire gained a 131 runs lead, Denton making 85, Whitehead 62, Hirst 46 and Ernest Smith 40. Warwickshire fought hard to save the game with T. S. Fishwick (86) being mainly responsible for holding up the home attack. Yorkshire required 164 to win in the final innings, but had only reached 86 when time ran out. Yorkshire returned to winning ways at Lord's. A first innings lead of 105 was gained and Yorkshire won comfortably by six wickets.

Yorkshire then beat Leicestershire at Leicester by ten wickets with Rhodes and E. Smith bowling out the home side for 162 and Haigh taking five for 52 as Leicester could only score 93 in their second innings. Yorkshire scored 241 thanks to Hirst (55) and Wainwright (47). Yorkshire also had the best of the game with Lancashire, who were bowled out for 96 with Rhodes taking eight for 43, after Yorkshire had scored 230 (E. Smith 56 and Hirst 50). The game was abandoned owing to the rain with Yorkshire 64 for six in their second innings.

Essex, at Leyton, were defeated by six wickets. Buckenham scored 52 out of Essex's 132 and the younger J. T. Brown took six for 57 with his fast bowling. The dangerous C. J. Kortright then replied with eight for 57 as Yorkshire gained a mere 20 runs lead thanks mainly to Tunnicliffe (43). In their second innings Essex were at one time 43 for eight but A. P. Lucas and Mead took Essex to 120. Requiring 101 to win, Yorkshire had four down for 60 but Denton (42) and Hirst (41 not out) were Yorkshire's saviours. Surrey's important visit to Sheffield was spoilt by the weather with the third day washed out.

D. L. A. Jephson with 109 and 48 from V. F. S. Crawford helped Surrey to a score of 242 and Yorkshire in reply were at one time 13 for four. Denton batted well for 96 after being dropped twice early on and acting captain E. Smith made 49 as Yorkshire fell only 47 short. Brockwell took seven for 78. Batting again Surrey struggled to 146, Rhodes taking six for 58 and when the match came to an unscheduled end at stumps on the second day, Yorkshire were 31 for one.

Two easy victories followed over Hampshire at Hull and against Derbyshire at Derby. In the first match Yorkshire gained a lead of 332 and the margin was an innings and 271 runs. There was only an innings and 24 runs to spare at Derby where Hulme with 7 not out and 35 not out was the home side's main run-getter, Rhodes taking eleven for 77 in the match and Haigh nine for 80. Rhodes also scored 53 for Yorkshire as they struggled to 195 with Tunnicliffe top scorer with 71. Hulme and Bagshaw took four wickets each.

The Somerset visit to Dewsbury provided a much better game with Yorkshire all out for 137 as Tunnicliffe was again Yorkshire's batting hero with 54. S. M. J. Woods with 49 and a last wicket stand of 37 took Somerset to a 3 runs lead. In their second innings Hirst played a remarkable innings of 106 out of 152 to take Yorkshire to 191 with Cranfield having match figures of thirteen for 159. Somerset, set 189 to win, were bowled out for 48 by Rhodes and Haigh.

Draws with Kent and Nottinghamshire were to follow with rain causing problems. At Leeds, Kent scored 230, P. C. Baker (89) and J. R. Mason (63) being their main scorers. Yorkshire could only reply with 132, Tunnicliffe (42) and Hirst (52) taking the score to 119 for four before the last six wickets fell for 13 runs. Blythe took five for 41 as Yorkshire got the worst of the wicket. Showers on the second day ruined the Nottinghamshire match at Scarborough where Nottinghamshire scored 279 after being 45 for four. Yorkshire, too, lost early wickets before Hirst scored 155 out of 227 in a brilliant exhibition. By the close, Nottinghamshire had lost six wickets for 72.

At Sheffield Yorkshire had little difficulty in defeating Sussex by an innings and 93 runs although Ranjitsinhji played two fine innings of 72 and 87, and his presence ensured huge crowds. Killick also scored 90 in the first innings of 232, while C. B. Fry with 42 in the second innings helped Sussex to score 164. Hirst took six for 49 in the first Sussex innings and Rhodes seven for 59 in the second. For Yorkshire, Tunnicliffe (54) and Denton (79) added 111 for Yorkshire's second wicket, Hunter making 41 and Hirst 71. Then in a ninth wicket stand of 161, Ernest Smith scored 116 not out, and Rhodes 79.

Hampshire scored 202 at Portsmouth, to which Yorkshire replied with 372, Tunnicliffe continuing his fine form with 138. In their second innings Hampshire reached a very respectable 299 with the Rev G. B. Raikes scoring 77 and A. J. L. Hill 70. Yorkshire won easily enough by six wickets. A draw with Worcestershire followed at Worcester with the home side gaining a first innings lead of 48 runs. Only Hirst (65) really got going for Yorkshire but for the home side W. H. Wilkes scored 90 and H. K. Foster 59 as they added 103 for the fifth wicket. In their second innings Yorkshire lost five wickets for 68, but Tunnicliffe, in an innings lasting 5 hours and 20 minutes, scored 158 and with Haigh (71) added 112 for the sixth wicket and with Hunter (58 not out) 160 for the ninth before a declaration was made at 349 for nine. Wilson took five for 116 for Worcestershire. Needing 302 to win, Worcestershire lost four wickets for 35 and eventually battled out for a draw.

Charles Oyston played in three matches for Yorkshire in 1900 and played occasionally until 1909. A left-arm slow bowler, he was born at Armley, Leeds in 1869, and played for Leeds for many years with success, having been professional at Wortley in 1894 and also with Armley. He was professional at Bingley in 1917 and in 1927 won the Leeds League bowling prize. A printer's bookbinder by trade, he died at Leeds General Infirmary in 1942.

The return match with Lancashire was looked forward to with great keenness. Each side had won eleven and drawn six matches. Yorkshire were dismissed for 235 with Hirst (59) and Tunnicliffe (51) batting with some success. At the end of the first day, Lancashire had replied with 63 for four and next day, thanks to A. C. MacLaren (52) and Cuttell (63), got to within 7 runs of the Yorkshire total. Yorkshire had dropped catches and on the last day had only scored 84 for the loss of eight wickets before Wainwright (50) played one of his best innings of the season after many failures. Haigh stayed with him for 80 minutes in making 19 and Yorkshire eventually reached 146 with Cuttell taking five for 51 and Sharp four for 51. Lancashire's fielding had been much better than Yorkshire's. Lancashire were 20 for one at the close and a draw kept both teams with 100% records.

The Gloucestershire match at Bradford was a remarkable game of cricket and was won in the end by 40 runs by Yorkshire. Three wickets were down for 172 with Denton out for 85 when T. L. Taylor (64) was joined by George Hirst, who scored a brilliant 111 in 100 minutes, and Yorkshire reached 409 long before the close of play. Gloucestershire soon had five down for 77 before Jessop joined Wrathall and scored 104 with fortune on his side. Rhodes took eight for 72 as Gloucestershire just avoided the follow-on. Yorkshire then lost three for 25 but Hirst hit 92 in 85 minutes. Gloucestershire were set 328 to win. Five wickets were down for 73 when Jessop came in again and this time he batted brilliantly, scoring 139 in less than 90 minutes and hitting no less than seven sixes off Wilfred Rhodes. He added 122 for the seventh wicket with F. H. B. Champain. From 272 for seven, Gloucestershire collapsed to 287 all out for Yorkshire to gain a creditable victory by 40 runs. Gloucestershire's gallant defeat was recompensed somewhat by inflicting on Lancashire their first defeat of the season in the next match at Old Trafford. This defeat was to cost the Red Rose County the Championship.

Rain also ruined Yorkshire's chances at The Oval where Surrey scored 360 with D. L. A. Jephson (121) obtaining his second century of the season against Yorkshire as he and Lockwood (98) had a partnership of 208 for the fifth wicket. Yorkshire lost two early wickets before Tunnicliffe (101) and T. L. Taylor added 201 for the third wicket and then Hirst hit 59. Taylor's 147 was his first century for Yorkshire. Yorkshire had a lead of 20 but rain had interferred with the match. At one stage Surrey were 5 for four in their second innings before Jephson again came to their rescue, batting an hour for 20 and saving the game for his side as they were dismissed for 52 just before the close. Another draw followed at Trent Bridge with Nottinghamshire having a 65 runs lead on the first innings and Yorkshire having lost two quick wickets in their second innings before the rain came down.

Wainwright's 50 out of Yorkshire's 171, with Mead taking six for 65, was a large enough total to gain a 106 runs lead over Essex, who collapsed to 65 all out. Yorkshire then declared at 42 for one and bowled out Essex again for 52. Rhodes took fourteen wickets for 68 runs. Reserve wicket-keeper Bairstow captured six victims. Rain ruined Yorkshire's chances on another wet pitch at Birmingham, where Yorkshire declared at 158 for two with Denton 85 not out and T. L. Taylor 50 not out in reply to Warwickshire's 84. In their second innings Warwickshire finished the match with a total of 43 for seven, Rhodes taking nine wickets in the match.

The next three matches were won too; Middlesex bowled Yorkshire out for 235 at Leeds, T. L. Taylor (74) and Hirst (77) putting on 132 for the fourth wicket. Middlesex battled hard against Rhodes and Haigh and thanks to some hard hitting from Trott (50), Yorkshire only led by 43 on the first innings. On a difficult pitch, Brown senior scored 27 out of Yorkshire's 96, C. M. Wells taking eight for 35, Yorkshire making their lowest score of the season. Haigh was unplayable bowling Middlesex out for 76; he took seven for 33. Lord Hawke with 79 and Hirst 108 in two hours, took Yorkshire to 305 to put them in a winning position after Rhodes had bowled Gloucestershire out for 101. Gloucestershire did a little better in their second innings being dismissed for 160, with Rhodes taking his match tally to thirteen for 103. Yorkshire moved from Cheltenham to

Taunton and defeated Somerset by an innings and 120 runs to make
sure of the Championship. Yorkshire's last match against Sussex at
Hove nearly resulted in defeat as Sussex took a lead of 54 and then had
seven Yorkshire wickets down for 117, but Taylor came to the rescue
with a timely 68 and Yorkshire were 145 ahead with two wickets left
when a thunderstorm finished play at tea-time on the last day.

Yorkshire had won the Championship with 16 wins and 12 draws,
with Lancashire runners-up with 15 wins, 2 losses and 11 draws.
Yorkshire beat the MCC at Scarborough to gain revenge for their
only defeat of the season at Lord's. Victors by 272 runs, their hero was
Lees Whitehead, who scored 62 not out in Yorkshire's first innings and
then took six for 45 as he and Rhodes dismissed the MCC for 105 in
their second innings. In the match against an England Eleven,
Wainwright, with 117, and Denton (88) were Yorkshire's batting
heroes, while Hirst took five for 53 when the England Eleven totalled
266, with Jessop scoring 95 in 50 minutes. After W. L. Foster had
scored 95, Yorkshire were eventually set 207 to win and the runs were
knocked off for the loss of three wickets, Brown senior scoring 54 and
Ernest Smith 45 not out.

Frederick William Elam was born in Hunslet, Leeds in 1871 and
played in two matches for Yorkshire – against Nottinghamshire at
Trent Bridge in 1900 – and against Worcestershire at Harrogate in
1902. An amateur with the Leeds Cricket Club, he was a right-handed
opening batsman who played with success for the Yorkshire 2nd XI
between 1900 and 1902 and was captain of the Leeds Cricket Club in
1908 and a member of the side for many years, at least until 1920. In
1918 he opened with Percy Holmes (107) for Yorkshire against an
England XI in a two day match and scored 86 against a side with
P. G. H. Fender, Jack Sharp, John Gunn and Coe in its ranks. He was
headmaster of St Michaels School, Headingley and died in Headingley, Leeds in 1943.

Whitehead had the distinction of heading the batting averages in
1900 although he only played in nine matches, scoring 321 runs at
53.50. He was followed by amateur T. L. Taylor, who averaged 42 for
801 runs. Hirst averaged over 40 for 1,752 runs and had a marvellous
season. Tunnicliffe also played at his best with 1,496 runs average 32.
Ernest Smith did well with both bat and ball in the 17 games that he
played in, while Denton scored 1,378 runs at 29.31. J. T. Brown also
scored over 1,000 runs but had a disappointing season by his own high
standards, while Wainwright could do little right to average only 20,
although he did score 912 runs at 20.26.

It was not the batting, however, that was Yorkshire's strong point;
it was the bowling of Rhodes and Haigh who dominated the scene
with Rhodes topping the national averages and for Yorkshire taking

240 wickets at 12.72. Haigh, slowing down a little and not taking so much out of himself was almost equally deadly with 160 wickets at 14.56 and these two virtually did all the bowling. Ernest Smith was very useful when available, taking 33 wickets at 23.06 each while Brown junior had his days of success.

So far as the fielding was concerned, Hunter was as sound as ever behind the stumps, while Tunnicliffe, with 70 catches, and Wainwright, with 37, both had a big hand in Yorkshire's success story by virtue of their brilliance close to the wicket.

The 1901 season opened as usual with a visit to Lord's. Frank Mitchell returned to the Yorkshire side, which had two debutants in E. Foster and Ringrose. Storer (107) helped MCC to a total of 241, Hirst taking seven for 55 which he followed up with 86 helping Denton (80) in a stand of 93 for the fifth wicket. Going in again 64 runs behind, the MCC batted poorly to be out for 120 with Hirst this time taking four for 28. Walter Mead bowled well to take four for 26 as Yorkshire won by six wickets.

Ernest Foster made his solitary appearance for Yorkshire in this match. He came from Bramley, Leeds and was 27 years old at the start of the 1901 season. Very little is known about this cricketer as he never appeared for the Yorkshire 2nd XI nor did he appear in the list of Colts' applications. He died at Leeds in 1956 at the age of 82.

William Ringrose was a left-handed batsman and right-arm fast bowler. He continued to play for Yorkshire until 1906 by which time he had taken 155 wickets at 20 runs each. Born at Ganton, near Scarborough in 1871, he had a big reputation in league cricket and was said to be one of the first bowlers to develop the out-swinger. Coached by Shoey Harrison, the old Yorkshire fast bowler, Ringrose went as professional to Sheffield United before joining Liverpool where he remained for several years. In 1903 he took 36 wickets for Yorkshire at 13.47 each and in his last full season, 1905, he took 73 wickets but in 1906 his health broke down and he was unable to continue to play county cricket. From 1907 to 1913 he was engaged by Forfarshire at Broughty Ferry and gave good service to the Scottish club. In 1913 a further injury finished his career but he came back to act as scorer to Yorkshire in 1922 and was official scorer to the Club from 1923 to 1939. He died at Crossgates, Leeds in 1943.

Yorkshire began the Championship season with a Western tour in which they defeated Gloucestershire at Bristol by ten wickets, Rhodes having match figures of fourteen for 141, while George Hirst with 64 was mainly responsible for Yorkshire having a comfortable first innings lead. At Taunton a thrilling game finished in favour of the visitors but only by one wicket. Somerset's L. C. H. Palairet, with 103, and S. M. J. Woods, with 60, helped Somerset to a handsome total of 349 to which Yorkshire replied in excellent style with 391 due to T. L. Taylor (97) and Tunnicliffe (80). S. M. J. Woods followed up his first innings with a very fine 90 while Robson with 58 and Gill (40) took Somerset to 281. Rhodes took his match figures to twelve for 182 and Yorkshire required 240 to win. After losing six wickets for 119, Yorkshire looked hopelessly placed, but a fine partnership between the reliable Wainwright (70) and Lord Hawke (52) took the score to 212 before Rhodes guided Yorkshire home.

Yorkshire also won their next eight county matches – a remarkable performance – starting their home programme at Dewsbury. Here Worcestershire gave a reasonable performance and Yorkshire were 8 for three before T. L. Taylor (44) and Wainwright (47) rescued the Champions. With nine wickets down for 144, Rhodes and Hunter took the score to 205. In reply Worcestershire lost three for 13 before Bowley (63) and W. H. Wilkes (109) added 106 for the fourth wicket and the tail wagged enough to give them a 13 run lead. Rhodes took his match aggregate of wickets to nine and Yorkshire ran out winners by 90 runs. Derbyshire were brushed aside in a summary manner – the winning margin being an innings and 282 runs.

Yorkshire introduced two new players to the side against Cambridge University at Fenner's where Cambridge did very well to score 395; H. K. Longman scored 150. T. L. Taylor (53) and F. Mitchell (87) along with Lord Hawke (69 not out) helped Yorkshire to 356. In their second innings only E. R. Wilson with 42 shone in an innings of 121 as Haigh took six for 48. At the close Yorkshire were only 34 runs short of victory with eight wickets left.

James Higgins who made his debut in this match played in nine matches for Yorkshire as a stand-in for David Hunter between 1901 and 1905. A native of Birstall he played for Dewsbury at one stage and died at his home in Wibsey, Bradford in 1954.

George Smith who played against Cambridge University also played once in 1906 against Warwickshire without batting or bowling. He may have played for Yorkshire 2nd XI but no George Smith was included in the list of colts called up for practice. He is believed to have been born at Thorp Arch in 1875 or 1876, and he died there in 1929 aged about 54. He was a joiner by trade.

At Old Trafford, Lancashire were dismissed for 133 on a pitch that had been fiery all season. Rhodes and Hirst were always difficult to play. Yorkshire lost five wickets for 44 before Hirst (40) and Wainwright (35) came to the rescue to help Yorkshire gain a one run lead. A brilliant display of catching – not evident in Lancashire's first innings – reduced Lancashire to 44 all out with Hirst quite unplayable as he took seven for 23. Yorkshire won by nine wickets. This was followed by an innings win at Leicester where Yorkshire's score of 348 was due to Brown (81) and Hirst (61) with plenty of help from the others in an attractive batting display. Rhodes finished the match with thirteen for 96.

There was a similar result at Bournemouth where Frank Mitchell with 100 and Hirst (81) put on 140 for the fifth wicket after Denton was out for 64. In reply to Yorkshire's 365 Hampshire were bowled out for 75, Hirst taking six for 42, and in the second innings succeeded in scoring 208. Middlesex at Lord's, hitherto undefeated, were well beaten by seven wickets after being subjected to another 100 from Frank Mitchell with help from Brown (73), T. L. Taylor (50) and Rhodes (41 not out) who was averaging over 30 in the Championship. P. F. Warner then carried his bat through the innings to score 73 out of 168 with the highest stand being for the last wicket; Rhodes finished with eight for 53. Following on, Middlesex did much better with Hayman (44) and G. W. Beldam (86) both batting well and then Hearne and Rawlin lifted Middlesex to a respectable 282.

Draws followed at Bradford against Surrey and at Edgbaston. Yorkshire then ran into another run of seven successive victories which really clinched the Championship; four were by an innings, one by 10 wickets and another by 245 runs. Rhodes took 55 wickets in those matches, including ten for 78 against Essex and six for 4 against Nottinghamshire, who were all out for 13 after Hirst was taken off after one over. Haigh took four for 8. In the second innings Nottinghamshire did score 173 thanks mainly to Iremonger (55 not out) and A. O. Jones (47). Hirst took six for 26. Essex failed to score three figures in either innings with Lord Hawke (60) and Frank Mitchell (52) taking Yorkshire to 252 and then at Nottingham, Denton with 73 helped Yorkshire to a score of 204, John Gunn taking five for 49 before the rain came that made Trent Bridge unplayable. At Sheffield, Kent lost by 212 runs, though they led on first innings by 17 runs, Frank Marchant scoring 111. Only Tunnicliffe with 64 batted well for Yorkshire as J. R. Mason took seven for 90 but in their second innings after losing six for 194, Wainwright with 65 helped Yorkshire to 309. In their second innings, Kent were never in the hunt and were all out for 80.

T. L. Taylor (58) and F. Mitchell (86) put on 127 for Yorkshire's fourth wicket at Glossop with Bestwick finishing with seven for 70, Yorkshire being dismissed for 213. Haigh took five for 55 in the Derbyshire total of 141 before Yorkshire reached 359 for five declared. Wainwright scored an unbeaten 108. Brown (71), opened with a partnership of 121 with Tunnicliffe (58) and Whitehead made 52 not out. Derbyshire were dismissed a second time for 186 with Haigh and Rhodes taking four wickets each. Sussex managed only 52, Hirst and Rhodes sharing the wickets at Bradford and Yorkshire lost three wickets before going ahead. They went on to 158 with Lord Hawke making the top score (36). In their second innings Sussex scored 155 with Ranji making 57 and Wainwright accounting for five batsmen. Yorkshire scored 562 against Leicestershire, T. L. Taylor (113) and F. Mitchell (122) being the leading run-getters after Tunnicliffe (91) and Denton (86) had paved the way with 119 added for the second wicket. Hirst also scored 61 and then proceeded to take seven for 21 in Leicestershire's first innings of 103 – after De Trafford (52) and C. J. B. Wood had put on 64 for the first wicket. Knight (76) and King (60) put on 124 for Leicestershire's third wicket in their follow-on but their final all out total was only 212; Rhodes taking six for 46. R. E. Foster (42) made top score at Worcestershire as his side collapsed for 156, then Tunnicliffe (57) and Denton (48) took Yorkshire towards the lead before F. Mitchell with 57 added 104 with Hirst for the fifth wicket. Hirst also took part in a stand of 146 with Rhodes (53) and Hirst went on to score 214 in 270 minutes at the crease. Facing 530, Worcestershire could only muster 162.

Somerset at Headingley appeared easy meat in the eyes of Yorkshire players and their followers. Yorkshire began well by bowling out the opposition for 87, of which Sammy Woods scored 46. Rhodes took five for 39. Yorkshire had lost six wickets before they took the lead. Lord Hawke then joined Hirst in a 56 stand before Haigh (96) and Rhodes (44) came together to add 118 for the ninth wicket. Yorkshire had a lead of 238 runs but L. C. H. Palairet (173) and Braund (107) put on 222 for the first before Palairet and F. A. Phillips (122) added a further 125 for the fourth wicket. Further fifties came from S. M. J. Woods (66) and V. T. Hill (53) and Somerset finally scored 630. Rhodes did take six for 145 but Hirst's lone wicket cost him 189 runs. In the second Yorkshire innings only Tunnicliffe with 44 stayed for long and Yorkshire were dismissed for 113 to suffer defeat – their first in the Championship since 21 August 1899 – by 279 runs. Cranfield took four for 35 and Braund four for 41.

Yorkshire had to follow on in their next match against Warwickshire at Bradford as Kinneir (123) and Charlesworth (99) were responsible for the visitors reaching 401; Rhodes took four for 118. In reply, Yorkshire had lost seven for 104 before Whitehead with 45 and Haigh (60) with help from Rhodes (30) took Yorkshire to 237; Frank Field took six for 92 in 50 overs. After losing two wickets for 23, Brown (134 not out) and F. Mitchell (116 not out) easily saved the game.

Nottinghamshire went down by an innings and 226 runs at Bramall Lane; J. A. Dixon made their highest individual score in the second innings with 44 as J. T. Brown, junior, returning to the side for his only game of the season, took nine wickets. Yorkshire made the huge total of 528 all out with Hirst (125) and Haigh (159) adding 205 for the sixth wicket in 130 minutes. It was Haigh's first century in first-class cricket and he batted for four hours in all. Lord Hawke (89) helped Haigh to add 146 for the eighth wicket. The Surrey match at The Oval was abandoned without a ball being bowled.

On a wet wicket at Hull, Jessop took the decision to put Yorkshire in to bat and a total of 186 put Yorkshire on top. F. Mitchell was top scorer with 43. Gloucestershire collapsed to 50 for nine before Kitcat, who carried his bat through the innings for 18, added 20 for the last wicket with Roberts. It was Yorkshire's turn to collapse and eight wickets went down for 91, then Lord Hawke took the score to 123 and set Gloucestershire 240 to win. On an improving pitch, Kitcat batted well for 40, Jessop made 48 and Board 57 but Rhodes was again in fine form and Yorkshire won narrowly by 55 runs.

A crowd of almost 31,000 saw the first day's play against Lancashire at Headingley, set aside for J. T. Brown senior's benefit. After losing three for 21, Brown (37) and F. Mitchell took the score to 70 and then Mitchell (106) with Hirst (58) put on a further 122 runs for the fifth wicket before further wickets fell to make Yorkshire 232 for eight. Lord Hawke with 55, helped by Hunter, took Yorkshire to 319 but playing time was curtailed owing to the size of the crowd. A. C. MacLaren (117) helped Albert Ward to add 134 for the third wicket and Ward, who batted too slowly for his 100, added a further 107 with A. Eccles (59). Lancashire's total of 413 gave them a 94 runs lead, with Rhodes taking three for 85 in 66.2 overs. The rest was of little interest.

Brown with 110 and T. L. Taylor (156) put on 152 for Yorkshire's second wicket and Yorkshire took their score to 439 in reply to Hampshire's 204, out of which Webb made 65 and E. C. Lee 54 not out. Hirst took six for 85, and in the second innings Hampshire were bowled out for 154 to lose by an innings and 81 runs. Yorkshire scored 363 at Sheffield against Middlesex with Denton (78) top scorer, and fifties coming from the bats of F. Mitchell, E. Smith and Lord Hawke. In reply Middlesex were 62 for three at the close. Essex (30 and 41) were brushed aside at Leyton, Hirst proving unplayable and making the ball swerve and lift in a disconcerting manner. He took twelve wickets.

Yorkshire's visit to Brighton was another surprise packet almost as remarkable as the Somerset game at Headingley. Sussex went in first and Killick joined Fry after Vine had lost his wicket with 66 on the board. C. B. Fry (209) and Killick (200) added 349 for the second wicket, which remains the record against Yorkshire. When Ranjitsinhji came in he scored 86 not out and Sussex declared at 560 for five. Yorkshire then lost four wickets for 6 runs; recovered to 39 for eight and again to 92 all out. Following on, Yorkshire easily saved the game by scoring 107 without loss in 81 laborious overs.

Yorkshire's last match was at Canterbury against Kent and Yorkshire scored 251 with Tunnicliffe (71), Denton (38), T. L. Taylor (41) and F. Mitchell (36) all in form. Kent at 172 for four were in a good position but after losing Burnup for 83 and Mason for 51 they collapsed to be all out for 206, Rhodes, at his best, took eight for 55. Frank Mitchell (47) and Wainwright (44) helped Yorkshire to 265 in their second innings and Kent needed 312 to win. The total was quite beyond their capabilities and they were dismissed for 63.

Hubert Myers, who made his debut in 1901, was a right-hand batsman and medium-paced bowler. He made his first appearance against Lancashire at Old Trafford, but did not play again until 1903 when he made two appearances. In 1904 he gained a regular place in the Yorkshire side and in 1905 proved a valuable member of the side. Unfortunately, although persevered with until 1910, he failed to improve and seemed to deteriorate each year until he was dropped after the 1910 season, when he scored over 900 runs. He was one of several cricketers of the early 1900s who failed to make the grade as Yorkshire cricketers and yet were capped and expected to replace the aging cricketers of the 'golden age' period. A medium-paced bowler with a decided swerve, he emigrated to Tasmania and became a player for Tasmania as well as acting as captain and being appointed coach to the Tasmania Cricket Association at Hobart. When he appeared for Tasmania in 1913–14 he played as an opening bat and also developed as a googly bowler. He died in 1944 at Hobart.

Yorkshire played several other extraneous matches in 1901, beating the South Africans at Harrogate early in August, and the usual Scarborough matches, in the first of which Rhodes hit his maiden first-class century. There was also a game against the Rest of England at The Oval, in which Jessop hit a quite extraordinary 233 in 150 minutes – Yorkshire lost by an innings.

Yorkshire, apart from their slip against Somerset, were as convincing as Champions as any side that had ever played in the Championship. A glance at the averages reveals no less than seven of the eleven reached 1,000 runs. Rhodes and Lord Hawke each scored over 800 runs with an average of at least 24 while Haigh managed 607 at 26.39. Only Hunter failed to average 20 of the regular members of the side. Frank Mitchell finished top of the batting averages with 1801 runs at 46.17, and without doubt he was the most reliable bat in the team, with Hirst deservedly second with 1,669 runs at 37.93.

With the ball it was very much the same as the previous year except that Rhodes led the averages with 233 wickets at 15.00 each with Hirst (not Haigh) next with 171 wickets at 16.30. Haigh's 56 wickets cost 21.41 each and J. T. Brown senior also took over 50. Wainwright's

*The County Champions of 1901. Back row: E. Wainwright, L. Whitehead,
W. Rhodes, D. Hunter. Middle row: G. H. Hirst, Mr E. Smith, Lord Hawke,
Mr F. Mitchell, J. Tunnicliffe. Front row: D. Denton, Mr T. L. Taylor,
J. T. Brown.*

total rose to 34 but he was rarely needed – a category in which could
be placed Ernest Smith. Rhodes also headed the national bowling
averages with George Hirst second.

Yorkshire had virtually the same side available for the 1902 season
except that their outstanding batsman, Frank Mitchell, was unavailable and Wainwright had virtually retired. They opened at Lord's
with a crushing defeat of the MCC by an innings and 71 runs just after
lunch on the second day. King was top scorer for the home side and
Washington, taking Mitchell's place, batted well for 43. There was no
chance of a finish at Leyton, the first two days having been lost to rain,
but Essex were all out for 89 with Haigh taking five for 32 and Rhodes
four for 44.

Snow and rain interrupted the Sussex game at Headingley where
Yorkshire recovered from 52 for three to 302 all out thanks to
T. L. Taylor (74) and Denton (99) adding 155 for the fourth wicket.
Fry (68) and Vine (52) gave Sussex a good start by putting on an
opening stand of 121 before Hirst and Brown senior took control and
dismissed them for only 232. Tunnicliffe scored 79 as Yorkshire went
on to declare at 182 for five and at the close the visitors were 126, with
C. B. Fry making 70. Nor could a finish be obtained at Fartown

against Leicestershire, who began well with a stand of 125 between C. J. B. Wood (72) and Whitehead (51) before Rhodes and Haigh bowled Leicestershire out for 228. When Yorkshire batted T. L. Taylor scored 114, Denton 58 and Hirst 45 before Yorkshire declared at 323 for six. Leicestershire were 10 for one at the close.

When victory at last arrived, it was especially sweet, Lancashire being dismissed for 72 and 54. Jackson took three for 5 and five for 8 and was quite unplayable. F. S. Jackson was also Yorkshire's batting hero with 33 as S. F. Barnes took six for 39, but most of Yorkshire's batsmen contributed to their all out score of 148, as they won by an innings and 22 runs. Denton scored 94 at Fenner's, where Cambridge escaped defeat due to the weather. Haigh's match figures were nine for 62 as the home side still needed 73 for victory and had lost seven second innings wickets.

Tunnicliffe was again amongst the runs at Bradford, his fine 127 helping Yorkshire to 337. Kent were all out for 100 and 129 in reply with C. J. Burnup, with 64 in the second innings, and J. R. Mason, 34 and 29, alone staying for long. Rhodes took six for 42 in the first innings but it was Jackson with six for 30 who did the damage in the second innings. There was no play at Dewsbury on the last two days where Yorkshire had scored 393 against Derbyshire.

The next game brought the highest praise to the Yorkshire team, who performed one of the greatest feats in the annals of the game at Headingley. The visitors were the Australians, probably the most powerful combination ever to visit our shores and hitherto unbeaten. They were dismissed in the first innings for 131, with Trumper top scorer with 38, and Hirst and Jackson taking four wickets each. Denton with 32 helped Yorkshire to 107 as Howell (six for 53) and Noble (four for 30) kept the Australians on top. The Australians were then bowled out for 23, their last six wickets falling for three runs. Hirst and Jackson shared the wickets. Washington showed fine nerve as he made 9 not out and Yorkshire won in exciting style by five wickets.

Yorkshire's misfortunes with the weather continued in the return at Chesterfield, Derbyshire being on the brink of defeat when the third day was all but washed out. Middlesex had little to offer at Bradford, their only stand of note being for the seventh wicket in the second innings when Rawlin (21) and R. O. Schwarz (27) improved Middlesex's position from 26 for six to 80 all out – seven more than they had managed in their first innings. Rhodes had match figures of ten for 56 and Haigh nine for 53. Victory was by an innings.

When playing and not hanging about pavilions, Yorkshire appeared to be as strong a side as ever but in the next match Somerset brought them down to earth as they had in 1901. Batting first,

Somerset had 44 on the board before losing L. C. H. Palairet for 25, but Braund went on to 31 before Rhodes got him and then the rest went down for 86 all out. Jackson finished with six for 29. Yorkshire reached 54 for three but after Denton had left for 20, Braund went through the rest of the side and Somerset gained a lead of 12 on the first innings. Somerset changed their batting order and Gill made the best score of 41 while Braund (34) and Palairet (24) took Somerset to 106. Haigh was Yorkshire's best bowler with six for 19. Yorkshire were set to score 119 to win but Braund captured nine wickets for 41 and Somerset were victors by 34 runs.

Warwickshire were never in the game at Birmingham, with Rhodes taking eight for 57 in the match and Haigh eleven for 66. Yorkshire's 208 took them to victory by an innings and 63 runs. The next match was the return with the Australians at Bradford and the visitors had both Trumble and Saunders in the team. On a bowler's pitch, Clem Hill (34) and Darling (40) took the Australians to 106, Rhodes taking five for 49. Hugh Trumble was at his best when Yorkshire batted taking six for 17. Yorkshire only scored 77 with Brown and last man Hunter joint top scorers with 14. Syd Gregory, with 42 not out, was the visitors' hero in the second innings as Haigh and Rhodes bowled the opposition out for 87 leaving Yorkshire needing 117 to win. On such a pitch, it was a very tall order and though Hirst and Washington (22) were the only batsmen to reach double figures, Yorkshire's defeat by 44 runs was not a disgrace, with Trumble this time taking six for 27.

A convincing win over Nottinghamshire at Hull followed and Surrey were thrashed at Headingley by an innings and 102 runs, but Yorkshire had to be content with a draw against Sussex at Hove, when Brann and Newham took centuries off the visiting bowlers. Yorkshire returned to their best at Park Avenue, scoring 504 against Essex. T. L. Taylor, with 60, took Yorkshire to 177 for five before Denton (127) and Hirst (134) came together to add 200 for the sixth wicket in 110 minutes. On the next day Haigh scored 55. On a good pitch, F. L. Fane batted with good judgement for $3\frac{1}{4}$ hours to score 106. Only Tosetti, with 56, gave him much support and with Rhodes taking seven for 123, Essex were forced to follow on 223 in arrears. They failed to avoid the innings defeat and were dismissed for 193. Rhodes took his total of wickets in the match to twelve, which cost him 195 runs. A heavy-scoring draw at Trent Bridge saw centuries for Nottinghamshire by J. A. Dixon and Iremonger but Yorkshire replied with 104 from Tunnicliffe and 120 from T. L. Taylor. At the end of the game Nottinghamshire were leading by 86 runs with eight second innings wickets in hand.

Fifties from Tunnicliffe, Denton and Hirst took Yorkshire to 253 at

Leeds against Gloucestershire, who were then dismissed for 46 and 116. Spry took eight for 83 with his leg-breaks but the visitors had no answer to Rhodes, who bagged twelve victims. Yorkshire were now on top of the table but Worcestershire gave a good account of themselves against a weakened side, Jackson, Hirst and Rhodes all being at Old Trafford for the Test. Yorkshire gained a 27 runs lead on the first innings, with Arnold scoring 92 for the home side and Haigh taking five for 90. This followed a brilliant 76 from Jack Brown, which with help from E. R. Wilson (63) took Yorkshire to 257, Simpson-Hayward and Arnold each taking four wickets. When Yorkshire batted again, Brown was again at his best with 91 while Washington scored 50, and Yorkshire at the close had scored 248 for eight with rain stopping play after two overs on the last day.

At Sheffield, Warwickshire were in a strong position at one time, dismissing Yorkshire for only 135 and reaching 114 for two at the end of the first day. In the end Warwickshire were left with 199 to make at a run-per-minute. After taking their score to 56 for two, Warwickshire, on a pitch now wearing, were unable to do anything with Rhodes's bowling as he took six for 33 in 22.3 overs with Yorkshire winning by 100 runs.

Tom Hayward's benefit match at The Oval produced a match of high scores, but initially on a wet pitch, Yorkshire were at a disadvantage with Lockwood bowling very well. Two wickets went cheaply, but helped by dropped catches, F. S. Jackson hit up 77, Haigh 62 and Lord Hawke 126. Yorkshire finally made 470. Surrey replied with 359 but were tied down and at one stage were in danger of following on. Hayward with 95 and Leveson-Gower (70) were Surrey's main scorers. The game then drifted to a draw.

Albert Ward's benefit at Manchester was the next game on the agenda and once again it was a draw but heavily in favour of Yorkshire, with the third day washed out. Rain remained to prevent any play at all in the next fixture at Leicester.

The pitch at Harrogate was very wet after almost a week of rain and with Yorkshire's three all-rounders away on Test duty, Worcestershire were dismissed for 82, Haigh taking seven for 38 and Oyston, making a rare appearance, three for 30. Only Tunnicliffe with 28 stayed for long as Yorkshire finished three behind on the first innings. Worcestershire batted a little better in their second innings and Yorkshire were set 134 to win. The pitch might have been getting easier but several chances were missed, Yorkshire going on to win by six wickets.

The Western tour began well with Yorkshire beating Gloucestershire by an innings and 102 runs at Cheltenham. Only Jessop with 42 out of 104 made much progress against Rhodes or Hirst and Yorkshire passed that total with only three wickets down. Gloucestershire only scored 55 in their second innings, Rhodes taking six for 34 and Haigh four for 10. The weather closed in again and play was possible on only one day at Taunton.

The last two matches comprised a southern tour of Middlesex and Kent and low scores were the order of the day. Middlesex, dismissed for 99, found Haigh and Rhodes almost unplayable, although MacGregor did score 27. Yorkshire were 92 for two at one stage with Washington and Denton both recording 39 before Bosanquet took six for 28 to confine the visitors to a 26 runs lead. C. M. Wells, 28 not out, alone played Haigh with any confidence as he took seven for 40 in Middlesex's 93 all out. Yorkshire won by four wickets. Moving to Catford, Kent collapsed, 71 all out, Rhodes having the remarkable figures of eight for 28. Yorkshire had five wickets down for 15 and young Washington was dropped early on before he attacked the bowling to score 59 not out, adding 50 with Wilfred Rhodes, Yorkshire scored 97, Alec Hearne taking five for 22. In their second innings Kent made exactly 100, then runs came more easily, Brown and Washington taking Yorkshire to victory by nine wickets.

Champions for the third season running with 13 victories and only 1 loss, Yorkshire also led on the first innings in 9 of their 10 drawn games. The fight over, Yorkshire met the MCC at Scarborough and surprisingly met with a reverse by 26 runs after the sides had finished level on the first innings. Yorkshire also played a drawn game against the Rest of England which was ruined by the bad weather after Tunnicliffe and Jackson had obtained fifties for Yorkshire.

When Yorkshire played Cambridge University at Fenner's, George Emanuel Lowe kept wicket for Yorkshire. He never appeared for Yorkshire again nor did he ever play for Yorkshire 2nd XI or appear in a list of Colts applications. He died in 1932 at Middlesbrough aged about 54.

Another player who appeared against Cambridge University was Horace Rudston from Hessle. An attractive right-handed batsman, he played in a few matches from 1904 to 1907 with 164 against Leicestershire in 1904 as his highest score, but he never achieved such success again. He played for Hull for many years and scored 111 not out in an opening partnership of 230 for them in 1921. In 1911 and 1912 he played for Hopton Mills. He was a joiner and undertaker in Hessle working for the family business and he died there in 1962 aged 83 and was buried in Hessle Cemetery.

Another fresh face was William Brown, younger brother of John Thomas Brown junior. He played for Darfield before becoming a professional with Barnsley from 1898 to 1904. He played only twice for Yorkshire – once in 1902 when he took three for 61 against Sussex at Hove and again in 1908 when he played against Ireland at Dublin. He was with Darfield for three years and also played for Mexborough and Mitchell Main. From 1918 to 1923 he took 363 wickets for Farsley where he was professional. He was a hard-working cricketer and lived at Darfield all his life although dying in Barnsley Beckett Hospital in 1945. His son Jack Brown was groundsman at Darfield for many years.

In a season of soft wickets, George Hirst headed the batting averages with 1177 runs at 39 runs each closely followed by T. L. Taylor with 1,373 runs, also at 39, while Denton averaged exactly 30 for 1,110 runs. Washington, in his first and last full season, exceeded four figures and looked a real find. Jackson batted well when available but Tunnicliffe, the fifth batsman to reach a four figure aggregate, and Brown were disappointing. The latter showed signs of his old form towards the end of the season and any criticism of John Tunnicliffe must be mentioned alongside his slip fielding which remained in the top bracket. Haigh also batted well and the tail was reliable with only Hunter failing to make a good score in the side.

The bowling was in the capable hands of Haigh, 144 wickets at

Irving Washington, who hit 1,000 runs in 1902, aged only 22, but who could not continue after this season because of illness.

216

11.43 and Rhodes, 163 at 12.17. They finished first and second in the first-class averages in a season ideally suited to their methods. The Hon F. S. Jackson also took 45 wickets at 12.60 and Hirst was the other bowler – comparative failure by his standards – but his 71 wickets only cost 17.42 each. Jack Brown's leg-breaks were not needed and Lees Whitehead hardly bowled at all, although as perpetual 12th man he was a godsend to the team. Hunter was as sound and reliable as ever behind the stumps.

After three seasons of unabated success, it was with some relief to many people that Yorkshire should drop to third place in 1903. It was one of the wettest seasons on record. The Yorkshire side were without T. L. Taylor for the whole season and F. S. Jackson only played in a few matches. Washington's illness ended his career.

Opening the season at Lord's, Yorkshire introduced three new players – all left-handed. Walker Wainwright was born at Rotherham in 1882 and was a useful batsman and medium-pace bowler who took six for 49 on his debut, but never repeated his form with the ball again. He lived in the Tinsley area of Sheffield and assisted Sheffield Collegiate for several seasons when their ground was at Tinsley and he was also engaged on the groundstaff at Lord's. From 1921 to 1939 he was an umpire and was coach at Winchester College for many years and he died in the Hampshire town in 1961.

William Herbert Wilkinson, a hard-hitting batsman, had an early opportunity to take over Washington's place as the left-hander in the Yorkshire side. His one weakness in his early days was that he was an indifferent fielder. He was born at Thorpe Hesley near Rotherham in 1881 and scored over 400 runs for Yorkshire in 1903 but did not appear again for them until 1905, and made only moderate progress until 1908 when he established himself with over 1,200 runs at an average of 28. He never repeated that form and after the 1910 season he was dropped from the side. After leaving Yorkshire he joined Mitchells & Butlers in Birmingham and was stocktaker in the offices there, staying until the end of the 1953 season, as well as being a regular member of the firm's cricket side. He played his early cricket with Sheffield United and also played soccer for them, making 25 appearances. His brother Bernard Wilkinson was a well-known Sheffield United soccer player and also played cricket for the same club. W. H. Wilkinson died in Birmingham in 1961 aged 80.

Frederick Ward was a slow left-arm bowler from Heckmondwike who first played for Yorkshire 2nd XI in 1901 and did moderately well with the ball for the second team in 1903, but the match v MCC was his solitary outing in first-class company. He played for both Heckmondwike and Dewsbury for many years and died in Dewsbury Infirmary in 1948.

Haigh made top score (44) against Essex at Leyton but another nine members of the Yorkshire side obtained double figures as they reached 240. Essex had six wickets down for 21 but Young hit hard for 35 and Essex avoided the follow-on by 6 runs. Tunnicliffe scored 62 in Yorkshire's second innings as they totalled 189 with Buckenham and Young each taking four wickets which left Essex needing 334. Hirst then took six for 34 to give Yorkshire a victory by 261 runs. A win over Gloucestershire by an innings and 142 runs saw Rhodes and Hirst in form, both taking eight wickets. When Yorkshire batted, Brown scored 125 with help from Hirst (38) and Rhodes (42) as they went on to score 313.

Taunton once again proved that Somerset are capable of surprising Yorkshire whatever the circumstances. Only Brown with 48 and Lord Hawke (29) made any sort of a show as Yorkshire were dismissed for 147. L. C. H. Palairet (43) and Braund (47) opened with a stand of 72 for Somerset who soon had seven wickets down for 111 before H. Martyn (62) and A. E. Newton (47) added 86 for the eighth wicket and Cranfield (30 not out) helped Somerset to reach 256. Hirst was Yorkshire's most successful batsman with 50 as Yorkshire were bowled out again for 190. Somerset finally won by six wickets. The next match at Worcester was drawn after Yorkshire had scored 518. Wilkinson, with 88, put on 149 for the fourth wicket with Hirst, who completed his 123 in two hours of brilliant batting, and then Lord Hawke hit 76 to put Yorkshire in an impregnable position. Wheldon, with 71, H. K. Foster and A. W. Isaac took Worcestershire to 278 with Rhodes taking eight for 87. Following on they were soon 5 for two before Arnold (83) and Wheldon (71) put on 149 for the third wicket. H. K. Foster (120) and R. S. Brinton (66 not out) added a further 156 for the sixth wicket and at the close Worcestershire had scored 381 to save the game in fine style.

Walter Bedford, a right-hand batsman and fast-medium bowler, was born at Barnsley in 1879 and died at Doncaster in 1939 aged 50. He played twice for Yorkshire in 1903 scoring 30 not out against Worcestershire and took two for 38 in the first innings against Cambridge University. He never played for Yorkshire again. A player by the name of Bedford played for Yorkshire 2nd XI from 1902–1904 and in 1903 two Bedfords played – one from Morley and the other from Rotherham; it is not certain which of the two was Walter.

A weak Yorkshire team accounted for Cambridge University at Fenner's by five wickets with Rhodes taking seven for 110 in the match and Denton scoring 101. The Lancashire match at Old Trafford ended in an even draw after Yorkshire had gained a lead of 130 on the first innings. Denton made 98 for Yorkshire but it was a last wicket stand of 108 between Lord Hawke and Whitehead that took

Yorkshire to 360. John Tyldesley (73) and A. C. MacLaren (53) put on 104 for Lancashire's fourth wicket before F. S. Jackson went through the tail to finish with seven for 61. Walter Brearley then took six for 81, only Denton (84) and Jackson (48) playing him with confidence and Yorkshire were all out for 215. Lancashire were 254 for three in their second innings, still needing 92 when stumps were drawn.

Yorkshire gave a very uneven display at Lord's against Middlesex. After Brown had scored 50 they collapsed from 130 for two to 157 all out, J. T. Hearne taking six for 39. Bosanquet was top scorer when Middlesex batted but eight batsmen got 29 or more and the home side led by 192 on the first innings. Brown scored well for Yorkshire with 55 but only Whitehead, with 60, could hold up the Middlesex attack as they dismissed Yorkshire for 240. Middlesex obtained the 49 needed for victory for the loss of one wicket.

At Bradford Yorkshire suffered their third reverse in the Championship at the hands of Sussex, who scored 558 for eight before declaring, with all the Yorkshire bowlers having astronomical figures. C. B. Fry made 234 and he added 105 for the second wicket with Killick (58) and 174 for the third wicket with Ranjitsinhji (93). Yorkshire then gave a dreadful batting display as they collapsed for 120. When they followed on, although they fought hard, only Lord Hawke, with 61 not out, caused problems to Sussex as they were bowled out for 258. During June Rhodes had taken four wickets for 395 runs, while Haigh had taken ten for 557 in the Championship since the middle of May. Hirst's absence through injury had not helped Yorkshire's cause.

A draw with Warwickshire at Birmingham produced little of interest. This was followed by a seven wicket win at Derby with Hirst back in the side. L. G. Wright, with 47 and 78, was Derbyshire's only run-getter of note. Ringrose took four for 13 in the first innings and three for 66 in the second and for Yorkshire Rhodes scored 69. When Yorkshire were set 145 to win, Denton scored 46 and Hirst 46 not out as they strolled to a win by eight wickets. Meanwhile a scratch Yorkshire side had inflicted another defeat on Cambridge University at Sheffield with Denton scoring 85. The 'varsity could only obtain 75 and 39, with Haigh and Rhodes bowling unchanged.

Making his first appearance for Yorkshire in the Cambridge match was 25-years-old John Thomas Newstead from Marton-in-Cleveland, a right-handed batsman and medium-paced or off-break bowler. He only played in two matches in 1903 but was given a further trial in 1907 and in 1908 did so well that he almost obtained the double for Yorkshire and became one of *Wisden's* 'Five Cricketers of the Year'. He was never the same force again and soon lost his place in the side, dropping out altogether after the 1913 season. Of all the players who failed to make it to the top in this period none was a greater disappointment then Newstead. He was playing for Middlesbrough at the age of 17 and played first for Yorkshire as a batsman but he never really developed into a reliable run-getter being somewhat slap-dash in his methods. He was an extremely accurate bowler, at his best on hard wickets. After retiring from county cricket, he joined Rishton and in 1914 took 94 wickets for them at 7.57 each. He later appeared for Lidget Green, East Bierley, Church and Haslingden. His son R. Newstead was playing for Rishton in 1935. J. T. Newstead died at Blackburn in 1952.

Victory by an innings and 130 runs over Kent at Headingley must have put Yorkshire into a better frame of mind. After losing four wickets for 65, George Hirst (120) added 151 for the fifth wicket with Fred Smith (55) in just over two hours and then Haigh and Hunter joined in a stand of 79 for the ninth wicket to take Yorkshire to 315. Kent had no answer to Hirst, who finished the match with nine for 76. Further success came by an innings at Trent Bridge where Nottinghamshire collapsed to 132 all out against Rhodes (seven for 40) before Yorkshire exceeded that by 232 runs. Yorkshire scored their 364 in 7 hours at the crease, but the Nottinghamshire bowlers recorded an overs-rate of 24 per hour. Wilkinson (64) and Hirst (99) added 143 for Yorkshire's fourth wicket and then Rhodes (63) and Walter Wainwright (41) also got amongst the runs. Nottinghamshire failed in the second innings too and were out for 169.

Fred Smith of Yeadon was a left-handed batsman who played in 13 matches for Yorkshire in 1903 scoring 294 runs at an average of 15. He was only 23 at the time but he never played again and died at Nelson (Lancashire) in 1905 aged 25 from pneumonia caught after returning to his new home from Bramley in wet clothes after playing as a three-quarter for them. He was qualifying for Lancashire at the time.

Yorkshire met with another reverse at Sheffield against Surrey who scored 280 with Holland making top score (90) while Ringrose on a pitch that became fiery, took four for 45. Only Tunnicliffe, with a fine chanceless innings of 97, and Denton faced Richardson and Lockwood with much confidence as Yorkshire collapsed to 182 all out – 98 was a big lead on this Bramall Lane pitch. Surrey put on 80 for the first wicket and finally succumbed to 169 all out, with Holland again Surrey's hero with 43. A target of 268 was never a likely one and only Tunnicliffe with 26 stayed long against Richardson (seven for 57) who was back at his best, Yorkshire being dismissed for 122.

At Dewsbury, Yorkshire overwhelmed Leicestershire by an innings and 280 runs with Denton (133) and Hirst (153) in fine form. Denton batted for nearly three hours for his score but Hirst made his runs in 2 hours and 20 minutes. C. J. B. Wood scored 61 out of his side's 164 with Haigh taking five for 31 and Hirst four for 66. In the second innings, Whitehead hit 39 but Ringrose was at his best to take six for 20 in 15.1 overs. Somerset had all the worst of a draw at Bradford after Yorkshire scored 417 for six declared. Hirst made 142 to continue his fine batting form, Brown 96 and Fred Smith 51. Almost a day was lost to the wet weather. Another draw occurred at Fartown where Worcestershire could only score 24 and 27 for six as Rhodes had match figures of 30-22-12-8 and Hirst 29.3-13-34-8. In only $3\frac{3}{4}$ hours of cricket Yorkshire got pretty near to a result by scoring 76 for one declared.

Yorkshire's fortunes suddenly changed as they won the next seven matches in a very convincing manner, their form being quite up to that shown during the last three years. George Hirst took 52 wickets in those seven games and Wilfred Rhodes obtained exactly the same number. Nottinghamshire were well beaten at Leeds where Brown, Tunnicliffe, Denton, Hirst and Rhodes all obtained fifties as Yorkshire scored 339. J. A. Dixon rescued Nottinghamshire with 77 but they went down by 164 runs when Hirst took his match figures to twelve for 113. Warwickshire put up a good fight at Hull after trailing by 70 on the first innings. Only Brown looked to be in form for Yorkshire as he scored 92 out of 151 for two and Moorhouse had match figures of eleven for 114. Warwickshire were set 211 to win and if anyone could have stayed with Quaife then they might have come nearer than 141 all out.

Gloucestershire, dismissed for 65 and 36 by Hirst and Rhodes were completely outgunned as Yorkshire scored 284 with Denton making 83, and Surrey did little better at The Oval, being dismissed for 84 and 73. Hirst and Rhodes had ten wickets each while Denton batted very attractively for 104 out of Yorkshire's 254. In John Tunnicliffe's benefit match at Park Avenue, Lancashire, after closing 97 for seven, recovered to score 233 thanks to A. Eccles (61) and Cuttell (51) who added 85 for the ninth wicket, Rhodes and Haigh taking five wickets each. Hirst with 58 and Brown (40) managed to give Yorkshire a five runs lead, Barnes taking four for 94. Lancashire were in real trouble at 88 for eight before Sharp hit a sound 56 to bring them up to 168. Yorkshire, set 164 to win — no easy matter on a suspect pitch — lost 111 for five but George Hirst was the man for the occasion and with 69 not out guided his side to an excellent victory. C. J. B. Wood carried his bat through the innings at Leicester for 118 out of 322 with much help from V. F. S. Crawford (77) and Gill (61). The two latter players each batted for some 50 minutes in all and Ringrose took five for 60. Brown (75) and Tunnicliffe (36) put on 112 for the first wicket and then Hirst came in and scored 93 in his most aggressive manner while Rhodes (72) and Lord Hawke (41 not out) took Yorkshire to a 93 runs lead. Leicestershire folded in their second innings for 106, with Haigh taking five for 27, and Yorkshire went on to an easy ten wicket win. Yorkshire also had an easy time at Headingley against Middlesex who were favourites for the title. Yorkshire batted first and were all out for 253 with Tunnicliffe scoring 77 and Hirst 52 while J. T. Hearne took six for 97. Middlesex were then dismissed for 79, with Rhodes taking six for 37 and Hirst four for 31. Yorkshire declined to enforce the follow-on; instead they batted again and scored 233 before declaring. Middlesex were set the enormous task of obtaining 408 to win and were quickly dismissed for 177. It was Middlesex's only defeat of the season.

The weather broke again and at Harrogate, where Ernest Smith made 47 out of 220, there was no play on the second and third days, while the Essex match at Sheffield saw Essex still needing 50 to win with two wickets left after Yorkshire had declared their second innings at 76 for three.

On their southern tour, Yorkshire had the worst of the draw at Canterbury where Kent declared at 181 for seven after taking a lead of 102. Blythe had taken six for 35 for Kent which he followed up with seven for 26 as Yorkshire's batting again failed. On the other match of the tour, Yorkshire's batting collapsed at Hove, with scores of 72 and 96, and Sussex won through by four wickets.

Yorkshire finished a mixed season with an innings victory over the MCC at Scarborough, Hirst, Jackson and Denton obtaining fifties. The match against C. I. Thornton's XI was drawn with further fifties for Yorkshire from Hirst and Denton.

Frederick Thomas Asquith played one match for Yorkshire at Sheffield against Gloucestershire. He learnt his cricket as a member of the Sheepscar Leather Works Club. He was later wicket-keeper for Hull CC for many years and was landlord of the 'Locomotive' in Hessle Road, Hull where he died in 1916 aged 45. He was buried in the Western Cemetery. He had appeared for Yorkshire 2nd XI from 1898–1901 and was quite a useful batsman.

James ('Jimmy') William Rothery was a right-hand batsman with a fine off-drive who batted in an artistic manner. He was born at Staincliffe in 1877. He made his debut at Scarborough in 1903 and, after steady progress in 1904, he gained a regular place in the side in 1905. He first played for Yorkshire 2nd XI in 1898 and he played for Harrogate from 1897 to 1909 scoring 3,299 runs at an average of 34.73. He continued to play for Yorkshire until 1910 and three times scored over 800 runs in a season, but never batted with the consistency needed to become a county cricketer and was dropped from the side after the 1910 season. He lacked the necessary determination and was temperamental. He moved to Scarborough in 1911 and in 1914 was with Wearmouth for whom he scored 712 runs at an average of 39.56 topping the league averages. He also played for Durham. He died in 1919 at Beckett's Park Hospital in Leeds as the result of war wounds, incurred while serving with the East Kent Regiment.

Henry Wilkinson played for Yorkshire for three seasons from 1903 and scored 847 runs for the County in 1904. He was a very useful right-handed batsman. Having been born at Hillhouse, Huddersfield in 1877 and educated at Western College, Harrogate, he went on to Cambridge University but failed to gain his blue. For Harrogate between 1894 and 1910 he scored 5,222 runs at an average of 21.77 and captained the club for eleven years. A schoolteacher by profession, he played his last first-class match in 1912 for C. B. Fry's XI and at one time played for East Stirlingshire. He played Rugby Union for Yorkshire and died in 1967 in Cape Province.

Yorkshire had to be satisfied with third place in 1903. To lose five matches surprised many people but there was a vast difference in the form of the side at the end than at the start of the season. The weather was very poor, though perhaps the main difference from the three previous seasons was the fact that Wilfred Rhodes lost his bowling form for the first time in his life. It is difficult to believe that, when one remembers his success in the previous year. Ringrose was nominally top of the Yorkshire bowling averages but he only took 36 wickets and it was Hirst who led the way with 121 wickets at 13.52. Haigh also took over 100 wickets while the Hon F. S. Jackson and Walker Wainwright both had their good days with the ball.

Yorkshire's batting was reasonably good, with George Hirst outstanding. He easily led the averages with 1,535 runs at 46.51, with Brown scoring 1,291 runs at 28, just behind Denton who averaged 30 for 1,443 runs. Rhodes was now in the all-rounder's category, scoring 947 runs at 25.59, while Lord Hawke and Tunnicliffe both had days of success. The fielding at times gave cause for concern and it was mainly amongst the younger members where the lack of consistency was noticeable.

The membership of the Club continued to increase though the target of 5,000 had not yet been realised. For the 1904 season, the team would be virtually the same, but J. T. Brown senior only played in two first-class matches before becoming ill.

A Time Limit Match at Leeds was won by Yorkshire by 71 runs but it was hardly a test as none of the four innings went up to the limit. Hirst made top score in each innings for Yorkshire and Ringrose, Hirst and Rhodes all bowled well and the first-class programme got off to a good start with an innings win at Fenner's with Hirst scoring 102 very quickly.

The Championship season began with a draw at Bradford.

Yorkshire scored 321 with Tunnicliffe (85) putting on 111 for the fourth wicket with Hirst (76), dropped catches helping Yorkshire to their large total. Leicestershire, in reply, had Whitehead to thank for avoiding the follow-on and when Yorkshire batted again they lost seven wickets for 91 before Rothery with 50 and Lord Hawke (100 not out), along with 17 from Ringrose, took Yorkshire to 269 for nine declared. Leicestershire were left with 385 to win in some four hours and they comfortably fought their way to a draw.

A high-scoring match at The Parks was drawn with Oxford University, who totalled 374, with J. E. Raphael scoring 201 in 270 minutes. Ringrose and Rhodes each took four wickets but the slow bowler conceded 129 runs in 32.4 overs. Tunnicliffe (77) and F. Mitchell (63) added 101 for Yorkshire's third wicket; Mitchell being back in the side for the first time since 1901. Hirst then scored 153, reaching his hundred in an hour and a quarter, and Yorkshire scored 426. The third day was washed out. A draw at Old Trafford had its interesting moments. Yorkshire lost eight for 126 before Rhodes and Haigh added 162 for the ninth wicket, and the visitors totalled 293. Lancashire reached 257 for four with Spooner scoring 126 and Sharp 52 but they were all out for 273, with F. S. Jackson taking six for 91. Yorkshire were 34 for two when the game was washed out. The Derbyshire game was also ruined by rain, and the match against Worcestershire resulted in a third successive draw.

There was little comfort to Yorkshire when they visited Lord's, for though Middlesex lost seven wickets for 76, they recovered to 214 all out. Yorkshire then failed dismally for 72 and would have followed on if Trott (four for 7) had been put on earlier. Warner alone batted well as Middlesex struggled to 95. Yorkshire, needing 238 to win, fought well but Hearne with six for 48 proved to be the match-winner as they were bowled out for 160.

Yorkshire's first victory took place at Bradford where the home team gained a first innings lead of twelve over Surrey. F. S. Jackson, driving splendidly, played a true captain's innings of 158 and Wilfred Rhodes scored 107 in 100 minutes at the crease. A declaration was made at 398 for seven. Surrey were then bowled out for 113. Yorkshire's improved form continued at Trent Bridge where Nottinghamshire, in spite of centuries from A. O. Jones and J. A. Dixon, finished the first innings 100 runs in arrears. Tunnicliffe with 119 and Denton (85) added 174 for Yorkshire's third wicket before Hirst, hitting very hard, scored 77. When Nottinghamshire batted again Rhodes and Haigh bowled Yorkshire to a ten-wicket victory.

A poor batting display by Yorkshire saw them all out for 220 on a good batting strip at Bramall Lane; Sussex passed that with only two wickets down, C. B. Fry (177) and K. S. Ranjitsinhji (148) adding 255 for their third wicket. They declared with a lead of 220 but Yorkshire were quite content to play for a draw. There was another high scoring draw at Worcester. The home county made 220 and 456 for seven in reply to Yorkshire's 447.

Two wins in June carried Yorkshire from level bottom to equal third in the Championship table. Five consecutive victories then took them up to second place, where they would remain for the rest of the season. At Leyton, Essex went down by nine wickets. Rhodes had the distinction of taking five for 68 in each innings and Yorkshire's Denton, Walker Wainwright, Hirst and Haigh all managed to obtain fifties. Against Somerset at Hull, Yorkshire's margin was down to seven wickets as L. C. H. Palairet helped Somerset to 302 in their first innings, a total Yorkshire passed by 26 runs. Haigh went on to take his match figures to nine for 147 as Somerset collapsed to 176 all out in their second attempt. Tunnicliffe with 50 helped Yorkshire to an easy victory.

At Leeds, Hampshire were dismissed for 62 and 36, with Rhodes (ten for 39) bowling unchanged with Haigh (ten for 49) on a pitch taking a lot of spin. F. S. Jackson had put Yorkshire on top with 73 out of his side's 194, scoring his runs at almost a run a minute, and in the second innings Tunnicliffe continued his fine form with 94 as Yorkshire totalled 274. The ultimate victory was by 370 runs. Warwickshire, at Birmingham, went down by an innings and 4 runs after being 147 for one and then 308 all out. At one stage Yorkshire had six down for 163 before Hirst (93) and Haigh (138) added 136 for the seventh wicket to help them to 419. Rhodes followed six for 95 with figures of six for 33.

Yorkshire were weakened by the absence of F. S. Jackson, Denton and Rhodes, all playing in the Gentlemen v Players match at Lord's, for the Derbyshire match at Sheffield and the opposition put up a good fight as they led by 59 on the first innings. All-round cricket by Haigh who followed five for 85 with 104 provided Yorkshire with victory by four wickets. At Harrogate, the Kent match was abandoned as the ground had been tampered with. It was very unfortunate for Schofield Haigh who scored 74 not out and took nine for 85; none of which would count in the first-class averages. In fact he would have completed the 'double' in Championship cricket, instead of having to be satisfied with that feat in all Yorkshire matches.

At Portsmouth, Yorkshire completed the double over Hampshire by an innings and 18 runs after Tunnicliffe (128) and Hirst (152) had added 258 for the fourth wicket in 165 minutes and Rhodes (98) and Rothery (70) added 152 in little more than an hour to take Yorkshire to 549. Webb (83) and E. M. Sprot (118) and A. J. L. Hill with 68 helped Hampshire to a respectable 331 but only Hill with 48 offered any real resistance in the second innings. Heavy scoring draws followed at Tunbridge Wells and The Oval, with Tunnicliffe obtaining centuries in each game, as did George Hirst. In three consecutive games they had each scored a century and taken part in partnerships of 258, 171 and 180 with one another.

Five more draws followed, mainly as the result of poor weather, but the Gloucestershire match was in an interesting situation with Yorkshire requiring 204 to win with nine wickets left in two hours. The Nottinghamshire game was drawn with Yorkshire 42 ahead with nine second innings wickets left after Lord Hawke had rescued Yorkshire with 59, putting on 67 with Hunter.

For George Hirst's benefit at Leeds, record crowds attended the match and the proceeds were a record as well. Yorkshire batted first after being put in to bat and they lost five for 143. Later Ernest Smith (98) added 130 for the eighth wicket with Lord Hawke (54) and Yorkshire eventually reached a formidable 403 in seven hours batting, although the Lancashire bowling was well below their usual standard and the fielding was poor. Lancashire then lost three for 9 and they eventually followed on 230 behind, with only A. H. Hornby (59) and Poidevin (40) offering much resistance to Hirst. A draw made Lancashire virtually sure of the title.

At Leicester, Yorkshire scored a formidable 414 with Rudston batting for $5\frac{1}{4}$ hours in making the highest score of his career (164) and adding 132 for the second wicket with Denton (85). Myers hit 73 quick runs. C. J. B. Wood scored 71 and then Knight (80) and Coe (70) put on 126 for Leicestershire's sixth wicket and the home side scored 310. Yorkshire tried to force the pace in their second innings with Rudston hitting 69 and Tunnicliffe 51 not out, but in the end Leicestershire had only $2\frac{1}{2}$ hours to chase 252 and the chase was never on as they lost seven wickets for 94.

At Sheffield, Yorkshire scored 309 against Middlesex with Denton making top score (91), before Rhodes (73), Ernest Smith (33) and Haigh (50) caused the tail to wag. When Middlesex batted, eight wickets were down for 269 before B. J. T. Bosanquet (141) and R. E. More (120 not out) added 128 in less than 50 minutes. Middlesex's 488 took less than $4\frac{1}{2}$ hours. In their second innings Yorkshire batted much better and defeat was avoided.

At Huddersfield, Warwickshire succeeded in inflicting Yorkshire's second defeat of the season in a thrilling game of cricket. On a treacherous pitch, Warwickshire did well to reach 164, mainly through a hard piece of hitting from Santall (51), he and Moorhouse putting on 71 for the seventh wicket. When Yorkshire batted, only Grimshaw, with 39, had any success on a pitch at its worst against Field and Hargreave and Warwickshire's lead was 48. Warwickshire fared worse against Rhodes and Haigh and Yorkshire needed 130 to win. Six wickets fell for 59 before Ernest Smith (22) and Haigh (28) took the score to 107. At 120 for seven, Yorkshire must have been favourites but Hargreave dismissed the last two men, Warwickshire gaining a sensational win by 6 runs.

Charles Henry Grimshaw (known as 'Harry') first played for Yorkshire in 1904 and had an extended trial in the following year, but never realised the promise he showed for the colts in 1905, when he averaged 50. He played for Yorkshire until 1908, and after leaving them he continued to play for Bowling Old Lane in the Yorkshire Council and in the Bradford League, heading both batting and bowling averages in the Bradford League in 1924, when he took four wickets in four balls against Keighley. In 1915 he made the record score in the Priestley Cup of 230 not out against Great Horton and took 1,273 wickets in the Bradford League, a record until beaten by M. C. Fearnley.

At Headingley, Yorkshire scored 379, after losing four wickets for 113, Hirst (140) and Rhodes (58) adding 114 for the fifth wicket in 65 minutes. In all Yorkshire batted for $4\frac{1}{2}$ hours, but Essex missed several chances on a helpful wicket. Essex then lost five wickets for 38. Following on 175 behind, Essex were 118 for six at the end of the second day. The third day was washed out by the rain. The Sussex match which followed produced a different type of draw. Hirst with 121 saved Yorkshire as they struggled to 292 in bad light. When Sussex batted they spent almost seven hours totalling 377, with C. B. Fry (229) dominating the play after he and Vine (53) had opened with a stand of 186. Yorkshire were 86 for three at the close.

The final Western tour saw Yorkshire get the better of a drawn game with Gloucestershire, rain preventing any play beyond the third innings. At Taunton, Somerset lost to Yorkshire by an innings and 152 runs with Denton (111), Haigh (81), Tunnicliffe (90), Hirst (71) and Rhodes (49 not out) all contributing towards Yorkshire's 472 for seven declared, as they averaged almost 100 runs per hour. When Somerset batted, Hirst took ten wickets. Both Hirst and Haigh managed to complete their 'doubles' in first-class cricket in this match.

Yorkshire also met the South Africans twice, almost forcing an innings victory in each game. In the Scarborough match Denton scored a century while L. J. Tancred with 101 saved the game for the visitors. Hirst was also at his best with the ball, taking five for 28. The MCC followed on against Yorkshire at the same venue but easily saved the game with P. F. Warner scoring 145 and A. C. MacLaren 114.

Yorkshire finished in second place with George Hirst easily heading the batting averages with 2,257 runs, average 55.04. Denton also did well with 1,919 runs at an average of 43. F. S. Jackson scored 858 runs with an average of 39.40, and Tunnicliffe had a good season with 1,650 runs average 36.66. Rhodes had his best season ever with the bat, scoring 1,251 runs at an average of 33. Haigh also passed his thousand runs.

The bowling was not as strong as in the past, with Haigh doing well and taking 118 wickets at 19.50. Rhodes also took 118 wickets at 20.14, but he was a pale shadow of his old self. Myers did very well with 78 wickets at 20.41 while Hirst took 114 wickets at 22.26. Thus three Yorkshire cricketers completed the double – a feat equalled by Booth, Drake and Hirst in 1913. In November 1904 came the sad news of the death of Jack Brown, whose career had halted suddenly at the start of the summer.

In 1905 therefore the County lacked both Brown and Frank Mitchell, otherwise the eleven was little changed. Yorkshire began the new season where they left off, on a Western tour, and a more convincing start could not have been made than the visit to Taunton. Batting first, Yorkshire soon lost their opening pair before Denton (107) was joined by Tunnicliffe (63) in a stand of 164, and at the close of play Yorkshire were 380 for seven with Rhodes 97 not out. He went on to score 201, his highest score, having been at the wickets for 225 minutes. He drove very well and Lord Hawke helped him to add 151 in 100 minutes. When Somerset batted, Hirst took eleven wickets and the home side lost by an innings. Going on to Bristol, Hirst (86) and Haigh (69) took Yorkshire to 338 but Gloucestershire lost four wickets with only seven runs on the board and a partial recovery only took them to 96. They followed on and their final score of 187 left them with an innings and 55 runs defeat.

At Worcester, Yorkshire's all-rounders were to the fore again with Hirst batting in his own typical fashion to score 108 and 59, both not out, as well as taking five wickets. Only Haigh (48) gave him much assistance in the first innings of 225. In the end Worcestershire required 361 and despite good batting by Bowley (165) lost by 65 runs. F. S. Jackson with 111 helped Yorkshire to a first innings score of 289 against Derbyshire and the score was sufficient to gain an innings victory.

Yorkshire's visit to Leicester provided plenty of interest. C. E. de Trafford with 58 opened with a stand of 73 with C. J. B. Wood, who helped Whitehead in a fourth wicket stand of 116 before Whitehead (56) was dismissed at 210. Coe then came in and scored 100 out of 167 added for the fifth wicket and when Leicestershire were out for 419. C. J. B. Wood had carried his bat throughout the innings for 160 not out in 6½ hours. Yorkshire were 74 for five at one stage but George Hirst took part in a sixth wicket stand with Haigh (31) that added 144 and then Myers (57) helped Hirst in a stand of 183. When Hirst was out he had made 341 in 7 hours, the highest individual score ever made for Yorkshire and he scored runs all round the wicket in a most brilliant fashion. He was last out at 515. Leicestershire lost seven wickets for 72 before A. E. Davis and W. W. Odell came together to save the match.

Moving on to Edgbaston, another draw resulted, with high scores once again the reason and not the adverse weather. Yorkshire returned to winning ways when Worcestershire visited Leeds. Denton scored 91 and H. Wilkinson, who led the side, 78 as Yorkshire scored 323. Cuffe, in a stay of $2\frac{1}{2}$ hours, was the only visiting batsman to shine, Haigh taking six for 36 in Worcestershire's total of 119. On a wearing wicket, Yorkshire batted again and Tunnicliffe when set drove very well to score 80 not out as Yorkshire were all out for 157. When the visitors batted again Haigh bowled Yorkshire to an easy victory. The Middlesex match at Lord's followed, with Middlesex in immediate trouble as they lost seven wickets for 77. J. H. Hunt with 41 helped them to reach 145, a total that Yorkshire passed with only three wickets down. Haigh bowled well on a pitch that was drying out to take six for 56, and when Yorkshire batted on an improving pitch, Denton was dropped twice and went on to score 102 in $2\frac{1}{4}$ hours. A lead of 130 was sufficient for Yorkshire to go on and win the match by seven wickets.

Yorkshire met the Australians twice during the season and at Sheffield the visitors made a score of 322, with Trumper (85) and Duff (61) putting on 122 for the opening stand inside an hour. Yorkshire made a good start with Tunnicliffe scoring 52 and F. S. Jackson 42, but from 106 for two they collapsed to 197 all out, Laver taking eight for 75. Haigh on a wearing wicket, helped by Myers and Rhodes, dismissed the Australians for 127 and Yorkshire needed 253 to win. Rhodes made 22 but Yorkshire were dismissed for 78, Howell taking six for 38. The return match at Bradford was drawn, much more in Yorkshire's favour, with Denton in particularly good form with 52 and 153 not out, the latter being a brilliant innings, and the highest made against the tourists that year. Rhodes with 70 and Grimshaw with 40 and 41 were also seen to advantage. Facing a Yorkshire total of 324, the Australians lost three wickets for 1 run and then seven wickets for 51 before Noble (75) and Armstrong (44) put on 102 for their eighth wicket and they managed to avoid the follow-on. Ringrose bowled splendidly to take nine for 76. Set 383 to win, Noble and Armstrong saved their side after four wickets had fallen for 96. A victory at Fenner's was a formality after Rhodes had taken six for 16 as Cambridge were dismissed for 35, but Yorkshire were 30 for four before Hirst scored 113 not out, adding 94 with Rhodes, who scored 46. G. G. Napier took six for 105 in Yorkshire's score of 243, and then Cambridge were dismissed for 161.

Yorkshire's visit to play the Champions at Old Trafford proved a traumatic affair. Lancashire batted first and thanks to R. H. Spooner (109) and Tyldesley (134) who added 223 for the second wicket, they reached 399. Only F. S. Jackson (34) and Denton (41) with a stand of 50 were able to play Walter Brearley (five for 31) and following on they scored 214 with Rhodes (65) badly bruised by the pace bowlers. Kermode with six for 70 assured the home side of a comfortable win.

Worse was to come. Lacking Jackson, Haigh, Rhodes and Hirst because of the Test Match at Lord's, Yorkshire went to Derby and were dismissed for only 123, with Warren taking seven for 57. Derbyshire then took a lead of 67. Yorkshire, in their second innings, made only 161 leaving Derbyshire with 95 to win – they won at tea-time on the second day by nine wickets. Yorkshire were now in third equal place with Lancashire and Surrey still unbeaten.

John Emanuel ('Jack') Elms played once for Yorkshire against Derbyshire in 1905. A right-hand bat and medium-fast bowler who switched to both off-breaks and leg-breaks, he took 2,000 wickets in the Yorkshire Council and for 47 years was player and coach with Sheffield United. He used to bowl at Bramall Lane from morning until night for 20 years, and in the winter used to paint the railings and sit on the trainer's bench at soccer matches next to George Waller and considered himself to be assistant trainer. A florist of some note, he had an allotment at Pitsmoor and he used to arrive at Bramall Lane with a button-hole at eight o'clock in the morning after being in his allotment since six. He died in 1951.

Yorkshire were in trouble from the start at Bramall Lane against Nottinghamshire, being dismissed before lunch for 61 with Wass taking seven for 28. Iremonger (37) and George Gunn (40) were within two runs of Yorkshire's score before they lost a wicket but only Rev H. Staunton (23) reached double figures for Nottinghamshire after that. Haigh bowled well to take six for 34 as Nottinghamshire doubled Yorkshire's score. H. Wilkinson with 81 and Denton (61) then put on 146 for Yorkshire's second wicket, and they finally reached 227 to set Nottinghamshire 167 to win. John Gunn took seven for 78. Rain then interrupted play and on a drying pitch Rhodes and Haigh bowled out the opposition for 39. At Dewsbury, Yorkshire gained a first innings lead of 15, Rhodes (54) and Haigh (34) adding 67 for the sixth wicket before Hargreave finished with five for 64 in Yorkshire's all out score of 153. Only Kinneir (50) stayed long for Warwickshire, with Rhodes taking five for 48. H. Wilkinson (31) and F. S. Jackson (25) opened with a stand of 42 when Yorkshire batted again and Haigh made 18 as Santall with five for 26 bowled out Yorkshire for 108. Warwickshire had no chance on the now treacherous wicket. Yorkshire were now in third place with Lancashire still unbeaten.

Yorkshire, at Headingley, scored 295 against Sussex, Denton, Hirst and Rothery all reaching the half-century. C. B. Fry scored 111 as Sussex struggled to get within sight of the Yorkshire score. Going in again Yorkshire collapsed in devastating fashion in their second innings as they lost six wickets for 48 before Denton (78) and Hirst (103 not out) put on 138 for the seventh wicket. A missed chance given by Denton could have resulted in a Sussex win. As it was the game was drawn.

Arthur Dolphin had made his debut for Yorkshire against Cambridge University at Fenner's at the age of 19. He showed great promise and eventually succeeded David Hunter as Yorkshire's regular wicket-keeper in 1910, keeping his place in the side until 1927 when he was replaced by Arthur Wood. Born at Wilsden nr Bradford, in 1885, Dolphin was considered one of the best wicket-keepers in the country, almost as good as Strudwick on his day, but he only played once for England, during the tour to Australia in 1920/21. He was the first Bradford League player to play for Yorkshire and lived most of his early life in Wilsden. After his playing career he became a first-class umpire. He died at his home in Heaton, Bradford in 1942 aged 56. His funeral was at Scholemoor Crematorium. A short, perky little man, ideally built for a wicket-keeper, he suffered from sciatica from time to time which may have affected his form behind the stumps.

Arthur Crowther, a right-hand batsman of ability who scored many runs in the Heavy Woollen area, played at Dewsbury in 1905 against Warwickshire, being bowled by Hargreave in each innings without scoring and never appeared again. He was then 26 years old but only played for Yorkshire 2nd XI in this one season. He started his career with Staincliffe in 1897 moving to Dewsbury, Batley, Queensbury and back to Staincliffe in 1907–09, then back to Batley before moving to Heckmondwike in 1912–13. In 1917–20 he played for Ossett. He was born at Leeds in 1878 and was working in Fox's Cotton Mill at Staincliffe when called out to play for Yorkshire.

Geoffrey Tattersall, who played for Harrogate from 1904 to 1913 and captained the club in 1911 and 1913, scored 2,728 runs for them at an average of 25.03, including three centuries. He was born at Ripon in 1882. He made one appearance for Yorkshire against Sussex at Leeds in 1905 when he scored 26 and 0, adding 58 with Denton for Yorkshire's third wicket in the first innings. He played Rugby Union for Yorkshire on 25 occasions as a centre and full-back and was in the Harrogate side that won the Yorkshire Cup in 1905.

At Hull, Yorkshire were dismissed for 77 and 162, the main reason for their defeat being the superb spin bowling of Colin Blythe, who took eleven for 89, four of his wickets being classically caught by Seymour at slip. Kent had a lead of 47 on the first innings but, needing 116 to win, lost four wickets for 31. A. P. Day and Blaker took Kent to a well-deserved six wicket win. Yorkshire were now down to fourth place in the table, having lost three more matches than chief rivals Lancashire.

Somerset provided an easy victory for Yorkshire at Harrogate, Rhodes scoring 108 after H. Wilkinson (67) and Grimshaw (71) had put on 144 for the first wicket. Haigh (70) helped Rhodes to add 117 for the sixth wicket and Myers hit hard for 75 as Yorkshire finished the day with 474. Somerset were then dismissed twice on the second day for 125 and 200, with newcomer Deyes taking five for 75 in the first innings.

This was George Deyes's first match for Yorkshire in which he did so well as a right-handed fast bowler, but his career in county cricket was very limited. He was living at Thirsk when called up by Yorkshire and subsequently played for Staffordshire, who considered that he and Sedgwick were better than most of Yorkshire's retained bowlers.

Revenge against Kent at Tunbridge Wells followed, with Ringrose taking six for 66 when Kent were dismissed for 142. Rothery with 51 and Rhodes (53) took Yorkshire into a lead of 97. In Kent's second innings of 174 Seymour scored 54 but Hirst was in fine form to finish with five for 43. Lord Hawke and Tunnicliffe took Yorkshire to an eight wicket win. Yorkshire were now in a run of seven consecutive victories which would bring them well back into the running for the title.

Against Hampshire, Rothery (118) and Denton (165) put on 119 for the second wicket in 70 minutes. Rothery scored his 118 before lunch, driving brilliantly and timing his leg-side shots well. Denton batted for $3\frac{1}{2}$ hours for his then highest score in first-class cricket. It was Rothery's first century for Yorkshire. Rhodes (48), Myers (54) and Hunter (38) took Yorkshire to an immense 491. On the second day, Hampshire were completely outplayed by the home side as they were dismissed for 172 and 152 with Myers taking nine for 80 and Hirst seven for 82.

At The Oval, Surrey, one of the sides above Yorkshire in the Championship, were expected to provide formidable opposition. Surrey bowled well to take four Yorkshire wickets with only 63 on the board and Yorkshire were fortunate to finish the day at 314 for eight with the Surrey bowlers not having the best of good fortune. When Surrey batted only Hayes (69) showed up well as they followed on. Myers took four for 59 as Yorkshire won by an innings and 108 runs. Yorkshire were now second to Lancashire in the table.

Yorkshire had little difficulty in beating Leicestershire at Sheffield in spite of Jackson, Hirst and Rhodes being on Test match duty. The left-handed Wilkinson played a good innings of 60 to take Yorkshire to 261. Leicestershire were 122 for two, then eight batsmen were tumbled out for the addition of fifteen runs. In their second innings, Rothery, Tunnicliffe, Myers and W. H. Wilkinson all obtained fifties in an attractive batting display, enabling Yorkshire to declare at 295 for eight. Leicestershire began their second innings well and C. J. B. Wood (44) and King (69) shared a second wicket stand of 77 to take the visitors to 106 for two but they could only obtain 174, to lose by 245 runs. At Trent Bridge, Rhodes and Haigh put Nottinghamshire out for 114 and Yorkshire passed that score with only three wickets down. Denton, Hirst and Myers all obtained fifties, Yorkshire making 343. Nottinghamshire, with Hardstaff scoring 51, batted a little better at their second attempt but 174 did not prevent an innings defeat.

Gloucestershire's visit to Bradford provided Yorkshire with another innings win with 118 runs to spare. The fixture at Hull against Hampshire was so badly affected by rain that not even the first two innings were completed.

On the county scene, there was no doubt that the Lancashire match at Bramall Lane was the game of the season. Yorkshire batted first and were in great trouble, with F. S. Jackson scoring 30 of his side's all out total of 76. Once again Walter Brearley had a field day as he took seven for 35. With Lancashire putting on 90 for the first wicket through A. C. MacLaren (51) and R. H. Spooner (42) the visitors appeared to be in a winning position, but apart from J. T. Tyldesley's 33, the rest of the Lancashire batting was undistinguished against Rhodes and F. S. Jackson. Brearley then shook Yorkshire with two quick wickets before Denton (96) and Jackson (45) took the score from 21 to 164, Denton playing brilliantly if having some luck. Jackson played a very restrained innings and then Rhodes came in to play a dashing 74 as Yorkshire scored 285 and put the Lancashire bowling to the sword. Cook took four for 51 but Brearley's six wickets cost 122 runs in 26.3 overs. Set 185 to win, L. O. S. Poidevin scored 40 and Tyldesley 26, but in defective light and on a deteriorating pitch, Lancashire were dismissed for 140 to lose by 44 runs.

Yorkshire were now narrowly behind Lancashire in the table which made their next match at Headingley against Surrey of especial importance. Surrey won the toss on what could be termed a slow 'turner' but Surrey lost six early wickets for 68 before J. N. Crawford (42) and Lord Dalmeny (41) rallied them to an eventual score of 171. Rhodes bowled very well to take six for 73 and Yorkshire were 100 for three at the end of the first day. Denton with 50, Hirst (38) and Rhodes (59 not out) took Yorkshire to 231, with Crawford taking seven for 90. The later Yorkshire batsmen, apart from Rhodes, found him unplayable. Surrey collapsed again to be dismissed for 91; Yorkshire needed 32 to win. The task could not have been easier, but they were reckoning without Knox who found life and lift and took five for 21 as Yorkshire limped home by five wickets. Yorkshire now had four matches to play and were still behind their Roses rivals in the Championship.

At Fartown, Ringrose took six for 79 as Essex were bowled out for 172. In reply Rothery (53) added 111 with Denton (134) for the second wicket in a fine batting display before rain interrupted the game. To make up time, Hirst, Rhodes and Haigh all scored quickly to take Yorkshire to 423 for six before declaring. The match was over by tea-time on the third day with P. Perrin scoring 29 – exactly half of the Essex total – with Rhodes taking six for 9 and Hirst four for 44. Essex lost their last eight wickets for 11 runs to lose by an innings and 193 runs. Before this match Yorkshire had three days without any cricket during the Test match, in which Lancashire had several players engaged. The Red Rose County lost at Bristol by five wickets. Gloucestershire seemed to have replaced Somerset as the western shire who were to blight the chances of title contenders! Yorkshire were therefore on top before the start of the Essex match. Three drawn matches would secure Yorkshire the title.

At Bradford only rain prevented victory over Middlesex with Yorkshire requiring 33 more runs to win with all their wickets in hand. At Leyton, Essex almost upset Yorkshire's chances in a remarkable performance. On the first day they scored 404 for six, F. L. Fane making 106 and McGahey 105, the final total being 521. Then in 105 minutes Yorkshire were dismissed for 98. Douglas took five for 31 and Tremlin three for 16, and Yorkshire had to follow 423 in arrears. Overnight, Yorkshire lost Rothery with 15 on the board and on the last day Yorkshire had to fight a rearguard action. With two down for 22, Tunnicliffe (59) and Hirst (90) fought hard to take the score to 158 in $3\frac{1}{4}$ hours before Tunnicliffe left, and when Hirst was out he had batted for 4 hours and fifty minutes. Ernest Smith, the hitter, then came in and batted for an hour without scoring. Yorkshire had saved the game with a score of 227 for seven, with Reeves typifying the Essex attack by this analysis – 36-24-37-2. The Championship was certainly coming across the Pennines back to Yorkshire.

Another draw at Hove completed Yorkshire's programme and the title was secured.

Having won the crown by dint of some dubious draws, Yorkshire produced the form which convinced the cricketing public that they were worthy Champions. Meeting the Rest of England at The Oval, the County gained a first innings lead of 18 and later set England 232 to win. Hirst and Rhodes bowled in brilliant style and dismissed the opposition for 166. Victory by 65 runs was very sweet indeed.

Yorkshire thoroughly deserved the Championship in 1905 although their margin over Lancashire was a small one. There is no doubt that as the season went on Yorkshire improved as a team whereas most of Lancashire's good work was done at the start. After 1 July, Lancashire won four games and lost three whereas Yorkshire won ten and were undefeated.

Schofield Haigh played over 500 times for Yorkshire up to the First World War, and obtained many wickets with his fast-medium bowling.

Hirst finished at the top of the batting averages with 1972 runs at 56.31, a really fine performance, invariably getting runs when they were wanted and scoring in an unrestrained manner unless the situation warranted it, as in the Essex match. Denton exceeded 2,000 runs with an average of over 45 and Rhodes's continual improvement as a batsman was quite remarkable. Tunnicliffe batted very well to complete his thousand runs, while Jackson, when available, was usually in good form. Rothery made a big advance with Haigh averaging over 20, too. Myers scored 664 runs at 17.42, just behind Lord Hawke and the very promising Grimshaw.

Haigh topped the bowling averages with 118 wickets at 14.53, with Rhodes taking 158 at 15.67. Hirst took 95 at 18.55 and Myers and Ringrose both took over 70. Haigh also topped the national first-class averages, and those five Yorkshire bowlers were all in the top 12 in the country, a remarkable record which can never have been bettered. One should remember that the England captain, Stanley Jackson, headed the Test bowling averages against Australia and was an additon to the Yorkshire attack when needed – a fact that speaks for itself.

HIS LORDSHIP RETIRES

THE NEW SEASON WAS HERALDED IN for Yorkshire with the knowledge that the finances were in a satisfactory state; the membership had never been better and a new benefit fund was launched to assist players if their allotted match was rain-affected. Season 1906 would no longer see Walker Wainwright or H. Wilkinson in the side and F. S. Jackson would only play in one match before retiring for good; also Ernest Smith would play in only two matches before he too would make his farewell. There was room for young players to come through to the Yorkshire team and a Young Players' Scheme, which allocated players to certain grounds was introduced.

Yorkshire were upset in their very first fixture at Lord's where the MCC won a keenly-fought game by 40 runs. The County, however, had no difficulty in winning their first Championship fixture at Southampton in spite of E. M. Sprot (66) and Phil Mead (60) adding 120 for Hampshire's third wicket. Hirst finished with six for 87 as Hampshire were bowled out for 198 and almost everyone made runs as Yorkshire raced away to a total of 421. Hampshire then lost five wickets for 74 before E. M. Sprot (109), with help from Badcock (39) and Langford (48), took Hampshire to 277. Yorkshire won by seven wickets.

The Cambridge match at Fenner's was nothing other than a humiliation for Yorkshire. C. H. Eyre with 153 helped his side to a total of 312. He made his runs in $3\frac{1}{2}$ hours and it was his highest score in first-class cricket. Haigh took five for 92 but Yorkshire's batting was worse than their bowling as P. R. May (seven for 41) bowled the Champions out for only 119 with Hirst (30) and Tunnicliffe (26) slowing down Cambridge's progress. With a lead of 193 Cambridge decided to bat again, obtaining 163. Yorkshire were then bowled out for 51 with May taking five for 25 and G. G. Napier five for 26. Cambridge University's victory was by 305 runs.

Returning to Catford for the game with Kent, Yorkshire played like their real selves with Hirst scoring 101 out of his side's 229. Apart from a stand of 88 for the second wicket between Humphreys and James Seymour, Kent were disposed of for 178 with Haigh taking four for 42 and Hirst four for 46. On a wicket that was deteriorating and in poor light, Yorkshire were dismissed for 137 with Denton (68), batting very well against the rampant Blythe (seven for 63), making almost half of Yorkshire's runs. Kent needed 189 to win, but some brilliant catches by Rothery and Grimshaw caused a sensational collapse and they were dismissed for 69, Hirst taking seven for 33.

Yorkshire then overwhelmed Leicestershire at Leeds, Denton scoring 108 in quick time as Yorkshire scored 244 before dismissing Leicestershire for 34 and 107. Hirst took twelve wickets in the match.

Benjamin Birdsall Wilson played in four matches for Yorkshire in 1906 without success, but was a regular member of the side from 1909 to 1914, proving himself a prolific run-getter, though he could be very slow at times and was indifferent in the field. He was born at Scarborough in 1879 and was therefore 26 when he first played for the County and he played for Scarborough for several years from 1905 onwards. A right-handed batsman, without any style, he later played for Pudsey Britannia in 1921, and then coached at Harrow for 11 years and afterwards St Peter's School at York. He died at Harrogate, where he had lived for many years, in 1957 aged 77. His son, B. A. Wilson, was also a useful cricketer and had trials with Yorkshire.

Hirst scored 104 out of 190 at Edgbaston against Warwickshire with Hargreave taking six for 81, after Warwickshire had scored 133 with Devey making 48 and Haigh capturing five for 21. The match was abandoned with Warwickshire 114 for five in their second innings. A visit to Oxford saw the University go down by an innings and 106 runs, with Grimshaw (85) and Hirst (169) adding 225 for Yorkshire's fourth wicket before a declaration at 358 for nine. R. G. Barnes with 77 was the only Oxford batsman to have any success as they were dismissed for 168 and 84. At the end of May, Yorkshire were one of four counties unbeaten at the top of the table.

At Stourbridge, Yorkshire beat Worcestershire by nine wickets with H. K. Foster alone defying the bowling of Hirst and Haigh. Rothery with 89 played a sound defensive innings while Rhodes scored 51 to place Yorkshire 113 ahead on the first innings. F. Bowley, with 74, helped Worcestershire to score 185 in their second innings, with Haigh taking six for 48, and Rothery shone with 38 not out as Yorkshire cantered to an easy win. Lancashire, at Bradford, were accounted for inside two days the visitors being bowled out for 67 by Hirst and Haigh. Only Hirst with 58 played Brearley with much confidence as he took six for 66 but Yorkshire gained a lead of 110. Lancashire, with R. H. Spooner (42) and Tyldesley (37), then put on 84 for the second wicket before Haigh with five for 35 caused a further collapse and Lancashire were all for 151, leaving the home side needing 42 to win. They lost four wickets in the process. Haigh's 57 wickets so far had cost him 565 runs at 9.91 each. Hirst had taken 65 wickets for 742 runs at 11.41 each.

Yorkshire's visit to Chesterfield saw Derbyshire defeated by the narrow margin of 33 runs. Good bowling by Warren and Bestwick dismissed Yorkshire on a good wicket for only 130. Derbyshire then gained a useful lead of 39. Yorkshire did better at their second attempt, after losing seven wickets for 138. Hirst and newcomer C. A. Midgley added 40 for the seventh wicket. Midgley batted for 2 hours and 40 minutes also sharing a partnership of 70 for the eighth wicket with Lord Hawke. Derbyshire were soon in trouble at 74 for five but a stand of 52 for the sixth wicket, dominated by E. M. Ashcroft (48), gave them hope before Haigh bowled him, Derbyshire were finally dismissed for 171.

Mr Charles Augustus Midgley, who made his debut for Yorkshire in the above match, was a capable right-hand batsman and medium-fast bowler who made just four appearances for Yorkshire in 1906 and met with success with both bat and ball. Born at Wetherby in 1877 he was a civil engineer by profession and died at Bradford Royal Infirmary in 1942.

Another newcomer to the Yorkshire team in this match was Fairfax ('Fairy') Gill who played in just two matches for Yorkshire in 1906 without much success. A right-handed batsman, it was thought that he could make a county cricketer but he preferred the security of working at the West Riding Registry of Deeds Office in Wakefield, where he lived throughout his life. He scored over 3,500 runs for Ossett and was a cheery, reliable cricketer, liked and respected by all. He died of wounds in 1917 at the General Hospital in Boulogne.

At Sheffield, Hampshire put up a good show after falling to Haigh (six for 31) in the first innings. Yorkshire lost three wickets with two on the board before Tunnicliffe (63) and Hirst (67) added 129 for the fourth wicket. Myers scored 44 as Yorkshire took a lead of 63. In their second innings, Johnston (58) and Mead (47) took Hampshire to 225. Yorkshire were set 165 to win and thanks to an admirable 72 from Denton, got home by three wickets.

Further success came Yorkshire's way at Lord's where Middlesex were thrashed to the tune of 281 runs. Denton scored 127 in his usual brilliant manner. Haigh, cleverly disguising his use of the slower ball, took seven for 46, giving Yorkshire a lead of 120. Deciding to bat again the Champions compiled 255 for five before declaring and setting the home side 424 to win. Middlesex were bundled out for 142, Haigh taking his wicket total to twelve.

At Bradford, Essex lost by nine wickets, Yorkshire now being the only unbeaten team left in the Championship. A draw at Trent Bridge followed, with the bat dominating the ball. Denton scored a century in each innings, the first Yorkshire player to perform this feat. Nottinghamshire began their second innings requiring 270 for victory but they were happy to bat out time. Another draw followed against Kent at Sheffield with honours even. Yorkshire had scored 287, five runs behind on first innings, and on the last day, Kent were happy to bat out time.

Another draw at Leyton followed with Essex scoring 231, thanks to

Rev F. H. Gillingham (89 not out) and F. L. Fane (65). Yorkshire gave a poor batting display and were 84 for nine before Myers and Hunter added 54 for the last wicket. In their second innings, rain having taken 3 or 4 hours out of the match, Essex were able to declare at 204 for seven, P. Perrin scoring 62 and Reeves 39 not out. Yorkshire then lost three quick wickets but Tunnicliffe and Hirst batted out time.

The match with Gloucestershire at Leeds was also drawn, rain washing out the first day's play.

Cecil Harry Parkin made his one appearance for Yorkshire against Gloucestershire when he scored 0 and took two for 23 in the first innings. He had taken 13 wickets for Yorkshire 2nd XI at 14.30 each, taking five for 31 against his native county, Lancashire, at South Shields four days before playing in the first team. After the Gloucestershire match he returned to the second eleven and played at Wath against Durham and at Halifax against Staffordshire, before playing in a 14-a-side match at Headingley. Playing for Hayley's XI he took eight for 67 in the first innings but never appeared for a Yorkshire side again. It was discovered that his birthplace was Eaglescliffe, 100 yards from the Yorkshire border at Yarm, where, it had been incorrectly stated, he was born. A right-hand batsman and fast-medium bowler who could switch to medium-paced off-breaks, he was similar to Sydney Barnes in some ways and was a natural bowler who would have been an asset for Yorkshire had he been able to play for them; his parents were in fact of Yorkshire ancestry. He eventually qualified for Lancashire and played for them from 1914 to 1926, also appearing in ten Test matches.

Yorkshire suffered their first defeat at Dewsbury at the hands of Nottinghamshire who had not beaten Yorkshire since 1896. Nottinghamshire batted first and were dismissed for 74. Yorkshire passed that score with half their wickets down, and went on to 151. In Nottinghamshire's second innings, A. O. Jones scored a brilliant 88 before the side collapsed and were all out for 170, Hirst taking seven for 70. Yorkshire only needed 94 to win but on a pitch that had helped the bowlers throughout, they crashed to 26 for eight and Haigh and Deyes then helped Yorkshire to 68 and defeat by 25 runs. Yorkshire had now dropped to second place behind Surrey.

At Brighton, Sussex totalled 282 with Killick (67), Robert Relf (63) and Cox (63) all amongst the runs. Yorkshire recovered from 29 for 3 to take their score to 357, Hirst scoring 122 as he added 145 for the fifth wicket with T. L. Taylor (69) who was back into the side after 4 years absence. When Sussex batted again six wickets fell for 55 before Killick (114) and H. L. Simms (45) added 81 for the seventh wicket and Sussex reached 194. Yorkshire won fairly comfortably in the end by six wickets, Denton scoring 42.

Easy victories over Derbyshire and Somerset followed and

Yorkshire were now joint top of the table with Surrey, but fell behind their opponents as Surrey defeated Worcestershire, while Yorkshire could only draw at Bradford against Sussex. Only Wilkinson with 67 was anything like his best as Yorkshire scored 212. Killick batted splendidly for Sussex to score 164, putting on 156 for their third wicket with Albert Relf and a further 139 with Robert Relf for the fifth wicket, Sussex gaining a lead of 128 runs. Yorkshire struggled to avoid defeat as they lost six wickets for 134. Lord Hawke (34) and Hunter (34 not out) combined to add 75 for the ninth wicket and Sussex needed 123 to win. Losing three wickets for 8 – all to George Hirst – Sussex finished at the close with 45 for five. Defeat at The Oval followed with Yorkshire very much the second best team, only Tunnicliffe batting at his best with 60 out of his side's 186. Walter Lees took five for 61 against his native county and Knox four for 61. Hayward with 76 and then Hayes (53) and J. N. Crawford (51) soon gave Surrey the upper hand and the home side gained a substantial lead. Yorkshire did better in their second innings with Rhodes (53) and Tunnicliffe (53) putting on 107 for the first wicket but only the reliable Hirst (87) stood up to the fast bowling of Knox who took six for 105 and Surrey won very comfortably.

A remarkable win inside two days was then inflicted on Worcestershire at Hull. Yorkshire, batting first, saw Rudston (50) and Denton (65) put on 97 for the second wicket but they had to settle for 271, Arnold taking five for 15. Yorkshire opened the bowling with Hirst and a newcomer called Sedgwick. Between them they dismissed Worcestershire for 25, Sedgwick having the sensational figures of 9-5-8-5. When they followed on Bowley scored 38, and W. E. C. Hutchings (31) helped Arnold (103 not out) to take Worcestershire to 207 for six, at which point Sedgwick performed the 'hat-trick' and finished with four for 69 as Yorkshire won by an innings and 10 runs.

Herbert ('Bert') Amos Sedgwick , who appeared in this Worcestershire match with one of the most remarkable debuts ever, went on to play against the West Indians at Harrogate and Lancashire at Old Trafford but never played again for Yorkshire. Born at Richmond in 1883, he was a right-arm fast bowler who was professional with Littleborough. In 1909 he went to live at Leek in Staffordshire and was professional with Knypersley in 1914, and used to open the Staffordshire attack with Sydney Barnes. When Barnes moved to Saltaire as professional Sedgwick joined the club at the same time. He was also professional with Walsall in 1926. He became managing director of Sneyd Engineering Co Ltd, in Sneyd Street, Leek. He died in 1957 at the North Staffs Royal Infirmary at Stoke-on-Trent, aged 74. On whether Sedgwick would have made a first-class cricketer for

Yorkshire it is difficult to come to any conclusion. He may have refused any terms offered to him but certainly he was worthy of a longer trial than he received.

Albert ('Alty') Farrar, a right-handed batsman, was educated at St James's School, Brighouse where he was living when he made his only appearance for Yorkshire against Somerset at Fartown in 1906. He showed good form when he played for Yorkshire 2nd XI from 1903 to 1906. He was also a Rugby League player for Rochdale Hornets and at one time kept the Albion Inn at Brighouse. He died in 1954 at Halifax General Hospital.

At Harrogate, the West Indians defeated Yorkshire by 262 runs although the County were without Hirst and Haigh. The visitors compiled 270 with Constantine (79) and Layne (63) adding 117 for the second wicket. Yorkshire were then dismissed for 50, R. Ollivierre taking seven for 23. Instead of enforcing the follow-on, the West Indians batted again to total 305 for six before declaring, P. A. Goodman scoring an unbeaten 102 in 90 minutes, Yorkshire went in requiring 526 to win but collapsed from 252 for four to 263 all out.

Roland Sutcliffe Leather made his only appearance for Yorkshire against the West Indians. A right-handed batsman who was in the Marlborough XI of 1898, he appeared for Oxford University without obtaining his blue. He appeared for the Yorkshire colts from 1900 to 1906 and in 1904 scored 108 against the Nottinghamshire Colts. He lived at Harrogate and played for the town club. He died in 1913 at Heliopolis (Egypt) aged 32.

For Tyldesley's benefit at Old Trafford, Yorkshire, by a steady batting display, scored 291 with Tunnicliffe scoring 82. Lancashire replied with 280 made at a much quicker rate, with Tyldesley (65) and Sharp (84) doing the bulk of the scoring. At the end of the second day, Yorkshire were 77 for five, then overnight rain made the pitch play much easier. Hirst scored 85 and added 64 with Ernest Smith (46) to take Yorkshire to 193. Needing 205 to win, on a pitch that was now drying out, Lancashire were in trouble from the start and were dismissed for 97, Rhodes taking five for 49. Yorkshire had won by 107 runs. Yorkshire were now slightly behind Surrey in the Championship race, Surrey having an additional victory to their name.

A heavy scoring match at Leicester produced a draw, with C. J. B. Wood scoring 148 out of Leicestershire's 425. Tunnicliffe (57) and Rhodes (119) opened with 108 for Yorkshire before Denton (80) joined Rhodes to add a further 164 for the second wicket, the total reaching 483. Leicestershire were 169 for five at the close. Rain prevented a result in the Middlesex game at Leeds, but Hirst and Myers bowled Warwickshire out for 79 and 85 at Harrogate.

Tunnicliffe (62) and Denton (95) put on 138 for Yorkshire's second wicket and Hirst hit hard for 68 before Yorkshire declared at 255 for eight, the victory being by an innings. At Sheffield, Yorkshire gained revenge against Surrey, Yorkshire recovering from 22 for three to 144 all out, due to 47 from the free-scoring Hirst. Holland with 40 took Surrey 10 runs ahead of Yorkshire, but Rhodes with 94 swung the game Yorkshire's way by taking them to 225, leaving Surrey with 216 to win. Only Hobbs and Hayward could do anything with Hirst or Haigh as the home side won by 102 runs and took over at the top of the Championship table.

Charles Henry Hardisty, a shortish right-hand opening bat similar to J. T. Brown in style and stature, first appeared for Yorkshire in 1906 without success but he played a number of useful innings over the next three summers. His fielding let him down. In 1911 he joined the Northumberland Club at Jesmond and stayed in the north-east for over 12 years playing for Consett, Wallsend and Ryton-on-Tyne. Professional at Wallsend in 1921, he later returned to Yorkshire and captained Horsforth CC, also assisting Leeds and Keighley.

Yorkshire had two games in which a single victory and avoidance of defeat in the other game would lead to the retention of the title. The Western tour had arrived and Gloucestershire at Bristol did not excel as they lost six wickets for 54 runs. Then C. O. H. Sewell (24) was joined by F. H. B. Champain (42) – brother of a future Bishop of Knaresborough – and they added 61 for the seventh wicket and Gloucestershire managed to score 164. Yorkshire batted poorly against Dennett who took eight for 86, only Ernest Smith (34) and Haigh (26 not out) making any sort of show, and eventually they were five runs behind on the first innings. Gloucestershire again started badly but recovered from 114 for five to add 52 for the sixth wicket through Jessop and Board, who went on to score a fighting 57. Gloucestershire were bowled out for 228. Requiring 233 for victory, Yorkshire soon lost Tunnicliffe and Denton, but Rhodes (52) and T. L. Taylor (41) put on 59 valuable runs for the third wicket and Rudston (40) and Ernest Smith (39) added 66 for the sixth wicket before Jessop caused Rudston to hit his wicket and bowled Smith. At 200 for seven it was anybody's game and the tension grew as last man Ringrose joined Myers with just eleven needed for victory. The tension had been building up throughout the day – the sort of excitement that only cricket can give. The runs were slowly knocked off until with two required Jessop succeeded in getting Ringrose lbw for 0 to give his side a one run victory. It was a defeat that would live on for Yorkshire as they became 'the team that lost the Championship by one run.'

At Bath Yorkshire compiled 368 against Somerset with George

Hirst scoring 111 while Rhodes (64) and Denton (67) put on 102 for Yorkshire's second wicket. Hirst then took six for 70, bowling Somerset out for 125. Ernest Smith, acting captain in place of Lord Hawke who was ill, went in again and Rhodes (115 not out) and Hirst (117 not out) put on 202 in an hour and a quarter for Hirst to complete his 2,000 runs for the season. As he went on to take eleven wickets in the match, he completed another remarkable feat as the home side were dismissed for 134. Yorkshire then completed the season with a five wickets win over the MCC at Scarborough with Rhodes (109) and Hirst (76 not out) knocking off 287 to win in 165 minutes with six wickets in hand. Myers had scored 85 and Denton 80 in Yorkshire's first innings total of 292.

By any standards Yorkshire had had a good season, only narrowly failing to finish top; an honour that went to Kent for the first time after winning their last 11 matches on the trot. Kent had played exciting cricket all season and it heralded a new age of attacking batting, brilliant spin bowling and the arrival of Frank Woolley.

Hirst with 2,174 runs at an average of 46.25 was again the best batsman in the team and he became the first and only player ever to score 2,000 runs and take 200 wickets in a season. This he performed for Yorkshire alone in first-class matches. Denton scored 1,905 runs at 36.63 and Rhodes 1,618 runs at 31.11, while Tunnicliffe also scored 1,232 runs and held 31 catches – he was now 40 years of age. T. L. Taylor, who played in less than half the matches, was the only other batsman to average 20 and this was one of the weaknesses in the side.

The bowling, like the batting, seemed to be one short for most of the time. Haigh with 161 wickets at 13.63 could not be faulted nor Hirst with 201 at 15.31. Both were magnificent and if Rhodes's 111 wickets did cost 22.87 – bearing in mind his batting ability and the 36 catches that he took, then it would be unkind to criticise him in any way. Yet as an all-rounder, he was certainly second best to George Herbert on all counts. Sedgwick and Deyes were hardly given sufficient opportunity and Ringrose, plagued by injury, retired at the end of the season. His fast bowling was not replaced. Myers went back, taking only 43 wickets at 31.65. The weakness in the Yorkshire side was obvious; the youngsters who had been expected to develop had failed to do so. The senior players were as capable as ever and had done a magnificent job.

The present Yorkshire team have been known to play the occasional benefit match at or near Bray in the county of Berkshire. In 1907 the Yorkshire side began their first-class season with a first-class match against All Ireland at Bray in Ireland and David Denton scored his only century of a very wet season not suited to his batting methods.

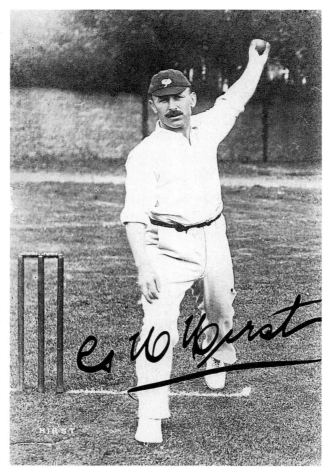

George Hirst, the great all-rounder, and the only man to take 200 wickets and score 2,000 runs in a season.

He made 149 in his usual attractive manner out of 292. G. P. Meldon scored 34 for the home side in their first innings of 102 and, following on, Sir Timothy O'Brien scored 60 not out, but Yorkshire won by an innings. The match at Lord's against MCC was a rain-ruined draw.

Lt Col Harold Swift Kaye, a right-handed batsman, appeared in 13 matches for Yorkshire in 1907 and several in 1908 without meeting with much success. He was in the Harrow eleven in 1899 and 1900 and went up to Sandhurst. Most of his cricket was for Yorkshire Gentlemen, the Household Brigade and Harrow Wanderers; later he became a member of the Yorkshire CCC Committee and was chairman of Marshall, Kaye & Marshall, woollen manufacturers of Ravensthorpe.

Yorkshire started their Championship programme as they had finished the previous season with a western tour playing Somerset and Gloucestershire. S. M. J. Woods with 25 was top scorer as Somerset were dismissed for 110 at Taunton, with Rhodes taking six for 61. Tunnicliffe (66) and Rothery (36) knocked off 50 of those in a first-wicket stand. Yorkshire finally totalled 181. In their second innings only Braund, who carried his bat through the innings for 42, played Rhodes with any real skill and Somerset could only muster 113, Rhodes taking another six wickets. Tunnicliffe was 26 not out as Yorkshire won by nine wickets. At Bristol, Gloucestershire made 145, Hirst taking six for 56. They then bowled out Yorkshire for 126 only Hirst with 46 making much of Dennett, who took six for 65. Yorkshire needed 135 for victory. Three down for 33, Yorkshire would have been in trouble but for Denton (77) who played with perfect judgement for two hours and so won the match for his side by three wickets.

Yorkshire came unstuck at Worcester where Worcestershire batted well to score 292, H. K. Foster scoring 63 and Pearson 65. On a fast wicket Yorkshire, 119 all out, gave a poor account of themselves. H. K. Foster again batted well for 54 when Worcestershire were dismissed for 139, setting Yorkshire 313 to win. Tunnicliffe (53) and Rothery (53 not out) batted well when Yorkshire went in again but only a stand of 82 between Myers (33) and Hunter (37) took Yorkshire to comparative respectability at 258 all out to lose by 54 runs.

At Old Trafford, the second day was lost to the rain and the Lancashire game finished in an even state. The Derbyshire match at Sheffield was abandoned without a ball being bowled and the Hampshire match that followed saw no play until four o'clock on the second day. Llewellyn (98) and Mead (37) took Hampshire to 209, after which Yorkshire were bowled out for 112, with Rhodes top scorer with 25. In their second innings Hampshire were 45 for six at the close. The important game at Trent Bridge against the leaders Nottinghamshire was virtually a wash-out.

Harold Harrison, a noted left-arm slow bowler in league cricket for many years, played in two games for Yorkshire in 1906. He began his career as a Horsforth schoolboy before joining Yeadon CC and he was discovered by Hubert Myers and coached by Harry Hayley. Around 1905 he took 100 wickets for Yeadon Albion at 2 runs apiece and he played with Yeadon in 1907 moving to Dewsbury in 1908–10. He was engaged by Rawtenstall, Enfield and then Laisterdyke. He lost his left eye during the First World War, but continued his cricket with Farsley from 1918 to 1920 and once took all ten wickets for Haslingden against Burnley. His last engagement was with Ayr in 1935 when he was 51 as groundsman and professional – before that there had been 11 years with Yeadon Green Lane as coach and groundsman.

The bad weather continued when Kent visited Headingley. Hirst (53) and Denton (45) took Yorkshire to a score of 150 but for Kent only J. R. Mason (25) and Woolley (18) could reach double figures as Haigh took six for 36. Yorkshire were 65 for four when the game was finally abandoned, the last day being washed out altogether. The Surrey match at Bradford was the same with no play on the last day. At Lord's there was even less progress as Middlesex scored 244 with P. F. Warner batting well for 84 as Haigh and Rhodes took five wickets each. Denton with 48 made top score in Yorkshire's total of 163 as Tarrant took five for 66 but Middlesex were only 57 for two when the match was abandoned.

At Hove, Sussex, with C. B. Fry (85) and Albert Relf (55) putting on 125 for the third wicket, finally totalled 223. Then Yorkshire were put out for 181, with Denton top scoring with 39. Sussex lost four quick wickets for 17 and were finally out for 110, leaving Yorkshire with 153 to win. In helpful conditions, Yorkshire fell to George Cox, his skilful left-arm slows taking six for 39 as Yorkshire were bowled out for 87.

At Dewsbury, Essex (142 and 109) were dismissed by Hirst with match figures of nine for 102. Yorkshire, with Myers scoring 37 and Hirst 39, were bowled out for 160 and, needing 92 to win, won by five wickets. Somerset were no match for Yorkshire at Leeds where there was no play on the first day. Hirst and Haigh shared the wickets when Somerset were dismissed for 93 and with Rhodes (40) and Denton (81) adding 123 for Yorkshire's 2nd wicket, the home side reached 260 for seven before declaring. Grimshaw with 46 and Myers 50 both attacked the bowling in order to make up lost time. Somerset, after an opening stand of 83 by L. C. H. Palairet (47) and Braund (34), were dismissed for 122.

Yorkshire scored 515 against Leicestershire with every member of the side scoring at least 22. On an easy-paced wicket Leicestershire replied with 249, but following on they fought back to 270 for seven by the close after being 137 for four. Coe with 72 not out and V. F. S. Crawford with 84 helped the home side to gain an honourable draw with Yorkshire dropping several catches.

What should have been a vital Championship match – against Nottinghamshire at Huddersfield – was abandoned without a ball being bowled, but at Leyton, Yorkshire returned to winning ways as Essex were dismissed for 69. Yorkshire soon went ahead, Denton, Hirst and Lord Hawke all making runs. Yorkshire's insertion of Essex had been successful and Essex were bowled out for 209 in the second innings with Rhodes and Haigh each taking four wickets.

William Ederick ('Eddie') Bates was a son of Billy Bates, the former Yorkshire and England all-rounder, and first played for Yorkshire against Essex and maintained his place in the side for the rest of the season, averaging 16 and showing some promise as a steady and sound batsman. In the following season, he kept his place throughout without doing anything of note, and was given further chances in the next few seasons before dropping out of the side in 1913. Here again Yorkshire had shown faith in one of their youngsters, but like so many others at this time, he failed to make the grade. One can only assume that the wrong choice was made. He had lived at Dalton as a young man but was allocated to Harrogate, later playing for Barnsley and Dewsbury before moving to Briton Ferry as professional in 1914. Here he qualified for Glamorgan after the war, and played for that county from their initial appearance in the Championship in 1921 until he retired in 1931. In 1908/09 he played soccer for Leeds City in 12 league matches and was the father of Eddie Bates, the Southampton inside-forward and later manager of the club.

The South Africans won a low-scoring game at Bradford with the highest scorer of the game being J. H. Sinclair with 37. He was in at the finish as the tourists won by five wickets. At Harrogate, Dennett took five for 77 for Gloucestershire and a fine display of hard hitting from C. L. Townsend with 61 saw the visitors lead by three runs. Yorkshire, after losing six wickets for 99, had a stand of 64 between Myers (63) and young Bates (71) to thank for their side reaching 236 in the second innings. Set 234 to win, Gloucestershire made a commendable effort through G. L. Jessop, whose innings of 89 was made in 45 minutes, but after being 158 for four they collapsed to 195 all out.

At Bramall Lane, Warwickshire had Kinneir to thank for reaching 107 as Haigh was quite unplayable with six for 27, which he followed up with seven for 13 on a rain-affected wicket that was not quite so difficult as the poor batting suggested. Yorkshire were 31 for six at one stage of their first innings before Rhodes (20) and Bates (38) and a very timely 29 not out from veteran David Hunter took them to 140. Santall took eight for 72 but Yorkshire won easily by ten wickets after putting the visitors out for 47. At Glossop, Derbyshire fared even worse with scores of 44 and 72, with Hirst taking eleven for 44 in the match and Wilfred Rhodes eight for 71. Yorkshire totalled 246 to gain an easy innings win with 130 runs to spare. Yorkshire's run of successes had taken them from the unfamiliar middle of the table up to second place in the Championship.

Leicestershire, at Hull, were dismissed for 60 and 54, with Hirst taking 15 wickets for only 63 runs and performing the hat-trick in the second innings. He took full advantage of a lively pitch. When Yorkshire batted Odell took eight for 40 with Bates making top score of 33 out of 114, and Yorkshire won by ten wickets. They followed that up with a nine wicket win over Lancashire at Headingley in a match which was played for the benefit of David Denton. Nearly 50,000 witnessed a fascinating game with Lancashire starting well with 92 for three on the board at lunch. R. H. Spooner made 32 and A. H. Hornby went on to score 55 but Rhodes (six for 71) and Hirst (four for 50) went through the rest of the side and Lancashire had scored 136. Yorkshire then lost five wickets for 39 before Rhodes with 69 and Wilkinson (43) pulled the game round, and they took a lead of 47 on the first innings. Lancashire were going well at 145 for four but H. D. Stanning was out for 42 and Hornby run out for 46 and they were dismissed for 179. Yorkshire made light work of scoring 133 to win by nine wickets. This was F. S. Jackson's last game for Yorkshire.

A draw at Edgbaston followed, with Warwickshire batting consistently well to score 343 and yet nobody reached 50! Tunnicliffe then batted for $4\frac{1}{4}$ hours for 141, taking part in a 77 opening stand with Rothery (40) and a second wicket partnership of 119 with Denton (58), and Yorkshire gained a first-innings lead of 64. Warwickshire were never in any danger of defeat and they declared at 260 for four, leaving Yorkshire an impossible task.

On a difficult Bramall Lane pitch, Middlesex struggled after P. F. Warner was Yorkshire's second victim for 42 with 90 on the board. Myers had one of his best days for Yorkshire and took six for 35, Middlesex being dismissed for 173, and by the close of play Tunnicliffe with a not out half century had taken Yorkshire to 134 for four. Next morning Tunnicliffe went on to score 75 and Rhodes hit brilliantly to score 66 and give Yorkshire a lead of 75. Hirst, making the ball swerve in a helpful cross-wind, was in top form and took nine for 45 as Middlesex were bowled out for 91. Yorkshire won by seven wickets.

The match with Surrey at The Oval was drawn with Surrey recovering from 140 for seven to score 294, with Walter Lees scoring 77 when Yorkshire were hampered by a wet ball. In reply only Hirst with 49 not out batted well as Lees and May took three wickets each to gain their side a lead of 132 on the first innings. Surrey then declared at 206 for five, Yorkshire being left with 255 minutes to obtain 339 to win. With two wickets down for 34, Tunnicliffe and Hirst were content to play out time.

One of the most remarkable games of the season was the return with Worcestershire at Bradford. On the first day, lacking Hirst and Rhodes on Test match duty and Haigh ill, Yorkshire could not take advantage of the conditions as Worcestershire scored 155. G. N. Foster with 51 and Pearson (42) put on 73 for the third wicket. Newstead took four for 62 and Wilkinson three for 36, but neither performed as the absent star bowlers would have done and Grimshaw and newcomer Atkinson failed to take a wicket. Against Arnold and Cuffe Yorkshire were bowled out for 62. When Worcestershire batted again on a pitch that was still lifting and turning, Newstead was quite unplayable as his analysis proves: 8.2-4-10-7. Worcestershire were bowled out for 28. Yorkshire needed 132 to win and at the close of the second day they had scored 52 for three. On the last day Wilkinson went on to score 32 but the rest were soon dismissed for 91, with Cuffe taking nine for 38 to earn Worcestershire their first-ever double over Yorkshire.

Harry Atkinson, who made his single appearance for Yorkshire in the above match, came from Sculcoates and died in 1959 aged 78.

A draw at Canterbury followed with Tunnicliffe scoring 45 out of Yorkshire's 147, a score Kent passed with only four wickets down. Seymour (52) and S. H. Day (51) were Kent's leading run-getters but on their dismissal Kent lost their last six wickets for 20 runs. After rain overnight Kent had 2¾ hours left to bat in on a drying pitch but they survived by good defensive play.

Sussex at Brighton gave Yorkshire a good game but Hirst proved his all-round abilities at Hove by bowling Sussex out for 186, taking five for 44. Killick with 68 was the only Sussex batsman to shine. Yorkshire lost four wickets for 86 but Hirst with 51 helped Bates (69) to take Yorkshire to a total of 273. When Sussex batted again they were all out for 215, leaving Yorkshire needing 129 to win. Four wickets were lost before George Hirst took his county to a five wicket victory.

In the last match of their southern tour, Yorkshire visited Bournemouth, where the home side treated the crowd to some festive batting after losing four cheap wickets. Captain White (73) and Stone added 149 for the fifth wicket and then Badcock (61) and Langford (43) put on a further 74 for the ninth wicket; Hampshire totalled 361. Tunnicliffe (51) and Wilkinson (74) put on 104 for Yorkshire's third wicket after two early wickets had been lost and Myers hit 41 at the end of the innings as Yorkshire were all out for 301. Hampshire then hit some quick runs with Mead (58) and Bowell (66) leading off with 109, while Captain White scored another 50. When they declared Hampshire had 221 for eight on the board. Yorkshire were set 282 in 160 minutes, and after losing four wickets for 75, Lord Hawke and Denton saved the match without difficulty.

Yorkshire's final match was at Scarborough where the MCC sprang a surprise to beat Yorkshire by 44 runs, but Yorkshire's position of equal second behind Nottinghamshire was a satisfactory summing up of the team's progress. In a very wet season, Hirst topped the batting averages with 1,167 runs at 31.54, just ahead of Tunnicliffe with 1,195 runs at 27.15, with Denton in third place with 25.63.

Rhodes scored 954 runs, but if those figures were comparatively disappointing the performances of Wilkinson, Rothery and Myers, as well as Bates in his first season, did give promise for the future.

On the bowling side, Haigh headed the bowling averages with 96 wickets at 12.31 which gave him second place in the first-class averages – an excellent performance particularly as he missed several games due to illness or injury. Newstead took 24 wickets at 12.91 and gave hope for the future but the brunt of the bowling was done by Hirst with 169 wickets at 14.44 and Rhodes who showed a great improvement on pitches that suited him with 164 wickets at 15.77. Deyes looked a useful fast bowler at times but Myers seemed to slip back even further on the soft pitches that did not suit him: 25 at 27.88 are not the figures expected from a Yorkshire bowler. Lord Hawke had now completed 25 years as captain of the Yorkshire side and on 14 July 1908 a valuable testimonial was presented to his Lordship, contributed by Yorkshire admirers from all walks of life both inside and outside the County.

The main change in the Yorkshire side in 1908 would be the absence of John Tunnicliffe who had retired after a first-rate career in which he had given solid service as an opening batsman and senior professional and as a slip fielder where he was unrivalled. The new season began with Yorkshire's first ever visit to Northampton. It was a remarkable game of cricket, Yorkshire scoring 356 for eight before declaring, but with rain falling, Northamptonshire could not start batting until 2.30 on the second day. Caught on a drying pitch they were dismissed in sensational fashion for 27 and 15, with Hirst taking twelve for 19 in 20.1 overs. By 5.40 the game had been completed with Yorkshire winning by an innings and 314 runs.

The MCC at Lord's and Cambridge at Fenner's did not suffer quite so badly but both matches resulted in innings victories for the County. At Bradford, Kent were dismissed for 77 and 46 with Haigh taking seven for 47 in the match while four Kent players ran themselves out. Only C. H. B. Marsham reached 20 in any one innings. Rhodes with 45 batted well for two hours as Yorkshire reached 101 and Yorkshire went on to win by nine wickets.

Essex at Leyton managed to draw with Yorkshire, compiling 226 and 226 for nine declared while Yorkshire were dismissed for 188 and were left with 265 to obtain for victory in just over three hours. They managed 210 for four. Back at Leeds, Hayes, with 58 out of 90, was the only batsman to play Haigh well as he captured six for 13 but Yorkshire only gained a lead of 23. Surrey did even worse at their second attempt as Hirst took six for 23. Yorkshire obtained victory by seven wickets.

Derbyshire at Chesterfield were defeated by 196 runs but they had performed better than most of Yorkshire's opponents. Yorkshire had three down for 14 before Wilkinson (56) and Hirst (58) put on 103 for the fourth wicket yet they were all out for 190. After L. G. Wright and Needham had an opening stand of 37, Derbyshire were dismissed for 102. When Yorkshire batted again, Rothery made 51, Denton 40 and Bates 41, but it was Hirst who took the main honours by scoring an unbeaten 128, a very fine innings that took three hours. Derbyshire were set 441 to win and made a valiant attempt to save the game. They reached 188 for four, then the remaining batsmen failed and Yorkshire won by 196 runs. After seven games played in the month of May, Haigh had taken 57 wickets at 7.26 and Hirst 44 wickets at 11.09, and Rhodes and Newstead had 13 wickets each.

Yorkshire made slow progress against Santall and Company at Edgbaston, batting for the whole of the first day for 278 for six – the total finally reached 339. Rain then interrupted play as Warwickshire were dismissed for 121, but following on, the midland county had little difficulty in saving the game after three wickets had gone for 39.

At Worcester, Yorkshire were intent on revenge after their beatings from Worcestershire in the previous season. Batting first, W. Rhodes made 39 but no one else batted well against Cuffe, who took five for 63, and Yorkshire were bowled out for 130. Worcestershire struggled in turn and lost their last five wickets for only 25 runs but they had built a lead of 67 runs. In their second innings Yorkshire soon had two down with only 19 on the board but Denton with 53 and Wilkinson (59) added 64 and other useful contributions took the Yorkshire score to 228. Worcestershire bowled well on a good pitch and it was thought that they would have a fair chance of scoring the 162 required for victory. They reckoned without the excellence of George Hirst's bowling, collapsing to 92 all out; Hirst took six for 34.

Lancashire's visit to Sheffield proved far from satisfactory for the Red Rose county who were well beaten by 193 runs in a little over two days' play. Leicestershire were thrashed by Yorkshire by an innings and 321 runs but the home side were unfortunate to be caught on a sticky wicket after Yorkshire had scored 389 for seven on the first day. Rhodes (50) and Hardisty (84) gave Yorkshire a good start with an opening stand of 93 and then Denton added 40 before Wilkinson (99) and Hirst (89) put on 146 for the fourth wicket. Wilkinson batted for four hours for his innings and on the following day Yorkshire were dismissed for 437. On the drying pitch, Rhodes was quite unplayable and took eight for 37 and Newstead ten for 29 as Leicestershire were dismissed twice for 58.

At Fartown, Northamptonshire were bowled out for 196 with Thompson scoring 87, putting on 86 for the last wicket with L. T. Driffield. When Yorkshire batted, Rhodes scored 140 in

$4\frac{1}{4}$ hours, with Denton (55) helping him to add 91 for the second wicket. Rothery with 36, Newstead (41) and Hunter (20 not out) helped Yorkshire to 347, but rain washed out the third day. At Lord's, Middlesex, hitherto unbeaten, were 57 for one after winning the toss but they were bowled out for 130, with only J. H. Hunt, who hit hard for 36, giving the score some respectability. Yorkshire lost four wickets for 47 on a bowler's wicket. Hirst, batting as only he could in adverse conditions, scored 50 and Yorkshire led by 27 on the first innings, Tarrant bowling well to take six for 59. P. F. Warner held the Middlesex second innings together but they lost seven wickets for 84 before Trott (24) helped Warner in a stand of 48. Warner was last man out for 76, Middlesex obtaining 153. Hirst was again Yorkshire's hero with six for 54. Requiring 127, Rhodes (40) and Hardisty (31) soon put 61 on the board and with Newstead hitting 29, Yorkshire won through by three wickets, with Trott taking five for 34 and nearly snatching victory as a crucial catch went begging.

Yorkshire were now in front of the field and Warwickshire's visit to Bradford was hardly likely to cause any consternation to Yorkshire followers. Warwickshire won the toss, but the Yorkshire fielding and catching on this particular day was below their usual standard, with the result that Warwickshire compiled a formidable 294. Yorkshire then batted in a similar manner to their fielders and were in real trouble at 112 for six, Denton scoring 35, before Rothery (58) was joined by the reliable Newstead (52) and took the score to 239. In their second innings Warwickshire were up against it, only Quaife (45) and Santall (38) batting with much confidence, as they were dismissed for 159. Yorkshire, needing 215 to win, lost wickets with regularity until they were 127 for six, but Denton played an admirable innings of 95 and then found a good partner in Myers; they added 74 and Yorkshire finally won by three wickets.

Yorkshire began badly at Trent Bridge losing five wickets for 35. Rothery and Denton took the score to 108 and with Newstead also scoring 29 Yorkshire finally totalled 179. Nottinghamshire managed to pass that score by 28 runs, Hardstaff making 81 in four hours on a perfect batting surface. Newstead in a fine spell of bowling took seven for 68 in 42.1 overs. He was again Yorkshire's hero when he came in at 220 for six in Yorkshire's second innings. After some initial luck he hit out brilliantly to score 100 not out, adding 154 with Hirst. Hunter, who was captain of Yorkshire in Lord Hawke's absence, certainly delayed his declaration too long in order that Newstead could complete his century, and he did not allow his bowlers time enough to dismiss Nottinghamshire, who finished a tedious day's play with 66 for four.

Somerset went down by nine wickets at Dewsbury. They began

badly by losing six for 52 before J. Daniell (42) and P. D. Banks (30) took the score to 113. In reply to Somerset's 160, Yorkshire were struggling too at 144 for eight, in spite of 53 from Denton, but Hirst with 58 and good support from Bates and Lord Hawke took Yorkshire to 240. Somerset gave a poor batting display as they were dismissed for 132. Denton then guided Yorkshire to a nine wicket victory.

At Dover, Yorkshire met Kent, a side at the peak of its form, having been unbeaten since their visit to Bradford. Rhodes (40) and Denton (47) added 72 for Yorkshire's second wicket and when Rothery came in Yorkshire were 117 for four. The latter then played the highest innings of his career (161), which was an admirable innings by any standards, and with Lord Hawke (43) helping him in a stand of 90, Yorkshire reached 401 early on the second day. Hardinge helped C. H. B. Marsham to put on 64 for the first Kent wicket but four were down for 92 before Woolley (43) and J. R. Mason (40) added 88 for the fifth wicket and Kent went on to score 242. Instead of enforcing the follow-on Yorkshire batted again and when rain finished the match in the middle of the afternoon, Yorkshire were 90 for three. Another draw took place at Fartown where Sussex totalled 290, George Cox scoring 51. In between showers of rain, Yorkshire replied with 164, with Rhodes making 53 and Wilkinson 44; the match was abandoned at lunch on the third day.

At Headingley, Wass with seven for 93 bowled Yorkshire out for 189, only Denton (50) and Wilkinson (45) showing much resistance although Wilkinson remained at the crease a long time. The pitch then became affected by the rain and Hirst, with seven for 51, dismissed Nottinghamshire for 113. In their second innings Denton (36) and Wilkinson (26) hit up 53 in half an hour as Yorkshire scored 132 at around a run a minute. Set 209 to win, Nottinghamshire had no chance on a now treacherous pitch, Hirst and Rhodes taking the home side to a 140 run victory. The Essex match at Hull saw the visitors score 42 for three but there was no further play after lunch on the first day.

At Sheffield, M. G. Salter with 52 was the only Gloucestershire batsman to reach thirty as the visitors were dismissed for 153 and 92, with Hirst taking eight for 70. This was Haigh's first effort at bowling since he had broken his finger and he showed he had lost little of his effectiveness by taking five for 19 in the Essex second innings. With the bat Rhodes scored 95 for Yorkshire as he put on 141 for the third wicket with Wilkinson (86), and a last wicket stand between Newstead (44) and Lord Hawke (50) added 87, as Yorkshire reached 340. The next match at Harrogate against Leicestershire was abandoned owing to rain in the middle of the last day. Rhodes with 122 batted well for Yorkshire, who scored 325 with Hirst (72) helping

Rhodes to add 102 for the fourth wicket. Leicestershire made a good reply in scoring 309 but they took a lot longer than Yorkshire to score their runs.

At Headingley, Derbyshire were dismissed for 127 with Newstead bowling very well and taking six for 43 in 36 overs, but Derbyshire batted for $3\frac{3}{4}$ hours for their modest total. Yorkshire then compiled 394 for eight before declaring, with B. B. Wilson, who was dropped three times, scoring 109 and adding 109 with Newstead (56) for the sixth wicket. Denton (59) and Wilkinson (79) had laid the foundations for Yorkshire's big total. When Derbyshire batted again, they soon tumbled to defeat.

Moving on to Old Trafford, Denton with 63 and Wilkinson (43) were again amongst the runs but Hirst (46 not out) was left stranded as the tail failed to wag in a total of 206. Lancashire, apart from a stand of 60 between Poidevin (35) and Sharp (33), were always second-best as they were dismissed for 144. Runs came even quicker in Yorkshire's second innings with Rhodes (39) and Hardisty (31) starting with a stand of 75. Denton hit brilliantly for 51 and Rothery scored 48 as Yorkshire reached 243 to set the home side 306 to win. R. H. Spooner did make 33 but the match was all over early on the last day with Lancashire out for 115. Newstead took five for 44 and Hirst four for 60. The experiment of starting the match on the Saturday was a huge success, with 35,000 watching the first two days.

The Middlesex game at Park Avenue swung first one way then the other before being drawn with Yorkshire needing 37 runs to win with two wickets left.

At The Oval Hirst (five for 58) and Newstead (five for 44) bowled Surrey out for 117 on a pitch that gave them some help. Yorkshire also struggled as the wicket became more lively, but Rhodes (33) and Hirst (32) helped them to a lead of 45 runs. Surrey had Marshal to thank for his 70 as once again the Surrey batsmen found Newstead difficult to play. He took five for 48. Yorkshire then knocked off the required total for victory on a pitch that had become easier. Gloom and fog accompanied by bad light caused a draw at Sheffield, where 24 for one was Worcestershire's reply to Yorkshire's 378, in which Rhodes scored 146 in 4 hours 35 minutes, Hirst (65) helping him to put on 156 in a fourth wicket stand.

Yorkshire outplayed Gloucestershire at Cheltenham; the home side could only reach 83 in reply to Yorkshire's 219 and Yorkshire batted consistently in their second innings to leave Gloucestershire with 359 to win. Once more Newstead was Yorkshire's hero as he took seven for 66 and Yorkshire proved victorious by 182 runs. Yorkshire's last two matches were drawn. At Taunton, where Somerset needed a further 286 to win with three wickets down for 64, Hirst took seven for 48 in the match. For Yorkshire Wilkinson, Denton and Rhodes had all scored fifties. W. T. Greswell had taken seven for 67 in the first innings of 210 and Robson five for 44 as Yorkshire made 240 for six in the second. Haigh bowled Sussex out at Hove for 105 and Yorkshire had taken the lead with three wickets down when the match was abandoned.

There was no disputing that Yorkshire earned the title by their overall superiority; they won 16 and drew 12 of their 28 matches and were also unbeaten in their extra matches. The three played in August onwards were a game in Dublin against All Ireland, the MCC match at Scarborough which was spoilt by rain, and the final match at The Oval against the Rest of England, when rain plus high scoring caused another draw.

David Denton finished on top of the batting averages with 1,852 runs at 41.15, slightly ahead of the reliable Hirst who scored 1,513 runs at 39.81. Rhodes also did well and had an average of over 32 for 1,574 runs, and Wilkinson had his best season with the Club to score 1,282 runs at 28.48. Hardisty made a welcome advance to score 733 runs and Newstead in his casual attacking vein showed that he had the capabilities to make a top-class all-rounder. Myers scored 537 runs at 19.88 but could not be classed as a batsman, while Rothery had a disappointing record and Bates did not improve as was hoped. Lord Hawke and Hunter both played valuable innings at times but Haigh had a poor time with the bat.

The County Champions of 1908. Back row: Newstead, Rothery, Mr Hoyland, Denton, Wilkinson, Bates. Seated: Hunter, Hirst, Lord Hawke (captain), Haigh, Rhodes. Front: Myers, Grimshaw.

Haigh topped the bowling averages with 93 wickets at 12.17, while Hirst took 164 at 13.65, figures which may be inferior to his 1906 record but in fact have rarely been equalled in first-class cricket. Rhodes took 100 wickets at 15.82 and Newstead 131 wickets at 15.94. Myers was the only other bowler to reach double figures in wickets, and his total of ten at 40.90 meant that he was no longer much use to Yorkshire as a bowler. The find of the season was undoubtedly Newstead, who became one of *Wisden's* 'Five Cricketers of the Year' and filled one if not two gaps in the Yorkshire side. Haigh and Hirst were first and second in the first-class averages, with Rhodes and Newstead both in the top six.

Three other players including Sir Archibald White made their debuts for the County in 1908. One was Haworth Watson, a right-handed batsman and wicket-keeper, who appeared for Yorkshire from 1908 to 1914 and proved himself a capable deputy to Hunter and rival to Dolphin. He was born at Barnoldswick in 1880 (although 1884 was given as his date of birth for many years – until long after his death) generally living in his native town. He was a newsagent in Skipton from about 1909 and was a member of the Skipton side that won the Yorkshire Council Championship in 1908. After leaving Skipton he was for some years a steward at the Broughton Road Bowling Club. When Hunter retired it was a toss-up whether Dolphin or Watson would get the wicket-keeping job. Watson died at his home in Doncaster in 1951.

Major William Booth made two appearances for Yorkshire in 1908. He started to play regularly for the County in 1910 and soon developed into one of the best all-rounders in the country, representing England in two Test matches. He was born at Pudsey in 1886 and was educated at Fulneck School, later playing for Pudsey St Lawrence as well as attending St Lawrence's church. He qualified as an electrician and was engaged at a large colliery, living at Wath-on-Dearne. He became captain of Wath Athletic Club in the Mexborough League. A right-hand batsman with a good off drive and cut, he usually scored quickly and steadily improved up to the war. He was best known as a tireless medium-fast bowler with a free, high action with late swing, a good off-break, and nip of the pitch. He played for Yorkshire 2nd XI from 1907. When war was declared he enlisted as a private with Leeds Pals (15th W Yorks Regt) and in 1915 became a second lieutenant, earning his commission the hard way. He was killed on 1 July 1916 near La Cigny (Lens) aged 29, in the same operation in which Roy Kilner was injured. He was best man at Roy Kilner's wedding and Kilner named one of his sons after him. At Pudsey, Booth lived near the Britannia Inn along with a brother and sister, the sister still keeping his room just as it had been some fifty years after his death.

The new season of 1909 – it proved to be a wet one – opened at Derby where Yorkshire gained a comfortable victory by an innings and 127 runs. Denton began the season well with 97 and Hirst (80) and Bates (81) followed by Myers (48 not out) all showed good form. Needham with 39 showed resistance to the Yorkshire attack but Newstead finished with four for 32. Morton with 52 took Derbyshire to 142 in the second innings as Newstead took four for 43. This win was followed by the visit of Northamptonshire to Hull where Yorkshire, batting first, spent the whole of the first day scoring 339 for eight. Hirst made 140 in a fine innings but it was the only hundred he would make during the season. Next day Yorkshire were all out for 363, but it was felt that a bigger effort should have been made to force the pace. Northamptonshire replied with 253, Thompson batting well to make 77 not out after he had taken seven for 98 in Yorkshire's innings. The run rate was so slow that there was no hope of a definite result.

At Bath Yorkshire again disappointed as Somerset made scores of 286 and 243 declared. Rhodes took six for 109 in Somerset's first innings but the bowling appeared to have lost its edge. There was little wrong with the Yorkshire batting as Denton (72), Hirst (66), Myers (91) and Newstead (42) took Yorkshire to a first innings lead of 82. After Somerset's declaration there was no other result than a draw possible.

The Western tour continued at Worcester where the home side provided another shock to the Champions, who seemed to have the game well in hand. Worcestershire scored 203 with Arnold (51) in form after Bowley and Pearson (44) had opened with a stand of 58. Yorkshire, with two down for 19, recovered well with Denton (53) and Wilson (39) putting on 79 for the third wicket and then Hirst (37) and Rothery (36) put Yorkshire almost level. Then Radcliffe and Haigh combined to take Yorkshire up to 254 and a further stand put Yorkshire 86 in front on the first innings. H. K. Foster and Arnold put Worcestershire in a strong position at 201 for four, then Hirst and Newstead brought Yorkshire back into the game as Worcestershire collapsed to 231 all out. Yorkshire needed 146 to win but Cuffe and Arnold bowled with such effect that Yorkshire had seven wickets down for 54. Newstead and Radcliffe rallied the cause with a partnership of 63, before a fine catch by Foster ended Yorkshire's hopes and they went down by 12 runs.

Sir Everard Joseph Reginald Henry Radcliffe was a forcing right-hand batsman who was educated at Downside and Christ Church,

Oxford and had three seasons with Yorkshire from 1909 to 1911. He was officially captain in 1911 but had led the side often in the two previous summers. He was never up to county standard as a player, but occasionally made some useful runs late in the innings. The Radcliffe family had lived at Rudding Park, near Knaresborough since 1824 where they remained until 1972, when the main residence was sold. Sir Everard died in 1969 aged 85 at St Trinian's Hall, Richmond having lived there for something like 20 years or more. He was a stockbroker in Newcastle-upon-Tyne at one time.

Yorkshire returned to winning ways over Essex at Leeds with Rhodes making 114 on a wicket helpful to bowlers and scoring his first 50 in an hour. Yorkshire scored 292. Haigh was unplayable, taking seven for 32, as Essex were dismissed for 90, with only F. H. Gillingham (40) and F. L. Fane, who carried his bat through the innings for 25 not out, being able to play him at all. Following on, Essex were dismissed for 114 with Hirst taking six for 43.

The visit to Northampton provided a comfortable win by eight wickets. Northamptonshire, lacking their best player Thompson, won the toss and gave a quite lamentable display as Hirst, Newstead and Haigh bowled them out for 138 on a good wicket. Only a last wicket stand between R. F. Knight (43) and Buswell (23 not out) earned them any respectability. Yorkshire had no difficulty in gaining a lead of 115 with East taking five for 66. Smith (85 not out) showed his talent as Northamptonshire, having lost five for 69, recovered to score 227. Rhodes and Rothery took Yorkshire to victory by eight wickets. Somerset's visit to Bradford saw a solid batting display from Yorkshire who scored 345 for nine declared with Rhodes (48) and Wilson (44) putting on 85 for the first wicket and Hirst (46) and Bates (44) taking Yorkshire to a good position. A wash-out on the second day and further rain saw the game abandoned with Somerset 21 for one in reply.

On a bowler's wicket at Old Trafford, Yorkshire were fortunate to have first innings but Walter Brearley bowled brilliantly, taking nine for 80, only Denton (48) and Hirst (21) playing him with any sort of confidence. With Yorkshire all out for 133 on a good pitch, rain then caused the pitch to cut up badly. A. Hartley with 31 was the only Lancashire batsman to reach 20. Haigh, in deadly form, took seven for 25 and Hirst three for 34; Lancashire were tumbled out for 89. Missed chances did not aid Lancashire's cause when Yorkshire batted again, but the visitors were all out for 78, with Huddleston having the remarkable analysis of 23.2-12-24-8, his off-breaks turning and lifting in an alarming manner. When Lancashire batted they were soon six down for 5. A stand of 22 between Heap and A. H. Hornby improved matters, but the end soon came with Lancashire all out 57. Hirst took six for 23. At this stage of the season Yorkshire, Surrey and Lancashire were in joint fourth position with the three southern counties, Middlesex, Kent and Sussex all unbeaten.

Prior to the Lancashire match, Yorkshire had lost to Cambridge University at Fenner's by six wickets. This proved to be Lewis Linaker's only match for Yorkshire. A right-handed batsman and left-arm medium-fast bowler, he was born at Paddock, Huddersfield in 1885, where he always lived, and played for Primrose Hill for many years. He died in his native town in 1961.

A draw on an easy Edgbaston wicket was inevitable after Warwickshire had taken 148.5 overs to obtain 376 in reply to Yorkshire's 500. Wilson (102) and Denton (140) put on 175 for Yorkshire's second wicket after Rhodes (45) had shared an opening stand of 90 with Wilson. For the home side, Kinneir (52) and Charlesworth (51) put on 96 for Warwickshire's first wicket and then Baker (74) and Willie Quaife (80) shared a stand of 139 for the third wicket. Rhodes bowled well to take seven for 83. Bad light stopped play before rain brought an abandonment with Yorkshire 89 for two in their second innings.

At Fartown, Yorkshire put Kent in to bat on what should have been a sticky wicket, but Kent survived the period until lunch when they were 119 for four. Seymour (62), A. P. Day (56), Hardinge (55), the last two putting on 100 for Kent's sixth wicket, and Huish, who played a vigorous innings of 46 helped Kent to 319. Radcliffe was blamed for putting Kent in, but another line of thought stated that the Yorkshire bowlers were out of sorts, otherwise they would have dismissed Kent much more cheaply. Yorkshire lost five quick wickets for only nine runs and the rest of the side only managed to bring the score to 69, with Fielder, bowling magnificently, taking six for 36. In Yorkshire's second innings, three wickets were down for 61 before Rhodes (101) and Hirst (61) added 149 for the fourth wicket, then three more wickets fell to make Yorkshire 219 for six. Bates and Newstead put on 51 and Haigh made a useful 23 not out to bring Yorkshire to 364, which meant that Kent needed 115 to win. Humphreys, with 59 not out, made that an easy task for Kent.

At Lord's, Hendren scored 71 out of the Middlesex total of 161 and Yorkshire had replied with 112 for four when the game was abandoned. Sussex were Yorkshire's next opponents at Sheffield and the home side, without Haigh, Hirst and Rhodes, batted first to score 489. Wilson (116) and Rothery (83) opened with a stand of 128 before Rothery's attractive innings came to an end. Wilkinson (103) and Bates (60) added a further 90 for the fourth wicket. When Sussex batted, Vine (44) and Cox (56 not out), Leach (39) and C. L. A. Smith (47) took Sussex to a score of 303. It did not prevent Sussex following on but bad light stopped play when Sussex were 91 for two. The result was another draw. Middlesex were now the only unbeaten team in the Championship.

Arthur Broadbent was born at Armley in 1879 and was a right-hand bat and medium-fast bowler who played for Yorkshire in three matches in 1909 and 1910. His three seasons for Yorkshire 2nd XI from 1908 were very successful and in his last year took 100 wickets at 13.20. He lived at New Wortley in his younger days but was engaged at Uddingston in Scotland in 1908 and 1909 taking 108 wickets at 7.53 in the former year. He played for Scotland from 1907 to 1912 and became a publican in Aberdeen where he died in 1958.

Yorkshire were back at full strength at Dewsbury for the meeting with Leicestershire. Wilson scored yet another century (109) and with Denton (129) put on 170 for the second wicket. Hirst dashed to 52 and the tail took Yorkshire to 410. Leicestershire made a solid reply with King (40), Coe (48) and V. F. S. Crawford (47) amongst the runs, but they were dismissed for 235, with Rhodes taking six for 68. When they followed on Rhodes took another six wickets, Leicestershire being bowled out for 154. Yorkshire won by an innings.

A fine game on a wet wicket at Sheffield followed against Surrey, despite a blank first day. Yorkshire had the fortune to bat first but were all out for 125 with only Newstead hitting boldly for 32, aided by Myers (18) making any sort of a stand. They added 53 for the eighth wicket. W. C. Smith took five for 54, but Surrey, in turn, were also soon back in the pavilion, all out for 62. Rhodes (22) and Wilson (12) then opened with a stand of 35 as Yorkshire took their score to 91. Rushby and Smith took five wickets apiece to leave Surrey needing 155 to win. They lost Hayward quickly and a threatened stand between Hobbs and Hayes never materialised; only J. N. Crawford with 33 held up Yorkshire's march to victory by 51 runs, with the last three wickets falling for a single. Haigh was again Yorkshire's hero with six for 35, taking twelve wickets in the match. Middlesex still led the table at the half-way stage, with Lancashire second, ahead of Kent and Yorkshire who were bracketed in fourth position.

Hard fought victories followed at Bradford over Nottinghamshire, who were outplayed almost from the start, and at Leicester where Yorkshire's first innings lead was 28 and the visitors finally won by three wickets. Lancashire had now gone to the top of the table followed by four clubs including Yorkshire in second place.

Yorkshire had to be satisfied with a draw in the return with Nottinghamshire at Trent Bridge where Denton batted brilliantly for 184 as he put on 122 with Rhodes (59) for the second wicket. The rest of the Yorkshire batting was undistinguished and they batted the whole day for 331 before declaring. Nottinghamshire also took a long time to score 188 with George Gunn carrying his bat through the innings for 91 after being at the crease for 4 hours and 40 minutes. Hirst bowled extremely well on a wet wicket to take five for 57 after three hours were lost through rain. Hirst then scored an unbeaten fifty as Yorkshire declared at 111 for four, but had insufficient time to force victory.

Two games against the Australian tourists were both drawn but the Yorkshire public at Bramall Lane had the satisfaction of seeing Cotter at his best as he took ten wickets in the game. The return at Bradford was ruined by rain.

Yorkshire met with further success over Warwickshire at Leeds. All round cricket from Rhodes (six for 59 and a hard hit 49) were largely instrumental in a first innings lead of 116. Yorkshire ended by needing 76 in the final innings, and hit off the runs for the loss of five wickets.

August opened with Schofield Haigh's benefit at Bradford, where once again the conditions were all in favour of the bowler. Rhodes (24) and Wilson started with a stand of 36 for the first wicket and the latter went on to score 47 as Yorkshire were 111 for four at the end of the first day. Next morning the home side were dismissed for 159, with Brearley and Heap each taking four wickets. R. H. Spooner with an attractive 47 was then largely responsible for Lancashire getting to 55 with one wicket down, but after that only A. H. Hornby (51) faced Rhodes (seven for 68) with any hope of survival. In their second innings, after Rhodes (25) and Denton (37) had taken Yorkshire to 86 before they lost their third wicket, another rot set in and Yorkshire were all out for 146 with Heap taking seven for 49. When Lancashire batted again they had little hope of getting anywhere near their target of 186, only Spooner with another fine knock of 30 making any sort of a show against the deadly Rhodes who took six for 40 and Haigh (three for 25). Yorkshire won by 100 runs. Yorkshire were now at their peak being in second place close behind Kent. Lancashire were third.

Lord Hawke returned for the Worcestershire match at Harrogate. Rhodes was an absentee and Hirst fell lame before the end of the game, but there was no doubt that Worcestershire thoroughly deserved their six wicket victory. Yorkshire went in first and were in no position to recover from 56 for six although the tail wagged to some extent, Haigh making 17 not out and taking the home county to 109. Cuffe bowled well as he often did against Yorkshire to take six for 35 in 31 overs. Worcestershire in their turn lost four for 59 but Cuffe scored a fighting 57 and W. B. Burns 30 as they gained a lead of 72 on the first innings. Haigh took seven for 46, and when Yorkshire batted again Hirst, with 87 in four hours, kept Yorkshire's flag flying. The County finished with 238, their innings having taken more than 155 overs.

Worcestershire were set to score 167 in 145 minutes and appeared to be in real trouble at 65 for four, but Pearson and Burns put on 102 and Worcestershire won by six wickets with 40 minutes to spare.

At Sheffield, Denton, with 130, took a weakened Yorkshire side to 293. His innings lasted for three hours and newcomer Drake (54) helped him to add 49 for the fifth wicket. Bestwick bowled well to take six for 88. In reply Derbyshire were soon in trouble, losing six wickets for 53 before L. Oliver and Warren, each with 24, added 39 and took Derbyshire to 108. Drake followed up his fine batting by taking four for 34. In the follow-on Drake soon took a wicket before Needham, Cadman, J. Chapman and L. G. Wright, all with usual contributions, put up a much better fight to take Derbyshire to 247. Yorkshire were set 63 to win, a target reached for the loss of five wickets. This was followed by a draw against Middlesex at Leeds, where Yorkshire needed 222 to win with all their second innings wickets standing when the game was abandoned at lunch on the last day.

Surrey at The Oval gave Yorkshire a real drubbing, which was remembered with a certain amount of shame by Yorkshire followers for many years. Surrey, after reaching 86 for four, were allowed to reach 273 all out. In reply Yorkshire were 200 for four, but collapsed to 223. Hirst and Rhodes brought the visitors back into the game by routing Surrey for 62, and thus Yorkshire needed 113 in the final innings. Rushby and Smith exploited the treacherous wicket to the full and an embarrassed Yorkshire were removed for just 26 – the lowest total recorded by the County to that date.

The greatly looked forward to game at Dover with Kent was washed out at 3.10 on the first day with Yorkshire's score at 100 for one. Moving on to Leyton, Essex were fairly comprehensively beaten early on the third day by 151 runs. For their final match of the season Yorkshire went to Hove. Rhodes gave a fine display after an uncertain start to record 199 in 4¼ hours. Wilson helped him in an opening stand of 82 before Rothery, with a fine 63, supported him in a third wicket stand of 147 and Yorkshire went into the second day to score 377. Robert Relf took five for 72, and followed that up by scoring 86 as Sussex in reply went on to 307 all out, after P. Cartwright (45) and Cox (53) had put on 89 for the sixth wicket. Newstead finished with seven for 77. With little to play for, Rhodes notched 84 in just over 2 hours and Hirst was 56 not out when rain set in at 4 o'clock and the game was soon abandoned. Thus the Championship season ended with Yorkshire in third place, which was just about right for them in the circumstances. They were by no means the lethal bowling side of the previous season and some of their 'star' players were frankly disappointing.

Yorkshire's final game at Scarborough against the MCC was another draw, with Rhodes scoring another century and Newstead taking seven for 156 in the match. For the opposition, King, W. B. Burns and Albert Relf all batted well but were outshone by Tarrant's 95. Burns was also MCC's best bowler with five for 47 in Yorkshire's first innings, in which they gained a lead of 79. At the end Yorkshire needed 104 to win with six wickets left.

Alonzo Drake played in seven matches for Yorkshire in 1909 and began his career in a promising manner, averaging 21 with the bat and taking 12 wickets at less than 21 runs each. He was born at Parkgate, Rotherham in 1884 and learnt his cricket and soccer with Aldwarke Park before moving to Alexandra Park for cricket, and Parkgate Albion for soccer, at the age of 14. He played soccer for Sheffield United from 1903–04 to 1908–09, in 95 games as an inside-forward scoring 24 goals. He possibly assisted Rawmarsh, Rotherham Town and Doncaster Rovers before that. He also played for Birmingham City for a short time before moving to Huddersfield Town in 1908/09, playing in the NE League and the Midland League in the following season. He also played for QPR. In 1907 he moved to Honley and married a local girl, taking up residence in the Allied Hotel owned by his father-in-law, and he started to play for Honley with success. He soon attracted the attentions of his county and in 1908 first assisted the Second Eleven before playing for the first team in 1909. He was given a regular place in the side in 1910, being then 26 years of age, but failed to grasp his opportunity and it was 1911 before he really came forward and clinched his place as a batsman who could bowl a little. Left-handed with both bat and ball, he was a confident, attacking batsman who in 1913 and 1914 advanced greatly as a clever left-arm medium-pace bowler. He could be unplayable on a helpful pitch, varied his pace cleverly and made the ball swerve at times. He was allocated to Harrogate in 1909 and later played with Barnsley. A strongly built all-rounder, he was rejected for military service at the onset of the First World War, having been in failing health for some time, and it was thought that his somewhat moody attitude was due to illness. He had been employed by Taylor & Littlewood of Newsome Mills near Huddersfield, where he was a wool operative as late on as 1918. In August of that year he was fit enough to take five for 64 against an England eleven at Bradford. Three days later he scored 66 not out against the Royal Artillery at Ripon for a Yorkshire XI. Yet on 14 February 1919 he died at his home in Honley aged only 34. Among his many ailments was thought to be cancer of the throat. His death, a particularly sad one for Yorkshire cricket, alongside the death of Major Booth, resulted in several changes to Yorkshire cricket. It is certain that Emmott Robinson would never have played for

Yorkshire; Kilner might never have developed his bowling and Waddington and Macaulay would not have come to the forefront in the way that they did. That of course is pure conjecture. It is fact that Yorkshire cricket was robbed of the services of two all-rounders who possibly might have been spoken of in the same breath as Hirst and Rhodes.

Wilfred Rhodes had the honour of heading the Yorkshire batting averages in 1909 with 1,663 runs at 38.67. He was soon to become an England opening batsman, breaking records with his partner Jack Hobbs. Denton was second with 1,765 runs at 37.18 and was dependable as ever in getting runs quickly and attractively. In third place was George Hirst, who perhaps was showing signs of his age with only 1,151 runs at 31.97, while B. B. Wilson scored 1,054 runs at an average of 23. There is little doubt that he remained a disappointment and still scored too slowly at times. In fact 1909 was his worst season for Yorkshire and he was no longer scoring runs so prolifically that he had to be chosen. Myers, Rothery, Bates and Wilkinson were all disappointing too and the weakness of the side was reflected in their performances. Haigh seemed to have lost his effectiveness as a batsman but the saddest decline was in Newstead with both bat and ball. Known as a hard-wicket bowler, his drop to 80 wickets at 21.62 was not surprising, but his batting average of 13.86 for 499 runs showed a marked deterioration.

With the ball, Haigh headed the bowling averages with 120 wickets at 13.34 and was also third in the first-class averages. On pitches that were tailor-made for him he was as deadly as ever. Rhodes was second to him with 115 wickets at 15.59 and had many good days as in the past, while Hirst's decline to 89 wickets at 20.30 was only seen as such by his own unique standards. Myers rarely bowled, and Hunter, in his last season, was still a capable wicket-keeper.

Lord Hawke was re-elected as captain for the 1910 season but he had made only eight appearances for the County in 1909, after which he reached the age of 49 and in 1910 he was to make only one appearance. Looking back it seems that the Yorkshire Committee feared the effect of a further period without a capable leader and had not the faith in E. J. Radcliffe to give him that authority.

THE END OF AN ERA

AFTER A SHORT TOUR OF SCOTLAND, Yorkshire began their first-class programme in 1910 with a match at Northampton which they won easily by 145 runs well inside two days. Rhodes with 41 dominated Yorkshire's first innings of 104. The home side were dismissed for 61 by Hirst (five for 30) and Newstead (four for 26). When Yorkshire batted again, Denton (66) and Drake (43) put on 69 for Yorkshire's third wicket and with Newstead scoring 35 Yorkshire reached 215. Northamptonshire were then bowled out for 113. Yorkshire then defeated the MCC at Lord's by 63 runs.

The Lancashire match at Headingley began with the visitors making a solid start and eventually reaching 229. In reply Yorkshire were caught on a pitch that gave some help to the bowlers but dropped catches aided Yorkshire as they recovered from 103 for nine to 152 all out, with E. J. Radcliffe (24 not out) and Haigh (27) at numbers ten and eleven being the two top scorers. When Lancashire batted again Hirst was at his deadliest, twice taking two wickets in two balls and hitting the stumps eight times as Lancashire were bowled out for 61. Hirst took nine for 23 and when rain stopped play, Yorkshire were 40 for two, needing 99 to win. The next match at Leicester was abandoned owing to the funeral of Edward VII on the second day and rain on the first day and part of the third. Yorkshire were then 51 for one.

At Bramall Lane, Somerset batted first and were bowled out for 153. Hirst this time took eight for 80 with seven of his victims bowled. In reply Yorkshire lost four wickets for 63 before Hirst (30) and Wilkinson (38) added 71 for the fifth wicket and Yorkshire managed to take a lead of 25 runs. Only Lewis who made a hard-hitting 56 out of his side's 116 did anything when Somerset batted again as Haigh took six for 34. Yorkshire knocked off 94 for the loss of four wickets to win by six wickets. Victory over Derbyshire at Chesterfield followed with the home side only scoring 82 and 154. All the Yorkshire bowlers took wickets. Yorkshire won by an innings and 142 runs, having scored 378 for five declared. Rothery (134) and Denton (182) added 305 for the second wicket, a record at the time for the County. Rothery batted for four hours and Denton's brilliant innings took $3\frac{1}{4}$ hours.

Yorkshire had to be satisfied with a draw against Hampshire at Bradford with rain finishing the match after lunch on the third day. Yorkshire lost seven wickets for 96 before Myers (50 not out) added 91 for the eighth wicket with Schofield Haigh. In reply to Yorkshire's

194 Hampshire, too, collapsed with seven wickets down for 61 before ending only 14 in arrears, with Hirst taking five for 53. When Yorkshire batted again Hirst scored 90. Yorkshire took their score to 232. When rain stopped play Hampshire were 65 for four.

Another draw followed at Trent Bridge where Yorkshire totalled 290 with Wilkinson making a painstaking 95 not out. Nottinghamshire were then bowled out for 136 with Newstead having his best performance for some time by taking five for 58. Yorkshire then lost seven wickets for 120 before recovering to declare at 200 for eight, setting Nottinghamshire 355 to win in 310 minutes. Nottinghamshire began well with A. O. Jones batting $2\frac{1}{2}$ hours for 116 including five fours in an over from Rhodes, but although Hardstaff scored 73 and John Gunn 50 not out, a shower of rain for 20 minutes put paid to Nottinghamshire's gallant effort and they finished with 317 for six.

Equal top with two other sides, Yorkshire lost that position at Dewsbury where Kent gained a comfortable eight-wicket victory after dismissing Yorkshire for only 81. E. W. Dillon held the Kent innings together with an innings of 138 and proved there was little wrong with the pitch as the visitors gained a first innings lead of 227. Yorkshire's second-innings total of 292 was not enough and Kent went on to win easily.

Essex then gained their first success over Yorkshire since 1899, outplaying the northern county who batted badly in the first innings with Rhodes carrying his bat through the innings for 85 not out out of 152. Essex lost three wickets for 36 but gained a lead of 125. On a wearing wicket, Yorkshire stood little chance and were bowled out for 130. Essex going on to win by ten wickets. For this match Dolphin had returned to wicket-keeping duties for the first time since 1907, superseding Watson who had been given the opportunity of taking over from Hunter. Dolphin quickly established himself and kept his place until 1927. Yorkshire followed that defeat with another at Fenner's, where Rhodes, Denton and Newstead were rested and Cambridge University won easily by nine wicket. Five fifties took the home side to 355, showing up the Yorkshire attack in the process. In reply Yorkshire had to follow on and lost three further wickets with only 39 on the board. Hirst scored 158 in less than three hours and in partnership with Myers (60) added 188 for the fourth wicket. Yorkshire were all out for 321 leaving Cambridge with 147 to win; a target they achieved for the loss of one wicket.

At Lord's a good game took place against Middlesex, who won the toss and scored 240. Thanks to Rhodes with 62 Yorkshire finished only nine behind on the first innings. Middlesex then hoisted 90 for the first wicket and as Tarrant went on to score 107 reached a total of 321. Rhodes took five for 57 and Yorkshire required 331 to win. They made a bad start by losing three wickets for 47 before Denton (95) and Hirst (137) came together and added 164 for the fourth wicket in $2\frac{1}{2}$ hours and then Myers (39 not out) joined Hirst in an 84 stand as Yorkshire scored 60 in the last half-hour to win with one ball to spare by two wickets.

After such a win it was a sad fall from grace that took them to Bramall Lane and defeat by Northamptonshire by five wickets. Yorkshire batted first and scored 288 with Denton (70) and Rhodes (56) putting on 135 for Yorkshire's second wicket. Northamptonshire at 163 for two looked on their way to a substantial lead with G. A. T. Vials scoring 100 in two hours, but a fine spell of bowling by Hubert Myers (six for 57) restricted them to a score of 237. When Yorkshire batted again they gave a wretched display, losing five wickets for 39 before reaching 132. Northamptonshire at 184 for five went on to win by five wickets.

A draw with Warwickshire followed at Edgbaston with York-shire's 125 being 60 more than the home side, as Major Booth took seven for 30. Yorkshire declared at 137 for six with Hirst (46) and Denton (40) both batting well but rain finished the match when Warwickshire had scored only 51 for two. At Headingley, Yorkshire returned to better form by defeating Worcestershire by 109 runs. The Worcestershire attack restricted Yorkshire to 194, but Haigh took six for 30 in Worcestershire's reply of only 139. Yorkshire were then dismissed for 104 leaving the visitors with 214 to make. On the drying pitch, Hirst and Haigh were unplayable after an opening stand of 21 as Worcestershire were bowled out for 50, Hirst taking seven for 28 and Haigh three for 8 in 10 overs.

At Bradford, Yorkshire gained another fine victory. Rhodes took five for 34 as Surrey were despatched for 158. In reply Yorkshire collapsed on a poor wicket to be all out for 89. Hobbs batted well to score 45 and Surrey's second-innings took the score to 72 for three before six wickets fell for only one run and in the end Surrey scored 87. Rhodes took six for 38 and then played a magnificent innings on the still helpful pitch, he and Bates putting on 77 for the first wicket in above even time before Bates left for 36. Rhodes continued brilliantly and was 88 not out when Yorkshire obtained their winning score of 158 for five obtained in only 36.1 overs.

Yorkshire then defeated Warwickshire at Fartown after scoring 387 with Rhodes (63) and Hirst (103) putting on 125 for the fourth wicket. Warwickshire replied with 319 with Quaife scoring 124. Yorkshire began the last day by scoring 197 for six before declaring, Hirst playing a captain's innings to score 88 in less than two hours. Only Quaife stayed long when Warwickshire batted again, losing by 172 runs after being dismissed for only 93.

Rain and bad light prevented Yorkshire from the chance of another victory over Nottinghamshire at Sheffield. Yorkshire were in good form with the bat and hit up 441 for eight before declaring. Wilson, restored to the side, played a solid innings of 108, with Hirst (76) and then Haigh (81 not out) and Booth (42) forcing the pace. Nottinghamshire replied with 212 with Myers taking five for 22. At the close Nottinghamshire had followed on and scored 15 for three.

The return match with Kent at Maidstone provided the home side with a much-desired double. On a pitch that had been wet for some time they scored 203, with Rhodes taking five for 43. Bates, in a stay of $2\frac{1}{2}$ hours for 56, withstood the Kent attack with Hirst (38) before Yorkshire collapsed completely to 120 all out, and when Kent batted again they finished the second day at 107 for two and in a strong position. The pitch on the last day was more treacherous than ever and against Haigh, who finished with seven for 65, Kent reached only 173. Yorkshire were then all out in 70 minutes for 78 with Blythe (six for 31) and Woolley (four for 41) bowling unchanged for each innings.

Derbyshire (75 and 62) were no match at Bradford for Hirst (five for 35) and Booth (five for 34) and in the first innings and Rhodes (five for 5) and Booth (three for 28) in the second. For Yorkshire Booth (54) and Hirst (53) put on 94 for the fourth wicket as they reached 238 to win by an innings and 101 runs by tea-time on the second day.

Sussex provided better opposition at Hull and made 196. Hirst was Yorkshire's main source of runs with 86 taking Yorkshire to a lead of 43 runs. Sussex then made 192 to set the home side 150 to win. Five wickets were down for 70, but Rhodes stood firm scoring 67 with 21-year-old Edgar Oldroyd making a promising debut with 33 not out as Yorkshire won by four wickets.

John Sharp's benefit match at Old Trafford attracted large crowds and saw Yorkshire well beaten by an innings and 111 runs. Yorkshire had three wickets down with only seven on the board before Hirst came in to score 46 and help to take Yorkshire to 103. When Lancashire batted chances were spilt by Yorkshire fielders with R. H. Spooner going on to score 200 not out in $6\frac{1}{4}$ hours having been dropped twice before he was 14. Tyldesley was also dropped twice although he scored only 32 while Sharp himself made 51 and when Lancashire declared at 395 for five, A. H. Hornby (60 not out) had added 123 with Spooner in 85 minutes. In their second innings Yorkshire were dismissed for 181 to complete a wretched three days for the Yorkshire visitors.

A heavy-scoring draw at Worcester saw 1,196 runs come from the bat with only 29 wickets going down. In Yorkshire's 412 Rhodes scored 87 and Haigh 87 not out and when Worcestershire batted R. E. Foster scored 133 in $3\frac{1}{4}$ hours, not having been seen in a first-class match since 1907. He came in with two wickets down for four. At 209 for nine Worcestershire seemed certain to follow on, but Burrows (53 not out) and Bale (32) put on 90 for the last wicket and Yorkshire had to bat again. At their second attempt Yorkshire scored 234 for four before declaring with Wilson scoring 115. Worcestershire were set to score 348 to win, a task they never attempted although Bowley (74) and Pearson (70) opened with a stand of 129 and H. K. Foster made 53, leaving them 251 for four at the close.

Yorkshire were outplayed by Leicestershire at Headingley, losing heavily by 259 runs. Leicestershire batted first and scored 278. Shipman, bowling fast, troubled Yorkshire batsmen as had several other fast bowlers this year, and they were bowled out for 130, with only Hirst earning many plaudits for an excellent innings of 66 as Shipman took five for 58; he took the first five wickets to fall, four being bowled. Leicestershire then declared at 256 for five. It was Jayes (seven for 57) who did the damage when Yorkshire set out to score 405. They were all out for 145.

At The Oval, Yorkshire recovered from 98 for four to score 266 all out. Surrey made a good start, then Ducat (153) added 121 for the fifth wicket with Hobbs (62) in 75 minutes. For the seventh wicket Ducat and Hitch put on a further 127 in less than an hour as Surrey totalled 437. Yorkshire were 7 without loss when rain caused the match to be drawn.

Middlesex inflicted another defeat on Yorkshire at Sheffield despite the visitors having the worst of the first day as they were bowled out for 72. Hirst took six for 41 and Booth four for 30. For Yorkshire, after three wickets had fallen for 64, Denton (68) and Hirst (65) added 97 in an hour before the last six wickets fell for 38 runs. Middlesex, 127 in arrears, started with a 137 partnership between P. F. Warner (78) and Tarrant (54). Rhodes took five for 73 as Middlesex were dismissed for 311, setting Yorkshire 185 to win. They lost Rhodes and Denton by the end of the second day and rain overnight left them with a treacherous pitch to bat on. Yorkshire were dismissed for 61 and Middlesex won by 123 runs. J. T. Hearne took twelve for 65 in the match.

At Harrogate, Essex made 272, with Hirst taking six for 70, in reply to which Yorkshire made 233. When rain came on the last day, Yorkshire had taken two Essex wickets with only 26 on the board. The journey down to Portsmouth for the Hampshire game providing an interesting game which Yorkshire finally won by six runs. Only Rhodes with 40 batted with confidence on a pitch that was drying out as Yorkshire were dismissed for 116. Hampshire took an 18-run lead as Hirst finished with seven for 56. When Yorkshire batted again they had seven wickets down for 139 before reaching 256 on a much better pitch for batting on. Hampshire wanted 240 to win. They then lost four for 26 on another rain-affected pitch before Captain White in a resolute innings of 90 brought his side back into the game. At the end of the match Bowell hit his wicket when facing Haigh and Yorkshire duly gained their narrow win.

Another rain-affected draw at Brighton saw Wilson complete centuries for Yorkshire in a total of 314. Sussex recovered from 9 for four to make 240. Yorkshire then declared at 133 for three and Sussex were 67 for two at the close. In their last match at Taunton, Yorkshire scored 196, which gave them a lead of 137 when Somerset were bowled out for 59, Hirst taking six for 34 and Haigh four for 24. Hirst also took three for 11 in Somerset's second innings of 25 for three before the game was abandoned, after a Yorkshire declaration at 48 for three.

Yorkshire finished the season in eighth place in the Championship table; their worst season since the early 1890s. A new scoring system had been introduced in 1910 in which the Championship would be decided by the percentage of wins to the number of matches played. (Under the old system, Yorkshire would have finished sixth instead of eighth.) The system was discarded for the 1911 season.

Another wet season meant that batsmen had a difficult season once again and only three Yorkshire players managed to reach their thousand runs. Top of the batting averages was the reliable Hirst, who scored 1,669 runs at 34.06. Rhodes, who had a comparatively poor season and had long periods of fairly low scores, obtained 1,355 runs at 28.22 and Denton, injured for a few weeks, scored 1,106 runs at 26.97. B. B. Wilson, who was dropped for a time during the season, scored 782 runs at 25.06 while Haigh had a much better season with 851 runs at an average of 23. Rothery, who looked such an accomplished player when scoring runs, scored only 634 at 22.64 and Myers, who improved a good deal, scored 918 at 21.34. Wilkinson and Bates both had their good days but neither improved and Newstead's batting, like his bowling, deteriorated immensely. Booth and Drake both showed promise with the bat, but the skipper (or acting skipper), E. J. Radcliffe, failed to average double figures.

The bowling averages were headed by George Hirst, who took 138 wickets at 15.52. He managed to gain sixth position in the first-class averages and his overall all-round abilities placed him in the highest category. Rhodes took 87 wickets at 18.26 and if this was poor compared with the previous season, he was still one of the best slow bowlers in the country. Haigh too dropped in aggregate, taking only 76 wickets at 20.02, but he did so much better with the bat that he could again be classed as an all-rounder. Newstead's aggregate fell to just 32 wickets at 21.12, while Booth in his first full season took 51 wickets at 21.37 and showed promise that he would develop into a top-class opening bowler. Drake was in the same category, but he took only 28 wickets at 22.28. The only other bowler to be mentioned must be Myers, who did have one or two successful days with the ball, but his 30 wickets cost 36.66.

For the 1911 season, E. J. Radcliffe would be fully captain of the side. There were other changes too with Myers, Rothery and W. H. Wilkinson all having played their last games for the County after promising starts that had not been fulfilled.

After a friendly match with Staffordshire, Yorkshire began the new season with a trip to Lord's where they won a hard-fought match by 45 runs. Yorkshire began well with Rhodes (59) and Wilson (87) opening with a stand of 134 but the rest of the batsmen failed to double this total and Yorkshire were dismissed for 265. The MCC batting was more impressive with Tarrant (127) putting on 191 for the second wicket with Phil Mead (82) as MCC made a total of 345. Yorkshire's second innings amounted to 338 with Denton scoring 84 and Haigh 56, the home side were set 259 to win. Tarrant (74) and Albert Relf (71) took the MCC score to 203 for six before Hirst (six for 55) went through the tail to dismiss the MCC for 213 and so gain victory for Yorkshire by 45 runs.

Yorkshire met with defeat in their opening Championship game at Leyton. C. McGahey (53) and J. W. H. T. Douglas (47) were mainly instrumental in Essex obtaining 208, a total that Yorkshire passed by seven runs. In their second knock J. W. H. T. Douglas (56) and F. L. Fane (82) gave the home county a good send-off with a stand of 109 for the first wicket, and Essex reached 257 with Hirst taking five for 66. In reply Yorkshire were never in contention and were bowled out for 119.

At Sheffield, Yorkshire showed much better form against Derbyshire with Rhodes scoring 100 in a fine innings lasting $2\frac{1}{2}$ hours. He put on 142 for the second wicket with Denton (70) and the all out score of 250 was enough to give Yorkshire an innings win. On a sodden pitch that was beginning to dry when Derbyshire batted, Hirst was unplayable as he took six for 24, supported by Haigh (three for 4). Dismissed for 61 the visitors were 124 for three at one stage of their reply but collapsed to 142. Further wins to make it eight victories consecutively then came Yorkshire's way over Somerset (twice), Worcester, Derbyshire (again), Lancashire, Warwickshire and Leicestershire.

Yorkshire gained only a 40-run lead over Somerset at Taunton as Somerset were bowled out for 138. In the second innings Denton with 120 – he reached his century in an hour and a quarter – and Booth (62 not out) enabled Yorkshire to declare at 393 for seven and then

Somerset, beset by illnesses and injury, were dismissed for 161. At Worcester, the home side were bowled out for 113 with Hirst bowling magnificently for nine for 41 – seven of them bowled – on a good wicket. Yorkshire replied with 535 with Booth making his highest ever score of 210 (as well as his maiden century). He added 233 for the sixth wicket with George Hirst, who scored 100. H. K. Foster then batted very well to score 112, taking Worcestershire to a score of 440, but Yorkshire went on to gain a ten-wicket victory.

In reply to Derbyshire's 215. Denton (13) and Drake (147 not out) added 193 for Yorkshire's third wicket. Drake's maiden hundred was somewhat fortunate for him as he was dropped three times. Yorkshire declared at 401 for four, and Derbyshire were then dismissed for 111. Rhodes took seven for 16, having caught the Derbyshire batsmen on a sticky wicket. Somerset went down at Leeds by ten wickets with Braund 55 out of their first innings of 130 alone halting the Yorkshire bowlers. After Yorkshire's 219, Somerset were dismissed a second time for 106. Yorkshire won soon after lunch on the second day by ten wickets.

In the middle of this run of success Yorkshire visited Fenner's and were beaten as usual by Cambridge University. Cambridge batted first and finished with 220. Yorkshire then lost seven wickets for 46 before E. J. Radcliffe (53 not out) added 65 for the last wicket with Bayes (36). Yorkshire were 63 runs in arrears. Cambridge were then dismissed for 206 with Rhodes taking six for 59 and Yorkshire must have fancied their chances of obtaining 270 to win, especially as they were 110 before their second wicket fell. However, carelessness was their downfall as at 200 all out they lost by 69 runs.

The Lancashire match was one of Yorkshire's best performances of the season. Yorkshire won the toss at Old Trafford and gave a poor display apart from B. B. Wilson, who scored 64. Walter Brearley took seven for 110 in the Yorkshire score of 199 and Lancashire took the lead with six wickets down. Then Hirst with the new ball went through the Lancashire tail and they were all out for 224, with Hirst taking six for 83. Batting again Yorkshire were in trouble with three down for 54 but Drake (85) joined with Hirst in a stand of 193 on a somewhat fiery wicket. Drake was missed twice early on, as was Hirst, who otherwise played a wonderful innings which virtually won the game for Yorkshire as they went on to declare at 376 for eight. Requiring 352 to win, Lancashire were dismissed for 192 to lose by 159 runs. Drake took six for 57.

Warwickshire at Edgbaston provided another outstanding game of cricket, with Warwickshire losing five wickets for 61 before Lilley (70) was joined by F. R. Foster who compiled the first century of his career in county cricket (105) and helped take Warwickshire to 317.

Rhodes (47) and Denton (83) took Yorkshire to 124 after Wilson had gone first ball and there was a further stand of 152 between Drake (83) and Hirst (85), and Yorkshire finished 30 ahead with Foster taking nine for 118 (seven of them bowled). By the close Warwickshire were in a strong position again with a century opening stand. But after the first wicket fell at 130, wickets fell steadily and they were dismissed for 245. Yorkshire batted very well in their fourth innings to win the match by four wickets on a pitch that gave some assistance to the bowlers.

C. J. B. Wood carried his bat throughout both innings for Leicestershire at Bradford, scoring 107 not out and 117 not out in 8 hours and 40 minutes batting. In the first innings Leicestershire scored 309. Rhodes (92) and Booth (71) batted well and Yorkshire gained a lead of 25 on the first innings. Leicestershire then lost five wickets for 46 but Wood, joined by Mounteney (96) put on 142 for the sixth wicket and in 80 minutes Leicestershire finally reached 296, with Hirst taking five for 68. Yorkshire were set to make 272 in 210 minutes, and thanks to David Denton, who scored 137 not out, the runs were obtained in 165 minutes.

At this stage of the season Yorkshire were top of the table, having lost only one game. The new points system gave five points for a win, with sides in a drawn game gaining three for a lead on the first innings and one for a deficit, with other draws not included. The percentage of points won to those possible determined the positions.

At Lord's, B. B. Wilson (125) helped Yorkshire reach a respectable score of 354, but Middlesex scored 425 in reply with E. S. Litteljohn and J. W. Hearne making centuries. Overnight rain and a drying pitch then helped Middlesex as Yorkshire were bowled out for 104, and Middlesex went on to win by nine wickets. With Kent also losing to Worcestershire, Yorkshire shared the top place in the table with Nottinghamshire, both sides having 80 per cent.

Yorkshire's match with the Champions at Bramall Lane was looked forward to with keenness but odd showers on the first day restricted Kent to 270 for five. The Yorkshire catching had not been up to its best standards and the following day Kent were all out for 324, with Hirst again bowling well to take six for 81. When Yorkshire went in, Rhodes (95) and Bates (58) put on 138 for the third wicket as Yorkshire were all out for 286. James Seymour with 100 not out in the second innings helped Kent to score 205 before lunch on the third day before declaring at 282 for six. Yorkshire had $2\frac{1}{2}$ hours left to obtain 321 but soon lost four wickets for 31 but Hirst (53 not out) and Booth (52 not out) had little difficulty in saving the day. Yorkshire were now second to Nottinghamshire in the Championship table.

At Dewsbury, Thompson (112) and Haywood (121) added 236 for Northamptonshire's fifth wicket as they took their score to 401, with

Rhodes taking six for 141 and Booth four for 49. Drake and Haigh were missing from the Yorkshire line-up being indisposed, and with rain curtailing play on the second two days, Yorkshire made only 88 for three before stumps were drawn.

Surrey were visitors to Headingley for a contest on a bowler's wicket which began with Surrey dismissing Yorkshire for 87. Surrey also collapsed to be all out for 103. Rhodes took six for 29. Yorkshire began much better in their second innings largely through Drake (74) but then a collapse occurred which resulted in the last seven wickets falling for 21 runs. Surrey were set 166 to win and got home by four wickets with Rhodes taking five for 54. Despite their defeat Yorkshire now stood on top of the Championship table.

An easy victory over Nottinghamshire followed at Trent Bridge with the home side soon dismissed for 141. Haigh took five for 51 and Hirst five for 69 and Yorkshire went into the lead for the loss of Wilson's wicket only. Bates (65) and Denton (83) added 137 for the second wicket to help Yorkshire to a total of 266. Nottinghamshire were soon 34 for six on the now rain-affected pitch, with B. J. Hind making highest score (23) in the only first-class game he played. They made a partial recovery to be bowled out for 98 and lose by an innings and 27 runs, Hirst taking five for 38.

Roy Kilner, elder brother of Norman and nephew of Irving Washington, was born at Low Valley, Wombwell in 1890 and was a left-handed batsman who hit the ball hard especially to leg and invariably scored at a fast rate unless conditions demanded otherwise. When Yorkshire lacked bowling after the First World War, he developed into a very useful left-arm slow bowler who bowled either orthodox left-arm slows or chinamen and googlies (he claimed to have invented the former term). He first played for Yorkshire 2nd XI in 1910 and was chosen in seven matches for the first team the following season, his debut being against Somerset at Taunton. Roy was allocated to Harrogate as a colt from 1911 and showed steady progress with both bat and ball. In the following year he gained a regular place in the side, which he kept up to the end of the 1927 season. Roy Kilner was one of the most popular cricketers ever to play for Yorkshire. His benefit of £4,106 in 1925 was the highest in county cricket up to the Second World War and his sunny disposition was in the direct line of Schofield Haigh to Maurice Leyland. His shortish stocky figure with bulging rear made him a popular figure for the caricaturist, but though his methods with both bat and ball often amused the crowd, he had that same awesome depth of steel possessed also by Leyland and Hirst that made him a man for the big occasion. Coaching in India during the winter of 1927/28 he caught some bug or other, possibly from shellfish he had eaten, and this developed into

Roy Kilner, a Test all-rounder, who achieved the double four times, bowling his slow left-arm.

enteric fever from which he died in April 1928 shortly before going back for practice with Yorkshire. It was reckoned that 100,000 people lined the streets of Wombwell for his funeral.

In the next match, Worcestershire, despite a stand of 109 for their fourth wicket, managed to reach 165, the last six wickets falling for 24 with Booth (six for 51) completing a hat-trick. Rhodes (92) and Drake (59) added 119 as Yorkshire took a lead of 100 runs. On a by-no-means-easy batting track, Worcestershire struggled to make 178, with

275

Hirst bowling exceptionally well to take six for 66 as Yorkshire went on to win by nine wickets. At Fartown, Hampshire scored 142, Hirst taking five for 54 and Booth five for 60. Then Wilson (86) and Denton (81) added 117 for Yorkshire's second wicket and really put them in the driving seat. A total of 355 gave Yorkshire an overwhelming lead. In their second innings, Phil Mead completely dominated the scene as he carried his bat for 120 not out in 234 — it was his third century of the week. Hartington bowled well to take five for 81. Yorkshire won by ten wickets, and now led the table comfortably over Middlesex.

At Hull, Yorkshire had defeated the All Indians by an innings and 43 runs. Denton and Haigh both contributed centuries towards Yorkshire's total of 385 with W. H. Micklethwait, playing his only match for the county scoring 44. In spite of playing a weak side, Yorkshire dismissed the opposition for 233 and 109. Lord Hawke returned for this match and also played against the MCC at Scarborough.

Yorkshire's next match with Essex at Sheffield was a draw in Essex's favour as they gained a lead of 122 on the first innings, replying with 392 to Yorkshire's 270. With only the last day remaining, Yorkshire soon cleared off the arrears with Rhodes (61) and Wilson (88) opening with a stand of 125 while Hirst hit 71 before Yorkshire declared at 333 for seven. Essex finished with 78 for two.

Yorkshire's fourth defeat of the season occurred at Northampton where Yorkshire had a thoroughly bad day in the field and Northants were fortunate to score as many as 316. Only Denton (59) and Hirst (49) were able to cope with a wearing pitch as Yorkshire replied with 250. In their second innings Northamptonshire were all at sea against Rhodes who followed up his eight for 92 in the first innings with six for 47 to dismiss them for 118. Yorkshire in turn collapsed to 140 all out, including 34 for the last wicket, as Northamptonshire won by 44 runs.

Yorkshire returned to winning ways at Headingley against Sussex; Denton scored a rapid 76 and Booth also moved quickly to obtain 44 not out as Yorkshire were all out in less than 3 hours for 225. When Sussex batted, Hirst was unplayable and took six for 34 as Sussex were dismissed for 102. Rhodes with 125 in $3\frac{1}{4}$ hours then played a masterly innings and Yorkshire finished with 282. Sussex were dismissed for 124 to lose by 281 runs. Hirst, with some help from the pitch, bowled at his very best to take seven for 20 in 17.2 overs. Yorkshire were in second place in the table with Kent on top.

Sir Archibald Woollaston White, Bart, played ten matches in 1911 when he occasionally led the side in Radcliffe's absence. He was a right-arm medium-pace bowler and right-hand batsman who had been in the Wellington College XI, but failed to get a blue at Cambridge. He had played in one match for Yorkshire in 1908. He was appointed captain of Yorkshire in 1912 when they finished Champions, and also led them in the following two seasons, and took part in two matches in 1920.

At Harrogate, the visitors Warwickshire batted brightly on the first day to score 341, and when Yorkshire went in four wickets fell for 119 before Drake (99) and Hirst (78) put in 142 for the fifth wicket in less than 90 minutes. F. R. Foster took for four 94 and then followed up a first innings 60 with 101 in 105 minutes as Warwickshire scored 225. Hirst took five for 26. On a wicket giving them help, Field (seven for 20) and Foster (two for 35) bowled Yorkshire out for 58. Yorkshire had now dropped down to fifth position in the championship.

At Hull, Yorkshire made a bad start against Nottinghamshire, losing half their wickets with only 48 on the board. Denton (74) and young Oldroyd (75 not out) added 84 for the sixth wicket and then Bates (63) joined Oldroyd in a further stand of 105 and Yorkshire reached 269. Both stands were at the rate of 80 runs per hour. In reply Nottinghamshire had five wickets down for 59 by the close of play, but next morning just avoided the follow-on and finally reached 146, with Booth taking five for 62. In the second innings Rhodes (55) and Wilson (68) put on 122 for the first wicket and Denton made a most attractive 101 not out which enabled Yorkshire to declare at 293 for six. Nottinghamshire were bowled out before tea on the third day for 191 with Yorkshire victors by 225 runs, and rising to third.

Yorkshire's Roses match at Sheffield was played for the benefit of Wilfred Rhodes and the game turned out to be a topsy-turvey one, with Yorkshire on top at the start as Lancashire were bowled out for 167, Rhodes and Hirst each getting four wickets. Rhodes (36) and Wilson (50) opened with a stand of 60 and then Wilson and Drake (54) added 80 for the third wicket and with Haigh hitting out to score 50 not out Yorkshire finally achieved a lead of 114. When Lancashire batted again, five wickets were down for 123 but Makepeace with a stubborn 55 and K. G. McLeod, who scored 121 in 2 hours, turned the game and Lancashire finally reached 364, with Rhodes taking four for 109. Yorkshire required 251 to win in three hours but after losing three wickets for 51, they were content to play for a draw, with Denton scoring 101 not out as they finished with 183 for six; an honourable draw for both sides.

At Leicester Yorkshire were bowled out for 153 and at the close of play, Leicestershire were 137 for five. Leicestershire built up a big lead, and when Yorkshire batted again after a torrential rainfall the drying turf became unplayable and they were dismissed for 47. J. H. King bowled magnificently on the treacherous pitch to take eight for 17 and record Leicestershire's only win of the season, Middlesex now headed the Championship table, with Yorkshire down to fourth position.

The leaders took advantage of a good wicket at Bradford to score 378, F. A. Tarrant scoring 207 in five hours. Yorkshire replied with 218, and instead of enforcing the follow-on, Middlesex batted again to reach 261 for five before declaring. Yorkshire were set 422 to win in 280 minutes, an impossible task. They lost three wickets for 30 in 40 minutes but a rearguard action was mounted and with Hirst scoring 75 in three hours, and support from Booth, Drake and Haigh, at the close of play Yorkshire were 280 for nine with the match saved.

Major John Wilson, DSC, AFC, who made 36 in this match, made nine appearances for Yorkshire in 1911 and 1912, but earned more fame as a steeplechase jockey. In 1925 he rode Double Chance to victory in the Grand National.

At The Oval, Rhodes (91) and Wilson (30) opened with a stand of 89 against Surrey and Denton scored 32 before Drake (54) and Hirst (87) added 100 for the fourth wicket. Yorkshire took their overnight score of 334 for six to 372 all out. After losing Hobbs for five, Hayward in an innings of 177 lasting almost four hours, put on 259 for Surrey's second wicket with Hayes (89) before M. C. Bird (83) and I. P. F. Campbell (51) added 112 for their fifth wicket. Surrey's total eventually reached 540. Yorkshire reached 158 for seven at the close, still ten runs behind.

Another defeat was suffered by Yorkshire at Portsmouth, where only Rhodes 55 and Bates 45 not out shone for Yorkshire in a poor batting display of 169. Hampshire took a 22-run lead, Hirst taking five for 49. On a deteriorating pitch, Yorkshire were dismissed again for 158, and Hampshire, requiring 137 to win, achieved their target thanks to a fine 62 in two hours from Stone. On a rain-affected wicket at Canterbury, Yorkshire found Blythe (five for 35) and Woolley (five for 39) quite unplayable, and were bowled out for 75 in 100 minutes. Kent did better through a brilliant display from Woolley, whose 57 was obtained in a faultless manner in 80 minutes batting. Kent were all out for 151, with Drake taking five for 36. Rhodes alone batted well for Yorkshire as they were dismissed for 79 in another dismal display as Blythe took six for 28. Kent went on to win by ten wickets.

Yorkshire's final Championship match at Hastings put their performances of the previous few weeks in perspective. After a wretched record of two wins in eleven matches, during which they suffered five defeats, they produced some splendid batting to reach a total of 522 for seven wickets before declaring. Drake (115) and Hirst (218) added 259 for the fourth wicket in 150 minutes before Hirst and Booth (39) added 111 in less than an hour. George Hirst's powerful display was made at more than a run-a-minute. Vine batted well in both innings for Sussex, but totals of 278 and 212 meant Yorkshire gained a fine victory by an innings and 32 runs.

Yorkshire's final match at Scarborough against the MCC provided a feast of runs with Rhodes taking pride of place with 128 and 115, to score two centuries in a match for the first time. Denton also scored 94 and 42 as Yorkshire compiled 387 and 225 for six declared. G. L. Jessop had scores of 59 and 117 not out; his second innings being compiled in 85 minutes. R. H. Spooner also scored 102 in 110 minutes in the MCC second innings of 334 for seven, which fell just five runs short of victory.

David Denton headed the Yorkshire batting averages with 2,161 runs at an average of 42.37 with the hard wickets suiting his style and methods admirably. Now aged 37, he showed no signs of his powers waning. Wilfred Rhodes was second with 1,961 runs at 38.45, another fine record, while George Hirst scored 1,639 runs at 34.14. Drake had his best season so far with 1,487 runs at 30.97 while Wilson's total of 1,455 was obtained at an average of 27.45, which for an opener was below Yorkshire standards. Booth was the sixth batsman to reach his thousand with 1,189 at 25.84. Haigh, who batted very low in the order as a rule, scored 906 at 24.48, which left Bates as the disappointment with 533 runs at 21.32; figures which were not up to the required standard, although he always appeared capable of getting runs when they were needed.

The bowling was a more important test of Yorkshire's abilities. In a hard-wicket season Schofield Haigh did well to head the bowling averages with 97 wickets at 17.36 each. He was as deadly as ever in conditions that suited him and could never be taken lightly at any time. Hirst bore the brunt of the work during the season as he finished with 130 wickets at 18.60, while Drake showed further improvement as he took 79 wickets at 22.18. Rhodes took 105 wickets at 24.06 – his deterioration being marginal considering the dry wickets. Booth with 78 wickets at 27.06 each was disappointing as so much was expected of him, but he was still only 24 years old.

Dolphin was now established as wicket-keeper, and perhaps the availability of a regular captain would improve the side, a luxury that had not been enjoyed since 1908, when Lord Hawke, even then, missed several matches. Yorkshire, who had led the Championship table for several weeks and always been in contention until August, finally finished seventh; they remained, however, a team to be feared by the other counties. The Yorkshire side was capable of improvement, and if all went well then Booth and Drake were well on the way to becoming the cornerstone of the side. Time would tell.

Yorkshire's three seasons of comparative failure had seen the membership decline in 1911 by 200 members and it was now only 2,500. In 1911 a winter practice shed had been erected at Headingley and was expected to prove a great benefit to the club.

Sir Archibald White was without Rhodes when he led the Yorkshire side out at Lord's for the first match of the season in 1912. The home side began badly with the score at 25 for six but the tail wagged as MCC scored 113. Hirst took five for 40. Yorkshire, in turn, lost eight wickets for 85, but the reliable Haigh (45 not out) added 43 for the ninth wicket and 62 for the last as they were finally out for 190. In their second innings, the MCC lost seven wickets for 72 but once again the tail came to the rescue and they finally managed 151, with Hirst again bowling in splendid fashion to take nine for 69. Thanks to the newcomer J. Tasker, Yorkshire, after losing six wickets for only 46, rallied with Tasker scoring 22 not out as the visitors got home by two wickets.

Yorkshire opened in the Championship with a match at Leicester where Yorkshire batted first and scored 344 with Rhodes making 78, Tasker 50 and Booth 75. Overnight rain aided the visitors and Leicestershire were soon bowled out for 143 with Drake taking five for 26. Following on, they did much better, but at 190 for seven the game seemed all over. Then a stand of 66 helped them to 317. Rhodes with 67 not out saw Yorkshire to the 117 they needed.

Hampshire at Sheffield were bowled out for 80, with Booth taking six for 31 and Hirst four for 46 and at the end of the first day, Yorkshire had replied with 330 for four, with Denton and Drake putting on 134 in 85 minutes for the third wicket, with Denton scoring 107 and Drake 65, and then Denton and Hirst (78) hit 113 in 55 minutes. On the following day the innings closed for 471. Hampshire batted much better in their second innings with Mead making 111 not out. Rain washed out the third day to rob Yorkshire of possible victory. Another draw followed at Fartown, where the South Africans fought back from a deficit of 147 on the first innings to reach 288 in their second innings, with the former Yorkshire batsman, Frank Mitchell scoring 91 not out. Pegler performed the hat-trick during Yorkshire's first innings of 317. Again rain hindered Yorkshire's chances of victory, robbing the first day of all but an hour's play.

The wretched weather continued at Leeds where Kent dismissed Yorkshire for 96 with Wilson scoring 36 as Woolley took six for 42 and then Kent opened with a stand of 101 with Humphreys scoring 64 as they finished at 103 for two, no play taking place on either the first or last day. A weak Yorkshire side then lost at Fenner's by four wickets after Yorkshire had led by 139 on the first innings. Yorkshire made 335, and Drake took five for 60 in the varsity's reply of 196. Extras with 24 was the Yorkshire top scorer in the second innings of 106, leaving Cambridge with 246 to win, a target they achieved by four wickets.

At Bradford, Yorkshire outplayed Lancashire to win by ten wickets after Wilfred Rhodes with 107 had played a masterly innings on a pitch with a certain amount of lift that Lancashire were able to exploit as Yorkshire were dismissed for 226. With the pitch drying in the hot sun, Drake took six for 33 as Lancashire were dismissed for 76, and then, on an easing pitch, they fell to Haigh (five for 25) for 165. Yorkshire won comfrotably inside two days.

Rain ruined Yorkshire's chances of victory at Dewsbury where Somerset were out for 73 in the first innings and were 45 for five in the second. Haigh took five for 14 in the first innings. For Yorkshire Wilson had batted well for 72 out of a first-innings 146. Yorkshire declared their second knock at 111 for eight. There was no play on the second day owing to rain. The next match at Sheffield against Surrey was abandoned without a ball being bowled. Another blank day followed against Essex at Huddersfield and in the time that was left Yorkshire scored 242, with Bates (64) and Hirst (59) both batting well. Essex were 76 before the second wicket fell, but their last seven wickets fell for nine runs, with Drake taking six for 35, including a spell of six for 7 which contained a hat-trick. In the end the wet conditions were the only victors.

Another draw followed at Bradford against the touring Australians but not before some fine cricket had been witnessed. Yorkshire started on the second day by scoring 155. On a treacherous pitch Haigh finished with five for 22 as the Australians scored only 107. Yorkshire slumped to 66 for seven before declaring and when the match ended the Australians were 35 for six, still requiring 80 to win, Schofield Haigh having taken six for 14.

At Lord's, Yorkshire met with their first Championship defeat in a well-contested game by four wickets. With the wicket at its worst, Yorkshire finished at 157, and Middlesex took a lead of 28 runs. When Yorkshire batted a second time Rhodes made 84 in a masterly innings of $2\frac{1}{2}$ hours, but they were all out for 166. Middlesex scored the 139 needed for six wickets. Yorkshire were now in sixth place in the Championship table with Lancashire leading the way.

Victory over Gloucestershire was obtained by 74 runs on a pitch always favouring the bowlers and with the second day lost because of the weather. Yorkshire were bowled out for 82 but Haigh was at his deadliest when Gloucestershire batted as he took nine for 25 and gained Yorkshire a lead of 14. In their second innings Denton made 60 before Yorkshire collapsed again for 170, but Gloucestershire were soon reduced to 61 for eight and were eventually dismissed for 110.

At Trent Bridge on a good pitch, A. O. Jones (96) helped Nottinghamshire to a total of 261. Yorkshire then batted poorly to be dismissed for 145. Yorkshire then dismissed Nottinghamshire for 132 on a pitch now deteriorating. Yorkshire required 249 to win, a tall order in the circumstances. But with 133 for four on the board Kilner playing a splendid innings as substitute to the injured Hirst, and scored 83 not out as he added 113 with Tasker (52), the youngest member of the side, and Yorkshire won well by four wickets. Northamptonshire were now on top of the table with Yorkshire in fifth place.

The leaders at Bradford were lucky to escape defeat as they were completely outplayed in a match where the second day was lost to the weather. With Rhodes on Test duty and Hirst still injured, Yorkshire declared at 241 for nine. Northamptonshire did not start their innings until 1.30 on the last day and they were soon dismissed for 74 and following on lost four wickets for one run, and at 5 for four J. S. Denton, the first-innings top scorer, had to retire hurt. An hour then remained with the wicket greatly helping the bowlers, but Northamptonshire avoided defeat by scoring 24 for seven, with Newstead taking four for 8 in 11 overs. Nor could Yorkshire gain winning points at Edgbaston, where the home side was completely outplayed until the third day, which was another blank. Warwickshire still required 205 to avoid an innings defeat, with seven wickets left. Yorkshire won the toss and Wilson made 150 while Denton went on to score 200 not out in 250 minutes as Yorkshire declared at 451 for three. In reply Warwickshire were out for 183, and following on had scored 63 for three.

The return match with the Australians took place at Sheffield with the Australians scoring 299. Yorkshire replying with 280, with Wilson (54), Denton (31) and Hirst (62) batting well. There was no play on the second day and the match finished with the visitors 3 for none in their second innings.

At Dewsbury, Yorkshire, on a bowler's wicket, were dismissed for 129, and Worcestershire finished the day on 85 all out, with Haigh taking five for 37. Yorkshire then occupied the second day in scoring 345 for nine declared with Hirst making 109 in spite of being missed before he had scored. Worcestershire were then dismissed for 175 leaving Yorkshire winners by 214 runs. Haigh took five for 57.

Yorkshire followed that win with a 247-run win at Bristol against Gloucestershire, who had Yorkshire in real trouble at 13 for three, but Denton (29) and Kilner (30) brought an air of respectability back in to the Yorkshire batting and they were dismissed for 134. Gloucestershire then lost five wickets for 29 before C. O. H. Sewell with 57 helped them to 132 with Haigh taking six for 6. Yorkshire then lost two wickets for ten runs before Denton, dropped when five, changed the complexion of the game with a fine 182 in 250 minutes. Yorkshire declared at 411 for nine. Bowling and fielding well. Yorkshire then dismissed the home side for 166.

There was no better performance by any side than Yorkshire's against Kent at Tunbridge Wells when most of the visitors' batsmen did well, especially Denton, who batted for $5\frac{3}{4}$ hours in brilliant fashion to score 221 as Yorkshire reached 543. Kent were 180 for three at the close of the second day, but on the last day, on a wicket showing signs of wear, they were bowled out for 310 with Haigh taking five for 62. Woolley batted well with 75 in the follow-on, but Yorkshire ran out worthy winners by an innings and 45 runs. Yorkshire were without Rhodes who was assisting the Players at The Oval, Kent having declined to allow Woolley to play in the same fixture. Yorkshire were now in second place behind Northamptonshire.

At Sheffield, Yorkshire scored 350 against Leicestershire before Booth, who had scored 71, followed with a splendid spell of bowling to take eight for 52 as Leicestershire were dismissed for 140. But on following on Wood and Knight opened their second innings with a stand of 183 and Knight went on to score 147. Leicestershire then collapsed to be all out for 324 and Yorkshire won easily enough by eight wickets. As Northamptonshire had been defeated by Warwickshire. Yorkshire went to the top of the Championship table.

A draw at Northampton, with Yorkshire gaining first innings points, was satisfactory to the visitors but it was another rain-spoilt match. Oldroyd (60) and Denton (111) added 164 for Yorkshire's second wicket and Yorkshire were dismissed for 330. The home side were all out for 233, with Booth taking five for 91 and Hirst four for 62. At the close of play Yorkshire were 27 without loss.

Yorkshire at The Oval scored 233 against Surrey with Drake making the top score of 54, but Surrey gained a lead of 34. Yorkshire then declared at 229 for six with Hirst making 94, and at the close Surrey were 93 for one.

At Southampton, a most remarkable game was won by Yorkshire by nine wickets, although such a result seemed impossible after the first day's play. Hampshire started by losing two wickets for 23 before Stone (73) left after a partnership of 109 with C. B. Fry, who then added 246 for the fourth wicket with E. I. M. Barrett, who scored 120 in $4\frac{1}{4}$ hours. C. B. Fry went on to score 186 as Hampshire finished their innings at 441. Yorkshire replied with B. B. Wilson (74) helping Denton to put on 197 for the second wicket; the latter scoring his 191 in $3\frac{1}{4}$ hours. Yorkshire made 492. Both sides had missed catches during the two innings. When Hampshire batted again Hirst (six for 47) and Haigh (three for 13) bowled them out for 95 and Yorkshire went on to win easily.

The next match at Bradford against Sussex was lost to rain after Yorkshire had scored 178 and Sussex 28 for two. Nor was much progress made in the Warwickshire match at Hull where the visitors scored 59 and 64 for three with Hirst taking four for 27 and Drake six for 25 in the first innings. For Yorkshire, Kilner (22 not out) was top scorer as Yorkshire were dismissed for 88.

At Old Trafford, Lancashire began well by scoring 347 with R. H. Spooner making 109. Rain had delayed the start and there were further interruptions, but by the end of the second day Yorkshire had been bowled out for 103. Following on, Yorkshire did not start their second innings until 3.30 but the wicket became treacherous at the end of the innings, by which time Denton had gone for a fighting 48. Yorkshire held on with 105 for seven.

Yorkshire easily beat Essex at Leyton. Only Perrin (74) showed any resistance to Booth, who took seven for 50 as Essex were bowled out for 129. After Yorkshire had made 278; Booth took five for 69 as Essex scored 187 and Yorkshire went on to win by ten wickets.

At Headingley Yorkshire recorded another win at Middlesex's expense. After heavy rains, Yorkshire batted $2\frac{1}{2}$ hours in making 92, with Hirst scoring 24 and Tarrant taking seven for 40. Middlesex improved on this by 18 runs, with Tarrant proving the best batsman with 35 as Drake took five for 23. In their second innings, Oldroyd (47 in 3 hours) and Denton (42) put on 69 for Yorkshire's second wicket before the tail took the total to 215. Middlesex needed 190 to win and they were soon dismissed for 90, with Booth at his best taking eight for 47.

At Harrogate, Rhodes made 176 as Yorkshire were out for 389 to Nottinghamshire. He then took five for 68 to ensure a big lead for Yorkshire as they bowled out the opposition for 161. When Nottinghamshire followed on on a rain-affected pitch, Drake finished with six for 24 for Yorkshire to win by an innings and 102 runs.

At Worcester there was another draw with not much play on the first day and some on the last two. Yorkshire bowled out the home side for 134. Yorkshire then travelled to Taunton and beat Somerset by an innings and 136 runs. After Yorkshire had scored 330 (Denton 82), W. T. Greswell with 23 out of 69 and Braund with 50 not out of 125 were the only home batsmen to succeed as Hirst took six for 30 and six for 37.

The Championship season finished with a draw at Hove with Yorkshire making 141 and Sussex 154 for eight. There had also been a drawn match with the South Africans at Sheffield in which the visitors led by 31 on the first innings.

At Scarborough, MCC made 153 with Booth taking six for 52 but Yorkshire, in wet conditions, could reply with only 124 as Drake made the top score of 35. After a blank second day and a further hold-up MCC replied with 84, with Hirst taking six for 40 and Drake four for 24. Yorkshire were left 100 minutes to score 116 to win, but were happy to play for a draw at 79 for six.

As Champion County, Yorkshire met the Rest of England at The Oval and met with a humiliating defeat by an innings and 122 runs. Yorkshire were bowled out for 167 by Hitch, and when the Rest batted, R. H. Spooner scored 130 in a very fine innings as the Rest gained a lead of 200. Yorkshire were bundled out for 78 with Douglas, bowling slower than usual, taking seven for 39 in a fine spell of bowling.

Yorkshire were worthy Champions in 1912, and had the club not had such poor weather which coincided with the home programme, adversely affecting the gates, then the season would have been considered satisfactory from all angles. The Club's annual report hoped that the membership would rise to 3,000 or even 3,500 in order to 'have an assured income which would go far in enabling it to meet with complacency any falling off of gate receipts due to exceptional causes.'

Once again David Denton headed the batting averages with 2,088 runs at 44.44. He was well ahead of Rhodes, who scored only 1,030 runs at 30.29 and B. B. Wilson with 1,453 runs at 28.49. Hirst had one of his poorest seasons with the bat, making only 1,119 runs at 26.08. Roy Kilner scored 570 runs at 22.80 and looked as though he would make a valuable member of the side and if Booth's batting went back his bowling was of rather more importance to the side. Oldroyd

County Champions again in 1912. Back row: Dolphin, Booth, Drake, Rhodes, Mr. Hoyland. Seated: Wilson, Denton, Sir Archibald White, Hirst, Haigh. Front row: Kilner, Oldroyd, Bates.

played some valuable innings, while Haigh and Sir A. W. White both batted well when runs were wanted quickly. J. Tasker was given plenty of opportunity and showed great promise without looking a player of real quality. Drake's batting went back with a poor average of 16.95, but he showed the making of a top-class all-rounder. Dolphin kept wicket well and showed qualities as a batsman at times.

With the ball Haigh bowled superbly in conditions that suited him and only Blythe of the regular bowlers headed him in the first-class averages. For Yorkshire he took 125 wickets at 12.06 each. Booth was second with 104 wickets at 15.37 and he had an excellent season and bore comparison as a fast bowler with any in the country. Hirst took 113 wickets at 16.91, a wonderful performance for a 41-year-old. Drake took 87 wickets at 18.72, which with any other county would have been considered first-rate. Rhodes' total of wickets fell to 45 at 22.15 – he had never done quite so badly before – but his bowling, fortunately, was seldom needed. Kilner showed signs of making a bowler.

The 1913 season opened for Yorkshire in a manner that destroyed any illusions of grandeur they might have possessed. At Old Trafford, they were defeated by Lancashire by an innings and three runs. Yorkshire found run-getting difficult with the ball coming through at varying paces and only Hirst, with 21 in a stay of two hours, looked at all at ease as Yorkshire were bowled out for 74, with Heap bowling wonderfully well in taking six for 16. The Yorkshire bowlers managed to dismiss Lancashire for 130, with Haigh taking five for 42 and Hirst three for 37, but the Lancashire bowlers did even better in Yorkshire's second innings which finished at 53, with Heap taking five for 23.

Yorkshire returned to something like their normal form at Bristol where they recovered from 43 for three to 271. Gloucestershire then lost four wickets for 17 before recovering in turn to 210, with Hirst taking six for 70. Rhodes (110) and B. B. Wilson (104) then opened with a stand of 197 in 135 minutes with the latter hitting well all round the wicket and Rhodes' cutting being seen to advantage. Yorkshire reaches 369 for five before declaring. Gloucestershire then collapsed for 200. Yorkshire's Western tour then furnished an innings win at Bath over Somerset, who were dismissed for 90 and 67. Drake took four for 4 and three for 3, while Booth took six for 39 in the second innings. When Yorkshire batted, Hirst, Booth and Haigh passed 50 as Yorkshire were dismissed for 289.

Returning home via Worcester, Yorkshire bowled Worcestershire out for 201, with Hirst and Booth taking four wickets each. Denton scored 92 in 105 minutes of brilliant batting for Yorkshire adding 99 for the first wicket with Hirst (53) as Yorkshire gained a first innings lead of 93. In the home side's second innings only H. K. Foster with 86 offered much resistance and they were dismissed for 178. Yorkshire requiring 85 to win, and soon obtained them with three wickets going down.

In spite of their bad start, Yorkshire stood in third position behind Kent and Nottinghamshire, who each had 100 per cent records. At Sheffield, Sussex were in trouble throughout their first innings with nine down for 98, but reached 135. Rhodes (59) and B. B. Wilson (77) opened for Yorkshire with a stand of 131 and Haigh scored a rapid 56 as Yorkshire finished with 317. Sussex scored 233 in their second innings with Booth taking five for 77 and Yorkshire went on to win by eight wickets after tea on the second day.

Yorkshire's trip to Fenner's finished in a draw, with Rhodes scoring 102 as the visitors made 266. E. L. Kidd (123) then dominated the Yorkshire bowling as Cambridge took a lead of 74 runs, with Rhodes taking seven for 98. Yorkshire batted much better in their second innings scoring 361 for seven before declaring with Drake getting 108. Cambridge University scored 184 for six to secure an honourable draw.

No match could have been looked forward to more keenly than the visit of leaders Kent to Park Avenue. Winning the toss, the visitors lost three wickets for 88 before Woolley (84) joined Hubble (55) to add 108 for the fourth wicket after which Kent collapsed to 251 all out before the bowling of Booth (six for 108). Denton with 85 rescued Yorkshire after seven wickets were down for 135 but it was a last-wicket stand between Booth (38 not out) and Dolphin (29 not out) that added 34 that really brought Yorkshire back into the game at 217. Kent then reached 275, leaving Yorkshire with 310 to win in 5 hours. Kent could not have started better with Fielder taking three quick wickets as Yorkshire's score was 41 for four but Hirst and Kilner came together to add 151 without being parted in three hours and in light that was far from good. Rain then came to ruin a good finish with Hirst on 102 and Kilner 50. Yorkshire remained third in the table with Kent leading from Nottinghamshire.

At Trent Bridge, as so often in the past, the bat was well on top of the ball with Wilson (80), Denton (148) and Kilner (76) as Yorkshire ran up 471. Nottinghamshire in reply spent over 6 hours in scoring 331, with George Gunn making 132. Booth took six for 99. Yorkshire declared at 112 for three and with only 90 minutes remaining, George Gunn reached 109 not out in 129 for three before stumps were drawn. At Headingley, against Leicestershire, Yorkshire soon lost five wickets for 58 before Kilner (104) and Booth (79) added 184, with Kilner making his first hundred in county cricket. Hirst took ten for 48 as Yorkshire won by an innings and 108 runs.

At Leyton, Essex recovered from a poor start to reach 233. Yorkshire made 271 and Essex at their second attempt were in real trouble at 64 for six before F. L. Fane (75) and C. D. McIver (85) put on 118 in 110 minutes as Essex reached 252. Booth was Yorkshire's best bowler with five for 94. Yorkshire were set 215 to win which they achieved for the loss of seven wickets, Rhodes making 97.

At Fartown, Worcestershire were well beaten by 213 runs after Yorkshire had scored a modest 213 which was enough for a first-innings lead of 66, with Booth taking five for 68. Yorkshire then declared at 215 for six before Worcestershire were bowled out for 68.

Yorkshire had to be satisfied with a draw at Lord's against Middlesex, who bowled half the Yorkshire side out for 125 before Booth with 107 not out in two hours of brilliant batting helped his side to 280. Middlesex in the end finished only 18 runs behind after Booth had gone through the tail to take five for 72. Early wickets for Middlesex caused Yorkshire to struggle to score 234, and Middlesex were set 253 in $3\frac{1}{2}$ hours, but gave up the chase after losing four wickets for 53 and finished at 186 for six. The Warwickshire match at Sheffield provided Yorkshire with a win by 89 runs. Yorkshire batted brightly to score 254 and Booth took six for 84 as Warwickshire finished 102 behind. Kilner then hit up 74 in 55 minutes with help from Holmes (36) and Yorkshire reached 195 to set Warwickshire 298 to win. Hirst, with five for 67, bowled Yorkshire to a comfortable victory. Yorkshire were still second in the table to Kent, who had suffered a defeat at the hands of Gloucestershire.

Percy Holmes made his debut in the Middlesex match at Lord's, but during 1913 and 1914 did little of note when playing in the first eleven. It was 1912 (when aged 25) that he first played for Yorkshire 2nd XI, and he was a late developer by today's standards. In 1919 he immediately got into the Yorkshire side and for several years was the senior and the quicker-scoring, more attractive, partner in that greatest of all county opening pairs of Holmes and Sutcliffe. Percy Holmes was a short, dapper right-hand opening bat, very quick on his feet and attractive to watch. He was 32 years old before he established himself in the Yorkshire side but then on until his retirement in 1933 he was one of the best batsmen in England. His Test career was rather disappointing, as he played only once against Australia when he made top score (30) against Gregory and McDonald at Trent Bridge and was then dropped from the side. When he retired from first-class cricket, he was professional at Swansea for a time and had one season (1947) as a first-class umpire, but later went as coach at Scarborough College until retiring due to ill-health in 1959.

The visit to Northampton provided another draw, with Northamptonshire batting all day for 305. Rhodes, not quite at his

Percy Holmes, the opening batsman for 20 years, who shared 69 opening century partnerships with Sutcliffe, including the world record 555 against Essex in 1932. (NCCC)

best, scored 110, adding 96 with Denton (55) for the second wicket, and Yorkshire reached 333. S. G. Smith scored 102 when Northamptonshire batted again and declared at 254 for seven. Yorkshire made little effort to obtain 227 to win and finished at 141 for three.

At Bradford, Yorkshire had little difficulty in beating Somerset by an innings and 25 runs. Braund (44 not out and 19) made the top score in each innings as Somerset were dismissed for 149 and 124, with Booth taking five for 80 in the first innings. For Yorkshire, Rhodes took two hours to score 56 and Hirst spent the same time scoring 90 not out as Yorkshire took their score to 298. Moving to Leicester, Yorkshire began well by Rhodes (152) and B. B. Wilson putting on 180 for the first wicket, and then Hirst scored 55 in two hours for Yorkshire to reach 405. On a rain-affected wicket, Leicester were soon in trouble at 29 for five before W. N. Riley reached an aggressive 100, at one time adding 60 in 40 minutes and hitting 24 off an over from Hirst. In spite of that display, Yorkshire bowled the home side out for 168, with Booth taking seven for 65. Batting again, Yorkshire scored 142 for six before declaring and Leicestershire were bowled out for 189.

On a pitch that always gave the bowlers a little help, Northampton-shire in the next match obtained 145 as Rhodes took seven for 45. When it was their turn to bat, Yorkshire's batsmen were never set and were soon dismissed for 107. Haywood (58) and Seymour (75) each attacked the bowling as Northamptonshire increased their lead of 232, with Booth taking seven for 64. Yorkshire then went in and lost four wickets with only 56 on the board before Kilner, who went on to score 91 and Hirst 30 put on 74 for Yorkshire's fifth wicket. They were 199 for seven at one stage but were soon all out for 212. Northamptonshire thus won by 20 runs, but many felt that if Yorkshire had shown more aggression they would probably have finished the winners.

A friendly match with Lancashire followed at Liverpool where the home side won by three wickets. Dean took nine for 62 and eight for 29 to take 17 wickets in the match.

Once again the Kent match was ruined by the weather, the second and third days being complete washouts. Yorkshire batted first and were dismissed for 100. James Seymour then treated the Tunbridge Wells crowd to a fine display of batting scoring 75 out of 127 with shots all round the wicket. At the end of the day Kent had been dismissed for 135 with Rhodes taking five for 42, the match being abandoned in due course.

Yorkshire's misfortunes continued at Bramall Lane where Glouces-tershire batted first and scored 157, with G. L. Jessop scoring 67 out of 83 in an hour, and Booth taking five for 55. Yorkshire, batting consistently, made 172, including 38 for the last wicket. When Gloucestershire batted again, five wickets fell for 49 before Jessop, with 40 out of 69, again saved his team in 37 minutes of batting as his side reached 124. This time Drake took eight for 59 and when Yorkshire set out to score 110 it was Drake with 45 not out who nearly snatched victory for the home side. Seven wickets were down for 50, but after Holmes was out for 16, it was Jessop who got the last two wickets to gain victory for his side.

Nottinghamshire arrived at Dewsbury and put on 94 for the first wicket, going on to 285. B. B. Wilson made 77 in 3¼ hours with hardly one scoring shot in front of the wicket. With Denton (55) he added 105 for the third wicket, but with nine down for 269 it needed Birtles with 34 not out and his captain to add 40, and earn Yorkshire first innings points. George Gunn then had the distinction of carrying his bat through the innings for 62 not out out of 176. Requiring 153 to win, Yorkshire taking great care, knocked them off in 3 hours with Denton (55) holding the fort as they won by five wickets.

At Hull, Yorkshire's up-and-down form continued when Surrey beat them by 57 runs. Hobbs with 64 was the only Surrey batsman to overcome the treacherous conditions and Yorkshire gained a lead of

27 runs. Surrey then lost three wickets for 30 but recovered to reach 266. Dolphin captured seven victims behind the stumps. With the game now running in Surrey's favour, Yorkshire lost five wickets for 58 before Drake (64) and Birtles (47) added 82 but Yorkshire were out for 182. Had Surrey's fielding and catching been better then victory would have been by a much larger margin.

Yorkshire's last match in July at Harrogate resulted in a win by 182 runs over Hampshire. Kilner, opening the innings scored 85 and B. B. Wilson made 81 as Hampshire dropped eight catches in Yorkshire's innings of 382. The Hon L. H. Tennyson scored 96 in a brilliant innings in which he was dropped twice early on and Hampshire reached 262. Batting again, Drake (63), Booth (74) and Hirst (62 not out) helped Yorkshire reach 291 at a fast rate. Hampshire were then dismissed for 229, with Drake taking five for 71.

At Leeds the Lancashire match proved to be exciting with Lancashire making 275 after losing six wickets for 134, Heap scoring 90 in a fighting innings before being run out. Yorkshire then themselves lost seven wickets for 131, when Hirst in typical fashion scored 78 not out and Lancashire's first innings lead was restricted to 56. When they batted again, Lancashire made 160 all out, in face of fine bowling from Booth, with seven for 77. Yorkshire had to obtain 217 in less than 150 minutes and after Haigh (67) and Wilson (48) added 108 for the third wicket in 50 minutes, Sir A. W. White was there at the end with 27 not out as Yorkshire won a fine victory by three wickets.

A draw with Warwickshire followed at Edgbaston. The home side totalled 336 after recovering 190 for seven. E. R. Wilson, playing his first match for the County since 1902, took six for 89, Yorkshire replied with 369, Haigh scoring 92 and Kilner and Rhodes each scoring 50. Warwickshire then declared at 142 for five and Yorkshire were 64 for two at the close.

A hard-fought win followed over Middlesex at Sheffield where the visitors started well with an opening stand of 109 but scored only 247. Kilner made 94 but Yorkshire were two runs in arrears at the end of their innings. Again Middlesex collapsed, from 138 when the fourth wicket fell to 180, with Booth bowling in brilliant fashion to take eight for 86. Rhodes batted three hours for 86 not out as Yorkshire scraped home with three wickets to spare.

An easy victory over Surrey at The Oval followed, with Yorkshire scoring 409 for nine declared in which Rhodes (90) and B. B. Wilson (51) opened with a stand of 109. Hirst played at his best to record 112 not out to put Yorkshire well on top. The Surrey batsmen failed against the very keen Yorkshire attack all of whom got amongst the wickets, and following on were all out for 213 leaving Yorkshire easy victors. For their next game at Bradford, Yorkshire gained an even more emphatic win over Essex. Kilner (85), Hirst (77), Haigh (69) and Booth (56) helped E. R. Wilson, who went to his first century in county cricket and was 104 not out at the close with Yorkshire declaring at 512 for nine. Essex scored only 115 and lost two early wickets in the second innings before F. L. Fane scored 130 and helped them to 349. Drake took seven for 69 and Yorkshire won by an innings and 48 runs.

Two draws on the southern tour finished Yorkshire's Championship season, with Hampshire at Bournemouth having the better of the game after scoring 315, with George Brown making 122. The last two Hampshire wickets aded 168. Hirst took four for 91 and when Yorkshire were dismissed for 249 he made 82, but no other Yorkshire player reached 30. Hampshire, on a slightly rain-affected pitch, made 200 for seven before declaring. Yorkshire then lost six wickets for 92 but Rhodes (66 not out) stood firm and they finished with 148 for six to earn a draw. Moving on to Hastings, for the benefit match of Joe Vine, Yorkshire spent the first day in amassing 292 for seven wickets with B. B. Wilson getting 108. Hirst went on to score 166 not out cutting, leg-hitting and pulling in his favourite manner as Yorkshire's total reached 374. Unfortunately, after Sussex had scored 40 for two there was further rain and no more play was possible.

Two other matches were played by Yorkshire, one being a drawn game at Harrogate against an England XI who sent Yorkshire in to bat but had to field all day as the home side scored 337, with Denton scoring 114. Rain restricted play on the second day when the England XI scored 106. They followed on and managed to save the match by scoring 196 for eight with Drake taking six for 45 on a drying pitch. The other game at Scarborough against the MCC was also drawn with MCC needing 86 to win with two wickets left.

The season of 1913 had been an excellent one with the weather generally speaking almost up to the golden summer of 1911. Yorkshire's second position in the Championship was well earned, and they showed up well on the fast, dry wickets, with Kent deserving winners in the end with the slightly better record.

Hirst headed the batting averages with 1,431 runs at 36.66, slightly ahead of Roy Kilner, whose left-hand batting was a joy for spectators; he endeared himself to the crowd with his methods and his 1,586 runs at 34.47 made him one of the most dependable cricketers in the side. Wilfred Rhodes scored more runs than anyone else with 1,805 at 33.42 while B. B. Wilson with 1,533 runs could never be overlooked by the opposition, although he still tended to bat too slowly at times Denton had a poor season by his standards with 1,264 runs at 26.89, but he still batted in an attractive manner and at the age of 39 one could expect a deterioration. Booth and Drake also scored over 1,000 runs which considering their bowling efforts was excellent. Haigh with 710 runs at 22.90 proved himself a valuable member of the side, even though his bowling was hardly needed and, at the age of 42, he had decided to retire from the game that he had graced so long, with his good humour no small asset in the Yorkshire team's unrivalled successes over almost 20 years. Sir Archibald White had his days of success with the bat and he led the side with a mixture of enthusiasm and discipline that earned the respect of the players. Dolphin too showed his batting ability on occasions and his wicket-keeping was as good as in the past.

Alonzo Drake headed the bowling averages with 115 wickets at 16.80 and was deadly on the wet pitches that suited him. Booth came second with 167 wickets at 18.52, and could claim to be the best fast bowler in the country. Not a strongly built man, he never seemed to wilt and there seemed to be nothing to stop him becoming the best all-rounder in the country, if he was not that already. George Hirst took 100 wickets at 19.59 and his swerve bowling could be as devastating as it was ten years before, even though at 42 years of age he needed the occasional rest from batting or bowling. Haigh took only 39 wickets at 20.28, but he had his days of success, while Rhodes with 81 at 22.44 showed a welcome improvement on the previous season. Kilner, with 18 wickets at 25 runs each, was clearly not required with three other left-handed bowlers in the side and the Yorkshire fielding was better than most of the other sides, even though they did drop catches on occasions.

The 1914 season began with Sir A. W. White again captain, but without the assistance of Schofield Haigh. Nor would Bates, Newstead or J. Tasker ever play for Yorkshire again.

Yorkshire started off at Northampton where the visitors obtained 378 with Denton starting well with 58 before Kilner (77) and White (51) consolidated. Northamptonshire made 117 and 105, as Hirst took six for 34 in the first Northamptonshire innings and Drake took six for 40 in the second.

The MCC at Lord's provided no contest for Yorkshire, who after scoring 292, with Hirst 77 not out, bowled the home team out for 39, no batsman reaching double figures. Booth took seven for 21 and followed that up with four for 21 in the second innings when Hubble scored 62 out of his side's 134. Drake had figures of three for 14 and five for 45. Leyton was the next venue where Essex made 259 after opening with a stand of 102 and ending with one of 59. Yorkshire lost Rhodes before B. B. Wilson (106) and night-watchman Dolphin (66) put on 124 for the second wicket in 85 minutes. Hirst (81) batted well as Yorkshire's score mounted to 441. Booth, who had taken six for 96 in Essex's first innings without much luck, then took the first six Essex wickets when they slumped to 42 for six, after which they took their score to 141, with Booth finishing with eight for 64.

A halt to Yorkshire's winning ways came at Southampton, where only Wilson with 56 stayed for long in Yorkshire's modest 232. Mead was Hampshire's hero as he scored 213 by careful watchful batting, although his fourth fifty came in 35 minutes. Hampshire scored 416. Yorkshire then had three wickets down for 114 but a very fine 168 not out in $5\frac{1}{2}$ hours by Denton saved the day as Hirst helped him in a partnership of 312 in $4\frac{1}{2}$ hours for the fourth wicket, when Yorkshire declared at 426 for four. At the close Hampshire had made 77 for three.

Back home at Bradford, Yorkshire met with their first defeat at the hands of Surrey, who began well with Hobbs reaching 100 out of 151 in only 75 minutes on a soft wicket, hitting five sixes. Hayes also scored well and played with fine judgement to reach 125 as Surrey were dismissed for 317, with Rhodes taking six for 109. The latter also proved Yorkshire's best batsman with 89 as Yorkshire finished 33 in arrears. When Surrey batted again, Hobbs batted brilliantly again with 74 out of 107 in 75 minutes as Rhodes (five for 56) helped dismiss Surrey for 189, to set Yorkshire 223 to win. Yorkshire lost eight wickets for 106, with B. B. Wilson scoring 51 before Hirst (55) and Birtles (40) came together to take the score to 188, when Birtles was run out. Surrey finally won by 28 runs.

On a good pitch at Bramall Lane, Yorkshire batted all day against Lancashire to score 381, with Kilner making top score (93). Lancashire put on 130 for the first wicket before collapsing to 219 for eight, after which James Tyldesley (62) and Huddleston (88) added 141 for the ninth wicket in 90 minutes as Lancashire finished 11 runs behind. In their second innings, Wilson (55) and Birtles opened with a stand of 115, with Birtles (104) scoring his first century for the County. Yorkshire declared at 299 for four. At the close, Lancashire were 130 for two.

Yorkshire failed at Leicester even to gain a first innings lead after being dismissed for 225. When Leicestershire batted J. H. King scored 114 not out but no one else met with success as Hirst took five for 94. This was a very fine innings following rain on a drying pitch. When Yorkshire batted again they declared at 132 for eight, and Leicestershire batted out time at 34 for two.

At Headingley, Derbyshire were soon in trouble, and were dismissed for 157. Thanks to B. B. Wilson (102) Yorkshire passed that score with only two wickets down and declared at 252 for nine. Rain had curtailed most of the first day's play and the second was a washout, and there was less than three hours playing time left when Derbyshire went in again but Rhodes, bowling at his deadliest, took seven for 19 and Yorkshire won by an innings and five runs with 35 minutes to spare.

Rain was partly to blame for the drawn game with Middlesex at Lord's as Middlesex scored 170 for five on the first day before the weather broke. On the next day they reached 243 for six, after which Drake went through the batting to take six for 54. On a drying pitch Rhodes scored a skilful 56 but Yorkshire were dismissed for 179. Middlesex, however, could not or would not force the pace against the keen Yorkshire attack as they batted for nearly four hours to score 172. Left with only two hours and 20 minutes to bat Yorkshire easily drew with 123 for four.

At Dewsbury, another draw was the result in favour of Warwickshire, with Crowther Charlesworth playing a great innings of 206 out of 283 in less than four hours. Warwickshire declared at 424 for eight. In reply Rhodes hit a steady 66, but, all out for 262, Yorkshire had to follow on. Rhodes (75) and Denton (88) enabled Yorkshire to declare with 345 for nine. Warwickshire were 85 for four at the close.

At Tonbridge Yorkshire gave a disappointing performance against Kent after being 114 for two at lunch they reached 227 and at the close of play Kent were 68 without loss. They were bowled out for 493 at the end of the second day. Rhodes bowled well to take five for 93 but there was no excusing the pitifully poor batting performance in Yorkshire's second innings, when they were bowled out for 117.

Yorkshire's sad loss of form was to continue with four draws, in only one of which they managed to gain first innings points and a further defeat from Kent. At Bradford Yorkshire were dismissed by Leicestershire for only 164 and 133 and but for blunders in the field must have lost. At least Yorkshire could claim that the Centenary match at Lord's had robbed them of Hirst, Rhodes, Booth and Dolphin. Leicestershire led by 39 runs, and when Yorkshire were 28 for six in their second innings defeat looked certain. Ernest Smith bowled well for Yorkshire to take six for 40.

At Trent Bridge, Nottinghamshire were all out for 213, and Denton (93) took Yorkshire to within 14 of the Nottinghamshire total. Iremonger made 109 and Yorkshire looked set for defeat but held out at 214 for six at the close.

Yorkshire may have been a little unlucky at Leeds against Essex. They failed dismally in the first innings and were bowled out for 150 with only B. B. Wilson, who was dropped twice, batting well for 77. In reply, Essex did little better, but a last-wicket stand gave them a lead of 50 as the fast bowler Whiting took five for 46 – all his victims being bowled. Yorkshire then lost five wickets for 125 before Drake (54), Booth (50) and Dolphin (56 not out) took them to 313 to set Essex 249 to win. In between the showers Essex reached 139 for seven before further rainfall finished the match.

There was no play at all on the second day of the Hampshire match at Hull after Yorkshire had gained a first-innings lead of 49 and declared at 142 for four, with B. B. Wilson having made 57 and Hirst 53 not out. Hirst took five for 24 and Drake five for 37 in Hampshire's 108. Hampshire in their second innings were 79 for seven.

Yorkshire's defeat at Bramall Lane at the hands of Kent was not surprising in view of the poor form shown in the last few weeks. Rain prevented play almost until lunch-time and the Kent bowlers made the ball fly when Yorkshire batted first. They soon lost five wickets for 44 but Kilner played a delightful innings of 50 as Yorkshire reached 101 all out. Kent fared little better against Booth (five for 43) and took a lead of only 25. When Yorkshire batted again they were all out for 105, with Blythe taking eight for 55. Humphreys scored 41 not out to guide his side to a five-wicket victory as Booth took five for 36 in Kent's total of 77 for five. Yorkshire were now 12th in the table.

At Huddersfield Rhodes (59) and Kilner (79) paved the way for Hirst to hit 105 not out in just over three hours in his usual style and with Oldroyd scoring 51 at a good rate Yorkshire were 346 at the end of the day. Northamptonshire were always struggling against Booth, who finished with seven for 69. In the second innings they were all out by the end of the second day for 192 and Yorkshire won by an innings and eight runs.

In the next match at Chesterfield Derbyshire were bowled out for 181, but with rain affecting the match, Yorkshire had scored only 224 for five at the end of the second day, Denton having made 77. On the last day Yorkshire reached 297. In Derbyshire's second innings, Drake took four wickets in four successive balls to finish with five for 6 in only three overs, Derbyshire's last six wickets all falling at 68, as Yorkshire won by an innings and 48 runs.

At Headingley, Nottinghamshire sent Yorkshire in to bat and dismissed them in 2½ hours for only 75. Nottinghamshire then lost four wickets for 31 before finally totalling 161. Yorkshire did much better in their second innings with Drake scoring 80 out of 96 in 90 minutes after Yorkshire had lost five wickets for 110. Yorkshire went on to score 286 and set Nottinghamshire 201 to win. Unfortunately for them a shower of rain on the morning of the last day livened up the pitch and Nottinghamshire were soon dismissed for 103.

In the next match at Bramall Lane, Yorkshire won before tea on the second day by the enormous margin of an innings and 155 runs. Denton (52) added 102 in 55 minutes with Hirst (107) for the fifth wicket. Hirst's innings took 100 minutes and then Booth (60) and R. C. Burton (47 on his debut) added 73 for the eighth wicket. Yorkshire were all out for 372. On the next day, Somerset were dismissed for 90 in 100 minutes, Booth taking five for 60 and following on scored 127 in about two hours, but they gave a deplorable batting display. Drake took eight wickets in the match and Booth seven.

Gloucestershire, at Harrogate, were also well beaten at teatime on the second day, by an innings and 118 runs. Gloucestershire began well with Dipper dominating the batting but wickets fell regularly at the other end and he had scored 92 when he was ninth out at 182. They were all out 185 and at the close of play on the first day Yorkshire were 165 for two. Wilson (102) and Kilner (79) eventually took their third wicket partnership to 119 and White (44) and Dolphin (55) later added 82 for the last wicket for Yorkshire to finish with a formidable 449. In two hours on the second day Gloucestershire were dismissed in less than two hours for 146.

Early in August the Lancashire match at Old Trafford saw the home side bat first and make 162. Yorkshire gained a lead of 28 on the first innings. In the second innings on a pitch that gave continued help to the bowlers, Drake took five for 33 and Rhodes four for 30 as the home side were dismissed for 83. Yorkshire knocked off 56 to win convincingly by ten wickets.

Yorkshire's run of success continued at Edgbaston where Warwickshire were beaten inside two days by 163 runs. Yorkshire lost their opening pair with four on the board before Denton (60) and Kilner (50) put the hundred up in less than an hour. The innings finished at 243. Warwickshire were bowled out for 110, Drake taking five for 48, and when Yorkshire batted again, Booth (60) helped hoist 60 in half-an-hour before the effects of the roller had worn off. Yorkshire were dismissed for 126, but on a pitch becoming even more helpful, Warwickshire had no chance and were bowled out for 96, with Booth taking five for 39.

Yorkshire's eighth Championship win on the trot was at Sheffield against Championship contenders Middlesex. Put in, the visitors were dismissed for 175 with Rhodes taking six for 68. At the close of play Yorkshire had scored 190 for four, and on the following day, Denton scored 129 in 4 hours and 20 minutes in an accomplished innings which put the needs of his side before any other consideration. With Drake (52) he added 107 for the seventh wicket and Yorkshire made a total of 345. Middlesex did better in their second innings with Hendren playing a superb innings of 121 but he received little support and they were bowled out for 255. Yorkshire needed only 86 to win, but Middlesex fought gamely after Booth (22) and Denton (25) had put on 42 for Yorkshire's second wicket. At 63 for six, Hirst hit hard for 18 but two more wickets fell before Yorkshire finally won by two wickets. Yorkshire had now risen to fourth in the table.

At Lord's against Surrey (instead of The Oval which had been occupied by the military authorities) Yorkshire came sadly down to earth against the future Champions. Surrey began well by putting on 290 for the first wicket before Hayward left for 116. Hayes joined Hobbs who left at 349 for two having scored 202 and at the close of play they had scored 434 for four. Hayes went on to score 134 as Surrey declared at 549 for six. Yorkshire followed on after being dismissed for 204 and were bowled out for 315 to lose by an innings and 30 runs. Denton had scores of 44 and 52 and in the second innings Wilson scored 95 and Kilner 54.

At Bradford, Yorkshire defeated Sussex by an innings and 183 runs with B. B. Wilson and Kilner (55) putting on 110 for Yorkshire's third wicket before Rhodes (113) joined Wilson and put on 271 in $3\frac{1}{4}$ hours. Wilson batted for over $5\frac{1}{2}$ hours for his innings of 208. Yorkshire were all out for 443. Sussex were soon bowled out for 111 with Rhodes taking four for 13 and Booth four for 34 and followed on to be dismissed for 149, with Yorkshire victors by an innings and 183 runs. Booth took five for 56.

Gloucestershire were bowled out at Bristol for only 94 as Booth took six for 48 and Drake four for 41. B. B. Wilson with 56 drove well and later Kilner, hitting powerfully on the leg side and driving well, scored 169 in a faultless display in which he and Holmes (61) put on 117 for the sixth wicket in 75 minutes as Yorkshire went on to total 405. In Gloucestershire's second innings Dolphin bagged five victims, as Booth (six for 41) and Drake (four for 40) bowled them out for 84 to gain victory by an innings and 227 runs.

Victory at Weston was by 140 runs, after Yorkshire had opened with 162; Denton making 52 in as many minutes as Yorkshire had 90 up in an hour on an easy pitch which cut up badly. When Somerset batted they collapsed for only 44 with Drake taking five for 16 and Booth five for 27. Yorkshire were dismissed for 112, and then Booth and Drake again bowled unchanged. J. D. Harcombe did have the temerity to hit Drake for 11 in one over but the all-rounder took all ten wickets at a cost of 35 runs.

Yorkshire's last match of the season with Sussex – the same opponents Yorkshire were to finish the 1939 season with – was drawn with Denton scoring 124 and Kilner 88 as they added 177 for the third wicket. Rhodes, Hirst and Holmes also got amongst the runs as Yorkshire totalled 461. At the end of the second day Sussex had replied with 316 for one and their second wicket partnership reached 249 before Jupp left for 113. Vine went on to score 175 in 4 hours and ten minutes as Sussex collapsed to 405 all out. At the close Yorkshire were 123 for five. Yorkshire therefore finished in fourth position in what had been an interesting season. They were not far behind Champions Surrey, although their bad spell of eight matches without a win ruined any hopes they might have had of making a real challenge.

Matches against an England XI at Harrogate and the MCC at Scarborough were both abandoned because of the war and the only other match played was against Lancashire at Hull which ended in a draw with Drake taking five for 53 and Rhodes scoring 106 not out. Yorkshire were 70 runs ahead on the first innings before rain had its final say.

Hirst headed the batting averages with 1,655 runs at 41.37, with Denton next scoring 1,799 runs at 35.27. B. B. Wilson scored 1,632 runs at 31.38 and Kilner, who had such a poor time of it at one stage, recovered well enough to score 1,329 runs at an average of over 30, with Rhodes scoring almost the same number at an average of 30. Booth and Drake might be considered disappointing with averages of 21 and 19 but each scored over 800 runs and they often batted very low in the order. Others to be mentioned are the three colts, Birtles, Holmes and Oldroyd, all of whom showed promise without getting near to gaining a regular spot. Sir Archibald White and Dolphin both did well at times and the latter's wicket-keeping was considered among the best two or three in the game.

Alonzo Drake had his best season with the ball, taking 158 wickets at 15.30 which left him in second place in the first-class averages. He bowled more overs than anyone else in the country apart from Tarrant and Kennedy. Major Booth was second with 155 wickets at 17.40, an excellent performance even by the highest Yorkshire standards, and Rhodes took 117 wickets at 18.03 which meant that Yorkshire had three bowlers in the top ten of the first-class averages. Hirst managed only 42 wickets at 29.61, which meant that he had completed one of his worst-ever seasons with the ball. He was, of course, almost 43 years old when the season ended so it was hardly surprising that his bowling should go into decline. All-in-all it was barely noticeable that the Yorkshire side had deteriorated in any way, but it did seem that the team needed one or two players to develop into the highest class of side.

Four seasons without county cricket would indeed ensure that there would have to be several changes in the Yorkshire line-up for the post-war resumption.

CONQUERING HEROES

THE FIRST WORLD WAR ROBBED YORKSHIRE cricket of one of the most promising all-rounders in the game in Major Booth. A hard-working cricketer who had just become an England player, he was bound to be missed when the new season began. Alonzo Drake, almost as effective as Booth, died early in 1919 as a result of illness, which might well also have affected his cricket prior to the war. Yorkshire also decided to dispense with the services of Benny Wilson, who was slow in the field and was 39 years old anyway, although a very dependable, if slow, batsman.

Sir Archibald White retired from the captaincy and he was replaced by D. C. F. Burton, who had played fairly regularly in 1914 without much success, and had appeared for Yorkshire in 1907 and once in 1909. He was born at Bridlington and brought up at Cherry Burton, where he learnt the game of cricket on his father's ground where the village played alongside six other members of the Burton family. He appeared for Cambridge University in 1907–08 but failed to obtain his blue, having been in the Rugby School side in 1904. In 1910–11 he had taken part in the first MCC tour to the West Indies, when he scored 334 runs at an average of 19.64. He was an attractive batsman who scored quickly when set and was a brilliant fielder at cover. He led the Yorkshire side with great enthusiasm and was noted for his coaching ability. He scored two centuries for Yorkshire during his three years as captain and led the side to the Championship in 1919. Cricket was always the greatest interest of his life and in 1956 he opened an indoor cricket school at Sunningdale with A. T. Barber as one of his co-directors, and continued to take an interest in it until his death in Surrey in 1971 aged 84.

The County Championship of 1919 was doomed to failure from the start with the games limited to two days each. Fortunately it was an exceptionally dry summer so that only 56 out of the 124 games arranged were drawn. Yorkshire opened their season at the Spa Ground, Gloucester, with the following side in its batting order: Rhodes, Holmes, Denton, Kilner, R., Hirst, Sutcliffe, D. C. F. Burton, H. M. Claughton, Dolphin, W. E. Blackburn and E. Smith. Sutcliffe and Blackburn had never played before while Claughton had appeared only once and Smith three times. The captain and Holmes had not established themselves in the side.

Yorkshire beat a weak Gloucestershire side by an innings and 14 runs, Rhodes (72) and Kilner (112) putting on 165 for Yorkshire's third wicket. Rhodes had a good match and took seven for 47 and four for 5 while Blackburn took three for 24 and five for 39.

Captain William Edward Blackburn was born at Clitheroe in 1888 (but disguised the fact that he was not born at nearby Sawley in Yorkshire) and was a right-handed batsman and fast bowler who took 45 wickets for Yorkshire in 1919 with five for 17 against Derbyshire as his best performance. He lost his place in the side at the end of June and lacked the necessary stamina to bowl in county cricket. He played in one game in 1920 and later lived at Bolton.

Herbert Sutcliffe was born at Summer Bridge, near Pateley Bridge, in 1894, being the son of William Sutcliffe, who played for Dacre Banks and Pudsey St Lawrence but was injured while playing rugby Union. This injury was aggravated by playing cricket and he died when Herbert was only three, having moved with his parents to Pudsey when a small child. Herbert's mother also died when he was only six, and he was brought up by three maiden aunts. When only 14 he played for Pudsey St Lawrence before moving to Pudsey Britannia, for whom he opened the innings along with Albert Simms, a

Herbert Sutcliffe, one of the greatest of all opening batsmen, who shared in prolific partnerships with Holmes for Yorkshire and Hobbs for England.

schoolmaster who helped him in his early career. He made steady progress for a season or two and in 1914 he was good enough to play for Yorkshire 2nd XI, for whom he averaged 35. During the war, in which he became a Second Lieutenant, he was stationed at York and sometimes played in the Bradford League under another name. He made some useful scores for Yorkshire in 1919 and was promoted to open the innings with Holmes at the end of June against Kent, when he made top score (20) out of 64 all out. At the end of July he and Percy opened with a stand of 279 against Northamptonshire at Northampton. He finished the season with 1,839 runs for Yorkshire at an average of 44.85 and headed the averages. A batsman with an unperturbable temperament, he was a fixture in the Yorkshire side until his retirement in 1939 (also appearing in 1945) and at Test level was the most successful in terms of figures of all the opening batsmen ever to open for England. A good businessman and owner of a sports outfitters in the middle of Leeds, he was the father of Billy Sutcliffe, a Yorkshire captain in 1956 and 1957. He died in 1978 at Cross Hills Nursing Home, near Keighley, at the age of 83.

Hirst scored a century against Essex in an even draw before Lancashire won fairly convincingly at Old Trafford by 140 runs. Makepeace scored 105 and 78 for Lancashire while the former Yorkshire player, Cecil Parkin took six for 88 and eight for 35, proving quite unplayable. Young Sutcliffe did have the satisfaction of making 26 and 53 in his first Roses match. Another victory by an innings followed over Warwickshire at Birmingham where George Hirst scored another century, and Rhodes' fine form with the ball continued with nine for 79 in the match.

Emmott Robinson made his first appearance for Yorkshire in this match and though he kept his place for most of the season it was not until the second week in August at Leicester that he did anything of note. He took five for 64 and three for 24 and along with Waddington was responsible for an easy innings win for Yorkshire. He also batted with success against Derbyshire at Chesterfield with a hard-hitting 94. Now aged 35 Robinson had been on the verge of the Yorkshire side for some ten years. He certainly grasped his chance well and maintained a regular place in the first team until 1931 when he retired. A native of Keighley, he was one of cricket's true characters. He had numerous professional engagements, including six years at Ramsbottom in the Lancashire League from 1908 to 1913. He was with Keighley in 1914 and moved to Pudsey St Lawrence in 1919, when his county career started. A right-hand batsman who could play whatever type of game that was required, he was also an accurate medium to medium-fast opening bowler who could never be treated lightly. For his age he was a first-rate fielder and possessed a first-class knowledge of the game. He became coach at a school near Morecambe after the 1931 season and was professional at Benwell Hill in 1934 and 1935, taking 115 wickets at 8.1 each and scoring over 500 runs in the former season. He was then aged 50. In 1936 he moved to Sunderland and his influence was responsible for his side winning the league title. From 1937 to 1939 he was a first-class umpire, and after helping with Yorkshire's coaching towards the end of the Second World War, he was appointed coach to Leicestershire in 1947 before returning to the umpire's list from 1950. He died in 1969 at his daughter's house at Hinckley at the age of 86.

Norman Kilner, the younger brother of Roy, made his debut against Nottinghamshire at Sheffield; he scored 39 in the second innings but played in only two other matches without success. Born at Low Valley, Wombwell, he played for Mitchell Main and Barnsley and was a sound opening or early order batsman who scored two centuries for Yorkshire and was given an extended trial for the county in each of the next four seasons and was considered Leyland's chief rival for a place in the Yorkshire team. After the 1923 season he left to qualify for Warwickshire and assisted them with success from 1924 to 1937, accumulating over 17,000 runs in his career at an average of 30.

Abraham Waddington came into the side on 2 July against Derbyshire. He made an immediate impact, taking four for 26 in 26 overs, and though he missed the next match at Trent Bridge he returned for the Essex game at Hull, when he took nine for 65 in the match and retained his place for the rest of the season. The winning of the Championship was due to his bowling more than anything else, as he finished the season with 100 wickets at 18.74 each. 'Abe', a somewhat wild and irresponsible character, was born at Clayton, Bradford, and when only 11 was playing in the West Bradford League for Crossley Hall. In 1913 he was a member of the Laisterdyke team which won the Bradford League championship. A left-arm fast or medium-fast bowler with a perfect action, he took 98 wickets at 12 runs each for Wakefield in 1914 and later returned to Laisterdyke where he was playing when first called upon by Yorkshire. During the war he served with the Bradford Pals and was wounded on Serre in 1916. On recovering, he was transferred to the Flying Corps. He was very successful for Yorkshire for several seasons but due to a shoulder injury in 1923 never quite maintained his form of the early 1920s and was not retained after the 1927 season. He was a goalkeeper with Bradford City before moving to Halifax Town and was good enough to represent Yorkshire at golf and to play in the Open Championship. After his career with Yorkshire he was playing for Bradford in 1928. A quick-tempered individual, he was often at the centre of controversy and captains found him difficult to keep under control. After a long illness he died in a nursing-home in Scarborough in 1959 aged 65. He was cremated at Scholemoor Crematorium, Bradford.

Yorkshire won six of the next seven Championship games after Waddington's debut and now led the table. In those matches Waddington took no fewer than 51 wickets. As Rhodes managed to take 46 in the same games, there was no denying that their attack was at the height of its powers. Against Hampshire at Dewsbury, both Rhodes and D. C. F. Burton (142 not out) compiled centuries as they added 254 for the seventh wicket and at Northampton Holmes and Sutcliffe each recorded centuries. In the very next game against Gloucestershire, Sutcliffe scored another hundred while Roy Kilner and Denton did likewise. Both these matches resulted in heavy wins by an innings, and Waddington took twelve for 126 against Gloucestershire at Leeds.

Making his only appearance for Yorkshire at Hull was Raleigh Charles Joseph Chichester-Constable, who was captain of the Yorkshire 2nd XI from 1926 to 1938. He became an honorary life member of Yorkshire CCC and served as committee member for Hull, being Deputy Lieutenant for Hull and the East Riding. He toured India, Ceylon and Burma in 1926–27; represented the Army *v* Navy in 1922 and led the Hull Town CC to the first Yorkshire League title in 1936. A wild erratic fast bowler, he played for the Yorkshire Gentlemen and for H. M. Martineau's XI.

Ambrose Causer Williams – known as Bill – had appeared twice for Yorkshire in 1911 without success and once in 1914 when he took two for 22 and three for 81 against Nottinghamshire at Trent Bridge. In 1919 he played in nine matches for Yorkshire, capturing 25 wickets at 18.88, but he will be remembered for his bowling in the match against Hampshire at Dewsbury, when he took nine for 25 in 12.5 overs, numbering Mead, who was bowled, amongst his victims.

In the Northamptonshire match at Sheffield, Geoffrey Wilson distinguished himself on his debut by making top score (27) in the first innings, rather more than twice any other player in the side. At the end of the second day's play Yorkshire were 189 for six in their second innings, which placed them only 125 ahead, but so well did Wilson bat that he scored 56 as Yorkshire reached 273, a score that ensured a Yorkshire win. Wilson again made top score in the drawn match with Leicestershire and helped his side recover from 88 for five to 215 as he scored 70 in 75 minutes. He went on to average 26 in the seven games that he played, but strange to relate, although he took part in three games for Yorkshire in 1921 and led the side to three consecutive Championships in 1922–24, he never batted in such a manner again and his overall record for the County was very poor. He was born in Leeds and was in the Harrow XI in 1912–14, scoring 173 against Eton in 1913 and leading the side in the following year. A brilliant fielder in the covers, he attained his blue at Cambridge University in 1919, and in 1922–23 toured Australia and New Zealand, scoring 142 not out against Victoria, which proved to be his only first-class century. A clothier in Leeds, he retired to Southsea in Hampshire and died there in 1960 aged 65. He resigned the Yorkshire captaincy at the end of the 1924 season following a disciplinary problem during the game with the runners-up, Middlesex, who threatened not to play Yorkshire in the following season.

Yorkshire suffered their third defeat of 1919 at Harrogate against Sussex, who were indebted to Albert Relf, but Holmes and Sutcliffe contributed another big stand in a draw with Lancashire, scoring centuries apiece as they put on 253 for the first wicket, and Yorkshire did not lose another match. They were hampered by the weather, however, which could have cost them the Championship had Kent defeated Middlesex in their last match of the season.

The batting averages were headed by Sutcliffe, only fractionally ahead of his partner Holmes, who scored 1,874 runs at 44.61. Hirst averaged 38 but had practically ceased bowling, and then came Denton and Rhodes, with Roy Kilner the sixth player to complete a four-figure aggregate. The skipper, Burton, scored 685 runs with an average of 25. Rhodes easily headed the bowling averages, as indeed he did the first-class averages, and bowled with the guile of old; indeed his bowling took a new lease of life. Rockley Wilson, coming into the side during the school holidays, captured 36 wickets at 16.58 and Kilner's 45 cost 17.02 each and left the impression that more use could have been made of his bowling. Waddington in his first season did remarkably well, while the only other bowler not already mentioned was Smith, who captured 31 wickets at 28 runs each and was useful at times. Dolphin kept wicket well enough to be considered almost in the same class as Strudwick and he had one or two useful innings to his credit.

Over 112,000 people came through the turnstiles during the season but the membership had dropped to less than 3,000.

Yorkshire commenced the 1920 season in splendid style by winning seven of their first eight matches and leading Middlesex on the first innings in a draw at Lord's. Their first victory over Derbyshire at Sheffield was by an innings and 223 runs. Roy Kilner scored 206 not out for the Champions and Rhodes took five for 15 in the match in 24 overs, with 14 maidens.

George Macaulay was one of two new players introduced into the Yorkshire side in this match. He took the wicket of L. Oliver and scored 15 not out and kept his place until the middle of June, when he took one for 102 in 20 overs against Surrey and did not play again.

George Macaulay photographed at Bramall Lane. He took 100 wickets in a season, ten times, and was a brilliant fielder.

Wisden reported that: 'he had neither the pace nor the stamina required'. Macaulay may have lost form during this first season, but he came back in the following season to maintain his place in the Yorkshire side until his retirement in 1935 with the outstanding record of having taken more wickets for Yorkshire than any other bowler apart from Rhodes, Hirst and Haigh. A combination of a right-arm medium-fast bowler and an off-break bowler, capable of opening the bowling or bowling off-breaks at a slow pace or at medium-pace, he was a very passionate cricketer who did not suffer fools gladly. He was a batsman of more talent than his record indicates; it is possible that he was not encouraged in that department in order to keep him in peak form for bowling. He was also an outstanding close-to-the-wicket fielder, especially to his own bowling, and he typified the Yorkshire cricket of the 1920s and 1930s. He was educated at Barnard Castle School and worked in a bank in Herne Bay where he attracted the attention of Sir Stanley Christopherson, who recommended him to Yorkshire. As a boy he played for Thirsk Victoria, where his uncles and great-uncles were prominent in the days of Freeman. Before playing for Yorkshire he had spells with Wakefield and Ossett and assisted one of the Ossett soccer sides as a professional. After leaving

Yorkshire he was professional at Todmorden in 1938 and 1939 and took nine for 10 in the Worsley Cup final against Ramsbottom. While stationed at Church Fenton with the RAF during the Second World War, he caught pneumonia while on duty in the Shetlands. He died at the RAF Station at Sullom Voe and was buried in Lerwick Cemetery on 13 December 1940. A memorial was unveiled in 1952 at Barkston Ash Church and his name was included among those who had died on active duty during the war. A plaque was placed outside his birthplace in Town End, Thirsk, in 1973.

The other new player against Derbyshire was Billy Featherby, who took none for 12, and in his other match at Worcester neither batted nor bowled. In the only two games that Featherby ever played for Yorkshire he played in a side that won by an innings, and he saw two Yorkshire players obtain a double century, Denton making 209 not out at Worcester. Featherby was still playing for Londesbrough Park in 1953, and there still are many Featherbys taking part in cricket in the Beverley area.

A 22-run victory over Lancashire at Bradford provided a first-rate game of cricket. Holmes (68) and Denton (54) took Yorkshire to 98 before the second wicket fell and Rhodes made a fighting 49 but Dick Tyldesley finished with five for 62 as Yorkshire reached 208. Dick Tyldesley was also Lancashire's sole batting star with 63 as Waddington (four for 59) and Rhodes (four for 47) dismissed Lancashire for 165. Emmott Robinson's stubborn 37 not out enabled Yorkshire to total 144 after losing six wickets for 70, while Dean took seven for 51. Lancashire needed 188 to win and at 141 for four seemed to be home and dry, but Robinson dismissed both Jack Sharp for 41 and James Tyldesley for 43 and the last six wickets fell for the addition of 24 runs. Emmott Robinson finished with the remarkable analysis of nine for 36 in 31 overs and 15 maidens.

Easy victories over Warwickshire, Gloucestershire and Worcestershire were followed by a convincing win by ten wickets over Nottinghamshire at Leeds, with Rhodes scoring 167 not out, helped by Sir Archibald White (55), who came into the side as captain in Burton's absence. George Gunn then batted four hours for 69 but Kilner went through the tail with three for 10 and 50 to win was a mere formality for Holmes and Sutcliffe.

By putting on 191 for the first wicket at Lord's, Holmes (149) and Sutcliffe (70) ensured that Yorkshire would be safe from defeat, and when Middlesex followed on thanks to Rhodes's five for 47 in 32.3 overs, Yorkshire seemed to be on the brink of victory. Two second-innings wickets fell for 35 but Hearne (133 not out) and Hendren (64) saved the day for their side, and F. T. Mann scored a defiant 70 as Middlesex finished at 314 for five. At Dewsbury, Holmes scored 141 in Yorkshire's second innings and Rhodes bowled at his best to take five for 20 in 21.1 overs and with Robinson taking four for 48 Yorkshire beat Essex by 206 runs.

At Sheffield, Yorkshire received their first beating of the season. It was by 204 at the hands of Surrey, for whom Hobbs scored 112 and 70 and Sandham 81 and 89. Rhodes bowled well to take ten for 139 in the match but Macaulay and Waddington proved to be expensive. Three run-outs ruined Yorkshire's chances in the second innings when at one point they were 32 for six. Burton (50) and Dolphin (47) made a stand but Yorkshire were always fighting a losing battle.

Victory over Leicestershire at Hull was mainly due to Waddington's twelve for 74. The result of the next match at Headingley took everyone in the cricket world by surprise. Brown and Bowell gave Hampshire a good start with an opening partnership of 183 before Bowell went for 95, and four runs later Barrett was out. Brown (232 not out) and Mead (122 not out) then added 269 for an unfinished third wicket stand before Hampshire declared at 456 for two. Kennedy (ten for 135) and Newman (six for 110) then bowled Yorkshire out twice on a wicket rain-damaged following a wet day on the Sunday. Yorkshire went down by an innings and 72 runs.

Rain ruined the Kent match at Sheffield after Kent had scored 36–0 and two easy wins followed. Northamptonshire at Bradford were routed for 67 and 51, while Derbyshire (74 and 74) lost by an innings and 71 runs. Waddington took eleven for 54 against Northamptonshire and Rhodes eight for 27 as Yorkshire won by 228 runs. At Derby Holmes scored 104 while Rhodes took a further eleven for 44.

Holmes carried his bat through the innings in the return with Northamptonshire at Northampton, making 145 not out and Yorkshire's bowlers performed another remarkable performance in dismissing the home side for 57 and 40. Waddington took thirteen for 48 in 32.3 overs while Robinson took six for 34 in 31.3 overs.

Yorkshire were then outplayed by Kent at Maidstone where L. P. Hedges made a brilliant 130 to record his first century in county cricket. He and Woolley (81) put on 160 for the fourth wicket while Hubble scored 91 as Kent totalled 447; Rhodes took five for 113. Denton played brilliantly for 145, adding 140 for the third wicket with Roy Kilner (79), while George Hirst made 62 before Yorkshire collapsed from 308 for four to 358 all out. Collins took five for 75 and when Kent batted again he scored a rapid 67 as Kent reached 177 on a wicket that was beginning to wear; Waddington took six for 96 and Rhodes three for 31. When Yorkshire batted again, only Holmes (36) and Denton (50) stayed for long as Woolley took five for 41, with Yorkshire going down by 121 runs.

After two drawn games, Yorkshire gained a good victory over

Warwickshire at Harrogate, but not before the visitors had gained a first innings lead of 95. In the second innings Waddington was at his most venomous as he took seven for 21 and Warwickshire were dismissed for 54, leaving Yorkshire with 150 to win. They achieved this target with four wickets in hand with Sutcliffe making a fighting 34 and Burton (21 not out) taking the score from 117 for six to victory in conjunction with Robinson (11 not out).

Holmes scored a century in each innings at Old Trafford against Lancashire, but Yorkshire's first innings of 253 took almost 146 overs. Parkin took five for 86 and all the batsmen struggled apart from Spooner, who saved Lancashire twice with scores of 62 and 63. Astill, with six for 46 gained Leicestershire a one-run lead on the first innings at Leicester, but rain prevented either side from batting again. Victory over Worcestershire was no surprise, but Yorkshire were unfortunate not to beat Sussex in their next match at Leeds. Rhodes, bowling brilliantly, reduced Sussex to 73 for eight but they just held out at 91 for nine with Rhodes taking eight for 39 in 23 overs.

The Middlesex match at Park Avenue was a surprise to the spectators. All out for 105, with Rhodes taking seven for 53, Middlesex had Yorkshire in real trouble at 69 for seven before Burton (36) and Dolphin (52) took Yorkshire to a 64-run lead, young Jack Hearne taking six for 52. Middlesex fought back, with Lee scoring a patient 48 and Hendren 56, but six wickets were down for 187 before Nigel Haig hit hard for a splendid 86 to put Middlesex on top. Wilson took six for 61 but a score of 198 would take some getting on the wearing pitch. Yorkshire were in real trouble at 54 for four and again at 112 for seven but Rockley Wilson (39 not out) held firm. With Kilner missing absent ill, a last wicket stand between Wilson and Waddington took the score from 140 to 193 before Stevens bowled Waddington for 25 to record an exciting win for Middlesex by four runs.

Sutcliffe carried his bat through the innings for 125 not out from a total of 307 against Essex at Southend, who were well beaten by 122 runs with Waddington taking eight for 71 in the match. A visit to The Oval followed and Surrey began well with Hobbs (76) and Sandham putting on 103 for the first wicket. Ducat also batted well for 62 not out as Surrey scored 325. Yorkshire fell 74 short of Surrey's score in spite of 62 from Sutcliffe and a fighting 81 from George Hirst. Surrey collapsed badly in their second innings for 110 with Wilson this time taking five for 29, and Yorkshire were set 185 to win. Holmes and Sutcliffe (59) gave them a good start with 51 as the opening partnership and at 106 for two Yorkshire were favourites, but Surrey fielded brilliantly and Fender took a great catch to dismiss Hirst (20) when the visitors were getting on top again. From 141 for six

Yorkshire collapsed to 153 all out for Surrey to record a fine win by 31 runs. That game may have cost Yorkshire the title; the next match at Brighton destroyed all chances as Sussex beat them by 162 runs. Yorkshire never got on terms with Sussex, who opened with a 166 stand from R. A. Young (94) and Vine (73). Yorkshire needed 369 to win in the fourth innings and at 101 for one were in the game, but after the dismissal of Holmes (80) and Denton (61), Yorkshire fell to 206 all out with Vallance Jupp taking five for 37. In the last match of the season Yorkshire gained suitable revenge over Hampshire at Portsmouth when Holmes and Sutcliffe (131) put on 347 for the first wicket and then declared at 585 for three, with Percy Holmes making a remarkable 302 not out in $7\frac{1}{4}$ hours. Hampshire batted very poorly with H. C. McDonell (64) alone exceeding 40 as they lost by an innings and 235 runs. Rhodes had match figures of eleven for 129.

Holmes was without doubt the outstanding batsman of the season with 2,144 runs at an average of 54.97. Kilner was second with an average of 36 while Sutcliffe and Denton completed 1,300 runs and averaged 33. Rhodes was only 17 short of his thousand, while Robinson showed a great improvement with 644 runs. Only Waddington failed to do himself justice with the bat. Rhodes was the outstanding bowler once again with 156 wickets at 12.87, but Waddington bowled exceptionally well to take 140 wickets at 16.67. Robinson performed well at times but Kilner managed only 27 wickets at 24.70. Rockley Wilson came into the side in August to take 49 wickets at 14.20 but the weakness in the side appeared to be that they were a top class bowler short of their norm. Fourth position was not to the liking of the Club but they were in contention until the last fortnight, and it was to everyone's satisfaction that E. R. Wilson, Rhodes, Dolphin and Waddington were chosen to tour Australia, while the secretary, Mr Toone, was appointed the tour manager.

Humphrey Ward's only game for Yorkshire was at Derby in 1920, when he played an innings of 10 not out and took part in an unfinished partnership of 27 with Roy Kilner for the fourth wicket. He also took a catch. He was a right-handed batsman and wicket-keeper who gained his blue at Oxford University in 1919 and in 1921 and in the following year went out to India. In Madras Presidency matches he scored 1,354 runs for the Europeans *v* Indians – more than anyone else – with an average of 37.61. He also appeared for Madras from 1926–27 to 1938–39 and took part in his last first-class match in England for Leveson Gower's XI in 1931.

Albert Judson, a right-arm fast-medium bowler, had a first-class cricket career of ten overs in the field against Kent at Sheffield between 1.20 and 1.45. He bowled one over for five runs, the match then being abandoned. He played for Bingley and Keighley for 23 years and was professional at the latter in 1924–26. For the two clubs he scored 3,553 runs and took 1,282 wickets. A railway clerk, he lived most of his life in Riddlesden but died at the Home for the Blind in Bingley in 1975 at the age of 89.

Yorkshire entered the 1921 season with one change in their make-up. David Denton, after 27 years of service, retired at the age of 46 while still at the height of his powers. His place would be difficult if not impossible to fill. The season began with left-hander Cecil Tyson in his place for the Hampshire match at Bournemouth.

Tyson had one of the most sensational careers in the history of the game. Facing a Hampshire score of 242, he came in at number three after Holmes and Sutcliffe had opened with a stand of 43. After putting on 79 for the fourth wicket with Rhodes (41) he dominated the rest of the innings to score 100 not out in a total of 220. Hampshire went on to score 287 in their second innings and thus set Yorkshire 310 to win in

Cecil Tyson, an all-rounder who scored 100 not out on his first-class debut for Yorkshire, but left owing to a disagreement over terms after three matches. He is seen here on the Tong Park ground.

less than $3\frac{1}{2}$ hours; a task they never attempted after losing their opening pair for 46. Once again Tyson batted well, displaying a watchful defence and producing cuts and leg-side shots to score a further 80 not out as Yorkshire batted out time at 151 for two. Tyson went on to play against the Australians at Bradford and Lancashire at Old Trafford, to finish his career with the County with an average of over 70. A left-handed batsman of undoubted class, the reason why he ceased playing for Yorkshire was money. He insisted that he would have been better off playing as a week-end professional and working down the pit during the week. Sadly he preferred that arrangement much to cricket's loss. He played his early cricket with Scarborough, and in that area, before taking a job at Tong Park for nine years as groundsman/professional which he filled with great satisfaction. He later moved to the pit village of Whitwood near Castleford after a short period at Bankfoot around 1919, where his form was such that he was considered the best batsman in the county. He also played for Castleford and had a long and varied career in league cricket. He moved to Glamorgan to appear for that county against the Australians in 1926. In order to qualify for the Welsh county he played with Gowerton, but for some reason returned north without playing again for Glamorgan. Also a very useful bowler, he lived at Whitwood for many years but died in Leeds General Infirmary in 1940 aged 51.

Against Hampshire too, Yorkshire brought in George Macaulay again but he did little of note. But at Edgbaston, after Yorkshire had been dismissed for 89, he came on as first change and proceeded to take six for 10 as Warwickshire collapsed from 47 for two to 72 all out. Yorkshire, still seeking their first win of the season, then scored 420, the chief run-getter being Edgar Oldroyd with 125. Oldroyd, who had been on the fringe of the side for many years, had played twice in 1920 but gained a place regularly after this timely innings. Yorkshire went on to win by 308 runs, with Rhodes taking six for 40 and Macaulay a further four for 55. Rhodes had already shown his best form by taking seven for 80 in 51 overs in the first innings of Lancashire in a game played at a pedestrian Roses pace.

Easy victories over Gloucestershire and Hampshire followed, in which Oldroyd made his place secure with 70 and 96 against Gloucestershire and another century at Sheffield against Hampshire. Sutcliffe was also in good form and in Holmes' absence he and Robinson put on 129 for the first wicket against Hampshire. Waddington, with six for 41 ensured a 258-run win over Gloucester-hire and against Hampshire Bayes was recalled to the side to take five for 83 and four for 103. Robinson again excelled with 100 at Hull against Derbyshire, after Yorkshire had stood at 48 for five, and in Derbyshire's second innings Macaulay ran riot to take six for 3 in seven overs as Derbyshire could total only 23. Yorkshire were now running Middlesex very close at the top of the table.

Defeat was to follow at Park Avenue against Kent, who outplayed the home side, most of whose batsmen, apart from Oldroyd, were out of form. This was followed by another thrashing by an innings and 72 runs down at Lord's and Yorkshire's only excuse was Sutcliffe's absence through lameness in their second innings. Kilner and Robinson alone batted up to their true form.

Rhodes, with 267 not out, scored his highest ever score against Leicestershire, and with Norman Kilner making his first century (112) for the County, Yorkshire compiled 560 for six declared. Rhodes finished with seven for 66 in the match as Yorkshire gained victory by an innings and 242 runs. Warwickshire fared little better at Sheffield, but Yorkshire's improvement did not continue at Headingley against Surrey, who won convincingly by 179 runs. Shepherd scored 115 in Surrey's first innings but it was Hobbs, playing in his only match of the season, and carrying his bat through the innings for 172 not out from a total of 294 who won the match for Surrey. It was one of his greatest innings and he completely dwarfed everyone else in the match. Macaulay bowled well to take ten for 142 but Yorkshire's batting let them down, with Fender taking six for 66 in the second innings when Yorkshire were all out for 153.

The next seven county matches were all won, five of them with an innings to spare. Oldroyd scored 127 not out against Gloucestershire, and Rhodes (104 not out) and Roy Kilner (166) added 276 for the fifth wicket at Northampton. The Kent match at Tunbridge Wells was a real dog-fight with Oldroyd's 81 and 83 being decisive against Freeman (eight for 115) and Woolley (seven for 113). For Kent, J. L. Bryan carried his bat through the innings for 82 not out from 157. At one stage Kent in the second innings were 216 for four but the rest of the wickets could add only 17 more runs, as Yorkshire won by 31. Robinson (five for 16) and Waddington (four for 13) skittled Derbyshire for 37 at Chesterfield and then Percy Holmes scored an attractive 150. Macaulay took six for 32 as Derbyshire were bowled out again for 103 and defeat by an innings and 237 runs. There was little doubt around this period that there was a vast discrepancy between the best sides and those at the foot of the table. Sussex certainly were not in this latter category but after Holmes had scored 74, Emmott Robinson added an effective 115 to bring the total up to 394 and Sussex were heading for an innings defeat at 151 for eight. Jupp was still batting and he went on to add 74 with Arthur Gilligan (35) and a further 70 with C. H. Gibson (27 not out) before Macaulay got one through his defence after he had made 153. Yorkshire won by nine wickets.

Yorkshire had already played a drawn match against the powerful Australians in May when Rhodes made top score (63) against them. At Sheffield in the return game, only Holmes with 26 and 43 was in anything like his best form and Yorkshire were dismissed for 126 and 113 to lose by 175 runs. Waddington took six for 139 in the match but Yorkshire's most successful bowler was E. R. Wilson, whose innocent looking slows enabled him to capture six for 58 off 33.5 overs.

Yorkshire showed up well against Nottinghamshire with victory by an innings and 48 runs, with Macaulay playing the best innings of his career to reach 125 not out, with Waddington (44) helping him to add 113 for the ninth wicket and then Allen (41 not out) finally helping him take the score to 438 before the declaration.

At Harrogate Yorkshire scored 548 for four declared against Northamptonshire with Holmes (277 not out) and Oldroyd putting on 160 for the second wicket before Oldroyd was run out for 71. Roy Kilner then scored 150 out of the 299 put on for the fourth wicket. Northamptonshire lost twenty wickets on the Thursday and the match was over before 3.30. Robinson (ten for 70) and Waddington (nine for 61) bowled unchanged as Northamptonshire scored 58 and 93 to lose by an innings and 397 runs.

Yorkshire had all the best of two matches ruined by the rain against Lancashire and Leicestershire with Yorkshire obtaining large leads of over 300 on the first innings. Holmes scored 132 against Lancashire while Robinson (135 not out) and D. C. F. Burton (110) put on 215 for the seventh wicket at Leicester. Lancashire were still nearly 200 behind when rain stopped play with Lancashire having lost three wickets and Leicestershire were even worse off at 260 in arrears with their second innings score at 72 for six.

Yorkshire won the return match with Nottinghamshire at Huddersfield with Rhodes (nine for 104) and Rockley Wilson (nine for 85) bowling out Nottinghamshire twice for 136 and 129. The game with Championship favourites Middlesex was spoilt for Yorkshire who were without loss when the rain came on the opening day with Middlesex all out for 82 – Wilson this time taking seven for 32 and thoroughly enjoying his summer holiday. His success continued at Park Avenue where Essex were dismissed for 66, as he took four for 4 in 7.1 overs. Yorkshire had declared at 292 for seven and after Essex followed on Waddington took five more wickets to finish with a match analysis of nine for 58. Essex went down by an innings and 80 runs.

There was more misfortune for Yorkshire at The Oval where Surrey were still 48 behind Yorkshire's first innings total of 388 with eight of their second-innings wickets down. Oldroyd scored 144 for Yorkshire, with Rhodes scoring 65 and taking six for 38 in Surrey's first innings of 129. Another draw followed at Leyton where Essex were putting up a better fight, but were only 145 runs on in their second innings with three wickets left. Rhodes was again in form with 102 not out. Yorkshire finished their season with a win over Sussex by 188 runs, E. R. Wilson taking seven for 67 in the first innings, while in the second Rhodes took five for 27 and Wilson four for 42. Stumper Allen stumped four victims and caught two others.

William Reginald Allen was 28 years old when he made his first appearance for Yorkshire when Dolphin was injured and he went on to play in 20 matches in which he acquitted himself very well to take 51 victims. He continued to act as Dolphin's deputy up to 1925, when he played in seven matches and in 1926 he was still the second eleven wicket-keeper. When Dolphin finished with Yorkshire in 1927, it was Wood who took his place, not Allen, and many thought that Allen should have had the first chance of succeeding Dolphin. Allen, a very tall and corpulent person, was then 35 years old, and it was more sensible for Yorkshire to go for the younger man in Wood.

John Thomson Bell, a native of Batley, was a right-handed opening batsman with a sound technique who played in two matches for Yorkshire in 1921 and in three innings failed to score a run. He also played in five matches in 1923, but in 1924 went to qualify for Glamorgan for whom he played from 1925 to 1931. In all first-class cricket he scored 12 centuries and averaged slightly less than 30.

Yorkshire had the satisfaction or annoyance of knowing that third position in the Championship was hardly worthy of their ability. Misfortune in several matches befell them and there was little doubt that at the end of the season they were as worthy to be Champions as any of their rivals.

Six batsmen obtained their thousand runs with Rhodes actually finishing on top. As he also took 128 wickets at 13.04 each, he could be said to have had a truly magnificent season.

Oldroyd at last made his place secure in the side, and if Holmes did better than Sutcliffe in the opening batsman role, it should be remembered that he was seven years older than his partner and had more confidence than Sutcliffe, who in comparison appeared to be feeling his way. Very much the quicker scorer, Holmes was a polished batsman and the finished product, whereas Sutcliffe had not yet achieved his potential. Robinson and Roy Kilner had good seasons with the bat and Kilner certainly improved with the ball. Burton performed well with the bat, frequently obtaining runs when they were needed.

With the ball E. R. Wilson took 51 wickets at 11.13 to head the bowling averages and certainly improved the performance of the side from August onwards, while Macaulay in his first full season proved himself to be deadly on pitches that gave him any help and he was quite prepared to do his utmost when conditions were not in his favour. Waddington too took his hundred wickets, and all-in-all the team could hardly be faulted. George Hirst at last appeared to be getting past his best and he wisely retired at the end of the season, by which time he had passed his 50th birthday.

Maurice Leyland (or Morris if you follow his birth details) was born at New Park, Harrogate in 1900 and made one appearance for Yorkshire in 1920 and a further five in 1921 when he obtained 52 not out against Leicestershire at Headingley, adding 140 for the seventh wicket along with Wilfred Rhodes, who was more than 23 years his senior. A left-handed batsman with a sound enough defence, he was essentially a forcing batsman and possessed some delightful off-side strokes. Leyland gained a regular place in the Yorkshire side in 1923,

The left-handed Morris Leyland (whose first name was always spelt as Maurice) scored over 1,000 runs every year from 1923 to 1939.

and he first appeared for England some five years later. Altogether he scored nine Test centuries and possessed the ideal temperament, invariably coming off against Australia when England were in trouble. He was also a brilliant fielder, shining in the outfield, and he bowled his left-arm slows, copied from Roy Kilner, with occasional success which never failed to surprise him. Leyland continued to assist Yorkshire until 1946 and became a much-loved Yorkshire coach after his playing days were over. As a boy he played for Moorside (Lancashire), where his father was professional, and from 1918 he was engaged by the Harrogate CC until 1923, and after he had retired from county cricket he assisted them again until 1950. Greatly respected as a man, he latterly suffered from Parkinson's Disease and he died at Scotton Banks Hospital near Knaresborough in 1967 at the age of 66.

The new season began with the highest hopes bearing in mind Yorkshire's form at the end of 1921. The team could not have had a less testing start with Northamptonshire, Glamorgan and Worcestershire being their opponents in the first three matches. Only Worcestershire succeeded in passing the three-figure mark in any innings, scoring 111, and Bowley made the highest score (36) against Yorkshire in the three matches; he was the only player to reach double figures twice in the same match. At Derby, the home side did made 130 and cause Yorkshire to bat twice, but they went down by 251 runs, and then came the return with Northamptonshire which resulted in another innings win. Thus, five matches and five wins, with Oldroyd (2), Holmes and Roy Kilner (2) all obtaining centuries. Macaulay took 25 wickets for 154, including six for 8 against Northamptonshire in the first innings and then six for 12 in the first innings at Cardiff. Rhodes took 17 for 125 and Waddington 26 for 240 (including four for 26 and seven for 31 against Derbyshire). Roy Kilner took 21 for 142. Remarkable figures – and a remarkable start. A nine-wicket win over Cambridge University was a formality.

Geoffrey Wilson had taken over the captaincy from D. C. F. Burton, and he had little difficulty in running the side. At Leicester, the home side actually took a first innings lead of 15 with 298, which took up a considerable amount of time as Rhodes' figures indicate: 42-21-45-3. To be honest, Yorkshire spent almost six hours in reply, with Rhodes scoring a valuable 90. The draw was followed by the Lancashire game at Sheffield, which was a triumph for the home side. When Hallows left at 165 for 66, he was the second Lancashire wicket to fall. Ernest Tyldesley dominated the rest of the innings with a great knock of 178 but no other batsman reached double figures. Lancashire finished with 307 and in reply Yorkshire failed by one run to reach that score with Sutcliffe (65) and Oldroyd (77) adding 92 for the second wicket. The skipper made a very useful 49 not out and Dick Tyldesley finished with six for 70. Lancashire then scored very slowly with Hallows (47) and J. R. Barnes (43) alone making any headway. They collapsed from 126 for four to 144 all out. Rhodes took four for 28 and Roy Kilner three for 25. Yorkshire, thanks to Herbert Sutcliffe (73 not out) knocked off the runs with six wickets to spare, Roy Kilner scoring a quick 47.

Holmes (208) and Oldroyd (138 not out) enabled Yorkshire to declare at 453 for two at Edgbaston with Warwickshire losing by an innings and 152 runs. Surrey did gain a first innings lead of 34 at Bradford with Hobbs scoring 52 and 71 and Shepherd 95 while Sutcliffe maintained his good form with 114 before being run out. Rain ended play with Surrey 133 for one in their second innings. At Lord's, Holmes (129) and Sutcliffe (46) opened with 100 in reply to Middlesex's 138; Yorkshire declared at 339 for seven and then bowled out the home side for 180.

Yorkshire's first downfall came at Sheffield where their powerful attack was rebuffed by George Gunn (74) and W. W. Whysall (93) in an opening stand of 158, and Nottinghamshire took a lead of 113 on the first innings. In a wretched display all round, Yorkshire lost inside two days by an innings and 75 runs' S. J. Staples taking four for 12 to complete Yorkshire's misery. That defeat meant that Yorkshire and Nottinghamshire shared top place in spite of the fact that Yorkshire had lost only once and Nottinghamshire three times. The importance of gaining a first-innings lead was paramount under the system of points which gave 5 for a win and 2 for a first innings lead. If one lost on the first innings then no points were obtained whether a side lost or drew.

Yorkshire now embarked on a run of 13 matches of which nine were won and the other four draws in which Yorkshire gained the first innings points. At Huddersfield, Percy Holmes again reached a double century at Warwickshire's expense, this time making 220 not out from Yorkshire's 495 for five declared. Warwickshire went down by an innings and 271 runs. Waddington took eight for 96 in the match and Macaulay seven for 51. Yorkshire certainly looked like Champions when they beat Kent by 10 wickets in Dolphin's benefit match at Leeds. Waddington bowled magnificently on the first day to take eight for 39. Yorkshire gained a lead of 110 before declaring with nine wickets down. The attack was in fine form when Kent batted again; only Woolley in a superb display of 77 could do anything at all as Kent were bowled out for 131.

Oldroyd and Rhodes each scored hundreds against Glamorgan at Leeds and Yorkshire's attack was again too strong for the modest Glamorgan side who lost by an innings and 103 runs. Only the weather prevented another easy win over Derbyshire at Sheffield.

Rhodes (six for 43) and Roy Kilner (four for 19) bowled Sussex out for 95 at Hull but when Yorkshire were dismissed for only 125 few would have thought that they would win with an innings to spare. It had been a wet and difficult pitch for the batsmen and when Sussex batted again it was agreed that Abe Waddington was quite unplayable, moving the ball off the seam and lifting nastily. He took seven for 6 in seven overs, only Street, with 10, reaching double figures. At the other end Kilner took his match figures to seven for 32. The match was completed in five hours play.

The next two matches against Worcestershire at Bradford and at Harrogate against Essex were both drawn heavily in Yorkshire's favour. Yorkshire lost seven wickets for 122 against Essex before Rhodes (108 not out) and Macaulay (101 not out) added 192 without being parted. Essex finished up with 105 and 149 for nine, but stoppages certainly prevented a Yorkshire win. Roy Kilner with eleven for 51 was in fine form for Yorkshire while Rhodes completed a good match with seven for 86. The return match with Kent at Maidstone resulted in an excellent win for Yorkshire by 166 runs, after a great start with Holmes (107) and Sutcliffe (92) putting on 143 for the first wicket. Needing 314, Kent were bowled out for 147. Yorkshire were slightly ahead of Nottinghamshire at this stage.

John Gunn had picked the Yorkshire match for his benefit game at Trent Bridge – a wise decision indeed with the sides locked together at the head of the table. Nottinghamshire won the toss and batted, and though Payton was the leading run-getter with 67 most of the others got amongst the runs and 257 was by no means a poor total. Rhodes bowled well to take four for 59.

Yorkshire lost three wickets for 40 before Sutcliffe (86) and Rhodes took the score to 147 but Yorkshire ended 35 runs behind on the first innings. Nottinghamshire began badly in their second innings and lost five wickets for 38 runs, mainly to Robinson, before Whysall (21) and W. Flint (19) took the score to 71. But Yorkshire's keen attack prevailed and the last five wickets fell for only three runs. Robinson, who had had a poor season so far, took five for 20 and Roy Kilner, bowling better than ever before, took four for 15 in 18 overs.

Yorkshire won and now led the table, and in their next two games Gloucestershire and Leicestershire were no match for the leaders as they lost with an innings to spare. Lancashire did manage a draw at Old Trafford, with Yorkshire needing three to win with the last men at the crease. Ernest Tyldesley alone mastered the Yorkshire attack, making 45 out of 118, with E. R. Wilson, on holiday from Winchester, taking three for 28 in 23 overs. Yorkshire took an hour less to score 122 but only Sutcliffe looked at home. In their second innings Lancashire lost four wickets for 42 before J. R. Barnes (28) and

James Tyldesley (55 not out) added 63 but no one else could withstand Macaulay's breakbacks as he took four for 16. Yorkshire were set 132 to win but they never looked like making them until E. R. Wilson arrived at the crease to join Rhodes. Yorkshire were unfortunate to be batting one short as Geoffrey Wilson had been taken ill after the Saturday's play with appendicitis and would be out for the rest of the season. Rhodes (48 not out) and E. R. Wilson took the score to 129 and perhaps they should have won with only three runs coming off the last five overs.

Yorkshire had little difficulty in beating Gloucestershire, in spite of being 106 runs behind on the first innings, with Parker taking nine for 36 in 70 minutes cricket as Yorkshire were bowled out for 66. Batting again 106 ahead, Gloucestershire collapsed in their turn for 58, only Dipper with 16 being able to play Rhodes (five for 24) while E. R. Wilson, captain in place of his namesake, took two for 7 in 11.1 overs. Needing 165 to win, Yorkshire lost four for 71 but Oldroyd (63 not out) and Robinson (39 not out) took them to a brilliant victory.

Defeat came in their next match at Bradford with Hampshire gaining a remarkable victory by five wickets. Holmes and Sutcliffe began on a rain-affected pitch by putting on 25 for the first wicket before Kennedy took seven for 28 and Boyes three for 25 to dismiss Yorkshire for 56. Tennyson opened with Kennedy and they put on 45 for the first wicket, with Tennyson hitting fiercely to score 51 while Mead made 26. Waddington finished with eight for 35 as Hampshire took a lead of 57 on the first innings. Rhodes (21) and Leyland (23) took Yorkshire to 116 as Boyes finished with six for 53 and Kennedy four for 45 but Hampshire knocked 60 off with some difficulty to win a notable victory. Rhodes scored a century at Lord's against Middlesex and Roy Kilner captured five for 38 in 37 overs but the game frittered away to a draw.

It was a fight for first innings points at The Oval where Surrey accumulated 339 with a solid batting display, Percy Fender being top scorer with 58. E. R. Wilson bowled well to take five for 91. Yorkshire lost Holmes at 57 but Sutcliffe (232) and Oldroyd (83) added 196 and Roy Kilner (89) took part in another partnership with Sutcliffe of 173. Sutcliffe batted for over seven hours and when Yorkshire declared they had scored 539 for five. Surrey scored 165 as the game turned into a tame draw. At Bournemouth, Yorkshire gained deserved revenge for their earlier defeat, but Hampshire had the best of matters at first. Yorkshire took a lead of 21 and in their second innings Hampshire collapsed completely against Kilner (six for 13) and Waddington (four for 24) and Yorkshire gained a surprisingly easy ten-wicket win after a draw had seemed certain earlier in the day.

By now Yorkshire were Champions but they had one further shock when they faced Sussex at Hove. Batting first on a wet pitch in heavy sunshine, Yorkshire collapsed from 18-0 to 42 all out; their lowest score of the season. Tate and Roberts each took five for 20. Sussex were dismissed for 95, a lead of 53. Yorkshire batted much better in the second innings and it was all struggle for the Sussex batsmen as Rhodes took six for 13 and gained Yorkshire a win by 92 runs. The last match of the season at Leyton against Essex was abandoned.

Yorkshire thoroughly deserved to finish County Champions with 19 wins and two defeats in 30 games. Their record was better than Nottinghamshire's who had 17 wins and 5 losses. Sutcliffe headed the averages with 1,909 runs at an average of 45.45, with Oldroyd close behind him. Rhodes averaged 40, which was a magnificent performance for a man of 44 who also headed the bowling averages with 100 wickets at 12.32 each. Holmes did not bat with quite his old consistency but made some huge scores, while Roy Kilner performed well too. Apart from those five with their thousand runs, Robinson scored 730 runs and took 52 wickets, and it was obvious that he could be relied on when all else failed. Geoff Wilson played some good innings too, as did Macaulay. Leyland and Norman Kilner shared the 12th man duties and both showed promise, although their performances were not outstanding. On the bowling side it was remarkable

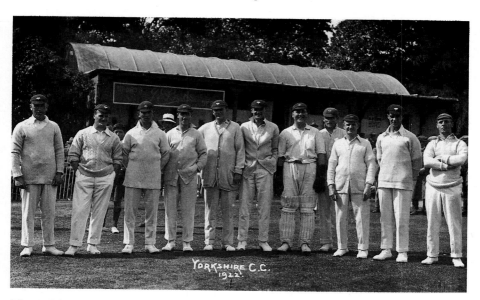

The Yorkshire team at Bournemouth in 1922. They went on to win the Championship. From left: Rhodes, Kilner, Leyland, Holmes, E. R. Wilson, Macaulay, Allen, Waddington, Robinson, Sutcliffe, Oldroyd. (NCCC)

that four bowlers should reach 100 wickets. Macaulay bowled even better than in the previous season with 130 wickets at 13.73, and Waddington's 132 wickets cost 15.83. Both had days when they were irresistible, but perhaps the most significant point about the bowlers was the vast improvement of Roy Kilner, who bowled more overs than anyone else and was the most economical bowler in the side. E. R. Wilson came in and captained the side when G. Wilson was ill, and he took 23 wickets in that refreshing manner of his and enabled some of the others to have a well-earned rest. G. Wilson was chosen to tour New Zealand with the MCC and G. G. Macaulay was chosen to tour South Africa.

Arthur Mitchell was 19 years of age when he first appeared for Yorkshire against Glamorgan at Leeds in 1922. He went in at number four and made 29 out of a stand of 69 with Edgar Oldroyd, who went on to score 143. He played in one other match in this season and twice played for the County in both 1924 and 1925. He played more often in the following two years and became a regular in the side from 1928 up to his retirement in 1939. He learnt his cricket at Wood Bottom, Baildon, and appeared in the Sunday School Friendly League before getting into Baildon Green 2nd XI at the age of 15 also getting into the first team in the same season. He was with Tong Park in 1921, moving to Saltaire in 1922 and 1923 and improved his fielding considerably under the captaincy of Newman Robinson, who had Mitchell fielding in many different positions particularly close to the wicket to Sydney Barnes. A sound batsman, very solid in defence, he had little to commend him from an aesthetic point of view but he was dependable and if runs were required quickly he would always oblige. As a fielder he was outstanding close to the wicket and had few peers at short-leg. A good runner between the wickets, he played in six Tests for England, and was essentially a good team man, although he had the reputation of being a taciturn individual. A noted coach after his playing days, he was the brusque, fearsome member of the Leyland and Mitchell team and was actually the first full-time County coach employed by Yorkshire in 1945. He was professional with Bowling Old Lane in 1946; and was with Hunslet in 1950–51 moving to Undercliffe in 1952, for whom he scored three fifties when in his 50th year. He died on Christmas Day in 1976, at Bradford, aged 74.

The 1923 season began with Glamorgan being beaten by nine wickets at Cardiff with Macaulay taking seven for 13 in the first innings and Roy Kilner eight for 26 in the second. Oldroyd with 194 and Holmes 50 took Yorkshire to an immense 282 lead at Worcester after Robinson (four for 41) and Roy Kilner (three for 9) had bowled Worcester out for 76. They managed 169 at their second attempt but lost by an innings and 113 runs, with Rhodes taking five for 35 and

Robinson three for 33. More impressive was their win by an innings and 229 runs at Bradford over Middlesex, who had the misfortune to be caught on a wet wicket. Holmes and Sutcliffe started with a 127 opening stand and then Rhodes, with 126, added 190 for the sixth wicket with young Leyland, who scored 79. Only Hendren held up the Yorkshire attack for long as Middlesex were dismissed for 122 and 60. Roy Kilner took nine for 42 in the match in 40.4 overs. The Whitsuntide match at Old Trafford saw Lancashire bat for nearly 100 overs in which time they were dismissed for 108, Kilner taking five for 33. At this stage of the season Roy Kilner had taken 27 wickets for 157 runs in 138.3 overs. In reply Yorkshire scored 126 for five with Sutcliffe making 48 in 34 overs less than Lancashire. There was no further play.

Macaulay and Roy Kilner were too good for Warwickshire (110 and 82), with Roy also making top score (60) for Yorkshire. A draw at Sheffield against Kent was all in Yorkshire's favour, with Rhodes taking six for 37 as Kent collapsed for 136 and they were 48 for five in their second innings, with Woolley out, but the loss of the second day prevented victory. Leyland with 62 not out and Robinson with 49 had enabled Yorkshire to declare at 180 for six.

At Derby, Yorkshire won by an innings and 126 runs inside two days with Roy Kilner taking eight for 69 in the match. Oldroyd (70) and Robinson (96) were the chief contributors to Yorkshire's 302 for nine declared. The Nottinghamshire match at Leeds saw Yorkshire suffer defeat for the first and only time in 1923 – by just three runs in a splendid game of cricket. It was a slow grind as Nottinghamshire scored 197 for eight at the end of the first day. Yorkshire finally dismissed them for 200 but were all out themselves for 134. When Nottinghamshire batted again a collapse against Rhodes (six for 23) and Kilner (three for 30) left them with a total of 95, leaving Yorkshire with 162 to win. At 133 for four Yorkshire were favourites to win, but Staples polished off the tail while Richmond took two quick wickets to gain Nottinghamshire the victory by the narrow margin of three runs. The last two wickets fell at 158, leaving poor Macaulay stranded with 17 not out. Victory for Nottinghamshire put them marginally ahead of their rivals at this stage of the season.

Then came a run of 13 victories which virtually won Yorkshire the Championship and left their opponents no doubts about their abilities. At Lord's, J. W. Hearne made a superb 175 not out and 289 seemed a formidable total when Yorkshire were dismissed for 168. Middlesex then made 102 with all the Yorkshire bowlers taking wickets. Yorkshire, set 224 to win, made an excellent start with Sutcliffe driving brilliantly and scoring 76 out of the 119 put on for the first wicket with Holmes. The latter played a defensive role and Yorkshire were almost there when he was dismissed for 89. Yorkshire's victory was by six wickets. After Northamptonshire were beaten by an innings and 60 runs, the next game was one of Yorkshire's best performances of the season. Against Surrey at Headingley, Yorkshire were in trouble at 35 for four before Leyland made a gallant 50, being seventh out at 124. Then came stands between Geoffrey Wilson (57) and Macaulay (30) and Wilson and Waddington (64 not out) which added 47 and 99 respectively, and the final total of 278 was respectable. Hobbs (78) and Shepherd (41) were the only Surrey batsmen to get on top of the bowling, apart from Fender (32) and Surrey were dismissed for 224 with Roy Kilner taking four for 78. Yorkshire were soon in trouble again and were dismissed for a paltry 129, leaving Surrey with 184 to win. Macaulay bowled Jack Hobbs for 19 but Sandham (49) and Shepherd (61) enabled Surrey to be in a good position at 127 for two before Robinson took three quick wickets, and then Kilner (six for 22 in 25.2 overs) accounted for the tail for Yorkshire to win by 25 runs.

Yorkshire got the better of Kent by 120 runs at Tonbridge. Kent needed 360 to win and after losing five for 32 were in a hopeless position. But as long as Woolley was there Kent were in with a fighting chance but after he was out for 138, Kent were dismissed for 244. Emmott Robinson bowled with fire to take seven for 26 while poor Waddington was mauled by the great left-hander to the tune of two for 116 in 27 overs.

A weakened side during the Test Trial at Manchester robbed Yorkshire of Holmes, Sutcliffe and Roy Kilner for the Essex match at Leyton, and they finished 99 short on the first innings. Essex gave a woeful exhibition in their second innings with only O'Connor (35) being able to play Rhodes on a drying wicket. Rhodes took five for 8 as Essex were bundled out for 64. Needing 164 on an improving pitch, Bell and Norman Kilner put on 117 and Leyland with 26 not out guided Yorkshire home by seven wickets.

Victory over the weak Northamptonshire side was a formality by an innings and 155 runs, Macaulay taking three for 11 and six for 18. Sussex met a similar fate at Leeds where Rhodes scored 88 and took eight for 60 in the two Sussex innings.

Yorkshire then beat Warwickshire at Hull by 96 runs but not before they had been 36 for five in the first innings and all out for 170. Warwickshire passed that total with six wickets down and went on to score 249. Yorkshire batted consistently in their second attempt and were able to declare at 311 for nine. Macaulay, with six for 54 was mainly responsible for Warwickshire being dismissed for 136. Holmes (199) and Sutcliffe (139) started off with 274 against Somerset at Hull, where the Yorkshire bowlers made Somerset follow on and lose by an innings and 130 runs. Essex too were well beaten at Dewsbury by 280 runs, with Robinson having match figures of eight for 49 in 37 overs. Rhodes scored a second innings 102 for Yorkshire, with Roy Kilner notching 72 and Sutcliffe 70. Yorkshire then scored 376 against Leicestershire at Fartown with Oldroyd top scorer with 81 and Leicestershire lost by an innings and 173 runs.

Yorkshire then met and beat Gloucestershire twice – by ten wickets at Sheffield and by an innings and 18 runs at Bristol. In the home match Holmes scored 122 not out, and at Bristol, where Gloucestershire were dismissed for 95, Rhodes took seven for 15. A draw with Nottinghamshire followed at Trent Bridge after the first day had been washed out. Roy Kilner took six for 42 in 38 overs when Nottinghamshire were dismissed for 131 and also made top score (42) when Yorkshire took an 85 runs lead. Nottinghamshire were 50 for five at the close. This was followed with another hollow victory over Worcestershire, who were bowled out for 42 with Macaulay taking five for 11 and Robinson four for 22. Yorkshire declared at 242 for two, with Oldroyd 84 not out and Leyland 77 not out, and then Worcestershire were dismissed for 163, with Macaulay taking five for 58.

In the Lancashire match at Bradford the visitors made a game of it up to the half-way stage. Steady batting took them to 188, and though Holmes scored 80 for Yorkshire, Dick Tyldesley bowled well to take seven for 71 and Yorkshire's lead was restricted to 25 runs. Batting again Lancashire gave an inept display and were dismissed for 73, and Yorkshire won very easily by eight wickets.

Victory over Leicestershire at Leicester was by an innings and 74 runs with Rhodes taking eight for 76 in the two innings and Roy Kilner seven for 69. Derbyshire actually headed Yorkshire by one run on the first innings in the game at Park Avenue. Yet Derbyshire took 60 overs longer to score 197 than Yorkshire did to get 196 with Holmes (45) and Sutcliffe putting on 90 for the first wicket. When Derbyshire batted again Carter scored 40 but they were dismissed for 121 and Yorkshire. needing 123 to win won by eight wickets with ease, Holmes scoring 52 and Sutcliffe 41. Hampshire then drew with Yorkshire at Leeds, Mead with 123 helping Hampshire to a lead of 81 on the first innings; but they batted for $7\frac{1}{2}$ hours to reach 327. Sutcliffe scored 87 when Yorkshire batted again and they did make an effort to win, declaring at 206 for five and setting 126 to win in 85 minutes. Unfortunately the rain returned and there was no further play. Robinson, with eight for 52 in the match and Rhodes, eight for 63, were altogether too good for Glamorgan and Yorkshire's 233 was enough for a win by an innings and 34 runs.

At The Oval Surrey compiled 360 against Yorkshire with Jardine (74 not out), Fender (53) and Hobbs (50) all enjoying themselves at

Yorkshire's expense. Roy Kilner took five for 93 and Rockley Wilson bowled 36 overs for 41 runs without taking a wicket. The innings lasted $7\frac{1}{4}$ hours and the fielding and field-placing according to Wisden 'recalled the Australian team of 1921'. Rain ruined the match which saw Yorkshire at 88 for two in reply. Roy Kilner was also the leading player at Portsmouth, taking five for 12 in the match as well as making top score (77) out of Yorkshire's 206 which was sufficient to win by an innings with Hampshire dismissed for 66 and 52. Macaulay was unplayable with five for 25 and six for 27. Only rain stopped a further win over Sussex at Hove with Sussex 48 for five in their second innings and still requiring 81 to win on a bowler's wicket. Robinson, Roy Kilner and Macaulay took all the wickets with Rhodes making top score in each Yorkshire innings with 30 and 43 not out. Yorkshire gained their 25th win of the season in the Championship by seven wickets over Somerset at Taunton, who did rather better than anticipated. Facing Somerset's 134, it was a last-wicket stand between E. R. Wilson (16 not out) and Dolphin (21) that finally put Yorkshire on top as they took the score from 149 for nine to 180. After being 52 for seven Somerset pulled round to 124 all out and Yorkshire lost three wickets in knocking off the runs for victory.

And so ended probably the best season in Yorkshire's history, or any county's history from a statistical viewpoint. Certainly Surrey's record of 23 wins out of 28 matches in 1955 was impressive but they lost five matches against Yorkshire's one. The opposition faced by Yorkshire in 1923 was certainly weaker than the sides that faced Yorkshire in the 1930s and in the early 1900s.

In other matches played during the season, Holmes and Sutcliffe, both with not out centuries, put on 238 for no wicket declared in the second innings against Cambridge University at Fenner's. Yorkshire won the match by 165 runs. Yorkshire compiled 430 for four declared against the rest of England at The Oval, where Holmes was unfortunate to be dismissed for 99 and Leyland (49) made the lowest score for Yorkshire. J. L. Bryan scored 109 for the Rest but rain ruined a game in which Yorkshire looked the better side.

Six batsmen scored their thousand runs in the season, with Holmes 1,884 runs leading the way from his famous partner, who scored 1,773 runs. Their averages were 40 and 39 respectively. Roy Kilner with a top score of 79 was third with 37 and Rhodes, Oldroyd, and Leyland – who gained valuable experience – were the others. Robinson scored 670 runs and had a much better season with the ball, taking 96 wickets at 15.61, and was a most important cog in the team make-up. Waddington and Macaulay both did better with the bat, and if Waddington's figures with the ball show a distinct deterioration, he did miss several matches with a shoulder injury which meant that he was never quite the same bowler again. Even so his 65 wickets cost only 17.92 each. Rhodes topped the bowling averages with 127 wickets at 11.49 each, but above Roy Kilner, who was again the most accurate bowler in the side as well as being a leading wicket-taker. His 143 wickets at exactly 12 runs each was a phenomenal performance and it is difficult to say whether he was more useful than Macaulay, whose 163 wickets cost only 13.53 each. A glance at the first-class bowling averages shows the top three in the Yorkshire bowling averages were also at numbers one, two and three in the country. The membership was still rising, being now well over the five thousand mark.

The 1924 season began with a rain-ruined tour of Scotland before taking the long journey from Broughty Ferry down to Cardiff for the Glamorgan match. Yorkshire scored 275 and the Welshmen were dismissed for 48 and 50. Kilner took nine for 42 in the match. Gloucestershire fared little better at Gloucester and were then dismissed for 68 and 42, with Macaulay having match figures of twelve for 40, Kilner taking six for 41. Oldroyd's 41 was the highest score of the game as Yorkshire reached 98 and finally won by eight wickets.

Oldroyd again showed himself to be Yorkshire's most reliable batsman by scoring 103, adding 102 for the fifth wicket with the so reliable Roy Kilner (50), the team finally scoring 262 against Surrey, who were 169 for seven when the weather in Leeds turned wet and there was no further play. Down at Northampton, Northamptonshire were all out for 84 with Macaulay taking six for 26 and Yorkshire replied with 159, with bowling hero Macaulay also making top score (25) and then in the second innings taking a further four wickets for 42. At this point he had taken 38 wickets at just over five runs apiece. Needing 49 to win, Yorkshire lost five wickets in obtaining them.

Nottinghamshire provided an excellent game at Bradford. Nottinghamshire were dismissed for 147. Macaulay taking four for 29, and when Yorkshire batted, Sutcliffe gave a fine display on a wet wicket to score 67 and take Yorkshire to a 14-run lead. Nottinghamshire then slumped to 92 all out, with Rhodes taking five for 30 and Roy Kilner four for 28 in 26.4 overs. Requiring only 79 to win, Sutcliffe's 21 was crucial as Yorkshire stumbled home by three wickets.

At Lord's, Yorkshire met with a crushing defeat against Middlesex by an innings and 152 runs. Clashing with the Test Trial, Yorkshire were without Kilner, Macaulay, Holmes and Sutcliffe, while Middlesex lacked Hearne and Hendren. Yorkshire opened with Geoffrey Wilson and Maurice Leyland but the batting failed and they were dismissed for 192. Middlesex in reply knocked up 173 for the first wicket, thanks to H. L. Dales (113) and H. W. Lee (70), and

G. T. S. Stevens (114) and F. T. Mann (79) put on 151 for the fifth wicket; the latter hitting Rhodes for four sixes as the weakened attack was thrashed for 465 for eight declared. In their second innings the disheartened Yorkshire side batted even worse to be bowled out for 121, only Leyland with 45 and newcomer Taylor (27) making much impression.

Interruptions from rain ruined the next match at Hull against Kent. Another draw followed at Sheffield against the South Africans who had much the worst of the proceedings being dismissed for 111, Roy Kilner taking four for 30 and Macaulay four for 47 after Oldroyd (67) and Rhodes (52) had helped Yorkshire to a total of 236. Sutcliffe was 67 not out when Yorkshire declared in their second innings at 142 for two. The tourists were 141 for six at the close of play.

One of the most remarkable matches took place at Headingley against Lancashire on 7 June. Lancashire spent over 90 overs in compiling 113 with Ernest Tyldesley scoring 29 as Macaulay took six for 40 in 33 overs and Roy Kilner took two for 28 in 26.2 overs. Oldroyd (37) and Roy Kilner (35) put Yorkshire in a reasonable position at 115 for five but Parkin (five for 46) and Dick Tyldesley (four for 69) ensured that Yorkshire's lead was only 17. Lancashire then spent a further 56 overs and 2 balls to score 74, with Macaulay taking four for 19, and Roy Kilner four for 13 in 23 overs with 16 maidens. Before the close on the second day, Sutcliffe was dismissed for three, and requiring only 58 to win, Yorkshire were 3 for three, before being dismissed for 33, Dick Tyldesley taking six for 18 and Parkin three for 15. It was a very spiteful wicket but the result was a real shock for the cricket world; especially that of Yorkshire. In spite of their disappointing form Yorkshire were still top of the Championship table.

The game at Edgbaston with Warwickshire was soon abandoned. At Chesterfield, Yorkshire lacked Sutcliffe and Kilner on Test duty but scored 169 with Holmes making top score of 46. Skipper G. R. Jackson scored 43 out of Derbyshire's 74 but the next highest score was seven, with Waddington taking four for 34 and Macaulay four for 21. Robinson (51 not out) and Oldroyd (35) helped Yorkshire to 205 in their second innings and Derbyshire required 301 to win, and scored 163.

Somerset were thrashed at Dewsbury by an innings and 202 runs inside two days with only J. C. W. MacBryan with 24 and 38 able to withstand the strong Yorkshire attack with four bowlers taking wickets. For Yorkshire, Herbert Sutcliffe scored 213 out of 434 for eight declared with Oldroyd (70) and Rhodes (56) giving him good support. Sussex at Sheffield were also beaten heavily, by 226 runs. Sussex were 18 for four at one stage but Tate hit hard all round the

YORKSHIRE COUNTY CRICKET CLUB,

Headingley Ground, Leeds.

SOUVENIR OFFICIAL SCORE CARD.

YORKSHIRE v. LANCASHIRE, Saturday, Monday, Tuesday, June 7, 9, 10, 1924.

LANCASHIRE.

	First Innings.		Second Innings.	
1	Makepeace b Rhodes	17	c Robinson b Kilner	9
5	A. W. Pewtress b Macaulay	20	b Macaulay	5
3	Tyldesley, E. lbw Macaulay	29	c Waddington b Kilner	2
4	Watson c Waddington b Rhodes	13	lbw Kilner	21
2	Hallows lbw Macaulay	5	lbw Rhodes	0
6	J. Sharp b Kilner	12	c & b Kilner	14
7	Iddon b Macaulay	1	b Rhodes	6
8	A. Rhodes c Oldroyd b Macaulay	1	b Macaulay	6
9	Tyldesley, R. c Holmes b Kilner	3	b Macaulay	0
10	Parkin lbw Macaulay	0	not out	2
11	Duckworth not out	0	c Robinson b Macaulay	0
	Extras	7	Extras	11
	Total	**113**	**Total**	**74**

Total runs at fall of each wicket
7 33 65 82 102 107 111 113 113 | 7 16 32 41 41 53 69 72 74

Bowler	Overs	Maidens	Runs	W'k'ts	Overs	Maidens	Runs	W'k'ts
Robinson	11	7	10	0	2	1	3	0
Macaulay	33	14	40	6	16·2	7	13	4
Kilner, R.	26·2	12	28	2	23	16	13	2
Rhodes	20	7	28	2	15	5	28	2

Umpires: Messrs. Chester & Warren.   Scorers: Messrs. Ringrose & Moore.

YORKSHIRE.

	First Innings.		Second Innings.	
1	Holmes b Parkin	10	lbw Tyldesley R.	0
2	Sutcliffe c Tyldesley R. b Parkin	0	lbw Parkin	3
3	Oldroyd b Tyldesley R.	37	b Parkin	3
4	Leyland run out	21	c & b Tyldesley R.	0
5	Rhodes lbw Parkin	18	c Makepeace b Tyldesley R.	7
6	Kilner, R. b Parkin	35	not out	13
7	Robinson c & b Parkin	1	run out	2
8	Turner lbw Tyldesley R.	2	b Tyldesley R.	1
9	Macaulay c & b Tyldesley R.	0	b Parkin	4
10	Waddington b Tyldesley R.	0	b Tyldesley R.	0
11	Dolphin not out	0	st Duckworth b Tyldesley R.	0
	Extras	6	Extras	6
	Total	**130**	**Total**	**33**

Total runs at fall of each wicket
3 10 68 87 97 115 120 126 130 | 3 3 3 13 13 16 23 32 33 33

Bowler	Overs	Maidens	Runs	W'k'ts	Overs	Maidens	Runs	W'k'ts
Parkin	27·2	9	46	5	12	6	15	3
Tyldesley, R.	27	9	69	4	11·5	6	18	6
Watson	7	2	9	0				

Commence Sat. 12, Mon. & Tues. 11-30.   Lunch 1-45 to 2-30.   Stumps drawn 6-30.

Printed on the Ground by Arthur Wigley. The Waverley Press, Woodhouse Street, Leeds.

A scorecard calculated to inspire nightmares in all true Tykes.

329

wicket to score 102 not out from a total of 192 and were only eight runs behind at the end of the first innings, with Robinson taking six for 87. Going in again Herbert Sutcliffe played another brilliant innings of 160, being helped by Holmes (83) in an opening partnership of 195, Yorkshire going on to declare at 343 for three.

Yorkshire gained first innings points against Essex who made a better fight of it than most of their brethren near the foot of the table. Requiring 163 to win Essex held out with 68 for six in nearly $2\frac{1}{2}$ hours batting.

The Middlesex match at Sheffield was the cause of Middlesex deciding not to play Yorkshire in the following season. Middlesex batted for almost the whole of the first day after being sent in first, recovering from 89 for three to add 174 for the fourth wicket thanks to Hendren, unfortunately run out for 99, and the Hon C. N. Bruce, who scored 88. The Yorkshire bowlers had been too vociferous in their appealing and the crowd got a little out of hand with the result that umpire Butt reported Waddington's behaviour to Lord's. (In due course the rift between the two counties was repaired with the result that the home match with Middlesex at Leeds in the following season was put aside for Roy Kilner's benefit, a match which broke all financial records.) In reply after the early loss of Sutcliffe, Holmes (61) and Oldroyd (54) took Yorkshire to 143 and then Leyland (51 not out) defended desperately as Rhodes (42) and Roy Kilner (37) got within striking distance of a first-innings lead, but Middlesex led by 24 runs as Haig took six for 79 in 45.2 overs. G. T. S. Stevens (63) helped Middlesex to a total of 268 when they batted again, but a draw was always the most likely result after Yorkshire had taken so much longer batting during their innings. At this stage Middlesex had taken over at the top of the table and clearly looked a better side than Yorkshire.

The return game with Essex resulted in an easy win for the Champions. After Essex collapsed to 132 all out, Sutcliffe, with 255 not out, batted brilliantly for Yorkshire, with a stand of 314 with Oldroyd (138) dominating the innings of 471 for five declared. Essex took the game into the third day but Rhodes (four for 16) mopped up the tail for Yorkshire to have an innings and 131 runs to spare.

With Test calls taking away Macaulay and Sutcliffe from the Yorkshire team and Woolley from Kent, the match at Maidstone lost some of its attractiveness, but the game itself once again proved that Yorkshire were not of the calibre of the two previous years. Ashdown and Seymour took Kent to 105 for one at one stage but Roy Kilner was at his best in taking five for 48 and the hard-working Robinson took four for 73 as Kent were dismissed for 230. Holmes with 59 was in good form for Yorkshire but Freeman's five for 39 ensured a first innings lead for Kent of 25 runs. In their second innings, Hardinge dominated play with a splendid 140 and Kent reached an impressive 273, with Robinson taking five for 84. This left Yorkshire some 4¼ hours to score 299 and in spite of a good opening stand between Holmes and Leyland (57) they never got on terms and were happy to play for a draw. Percy Holmes scored 105 not out in Yorkshire's total of 196 for three.

Somerset at Weston-super-Mare were outclassed by a Yorkshire weakened by test calls, with only R. A. Ingle with 42 and 50 withstanding the wiles of Wilfred Rhodes, who took four for 49 and five for 28 after he had rescued Yorkshire with 100, not a bad all-round performance for a 46-year-old. A disappointing draw took place at Trent Bridge with Macaulay taking six for 72 as Nottinghamshire scored 216, and then Holmes scoring 112 as Yorkshire reached 206 for nine before the game was abandoned.

At Bradford, Holmes obtained another century (118 not out) in a declaration at 248 for three as Glamorgan were beaten by an innings and 26 runs. At Headingley there was a rain-ruined game with Gloucestershire, and at Huddersfield, after Holmes scored 107 and Oldroyd 58 as Yorkshire scored 300 for seven in a solid batting display, Derbyshire following on with 111 (Rhodes six for 25) were saved by a rain-ruined third day as they progressed painfully to 78 for eight.

Maurice Leyland scored 133 not out in the Old Trafford Roses match, adding 75 with Sutcliffe who batted brilliantly for 90. Yorkshire took their score to 359 and Lancashire replied with 78 for two before more rainfall prevented any further play. It had been a wretched season for weather. The next four games all resulted in comfortable victories for Yorkshire, with Abe Waddington returning to something like his best form with seven for 43 at Leicester, where Percy Holmes scored 90 in a nine-wicket win. Warwickshire lost by ten wickets, with Macaulay having a match analysis of eleven for 123, and Sutcliffe was dismissed one short of his hundred. Northamptonshire also went down by ten wickets at Dewsbury, with Jupp scoring 40 and 59 as Macaulay and Rhodes each took eight wickets. The Leicestershire game at Park Avenue was a much better game with Rhodes making top score (36) as Yorkshire struggled to 119, Astill taking six for 45 in 36 overs. Macaulay with seven for 31 was unplayable on a drying wicket as Leicester replied with 71. Holmes (48), Oldroyd (38) and Robinson (56) put Yorkshire in a strong position at 135–3 and Yorkshire reached 203. E. W. Dawson (48) and Geary (63 not out) made a brave fight of it but Waddington, with five for 57, ensured victory for Yorkshire by 92 runs.

Middlesex stood on top of the table on 20 August but they lost on the first innings to Kent. When rain finished the game Middlesex had compiled 334 in their second innings and would probably have won but for the weather. Meanwhile at Harrogate, a 'no result' in which Yorkshire scored 291 for two declared with Oldroyd (122 not out) and Leyland (100 not out) adding 205 in an unfinished stand, put Yorkshire on top. Hampshire replied with 137 for seven. At The Oval Surrey outplayed Yorkshire by scoring 209 and bowling out Yorkshire for 100. Yorkshire had recovered from 40 for seven, with Macaulay scoring 34 not out. Sandham, who scored 72 in the first innings, was again prominent when Surrey batted again, making 60 out of 202. Roy Kilner followed his five for 58 in the first innings with five for 95 as Surrey set Yorkshire 312 to win. In spite of a fighting 51 not out from Rhodes and 41 from Roy Kilner, Surrey bowled Yorkshire out for 202. Meanwhile Middlesex had bowled out Gloucestershire for 31 at Bristol and seemed on the road back to the title, but they reckoned without a magnificent 174 not out from Walter Hammond and another hat-trick in the match from Parker; Gloucestershire went on to win by 61 runs.

With two matches to play Yorkshire were in no position to relax but Hampshire at Portsmouth offered little resistance, being dismissed for 74 and 97 as Roy Kilner took eleven for 48 in 48 overs while Macaulay took eight for 84. Victory in the final match at Hove would ensure that Yorkshire were Champions once again. There was never any doubt about Yorkshire winning after Sussex were bowled out for 60. This time Kilner took five for 18 and with Percy Holmes scoring 88 and Oldroyd 42, Yorkshire were well ahead with only one wicket down. After a declaration at 253 for nine, Roy Kilner did even better with seven for 37 as Sussex collapsed for 83. At Lord's Surrey were well on top of Middlesex at 221 for two when rain ruined the match.

Yorkshire therefore finished Champions for the third season running but there was an uneasy feeling that all was not well with the team and Geoffrey Wilson decided to resign from the captaincy. In his place would be a Major Lupton, a strong disciplinarian but by no means a good cricketer at the age of 46. Meanwhile Yorkshire beat the MCC at Scarborough with Macaulay taking six for 30 in the first innings and Waddington six for 87 in the second, while Sutcliffe with 108 was Yorkshire's best batsman. At The Oval, Woolley with 202 helped the Rest to a monumental 524 for eight declared as Yorkshire lost by an innings and 124 runs.

Sutcliffe topped the batting averages with 1,720 runs, average 47.77, and showed himself to be the best batsman in the team. He was to prove himself next to Hobbs as perhaps the best batsman in the game while touring Australia in the forthcoming winter, when he was accompanied by Roy Kilner. Holmes was not far behind Sutcliffe, averaging 35, and Oldroyd scored 1,607 runs – three less than Holmes – to average 34.93. Leyland showed steady progress to average over 30 and Robinson narrowly failed to reach a four figure aggregate. Rhodes managed his thousand runs with a 26.41 average but Roy Kilner was very disappointing with the bat and averaged only 17.90.

With the ball Macaulay had another wonderful season with 161 wickets at 12.26 and Kilner was never far behind him with 134 wickets at 13.01. They also occupied the first two positions in the national averages. Rhodes, bowling fewer overs, took 96 wickets at 14.79 while Waddington and Robinson had their days of success, although Waddington did appear to be less dangerous.

Major Arthur William Lupton was born at Bradford in 1879 and made one appearance for Yorkshire in 1908. A member of a firm of wine merchants in Bradford, he was the son of a former Lord Mayor of Bradford and was living in that city when appointed captain of Yorkshire, a post he held for three years. A well-known Bradford club cricketer who played for the Yorkshire Gentlemen, he was a right-arm fast bowler and left-handed batsman who was in the Sedbergh XI at one time. During his three years as Yorkshire skipper he installed discipline into the team that was perhaps previously lacking but he had little influence over the tactics of the side and he was well past his best as a player to be anything but a passenger in that category.

Yorkshire started the new season at Cardiff and the only cricket occurred after 4.30 on the opening day. Against Gloucestershire at Bristol, Yorkshire were dismissed for 166. Parker took five for 49 in 38.1 overs, but Kilner (four for 24), Macaulay and Rhodes bowled Gloucestershire out for 82, and in their second innings Yorkshire declared at 77 for four. The home side were then dismissed for 42, with Macaulay taking six for 30 and Kilner four for 10. Further victories came over weak opposition in Worcestershire, Northamptonshire and Derbyshire with Holmes, who had begun the season well, continuing to show good form with 71 against Worcestershire and 125 at Chesterfield against Derbyshire. Sutcliffe and Oldroyd also scored 50s at Worcester where the home side made a respectable 213 (Pearson 70) which Yorkshire headed by 82 runs. In their second innings Worcestershire scored only 65, George Macaulay taking seven for 20. Oldroyd (96) and Leyland (66) added 143 for the third wicket against Northamptonshire at Sheffield and then Emmott Robinson completed a fine century (112 not out) as he added 91 for the last wicket with Dolphin (39). Rhodes took four for 40 in the first innings, and when Northamptonshire followed on Robinson took five for 44. Yorkshire scored 330 for seven declared at Chesterfield and Derbyshire failed twice against Macaulay, seven for 13 in 24 overs and 16 maidens, and Waddington, who took four for 25 in the second innings.

Only 50 minutes were possible at Leeds against Kent, then Yorkshire were at last headed on the first innings – at Fenner's by Cambridge University, where Robinson took six for 72 but Duleepsinhji produced some classic strokes in scoring 53 and 70. Yorkshire fell short of Cambridge's 192 by 31 runs. Cambridge scored 214 at their second attempt, Waddington taking six for 39, and Yorkshire played out time at 193 for five.

In this game Cyril Turner made his debut for Yorkshire. He was a very capable left-handed batsman and very useful right-arm medium-pace bowler who was on the verge of the side until 1933, but played only two full seasons in his career, although he was for some eight years a regular member of the Yorkshire 'squad', uncomplainingly taking the 12th man role. An ideal team man, he was well-liked by everybody, and was a first-rate coach after his playing career. A brilliant close-to-the-wicket fielder, he dovetailed into the Yorkshire side when they were in their prime without any apparent weakening of the team. He was confined to a wheelchair in his latter days.

The Lancashire match provided little in the way of excitement for the huge attendance except the fight for first innings points. Holmes (51) and then Rhodes (59) and Robinson (45 not out) took Yorkshire to 232 after a delayed start. Lancashire's lead was due to the left-hander Charles Hallows, who batted for 5 hours and 20 minutes for his 111 not out. In their second innings Yorkshire finished at 186 for six with Rhodes again making the top score of 54 not out.

At Birmingham, Yorkshire beat Warwickshire by 142 runs after taking a first innings lead of 70. In the second innings, Holmes and Sutcliffe put on 199 for the first wicket. Holmes was dismissed for 79 but Sutcliffe went on to score 130 before Yorkshire declared at 275 for three. Warwickshire were dismissed for 203 with Roy Kilner taking six for 62.

The Middlesex match provided Yorkshire with a deserved victory over their great rivals at Lord's in a game made memorable by the fact that Percy Holmes beat the record highest individual score ever made on the ground, William Ward's 278, by scoring 315 not out, batting brilliantly for 410 minutes and producing every stroke in the book. Sutcliffe made 58 in an opening stand of 153, and after Leyland scored 61 Macaulay (21 not out) helped Holmes in an unfinished seventh-wicket stand before Yorkshire declared at 538 for six. That score gave Yorkshire a lead of 420 on the first innings, Robinson having taken five for 52. In the second innings, Stevens (65) and J. W. Hearne (91) took Middlesex to 271, with Macaulay taking four for 94. There was another easy victory over Gloucestershire at Bradford where Gloucestershire were dismissed for 137 and with Holmes again in great form with 78, Yorkshire eventually scored 365 (Leyland 131 not out).

In their second innings, Gloucestershire were dismissed for 229 and four wides were sufficient to give Yorkshire a ten-wicket victory. At this stage of the season Yorkshire were going through a spell where they had 12 consecutive wins; six by an innings and three by ten wickets.

At Sheffield, Nottinghamshire provided a fine and even game of cricket which Yorkshire won by five wickets. Nottinghamshire were dismissed for 139 and Yorkshire lost eight wickets for 117 before Waddington with 31 not out ensured that they went ahead on the first innings. In their second innings Macaulay was too good for the Nottinghamshire batsmen as he took seven for 76 and Yorkshire got home by five wickets.

At Huddersfield, Glamorgan totalled 246, Waddington taking seven for 96. Holmes (130) and Sutcliffe (121) then opened with a stand of 221 and then Oldroyd retired hurt with 41 before Robinson scored 108 not out and Macaulay 71 as Yorkshire declared at 579 for six. In Glamorgan's second innings Macaulay took seven for 81 and Waddington three for 98. Leicestershire and Hampshire were both completely outplayed at Hull. Holmes and Sutcliffe put on 272 for the first wicket against Leicestershire with Holmes scoring 194 and Sutcliffe 129. Yorkshire declared at 451 for three and Macaulay, with six for 34, bowled out Leicester for 85. In their second innings, in which they scored 206, Kilner took five for 56 and Waddington four for 67. Macaulay and Kilner dismissed Hampshire for 139 in the next match and in reply Yorkshire stood at 142 for six before Rhodes (91), Macaulay (63) and reserve 'keeper Allen (95 not out) took the final score to 408. Hampshire were dismissed for 153 in their second innings, Macaulay taking six for 73.

Surrey, with 81 for two on the board at Bradford, collapsed dramatically after Sandham was dismissed for 34 and reached only 105, with Macaulay taking five for 36. Holmes with 86 dominated the Yorkshire innings as Yorkshire took their total to 233. Surrey did rather better in their second innings with 175 but Macaulay finished with a further six for 68 to take his total of wickets to 64 taken during the month of June. Yorkshire won easily by ten wickets and followed this up with a win by an innings and 159 runs over Derbyshire in two days at Leeds.

After the Hull 'Festival' came the Harrogate Festival with wins over Somerset and Worcestershire. A score of 414 for nine declared against Somerset included another victory from the old veteran Rhodes, 114 not out this time, while Oldroyd scored 86 and Kilner 59. The Major too made his highest score of the season, 31 not out as he added 57 in an unbeaten last-wicket partnership. Somerset were 266 short on the first innings, with Robinson taking five for 65. Following on they were all out for 116 on the second day and Yorkshire had won by an innings and 150 runs. Worcestershire did rather better, compiling 215 and 235 with Root as their hero with 44 not out and 53 not out. Significantly their sixth wicket fell at 85 in each innings so the tail did much better than the earlier batsmen. Macaulay had match figures of ten for 167. Once again the Yorkshire openers failed but Oldroyd (51) and Leyland (138) along with Rhodes (65) and Macaulay (46 not out) took Yorkshire to 438 and they won easily by nine wickets. Their twelfth and last victory on the trot was against Kent at Maidstone in a splendid performance from both sides – the margin being 110 runs in the end. Kent went into a 63-run first-innings lead, Waddington with six for 90 being the best of the Yorkshire bowlers. In their second innings, steady contributions all down the order allowed Yorkshire to reach 333, to leave Kent with 271 to win. Apart from the left-handers, Woolley (52) and Chapman (32) the Kent batting failed and they were all out for 160. Kilner took three for 21 and Robinson three for 32 while Macaulay was hit for 75 in 14 overs, mainly by the brilliant Woolley.

Such a splendid performance by Yorkshire just about took them to the Championship title; there would have to be a remarkable change in form if any other side was to catch them. Yorkshire had the best of the draw with Essex at Sheffield but they were without Holmes, Sutcliffe, Macaulay and Kilner, who were playing for the Players against the Gentlemen at Lord's.

Another draw with Nottinghamshire followed. On a good Trent Bridge wicket Yorkshire took their score to 386 thanks mainly to Roy Kilner (90), Robinson (58 not out), Rhodes (57) and Oldroyd (54), but Nottinghamshire finished only 74 in arrears with Rhodes taking four for 60. Yorkshire then declared with 142 for four but rain took a hand and Nottinghamshire were set 217 to win in 110 minutes. In his benefit match George Gunn saved Nottinghamshire by scoring 49 as Nottinghamshire slipped to 103 for nine, Waddington taking six for 59.

The Champions were back on the winning track at Kettering where Northamptonshire were dismissed for 107 and 42; Macaulay took nine for 59 in the match and Kilner five for 35. Yorkshire declared with 259 for five on the board with Oldroyd scoring 109 not out and Rhodes 55.

For Roy Kilner's benefit against Middlesex at Headingley, Percy Holmes was delayed on his train journey to Leeds, and Leyland took his place at number one. The move came off as he and Sutcliffe put on 218 for the first wicket. Leyland made 110 and then Sutcliffe, joined by Holmes at number four, added 135 for the third wicket before Holmes was out for 50. Sutcliffe went on to score 235 and Yorkshire declared at 528 for six. Rain then held up play but Middlesex were dismissed for

336

184. In their second innings they reached 149 for four, after being 59 for four at one stage. The Lancashire match at Sheffield was also drawn, with Lancashire leading by 43 runs on the first innings. Makepeace (90) and Hallows (79) gave Lancashire a good start by putting on 171 for the first wicket but Lancashire batted for $7\frac{1}{4}$ hours for their all-out score of 320. Holmes (41) and Sutcliffe (62) opened with 86 for the first wicket but only Leyland (80 not out) batted well and Yorkshire were bowled out for 277. At the close Lancashire were 74 for six with Roy Kilner having taken five for 14 in 14 overs.

Leicestershire also gained first innings points too at Leicester, where rain prevented a result. Yorkshire beat Warwickshire by an innings and 56 runs at Dewsbury with Sutcliffe contributing 206 and Kilner 124, the pair taking part in a stand of 173 for the fifth wicket. Sutcliffe batted for 260 minutes and Kilner for just over two hours in an attractive partnership and Yorkshire were able to declare at 507 for eight. Santall hit seven sixes in his 100-minute innings of 119 not out for Warwickshire, but they collapsed for 128 in their second innings.

The Essex match at Leyton was another ruined by the weather. Yorkshire then defeated Sussex by 23 runs at Bradford in a match that had a remarkable finish. Yorkshire were bowled out for 119, but Sussex did even worse as they were dismissed for 87, with Kilner taking five for 14 in 15.2 overs. Yorkshire did much better in their second knock and finished up with 230, which left Sussex with 263 to win. Ted Bowley (105) and Tate (39) started with a stand of 79, before R. A. Young (42) helped Bowley to take the score to 186, and at lunchtime on the third day Sussex needed 40 to win with six wickets left. Macaulay then made a superhuman effort and in 5.3 overs took five for 8 to finish with seven for 67 as Sussex were dismissed for 239.

Both the Hampshire match at Southampton and the Surrey game at The Oval were ruined by the weather, but Holmes did have time to make 159 against Hampshire. Yorkshire's return with Sussex at Hove ended in a nine-wicket win for Yorkshire. The final match at Taunton only just went into the third day with Yorkshire winners by ten wickets. At the end of the season Yorkshire met the MCC both at home at away, winning the Lord's game by ten wickets, Holmes scoring 134 and Macaulay taking eleven for 104 in the match, and drawing the other game at Scarborough, where Yorkshire declared at 450 for six, Sutcliffe contributing 171 and Kilner 100 not out, and then bowled out the MCC for 161, with Macaulay this time taking five for 32. Soon after Yorkshire began batting again the match was drawn, rain having taken its toll during the game.

With an unbeaten record throughout the season, Yorkshire had just one more match to negotiate, against the Rest of England at The Oval. The Rest batted first and Hobbs scored 106, adding 138 with Woolley

(64) while A. W. Carr (60), V. W. C. Jupp (61 not out) and P. G. H. Fender (56) all scored attractively as they reached 430. Macaulay took seven for 135. When Yorkshire batted, Sutcliffe batted well to make 124, and Kilner made 61 not out as Yorkshire were bowled out for 313. In their second innings the Rest made 252 for four declared, with Woolley scoring very quickly for his 104 and A. W. Carr making 83. Yorkshire finished with 112 for three, with Sutcliffe 50 not out, but rain finished the match early with Yorkshire possibly saved from defeat and thus keeping their unbeaten record.

Holmes and Sutcliffe headed the batting averages; each scored over 2,200 runs, Holmes averaging 58 and his partner 55.90. Leyland again showed improvement to score 1,560 runs at 42.16 and Rhodes scored over 1,200 at 41.09. In comparison with the others, Oldroyd showed a slight falling off, but even so 1,262 runs at 36.05 represented a good season's work. Robinson failed by only 68 runs to score his thousand while Roy Kilner just reached his at an average of 30.36, which was a distinct improvement. Macaulay almost reached the status of all-rounder with 594 runs at 24.75, and all the tail-enders played at least one useful innings.

The batting averages were those of a team that had completed an outstanding season. To play 36 matches without a single defeat was a magnificent record in what one might term a drier than average summer. The bowling averages show that Macaulay, with 200 wickets at 14.93 each, had a wonderful season, while Roy Kilner took 123 wickets at 17.72. He was a very economical bowler and bowled more than twice as many overs as Wilfred Rhodes, whose 57 wickets cost less than 20 runs each. Waddington took 105 wickets at 20.23 and on some days he was as dangerous as ever, while the hard-working Robinson's 79 wickets cost 23.30 each. There is little doubt that as a team Yorkshire were beyond criticism, and if their scoring was slow at times it was usually quicker – sometimes much quicker – than the teams they opposed. More people paid through the gate than ever before, the grand total being 326,239.

SHORTAGE OF BOWLERS

THE NEW SEASON OF 1926 OPENED with a ten-wicket win at Leyton. Yorkshire lost four early wickets for 47 before Oldroyd (65) was joined by Rhodes and they took the score to 188. Waddington made a timely 55 as he helped Rhodes to complete his century and go on to 132 as Yorkshire totalled 359. Kilner took ten for 116 in the match while Macaulay took six for 98. At Ilkeston, Yorkshire had the better of a draw with Derbyshire with the Monday lost to the weather so that the likelihood of Yorkshire winning was never on. Macaulay took six for 34 as Derbyshire collapsed to 108 all out and Kilner took for for 25 in 24 overs.

After another draw at Cambridge, Yorkshire moved to Worcester where a total of 84 for six was all that Yorkshire could show with less than three hours possible on the second day; Percy Holmes scored 44. Yorkshire showed little mercy against Leicestershire whom they dismissed for 82 and 118. Macaulay followed up six for 22 in the first innings with five for 15 off a total of 41.5 overs. Rhodes had match figures of seven for 70. For Yorkshire, Sutcliffe scored 60, Leyland 50 and Waddington 49 not out as they declared at 295 for eight. At Harrogate against Essex, Macaulay took a further five for 17 while Kilner finished the match with seven for 68 as Yorkshire won by an innings and 124 runs. For Yorkshire, Holmes (86) and Sutcliffe (48) opened with 102 for the first wicket and Oldroyd (81), Leyland (41) and Rhodes (61 not out) took Yorkshire to a formidable 398.

A series of dropped catches by Lancashire fielders helped Yorkshire to a score of 326 against their Red Rose opponents. Oldroyd with 64 and Kilner (85) were the chief run-getters but the skipper himself made 28 useful runs. In reply only Ernest Tyldesley (52) in partnership with J. R. Barnes (37) batted well as they rescued Lancashire from 49 for three to 114 before they collapsed to 159 all out. Rhodes took four for 20 and on a rain-affected pitch, Yorkshire, with ten catches – four by Holmes – dismissed Lancashire in the follow-on for only 73 to win by an innings and 94 runs.

The Warwickshire match at Edgbaston proved to be another easy win for Yorkshire who scored 326 for six before declaring. Sutcliffe with 102 and Oldroyd 104 added 191 for the second wicket. Kilner and Rhodes both reached their forties and those two also were the star bowlers as Warwickshire were bowled out for 162 and 65, but the home side had by far the worst of the wicket after rain had caused hold-ups. Each took nine wickets as Yorkshire confirmed their position at the top of the table. At Sheffield a masterly innings of 94 not out from Woolley saved Kent who were able to set Yorkshire 201 to win. With only 100 minutes left Yorkshire scored 71 without loss.

Yorkshire were in trouble at Huddersfield against Somerset with six wickets down for 130 but Robinson batted well to score 85 and in partnership with Macaulay (108) added 102 for the seventh wicket. Macaulay's valuable innings lasted over two hours and contained some splendid driving. When Somerset batted they collapsed from 52 for nought to 144 all out with Rhodes taking six for 29, and he followed that up in the second innings with eight for 48; brilliant bowling indeed for a man of 48 and it was no surprise that he was called up later to the England side in the successful bid to regain the Ashes. He had now taken 40 wickets at just over eight runs each. With an innings and 39 runs to spare in that game, Yorkshire did even better at Hull against Glamorgan who went down by an innings and 118 runs. Dismissed for only 52 (Macaulay six for 29 and Robinson four for 23) Glamorgan were passed by Holmes (62) and Sutcliffe without loss and Yorkshire declared at 265 for six. Glamorgan got 95 in their second attempt, with Macaulay taking six for 42 and Rhodes four for 31. The Nottinghamshire game at Leeds was abandoned without a ball being bowled.

A high-scoring match at Lord's gained Yorkshire first innings points. Macaulay again bowled well as Middlesex obtained 250. Holmes (73) and Sutcliffe gave Yorkshire a sound start while Oldroyd (42) helped Holmes to take the score to 158 after which Kilner, dropped four times, played brilliantly until he had obtained his century but then surprisingly slowed down as he reached 150 out of Yorkshire's 415. Middlesex looked in real trouble at 199 for six but Hendren played a brilliant innings of 213, never neglecting a scoring opportunity, and the home side saved the match comfortably. Macaulay again bowled well to take six for 84 but the only other bowler to meet with any success was the rarely used Oldroyd who took three for 32. At Hull Yorkshire gained a first innings lead of 41 and then took five Gloucestershire second-innings wickets for only 59 runs but rain ruined Yorkshire's chances of victory. Oldroyd took four for 14 in Gloucestershire's second innings.

At Sheffield, both Yorkshire and Surrey were weakened by Test calls but it did not prevent Yorkshire from gaining a huge victory by an innings and 13 runs. Leyland and Arthur Mitchell put on 192 for the first wicket, with Mitchell making his first big score (89) for the County, while Leyland scored a valuable 133. Yorkshire obtained 398 and Surrey made a dreadful start with Sandham being run out for one and losing three wickets for only 77. Shepherd (91) and Douglas Jardine (82) then added 150 for the fourth wicket but only Fender (26) could hold up Yorkshire's bowlers as they enforced the follow-on. Jardine was again in form in Surrey's second innings but they were

Edgar Oldroyd, a faithful servant from 1910 to 1931, who hit 1,000 runs in ten of those seasons.

dismissed for only 157 with Crawford taking five for 59 and Rhodes four for 41.

During June, Yorkshire had also met the Australians twice at Bradford and Sheffield. The latter match had been ruined by the rain, while a thunderstorm spoilt the Bradford match where Crawford took four for 38 when the Australians were bowled out for 177. In reply, Grimmett took six for 87 as Yorkshire were dismissed for 155, with Mitchell making top score with 46. Andrews (78) and Collins (77 not out) were both in form as the Australians compiled 243 for three declared before the storm set in. In the other game the Australians scored 146 for six, with Macartney scoring 54.

Yorkshire compiled a mammoth 428 for nine at Blackheath against Kent but were criticised for batting on on the second day when rain prevented a prompt start. Hardinge (47) and Ashdown (72) put on 112 for Kent's first wicket but they only just managed to double that score on a helpful wicket, and following on they were 42 for none at the close. At Dewsbury, Sussex were dismissed for 181 with Bowley scoring 40 and Rhodes taking four for 58 on a pitch that gave increasing help to the bowlers. Sutcliffe batted for two hours for his 52 and helped Oldroyd to take the score to 110 for two before he was out. Oldroyd defending with great skill, batted for $4\frac{1}{2}$ hours for his 135, receiving help from Kilner (41) and Rhodes (70). Yorkshire declared at 385 for seven. In their second innings Sussex batted badly and collapsed from 85 for two to 113 all out; Kilner taking five for 35.

Two more draws followed with Yorkshire perhaps unlucky not to beat the weak Northamptonshire but having the worst of the draw with Derbyshire, but Yorkshire were far from having their best side out because of the Test match and the Players *v* Gentlemen game. At Northampton, Yorkshire reached 448 for seven before declaring with Mitchell scoring 189, his first century in first-class cricket. Northamptonshire replied with 224, with Waddington taking six for 53. Following on, Northamptonshire were doing very well at 262 for four but Wilfred Rhodes caused a quick collapse and they were all out for 306. Rhodes took seven more wickets for 102. Set 83 to win in an hour, Yorkshire were 68 for six at the close with Clark having taken all six wickets for 24 runs. At Sheffield, Derbyshire recovered to total 369 and caused Yorkshire to follow on 160 runs behind. Yorkshire fought hard in their second innings and at the close were 212 for five. They had obtained a point.

At Bradford, Middlesex made a good start with Hearne, opening the innings, scoring a competent 134, and were all out for 295. In reply, Holmes (128), Leyland (67) and Kilner (44) took Yorkshire into a 76-run lead on the first innings. By lunch on the third day, Middlesex were 51 for two, but they collapsed against the left-arm slows of Kilner, who finished with eight for 40. Yorkshire went on to win by ten wickets. At Bournemouth, Leyland with 118 helped Yorkshire to 237 on the first day. Hampshire finished 63 behind on the first innings. Holmes (108) and Oldroyd (109) enabled Yorkshire to declare at 251 for two and leave Hampshire with 314 to win in around $4\frac{1}{2}$ hours. After they lost two wickets for 60, Newman (58 not out) and Mead (47 not out) batted out time.

Appearing in both matches against Hampshire was Ernest Smith, a left-arm medium-pace swing bowler who was very accurate in line and length and also a useful right-hand batsman. In 1912–20 he played regularly for Yorkshire 2nd XI and was one of the most successful bowlers in their side. He first played for Yorkshire in 1914 against Cambridge University and at Bradford against Leicestershire in his first county match he took six for 40. Playing in three matches that season, he took part in 11 in 1919. He did not play for Yorkshire again except for these two matches in 1926, but he did an excellent stop-gap job for Yorkshire, being 38 years old at the time.

At Trent Bridge, Nottinghamshire batted well to score 265, and when Yorkshire batted Holmes made 77, but seven wickets were down for 152. Waddington (41) and Major Lupton (43 not out) made a noble effort to gain first innings points for Yorkshire but they finished 20 short. Nottinghamshire batted badly in their second innings but reached 156. With only 105 minutes left to obtain 136 to win, Yorkshire made no effort to go for the runs, obtaining 53 for one

in 29 overs. (Food for thought in the *Wisden* statement that there was
1¼ hours left for play. One wonders why a better effort was not made
to get the runs – particularly as 29 overs were bowled).

The Gloucestershire match at Bristol saw Yorkshire back to full
strength and also back in form. In Gloucestershire's total of 170
Macaulay took six for 49. Yorkshire's score of 279 gave them a very
useful lead of 109. Macaulay was unplayable in the second innings as he
took eight for 43 out of Gloucestershire's total of 68.

The Lancashire match at Old Trafford proved a great attraction
with the two northern sides fighting it out at the top of the table.
Lancashire were 297 for two at the end of the first day's play with
Hallows (41) and Makepeace (126) alone back in the pavilion. On the
Monday, after nine hours play, Lancashire declared with 509 for nine
on the board, with Ernest Tyldesley having made 139 and Watson 92.
Rhodes took seven for 116. Holmes and Sutcliffe then put on 183
before the close of the second day and took their partnership to 199
before Sutcliffe went for 89. Oldroyd went at 218, when dropping on
to his stumps after being hit on the head by McDonald; a blow that put
him out of the Yorkshire team for the rest of the season. Holmes went
on to score 143 as Yorkshire were dismissed for 352.

The Leicestershire match at Leicester saw Yorkshire record a score
of 473 for six declared with Sutcliffe (200) and Leyland (116)
partnering each other in a stand of 248 for the second wicket.
Leicestershire had scored 220 for five by the close of the second day,
and the third day was a wash-out. Two further draws followed
because of the poor weather. At Sheffield, against Warwickshire,
Yorkshire were denied victory when there was again no play on the
last day. At Leeds, Northamptonshire fared none too well against the
fiery Macaulay, who took six for 26 in 25 overs. Yorkshire obtained a
lead of 51, but there had been no play on the first day, and as the third
day went by the board too, Yorkshire had to be satisfied with first
innings points.

At Bradford, Worcestershire were no match for Yorkshire, who
dismissed their visitors for 89 with Kilner taking four for 42 and
Waddington three for 9 in 12 overs. Holmes and Leyland put
Yorkshire in front without losing a wicket, and Yorkshire declared at
241 for five on the third day, having lost the second through rain.
Worcestershire did little better in their second innings and were
dismissed for 124 to give victory to Yorkshire by an innings and 28
runs. Kilner took five for 48 in 33.5 overs. The Hampshire match at
Harrogate was also spoilt by the weather, with no play on the first day.
Hampshire batted first and were all out for 121. Yorkshire replied with
262 for nine declared, but heavy rain then ruined Yorkshire's chance of
victory. At this stage of the season, Yorkshire still led the way but their

343

lead was only by two points, Yorkshire having four matches left to Lancashire's three.

At The Oval, Yorkshire gave a dour batting display with Holmes (51) and Sutcliffe (71) opening with a stand of 105. A dogged innings from Rhodes which brought him 96 helped Yorkshire to a score of 274. In reply Surrey's Jack Hobbs batted for 4 hours and 40 minutes for his 102, Jardine helping him add 110 for the fourth wicket. Fender with 72 and E. R. T. Holmes (34) then came together to put Surrey in the lead and they declared at 355 for nine. Yorkshire then went in to bat and Holmes and Sutcliffe knocked up 265 without loss, each recording a century. This failure to gain more than a point cost Yorkshire the Championship as they dropped back to runners–up spot.

Yorkshire beat Sussex at Hove with Waddington taking six for 49 as Sussex were bowled out for 148. Sutcliffe (94) and Kilner (62) rescued Yorkshire from 41 for three, but they eventually reached only 230. Tate was top-scorer a second time as Sussex were all out for 217, and Yorkshire made light work of their task of knocking off 139 to win by eight wickets. Another victory followed at Swansea where Leyland (191) and Robinson (124) not out) added 276 for Yorkshire's sixth wicket as they eventually declared at 420 for six. Glamorgan fought back well with Yorkshiremen Bell (59) and Bates (66) putting on 109 for the second wicket and C. F. Walters played a fine innings of 69. Robinson took five for 56 but could not stop the Welsh county from compiling 308. Yorkshire then scored 154 for seven before declaring with Kilner hitting out on a drying pitch for 52, and Glamorgan were ignominiously treated as they were dismissed for 76. Macaulay, with seven for 32, was quite unplayable in the conditions.

Centuries from J. C. W. MacBryan and M. D. Lyon at Taunton must have surprised the visitors, for whom Robinson took six for 87 in Somerset's total of 329 for eight declared but there was no time for a result on the first innings. By this time the Championship had been won anyway and Yorkshire had to be satisfied with second place. Unbeaten once again, they had had a fine season and had the better of Champions Lancashire in the one game that was finished between the two sides. Perhaps it was a relief to everyone that after four years at the top, there should have been a new Champion County. At Scarborough, in the last game of the season, Sutcliffe celebrated by scoring a century in each innings against the MCC while Holmes and Leyland each batted well. Macaulay took six for 82 in MCC's first innings, with G. T. S. Stevens scoring 100.

A player who made his debut for Yorkshire in 1926, when he appeared against Worcestershire at Bradford without having an innings, was Wilfred Barber. A late developer, he did not play for

344

Yorkshire 2nd XI until 1926 when he was 25 years old, but he averaged 40, scored 600 runs and made 108 against Northumberland at Jesmond. An orthodox opening batsman who usually went lower down the order for Yorkshire, he had few opportunities, and it was 1932 before he commanded a regular place in the side. He then gave eight seasons of loyal service, always performing to the needs of the side, batted attractively and was brilliant in the outfield and a very safe catch. After the Second World War he played with Lidget Green, King Cross and Mirfield and became coach to the North Riding Educational Authorities at one time. A modest, kindly man, he played in two Tests against South Africa in 1935.

Six players managed to score over a thousand runs for Yorkshire in 1926. Sutcliffe scored 1,672 runs at 59.71 while Holmes averaged 48 for 1,792 runs. Oldroyd averaged 44 and missed part of the season due to injury while Leyland's aggregate of 1,561 runs at 40 was also an excellent season's work. Rhodes and Kilner were all-rounders of the highest class, with Rhodes finishing on top of the bowling averages with 102 wickets at 15.00. Robinson, Macaulay, and Waddington all did well at times with the bat and only Dolphin and the captain could be classed as tail-enders. Mitchell averaged 33 and showed his ability when he came into the side.

Macaulay had a fine season with the ball with 133 wickets at 16.15, but he was not as effective as in the previous season. However, he could claim sixth place in the national averages with Rhodes in first place. Kilner took 97 wickets at 19.69 and had some very effective days, although he appeared to have deteriorated slightly, while Waddington too was very expensive at times. Robinson's 57 wickets cost him 25.50 each, but his value could not always be equated in figures. Behind the stumps, Dolphin, now aged 40, had hardly declined at all. By any standards but their own, Yorkshire had had a wonderful season, but the cynic could point out that they had drawn more matches in a season than any Yorkshire side had done previously.

Yorkshire began the new season (1927) at Fenner's with Oldroyd soon back amongst the runs after his injury with 114, while Leyland scored 54 and 77 not out. Duleepsinhji scored 101 and the University shared the honours with Yorkshire. Down at Gloucester, the home side were dismissed for 189 with Waddington taking five for 51 and then Holmes and Sutcliffe started the Championship season with an opening stand of 274. When Sutcliffe left for 134, Holmes went on to a score of 180 before Kilner came in and scored 90 not out as Yorkshire declared at 468 for five. Hammond batted splendidly when Gloucestershire went in again, but his 135 could not prevent an innings defeat. The short trip over the Severn brought Yorkshire another innings win at Cardiff. Batting first Holmes with 107 and Macaulay 57 took Yorkshire to 236. Glamorgan could not master the Yorkshire attack in which Robinson took six for 37 and three for 56 and Macaulay four for 31 and seven for 40.

Back at home in Dewsbury, the return game with Gloucestershire resulted in another innings win with Oldroyd (110) and Macaulay (76) helping Yorkshire to a total of 318 after being 144 for six. The visitors collapsed to 134 all out with Rhodes taking six for 20 and in their second innings they reached 182, with Macaulay taking five for 38. Yorkshire's fourth win of the season, all by an innings, was at Leeds against Worcestershire. Macaulay took seven for 17 in 20.2 overs and Robinson three for 27 as Worcestershire were routed for 46. Yorkshire did not do much better, losing seven wickets for 94 before Macaulay (67) and Waddington (114) added 163 for the eighth wicket, Fred Root taking seven for 82 in Yorkshire's total of 291. Worcestershire's second-innings total was only 81. Macaulay took five for 33 and Robinson five for 38, bowling unchanged throughout the match.

At Hull, Yorkshire lost to Warwickshire by eight wickets – their first defeat of any kind since 1924 – and it was a shock to all cricket followers. Yorkshire batted first, with Holmes (46) and Oldroyd (67) adding 120 for the second wicket, but they were all out for 272. In reply Warwickshire lost three for 102 before Quaife (59) and Parsons (136) added 142 for the fourth wicket, the latter driving imperiously to all parts of the ground. The Warwickshire tail wagged well, and a score of 393 put the Midlanders 121 in front. Kilner finished with five for 87 in 51.5 overs. Only Holmes (49) and Kilner (36) batted well in the second innings. Needing only 42 to win, Warwickshire got home by eight wickets.

At Sheffield, the bat was always on top of the ball, and there were two delays for bad light, as Hampshire were left 308 to win in 195 minutes, after they only just avoided the follow-on. They batted out time at 182 for three. Yorkshire regained their winning ways at Leeds where Surrey were dismissed for 172. Rhodes took five for 59 and Kilner four for 30, and although Yorkshire lost Holmes without a run on the board, Sutcliffe (176) took part in century stands with Oldroyd (52) and Leyland (70) and Yorkshire scored 333. Surrey could score only 203 in their second innings, Kilner taking five for 76 and Yorkshire went on to win by ten wickets.

At Huddersfield, Northamptonshire at 89 all out, looked to be very easy meat to the home spectators but this was a recovery from 40 for seven. Emmott Robinson bowled better than he had done for many years as he took eight for 32. After Holmes (33) left at 87, Sutcliffe (79) put on 54 with Oldroyd who went on to score 110 and Yorkshire reached 315. In their second innings, Northamptonshire recovered again with V. W. C. Jupp scoring 105 but their score of 286 was not enough to escape a seven-wicket defeat inside two days.

When Yorkshire went over to Old Trafford for the annual Roses match, both sides were locked together at the head of the table with 53 points out of a possible 64. Yorkshire were without Percy Holmes, whom they replaced with Kennie. Yorkshire were in trouble from the start and five wickets were down for 58, including Sutcliffe for nought and Leyland for five; both to McDonald, who made the ball lift disconcertingly. Oldroyd made a brave 34 and Kilner 27 but it was left to Rhodes to make a real stand and he compiled a patient 44 before Yorkshire were dismissed for 166. McDonald took five for 68. Lancashire then spent 151.5 overs in scoring 234 to put themselves in the driving seat. Kilner had the bowling analysis of 53-28-46-3. When Yorkshire batted again Sutcliffe made the top score (38) but after Rhodes (29) was run out the innings was soon over all out for 153 leaving Lancashire with 89 to win. This time McDonald took six for 67. Lancashire got home with eight wickets to spare.

George Kennie, surprisingly chosen for this match in place of Holmes, assisted Yorkshire 2nd XI from 1925–27 without any success, but was a brilliant fielder and when he appeared for Yorkshire it may have been purely as a stop-gap when Holmes was taken ill very suddenly and Kennie was the only player available at Old Trafford at the time.

Yorkshire's fall from grace continued when Warwickshire gained first innings points after Kilner (67) and Robinson (65) had helped their side to a first innings of 358. In reply Parsons (81) and Norman Kilner (65) battled hard to gain the lead which Warwickshire attained with the last pair at the wicket. Yorkshire also lost on the first innings against Sussex at Sheffield. Yorkshire reached 260, and Sussex gained a 47-run lead, with Macaulay taking five for 74. Holmes and Sutcliffe then opened with a partnership of 141 and Leyland knocked up 91 not out before Yorkshire declared at 323 for five but Sussex had no chance of going for a win and finished with 92 for two.

Thomas Alec Jacques (always known as 'Sandy') was a right-arm fast bowler and useful hitter who played for Yorkshire for the first time against Warwickshire, and he continued to play for the County from time to time up to 1936, sometimes playing as a professional, and he claimed never to have been a member of a losing Yorkshire side. A farmer by occupation, he was universally liked and was highly thought of in cricket circles.

At Bradford, Somerset were well beaten with an innings to spare after Holmes (126) and Oldroyd (111) had added 192 for Yorkshire's second wicket and Yorkshire declared at 486 for seven. Somerset had little to offer as they followed on 346 behind but they did manage 194 in their second innings. At Lord's, Yorkshire suffered their second defeat after some accurate swing bowling from Nigel Haig (seven for 33) had reduced Yorkshire to 81 all out. H. W. Lee (52) stayed for a long time and Haig himself scored 25 to ensure that Middlesex gained a lead of 97 runs as George Macaulay took five for 47. When Yorkshire batted again Kilner hit hard for 53 but along with Holmes, Sutcliffe and Leyland, fell victims to the gentle leg-spin of young Jack Hearne, leaving Middlesex to score 165 on a good pitch. Middlesex did lose four wickets for 120 but Hendren, with 68 not out, saw his side home to a six-wicket win. Rain spoilt the game at Portsmouth where Yorkshire were 156 for three in reply to Hampshire's 521 for eight declared. Left-handers George Brown (204) and Phil Mead (186) added 344 for Hampshire's third wicket with four Yorkshire bowlers completing their 'centuries'.

Further draws occurred at Tonbridge against Kent, where Yorkshire replied with 131 to Kent's 243 with Rhodes (31 not out) making the top score; at Bath, where Somerset had time to score 145 for seven in $3\frac{1}{2}$ hours play before rain ruined the game; and at Harrogate, where Macaulay took six for 52 and Rhodes four for 44 as Glamorgan were bowled out for 138. Yorkshire could only make 27 for one in reply. This game followed a similarly abortive game at Bradford against the New Zealand tourists, who had scored 133 for seven (Rhodes four for 29) in reply to 377 from Yorkshire when the heavens opened once again. Percy Holmes carried his bat through the innings for 175 not out and Leyland scored 118.

Five games on the trot had been ruined by the rain and there was to be a sixth when all but the last hour on the Tuesday of the important Nottinghamshire match at Bradford was spoilt by more rain. The match, played for the benefit of Edgar Oldroyd, was otherwise a success. Geroge Gunn (48) opened with Whysall and they put on 186 for the first wicket. Whysall, dropped twice on 35 completely dominated the rest of the innings making a splendid 184 marked by drives and fine leg-side shots. Nottinghamshire were all out for 343, Macaulay taking four for 78 and Kilner four for 81. In reply, Yorkshire started well losing only one wicket with 142 on the board, but the tail collapsed and the innings was completely dominated by Herbert Sutcliffe, who was at his best in scoring 169 out of 320 all out. That completed the match. Yorkshire then accounted for Essex at Leeds by seven wickets.

Nottinghamshire had now taken the lead in the table with Yorkshire trailing behind Lancashire with the next match proving to Yorkshire followers that their attack had lost its old edge. Yorkshire batted very well with Maurice Leyland playing an outstanding innings of 204 not out; he completely mastered the Middlesex attack and received good support from Oldroyd (88) and Holmes (53). On a good Sheffield pitch, Middlesex were at one stage 209 for three with Hendren (127) on top of the Yorkshire attack, but they collapsed to 302 with Kilner taking five for 80. Following on, N. Haig (80) and Lee (55) put Middlesex on top with a 116 stand and with Hendren scoring a further 62 not out they saved the game easily at 218 for two, with Yorkshire employing ten different bowlers. At Worcester the second day's play was lost to the poor weather. Robinson (96) and Macaulay (56) with a 99-run stand for the seventh wicket were mainly responsible for Yorkshire's 328 and the home side were dismissed for 199. At the close Yorkshire were 18 for two in their second innings. Nor could Yorkshire gain much satisfaction in their match with the leaders at Trent Bridge. Whysall repeated his high scoring with 163 out of Nottinghamshire's 298, and Yorkshire's weakened side finished 121 behind on the first innings. Whysall (74) again batted well in the Nottinghamshire second innings and they were able to declare at 224 for six. Yorkshire were set 346 in 280 minutes but with showers interrupting play, they made only 72 for none with Leyland 50 not out.

Yorkshire returned to winning ways at Northampton but it was a remarkable game. Northamptonshire scored 164 in their first innings but the pitch deteriorated as the match went on with frequent interruptions for rain and when Yorkshire batted it was unplayable. Holmes (22) and Sutcliffe (31) gave Yorkshire a good start with 51 for the first wicket but a sensational collapse meant that Northamptonshire had a lead of 97 on the first innings, with Jupp taking seven for 21. Northamptonshire did little better against Macaulay (five for 34) and Rhodes (four for 52) and their dismissal for 100 meant that Yorkshire required 198 to win. On a pitch still giving assistance, Sutcliffe took the bull by the horns and scored 60 out of 89 with Holmes, who went on the defensive in contrast to his partner but did not neglect any scoring opportunity while wickets fell at the other end. Holmes finished with 75 not out in Yorkshire's winning score of 200 for five, a fine achievement.

In poor conditions at Headingley, Sutcliffe played a brilliant innings against Lancashire after three wickets had gone down for 35 to McDonald. He went on to score a chanceless 95 as Yorkshire were dismissed for 157. Lancashire also lost early wickets with four down for 99 before Ernest Tyldesley, giving a top-class display, scored 165, adding 164 for the seventh wicket with Iddon (77), and this enabled Lancashire to declare at 360 for eight. Yorkshire started badly once again, losing four wickets for 75, but Sutcliffe played another fine innings and this time reached 135, effectively saving the match for Yorkshire. Rhodes (43), Robinson (43 not out) and Macaulay (61 not out) hit out and Yorkshire were 314 for six at the close.

Further draws followed which made this one of the wettest seasons ever. At Leicester, Mitchell scored 105 out of Yorkshire's 282 and Leicestershire got within six of Yorkshire's score, with Kilner taking five for 84. In a painstakingly slow game, Yorkshire then made 139 for three but the weather was certainly not to blame for this draw, as there were three full day's play. In the return game at Sheffield, Yorkshire scored 291 for four but rain prevented any further play. The Derbyshire match at Hull saw Derbyshire recover from 8 for five to 81 all out, with Macaulay unplayable as he took eight for 37. Yorkshire gained the lead for the loss of Mitchell and with some useful scores from the tail made 228. Derbyshire's 252 meant Yorkshire needed 106 to win with most of the last day available. After scoring 32 for none, Yorkshire had to give up the chase following several showers and the match was drawn. Worse was to come at Bradford when the Kent match was abandoned without a ball being bowled.

Macaulay and Kilner skittled Derbyshire at Chesterfield for 157 and Yorkshire were 92 for five when the match was abandoned. At The Oval Surrey compiled 341 for eight declared, with Hobbs scoring 150 and Percy Fender 100 not out as Rhodes took four for 72. When the game was completed Yorkshire had 143 for one on the board with Sutcliffe out for 64 and Holmes 73 not out. Matters were no better at Leyton where Leyland with 127 helped Yorkshire to a score of 249 for five declared. Essex had replied with 128 for five to make it a fourth 'no result' in a row. Yorkshire's final match was at Hove where Sussex totalled 221. Macaulay took five for 83. Kilner (91 not out) was top scorer in Yorkshire's reply of 302, a lead of 81. In their second innings Sussex batted poorly and could only muster 120, Kilner taking five for 21 in 21.1 overs to complete a fine all-round performance. Yorkshire won easily by nine wickets. At Scarborough Yorkshire also beat the MCC by eight wickets with Robinson taking five for 37 in the first innings and Macaulay seven for 76 in the second.

Lancashire finished Champions but only because Nottinghamshire lost their last match of the season at Swansea against Glamorgan, who had not won a single victory until then. Yorkshire were third and deserved to be no higher.

Holmes and Sutcliffe both averaged over 50; Holmes scoring 1,774 runs and his partner 1,814. Leyland finished third, averaging almost 40, while Oldroyd scored 1,390 runs at 37.56. There was little wrong with the batting as Kilner also scored over 1,000 runs and Macaulay batted better than he had ever done with 678 runs, average 25. Robinson and Rhodes – especially the latter – showed a marked deterioration, but they both played valuable innings as did Waddington. Mitchell, with fewer opportunities, was disappointing and Dolphin and the skipper did very little with the bat.

Macaulay headed the bowling averages with 129 wickets at 18.15 each. There was very little falling off, if any, and he occupied fourth place in the national averages. Rhodes with 82 wickets at 19.92 also had a good season, especially so for a cricketer within a month or so of his 50th birthday. Robinson, with 77 at 20.14, had a better season than any since 1923, while Jacques 25 wickets cost 21.36. Kilner did not bowl as well as in the past, but he did take 86 wickets at 23.34 and Waddington's falling-off was not entirely unexpected. He had one or two good days but they were fewer than in the past and he left the County at the end of the season. Dolphin also was not re-engaged, and with the skipper also giving up, the team would have a new look for 1928.

There was another problem regarding the captaincy. At a meeting of the County Committee held in November, Herbert Sutcliffe was elected captain for the following season. This evidently affected members in two ways; some objected to a professional being given the job. Others protested that if the captaincy passed to a pro it should go to the senior professional, namely Wilfred Rhodes. Unlike recent problems, this one was smoothed over as Herbert Sutcliffe declined the honour of being captain, and in his place Captain W. A. Worsley was asked. He accepted the captaincy of the Yorkshire County Cricket Club.

Already lacking the former captain, A. W. Lupton, and Dolphin and Waddington, Yorkshire were further depleted just before the season began when Roy Kilner died from a rare virus that he had caught while coaching in India. A more popular and lovable cricketer it was hard to imagine than Roy, many boys in Yorkshire being named after him in the 1920s. Aged 37, he was badly missed as a cricketer, as well as a man of humour and happiness.

The side that journeyed to Worcester to play the first match of the 1928 season was as follows: Capt. W. A. Worsley, T. A. Jacques, Holmes, Sutcliffe, Oldroyd, Leyland, Mitchell, Macaulay, Rhodes, Robinson and Wood. Worcestershire surprised everybody by scoring 402, after being 228 for six at one time. Holmes scored 88, putting on 95 with Leyland, who went on to score 247 in just over five hours. He added 125 with Mitchell (34) and 198 with Rhodes who scored 100 not out. Worcestershire, with J. B. Higgins (101) and Wright (71) opening with 135 for the first wicket, saved the match with ease and were 203 for three at the end.

Moving on to Leyton, Yorkshire compiled 514 for six with Holmes (136) and Sutcliffe (129) opening with a stand of 268. Leyland (133 not out) and Mitchell (71) then added 168 for the fourth wicket. Essex replied with 226 after being 173 for two at one stage. Macaulay took five for 83 and Rhodes four for 60. When Essex followed on they

Roy Kilner died of enteric fever just before the 1928 season, less than two years after playing his last Test.

reached 223 for two without any difficulty with O'Connor scoring 130 not out. The journey to Hull was interrupted with a call at Fenner's where Yorkshire scored 224 for five on a very slow pitch. Cambridge's batting was a disaster as they were dismissed for the lowest score of the season – 30 – and Emmott Robinson took eight for 13. Following on Cambridge fared a little better and in a rain-ruined game scored 41 for five. Leyland, who was being used as a successor to Roy Kilner, took three for 13 and the newcomer Shackleton two for 25. At Anlaby Road in Hull, Sussex obtained 247 with Cook scoring 105 and Robinson taking five for 74 and Leyland three for 66. Yorkshire were 49 for one and another 'no result' had been recorded.

For the visit to Northampton half the time available was again lost to the weather and the main interest was in the winning of first innings points. Northamptonshire, with three down for 23 staged a recovery but 164 was not a large total to face. Rhodes bowled well on a pitch that suited him to take five for 37 but when Yorkshire batted only Oldroyd (40) and Leyland (35) looked like staying for long and Yorkshire had little hope of topping Northamptonshire's score on a pitch that was worsening.

The Roses match at Bramall Lane saw Lancashire bat first to make 385, batting almost until lunch-time on the second day, Rhodes finished with four for 56. Holmes (79) and Sutcliffe (140) opened with 142 and Mitchell (74) shared a 123 stand with Sutcliffe, who batted for $4\frac{1}{2}$ hours. Steady runs came from the tail with Wood scoring 39 and Robinson 30 not out as Yorkshire totalled 473. Lancashire then batted out time.

At Edgbaston, Yorkshire scored 446 for six against Warwickshire with the eight batsmen scoring between Holmes' 91 and Macaulay's 22; the opening pair putting on 166. By this time seven hours and 20 minutes of playing time had been used. Tiger Smith (99) and Norman Kilner (50) opened in their turn with 118 and with Parsons scoring 81, Warwickshire were finally dismissed for 367 after another seven hours had gone.

The first result of the season occurred at Lord's. Once again Yorkshire's batting was at its best. Holmes and Sutcliffe opened with 158 before Sutcliffe left for 73 while Holmes made 105 our of 211 before Oldroyd (108) and Mitchell put on 170 for the fourth wicket. Mitchell scored 55 in an hour on Monday morning. At the end of the day Middlesex had lost only five wickets but on the Tuesday they collapsed to 261 all out; and in their second innings they could score only 130. On a slightly worn wicket Rhodes bowled magnificently to take seven for 39 while Macaulay took his match analysis to six for 75.

Captain R. T. Stanyforth, who was born at Chelsea in London in 1892, was a right-handed batsman and wicket-keeper who played three times for Yorkshire in 1928, taking two catches. He appeared for Eton in 1911 without obtaining his flannels and failed to gain his blue at Oxford University. He toured with several teams abroad, including Argentine in 1926–27 and captained the team to South Africa in 1927–28. He also toured West Indies in 1929–30 and Egypt in 1932. He took part in four Tests in South Africa catching seven and stumping three victims, and was the first player to captain England without taking part in county cricket. In his first-class career he took 93 victims. He won the MC in the First World War where he had a distinguished army career with the 17th Lancers. A trustee of the MCC at the time of his death, he became a Patron of the Yorkshire CCC in 1961 and died three years later at Kirk Hammerton Hall at the age of 71, having lived there for several years. He was the author of 'Wicket-keeping'.

Yorkshire put Hampshire in after winning the toss at Southampton and three wickets fell for 50 before Mead (118) and A. L. Hosie (155) came together to add 240 for the fourth wicket. Hosie batted over five hours and Hampshire's final score was 391, the hard-working Robinson taking seven for 110. Yorkshire lost three wickets for 32 but Leyland kept the innings together with a fighting 95. Macaulay (54 not out) and Captain Worsley (60) then came together to add 94 for the eighth wicket during which the follow-on was saved and Yorkshire reached 318. Rain prevented any chance of a result. This game was followed by the return game with Hampshire at Bradford. After only 40 minutes cricket took place on the Saturday Hampshire's first innings reached 204. After gaining a first innings lead, Yorkshire made every effort to win the game and Hampshire were dismissed for 169 at the close, with Robinson again Yorkshire's hero with seven for 63. Robinson was having his best-ever season for Yorkshire with the ball at the age of 44.

Yorkshire produced form more in keeping with their reputation when they defeated Leicestershire at Leeds by an innings and 28 runs. Rhodes bowled at his best to take six for 55 in 40 overs and Robinson took three for 44 in 42.3 overs. Oldroyd with 101 and the worthy Robinson (73) added 148 for the fifth wicket and Yorkshire took at lead of 149 runs. Leicestershire again had no answer to Rhodes and Robinson, while Turner, making a rare appearance for Yorkshire, took three for 3. It was a satisfying win for Yorkshire as they were without Sutcliffe, Macaulay and Leyland because of the Test Trial.

Frank Dennis, a brother-in-law of Len Hutton and uncle of Simon Dennis, first played for Yorkshire in 1928, at a time when Yorkshire had lost Waddington and Kilner and both Rhodes and Robinson were approaching the end of their careers. A right-arm fast-medium bowler, he made an immediate impact when he came into the Yorkshire side against Hampshire at Bradford. He did little of note during the rest of the season but was given a thorough trial in 1929 when he took 82 wickets at 21.82 each and was to receive his county cap. Unfortunately he was never to approach such form again and played only spasmodically after 1930; last appearing for the County in 1933. An honest, hard-working cricketer, he took 154 wickets for Yorkshire at 29.33 each and as an aggressive left-handed batsman, played several notable innings. In 1948 he emigrated to New Zealand to take up fruit farming in Christchurch and he became a selector for the Canterbury Cricket Association.

Yorkshire gained a further success at Hull against Worcestershire who were bowled out twice for 169 and 106, only Tarbox and King holding up the Yorkshire bowlers. In fact so deadly were Yorkshire with the new ball that Worcestershire were 20 for six and 31 for six in their two innings. Macaulay had match figures of eleven for 98 while

Robinson took eight for 143. Yorkshire declared at 295 for five with Oldroyd having scored 119 and Sutcliffe 79; the pair having added 162 for the second wicket. A drawn match with Kent at Dover would have provided a good finish if the weather had kept fine on the last day. A Yorkshire score of 242 (Mitchell 115) was passed by Kent by only 30 runs. Macaulay took five for 107 and Robinson four for 100. In their second innings Holmes and Mitchell both batted well again for 59 each before Yorkshire declared at 283 for nine. Set 254 runs to win, Kent were 65 for three at the close.

In 4½ hours play, Yorkshire scored 387 for two against Glamorgan, with Sutcliffe scoring 147 not out and Leyland 189 not out, which took him only 205 minutes as they put on 323 unfinished for the third wicket. Regrettably for Yorkshire it rained at Huddersfield for the next two days and there was no further play. The Nottinghamshire match at Sheffield was also delayed by the rain and when Nottinghamshire batted first they were in trouble against Robinson and Macaulay as they collapsed to 134 all out. Oldroyd (28) and the in-form Leyland (62) took Yorkshire to 103 before the third wicket fell but then Larwood bowled at his best to take six for 24 and Yorkshire were skittled out for 125. Whysall (107) and Payton (117) were in much better form in Nottinghamshire's second innings on an improved pitch and Nottinghamshire were able to declare at 329 for nine. Yorkshire were set 320 to win in 210 minutes but gave up after losing Holmes and Oldroyd to Larwood, and Sutcliffe (95) and Leyland (49) were content that Yorkshire would draw with their score taken to 198 for four.

The match with the West Indians at Leeds was won comfortably enough by Yorkshire. Sutcliffe and Barber each scored 98, the latter showing abundant promise before being bowled by Constantine. Facing 284 the visitors were in difficulty against the spin of Rhodes (four for 37) and Leyland (three for 35), but Martin (60) and Constantine (69) scored well to take the West Indian total to 208. Martin batted for 3½ hours and Constantine for 28 minutes. In showery weather Yorkshire declared at 172 for one with Holmes 84 not out and Mitchell 51 not out and the opposition slumped alarmingly in their second innings to be bowled out for 58. Macaulay took six for 30 and Robinson three for 28 and Yorkshire won by 190 runs. At Bradford another high-scoring game with Surrey resulted in another draw. Leyland was again in his best form when Yorkshire compiled 406, and facing that formidable total Surrey collapsed to 96 for five before Jardine (157) and Fender (177) joined in a remarkable partnership that added 294 for the sixth wicket. In the end Yorkshire could only bat out time.

Yorkshire returned to winning ways at Derby where Guy Jackson with 85 led Derbyshire to a respectable 234 with Robinson taking four for 47, his best bowling for the County. Holmes and Sutcliffe then put on 125 for the first wicket before Holmes left with 67, whereupon Mitchell (91) helped Sutcliffe to take the score to 213 before the opener was out for 111. Leyland joined Mitchell and the pair put on a further 183 with Leyland (149) in superlative form, although both players gave chances. Yorkshire declared at 485 for eight. Leyland's aggregate for Yorkshire now stood at 1,299 in 13 innings. Storer with 57 and Townsend with 35 tried their best for the home side, but all out for 199 they lost by an innings and 52 runs. Macaulay took five for 76 and Leyland two for 39 to complete a good all-round performance.

At Trent Bridge 1,080 runs were scored in the three days for the loss of 17 wickets. Holmes and Sutcliffe put on 184 for the first wicket in the first innings and in the second were at 210 for none at the end of the match. Sutcliffe scored two separate centuries while Holmes scored 83 and 101 not out. For Nottinghamshire, Whysall scored 166 but the weakened Nottinghamshire side, lacking Larwood, Sam Staples and George Gunn, finished 170 behind on the first innings. So good was the pitch that forcing the follow-on was not considered worthwhile. At Sheffield Yorkshire beat Essex by an innings and 215 runs after batting first and scoring 512 for nine. Oldroyd scored 112 – he had been the third Yorkshire centurion at Trent Bridge. Essex were dismissed for 193 and 104. Rhodes took eight for 36 in the match.

The heavy-scoring type of game such as the Nottinghamshire match at Trent Bridge was repeated in the Middlesex match at Headingley, and was becoming all too common throughout the country. In this game Hendren (169) and F. T. Mann (122) put on 202 for the fourth wicket after Nigel Haig had made 77. Middlesex reached 488, with Macaulay taking six for 130. Yorkshire's batting came unstuck for once with seven wickets going down for 143 before Robinson (70 not out) was joined by Arthur Wood, who went on to score 62; the pair put on 127 for the eighth wicket but it did not prevent Yorkshire following on 185 behind. The match finished with Yorkshire saving the game comfortably with the score at 290 for one, when Sutcliffe was bowled by Lee for 104 leaving Holmes undefeated with 179.

Yorkshire returned to winning ways against Northamptonshire by 10 wickets at Harrogate. Early shocks saw Yorkshire reduced to 131 for six before Mitchell (91) and Rhodes (61) were associated in a stand of 117 runs, and Yorkshire totalled 287. In reply Robinson (five for 52) and Macaulay (five for 58) bowled Northamptonshire out for 125. Following on, they made 172, Rhodes taking five for 57 with his uncanny accuracy.

At Old Trafford, Yorkshire's opening partnership of Holmes and

Sutcliffe completed their 55th century partnership together before Holmes left for 54 out of 134. Sutcliffe went on to score 126, but there was little support as Yorkshire were dismissed for 352. Ted McDonald took six for 144. At the close of play on the Monday, Lancashire had replied with 244 for three with Watson scoring 110 and Makepeace 81 not out, but Tuesday's play was completely washed out. At Leicester, Leicestershire scored 390, Armstrong batting for 6 hours and 40 minutes for his 186. Rhodes finished with six for 160 but he bowled 69.3 overs altogether in a dour batting exhibition. Yorkshire were then dismissed for 234 in a poor batting display in which Mitchell scored 55 but the next highest scorer was Extras with 31. Following on Holmes (110) and Sutcliffe (119) put on 227 for the first wicket and Yorkshire finished with 273 for four at the close.

Horace Fisher played in two matches for Yorkshire in 1928, against Northamptonshire at Harrogate and at Leicester in neither of which he took a wicket. He was a very useful left-handed batsman and left-arm medium-pace (as opposed to slow) bowler. In the one match he played in the first team in 1929 he again failed to take a wicket and he did not play at all in the 1930 season. In 1931 he appeared twice for the County and in 1932 he did play in eight matches for the first team, averaging 23 with the bat and taking 22 wickets at 14.09 each actually heading the bowling averages in county cricket for Yorkshire. In that season against Leicestershire at Bradford he took six for 11 in 17 overs and in his next match took five for 12 against Somerset at Sheffield, when he performed the hat-trick. In the next two seasons he did not play at all in the first team although continuing to perform well for the 2nd XI and this was probably due to his professional engagements on top of the fact that Verity had made the left-arm slow bowler's niche in the side his own. Fisher, from mining stock was a law unto himself and it was said that when he was recalled to the Yorkshire side in 1935 when Verity was chosen for England, he demanded his Yorkshire cap and got it. He certainly played in all but eight matches for Yorkshire in that season and he replaced Verity against Middlesex at Lord's when Verity was playing for England in the first Test at Trent Bridge. Yet Fisher's first regular season for Yorkshire was a sad and dismal failure by Yorkshire standards. He scored 325 runs at an average of 13 and his 51 wickets cost 28.07 each (eight of those came in the matches against the Universities). He faded from the scene; enjoyed a tour to Jamaica where he finished second in the batting averages; and took just nine wickets for the county in 1936. He never played again for Yorkshire although, at league level he continued to enjoy a successful career. Horace Fisher was a remarkable cricketer by any standards. Obstinate to a degree, his career with Yorkshire could and should have been much more successful. But he did perform the first lbw hat-trick in first class cricket and in his only full season with Yorkshire they did succeed in winning the Championship.

The Warwickshire game at Park Avenue was another ruined by the rain. Parsons with 73 defied the Yorkshire bowling as his side scored 244, Robinson taking six for 87, and then for Yorkshire Percy Holmes played one of his highest scores for the county when he made 275 in 310 minutes out of a total of 540 for seven. In reply Warwickshire finished with 21 for two so the weather could well have robbed Yorkshire of another victory. At Dewsbury, Rhodes bowled out Derbyshire by taking seven for 55 in Derbyshire's score of 126 and the home side gained a lead of 287, thanks to Herbert Sutcliffe's 138 in which he added 225 for the second wicket with Oldroyd (97). Derbyshire batted better in their second innings but Yorkshire were victors by an innings and 22 runs; Bedford taking six for 91. Two more rain-stricken draws followed with Macaulay taking six for 86 against Kent and Oldroyd notching a century at The Oval with Hobbs returning the compliment before the third day was washed out.

The journey to Eastbourne brought fine weather but another draw against Sussex, who saved the match by scoring 490 in their second innings. Yorkshire began well with Holmes (63) and Sutcliffe posting 141 for the first wicket. Oldroyd with 50 helped Sutcliffe (228) in another three figure stand before Barber hit 41 not out to take Yorkshire to 429 for four declared. Sutcliffe's beautiful innings lasted for five hours. In reply Sussex failed dismally to be dismissed for 131 with Robinson taking four for 35, and they were in further trouble with two wickets down for 127. Then Duleepsinhji, in an innings lasting three hours, scored 150, but it took Tich Cornford, with 82 – his highest score – and Hollingdale with 36 not out, to take Sussex to 490, and the game was safe.

In their last match, Yorkshire, thanks to 162 not out from Edgar Oldroyd, totalled 433 and then dismissed Glamorgan for 167 and 154. Macaulay took seven for 57 in the first innings and Rhodes six for 56 in the second to complete Yorkshire's eighth win of the season in the Championship. Yorkshire then completed the season with a high scoring draw at Scarborough in the MCC match.

Fourth position in the Championship was just about right for Yorkshire, who were obviously one bowler at least short of what was required.

Sutcliffe averaged 80 and scored 2,418 runs in spite of missing several matches, while partner Holmes also passed the 2,000 mark with an average of 58.16, slightly behind Leyland who scored 1,554 runs at an average of 59.76. Mitchell had his best season so far and scored 1,308 runs at 50.38, with Oldroyd just behind him, while Robinson scored 911 runs at 45.55. Barber showed promise and averaged 32 while

Rhodes admittedly fell away. Wood batted better than any previous Yorkshire wicket-keeper had done, with Macaulay pulling his weight as a tail-ender.

The bowling was in the hands of Rhodes and Robinson – the two veterans – and Macaulay, who was still in his prime. The workload was spread very evenly with all three bowling at least 1,150 overs and taking 112, 111 and 117 wickets respectively. Their averages varied from 19.21 by Rhodes – a wonderful performance by a 50-year-old – to 22.60 by Robinson, now aged 44, to 23.75 by Macaulay, for whom the season was a disappointing one by his high standards. Emmott Robinson, of course, had never bowled better and though the other bowlers failed to do themselves justice there was still hope that Dennis might become the opening bowler that was needed, and while Leyland was no substitute for Kilner, he did have a successful first season with the ball. Jacques, it was hoped, might still become a good fast bowler, but several others were tried without raising too many hopes for the future.

Captain Worsley, a right-hand batsman, captained the side at the age of 38 as well as could have been expected. A cheerful leader, he fielded well for a man of his age not used to the arduous days in the field and if his batting was disappointing, he was respected by all. He also captained the side in 1929 and batted with rather more assurance, but he retired at the end of that season in which he took Yorkshire up to second equal in the Championship. In 1908 and 1909 he had been a member of the Eton XI. After captaining Yorkshire in 1928 and 1929 he joined the committee in 1931 as a member for the North Riding and became president of the Club in 1961, a position he held until his death in 1973 at the age of 83. He was President of the MCC in 1961–62 and was Lord Lieutenant of the North Riding in 1951–65.

The new season of 1929 opened with two draws at Fenner's and at Lord's, against the MCC. Cambridge followed on, but M. J. Turnbull played a magnificent innings of 167 not out after G. C. Grant (88) and S. A. Block (90) had tired the bowlers. At Lord's Yorkshire scored 359 for five by the end of the first day, Oldroyd scoring 147 to add to 111 he scored at Cambridge. There was no further play. Another draw took place at Oxford, against whom Yorkshire had not played since 1906. Yorkshire declared with 378 for eight on the board with Oldroyd (97) and Mitchell (81) opening with a stand of 173 – their third century stand of the season in consecutive innings, which is probably unique for a pair of reserve openers – they were only there through the absence of Holmes and Sutcliffe. Oxford University were then bowled out for 168, and following on, scored 313 in their second innings. Set to get 104 in an hour, Yorkshire were 93 for six when stumps were drawn.

A newcomer to the Yorkshire team against Cambridge was E. R. Sheepshanks, the previous year's Eton captain. He never played for Cambridge University nor did he ever appear for Yorkshire again; he died while covering the Spanish Civil War for Reuters in 1937.

W. E. Harbord, an attacking middle-order right-hand batsman, who appeared in two matches in 1929 against MCC and Oxford University, was also in the Eton team, appearing as an opening batsman in 1927 and for Oxford University in 1930 without obtaining his blue. In 1930 at Oxford, he scored 109 for Yorkshire against Oxford University. He played the last of 16 matches in 1935. He scored 104 not out for Minor Counties v Australians in 1934 and served on the Yorkshire Committee for many years, becoming a vice-president.

Another debutant against Oxford University was W. E. Bowes, a right-arm medium-fast bowler who took two for 28 off 21 overs in Oxford's first innings, bowling H. M. Garland-Wells and E. M. Wellings for 0. He was then on the ground staff at Lord's, but played in 11 matches for Yorkshire, taking 45 wickets at 19.22, and in the following season he took 76 wickets. He gained a regular place in the Yorkshire side from 1932 and was one of the best fast bowlers in the game until his retirement in 1947. Born at Elland in 1908, he came to Leeds with his parents when his father, who worked for the Lancashire and Yorkshire Railway moved to Leeds when he was a small boy. Bowes learnt his cricket with the Wesleyan Sunday School League in Leeds and played for both Armley Park Council School and West Leeds High School before joining Kirkstall Educational. A tall, strongly built fast bowler, he could make the ball lift disconcertingly and was a dangerous bowler to face if there was life in the pitch. Slow moving in the field and a very poor batsman, his glasses gave him an unathletic look, but he had a very active cricket brain which as he developed turned him into a bowler who could control his bowling in an intelligent manner, making use of variations in pace. He could move the ball both ways. He was almost as deadly as Verity as a bowler for Yorkshire and the pair were the main reasons for Yorkshire's success in the 1930s. During the Second World War, he spent three years in a concentration camp when he lost a lot of weight and appeared to be a shadow of his former self. He soon recovered and spent two more successful years with Yorkshire in 1946 and 1947, and after retiring from cricket, he became an excellent cricket reporter with the *Yorkshire Evening News* and the *Yorkshire Evening Post*, and he was also the author of several cricket books. He lived at Menston for many years and played for the local club in 1945. His son W. A. J. ('Tony') Bowes was also a very good medium-fast bowler who played with success for Yorkshire 2nd XI and York as well as in the Bradford League and was a noted coach and groundsman at

Guiseley. Bill Bowes, a very popular cricketer and character in Yorkshire cricket circles, died in 1983 aged 79 at Otley after a heart attack at his home in Menston.

Yorkshire began their Championship season with a visit to Leyton where an innings win for Yorkshire was completed after lunch on the last day. Essex were in a good position at 117 for one but Robinson, Macaulay and Rhodes each took three wickets as Essex collapsed to 195 all out. Leyland (134) was the backbone of Yorkshire's innings of 299 for seven declared. Only Hipkin with 43 held up Wilfred Rhodes as he took nine for 39 in one of his best pieces of bowling in his career.

The Lancashire match at Old Trafford was a draw after Lancashire had scored 305, recovering from 123 for seven thanks to Charlie Hallows, who carried his bat through the innings for 152 not out. Yorkshire took 34 overs less to score 42 runs more, and Lancashire batted out time. At Edgbaston, Warwickshire batted over nine hours for 536 for seven with E. J. Smith scoring 142 and Santall 109. Yorkshire replied with 367 for six. Everyone who batted in the match reached double figures.

At home to Kent, Dennis bowled out the visitors for 125 by taking five for 42 but Yorkshire led that total by only one run, with Rhodes coming to the rescue with 53 not out after Yorkshire were 52 for six. Going in again Kent's batting failed, with Rhodes taking five for 46 and Leyland three for 23. At this stage of the season Wilfred Rhodes had a batting average of 169 and had taken 30 wickets at less than 16 runs each. He was now 51 years old. Yorkshire knocked off the 140 needed for victory for the loss of Holmes (47) and Sutcliffe (41), who had put 95 on for the first wicket.

Rain ruined the Glamorgan game at Cardiff with Leyland taking five for 44 and Rhodes four for 30 as Glamorgan were skittled for 146, and Yorkshire gained the lead. Also drawn was the Sussex match at Leeds with Rhodes scoring 43 not out and 55 not out. Macaulay took five for 54 as Sussex were dismissed for 261, and then Bowley with six for 72 was responsible for Yorkshire being all out for 205. Bowley then scored 70, but Dennis bowled well to take five for 61 as Sussex reached 285. Yorkshire were set 342 to win in three hours and until Rhodes joined Robinson (55 not out) it was a disastrous performance by Yorkshire who were then 12 for five. They recovered to hold out at 128 for five. Rhodes now had an average of 267.

Another draw followed against Northamptonshire with Holmes carrying his bat through the innings for 110 as Yorkshire made 219, Clark taking five for 38. On a drying pitch, Woolley also carried his bat through the innings for 38 not out out of 102 as Dennis took six for 42, and a declaration from Yorkshire at 58 for four did not enable the side to have hopes of victory.

At this stage of the season, Derbyshire were on top, followed by

Lancashire and Middlesex with Yorkshire down in seventh position. The Nottinghamshire game at Sheffield was keenly contested although Sutcliffe and Leyland were missing from the home side and Larwood from the Nottinghamshire side, all playing in the Trent Bridge Test. Nottinghamshire were dismissed for 157 and Yorkshire to gain a lead of 48 runs. Nottinghamshire made a good start but collapsed to the bowling of Wilfred Rhodes, who was at his best in taking seven for 38. Yorkshire, needing only 97 for victory, lost five wickets for 54, but Barber saw them home with 46 not out – his most successful match to date considering the circumstances.

Yorkshire were out for 197 at Lord's, but thanks to some brilliant fielding and catching Middlesex failed by 31 runs to take the lead. Barber batted well to score 64 out of Yorkshire's second-innings total of 227 but Hearne made sure the game was drawn. Northamptonshire, all out for 94 at Northampton thanks to Frank Dennis's excellent five for 12 were never in the hunt with Yorkshire going well ahead with only one wicket down, Sutcliffe compiling 150 in $4\frac{1}{2}$ hours. Yorkshire declared at 409 for eight and Northamptonshire, all out 277, never looked like saving the match.

Gloucestershire, Lancashire and Nottinghamshire now led the table with 69 points each, Kent 66, Middlesex 64 and Yorkshire 62 were all in close contention so the visit to Tonbridge was of the utmost importance, especially as Sutcliffe and Leyland were on Test match duty.

Yorkshire's subsequent defeat by an innings and 76 runs came as a rude awakening to their followers, but rain over the weekend was certainly in Kent's favour. Batting first, the home side, thanks to Hardinge (137) and Woolley (131) who added 239 for the second wicket, reached 471 for nine declared, with Rhodes finishing with seven for 116, taking advantage of a drying pitch after the weekend. Yorkshire found Freeman (six for 53) difficult to play as they struggled to 108 all out, but batted much better on following on, and made a respectable 287. Freeman took six for 118. With Barber also absent from the line-up, Yorkshire brought back Shackleton into the side and introduced Broadhead as an opening batsman, for his only game.

The next four games were all drawn. The Derbyshire match saw Yorkshire gain an advantage with a lead of 83 on the first innings but rain stopped play before lunch on the last day with Yorkshire 37 for three in their second innings. There was no play at all on the opening day at Leeds against Surrey who were 168 behind on the first innings after Rhodes had taken five for 324. Steady batting from Yorkshire's opening pair and a hard-hit 60 not out from Macaulay had put Yorkshire in the driving seat but Surrey were 137 for one when stumps were drawn. Yorkshire could not blame the weather for failing to beat Worcestershire, where four dropped catches were expensive. It was a good match at Fartown with Yorkshire scoring 238 (Root seven for 65) but Worcestershire gained a lead of 14. A newcomer, Frank Greenwood, was in good form when Yorkshire batted again making 65 and Yorkshire were able to declare at 267 for nine, leaving Worcestershire requiring 254 in even time. At the close they were 118 for seven, so the dropped catches were indeed crucial.

Frank Greenwood, a member of the Oundle XI in 1922 and 1923, was a solid looking right-hand batsman who had an aggressive outlook. He certainly impressed on his first appearance for the county at Fartown, and in his next match against Glamorgan at Hull, he attacked the bowling to such an extent that he completed 104 not out in two hours and looked a player of class; as indeed he did against Middlesex at Bradford in August when he made top score for Yorkshire with 62. He finished the season with 274 runs at an average of 39.14. In 1930 he averaged 29 in his 11 games and was appointed captain of Yorkshire for the 1931 season, when he led the side to the Championship, showing talent as a batsman and as a leader with a certain individualism which made him very much his own man. Re-appointed for the 1932 season, he could play in only a few matches owing to business calls and he never played for Yorkshire again. There can be no disputing that he was probably the best cricketer that Yorkshire had ever appointed to lead the side until Norman Yardley took charge, and though he does not appear to have played much cricket after his short county career he distinguished himself at league level with Slaithwaite and Huddersfield up to 1938. He later lived in the Isle of Man for several years.

The Nottinghamshire match which followed at Trent Bridge was an example of everything that was wrong with county cricket at that time. In three full day's play, Yorkshire scored 498 and Nottingham-shire replied with 190 for four in 160 overs. Percy Holmes, whose slowness was excusable as his side had to recover from 130 for six, scored 285 for Yorkshire. Rhodes (79) helped Holmes to add 247 for the seventh wicket. Further comment is unnecessary except to state that Rhodes had bowling figures of 35-29-11-0 and Turner bowled 24 overs for 25 runs.

At Hull, Glamorgan batted first to score 297 with the Yorkshire-born Bell making top score (58), and when Yorkshire lost two wickets for 15 Glamorgan appeared to be in charge. It proved an illusion as Oldroyd (168) and Barber (114) added 213 and then Greenwood (104 not out) helped Barber in a stand of 187 before Yorkshire declared at 437 for four. The batting display was in contrast to that at Trent Bridge. Yorkshire then dismissed Glamorgan for 86, Rhodes taking five for 41 and Dennis four for 18. Two further victories were

363

recorded over Essex at Bradford by ten wickets and over Warwickshire at Harrogate by four wickets. Macaulay had match figures of ten for 98 and Sutcliffe scored 133 not out to put Yorkshire on the winning track at Bradford. Only Warwickshire displayed some good cricket at Harrogate, where the home side were 57 in arrears at the completion of the first innings. Bowes took five for 52 and Macaulay four for 21 as Yorkshire were set 175 to win, and they got home by four wickets with Sutcliffe (82 not out) playing a great innings. Their spurt of success had placed Yorkshire in second place in the table, three points behind Champions Lancashire.

Leicestershire got the better of a drawn match at Dewsbury by compiling 298 with Bowes in fine form once again, taking eight for 77 in 42.1 overs. On a rain-affected wicket, Yorkshire lost five for 56 but avoided the follow-on, and eventually were happy to play out time. At Bradford, the Lancashire match was ruined by the weather, but Yorkshire were well on top when play finished on the last day at 2 pm. Lancashire were all out for 192 with Leyland taking seven for 52. Sutcliffe made sure of first innings points with 106, helping Yorkshire to a score of 285 for seven after which there was no further play.

The South Africans visited Yorkshire twice during the season and at Sheffield, I. J. Siedle and B. Mitchell compiled centuries as the South Africans scored 441 for five, with Yorkshire replying with 338. Sutcliffe (113) and Mitchell (126) put on 172 for the second wicket. At the close the visitors led by 380 with two wickets to fall. In the return game, Barber scored a century for Yorkshire, ensuring a lead of 70, but the match was easily drawn. Yorkshire also played against an England XI at Sheffield, A. T. Barber (100) and Oldroyd (143) putting on 203 for the second wicket before the game was abandoned.

At Leicester, the home side batted all the first day for 215 all out, and further stoppages for rain did not help Yorkshire's cause as they failed by seven to equal Leicester's total. There was no time for any other result but a draw. Back at Headingley, Yorkshire were all out for 369 against Hampshire whose batsmen did not put up much of a fight against tight Yorkshire bowling and the match was over well before lunch on the last day with Yorkshire victors by an innings and 18 runs. Robinson completed a fine all-round display with 64 and four for 47 and six for 62. The positions at the top of the table were now as follows with each side due to play 28 matches in all:

	P	W	L	DW	DL	NR	Pts
Lancashire	24	10	3	6	4	1	126
Gloucestershire	23	13	4	1	3	2	126
Nottinghamshire	22	11	2	3	4	2	123
Yorkshire	22	8	1	7	4	2	119

The tightness of the situation was obvious with Nottinghamshire meeting both Gloucestershire and Lancashire in a week's time. Yorkshire's next match against Derbyshire at Sheffield left the visitors with 331 to win in $4\frac{1}{2}$ hours but at 121 for two rain set in so that each side was robbed of a possible win. Derbyshire were 61 behind on the first innings, in which Macaulay took five for 62 and Dennis four for 45, and Holmes made 100 before Yorkshire declared at 269 for five.

At Bradford, Yorkshire rose to second place behind Nottinghamshire in the table when they comfortably beat Middlesex by 196 runs in spite of the absence of Leyland and Sutcliffe. Only Oldroyd (55) coped well with the difficult drying pitch after Yorkshire were put in to bat but a final score of 213 was ultimately satisfactory. With Hendren (86 not out) alone able to cope with the conditions Middlesex were bowled out for 154, with Bowes taking five for 48, and Yorkshire's reply put them in a winning position as they took their lead to 288 before declaring with seven wickets down. Middlesex were bowled out for 92 for an easy win.

Stubborn resistance from Hampshire and a session of rain finally robbed Yorkshire of the chance of victory at Bournemouth. Yorkshire passed Hampshire's 259 by the end of the second day, when with a lead of 11 and with only three wickets down they declared. Oldroyd scored 100 not out and Leyland 104 as they added 194 for the third wicket. On a pitch giving the bowlers help, stubborn batting robbed Yorkshire of a victory chance as Hampshire reached a total of 233. Meanwhile, Nottinghamshire had beaten Gloucestershire after

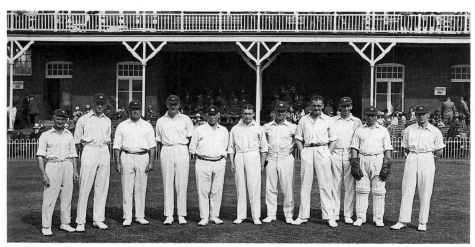

Yorkshire at Scarborough in 1929 against MCC, the last of George Hirst's 718 matches for the County. From left: Robinson, Dennis, Rhodes, Captain W. A. Worsley, Hirst, Greenwood, Leyland, Macaulay, Mitchell, Wood, Barber.

having by far the best of a draw with Lancashire, and had a clear lead at the top which they were not to relinquish.

In the next match at The Oval, Yorkshire did their chances no good by batting a long time for 304, with Oldroyd scoring 140 in $5\frac{1}{2}$ hours. Surrey, in less time at the crease, had a lead of 104 on the first innings with Sandham scoring 187, Yorkshire's bowling looking somewhat limited. Yorkshire had little difficulty in saving the match with Holmes (142) and Sutcliffe (123 not out) putting on 241 for the first wicket, and they finished the match with 315 for one.

At Worcester the home side failed against Bowes (four for 51) and Dennis (three for 4) and though Root had two early wickets, Yorkshire's Mitchell batting confidently scored 122 not out in three hours to take his side to 307 for seven declared. Dennis with five for 58 and Bowes three for 81 took Yorkshire to a ten-wicket victory early on the last day. Travelling to Hove for their last match against Sussex with the title won and lost, Yorkshire dismissed the home side for 169, but Sussex led by 17 on the first innings, with Tate taking four for 52. A Sussex score of 265 set Yorkshire 283 to win in $3\frac{1}{2}$ hours. Holmes (61), Leyland (43) and Robinson (40) put up a fight before Tate took the new ball to dismiss the last two batsmen for Sussex to earn victory by 78 runs.

Yorkshire therefore finished equal second to Nottinghamshire, who were worthy Champions, but Yorkshire's performances gave greater hope for the 1930s.

Yorkshire's batting was again the side's strong point with Sutcliffe again being the side's best batsman with 1,485 runs at 55. Leyland scored 1,407 runs at 42 and Holmes 1,724 at 41. Oldroyd showed no falling-off with 1,470 runs at 40.83 and Robinson also completed his thousand runs. Mitchell fell away a little being not always completely fit, but he was back to form by the end of the season and he was rated one of the best close-to-the-wicket fielders in the country. Barber scored 845 runs at 32.50 while Rhodes and Wood each scored over 600 runs. Captain Worsley resigned from the captaincy in the knowledge that he had played his part well and made one or two valuable contributions with the bat.

Wilfred Rhodes again headed the bowling averages with 100 wickets at 18.01 followed by Bowes with 45 wickets at 19 and Dennis, who took 82 wickets at 21.82. A successor to Rhodes and the continued improvement in the two fast men would ensure Yorkshire's future. George Macaulay took 102 wickets at 22.60 and worked hard throughout the season while Robinson's 82 wickets at 24 each were typical of that great trier. Leyland with 48 wickets at 27.41 each had his days of success without quite qualifying to be reckoned as an all-rounder. The future at least looked brighter than for a few years.

THE TRIUMPHANT THIRTIES

THE SHORTAGE OF BOWLING THAT troubled the Yorkshire side in the late 1920s was remedied in 1930 when Hedley Verity made his first appearance for the team. He came into the side at Fartown in a friendly match with Sussex along with another Leeds-born player, wicket-keeper Syd Buller. It was Buller's only match for Yorkshire but he did go on to play for Worcestershire and become one of the foremost umpires of his day, before he died in a Birmingham hospital after collapsing on the field of play during a Warwickshire *v* Nottingham-shire match at Edgbaston in 1970.

Verity, born within a few hundred yards of the Headingley ground, took three wickets against Sussex, but they cost him 32 runs each and Wilfred Rhodes returned against Essex at Dewsbury in a match in which the bat was well on top of the ball.

At Hull against Leicestershire, Verity took four for 45 and four for 15 and helped Yorkshire to an innings victory, with George Macaulay taking six for 11. Verity played only 12 matches during the season and it was not until the Gloucestershire match at Bristol that he actually bowled in harness with Wilfred Rhodes, now 52 years old and in his last season of county cricket. Gloucestershire, without Hammond, were thrashed by an innings and 187 runs, the two left-armers distinguishing themselves. Verity went on to head the first-class bowling averages with 64 wickets at 12.44 each. A notable start, he bowled slightly quicker than his predecessor and was much taller. Though he lacked experience, he had mastered the art of slow bowling in the Yorkshire nets and in various leagues with Rawdon, Accrington and Middleton (Lancashire).

As deadly as the more recent Underwood on a bad wicket, he bowled more in the manner of the orthodox left-arm slow and was a master of flight. During his ten years with Yorkshire he headed the bowling averages in his first and last seasons and was never lower than third in any of the other years. He was a very useful batsman – he actually opened for England against Australia in 1936–37 and a safe catcher. He died of wounds at Caserta in Italy in 1943 at the age of 38. He was respected and loved by all who came into contact with him.

It matters little whether one considers 1930 to be the start of the 1930s or the end of the 1920s; the arrival of Verity heralded a new era for Yorkshire cricket. In an exciting season, often plagued by persistently poor weather, Yorkshire finished third in the County Championship, only five points behind the unbeaten Champions, Lancashire. During a dreadful period in July, only one match reached a third innings and two games were abandoned without a ball being bowled.

This was Alan Barber's only season as captain of Yorkshire before becoming a schoolmaster and later headmaster of Ludgrove Preparatory School at Wokingham where he devoted the rest of his life. One of the well-known Sheffield family of Barbers who had close connections with cricket, A. T. Barber was considered the best captain and the best cricketer that the County had had since Burton and Yorkshire's immediate success in the early 1930s was due in no small measure to his astute leadership. Barber, a member of the Shrewsbury School and Oxford University cricket elevens, was a fine all-round games player and played soccer for Barnet and the Corinthians.

The following season saw Yorkshire's first of three consecutive Championships. Such was their domination that Yorkshire won 54 matches and lost only six in the three seasons. Only in 1933 did Yorkshire appear to be seriously challenged by another county when Sussex finished only 5.21 per cent behind them at the end.

In 1931, under Frank Greenwood, a Huddersfield industrialist who gave up the captaincy owing to business in 1932, Yorkshire lost only one match. This was a game in which rain ruined the first two days and both sides declared at 4 for none. Greenwood and Beverley Lyon, the Gloucestershire skipper, were reprimanded by the authorities for making a farce of the County Championship. Yorkshire came unstuck in that particular game but they tried a similar ruse against Northamptonshire later in the season which was successful. (Alas, many Championship matches in the present age are played under more farcical conditions with full approval of the game's legislators!)

The season had a wretched start as far as the weather was concerned. Yorkshire began with two innings victories but lost no less than ten days of cricket in the next seven matches, including that controversial match with Gloucestershire. Fortunately, they followed that with five consecutive innings victories and ran out Champions, with Sutcliffe having a marvellous season.

Sutcliffe topped the first-class averages while Verity and Bowes, backed up by Macaulay and the veteran Emmott Robinson were far too strong for the opposition.

Two newcomers were tried for Yorkshire in this season. One was Arthur Booth, who came in as a replacement for Verity and whose only wicket was Frank Lee's at Taunton; he was not to play again for Yorkshire until 14 years had elapsed. It was also Edgar Oldroyd's last season in first-class cricket. Now aged 42, he still averaged over 30 and as a number three batsman was a model of consistency. He was considered by many opposition bowlers to be one of the most difficult

batsmen to dismiss in the county game. After his retirement he joined
Pudsey St Lawrence where he opened the batting with Len Hutton,
and in 1933 became the first Bradford League batsman to complete
1,000 runs in a season. A successful businessman – he was a rag-
merchant at Batley – he went to live at Harrogate before retiring to
Falmouth in 1960. He died a comparatively wealthy man at Truro in
1964.

If the inclement weather at the start of 1931 upset that season;
Yorkshire's next season was affected both by bad weather and by bad
play. They began by losing to Lancashire at Park Avenue by an
innings and 50 runs in spite of Hedley Verity's eight for 59. Sibbles
replied with seven for 10 in 20.4 overs, a remarkable bowling analysis,
and after the follow-on he finished the match with twelve for 68.
Yorkshire, inevitably caught on a sticky wicket, were dismissed in the
first innings for 46, of which paltry total Herbert Sutcliffe scored 27.

Two abandoned matches came each side of a nine-wicket win over
Somerset at Bath before Yorkshire lost again to Hampshire at Leeds by
49 runs. Sutcliffe reached 104 not out of his side's 170 all out and
Yorkshire's only excuse for a poor batting display was Percy Holmes'
absence in the second innings due to illness. Yorkshire then lost on the
first innings at Hull and with 38 points only obtained out of 105
Yorkshire occupied a lowly position in the table. Even so Sutcliffe was
averaging almost 90 and Verity's 22 wickets cost less than 13 runs each.

The possibility of Yorkshire's poor form continuing proved to be
an illusion. A. B. Sellers, now virtually captain of the side in
Greenwood's absence – the latter playing in just three of the
remaining Championship fixtures – led them to victory in 18 of their
last 21 matches, and as well they had the better of the three drawn
games played. Amongst these successes were the 555 for the first
wicket by Holmes and Sutcliffe at Leyton, with Verity taking five for
8 in the Essex innings as they followed on 477 behind; a score of 270 by
Herbert Sutcliffe against Sussex at Leeds; Barber and Leyland adding
346 for the second wicket against Middlesex at Bramall Lane; all this
followed by eight for 39 by Verity at Northampton. There was
magnificent batting in the Gloucestershire match at Bradford, where
Sutcliffe and Wally Hammond played unforgettable innings in a
match containing almost 1,300 runs. Then to top them all, Hedley
Verity's ten for 10 v Nottinghamshire at Headingley cannot be
overlooked.

There was also a revenge win by an innings at Old Trafford, with
Herbert Sutcliffe notching his seventh century of the season – he was
to score four more. He finished the season with 2,883 runs in all
matches with an average of 80. There was an opening partnership of
169 between Sutcliffe and Leyland, with Leyland notching 113 with

Scoreboards registering two Yorkshire world records for opening stands. On the left, Brown and Tunnicliffe with their partnership of 554 against Derbyshire at Chesterfield in 1898, and on the right Holmes and Sutcliffe after beating the record with 555 against Essex at Leyton in 1932.

Herbert less than half that number. That was remarkable in a season when Sutcliffe was so dominant, and during a period in which for three years from 1930 to 1932 he headed the first-class averages. In fact, not since Ranjitsinhji or Grace had one player so dominated the batting averages in such a manner.

Nor did Yorkshire's individual performances stop there. Bill Bowes took nine for 121 in 44 overs against Essex at Scarborough, followed by 194 by Sutcliffe, this time batting at number four in the order.

At Bradford another left-arm slow bowler, Horace Fisher, took six for 11 in 17 overs against Leicestershire while Verity himself conceded ten runs in his two overs! In the next game Fisher took five for 12 and then hit 76 not out against Somerset. There was no denying Yorkshire's greatness. Sutcliffe, Leyland, Holmes, Mitchell and Barber all reached their 1,000 runs, while Brian Sellers in his first season scored over 800.

A native of Keighley, like his father who had played with distinction for the side in the 1890s, Arthur Brian Sellers was a natural leader who made himself into one of the best close-to-the-wicket fielders in the side. By sheer determination, he became more than a useful batsman and invariably obtained runs when they were needed. Educated at St Peter's School, York, he was captain of the side in 1923 and 1924 although he had got into the team as an off-spinner. He played with Keighley and became their captain in 1930 and took over as Yorkshire captain two years later when Greenwood was unable to

YORKSHIRE v. NOTTINGHAMSHIRE, at Headingley

Sat. Mon. and Tues., July 9th, 11th, and 12th, 1932.

NOTTINGHAMSHIRE.	1st Innings		2nd Innings	
1. Keeton b Rhodes	9	c Macaulay b Verity	21
2. Shipstone b Macaulay	8	c Wood b Verity	21
3. Walker c Barber b Bowes	36	c Macaulay b Verity	11
4. A. W. Carr c Barber b Verity	0	c Barber b Verity	0
5. Staples (A.) b Macaulay	3	c Macaulay b Verity	7
6. Harris lbw b Macaulay	35	c Holmes b Verity	0
7. Gunn (G. V.) b Verity	31	lbw b Verity	0
8. Lilley not out	46	not out	3
9. Larwood b Leyland	48	c Sutcliffe b Verity	0
10. Voce b Leyland	0	c Holmes b Verity	0
11. Staples (S.) b Leyland	0	st Wood b Verity	0
Extras b 8, lb 6, w 2, nb 2.	18	Extras b 3, nb 1.	4
Total	234	Total	67

Total runs at fall of each wicket
15 35 40 46 67 120 159 233 233 234   14 44 47 51 63 63 63 64 64 67 67

Bowler	Overs	Maidens	Runs	W'kts	Overs	Maidens	Runs	W'kts
Bowes	31	9	55	1	5	0	19	0
Rhodes	28	8	49	1				
Verity	41	13	64	2	19.4	16	10	10
Macaulay	24	10	34	2	23	9	34	0
Leyland	8.2	3	14	4				

Umpires: Scorers:
Messrs. Baldwin & Reeves.   Messrs. Ringrose & Carlin.

YORKSHIRE.	1st Innings		2nd Innings
1. Holmes b Larwood	65		
2. Sutcliffe c Voce b Larwood	0		
3. Mitchell run out	24		
4. Leyland b Voce	5		
5. Barber c and b Larwood	34		
6. A. B. Sellers b Staples (A.)	0		
7. Wood b Larwood	1		
8. Rhodes c Staples (A.) b Voce	3		
9. Verity b Larwood	12		
10. Macaulay not out	8		
11. Bowes not out	1		
Extras b 5, lb 5.	10		
Total for 9 wkts. dec.	163		

Total runs at fall of each wicket
1 37 121 123 125 128 135 152 154

Bowler	Overs	Maidens	Runs	W'kts	Overs	Maidens	Runs	W'kts
Larwood	22	4	73	5				
Voce	22	2	52	2				
Staples (S.)	7	2	8	0				
Staples (A.)	11	3	20	1				

HOURS OF PLAY—1st & 2nd Days, 11-30 to 6-30; 3rd Day, 11-30 to 6-0.
Luncheon Interval, 1-30 to 2-10 each day. Tea, 4-15.

The scorecard after a record-breaking bowling performance at Headingley in 1932. Nottinghamshire are all out in their second innings for 67 and Hedley Verity has the best innings analysis in first-class cricket: ten for 10.

play because of business. Sellers was to be officially appointed captain at the start of the 1933 season and went on to lead the side until 1947. During that period Yorkshire's success was guaranteed. Some would say that the team of the 1930s hardly required a captain, but Yorkshire cricket has always needed a strong disciplinarian and in Brian Sellers they had the ideal man. He was never up to county class as a batsman but his qualities of leadership and sheer guts meant that his position in the side was never questioned. He became an active member of the Yorkshire committee succeeding Clifford Hesketh as chairman of the cricket committee in 1959 and being elected as a vice-president in 1980.

A controversial figure in the politics of Yorkshire cricket, many accused him of living in the past. An outspoken personality, forthright in his views, he perhaps bore much of the blame for some of the Club's unwise actions. Always approachable, his heart was never far from his love affair with Yorkshire cricket and his later years were saddened by Yorkshire's problems and his own sufferings from arthritis and hip trouble. He also served on the MCC Committee from 1969 and his views on most aspects of cricket were invariably newsworthy. He died at his home at Eldwick, near Bingley in 1981 aged 73. His brother Godfrey, who survived him, also served on the Yorkshire committee.

The 1932 season also saw T. F. Smailes introduced into the Yorkshire side. Frank Smailes, a native of Ripley, near Knaresborough, was educated at Pocklington School and started playing with Ilkley at the age of 16. Coached by his father, a cattle dealer in Otley and by his elder brother, he eventually followed the same line of business. A hard-hitting left-handed batsman and a fine right-arm medium-pace opening bowler who could turn to off-breaks when required, he was a natural successor to George Macaulay and went on to play for England. As a youngster he followed brother George to Harrogate Cricket Club before becoming a professional with Forfarshire in 1931. He returned to play for Brighouse and gained a regular place in the Yorkshire side in 1934. The Second World War certainly affected his career but he continued to play for Yorkshire until 1948 when he became professional at Walsall for five years. He gave up county cricket as varicose veins were affecting his form and he kept the 'Sportsmans Arms' at Wath near Ripon. He died after a long illness in 1970.

The third great season was even more of a walkover for the Yorkshire side, the only sad aspect about that 1933 season being the sad falling-off of Percy Holmes. He played throughout the season but averaged less than 20, although he did score 929 runs. In comparison Herbert Sutcliffe had a poor season too but it was only by his own very high standards that one could discern any real deterioration. He still managed to average 48. One could not fault the other batting, with Leyland and Mitchell heading the averages while Barber scored nearly 1,600 runs. The bowling, in the hands of Verity, Macaulay and Bowes was again the strength of the side, and although Yorkshire did have a bad time in August, the Championship had been won very easily by then.

Kenneth R. Davidson, made his first appearance for Yorkshire in 1933 as an amateur and in the following season scored 1,241 runs as a professional with two centuries to his name. He scored 128 against Kent at Maidstone at a time when Leyland, Verity and Bowes were playing for England and Sutcliffe and Macaulay were absent too. it proved one of several sound innings he played for Yorkshire but after playing two games in 1935 he decided, in spite of being capped, that it was perhaps too late at the age of 29 to embark on a professional career. A man of many parts he was a very fine badminton player who helped to promote the game in the United States. He went on to play cricket for Scotland in 1938. He was killed in an air disaster at Prestwick on Christmas Day, 1954.

Yorkshire dropped to sixth place in the Championship in 1934, which was their worst season since 1911. Their final record of 12 wins and seven losses compares unfavourably with the previous season's 19 wins and only three losses, yet during the Tests against Australia Yorkshire lost six of their matches. In fact not since 1912 had Yorkshire won the title when the Australians were visitors. The batting was strong with six batsmen topping the thousand mark and skipper Sellers missing by only nine runs. Three bowlers, Bowes, Verity and Smailes, all captured 100 wickets and George Macaulay took 55 wickets. Furthermore, four other bowlers took 20 wickets or more. It may have been a poor season by their own high standards but Lancashire, the eventual Champions, were defeated by an innings and three runs at Sheffield. When it is remembered that the two leading batsmen for England were Leyland and Sutcliffe, and Verity and Bowes were the leading wicket-takers, then their absence from the Yorkshire side can be seen to be crucial. Mitchell, opening the innings instead of Holmes, headed the batting averages.

Five newcomers actually turned out for Yorkshire in 1934. Herbert Hargreaves, a fast-medium bowler, continued to play occasionally for Yorkshire up to 1938 his 55 wickets costing less than 21 runs each. J. H. (Jackie) Pearson was a fine opening batsman who made three appearances for Yorkshire, once in each season from 1934 to 1936, and made top score of the match against Northamptonshire at Kettering in 1935. Tom Bottomley played several games for Yorkshire in 1934 and one match in 1935.

The two other new players were better known by far. Ellis

Robinson, a brilliant close-to-the-wicket field, hard-hitting left-handed batsman and a very promising off-break bowler, first played for the side when George Macaulay fell ill. He helped Yorkshire to a ten-wicket win at Worcester by taking four for 81 on his first bowl for the County and then took four for 86 against Nottinghamshire. He developed steadily and gained a regular place in the Yorkshire side in 1938. The war robbed him of his best years, and although he was successful in 1946, a wet season that suited his bowling admirably, he never again showed such form and left Yorkshire in 1949 to go to Somerset. He became an honorary life member of the County Club in 1982 and still keenly follows their fortunes.

The most famous newcomer was a certain Hutton, L., who had played with success in the Second XI and was thought highly of by his mentor, Herbert Sutcliffe, and by coach George Hirst who claimed from the start that there was nothing he could teach him about the art of batting. An inconspicuous start to his first-class career – run out for nought at Fenner's – was followed by half-centuries at The Parks and at Edgbaston, and his first century for the County duly followed at Worcester when he reached a fruitful 196. He also showed promise as a leg-break and googly bowler which had he had a stronger constitution would have been made more use of by Yorkshire. His development was steady but sure, although his form in his first full season, 1936, was a disappointment. In that season he scored 1,282 runs at an average of just under 30, but such were the high expectations of him that even at the age of 20 miracles were anticipated.

The following season saw Hutton at last realise expectations. He did fail against Jack Cowie on his Test debut against New Zealand – 0 and 1 – but he was retained for the second Test and duly came up with a century. His future assured, the criticism he endured from critics who claimed that he did not score quickly enough were now in the background. Confidence came into his game and the master batsman, so long expected, at last came to fruition. Above medium height, he was an orthodox and classical opening batsman with an off and cover drive that photographs show was unsurpassed even by Hammond. A fine batsman on all types of pitches, he succeeded Sutcliffe as the best batsman in the side, and after the Second World War he became for a few years the only reliable batsman in the Yorkshire team.

He filled a similar role for England when Denis Compton developed knee problems and lost his old swashbuckling form. Hutton eventually became England captain, regained the Ashes from Australia, kept them while touring Australia, and was eventually knighted for his services to cricket.

In 1935 Yorkshire regained the Championship in a season when

374

South Africa had a full tour of England and no fewer than six members of the Yorkshire side faced them during the Tests. There were never less than three playing in any one of the three Tests, so Yorkshire did very well to have such a successful season.

They lost only one match – an infamous match at Fartown where Essex bowled them out for 31 – and only Derbyshire offered any real challenge to them. When the two sides met at Scarborough in the middle of August victory for Derbyshire would have put them marginally ahead of Yorkshire. As it turned out, Yorkshire won easily by ten wickets in two days, although the visitors were short of Worthington who had only three to his name in the first innings when he had to retire. For the victors, Sandy Jacques made his only Championship appearance of the season and took four for 35 in the first innings while Cyril Turner took seven wickets in the game.

Without doubt this 1935 season was one of Yorkshire's best, and if Bowes and Verity – the latter took 199 wickets in all matches for Yorkshire – bore the brunt of the bowling, Smailes did take 96 wickets and Horace Fisher 51. The batting was consistency itself, with Sutcliffe topping the averages with 2,183 runs and Barber, Leyland, Mitchell and Wood all exceeding the four-figure mark.

The only newcomer to the side was that remarkable character Paul Gibb, a dour opening batsman and very competent wicket-keeper. The elder son of a railway executive, he was in the St Edward's School XI at Oxford in 1929–31 and was later in the Cambridge University XI in 1935–38, scoring a century against Oxford in 1938. He also played in six matches for Yorkshire in 1935, more than in any other season and on his debut scored 157 not out against Nottingham-shire at Bramall Lane. He helped Herbert Sutcliffe to add 178 for the sixth wicket and put Yorkshire in a strong position. Gibb toured Canada in 1933; captained Yorkshire in Jamaica in 1936; toured with the MCC side to South Africa in 1938–39 where he was a big success, and went to Australia as first-choice wicket-keeper in 1946–47. He quickly lost his England place to Godfrey Evans, and severed his connection with Yorkshire, for whom he averaged 32 in a short and chequered career. He moved to Essex as a professional in 1951, where he performed creditably and became a first-class umpire in 1957 staying on the list for ten seasons. He also spent some time coaching in South Africa, and died after collapsing in Guildford Bus Station in 1977. He had been working as a bus driver.

Splendid performances abounded in 1935. Early in the season Cyril Turner took seven for 54 at Gloucester as the home side slumped to 128 all out, but Yorkshire were doing worse at 74 for seven before Arthur Wood (64 not out) added 47 with Verity and 45 with Smailes.

Barber's attractive 191 against Sussex at Leeds was followed by Bowes taking eight for 40 against Worcestershire at Sheffield before Sutcliffe scored 200 not out.

At Lord's, in a rain-ruined match, Middlesex were 32 for eight before Jim Smith scored a hard-hitting 57 and then Mitchell and Barber put on 207 for Yorkshire's first wicket. Verity had eight for 28 at Leeds against Leicestershire (55 all out), while Bowes took eight for 18 and eight for 17 against Northamptonshire at Kettering and went on to take seven for 58 in the next innings agaist Essex at Colchester.

Wilf Barber then scored 255 against Surrey at Bramall Lane, before Bowes, again in outstanding form, took six for 16 and six for 83 at Bradford against Lancashire, who scored only 53 in their first knock. In the next match at Leicester Herbert Sutcliffe compiled 212. At The Oval, Verity took six for 24 as Surrey collapsed to 44 all out, but rain saved the southerners. In the Test series, Leyland and Mitchell each averaged 56 or more and Sutcliffe and Barber both played good innings. Inevitably, Verity headed England's bowling averages and Bowes took the most wickets. It was a memorable season even by Yorkshire's pre-war standards.

Yorkshire had the satisfaction of defeating the Rest of England at The Oval at the end of the season, the winning margin being 149 runs. Hedley Verity took ten for 84 in the match and Maurice Leyland, in a low-scoring game, made 58 and 133 not out. George Macaulay retired at the end of the season, his last appearance being against Leicestershire at Headingley.

During the following February and March Yorkshire were invited to tour Jamaica under Paul Gibb's leadership, and they had the satisfaction of defeating Jamaica once and acquitting themselves well in the other two matches against the home team. George Headley scored one century and made 266 runs at an average of 53.20 in the three-match representative rubber. That average was more than doubled by Yorkshire's most successful batsman, Arthur Mitchell, who also headed the bowling averages with three wickets at 16.33 apiece – more wickets than he ever took in England. I. Barrow, R. L. Fuller, L. G. Hylton, E. A. Rae, C. C. Passailaigue, V. A. Valentine, H. H. Johnson and D. P. Beckford were other well-known Jamaican cricketers to take part in the series. Hedley Verity, besides being Yorkshire's most successful bowler, had the satisfaction of scoring his only century, 101, in the last match at Sabina Park, Jamaica suffered their first home defeat for ten years.

The new season opened with a draw against Essex, who battled hard after Leyland had compiled 263. The score was 3 for two when he went out to bat, and he added 247 with Len Hutton for the fourth wicket. Defeat at Stourbridge followed, Yorkshire collapsing from 68 for two to 106 all out when needing only 118 to win. Dick Howorth took five for 21 after Verity had match figures of thirteen for 88.

In what proved to be one of the wettest seasons on record, Yorkshire did play as well as ever for most of the time, and Verity with six for 52 and nine for 48 was irresistible in the return match with Essex at Westcliff. Champions Derbyshire did make Yorkshire follow on, and Gloucestershire bowled them out for 66 at Bristol, but only one further match was actually lost, against Kent at Dover by nine wickets.

Leyland easily topped the batting averages but Sutcliffe, Mitchell and Hutton all exceeded the 1,000 run mark. Barber failed by only seven runs and four other players scored over 700 runs. Apart from Bill Bowes, the team had no tail at all.

Nor could the bowling be faulted, with Bowes and Verity occupying fourth and second places in the first-class averages, and Frank Smailes, who took 125 wickets, finishing as high as seventh. It is easy to blame the poor weather for Yorkshire's poor showing but Yorkshire did suffer more than most, and led as often as 12 times on the first innings without winning the match.

There were several newcomers in the side, including Norman Yardley, who did well enough to suggest that he would become a welcome asset following a promising start with Cambridge University. An innings of 89 was his best innings in the last match of the season. Born in Barnsley in 1915, he was in the York St Peter's School eleven from 1930 to 1934, playing for the Yorkshire Colts while still at school. He was captain in his last two years and appeared for the Young Amateurs against the Young Professionals at Lord's when he scored an aggressive 189 against a side containing Denis Compton. He went on to play in the Cambridge University XI from 1935 to 1938. A hard hitting batsman, very strong on the leg-side, he could also bowl seamers with outstanding success at times and was a very good fielder. When he ultimately succeeded Brian Sellers as the Yorkshire captain in 1948, he led Yorkshire to a shared Championship in 1949 and had the misfortune to contend with the powerful Surrey side in the 1950s. He did lead Yorkshire to the runners-up spot on four occasions up to his retirement in 1955. He was certainly the best amateur to captain the side and he captained England for several seasons with some success.

A fine judge of a declaration, he was well-liked by his players, if perhaps lacking the sheer dynamism of his predecessor. He created something of a sensation by dismissing Don Bradman in Tests during the unsuccessful tour of Australia in 1946–47 and one felt that he could have been made more use of as a bowler particularly when he himself was captain.

A wine merchant by profession, he served on the Yorkshire

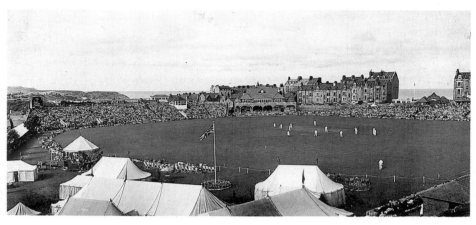

A view of a well-packed Scarborough ground before the grandstand was built.

committee after his playing days were over and acted as president from 1981 until he resigned at the start of 1984. During the most difficult and darkest period of the Club's history, he conducted affairs in a fair and unbiased manner. Alas, he should never have been burdened with the politics of Yorkshire cricket in the 1980s.

Yorkshire had a splendid season in 1937. Only two matches were lost: to Middlesex at Lord's by an innings and 22 runs when Bill Bowes was injured, and a five-wicket defeat at Bramall Lane by the old enemy for whom Jack Iddon took nine for 42 in the second innings.

After an opening ten-wicket win over Lancashire, Yorkshire had scores of 496 for eight and 566 mounted against them – by Warwickshire at Edgbaston and by Sussex at Bramall Lane – before winning four matches in a row. Robinson and Verity each took ten wickets in a match, at the expense of Gloucestershire and Worcestershire.

Skipper Brian Sellers (109) and Frank Smailes had a 125-stand at Park Avenue against Kent, after Yorkshire had collapsed to 48 for five, Sellers making his third century for Yorkshire, and Smailes followed his 65 with 80 not out and then took five for 16 in Kent's second innings. Kent recovered from 1 for four and then from 42 for eight before doubling the score for the last wicket. They finally lost by 287 runs.

Meanwhile Len Hutton had moved into what one might term top gear for the first time in his career. A score of 136 at Tonbridge was followed by 271 not out at Sheffield against the strong Derbyshire attack. With Sutcliffe the first-wicket partnership brought 181 and the pair put on 315 at Hull against Leicestershire in the next match. A total of 560 runs in two completed innings was followed by his first Test failure at Lord's. If he had been prone to any big-headedness that Test match must have been a salutary lesson to him. Such is cricket. After that Test, a bus-ride away at Ilford a first-wicket partnership of 109 against Essex saw Hutton scoring yet another century. In the next match against Surrey at Bradford, Hutton reached only 67 but it was out of 118 for the first wicket again with Herbert Sutcliffe, who scored 138.

The new Hutton, a confident, dominating batsman, went on to top the Yorkshire batting averages with 2,448 runs at 62.76, well ahead of Sutcliffe, who also topped the two thousand mark, which at the age of 42 was a tribute to his fitness in a season in which he played in every match for Yorkshire and batted 52 times. Barber, Leyland and Mitchell each averaged 37 as well as achieving the statutory 1,000 runs. That alone proves the strength of Yorkshire's batting but to them should be added the names of Yardley, who averaged 41 and scored 783 runs, and Turner, Wood, Smailes and the skipper himself who all scored over 800 runs.

Verity had another great season with the ball, taking 185 wickets in all matches for Yorkshire while Frank Smailes took 120 wickets at 22.75 each. Bill Bowes had a relatively poor season for him, but he did finish up with 78 wickets at less than 20 runs each; the same number as Ellis Robinson. Turner, Hutton and Hargreaves all had their moments and the close-to-the-wicket fielding was as tight as ever with seven fielders taking 20 catches or more.

Middlesex had a good season, too, winning 15 out of their 24 matches, and finishing second in the table, and at the end of the season their skipper R. W. V. Robins issued a challenge to Yorkshire to a four-day match at The Oval. This would take the place of the Rest of England match and was duly accepted by A. B. Sellers. The match was played and resulted in an innings victory for Yorkshire, for whom Hutton scored another century and Verity took eight for 43 in Middlesex's second innings. It was an eminently satisfactory conclusion to the season.

Four new players made their first appearance for the county in 1937 but none of them ever became regulars. One was Jack Hampshire, father of the Yorkshire and England batsman, John and Alan. He was a medium-fast bowler played in three matches in 1937 for Yorkshire taking five wickets at 21.80 each. His last victim in first-class cricket was Denis Compton and he was not called upon again. He also played as a centre-half for Bristol City and for Manchester City. Another with a famous son was Horace Brearley, father of the Middlesex and England captain, Michael J. Brearley. He was a useful batsman who scored eight and nine in his only match for Yorkshire, against Middlesex at Sheffield. He appeared twice for Middlesex in 1949.

Yorkshire's success continued in 1939 with Middlesex once again in the runners–up spot. It was an emphatic margin of victory, Yorkshire losing just twice during the season, to their main rivals and to Surrey, both in successive weeks in London. The Middlesex defeat was suffered with Yorkshire at full strength in one sense, but Paul Gibb had to retire hurt when he was four in the first innings, and in the second innings as well as Gibb's injury, further mishaps caused Leyland to retire hurt at one and Hutton could not bat either. The defeat in such circumstances was hardly a disgrace. In the other defeat, Yorkshire were without Bowes and Verity, who were on Test duty while Gibb and Hutton were both injured.

A busy season was notable for the fact that no fewer than seven Yorkshire players were chosen to play in the Test matches, which were notable for the record score of 364 by Len Hutton; a record stand between Hutton and Leyland that amounted to 382 runs, and fine bowling from both Bowes and Verity, who headed the England bowling averages. Arthur Wood, on his Test debut, helped Hardstaff add 106 for England's seventh wicket at The Oval, while Gibb and Smailes had the frustrating experience of being chosen in the squad for the Old Trafford Test without a ball being bowled because of rain.

Hutton again topped the Yorkshire averages, but Test calls and injuries prevented him from playing more than half of Yorkshire's Championship fixtures. Considering the chopping and changing that went on Yorkshire's title win was more creditable than ever.

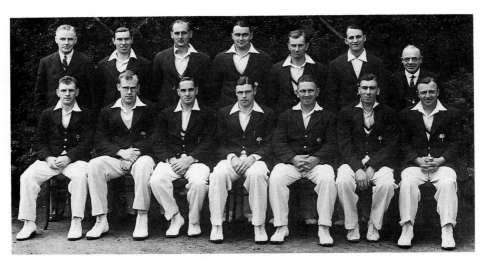

The County Champions of 1938. Back row: Mr Ringrose (scorer), Robinson, Verity, Smailes, Turner, Hutton, Mr Heyhirst (masseur). Seated: Barber, Bowes, Sutcliffe, Sellers, Leyland, Mitchell, Wood.

Hutton, Leyland, Sutcliffe, Mitchell, Barber and the skipper all passed the 1,000 runs mark, only Sellers failing to average 30. Smailes also reached his thousand in all first-class matches to complete the 'double' for the only time in his career.

The bowling was again very much to the fore, with Verity and Bowes taking their 100 wickets at less than 15 runs each. Robinson became the fourth bowler to take 100 wickets, for the first time in his case. Leyland's chinamen accounted for a further 61 victims and Turner and Yardley were around to take the odd wickets when necessary.

Ken Fiddling came in as a reserve wicket-keeper at Harrogate when Scotland were the visitors and in 1946 played for most of the season showing promise, but was not retained after the end of the season. From 1947 to 1953 he kept wicket for Northamptonshire and played most of his league cricket with Bingley, Bowling Old Lane, and Lightcliffe. He was at one time an executive with a firm of tailors.

Arnold Hamer played a couple of times for Yorkshire in 1938, batting at number ten against Essex and Gloucestershire and dismissing Nicholls in Essex's first innings. Then only 21 years old, he never played for Yorkshire again, but for some time was a full-back with York City. He was invited to play for Derbyshire in 1950 and proved to be one of the best batsmen ever to represent the county scoring over 15,000 runs up to his retirement in 1960. He played several important innings against Yorkshire and was a sound, reliable opening batsman with a fine defensive technique. He returned to league cricket and in 1963 headed the Bradford League averages for Spen Victoria after which he retired and was at varying times a licensee.

James Smurthwaite played a few times for the County in 1938 and 1939. His main claim to fame was to dismiss five batsmen for just seven runs after the Popes had bundled Yorkshire out for 83 in 1939. He bowled medium-pace in-swingers and off-breaks and with Frank Smailes (four for 11) shot out Derbyshire for 20. In the second innings Frank Smailes took all ten wickets for 47 runs.

There is no doubt that the most noted debutant was Harry Halliday, a native of Pudsey who was 18 years old when he appeared against Glamorgan at Cardiff. Yorkshire had lost four wickets for 42 when Halliday went out to join Leyland and helped him to take the score up to 129 with a solid 36. He played in seven further first team matches without success and it was eight years before he returned to first team duty. He became a dependable opening or middle order batsman who never quite fulfilled his pre-war promise but kept a regular place in the Yorkshire side until 1953. He had played his early cricket with Pudsey St Lawrence and during the war batted with great success for the British Empire XI. Halliday was also a good slip fielder, but put on weight in later years, and his medium-pace seamers made him a useful change bowler. A noted coach, he often went to South Africa, and was also coach with Workington, Cumberland and Scarborough College. He died in Pinderfields Hospital, Wakefield, in 1967.

The war which had been imminent for many months hardly affected the attendances at cricket matches in the last season before its outbreak, but the wretched early season weather certainly did. The season began with a win over Kent followed by a six-wicket defeat at Bradford against Gloucestershire, for whom Charlie Barnett scored 90 in an hour out of 132 as Gloucestershire knocked off 190 at two runs a minute. Verity was hit for 33 in three overs and Bowes conceded 59 runs in 8.2 overs. This was followed by a run of five successive victories by an innings in the Championship. Of the 100 wickets that the Yorkshire bowlers took in those five games, Verity took 31 and Bowes 30. At the same time Yorkshire lost only 31 wickets, yet Herbert Sutcliffe compiled 690 runs and Hutton 480. Against Hampshire at Sheffield, the opening pair put on 315 for the first wicket before the elder statesman was out for 116, at which stage Len Hutton was just short of 200. The fifth of the victories was against runners-up Middlesex, and in that game Sutcliffe helped Leyland (180 not out) add 301 for the third wicket. Herbert Sutcliffe's 175 was his fourth century in a row for Yorkshire. Middlesex had to follow on 368 runs in arrears and they lost before 5 pm on the second day, with Bill Bowes finishing the match with eight for 50 and Verity eight for 37.

Rain ruined the next two games but at Trent Bridge, Nottinghamshire, set 233 to win, were 3 for four after 6.6 eight-ball overs when rain put an end to Yorkshire's prospects. Smailes and Smurthwaite's remarkable game with Derbyshire followed a win at Bradford over Glamorgan, where Hutton scored a brilliant 144 and Verity took fourteen wickets for 68 runs.

With Yorkshire back at full strength at Bristol, Tom Goddard had analyses of six for 61 and seven for 38, outshining Hedley Verity as Yorkshire went down by seven wickets and Gloucestershire completed a worthy double over the Champions. Yorkshire's overall lead was almost unassailable; true they did have their bad days, such as a 16-run defeat at Stourbridge against Worcestershire, where Reg Perks took nine wickets and the Yorkshire batting failed twice, collapsing in the first innings from 84 for four to 91 all out and in the second from 68 for four to 113 all out. The game was all over by 3 pm on the second day.

A magnificent win at Headingley in the rain over Lancashire with Hutton scoring a brilliant 105 not out put the world to rights. This followed a remarkable spell of bowling by Ellis Robinson, who took eight for 35 as Lancashire collapsed from 75 for three to 92 all out.

Brian Sellers leads out Yorkshire against Lancashire at Headingley in 1939.
Following are Yardley, Leyland, Robinson, Wood, Turner and Barber.

Robinson then took six for 34 against Leicestershire, and in the second innings Johnson took five for 16 to see Yorkshire home by 97 runs. A revenge win over Worcestershire at Bradford followed, with Hutton reaching 109 and then taking five for 58 with his leg-breaks. Yorkshire's fourth and last defeat took place at Sheffield against Essex, who beat a weakened Yorkshire side by an innings and 84 runs. The home side were without Hutton, Wood, Leyland, Mitchell and Bowes.

With the war likely to break out at any time, Yorkshire finished the season with three easy victories; the last match against Sussex contained a remarkable innings of 198 by George Cox junior, but centuries from Hutton and Yardley gave Yorkshire a six-run lead. Hedley Verity then took seven for 9 in exactly six overs and in an unreal atmosphere Yorkshire gained a nine-wicket victory. It would be Verity's last appearance in first-class cricket.

At the end of the season Hutton headed the Yorkshire averages with 2,316 runs, at 59.38, with Sutcliffe following, also with a high average of 54.46. Hutton had averaged 96 against the West Indies in the Tests as he completed another great season.

Leyland, Barber, Mitchell and Norman Yardley, a regular member of the side for the first time, all completed their 1,000 runs with only Mitchell at 29.70 failing to average 30. Hedley Verity topped all the averages, his 189 wickets for Yorkshire costing exactly 13 runs each. Bowes was close behind him with 107 wickets and Robinson with 120 wickets at 19.07 had his best season to date. Hutton garnered 43 wickets when he was allowed to bowl at 18.06 each and only Frank Smailes, with only 50 wickets and just over 300 runs, had a disappointing time. Cyril Turner, who had made the substitute's bench his own for well over a decade, had his successful days with both bat and ball. Yorkshire were indeed lucky to have such a valuable reserve.

There were only two additions to the Yorkshire ranks in 1939. One was Willie Watson, son of the old Huddersfield Town wing-half and a noted footballer himself with Town and with Sunderland. He was later to enter football management and eventually moved on to South Africa, where he became a coach and ground manager in Johannesburg. He was only 19 when he appeared for the first time for Yorkshire but he headed the second team averages after opening his second team career with three successive ducks in 1938. He was very highly thought of at that time and his stylish left-handed batting along with his golden hair soon caught the eye.

The other newcomer was George Cawthray who played only twice in 1939, and it was to be a further 13 years before he played again in two matches without achieving anything of note. He became the groundsman/professional at The Circle, Hull in 1946 living in a bungalow at the side of the ground and he gained a good reputation, so much so that he joined the Leeds club in 1963 as their professional and tended the Headingley pitches – cricket and rugby – until his retirement in 1978. A highly regarded league cricketer, he continued to help prepare and cure the problems of crickets grounds in the Leeds area well into the 1980s and he was often to be seen in or around Headingley doing any job required of him.

And so ended a decade for Yorkshire that has never been bettered by any county in the history of County Championship cricket. The Golden Age of cricket is recognised as the period between the early 1890s up to the end of the Edwardian era. Since then the only possible repeat of such an age had to be the late 1930s, when English cricket abounded with so many potentially good batsmen, most of them with attack in mind. Tragically the on-set of war changed the outlook of cricketers; an equalitarian society was to arrive; there would be an increase in professionalism and of 'professionalism': the amateur would disappear and the game would change, sometimes for the better but sometimes it would change so much that it would no longer be cricket.

YARDLEY IN CHARGE

THE SECOND WORLD WAR DISRUPTED cricket as the First had. In fact it followed very much on the same lines. League cricket in Yorkshire made the Bradford League very much a centre of the game as in the first war. Cricket was better organised and a glance at the wartime *Wisdens* give a clear indication of this improvement. There were four seasons without any first-class cricket in England but in 1945 the Australian Services provided a series of 'Victory Tests' against England which proved very popular with the public. The visitors acquitted themselves very well against a more or less full England team and yet only three or four of the Australians would ever play first-class cricket to any extent and few would ever make the Australian Test side.

Yorkshire were fortunate that only Hedley Verity would be missing from the 1939 Championship side, although both Arthur Mitchell and Herbert Sutcliffe would retire before the game returned to normal.

The only other first-class matches to take place in 1945 apart from the Victory Tests were a couple of games during the Scarborough Festival; two matches in Yorkshire against the RAF and against Lancashire – the former was really part of the Scarborough Festival – and two matches at Lord's, England *v* Dominions and Over 33 *v* Under 33. No Yorkshire player took part in the first match at Lord's which proved to be a first-rate game of cricket while in the other Halliday represented the Over 33s at the age of 25 and Watson, who made 80 not out, played for the Under 33s while four weeks younger than Halliday.

Yorkshire took part in several two-day matches in 1945 and the Lancashire game at Bradford, known as the Hedley Verity Memorial Match, was played in aid of his family and produced about £3,000. Bill Bowes, who had been a prisoner of war in Germany, was no more than a shadow of his old self but he took three for 22, while Arthur Booth made his first appearance in the side since 1931 and had the satisfaction of dismissing Cyril Washbrook after he had made the highest score in the match of 97. Alec Coxon also played his first match.

Against the RAF at Scarborough Ted Lester opened the innings with Len Hutton, and at number five in the batting order was Herbert Sutcliffe, who actually made his final appearance for the County.

The coming season of 1946 was a wet one and bowlers' wickets were the norm. Yorkshire began with an expectancy that was well warranted. In spite of the absence of Verity; in spite of the doubt about

385

Bill Bowes' fitness and the fact that Booth and Coxon were really unknown quantities, the bowling from the start proved to be the strength of the team. Bowes, bowling even more intelligently than ever, conserved his energy. If he had deteriorated as a bowler it was purely because his pace had been reduced but that would have happened anyway after six years away from the game. With Smailes and Coxon, too, Yorkshire had a strong opening attack while the two spinners had a summer that suited them down to the ground. Robinson had his best season in the game and took 149 wickets for Yorkshire at 14.52 while Arthur Booth in his first full season topped the first-class averages with 111 wickets at 11.61 each. From the start Booth showed that he had mastered the craft of spin bowling to such an extent that he was soon awarded his cap at the age of 43. He had no pretensions to either bat or field at either first-class or even club standard nor did his small schoolboyish stature give him any credibility as an athlete. But he proved himself not merely a worthy member of the side but in later years shone as a coach and a speaker on cricket who could cause an audience to roar with laughter, and yet he never took cricket as being other than the most important aspect of life.

The attack was the best in the country and Bowes' ability to get rid of the important early batsman combined well with Alec Coxon's natural aggression. Leading the side was the ever-enthusiastic Brian Sellers; now close on 40 but still able to throw himself about the field to take 21 catches during the season.

The batting of the side was a different proposition altogether. There

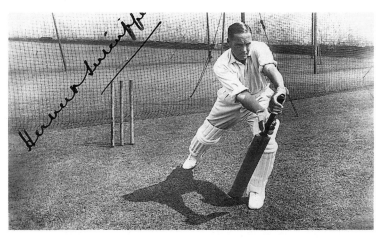

Sutcliffe in the nets. An imperturbable batsman, he made over 50,000 runs in his career, most of them in his 602 matches for Yorkshire.

was a doubt about Hutton himself. He had suffered a very bad arm injury while in the army and this resulted in a series of operations which left him with a left arm some two inches or so shorter than his right arm. This injury might well have affected his batting and might have undermined his confidence when facing the fearsome pace of Lindwall and Miller, and he was rarely seen to hook in the post-war period. If his technique was curtailed in any way, then it was barely apparent to the most discerning onlooker, most of whom were adamant whether they had seen the pre-war Hutton or not, that his style, technique and stroke-play was the richest talent that could be seen at the top level of cricket. Whether one should attempt to compare him with Hammond or Hobbs is not within the scope of this book; but certainly one could utter his name in the same sentence without rebuke.

Inevitably, Hutton batted consistently well in a wet year and topped the Yorkshire batting averages with an average of 52 and not unexpectedly was head and shoulders above the other batsmen.

It should be remembered that Herbert Sutcliffe had retired and Arthur Mitchell did likewise, having taken on the job of coach to the Yorkshire CCC – the first full-time coach to be appointed. Mitchell was aged 43 but he was younger than Leyland and Barber; both of whom played regularly in their final seasons.

Maurice Leyland had put on a lot of weight and seldom looked the top-class player of pre-war days. He managed only 590 runs for the County but when he did get any runs, such as an 88 at Bradford which was more than double any Kent batsman's score, or when he scored 41 not out at Manchester, it was generally when they were badly needed. The latter innings against Lancashire was typical of him as Yorkshire had lost five wickets in their second innings and were still 96 runs behind Lancashire. In tandem with his equally immovable captain, he saved the game and prevented Lancashire from going above Yorkshire in the table. Leyland also became a Yorkshire coach after his playing days and his kindly, humorous manner contrasted starkly with the brusque Arthur Mitchell, who did not suffer fools gladly. A native of Harrogate, Leyland went back there, where he developed Parkinson's disease, but he continued to have a smile and a kind word for everyone before dying in a Harrogate hospital in 1967.

Wilfred Barber, a sparse figure, was the second best batsman in the side and his classical stylish batting came perhaps more into its own than in his younger days when he was often in the background of a tremendously powerful batting line-up. Barber held the side together when a heavy defeat looked likely at Taunton after Somerset had scored 508 and his innings of 67 on a wretched Park Avenue pitch undoubtedly won his side eight points in a one-day match when no one else passed 15. Barber, a native of Cleckheaton, was brought out by the Gomersal Cricket Club and it was many years before he gained a regular place in the Yorkshire side. A loyal servant to Yorkshire cricket, he was a first-rate outfielder and became groundsman and coach at Ashville College near Harrogate in 1961.

Gibb and Sellers also batted well at times but Yardley was disappointing, and the large crop of youngsters who played, while gaining valuable experience, did little to justify a regular place.

Behind the stumps, Fiddling looked as though he might take over from the worthy Wood, while Gibb did well enough to go to Australia. Surprisingly neither were to play for Yorkshire again.

Arthur Wood was also to retire at the end of the season. A successful career began in 1927 and when accepted into the side as Dolphin's successor, he became a competent wicket-keeper, earning a place in the England team in 1938 and 1939. He was also a reliable batsman, capable of defending or attacking as the case demanded, and his happy approach to the game endeared him to spectators. A useful footballer, he also shone at golf, billiards and snooker. At one stage of his career he had played in 222 Championship matches for Yorkshire in succession.

There is little doubt that Yorkshire deserved to win the Championship, only Middlesex and Lancashire offering any real challenge. Yorkshire outplayed Middlesex when they met and when they were up against it as they were at Old Trafford, Yorkshire displayed their

Yorkshire continuing where they left off, as the first-post-war county Champions in 1946. Back row: Mr Walker (scorer), Beaumont, Whitehead, Wilson, Coxon, Smithson, Mr Heyhirst (masseur). Seated: Turner, Leyland, Yardley, Gibb, Barber. Front row: Jakeman, Booth. Some regulars were absent: Sellers, Hutton, Bowes, Robinson and Smailes. (A Wilkes and Son)

true spirit in fighting off defeat. Their only defeat was at Bournemouth in the penultimate match of the season when the Championship was won and when Hutton and Bowes were both absent, as well
as Yardley and Gibb.

A wonderful summer of cricket followed the depressing defeat
inflicted by the Australians during the winter on the MCC tourists.
Almost humiliated by a powerful team, ably led by Don Bradman,
Walter Hammond's England side were well beaten throughout
although all the leading batsmen, apart from the unfortunate skipper,
managed some creditable performances, including Hutton who
topped the batting averages. Norman Yardley did well enough to be
considered as the next England captain while Paul Gibb faded from the
scene, to return later as a solid Essex professional in 1951 and to become
a leading umpire.

The weather in 1947 was glorious. Batsmen dominated as rarely
before with both Edrich and Compton leaving Tom Hayward's
record aggregate of runs in a season behind and helping Walter
Robins lead Middlesex to their first County Championship since
1921. Yorkshire had their worst season since 1911 – another year
noted for its big scores and dry wickets.

The side was full of untried youngsters and the batting had to rely
on Len Hutton, who was head and shoulders above his colleagues and
dominated in a manner never seen before in the County although a
certain other batsman was to tower over his team-mates in the future.

Defeat at Lord's by a weak-looking MCC side was hardly a worry
and Hutton's 197 at Swansea was about as many as Glamorgan made
in both their innings. Yorkshire won that match by an innings and 115
runs before tea on the second day. Vic Wilson had shown
determination and Norman Yardley batted well too. At Park Avenue
for the Sussex game, a first innings collapse saw the last nine wickets
fall for 63 runs and Sussex obtained a 31-run lead which Yorkshire
wiped out without loss. Hutton went on to score 106 and at 184 for
three Yorkshire were in a strong position. Alas that quickly changed to
209 all out and though Bowes made inroads into the Sussex batting,
John Langridge stood firm and the visitors finally won by three
wickets.

Another win over Glamorgan followed, with Yardley scoring a
fine century at Bramall Lane, after which Hutton and Watson had
opening stands of over 100 against Lancashire at Old Trafford.
Yorkshire had by no means the worst of a draw.

Bill Bowes took six for 23 at Edgbaston and another fighting 67
came from Vic Wilson, perhaps the least considered of the talented
youngsters that Yorkshire would place into the melting pot of first-
class cricket. All out for 47, Warwickshire never recovered. Hutton's

brilliant early form had a reaction when he had a run of low scores and failure against Gloucestershire at Bristol saw further dreadful collapses as nine wickets fell for 46 runs (nine for 28 runs in the two innings together).

When fit and available Bowes bowled almost as well as ever but the hard pitches did not suit Smailes or Robinson, while Wardle, in his first full season, was somewhat disappointing. Coxon always worked hard but it was a wretched spell of four successive defeats at the height of summer that really made the Yorkshire membership realise that it might be a long time before Yorkshire returned to their rightful place. Failure in those games had compensations. Gerry Smithson, an attractive left-hander, made a magnificent 107 not out against Surrey at Park Avenue, which he followed up with a brilliant 98 at Bramall Lane in the Roses match.

Bill Bowes' benefit match at Headingley against Middlesex saw Wardle take seven for 66 and follow that up with a fighting 35 after Yorkshire took a lamentable 48 for six to 186 all out. Poor Watson, who had performed well early in the season, had a run of 0, 1, 0, 1 against Middlesex and Kent.

Further failures were to follow but such is the learning process of young batsmen that Watson's bad run must have been forgotten when he scored 153 not out at The Oval. He went on to complete his 1,000 runs for the season and joined Norman Yardley in that respect as well as Hutton. It was a far cry from the 1930s when five or six batsmen at least would expect to reach four-figure aggregates.

Smithson scored 169 against Leicestershire as Yorkshire won their first match early in August for eight weeks by an innings and four runs.

An honourable defeat at Park Avenue against Gloucestershire followed. Ted Lester made a fighting 55 after George Emmett had put his side in the driving seat with top-class knocks of 64 and 113; his cutting and driving being a delight to behold. Again, sadly, the Yorkshire batting collapsed from 204 for six to 227 all out when striving to obtain 236 to win. A feature of the game was the fine bowling of Ron Aspinall, who had a match analysis of eight for 140 in 49 overs.

At his home ground, Scarborough, Ted Lester put on 91 with Watson for the first wicket against Derbyshire; 85 for the second wicket with Smithson; and went on to score 127 while Norman Yardley, acting as skipper, made a very quick 177. The Yorkshire batting was on the upgrade at last and with Watson contributing 147 in the next game at Worcester, Yorkshire won easily in the end by 269 runs with the spinners playing their part.

Skipper Brian Sellers scored his third fifty on the trot against

Warwickshire at Leeds after Halliday had made a painstaking 97. At Northampton, Lester graced a glorious match with scores of 126 and 142, scoring at a phenomenal rate against C. B. Clarke's leg-breaks. Batting on pitches so suited to his unorthodox style, Lester actually headed Len Hutton in the averages, but he never really showed such form again for the County. However, he was a dangerous opponent at all times and he did repeat his feat of two centuries in the same match in the following year against Lancashire at Old Trafford.

Don Brennan came into the side in 1947, gaining a regular place in the side for seven seasons, and was the first amateur ever to keep wicket regularly for Yorkshire. A stylish and at times brilliant keeper, especially standing up, he was good enough to keep Godfrey Evans out of the England team in 1951, and at his best was quite without peer. A native of Eccleshill, Bradford, he played with them in the Bradford League, having been educated at Downside where he was in the eleven in 1937. In 1951–52 he toured India under Nigel Howard's captaincy. At one time he served on the Board of Bradford Northern Rugby League Club and was a member of the Yorkshire CCC committee for several years. He died in 1985 after a long illness which he bore with fortitude. Never frightened of expressing his opinion, he sometimes overstepped the bounds of reason but behind a vitriolic exterior was a kind heart and he bore no malice.

Another amateur to appear in 1947 was the Nice-born Geoffrey Keighley, who was the last non-Yorkshireman to play for the County, although his parents both came from Bradford. An Oxford University blue, he was a sound and reliable opening batsman who had he remained in England instead of going to New South Wales could well have become the eventual Yorkshire captain.

Yorkshire showed better form in 1948 and rose from eighth to fourth position in the table. Since the war there had been other cricketers to have come on the scene who failed to make the grade with Yorkshire. Freddie Jakeman, an attacking left-hander from Holmfirth played several games in 1946 and 1947 before joining Northamptonshire, for whom he scored 1,989 runs at an average of 56 in 1951. He scored 258 not out *v* Essex amongst his six centuries but later faded from the scene. There were also the two fast bowlers, Aspinall and Whitehead, both highly thought of. Two who succeeded were worthy stalwarts Wilson and Wardle.

J. Victor Wilson, a powerfully built, strong and tall left-hander from Scampston near Malton, became the established number three batsman in the Yorkshire side after a long apprenticeship in the Bradford League during the war and with the second team. Ever reliable, he was the true successor to Oldroyd and Mitchell; acting as

W. G. Keighley, Yorkshire's last foreign-born player. He was born at Nice in France and played from 1947 to 1951, and had the attributes to be captain. He now lives in Australia.

the fulcrum of an innings attacking or defending as the occasion demanded. A resolute figure in all circumstances, he never conquered his fast-footedness against spin, especially the back-of-hand variety, but if he looked a novice at times, he had a tenacity that was entirely admirable and a doggedness that was bred beneath the rolling wolds of the North and East Ridings. He lacked the style of Willie Watson, and was never in his class as a batsman, but he made himself into a very good county batsman and his straight-driving against the quicker bowlers when he became set was devastating. He also had a square-cut-cum-drive which was purely Vic Wilson, a magnificent and powerful stroke which garnered him many runs. A reliable out-fielder with a strong throw in his younger days, he developed into a top-class close-to-the-wicket fielder perhaps the best of a brilliant band who could muster Close, Trueman, Lowson, Hutton and Wardle in its ranks. Wilson specialised in the short-leg and gully positions. He became Yorkshire's first professional captain of modern times when he led them to the Championship in 1960 and again in 1962 after which he retired a respected figure and like a true yeoman, went back to his farming. He continued to play league cricket with Wakefield until 1968.

John Wardle was a different cricketer altogether. Born at Ardsley, near Barnsley, he was brought up at nearby Brampton and played for Wath Grammar School with outstanding success. In 1942 he took 113 wickets for Denaby, a record for that club, and moved to Eccleshill in the Bradford League. A hard-working cricketer with plenty of natural ability, he soon became the natural successor to Hedley Verity, but unlike any of his great predecessors he had also developed the chinaman and googly. This was hardly to the liking of Yorkshire's coaches, captain or committee, who saw no reason to change the orthodox methods that had been so successful for generations. When allowed a free hand to utilise his unorthodox style, as in the triumphant tour of South Africa under Peter May in 1956–57, he was remarkably successful. But even on that tour he was restricted by his captain.

However one judges Wardle's bowling, one always felt that he was a great bowler whatever method he employed. His bowling figures prove that. As a hitter and reliable tail-ender, he played some astonishing innings and at the highest level he proved himself to be an England bowler, although he suffered in comparison with Tony Lock who was often preferred in conditions more favourable to him, a fact that rankled with Wardle, who always claimed that Lock was a 'chucker' anyway; a view that history has proved to be accurate.

Wardle's sad dismissal in 1958 during Ronnie Burnet's term of captaincy was at the time and afterwards proved to be a correct decision. Of that there is little dispute. Whether the lack of apparent discipline in the side in the 1950s could have affected his career in any way is now a matter of conjecture. Certainly it was the first and most important of the 'incidents' in Yorkshire cricket which the game of cricket would have been better without. Certainly, Wardle proved by his exploits in the Lancashire League with Nelson and Rishton that he had many years of bowling left in him at the top level. Happily the breach between Wardle and Ronnie Burnet and the County Club was repaired to such an extent that Johnny was made a life member and he accepted the offer to help with the 'throwing' problems of Geoff Cope and with the coaching of young bowlers. Much more sadly, after helping for several years to improve the Doncaster Town square, he developed a brain tumour and died in 1985 at his home at Fishponds, Hatfield. He had developed a cricket school there, had the fishing and shooting rights to let out and developed a night club which proved successful.

Yorkshire finally finished in fourth position in 1948 but they won only one of their last four matches. They also lost twice in succession late in May, at Edgbaston and at Bristol, where Charles Barnett's 141 helped Gloucestershire to knock off the 392 to win for the loss of only four wickets. A couple of wins instead of these losses would have left Yorkshire as Champions.

Of the three teams above Yorkshire, Surrey and Middlesex were each beaten twice, and the eventual Champions, Glamorgan, had the worst of the draw in the only game played between the sides.

Certainly the batting showed a welcome improvement, with Hutton averaging over 90, although his appearances were limited owing to Test calls. Watson, Halliday and Lester all passed the thousand mark and Wilson was only 51 short in all matches. Lacking England skipper Norman Yardley too for many matches, Yorkshire's performance was really a good one and at full strength they were probably the strongest county side. Wardle took 129 Championship wickets at 17.62 each while Coxon showed himself to be an all-rounder of some quality and actually played at Lord's in the second Test, where he bowled his heart out and dismissed Australia's opening pair in the first innings.

A. B. Sellers finished his career in 1948, leading the side in Yardley's absence and helping young Sutcliffe on his Championship debut to put on 82 for the sixth wicket against the eventual Champions and reaching a top-scoring 91. A legend in his own life-time, Brian Sellers could look back on a courageous career where he had led the County in perhaps the most successful period of the Club's history.

William Herbert Hobbs Sutcliffe made his debut for Yorkshire after two fine performances for the Colts against Northumberland. He had a similar temperament to his father, with a sound defence, and like him performed well on pitches that were giving help to the bowler. He had ten years with Yorkshire during an era when Yorkshire's batting could claim to be the strongest that the County had ever possessed. He was only 21 in 1948 and it was five years before he could command a regular place in the side. Born at Pudsey, he was educated at Rydal where he captained the side in 1944, and excelled as a leg-break bowler as well as batsman.

Kenneth Smales an off-spinner and useful batsman, played in ten matches in 1948 aged only 20, after showing early promise. He played in only three further matches in 1950 before joining Nottinghamshire. Perhaps he did not quite live up to his early promise as top-class off-spinners were plentiful at the time and it was natural that he should try his luck with another county, where he did take over 100 wickets in 1955. Smales became secretary of Nottingham Forest Football Club.

The season of 1949 saw Yorkshire, with Yardley at the helm, share the County Championship title with Middlesex, winning their last six matches in a manner befitting Champions. It was a remarkable season with Frank Lowson, Brian Close and Fred Trueman all making their debuts against Cambridge University at Fenner's. The trio all went on to play for England and in that particular season, Lowson, a carbon copy of Hutton in many ways, scored 1,678 runs; Close performed the double in all first-class matches, while Trueman, although taking only

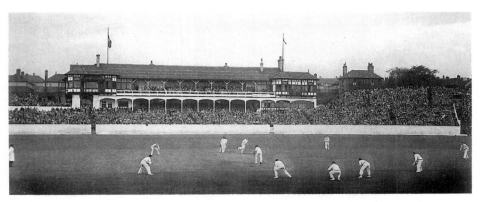

Another packed ground – at Park Avenue, Bradford, for the match against the New Zealanders in 1949.

31 wickets, became the white hope of English cricket as a fast-bowling prospect who might emulate the Australian fast bowlers. Such a hope was eventually realised, but in those days he was a raw talent indeed. The classic fast bowler's action was ever in evidence, and the sheer speed had spectators gasping at times, but the control and harnessing of his powers was several years away as yet. Yorkshire's success was due mainly to the advance made by Coxon and Wardle, who each completed 100 wickets, and in the last match of the Championship campaign took five for 17 and five for 15 respectively against Glamorgan, who were bundled out for 69 at Newport.

It was one of England's better summers, and Yorkshire's batting strength, while relying on Hutton, had Wilson dropping into the regular first-wicket down spot and finishing second to Len in the averages. Lester had a good season too, and skipper Yardley reached his thousand runs together with Frank Lowson, who in his first season averaged over 35. Only Watson disappointed, and his conflicting interests of cricket and soccer may have restricted his advancement. One of the handsomest left-handers ever to have graced the game, he was equally adept with the ball at his feet and his ball control could never be faulted, even if at times in soccer he appeared to lack commitment. Similarly at cricket, the game appeared to come too easy to him at times. He will be remembered chiefly at cricket for his magnificent back-to-the-wall innings at Lord's in 1953, when he defied the Australian attack and helped England towards the eventual recapture of the Ashes. He proved then that he had the ideal temperament.

Hutton batted magnificently throughout the season and he was at his zenith during June, when he scored 1,294 runs, which remains the

395

Yorkshire, Champions again in 1949. Back: Halliday, Mr Heyhirst (masseur), Close, Sutcliffe, Wilson, Mason, Mr Walker (scorer), Lester. Seated: Robinson, Hutton, Yardley, Brennan, Watson. Front: Lowson, Barraclough. (A. Wilkes and Son)

highest number ever scored in one month. Innings of 201 and 91 not out against Lancashire at Old Trafford were followed by 104 and 76 at Park Avenue against Northamptonshire, yet such are the vagaries of the game that he had the doubtful distinction of obtaining nought at Headingley in the Test against New Zealand, following it up with a pair against Reg Perks at Worcester.

Yorkshire met with only two defeats, losing at Bramall Lane to Worcestershire and Roly Jenkins by 186 runs, but Hutton, with 78 not out in the first innings, carried his bat through the innings for the first time. In the other game at The Oval, a weakened Yorkshire side was well beaten by Surrey. Yorkshire did have other bad days, none more so than at Headingley against Sussex when James Langridge and George Cox junior put on 326 for the fourth wicket to save the game after being behind on the first innings by 319 runs. This was on a typical batsman's paradise where some of Yorkshire's dullest matches were played. Their only success at Headingley in this season was against Somerset.

Don Brennan advanced as a wicket-keeper and had perhaps his best season with the County while Hutton and Coxon were reliable close-to-the-wicket fielders. Ellis Robinson, who was granted a testimonial of £1,500, had a poor season while Halliday, a reliable team man, was rarely at his best.

Apart from the three talented players already mentioned, there were four other players who made their initial appearances in 1949. The best known was Edric Leadbeater, leg-break bowler who could bat without having all-round pretensions. He was a brilliant out-fielder which made him into a valuable member of any side he played with. He never quite established himself in the Yorkshire side but had two full seasons in 1950 and 1951 and was good enough to visit India, Pakistan and Ceylon in 1951–52 with the MCC. In fact he appeared in Tests there although never capped by Yorkshire. In his two full seasons with Yorkshire he obtained over 80 wickets in each but never had much success after that and he dropped out of the side after the 1956 season. He played for Warwickshire in 1957 and 1958, and later broke numerous records in the Huddersfield League.

Jack Firth was another to move to another county. He kept wicket for Yorkshire in several matches in 1949 and 1950 and went on to play for Leicestershire from 1951 to 1958. In 1952 he dismissed 85 victims for Leicestershire, which was then a record for the county. He appeared for York City as a footballer.

The following year, 1950, saw Yorkshire in third place behind joint Champions Lancashire and Surrey. They lost to Lancashire at Bramall Lane on a turning wicket after making a gallant effort for victory. A little more discipline from some of the younger players might have resulted in victory. The other defeat, again a game they should have won when chasing 299 against Derbyshire, was due to a collapse from 182 for one to 219 all out. Bert Rhodes finished with six for 74 after Len Hutton had scored 107, reaching his century in 73 minutes. On the whole it was a good season for Yorkshire but they were without Close on National Service for most of the season and Willie Watson, who played only during August as he had been on World Cup soccer duty. Wardle had his best season to date with 172 wickets at 16.30 while Coxon also took over 100 wickets. Leadbeater showed a big advance as a bowler but only Trueman and Whitehead gave much support. Watson actually headed the batting averages, while Hutton averaged over 50 and Frank Lowson completed his 2,000 runs. The skipper also reached his thousand runs as did Wilson, Halliday and Lester. The first two were models of consistency and the batting as a whole was the best in the country.

Norman Horner made two appearances for Yorkshire in 1950 and looked a batsman of distinct promise, but the amount of batting talent in Yorkshire persuaded him to join Warwickshire, where from 1951 onwards he scored over 18,000 runs in an attractive manner and proved a very dependable servant to the club. He became a good groundsman and landscape gardener.

Another new player in 1950 was Robert Appleyard, who played in only three matches but topped the Yorkshire bowling averages with 11 wickets at 16.09. His debut for the Colts saw him take four for 29 in 24 overs as Cheshire compiled 311 for six, a remarkable bowling performance. He was soon drafted into the first team, helping Yorkshire to a seven-wicket victory at The Oval. Even at that stage of his career he showed a maturity beyond his years and his lack of experience at the top level was never in evidence.

It proved to be another good year in 1951 with Yorkshire finishing second to Warwickshire in the table. They would not claim to be other than second-best to the midlanders, who completed the double over them, dismissing them for 49 at Fartown and inflicting an innings defeat at Edgbaston, where the visitors lacked Hutton, Lowson, Watson and Brennan on Test match duty at Headingley, while Appleyard was also absent.

Yorkshire began the season without Alec Coxon, whose fiery temperament had got the better of him, and Brian Close who was absent on National Service. It was to the credit of the side that they should do so well without two such players. Appleyard bowled magnificently throughout the season. Even his keenest followers would not have anticipated that he would take 200 wickets in his first full season; a feat never accomplished before in first-class cricket. Wardle also reached 100 wickets and Fred Trueman had his best season to date, as also did Eddie Leadbeater. Considering the Test calls that affected the side, Yorkshire did very well indeed and although Hutton continued to be their best batsman, Vic Wilson and Frank Lowson were never far behind. Perhaps Yorkshire's most remarkable performance was to beat Somerset by 50 runs at Bramall Lane after following on 157 runs behind. The side's other defeat was suffered by a mere eight runs at Scarborough against Worcestershire, when Hutton, Lowson, Watson, Yardley and Brennan were all absent and Michael Crawford captained Yorkshire on his only appearance for the County. Crawford was a good batsman who captained the Leeds Cricket Club from 1947 to 1962. He was in the Shrewsbury XI in 1936–38 and on going up to Cambridge University, gained a soccer blue.

John Ashman took Wardle's place against Surrey at Headingley, when the latter was on Test duty, and took four for 116, but never played for Yorkshire again. He went on to assist Worcestershire in 1953 and 1954 without fulfilling expectations.

Roy Booth also first played for Yorkshire in 1951 and was a first-rate wicket-keeper and very capable batsman who was expected to take Don Brennan's place after his retirement. He played throughout 1954 for Yorkshire but was dropped from the side half-way through the following season. He never quite settled in the side or showed his best form so he moved to Worcestershire, where he was a valuable member of the team from 1956 to 1970 and twice had over 100 dismissals in a season. He later went on to become an important member of the Worcestershire committee.

Two other players began their careers with Yorkshire in 1951 who had significant contributions to make. Ray Illingworth played at Headingley against Hampshire and came in to bat to face a rampant Cannings with 40 for four on the board. By scoring 56, he helped Norman Yardley to add 136 and steer Yorkshire to a 10-wicket win.

Douglas Padgett was only 16, the youngest ever to play for the County, when he made 25 not out against Somerset at Taunton. He lived at Idle and was only 13 when he played in Idle's first team. A sound, patient, classical batsman, Padgett followed Arthur Mitchell as Yorkshire's coach, a post he still holds. Quiet and unassuming and possessing an excellent technique, he never quite realised the high expectations that were held of him, but he did appear for England and scored over 20,000 runs for Yorkshire. A very fine outfielder too, he did not obtain a regular place in the Yorkshire side until 1956.

Surrey's seven-year dominance of the County Championship began in 1952 as Yorkshire had to settle once again for the runners-up position. They won 12 matches and lost only two, a very fine performance when one considers that they were without Appleyard, not for one game, but for the whole of the season due to illness.

Fred Trueman was on National Service for most of the season, although he did play regularly for England. When available he bowled with tremendous pace and fire but was unable to play in either June or July.

Raymond Illingworth in action.

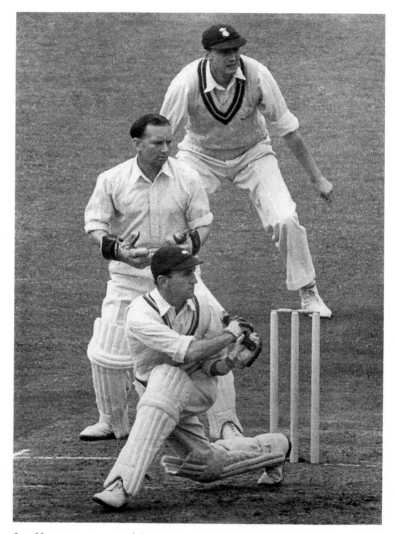

Len Hutton sweeps powerfully to leg against Surrey (wicket-keeper
A. J. McIntyre) in 1951. Hutton was the leading opening batsman in England for
many years after the Second World War. (NCCC)

There is little doubt that Yorkshire's main strength was in their batting, with four batsmen averaging over 40 and four others scoring over 1,000 runs, including Brian Close who completed the 'double' for the second time, and yet such was his talent that he left many people with the impression that so much more should have been forthcoming from him.

400

The absences of Appleyard and Trueman were very difficult to overcome. The committee certainly did their best to fill the gaps. George Cawthray was recalled for two games for the first time for 13 years and Peter Brayshay also played twice in spite of being 35 years of age. J. M. Cownley, B. Hall, Eric Burgin and G. H. Padgett were all newcomers who took the new ball for Yorkshire while Bill Foord and W. E. N. Holdsworth were both given extended trials.

Perhaps Eric Burgin, who had a long and successful career in league cricket, could have been given a longer trial. An intelligent in-swing bowler, he played in only 12 matches in all for Yorkshire in 1952 and 1953. In the Roses match at Old Trafford in 1952, he took five for 20 as Lancashire were skittled out for 52 and in the following season took the wickets of Morris and Hill in the match against the Australians at Bramall Lane. He was also a fine centre-half and captain of York City for a time; a position he gave up on a point of principle.

Bryan Stott also made his first appearance in 1952 but it was another four years before he gained a regular place in the side.

In 1953 Yorkshire lacked Bob Appleyard for the whole season while Brian Close played in only two games owing to cartilage trouble, and it was no surprise that Yorkshire should have a disappointing season. But to drop to 12th position and suffer their worst-ever season was a little too much for their followers to have to stomach.

It was obvious where the weakness in the side lay. Apart from the two cricketers already mentioned, Trueman, still in the RAF, took part in only ten matches. That meant that the brunt of the bowling had to be borne by Johnny Wardle, who bowled over 1,100 overs in the Championship and took 101 wickets at 22.77 each but received very moderate support. Apart from Foord, who took 54 wickets at over 25 runs each, the only other bowler to play regularly was young Illingworth, who always did his best but whose state of development as an off-spinner was still in its infancy. Foord played in more matches that he had ever played before and though successful at times he was a liability in the field and made no impression with the bat and he never played for Yorkshire again, even though he was only 29. He was a tower of strength to the Scarborough CC for over 20 years and it is probable that more could have been made of his services as his bowling undoubtedly improved and his string of successes in the Yorkshire League prove that he was one of the best bowlers in the county. Perhaps the likeliest of Yorkshire's bowling prospects was Mike Cowan. He bowled left-arm fast with some success especially against Gloucestershire where he finished with eleven for 101 and was mainly responsible for Yorkshire's innings victory.

If Yorkshire were weak in bowling, there was nothing wrong with their powerful batting. Hutton, besides having a triumphant season as England captain, winning the Ashes from Hassett's side, had time to head Yorkshire's batting with an average of over 60. Lowson and Watson also averaged over 40 and the former had one of his best seasons, scoring a fine 259 not out at Worcester. Six batsmen reached their thousand runs and three others managed to score over 750 runs.

Ken Taylor made his first appearance in 1953 at the age of 17, and although he failed with the bat and did not bowl, he gave spectators an occasional glimpse of brilliance in the field. He was a long time maturing.

Yorkshire's sad season ended with the followers satisfied that bad luck with injuries was the main reason for their low position. There could be no disputing that, but there appeared to be something wrong with the spirit of the side at times and there was a lack of ability to force victory when apparently in a winning position.

At the end of the season, Don Brennan decided to retire from first-class cricket as did the hard-working Harry Halliday, somewhat overweight for a player of 33, although he did take 32 catches in 1953 for Yorkshire and his medium-pace off-breaks and seamers often proved useful. He was granted a testimonial at the close of the following season which totalled £2,500.

There was no reason why Yorkshire should not recover their old position if all their players were fit for the 1954 season. In fact, Yorkshire had a good season by any standards apart from their own, and in an abominable summer, finished second in the Championship, inevitably to Surrey. A bad run in July cost them the title, when an exciting match with Glamorgan at Neath was ruined by the rain and this was followed by an innings defeat at Trent Bridge where Dooland's and Goonesena's leg-breaks accounted for all but two Yorkshire wickets.

After another rain-ruined match with Worcestershire at Bramall Lane, Arnold Hamer with 147 not out helped Derbyshire to a six-wicket win, with Yorkshire's fielding lapses costing them the game. Yorkshire did lose again in August at Headingley to Middlesex by 96 runs on a spinner's wicket but their position below Surrey was really due to that bad run.

Appleyard and Trueman returned and both bowled magnificently, while Wardle also reached the coveted hundred wickets in County Championship matches. Close's more mature mixture of medium-pace bowling and off-breaks made him a useful all-round performer, but Illingworth's off-spin was not often utilised and his all-round abilities were not really in evidence. Hutton missed more than half the Championship programme but still managed to head the batting averages, although Frank Lowson headed him in all Yorkshire

Vic Wilson, Ray Illingworth, Brian Close and Ted Lester on their way to the nets in 1954.

matches. Lester had one of his better seasons and along with the three left-handers, Wilson, Watson and Close, obtained his thousand runs. Billy Sutcliffe batted well when he was needed and the side was in every respect the equal of the Champions.

Joe Lister, a nephew of George Macaulay and the present long-serving secretary of the club, made two appearances as a batsman in 1954. He was shortly to move to Worcester where he served as secretary for many years before moving to Headingley in 1971.

James William Cammish, a leg-spinner from Scarborough, also played in two matches and was a member of the side that beat Surrey

Yorkshire's three great post-war bowlers: Fred Trueman, Johnny Wardle and Bob Appleyard, all outstanding Test players. (Central Press Photos Ltd)

at The Oval. He had previously played for Auckland during the 1950–51 season with success and after playing for Scarborough and Leeds, returned to New Zealand.

Three seam bowlers were also introduced into the Yorkshire side in 1954, the most successful being Melville Ryan, a hard-working, willing opening bowler who played only four full seasons with the County. Tall, well-built and with a good action, he steadily improved until he became Trueman's partner by right. He retired from first-class cricket in 1965 and served on the Yorkshire committee for a time.

During the winter Len Hutton went out to Australia in an endeavour to keep the Ashes and after a traumatic defeat in the Brisbane Test match, succeeded in defeating the Aussies. Appleyard and Wardle acquitted themselves well in the Tests although they suffered from lack of opportunity, while Vic Wilson, who went virtually as twelfth man, never playing in a Test, fielded in that reliable manner of his that made him so valuable to his skipper.

The high hopes that Yorkshire had of improved successes were realised in 1955 when the County won 21 out of their 28 games and lost five. There was one drawback: Surrey also lost five matches but succeeded in winning as many as 23 games, so that once again Yorkshire had to be satisfied with the runners-up position. It was a hot dry summer, and Yorkshire had only once surpassed their number of 21 victories before in one season, way back in 1923 when they won 25 matches.

Yorkshire began with six successive victories but then lost to Sussex at Hove by 21 runs and to the Champions at The Oval by 41 runs. This was followed by a humiliating defeat at Park Avenue at the hands of Hampshire, who won by an innings and 43 runs. To bounce back after

A great short leg catch by Fred Trueman at Bradford in 1955 to get rid of Desmond Eagar of Hampshire. (Yorkshire Post)

those three defeats, all in the absence of skipper Norman Yardley showed the spirit of the side. Acting skipper Hutton did make top score against Sussex in the first innings with 54 but he followed that up with 0, 0, 1, 17 and 4 before making 85 against Kent at Hull when Yorkshire returned to winning ways. Len Hutton was by no means fit at this stage of the season and he gave up the England captaincy. In fact he was to play in just four more county matches and on his last home appearance he brought back memories of his greatest days by scoring 194 and putting the leg-spin of Bruce Dooland to the sword, driving in his old manner.

Apart from Hutton's absence in all but ten of Yorkshire's matches, Bob Appleyard too was injured and he played in only one match after the end of June. The fact that he took 73 wickets at 11.54 each showed how valuable he was to Yorkshire's needs. Wardle and Trueman did all that was asked of them but those two, as well as Appleyard, Close, Lowson and Watson, all had Test calls upon them.

Mike Cowan bowled well too, and at Headingley against Surrey he took five for 15 in Surrey's second innings. This match was a remarkable game of cricket. In the first innings, Trueman and Appleyard reduced Surrey to 119 for eight before Lock (55) and Laker (81) helped Surrey to a respectable 268. In reply Yorkshire struggled in deteriorating light to finish 102 behind, and then in truly appalling light on the second evening, Surrey were 27 for seven before reaching 75 all out on the third morning. In now perfect light, Yorkshire gained a comfortable victory by six wickets thanks to sound batting from Lowson (52), Vic Wilson and Willie Watson (51 not out). Many who watched that second day's play will always claim that the umpires must have been upset by the belligerent attitude of some of the Surrey side. Even Mike Cowan never quite understood why the game was allowed to continue in such conditions. In 1889, a Surrey *v* Yorkshire match was described as the 'Gaslight' match as it was played in such dismal light. At Headingley that evening, lighted matches in the Grandstand shone like beacons; the gloom had a sometimes pinkish shade which turned yellowish as it grew towards evening; it was in the days before the clean air act was enforced. In those days Yorkshire and Surrey were greater rivals than the War of the Roses combatants.

Yorkshire's batting averages were led by Watson, who averaged almost 57 in the Championship, but Wilson, Sutcliffe, Close and Lowson all reached their 1,000 runs in all matches. Skipper Yardley scored 904 and young Illingworth 980 while Hutton managed 535 and Padgett 571, the latter playing in half the fixtures. Illingworth and Sutcliffe showed a welcome improvement, both scoring runs when they were needed. Sutcliffe, indeed, batted occasionally in a manner reminiscent of his father. During the season Jimmy Binks, who was

Jimmy Binks, long-serving wicket-keeper, in the nets. His career for the County ran from 1955 to 1969, during which time he appeared in 412 consecutive County Championship matches. (NCCC)

born in Hull, replaced Roy Booth behind the stumps and the new wicket-keeper was an immediate success. He was never a demonstrative keeper but was as reliable, sound and consistent as any in the past and missed only one match (in 1964) up to his retirement after the 1969 season. His batting was never in the highest class and this probably prevented him playing more times for England, but he did improve towards the end of his career and even opened for England against India on one occasion. In his second and final Test match for England he took five catches in the first innings at Calcutta.

Of three players to enter the Yorkshire scene in 1955 Robert Platt was most successful. He made his first appearance for Yorkshire at Bramall Lane against Sussex when he took four for 70 and although he played only two full seasons for the Club, he was a valuable member of the side when injuries were not affecting him. A hard-working medium-pace bowler with a lolloping run-up and somewhat awkward action, he could be very deadly when conditions suited him and he bowled intelligently at all times. He went on to captain Yorkshire 2nd XI in 1968–71 and later served on the Yorkshire committee.

In several ways, 1955 ended an era in Yorkshire cricket. Not only had Len Hutton retired after a distinguished career, but Norman Yardley also retired. He had been a very good batsman – not quite in the top bracket – a very useful medium-pace bowler who took many a wicket when it was needed, and a very fine fielder in his younger days. As a captain he had given valuable service since 1948 and had led Yorkshire to a shared Championship in 1949 and to runners-up position on five other occasions. He succeeded A. B. Sellers, arguably the finest county captain in the history of the game, and the captain who beat him three times to the title, W. S. Surridge, was another captain in the same mould as Sellers.

Norman Yardley, at times, was criticised in his capacity as skipper as perhaps being too lenient with some of his players; especially the younger ones and without doubt he did not have the same force of personality as the two other captains mentioned. On the other hand his fairmindedness, his timing of declarations and the manner that he played his cricket could not be faulted. He was a true gentleman in an age when dedicated professionalism was only beginning to give way to winning at any cost. Norman Yardley had little time for the latter way of playing cricket. He later served on the Yorkshire committee and succeeded Sir Kenneth Parkinson as president of the Club in 1981 before retiring in 1984.

Ted Lester lost his form and went into the 2nd XI in 1955 where he remained for the following season too, receiving a testimonial of £3,000. With his brilliant outfielding and unorthodox batsmanship – his late-cut was a delight, while no one hit the ball harder when he was in form – he scored his runs all round the wicket and could score very quickly indeed. He later became the 2nd XI captain and then the first team scorer.

REVIVAL UNDER BURNET

IN THE REMARKABLY WET SEASON of 1956, Yorkshire, led for the first time by Billy Sutcliffe, fell away badly to finish in seventh position in the table with only one more victory than defeat in the final tally. One could sympathise with the side when victory was in their grasp on several occasions without them being able to force it; opponents twice avoiding defeat with their last pair at the crease. However, one felt that the side did not play up to its full potential. Sutcliffe endeavoured to lead to the best of his ability but there was little doubt that the extra responsibility affected his batting form, as an average of 16.84 in the County Championship proves.

One can easily look back and think that Billy Sutcliffe was saddled with the captaincy too early in his career, and some rather torrid comments from the Yorkshire spectators probably affected him, as well as some of his team.

Bob Platt actually finished top of the bowling averages with 26 wickets at 12.61, but Trueman could only take 33 wickets at 25.54 each in the Championship. Fortunately, Illingworth showed a big advance and took 100 wickets for the first time – 103 at 13.08 each – joining Wardle (146) and Appleyard in this respect. Watson headed the batting averages with Lowson, Wilson and Padgett – for the first time – recording 1,000 runs. Taylor showed a big improvement and the youth of the side were beginning to show their metal at last.

If Yorkshire's supporters appeared to be more truculent it was in many ways due to the fact that decades of success, off-set by short periods of comparative failure, seemed to have altered into a period where an outright Championship-winning side had not been seen for over ten years. One had to go back to 1892 for such a period of desolation. In fact five seasons had been the longest period without a title win since then.

This season saw five newcomers in the side but only one, Brian Bolus, went on to command a regular place before he was dropped from the side, perhaps prematurely, after the 1962 season. John Brian Bolus came from Whitkirk, where he learnt his cricket. A sound early order batsman, he was no stylist, but hit powerfully all round the wicket and possessed a good defence. Also a dependable catch, he was a useful left-arm bowler and after leaving Yorkshire, he went on to play for England with an average of over 41 in his seven Tests. He toured India with the MCC in 1963–64 and represented Nottinghamshire with success from 1963 to 1972, and Derbyshire from 1973 to 1975, thus gaining his county cap with three counties. He captained

Nottinghamshire and Derbyshire, and in his first-class career scored 25,598 runs at an average of 34.03 including 39 centuries. The presence of Stott and Taylor as Yorkshire's openers tended to restrict his play and he rarely played to his true potential, or secure a regular niche in the batting order. His average for Yorkshire was less than 30, although he did play some fine innings for the County. Never afraid to express his opinions, he had a tendency to take things to heart if matters were not going his way. After retiring from first-class cricket, Bolus played with success for Bradford, Brighouse, Cleckheaton and Farsley.

Another newcomer was Harold Dennis Bird, who played in one match against Scotland in 1956 at Hull and went on to play in 13 matches in 1958 and 1959, scoring 181 not out against Glamorgan at Park Avenue in the latter season. That innings was the highest of his career, and he was left out of the next match much to his chagrin. He joined Leicestershire in the following season, scoring over 1,000 runs but he averaged only 21 and he soon faded from the first-class game. He gained a good reputation as a coach, particularly with young players, and coached with success in South Africa. Yet he will always be best known as an umpire who was recognised throughout the game as probably making fewer mistakes than any of his colleagues, whether at county or at Test match level. 'Dickie', a celebrity in his own right, never lost his Barnsley mannerisms and became a noted raconteur both at cricket dinners and on television. He learnt his cricket with the Barnsley CC and played for Barnsley Boys at soccer at which he shone and might have made a career at soccer but for a knee injury.

William (Billy) Oates, made just three appearances for Yorkshire without much success but later played for Derbyshire. A very useful, attractive middle-order batsman and fair medium-pace or off-break bowler, he joined Derbyshire in 1959 and twice passed the 1,000 runs in a season for them, with 1961 as his best season when he scored 1,288 runs at an average of 33. In 1965 he dropped out of the side and played as a league professional.

Billy Sutcliffe retired from county cricket after the 1957 season, when he manfully led the side to third place in the Championship behind Surrey and Northamptonshire. He had struggled to find his batting form and his final average of 20.61 gives an indication of the stress that it caused him. It was sad that at the age of 30 business commitments caused his retirement from the game.

Yorkshire never challenged the top place, Surrey proving themselves almost invincible, but were a capable side. Lowson headed the batting averages but injuries and varicose veins were bringing his career to a close, while the results of illness and injury were also beckoning for Appleyard, whose 69 wickets cost 21.42 each – he was to finish a lowly sixth in Yorkshire's bowling averages. It was also Watson's last season with the County, although he scored 1,455 runs at an average of 41.57. He thereafter spent another seven successful seasons with Leicestershire.

Fred Trueman, with 99 wickets at 15.21 each, headed the bowling averages for Yorkshire in 1957. He had been around for some nine seasons and was still only 26 years old. He had bowled very fast at times during his career but his spasmodic success had not brought him to the forefront of fast bowlers. That was yet to come and 1957 was the start of his maturity, when he showed that he had mastered the art of bowling. No longer a tearaway fast bowler, he now had full control of his bowling abilities and no batsman was safe from variations of pace and swing which were to keep him in the forefront of Yorkshire cricket for the next decade and result in the Championship returning to its rightful place on seven separate occasions. Yorkshire would reap fully the benefit of Trueman's greatness.

There were only two newcomers to Yorkshire cricket in 1957 but each was to have a significant effect on Yorkshire cricket. David Pickles was a native of Halifax, a most unlikely spot to unearth a fast bowler (not many cricketers have played for Yorkshire from Halifax since the days of Tom Emmett). He was certainly fast. He played his first match with the County at Scarborough when he took three for 39 in a rain-ruined match with Gloucestershire. He kept his place in the Yorkshire side for the rest of the season, taking 37 wickets at 17.56 each to take second place in the Yorkshire bowling averages, just below Trueman himself. His extreme pace astonished spectators and players alike, and he was hailed as another Trueman – another fast bowler to reap revenge on the Australians. Alas, it did not continue. Attempts were made to modify his action. Some coaches stated that it was a necessity if he were to play regular county cricket; others claimed that it ruined him. The truth lies somewhere between the two but Pickles, although persevered with during the 1958 and 1959 seasons was never the same bowler again. His 13 wickets for the county cost 41.38 each in 1959. A sad episode; David Pickles will be remembered by many who saw him as he goes into the ranks of 'might have beens'.

The other newcomer was Don Wilson, a tall angular youth with an endearing enthusiasm and a refreshing vigour that quickly made him a popular figure to spectators. When aged 19 he was recommended to Yorkshire by Len Hutton. He made his debut as a slow bowler at Paisley and steadily developed. Though few would claim that he belonged to that great line of Yorkshire left-arm slow bowlers, he did become Wardle's successor, and commanded a place in the Yorkshire side until 1972, when he lost his form. He retired eventually from the game after the 1974 season. A very hard-hitting left-handed batsman, capable of winning a game off his own bat, he was also a brilliant fielder and was always an important cog in the side.

The season had started reasonably well; but two defeats at Chesterfield and Bramall Lane against Glamorgan were very disappointing and at Old Trafford, Lancashire saved the match with the last pair at the crease. An innings defeat from Surrey at The Oval showed up the weakness of the side, only the left-hand batsmen showing up well. In that match Yorkshire stood at 145 for one in the second innings, yet the side collapsed to 174 all out, Eric Bedser taking five for 27. In the return game at Park Avenue, Yorkshire narrowly averted defeat. A run of four victories at the end of July revived the side but there was at times a lack of fight in the team. In a wet season which helped the bowlers, five batsmen reached 1,000 runs: Watson, Illingworth, Stott, Close and Vic Wilson, while Illingworth finished with 92 wickets, completing the 'double' in all first-class matches. Wardle finished with 104 wickets for Yorkshire at 18.83 each. Bryan Stott scored 1,362 runs in all matches at an average of 33.22 and he made 181 against Essex at Sheffield, which he followed up with 139 at Hull against Leicestershire. There were some exciting matches, especially on their end-of-season western tour, where Gloucestershire gained a two-wicket win at Cheltenham with 35 wickets falling to the spinners in less than two days. In the last game of the tour, Yorkshire, facing defeat at Cardiff, fought back to take Glamorgan's last nine wickets for 38 as they got home by four runs.

While Yorkshire were a disappointment, their 2nd XI, under the captaincy of Ronnie Burnet, finished top of the Minor Counties Competition and by virtue of a draw at Scarborough against Warwickshire 2nd XI were declared Champions. Burnet had become captain of the side in 1952 when it began to show a steady improvement. That 1957 side provided the nucleus of the team that Vic Wilson and Brian Close were eventually to lead to success.

The 1958 season opened with Ronnie Burnet leading the Yorkshire side at the age of 39. He was by no means lively in the field – although a very hard-hitting batsman, but he came with a good reputation as a disciplinarian who always put the interests of his team first.

Ronnie Burnet was absent from the first seven matches of the 1958 season, in which a victory over Somerset was the only clear-cut success. An eight-wicket defeat at Headingley against Lancashire followed by two rain-hit draws preceded the Northamptonshire game at Park Avenue, where Northamptonshire reached 196 for four before rain finished the game. A further abandonment followed against Nottinghamshire at Hull when the match was given up as early as 12 o'clock on the second day.

At Bramall Lane, Yorkshire shocked the Championship leaders,

Surrey, by defeating them quite comprehensively by 249 runs. Ken Taylor scored 104 in the second innings and that was the only innings in the game that surpassed the half-century mark, while Fred Trueman had nine for 58 in the match. Two further draws followed in what was one of the wettest seasons ever, and then came a nine-wicket defeat at Northampton where Yorkshire fell for 67 and 65, George Tribe following up a remarkable seven for 22 with the even better figures of eight for 9; one of the finest match analyses in the history of Championship cricket. Burnet recorded his first 50 against Sussex at Park Avenue where Stott and Taylor opened with a first innings partnership of 222. Yorkshire gained an eight-wicket victory. An innings defeat which provided Surrey with suitable revenge at The Oval was followed by a further defeat at Worthing against Sussex. Then came a comfortable eight-wicket win over Kent at Maidstone, followed by an innings victory at Sheffield over Somerset. It provided Phil Sharpe with his first century for Yorkshire (141) but the game will be remembered as the last match in which Johnny Wardle ever played for the County. He took six for 46 and two for 29.

Wardle was suspended on the advice of skipper Burnet after that match, the first 'split' in the Club occurred when he received a large sum from a daily newspaper in which his life story and his row with Yorkshire was relayed throughout the cricket world. Wardle had been chosen to tour Australia, but his invitation was withdrawn, and at the end of the season the services of J. H. Wardle, along with those of Frank Lowson and Bob Appleyard were no longer required by Yorkshire. Lowson and Appleyard were awarded testimonials but Wardle's first-class career drew to its conclusion. Yorkshire went on to finish 11th in the table and they won only two of their last eight matches following Wardle's dismissal, but five were ruined by the weather, including yet another game that was abandoned without a ball being bowled.

Wardle finished second in the Yorkshire bowling averages with 86 wickets at 15.29, while Appleyard took 22 wickets at 16.70 but was only able to play in nine matches. His career lasted for nine seasons in which he failed to play at all in one season and in two others played in only one match and in another only three matches. In only four seasons did he play in over half of Yorkshire's matches. Frank Lowson averaged only 19.81 and he dropped out of the side in July.

Frank Lowson was the son of a Dundee footballer of the same name who came south after being signed by Bradford Park Avenue. When 11 he played in the Bradford Grammar School XI and later played with Bowling Old Lane in which area he lived. His resemblance to Hutton as a batsman was uncanny and he looked a very good player indeed when in an attacking mood. Had he possessed a stronger

Frank Lowson straight-driving. He opened the Yorkshire batting with Len Hutton, and made his Test debut with Hutton at the other end – they put on 99. Brennan made his debut in the same match.

physique he would no doubt have stayed longer in the game, but his varicose veins caused him problems. When he left Yorkshire after the 1958 season, he went full time into the insurance business. For several years he was a successful professional with Brighouse in the Bradford League and in 1963 became only the fourth Bradford league player to pass 1,000 runs. Lowson died in 1984 after a long illness.

It was a relief to get this wet and sad season out of the way but two batsmen, both left-handers Stott and Close, reached 1,000 runs, with Taylor and Vic Wilson not far behind. Fred Trueman took 84 wickets at 11.41 each and Ray Illingworth's 81 wickets ensured his place as Appleyard's successor, indeed he had made his first appearance for England against New Zealand. Apart from the captain, two other players made their debuts in 1958. Philip Sharpe, a schoolboy prodigy who had appeared for Yorkshire 2nd XI in 1955, developed steadily and received his cap in 1960 at the age of 23.

A somewhat fast-footed batsman, he specialised in the cut and was a strong leg-side player at his best on fast pitches. Perhaps he never reached the peak expected of him but in 1962 he was at his best, scoring well over 2,000 runs. He also succeeded at Test level with a high

413

average of 46.23 from his 12 matches. He would undoubtedly have played more often had he been more consistent at county level, as he had an untroubled temperament. Apart from his batting, he was an outstanding slip fielder, and had a higher average of catches per match than any other Yorkshire cricketer. After leaving Yorkshire in 1974 he played for Derbyshire for two seasons. He finished his career with over 22,000 runs to his name at an average of 30. He was also a Yorkshire county hockey player and a member of the York Light Opera Company for many years.

Jack Birkenshaw, who played for England Schoolboys in 1956, made his debut for Yorkshire against Sussex at Worthing. An off-spin bowler of great promise, he would have made a very good Yorkshire cricketer but the presence of Illingworth gave him very little scope. He was also a handsome left-handed batsman, but he was slow to develop and never appeared to gain the confidence that his technique should have endowed him with and he could not quite be classed as an all-rounder. At the end of the 1960 season, Birkenshaw left Yorkshire to join Leicestershire, where he gave good service for 20 years, both on and off the field. He was a noted cricket coach and in the winter set up various coaching schemes for Leicestershire. Dedicated to the game, he received a record benefit for a Leicestershire player in 1974 with £13,000, and he played in five Tests for England touring Pakistan, India, Sri Lanka and the West Indies in 1973–74. He appeared a few times for Worcestershire in 1981 before becoming a first-class umpire in 1982.

Ronnie Burnet began the 1958 season with a very young and inexperienced side. The immediate loss of Wardle, Lowson and Appleyard placed Yorkshire in the position where they had to rely on youth. Senior professional was Vic Wilson, who was in wretched form for most of the season and lost his place in the side for a time, with the result that Close, Trueman and Illingworth (26 when the season started) were the only experienced players.

After beginning with a comfortable win at Middlesbrough over Nottinghamshire, Yorkshire, in spite of two fine knocks from Padgett, were quite outplayed by Lancashire at Old Trafford. Barber and Pullar were in scintillating form as the Red Rose county looked the team who might at last offer a challenge to the all-conquering Surrey. A solitary victory over Glamorgan was Yorkshire's only success in the next five matches, with left-hander Stott in particularly good form with 94 and 130 not out at Hull against Hampshire, who were beaten by four wickets. In an exciting finish Yorkshire, set 198 to win, reached 115 for one and then collapsed to 139 for five before Burnet and later Trueman contributed match-winning stands with Stott as he reached his fourth half-century in the week.

Yorkshire went to The Oval with high hopes and the main difference between the sides was a stand of 150 between Ken Barrington and John Edrich (76) after which only Close (52) reached a half century during the game. Bob Platt was in fine bowling form and took ten for 87 in the match. Yorkshire were still very much in contention in their second innings at 91 for two, needing 220 to win, but Lock and Eric Bedser put Surrey back on top as Yorkshire could add only 42 more runs. An inevitable draw at Trent Bridge followed, Nottinghamshire being saved by Norman Hill (167) and J. D. Clay (137) but not before Padgett (139 not out) and Close (154) had put on 252 for Yorkshire's third wicket. Mel Ryan reduced Nottinghamshire to 12 for four to finish with five for 45 as Nottinghamshire followed on 267 behind.

Easy victories followed over Sussex, Warwickshire and Essex with the bowlers taking most of the honours but Raymond Illingworth did score a match-winning 150 at Colchester. A 28-run defeat at Bournemouth was no disgrace, with timely declarations by both captains resulting in a good finish.

At this stage of the season, Yorkshire led the table, a tribute to Burnet's ability to get the best out of his youthful attack. At Chesterfield a splendid 144 from Ken Taylor, after Bob Platt had surprised everybody with a fighting 57 not out, which helped to save the follow-on, helped Yorkshire to reach 304 for four and win a fine victory. Doug Padgett made 88 and 62 not out against Essex at Scarborough, where Yorkshire won through by 69 runs. A drawn game at Headingley with Gloucestershire saw Vic Wilson in fighting form with 99 not out, but the much looked-forward to return clash with Surrey at Park Avenue placed Yorkshire's position in true perspective. An innings of 54 from the master, Peter May, was exceeded by the worthy Tom Clark (56) in Surrey's knock, with only Ken Taylor with 28 and 78 being able to withstand the fiery bowling of Peter Loader (twelve for 99) as Yorkshire lost by 48 runs. Yorkshire were now two points behind Surrey and Warwickshire at the top, and they were 16 points behind when a further defeat was suffered at Northampton where Frank Tyson and (inevitably) George Tribe in their contrasting styles reduced Yorkshire's batting to a shambles after Raman Subba Row had scored 183 not out to put the midlanders on the road to victory. Yorkshire lacked both Trueman and Illingworth at this stage of the season, Trueman bearing the brunt of the England attack and Illingworth making a bid to become England's off-spinner and all-rounder. An easy victory over Leicestershire at Grace Road followed, and then another abortive draw at Bramall Lane with Lancashire, Close making a painstaking 128.

At Scarborough, Yorkshire returned to winning ways by four

wickets after being set 225 to win by Middlesex. Off-spin had tended
to have the upper-hand throughout, with Titmus (five for 21) and
Bick (five for 22) bowling out Yorkshire for 84. Stott and Taylor put
on 95 in Yorkshire's second knock and Padgett held the dangerous
Titmus at bay, his 62 not out seeing Yorkshire to a four wickets win
and putting his County only two points behind Surrey – but the latter
had two games in hand as well. Yorkshire, with six games left to
complete their programme, had a brilliant victory over Kent at
Headingley. Illingworth played a fighting innings of 74 not out and
Close scored 52 as well as taking eight for 41 in Kent's second innings,
with young Don Wilson taking five for 67. The latter then pulled off
victory for Yorkshire with a hard-hit 34 as they reached a winning
total of 247 for eight in some $2\frac{1}{2}$ hours, after Burnet had declared 134
runs behind. This was a victory engineered out of nothing by a team
that exhibited fighting spirit to the full. Burnet may have looked slow
in the field, and may have looked out of his class with the bat, but he
had an uncanny knack of getting the best out of his young players.
Even his most critical detractors had to agree to that.

A good win at Lord's started a famous run-in for Yorkshire on a
south/west tour that will never be forgotten by those members and
supporters who were privileged to watch the fight for the title. Bryan
Stott and Brian Bolus were both in good form at Lord's but Trueman,
four for 23 in the first innings, was well-supported by Raymond
Illingworth, who bowled Peter Parfitt, top scorer in each Middlesex
innings, and took three for 38 and four for 30 in 47 mature overs.
Yorkshire were now back on top with eight points to spare over
Warwickshire, the table reading thus:

	P	W	L	D	T	Pts
Yorkshire	24	12	5	7	0	178
Warwickshire	25	12	8	5	0	170
Gloucestershire	24	10	9	4	1	158
Surrey	23	10	4	9	0	156
Glamorgan	25	11	7	6	0	156

The western part of the tour started at Bath and Yorkshire, without
Trueman and Illingworth on Test match duty, called in Birkenshaw
and Stead, an extra bowler. Alas, Yorkshire were outplayed, although
Close (128 and 34), Padgett and Taylor were in good form and Close
and Don Wilson bowled well. Lack of experience showed itself at
times and one felt that the defeat – a small margin of 15 runs – should
have been avoided. At Bristol an innings defeat left no doubt that
Yorkshire had a long way to go to become Champions. Yorkshire
were dismissed for 35, only Bolus with 12 not out and 91 shaping in
any way against Tony Brown, who took seven for 11 and three for 54.

Two successive defeats left Yorkshire in third place with the positions as follows:

	P	W	L	D	T	Pts
Gloucestershire	26	12	9	4	1	186
Warwickshire	27	13	9	5	0	184
Yorkshire	26	12	7	7	0	178
Surrey	25	11	4	10	0	174

Fortunately for Yorkshire, Surrey were also far from infallible, but were still favourites to win the title especially as they defeated Gloucestershire in a thrilling match by 89 runs when Lock and Laker shared 19 of the 20 wickets, the other being a run out.

At Worcester, the return of the Test players strengthened Yorkshire's team and both played a big part in a four-wicket win. Bryan Stott batted through the innings with 144 not out.

And so to Hove for the final match. On the last day Yorkshire were in a seemingly hopeless position with Sussex fighting to save the game and reaching 311 before being dismissed. Yorkshire then required 214 runs to win and this target was achieved in 28½ overs. It was a stand of 181 between Stott (96) and Padgett (79) that won the game for Yorkshire, but Illingworth had played his part with an innings of 122 and he also took wickets during the Sussex second innings. Don

Yorkshire at Lord's in 1959, the year they broke Surrey's run of seven consecutive Championships. Back row: Mr Allcock (masseur), Bird, Bolus, Binks, Wilson, Platt, Stott, Birkenshaw, Padgett, Sharpe. Front row: Illingworth, Wilson, Burnet, Close, Trueman. (Central Press Photos Ltd)

Wilson also made important contributions as did young Birkenshaw with four catches and a fighting 38. Surrey meanwhile were only hanging on to a draw against Middlesex, and so the Championship returned to Yorkshire for the first time since 1946 (not forgetting the shared title of 1949). They went on to beat the MCC in convincing manner by seven wickets at Scarborough and then following on against the Rest of England at The Oval, some 224 runs behind, they amassed 425 thanks largely to Close (86) and Vic Wilson (105) – and then Close and Illingworth bowled out the Rest for 135 runs to record a fine 66-run win. Remarkably all the Rest wickets fell to catches and a single stumping, which indicates how well the side fielded. The season was an unforgettable one for the players as they were not expected to be in contention at all for the title and few would dispute that they did have a little fortune at times. Yet Ronnie Burnet's contribution to the Championship was immeasureable. He averaged only 11.47 with the bat; took only six catches and captured only one wicket in two overs. But few who watched that side would deny that he had a tremendous hand in leading the team to success. He retired from the scene, satisfied that his two seasons with Yorkshire had shaken the side by the neck and had exceeded all the hopes and expectations that could have been anticipated. He had proved to all by his own enthusiasm and reliance on team spirit that a young side could win the Championship by playing positive cricket and by seizing the initiative in unlikely situations.

The bowlers fulfilled the highest expectations, with Trueman topping the averages with Illingworth close behind him. Padgett and Stott both achieved their 2,000 runs, while Close and Taylor also passed the thousand mark. Illingworth proved to be a top-class all-rounder and finished top of the batting averages with nearly 1,500 runs. Bob Platt earned his cap, taking 85 wickets at 22.35 each and Don Wilson's never-say-die attitude was infectious. Bolus produced some fine performances, and if Sharpe was disappointing with the bat, his slip fielding was of the highest class. Birkenshaw, Ryan and Taylor, too, all bowled well at times and Binks was his usual high standard behind the stumps.

PROFESSIONALS TAKE OVER

YORKSHIRE FINISHED WORTHY CHAMPIONS in 1960 in Vic Wilson's first season as captain. He was the first professional captain to be appointed by the Club since Tom Emmett in the early 1880s and at the time there were doubts about his batting form, which had deteriorated since 1955. Everything he did as captain was in the interests of the side, if at times he had to be persuaded to take a more positive course of action, and he tended to let certain situations drift. In the match with Northamptonshire (now without George Tribe), he put Yorkshire on the road to victory with a fighting 48, and against Sussex at Middlesbrough he rallied the side from 80 for four to a score of 381 with a battling 72. At Lord's he came in at 8 for four and made top score (24) against Middlesex and at Trent Bridge appeared with the score on 23 for four and his 59 helped Phil Sharpe to put on 122 for the fifth wicket. At Leicester he came in with Yorkshire at 127 for six and made a valiant 77, enabling his side to reach 318 and force an innings victory. He became the seventh man in the team to reach 1,000 runs – admittedly at a very modest 27.27 average – but at the age of 39 his fielding and catching remained superlative. All fielders drop catches; and even Vic was known to miss an absolute sitter at times; but by and large, he was the most reliable of all Yorkshire's close to the wicket brigade, amongst whom were some to rival the great Surrey close catchers of the 1950s. In 37 matches for Yorkshire he took 32 catches, behind Close (44 catches) and inevitably Sharpe (36 in only 24 matches).

The fielding and catching was the main secret of Yorkshire's success, along with the consistent batting led by Stott, Padgett and Close, who with Taylor, Bolus and Sharpe – the two latter for the first time – all reached 1,000 runs. Illingworth was a tower of strength and actually became the eighth Yorkshire player to pass 1,000 runs during the season in all first-class matches. Ryan and Platt gave adequate support to Trueman, while Don Wilson, Cowan and Close all took over 50 wickets. Fred Trueman headed the bowling averages and was by a long way the best fast bowler in the country. Along with his 150 wickets at 12.72 for Yorkshire, he took 25 wickets against South Africa in the Tests. The season culminated in a 137-run victory over the Rest of England at The Oval and though Yorkshire did lose six Championship matches during the season even in those they had their moments of glory.

At Hove in the first match of the season, Stott (138) and Taylor (130) put on 281 for none before Yorkshire declared and the eventual defeat was by 32 runs after Sussex declared at 250 for two. Six victories followed before spin proved Yorkshire's undoing at Headingley in the Roses match. Leg-spinner Tommy Greenhough had eight for 61 and with the help of Bob Barber and Jack Dyson, caused Yorkshire's batsman to fail twice. Further victories followed, including a nine-wicket win at The Oval where Close made a monumental 198 and Trueman took 14 wickets for 123 runs in 58 splendid overs. Yorkshire lost at Northampton by six wickets and were beaten by Essex in a close match at Headingley by 57 runs where Trevor Bailey bowled his seamers in immaculate fashion. Nor could Yorkshire prevent Lancashire performing the double at Old Trafford, but at one stage Yorkshire were 89 for seven in their second innings and only seven runs in front. In the end Lancashire struggled to 81 for eight to gain a two-wicket victory. Yorkshire also lost to Glamorgan at Swansea but victory at Edgbaston ensured the title for Yorkshire. In that game, Bryan Stott and Brian Bolus put on 152 for the first wicket, Stott going on to make a huge 186.

In the following season, Yorkshire again played the maximum number of county games (32) and had an eventful season although the weather was far from good. They won seven of the first nine matches and gained the first innings lead in the other two games.

Brian Close scored 111 against Lancashire at Old Trafford after Ken Taylor had taken six for 75 in Lancashire's first innings, and a comfortable ten-wicket win was assured as Illingworth took eight for 50 and Lancashire's last seven second innings wickets fell for only 27 runs. At Bramall Lane Taylor was again in evidence with 159 against Leicestershire and Trueman followed up his seven for 45 with five for 13.

A most remarkable game took place at Worcester where Yorkshire lost Don Wilson, who broke his arm and was out of the game for several weeks. Yorkshire began their second innings requiring 190 to win but lost seven wickets with only 86 on the board. Binks made a defiant 46 and helped Illingworth to add 60 runs for the eighth wicket but when Wilson came out to bat, one-handed, Yorkshire still required 37 to win. Helped by Bob Platt, Wilson played a variety of remarkable strokes and won the match for his side with 29 not out.

Keith Gillhouley was introduced into the side in place of Wilson for the very next match, and proved a good deputy for Don Wilson, maintaining his place in the side through the season but he never played for Yorkshire again.

Another spinner made his first appearance for Yorkshire in the one-wicket win at Worcester was Brian Bainbridge of Middlesborough. An off-spinner, he took three for 52 in Worcester's second innings and followed that up with six for 58 and six for 53 in the Essex match at

Harrogate. Later in the season he took part in two further matches and had the distinction of heading the Yorkshire bowling averages with 19 wickets at 19.19 apiece. Knowing that Illingworth would always block his path into the County team he only made one further appearance for Yorkshire, in 1963.

Yorkshire were then outplayed by Surrey at The Oval, Bernard Constable establishing a first innings lead of 235 for his side. Thanks to centuries from Bolus and Close, Yorkshire succeeded in saving the match. In the following game at Bristol, skipper Vic Wilson made top score in each innings (53 and 30) but that was not enough to save his side who went down to Gloucestershire by eight wickets.

Yorkshire soon returned to winning ways and Northamptonshire were defeated twice and Somerset once. In the match at Northampton, Padgett reached 112 not out in Yorkshire's total of 430 for three declared as Northamptonshire went under by an innings and 152 runs. A thrashing for Derbyshire at Chesterfield followed and then a high scoring draw at Taunton before Yorkshire returned to meet Sussex in an exciting match at Park Avenue.

Yorkshire declared 132 behind in a game that suffered because of rain. A further declaration from Sussex left Yorkshire needing 200 to win. At 27 for four Yorkshire's position looked very unsafe but Illingworth scored a fine 59 and Vic Wilson with 46 not out steered them through to a noteworthy win by two wickets. At this stage Yorkshire were in second place, slightly behind Middlesex and just in front of Hampshire, in what appeared to be a three-horse race. A comfortable win over Gloucestershire at Scarborough placed Yorkshire at the head of the table, but Surrey had the best of the draw at Headingley and another draw followed at Hove in spite of centuries from Taylor and Bolus. Then Yorkshire were without both Close and Trueman on Test match duty as Leicestershire overwhelmed them by 149 runs, in spite of Peter Kippax taking five for 754 in their first innings. Two further draws did not help Yorkshire's bid to retain the title and the side had slipped down to third place with Hampshire now leading the way. At Trent Bridge, Stott, Bolus and Taylor all notched up centuries and Nottinghamshire conceded defeat by 207 runs. Yorkshire returned to equal top place and recorded further victories at Park Avenue over Worcestershire and at Southend against Essex. Taylor scored 141 at Bradford while Trueman added another 18 wickets to his growing tally.

That Southend match was the start of a southern tour which took in Dover, Lord's, Edgbaston and finished at Bournemouth for a match with Championship contenders Hampshire. Yorkshire battled hard at Dover and took a first innings lead of six but on a turning wicket, Kent's batting proved more consistent and they won through by 69 runs. Further disaster struck at Lord's, where Yorkshire were set 300 to win. Stott and Bolus gave them a good start with 117 for the first wicket but collapse set in and only 97 runs were added, and Middlesex won by 85 runs. Yorkshire nearly lost at Edgbaston, too, in a game which gave Hampshire the title. Though Ken Taylor made his highest ever score (203 not out) for Yorkshire, they lost five for 59 in the second innings when set 270 to win, and they had to settle for a draw. It had been a sad end of the season for Yorkshire, so with Hampshire declared Champions, and deservedly so, for the first time in their history, the two met in the final match at Bournemouth. Stott (75) and Bolus (100) gave Yorkshire a good start with 141 for the first wicket and from that point they never looked back. Illingworth bowled magnificently to take twelve for 102 in the match and Yorkshire won by 58 runs.

At the end of the season, eight players had reached their thousand runs and Close, Bolus and Padgett all passed the 1,800 mark. Illingworth and Trueman each took over 120 wickets, while Platt and Ryan gave adequate support along with Gillhouley and Close. Two newcomers were Chris Balderstone and John Hampshire, who made a promising 61 on his debut against Leicestershire.

The new season, 1962, began with Vic Wilson again their captain and a good start was made with these successive victories, in one of which, at Edgbaston, the worthy captain himself scored 134 to put Yorkshire in an impregnable position. Three draws were to follow, in none of which were Yorkshire in a winning position, and then remarkably three successive defeats, Trueman being absent from two of them. Surprisingly Yorkshire soundly beat Lancashire by three wickets, Trueman taking five for 29 in Lancashire's second innings as Lancashire slumped to 112 all out.

Bryan Stott was then prominent with 145 in an innings win over Derbyshire at Hull, but Yorkshire's inconsistent form continued as they fell by six wickets at Northampton with Trueman absent. This was followed by a draw with Derbyshire at Chesterfield and at this stage Yorkshire stood in fifth place, a considerable distance behind leaders Warwickshire.

At the end of June, Yorkshire had a remarkable match with Hampshire at Park Avenue. Vic Wilson had made top score in each innings (51 and 45) for Yorkshire but only three players in the match reached fifty and Derek Shackleton had taken twelve wickets for 145 runs as Hampshire set about their task of obtaining 163 to win. Although wickets did fall from time to time, Jimmy Gray with 78 seemed to be guiding them to a comfortable victory and at 156 for five the game was all but over. But in one of the most remarkable turn arounds in county cricket history, Hampshire inexplicably collapsed and were all out for 157, and Yorkshire turned out to be winners by five runs. Ray Illingworth finished with figures of five for 33 in 22 overs.

Fred Trueman's benefit match followed against Surrey at Bramall Lane but there was never any hope of a definite result, in spite of two centuries from Sharpe and Padgett. After a draw with Essex, Yorkshire journeyed to neighbouring Worksop where they won comfortably by 180 runs after Trueman had wrecked Nottinghamshire's first innings by taking eight for 84. Sharpe had a century in this match and repeated that feat in a drawn match with Northamptonshire at Bramall Lane. Two further draws took place, at Headingley against Nottinghamshire and at Taunton. In both games runs were very plentiful and in the absence of Trueman Peter Wight scored 215 for Somerset. For Yorkshire, Ken Taylor scored 163 against Nottinghamshire and helped Vic Wilson (134) add 116 for the eighth wicket while at Taunton, Sharpe and Close both obtained centuries. At this stage Phil Sharpe, having his best-ever season, had scored four centuries in five matches for Yorkshire. Yorkshire now stood in fourth position in the table, well behind Worcestershire who had overtaken Warwickshire at the top.

Spinners Don Wilson and Illingworth ensured victory at Bristol over Gloucestershire after Doug Padgett had carried his bat through the first innings with 115 not out and Illingworth (six for 26) had a field day at Bramall Lane against Essex, who lost by an innings and 44 runs. For Yorkshire, Brian Close made a timely 142 not out.

A splendid victory over Kent at Middlesbrough by three wickets was largely due to Ray Illingworth's 51 and 84 not out – he added 66 for the match-winning eighth-wicket stand with Don Wilson – after he had taken five for 52 in Kent's second innings score of 136. It was a good fight back after Peter Richardson had made 162 to help Kent towards a first innings lead of 93. Then came a draw at Old Trafford with Sharpe again shining with 112 and 60 not out while John Hampshire scored 71 not out as an opener. Yorkshire were still in fourth place but were close behind the leaders. They then achieved a hard-fought victory over Sussex at Scarborough after showing a deficit of 46 on the first innings. They set Sussex 193 to win, and Ray Illingworth took five for 10 in 12.4 overs to dismiss Sussex for 99.

Comfortable victories over Leicestershire at Bradford where Mel Ryan took ten for 77 in the match, and at Gllingham against Kent really gave Yorkshire hopes of the title as they took over at the top, but the return game with Champions Hampshire at Bournemouth needed to be saved by the visitors with their last two batsmen at the crease and still requiring 52 for victory. This time Illingworth scored a century, and he again reached three figures at The Oval, where Surrey made no effort to get 358 to win. Yorkshire's methods were not without criticism as they spent almost one and a half days compiling 416 and Surrey's target, at the rate of 116 per hour, was hardly reasonable.

A draw at Leicester meant Yorkshire by now had lost their top spot; Worcestershire led the table but had finished their programme, so that Yorkshire had to win their last match at Harrogate against Glamorgan if they were to finish Champions. Glamorgan, put in to bat on a drying wicket, collapsed to 65 all out, Don Wilson taking six for 28, but only Taylor with a splendid 67 made much headway for Yorkshire, who replied with 101. Rain then took a hand and no play was possible on the Thursday, and in ordinary circumstances there would not have been much hope of play on Friday either but for help from voluntary labour who helped to dry the pitch. Crowds of 10,000 saw each of the day's play and it was estimated that 5,000 came on the blank day. When play did start, Wilson with four for 3 and Illingworth and Close with three wickets each caused another Glamorgan collapse and Yorkshire, set 66 to win, won fairly comfortably in the end and so took the title again.

Vic Wilson, in a season in which he scored 1,226 runs at a modest average of 23.62, decided to retire at the age of 41 to close a successful career in a suitable manner.

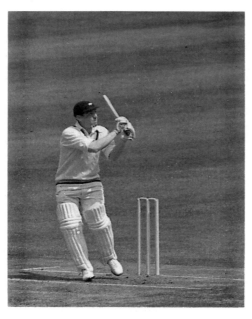

Ken Taylor hooking at Lord's in 1962. He played over 300 games for Yorkshire, topping 1,000 runs in a season six times. (Sport and General)

424

YORKSHIRE V. GLAMORGAN

Wednesday, Thursday and Friday, 5th, 6th, 7th September, 1962

(This card does not necessarily include the fall of the last wicket)

COUNTY CHAMPIONSHIP MATCH
OFFICIAL PROGRAMME 4d.

Intervals:
Lunch 1-30 to 2-10 p.m.
Tea 4-15 to 4-35 p.m.

Umpires : T. Drinkwater & A. E. Rhodes
Scorers : E. I. Lester & H. Jeffries

1st Day—11-30 a.m. to 6-30 p.m.
2nd Day—11-30 a.m. to 6-30 p.m.
3rd Day—11-30 a.m. to 6 or 6-30 p.m.

(The new ball may be taken after 85 overs, at the option of the Captain of the fielding side)

Harrogate C.C. "Grand Prize Draw"—Prizes include a Week in Paris (or £50), £25, £10, 3 x £5, Cigs., Spirits, etc. Tickets 6d. each obtainable from licensed bars, tea bars and main score box. Drawn here on Thursday afternoon. Proceeds for ground improvements etc. Your kind support welcomed.

FREDIE TRUEMAN'S BENEFIT : A collection will be taken during the course of the afternoon's play on Wednesday and Thursday, and your generous support is solicited.

YORKSHIRE

First Innings:

1. Taylor, K. F.	caught Evans bowled Shepherd	67
2. Hampshire, J. H.	bowled Ward	4
3. Sharpe, P. J.	caught Jones, A. bowled Ward	13
4. Close, D. B.	run out	0
5. Stott, W. B.	bowled Wheatley	5
6. Illingworth, R.	l.b.w. bowled Wheatley	0
7. Wilson, J. V. (Capt.)	bowled Wheatley	1
8. Trueman, F. S.	bowled Wheatley	8
9. Wilson, D.	caught Evans bowled Jones, I.	1
10. Binks, J. G. (w/k)	not out	0
11. Ryan, M.	bowled Jones, I.	0

Extras : 2 B. L.B. W. N.B. — 2

TOTAL 101

No. of Overs : 52

1	2	3	4	5	6	7	8	9	10
17	35	44	64	78	85	96	100	101	

Analysis of Bowling :

	Ov.	Mds.	Runs	Wkts.	N.B.	Wides
Jones, I.	2	3	6	2		
Wheatley	17	9	21	4		
Shepherd	24	15	35	1		
Ward	9	1	37	2		

Average runs per Over : 2.06

Second Innings:

bowled Jones, I.	0
not out	24
caught Lewis bowled Shepherd	12
caught and bowled Ward	13
not out	9

Extras : 8 B. L.B. W. N.B. — 8

TOTAL 66

No. of Overs : 18.1

1	2	3	4	5	6	7	8	9	10
0	18	23							

Analysis of Bowling :

	Ov.	Mds.	Runs	Wkts.	N.B.	Wides
Jones, I. J.	5	1	9	1		
Wheatley	5	1	10	0		
Shepherd	7.1	2	19	1		
Ward	4	0	20	1		

Average runs per Over : 3.6

GLAMORGAN

First Innings:

1. Parkhouse, W. G. A.	l.b.w bowled Ryan	0
2. Hedges, B.	bowled Wilson, D.	13
3. Jones, A.	caught Sharpe bowled Wilson	11
4. Lewis, A. R.	l.b.w. bowled Illingworth	0
5. Walker, P.	caught Stott bowled Wilson	6
6. Pressdee, J.	caught and bowled Wilson	15
7. Ward, D. J.	caught Wilson, V. bowled Illingworth	4
8. Evans, D. L. (w/k)	not out	6
9. Wheatley, D. L.	caught and bowled Wilson, D.	5
10. Wheatley, O. S. (Capt.)	caught Wilson, V. bowled Illingworth	3
11. Jones, I. J.	caught Close bowled Wilson, D.	0

Extras : 2 B. L.B. 2 W. N.B. — 2

TOTAL 65

No. of Overs : 50.3

1	2	3	4	5	6	7	8	9	10
1	18	19	26	46	47	53	58	65	65

Analysis of Bowling :

	Ov.	Mds.	Runs	Wkts.	N.B.	Wides
Trueman	6	3	7	0		
Ryan	2	2	4	1		
Illingworth	21	8	28	3		
Wilson, D.	19.3	10	24	6		

Average runs per Over : 1.28

Second Innings:

l.b.w. bowled Illingworth	9
l.b.w. bowled Wilson, D.	13
caught Close bowled Wilson, D.	9
caught Wilson, D. bowled Illingworth	17
caught Sharpe bowled Wilson, D.	14
l.b.w. bowled Illingworth	8
not out	19
caught Sharpe bowled Close	8
caught Stott bowled Wilson, D.	0
caught and bowled Close	0
bowled Close	0

Extras : 4 B. L.B. W. N.B. — 4

TOTAL 101

No. of Overs : 92.2

1	2	3	4	5	6	7	8	9	10
15	27	43	43	62	62	72	101	101	

Analysis of Bowling :

	Ov.	Mds.	Runs	Wkts.	N.B.	Wides
Trueman	11	6	15	0		
Ryan	3	2	0	0		
Illingworth	27	16	29	3		
Wilson, D.	31	17	48	4		
Close	1.2					

Average runs per Over : 1.1

The scorecard for the Championship match at Headingley against Glamorgan in 1962. Ken Taylor scored two-thirds of Yorkshire's first-innings total.

The batting was strong in depth with Phil Sharpe scoring 2,201 runs at an average of 40.75 to top Yorkshire's batting averages, while Padgett (1,750) and Illingworth (1,610) were next in aggregate. Close finished second in the averages with 1,438 runs, average 36.87.

Trueman again headed the bowling averages with Illingworth just behind him while Don Wilson took 97 wickets at 21.63 each. Ryan was the next best in total with 81 wickets at 24.22, but Platt, Taylor and Close all had days of success. Binks was his usual reliable self behind the stumps and the fielding was first-rate.

Three more newcomers came on the scene in 1962. Each was to have a significant part in the future of Yorkshire cricket.

Richard Hutton was the elder son of Sir Leonard Hutton and was born at Pudsey. Tall and upright, his stance at the wicket was similar to his father's and the off-side strokes he displayed were also in his stylish manner, but he lacked the defence of his father. He was also a very capable right-arm medium fast bowler who put plenty of effort into his delivery and at his best, bowled straight and not unlike Brian Statham in his approach to the stumps. A member of the Repton eleven he also played for Cambridge University in 1962–64, and first appeared for Yorkshire against Sussex at Scarborough. He impressed sufficiently to represent the Gentlemen against the Players in the same season. He gained a regular place in the Yorkshire side in 1965 and he continued to play until 1974. He perhaps did not realise the promise that he showed in his early years. He became a stockbroker and accountant after his retirement.

Tony Nicholson, a native of Dewsbury and for five years a policeman in Salisbury, Southern Rhodesia, was a right-arm medium fast bowler with an unusual action who gave great service for Yorkshire from 1962 to 1975. No batsman and slow in the field, he was a thoroughly wholehearted bowler, perhaps the best of Trueman's many partners for bowling 'into the wind'. He made his debut at Westcliff-on-Sea at the start of July and took four for 50 while bowling in harness with Ryan. Against Nottinghamshire at Head-ingley, he again took four for 50. He quickly gained a regular place in the Yorkshire side in the following season and was capped in the October of that year. After retirement from county cricket he became coach and professional to Marske in the North Yorkshire and South Durham League but he had trouble with circulation in his legs and gave up active participation in the game. He went to live at Ripon and died in Harrogate Hospital in 1985 aged 47.

Geoffrey Boycott made his debut against the Pakistanis, being dismissed by A. D'Souza, a medium-pace bowler, for just four runs in each innings. He played in four other matches and scored 47 against Derbyshire as his best score.

In 1963 Brian Close took over the captaincy, and in a wet season led the team to another deserved Championship. They won two more matches than any other county and lost but three, the same number as Warwickshire.

A seven-wicket win at Northampton was notable for the fact that Close scored 161 and 53 not out while Trueman scored his first century (104). All the bowlers had some success and Binks took seven victims behind the stumps. In this match John Waring made his first appearance for Yorkshire. A tall, strongly-built medium-fast bowler, he finished second in Yorkshire bowing averages with 13 wickets at 15.07 each. He went on to play spasmodically for Yorkshire until 1966, in which season he took 25 wickets at 21 runs each, and in 1967 appeared once for Warwickshire.

A draw with Kent was followed by a complete humiliation of Warwickshire at Edgbaston who were bowled out for 35 and 55, Trueman taking ten for 36 and Ryan seven for 42. Trueman followed up that fine bowling by taking eight for 45 at Park Avenue as Gloucestershire were dismissed for 80 before rain ruined Yorkshire's chances. The strong Hampshire side shocked Yorkshire at Headingley by defeating them by 130 runs, but at Gravesend Yorkshire returned to form with a 22-run win, but it was very close as Kent, chasing 252, reached 205 for five before Wilson finished with the remarkable analysis of 8.4-0-72-4.

In Championship style the Yorkshire side accounted for Lancashire, Somerset and Derbyshire with an innings to spare; a fine feat when it is remembered that Yorkshire were without Close and Trueman on Test match duty while Ray Illingworth was injured at the time. The Lancashire match will be remembered for Boycott's first century for his County. Along with Bryan Stott (143) in a fourth wicket stand of 249, Boycott scored 145, with the cut and his off-side play being especially prominent. In the match against Derbyshire, Padgett and Sharpe both recorded centuries and Tony Nicholson took nine for 69 in the match. A series of draws followed with victory over Glamorgan at Bramall Lane Yorkshire's sole success until July. In that game Close had a match analysis of ten for 74. Yorkshire stood in second place in the table; two points behind Sussex, who had a match in hand.

At Headingley, Yorkshire dismissed Middlesex for 47 with Tony Nicholson taking five for 7 and Don Wilson four for 11 but it did not prevent Middlesex winning easily by six wickets after Yorkshire had declared at 147 for seven in their second knock. Two draws with Surrey were played before and after a key game with the leaders at Park Avenue, where Sussex were well beaten by ten wickets, Nicholson continuing his fine form by taking five for 26 in the first innings before Don Wilson took six for 22 in the second to complete

Sussex's sad performance. Yorkshire had now drawn level but Sussex still had a match in hand. Against Surrey at Sheffield, John Hampshire completed a fine 120 to record his first century for the County and then in the next match, he had the satisfaction of taking seven for 52 as Glamorgan lost at Cardiff by an innings and 66 runs. At Worcester, Yorkshire were soundly beaten by the home side by an innings and 57 runs but they were without Sharpe, Close and Trueman on Test duty. Returning to form against Warwickshire at Scarborough, Yorkshire opened with their two promising youngsters, Boycott and Hampshire, Boycott remaining there for the rest of the season. Illingworth, with 49 and five for 35 was returning to his best form, and in the next game Boycott reached his second hundred of the season against Lancashire with Sharpe also reaching three figures. Rain, alas, ruined Yorkshire's chance of victory but with Sussex faltering badly, Yorkshire now had 18 points to spare at the top over Glamorgan. A comfortable win over Derbyshire at Headingley was followed by a draw at Park Avenue with Nottinghamshire, where Brian Bolus made 114 in Nottinghamshire's second innings. Rain alone saved Nottinghamshire and it was rain again at Lord's and at Clacton where Nicholson took another six wickets.

Yorkshire finally won the Championship at Scarborough, where Leicestershire were no match for them. Yorkshire lost only five wickets in beating their opponents by an innings and 111 runs. Boycott scored 165 not out and Illingworth completed Leicestershire's misery by taking five for 13, following that up in the return game at Leicester with three for 40 and six for 13.

Outside the Championship Yorkshire had the satisfaction of defeating the West Indians at Middlesbrough, Trueman taking ten for 81 in the match, but at Bramall Lane the visitors gained revenge by an innings and two runs as the Sheffield crowd saw a glimpse of Gary Sobers at his best as he scored 100 not out. The Gillette Cup was introduced in this season, and Yorkshire defeated Nottinghamshire at Middlesbrough before going out to Sussex, the eventual winners, in the second round. Their defeat by 22 runs took place at Hove with 562 runs being scored in the game.

Geoffrey Boycott headed the Yorkshire batting averages with 1,446 runs, average 46.64; he was the only Yorkshire player to reach his thousand runs although John Hampshire finished only five short. Trueman headed the bowling averages with 76 wickets at 12.84, while Nicholson, Illingworth, Don Wilson, Close and Ryan gave him good support and produced a well-balanced attack.

Bryan Stott announced his retirement in the middle of the season and then had the misfortune to suffer appendicitis, and he did not appear again. He went to Aireborough Grammar School and captained Yorkshire Schoolboys, played for England Schoolboys and for the Yorkshire 2nd XI when only 16. A forcing left-handed batsman and brilliant outfielder, he played in the same manner and style as Maurice Leyland, although he lacked the all-round strokes of the England batsman. He played a few games for Yorkshire from 1952 but did not get a regular place in the side until 1957. He scored over 9,000 runs at an average of over 31 during his comparatively short career with the County, retiring owing to business reasons. He joined the Yorkshire committee as Wharfedale representative in 1982 and served on the cricket committee.

The 1964 season will be remembered for its excellent weather but Yorkshire had to be satisfied with fifth place in the Championship, their worst season since 1958. In early May they introduced Geoffrey Hodgson from Huddersfield into the Yorkshire side in place of Jimmy Binks who had been chosen to play for MCC *v* Surrey at Lord's. This was the first game that Binks had missed for Yorkshire since entering the side in June 1955; a phenomenal record. Hodgson, by some, was considered as good a wicket-keeper as Binks. He went on to play for Lancashire in 1965 but on medical advice gave up any attempt to play regularly owing to a bad back.

Boycott, Hampshire and Nicholson were all capped during the previous winter so that the side had a nucleus of young players, with Trueman and Close the oldest members of the side at 33. The future appeared to be very healthy. A defeat from Kent was no disgrace at Park Avenue, where rain prevented a proper finish. Close was run out for 67, and took six for 29. A good win at Headingley followed with Boycott (151) taking Yorkshire to a first-innings lead after Middlesex had recovered from 89 for six to 309 for six thanks to centuries from John Murray and Wakefield-born Don Bennett. Ray Illingworth with six for 50 proved Yorkshire's match winner, and a ten-wicket victory was well-deserved.

A 236 stand between Boycott (131) and Taylor (153) put Yorkshire in a strong position against the old foes, but Geoff Clayton saved Lancashire after two more declarations in an endeavour to make a game of it. Further abortive draws followed, some because of the weather. Boycott scored 151 not out against Leicestershire, adding 205 with Sharpe (79 not out) and in the return game at Park Avenue John Hampshire scored 150 against the weak Leicester attack. That was Yorkshire's seventh consecutive drawn game plus an eighth if one includes a splendid match with the Australians at Bramall Lane. After a Norman O'Neill hundred, Yorkshire had to follow on 182 in arrears but a fine second wicket stand between Ken Taylor and Doug Padgett

(70) added 197 and Taylor went on to make 160. In the end the visitors were fortunate to draw, having lost seven wickets while still 46 runs behind.

Barry Wood made his first of five appearances for Yorkshire but gave little indication that he would become the player he did. A younger brother of Ronald Wood, the left-arm slow bowler, who appeared for Yorkshire in 1952–56, he was a fine opening or middle-order batsman, a very mean seam bowler and a wonderful fielder anywhere, especially close to the wicket. He was a competitive cricketer, and had he persevered with Yorkshire he would have eventually made the side, but he joined Lancashire in 1966 and played there until 1979, when having received a record benefit of over £62,000 he left for Derbyshire, where he played in 1980–83. He played in twelve Test matches for England and toured abroad several times.

Yorkshire returned to winning ways with an innings victory over Glamorgan at Headingley, where Tony Nicholson had match figures of twelve for 73 and in the first innings only a last wicket stand of 12 took Glamorgan up to the respectability of 55. Further draws at Park Avenue with Surrey, after Brian Close (100 not out) and Fred Trueman (50) had saved Yorkshire, who were still only 39 runs ahead with seven second innings wickets down. Yorkshire were now in sixth place in the table. Somerset then saved the match at Bath with their last pair at the crease and still needing 69 for victory. Yorkshire were without Boycott, Taylor and Trueman for this and the following game at Edgbaston, where Warwickshire bowled Yorkshire out for 54 with Barbadian Rudi Webster (seven for 6) taking advantage of a lively pitch. This defeat placed Yorkshire in ninth position, but victory at Swansea came with Yorkshire back to full strength.

After another draw with Derbyshire, an eight-wicket win over Nottinghamshire was followed by another rain-spoilt game at Bramall Lane against Northamptonshire. Then came a fine win over Worcestershire at Scarborough and innings victories over Lancashire and Nottinghamshire which helped to revive Yorkshire's Championship hopes. Tony Nicholson took six for 82 in Worcestershire's first innings, five for 27 in Nottinghamshire's first innings and seven for 32 in Lancashire's second. Yorkshire thoroughly out-played their northern neighbours in every department of the game, and had now risen to third place in the table but Warwickshire and Worcestershire still had a clear lead.

Fred Trueman shone with top score (77) and five for 49 in Gloucestershire's first innings to place the western county in a hopeless position at Bramall Lane, but they fought hard and defeat was avoided.

John Hampshire's 110 and 40 not out ensured victory over Hampshire at Portsmouth, and after a further rain-soaked draw with Sussex came a remarkable victory over Kent at the Crabble Ground at Dover. It was a game completely dominated by Raymond Illingworth, who came to the crease with Yorkshire's score at 41 for four. Close helped him to add 110 for the fifth wicket, after which he completely took charge and went on to score 135 before being last out. He then proceeded to take seven for 49 and seven for 52. To take seven wickets in each innings of a first-class match and also to score a century is a feat that has been performed on very few occasions. Rhodes, Hirst and Woolley never did as well.

John Edrich put Surrey on the road to victory at The Oval with 124 and 53 as Yorkshire went down by 57 runs. Warwickshire then had the better of a drawn game thanks to Tom Cartwright's bowling and centuries from Ibadulla and Bob Barber, but Yorkshire finished the season in remarkable fashion with an innings and 294 runs win at Bristol against foot-of-the-table Gloucestershire. Boycott scored 177 and then all five Yorkshire bowlers contributed to Gloucestershire's dismissal for only 46 and 84.

Although fifth position was disappointing by Yorkshire standards they were seldom at full strength, with at least four players taking part in Test matches and with Boycott and Nicholson injured on occasions.

Six Yorkshire players reached the thousand-run mark, while Binks had 826 to his name – a big improvement. Boycott easily headed the batting averages with 1,639 runs, average 60.70, and the bowling was headed by Nicholson, with 76 wickets at 15.69 each. Illingworth performed the 'double' and was a tower of strength. Wilson took 93 wickets but Trueman fell away to take only 75 wickets at 20.82 and herein lay the real deterioration in the team. He had been the spearhead of the attack for so long that it was not surprising that he should have a comparatively poor season. Yet he was still England's best bowler, and headed the Test averages against Australia as well as taking the most wickets.

In the Gillette Cup competition Yorkshire lost at Lord's to Middlesex by 61 runs in their only game.

The new season opened where the previous one left off with an innings victory over Gloucestershire who could only score 74 and 65, and Trueman showed a welcome return to his best form with nine for 48 in the match. Sussex held out for a draw at Park Avenue after being in a seemingly hopeless position in their first innings at 4 for five after Yorkshire had made 234. On a pitch that suited bowlers, Northamptonshire lost by 82 runs at Northampton, Illingworth taking six second-innings wickets for 39, and he took eight for 20 at Headingley against the Champions in a game ruined by rain.

A remarkable performance by Hampshire came at Middlesbrough. Derek Shackleton took six for 64 as Yorkshire reached only 121, Fred Trueman scoring 55 of those, and then Hampshire collapsed to take a four-run lead. When Yorkshire batted again they reached seven without loss but a few overs later the score stood at 8 for six and it took Don Wilson (7 not out) to 'revive' the home side from 13 for eight to 23 all out. It was Yorkshire's lowest total in their history. David White, the Hampshire pace bowler, took six for 10 and Hampshire went on to win by ten wickets.

Three drawn matches and an innings victory over the New Zealanders followed, with Close scoring 115 and taking five for 69 in the Kiwis second knock. Then came another defeat at Swansea where on a typical spinner's wicket Glamorgan deserved their 31-run win. Two draws followed and then Northamptonshire won at Headingley by 58 runs, after Yorkshire had led on the first innings. This time it was the fast bowler David Larter, with twelve for 80, who wreaked havoc amongst the Yorkshire batsmen, who had certainly had a wretched season so far.

At this stage of the season Yorkshire were in fifth place and only ten points behind Middlesex and Northamptonshire, the joint leaders. In fact every county had won and lost at least one match except for Surrey, who were at the foot of the table without a win to their name. They remedied that by beating Yorkshire by three wickets at Park Avenue in spite of centuries from Hampshire and Close that enabled Yorkshire to declare and set Surrey 207 to win.

Down at Hove, Trueman took thirteen for 77 but another rain-affected draw resulted. Yorkshire journeyed to Gillingham and played in much better form. Skipper Close had a fine match, taking 11 wickets in a close win. Middlesex saved the game at Scarborough after Trueman followed his five for 32 with 101, adding 147 with Peter Chadwick (59) for the eighth wicket. Yorkshire seemed to be cruising to victory but John Murray's 132 not out saved the day for Middlesex.

Yorkshire narrowly escaped defeat at Bradford against Essex for whom Barry Knight took ten for 90 in the match. Yorkshire had their last pair at the crease at the end and were still a run behind Essex's first innings score. Gloucestershire escaped defeat at Lydney, but Lancashire's visit to Bramall Lane proved very beneficial to the home side who won easily by seven wickets after declaring their first innings at 194 for three with Hampshire 110 not out and Padgett 72 not out. Trueman took seven for 59 in the match and Don Wilson six for 41. A draw at Portsmouth against Hampshire was followed by a surprising win at Headingley, where Leicestershire were left 328 to win. They seemed to be on their way to a comfortable draw when they put on 124 for the first wicket, but they collapsed in sensational fashion to be dismissed for 179. Yorkshire were now no higher than sixth. They nearly lost to Surrey at The Oval, but finished their season with victories over Essex and Somerset (twice) and a couple of rain-struck draws. Dick Hutton was in particularly good form at this stage and in the three victories had five wickets in an innings in each game. Yorkshire's final position of fourth may have been a slight improvement on the previous year but they were never in contention for the title and their actual record was inferior to 1964.

Boycott again headed the batting averages with 1,215 runs at 35.73, but he failed to reach three figures in any innings, while Hampshire finished next to him scoring 1,424 runs average 31.64. Sharpe, Close and Padgett all reached their thousand runs and Illingworth scored 916 runs as well as taking 94 wickets at 16.59 to finish second to the revitalised Trueman in the bowling averages. Fred bowled magnificently at times, taking 121 wickets at exactly 13.00 runs each. Don Wilson, Richard Hutton and Brian Close all took over 50 wickets, Close's being the most expensive at 20.98.

The Gillette Cup saw Yorkshire defeat Warwickshire in the semi-final by 20 runs after defeating Leicestershire and Somerset with ease in the earlier rounds. Yorkshire went on to score 317 for four in the final after being put in to bat by Surrey, and Yorkshire won very easily by 175 runs. Although Boycott did not achieve three figures on the first-class scene, he made up for it in this match by scoring a brilliant 146 and adding 192 for the second wicket along with his skipper, who reached 79. Illingworth took five for 29 as Surrey were dismissed for 142.

Brian Close was retained for the 1966 season with only Mel Ryan missing from the previous year. Boycott and Taylor each recorded centuries at the expense of the MCC and victory against Gloucestershire inside two days at Middlesbrough saw the new 65-over limitation rule inflicted on the public for the first time. In this game neither first innings reached the limit but Ken Taylor with 47 and 23 not out was by far the most successful batsman as Yorkshire won by seven wickets. Don Wilson was very economical in taking nine for 30 in 31 overs during the match.

Somerset, bowled out for 70 in their second innings, with Wilson taking five for 40, were well beaten by eight wickets, and after rain interfered with the return Gloucestershire match, Yorkshire had an easy win over Lancashire by ten wickets after bowling out the old enemy for 57 in their first innings, Trueman taking five for 18. Close made top score (48 not out) in this match at Headingley following a century at Bristol. Illingworth's eleven for 126 at Leicester was largely responsible for a comfortable seven-wicket win and then came an even draw at Lord's with Peter Parfitt (43 and 114 not out) taking most of the honours. Yorkshire were now level on top of the table with Worcestershire with Warwickshire only two points behind.

A win at Edgbaston was mainly due to an unbeaten 136 from Boycott while Ray Illingworth's six for 66 in the second innings ensured victory. In their first innings at Chesterfield, Derbyshire collapsed to 89 in reply to Yorkshire's 258 for six – an innings victory was inevitable. Rain ruined the Hampshire match at Park Avenue and at Headingley Sussex inflicted on Yorkshire their first defeat, by 22 runs.

The return with Derbyshire at Bramall Lane proved a triumph for Tony Nicholson who was quite unplayable on a seamer's wicket. He took five for 12 and four for 12 in a total of 37.4 overs, a real tribute to his accuracy. Yorkshire then had the worst of the game at Worcester, where Ron Headley made a fine 137 but Ken Taylor (86) and Padgett (51) saved the day. Two further comfortable wins were recorded over Somerset at Bramall Lane and at Park Avenue against Essex. Again Trueman and Nicholson bowled splendidly in suitable conditions with Trueman taking eight for 37 in Essex's first innings, and Nicholson six for 32 in the second. Yorkshire now had a margin of 40 points over Kent at the top of the table.

Boycott scored 164 at Hove, but Yorkshire were unable to force a win, and there followed defeat at Headingley against Northamptonshire, Yorkshire losing by 66 runs. Boycott returned to form at Sheffield with hundreds in each innings and only Bolus (90) put up much resistance for Nottinghamshire. Yorkshire then had a good win over Middlesex at Sheffield, Don Wilson taking six for 22 in the second innings for victory by 120 runs. Nottinghamshire were then defeated by ten wickets at Worksop, Wilson adding a further nine wickets to his total, while Close made an aggressive 115 not out to put his side well on top.

Lancashire were beaten by 12 runs at Old Trafford after declaring at 1 for none in their first innings, with Yorkshire forfeiting their second innings. Set 146 to win Lancashire fell under the spell of Illingworth, who took five for 33. Rain spoilt Yorkshire's chances in their next two games and a visit to The Oval proved unproductive. Close, celebrating his being chosen as England captain against the West Indies at The Oval the following week, took six for 47 as Surrey collapsed to 189 all out, but the visitors were 74 behind on the first innings. Set 173 to win Yorkshire fell for 151 to lose by 21 runs. Yorkshire, well on top all season, now had only 18 points to spare over Worcestershire.

A two-wicket win at Scarborough over Glamorgan placed Yorkshire in a much better situation. The match was played on a very poor pitch where batsmen struggled to achieve a rate of two runs per over and Glamorgan were dismissed for 137 but Yorkshire finished 13 runs to the bad. Glamorgan fared even worse in their second innings to be dismissed for 91, with Tony Nicholson taking four for 28. Yorkshire were set 105 to win and it was almost ten past seven before Yorkshire could claim a hard-earned win.

Only four games were left and Yorkshire were 28 points ahead but at Northampton, Yorkshire, lacking Close, Illingworth and Boycott on Test match duty, were beaten after a hard struggle by 34 runs. Set 268 for victory, Yorkshire never looked like winning until the end of the innings when having recovered from 108 for six they finally reached 233, thanks to Don Wilson (52) and Tony Nicholson (41). Back to full strength at Hull against Warwickshire, Yorkshire seemed to be moving satisfactorily with a four-run lead on the first innings, but Warwickshire were set only 106 to win. They took a long time to reach their target but Neil Abberley carried his bat for 54 not out and Warwickshire got home by three wickets. Only six points now separated Yorkshire from Worcestershire.

Both counties' next match was spoilt by the rain but not before Close had taken six for 27 against Surrey, so the stage was set at Harrogate with Kent as visitors and Yorkshire needing an outright win to secure the Championship.

Geoff Boycott put Yorkshire on top with 80 as they reached a respectable 210 and as Kent finished 91 behind, thanks to Trueman (four for 25) and Nicholson (three for 36), Yorkshire seemed strongly placed, but they collapsed badly at their second attempt. Needing 202, Kent took their score to 143 for three before Illingworth (five for 55) struck and Kent subsided to 176 all out. Victory by 24 runs and the Championship for Yorkshire. Had Yorkshire lost the game, Worcestershire would not have overtaken them as they were soundly beaten by Sussex.

In what had been a wet season, Yorkshire's batting was unpredictable at times and only Boycott, who headed the averages again but only with 38.55, and Close batted consistently. Padgett, Taylor and Hampshire all reached their thousand runs and Sharpe missed only by 12.

The bowling was much more satisfactory with Nicholson leading the way with 113 wickets at 15.50, just ahead of Illingworth with 96 at 15.78. Both Trueman and Don Wilson reached their 100 wickets too at just over 17 runs each and Close backed them up with 54 wickets, often taken when most needed. There was no doubt where the strength of the side lay, but it was a season of damp pitches which proved very helpful to the bowlers. Binks was in fine form as ever behind the sticks and Sharpe and Close both took over 40 catches. The close fielding and catching was magnificent at times.

Close led the side from the front in his own fearless manner and could hardly be faulted. He batted bravely at all times and close to the wicket was brilliant; if he had a fault it was that he might have given the younger players more to do – a criticism that was to be levelled at him in the future.

There were three newcomers to the Yorkshire side in Cope, Old and Leadbeater but none of them made any impact although all had done well for the Colts.

In the Gillette Cup, Yorkshire went out in their first match at Taunton, losing to Somerset by 40 runs.

The new season (1967) began with a convincing win over the MCC at Lord's in which John Hampshire scored a century and a newcomer, Peter Stringer, took four for 10, dismissing Milburn, Parfitt, Lewis and David Steele in his opening spell to leave MCC floundering at 23 for seven. Stringer also took four for 33 at Harrogate against Glamorgan but never quite lived up to that start. He played for Yorkshire during the following two seasons without much success and eventually went to live for a time in South Africa.

Boycott reached 102 against Glamorgan in a drawn game and a similar result was to spoil the game at Bradford against Kent, where this time Boycott was twice dismissed for 0 by Norman Graham. Yorkshire were dismissed for 40, Graham taking six for 14 in 23 overs with 16 maidens. When rain ended play in their second innings, Yorkshire were in a hopeless position. Their first success was at Hull against Worcestershire where with a useful lead of 38 Yorkshire's Illingworth caused Worcestershire to collapse to 74 all out as he took six for 34. Set 37 to win, Yorkshire lost five wickets in doing so. In the middle of two games abandoned without a ball being bowled, Yorkshire beat Nottinghamshire at Park Avenue in a game in which there were three declarations. Yorkshire won by five wickets but there were some who were incensed at the methods used to reach that situation.

There was no criticism of the antics used at Kidderminster against Worcestershire. Worcestershire scored only 119 in their first innings, Yorkshireman Duncan Fearnley making top score (33) and Boycott (60) and Taylor passed that score without loss. Taylor went on to score 162 and a lead of 199 was established with only four wickets down. Worcestershire fared a little better at their second attempt but there was a margin of an innings and two runs.

At Lord's Yorkshire were forced to follow on and in their turn lost by an innings and 58 runs. Further defeat followed in the next match at Bath but Yorkshire lacked Close, Illingworth and Boycott to the Test match with India. An 80 runs defeat was disappointing but not unexpected in the circumstances. A visit to Swansea was not expected to be successful either, but Glamorgan could make only 141, and it was the young bowlers that Yorkshire had to thank; Cope, Chris Old and Nicholson all taking three wickets, Yorkshire went on to win by 10 wickets and to move up to third in the table.

A nine-wicket win at Bristol was followed by three successive innings wins and Yorkshire were looking good for another title. Boycott followed up 98 not out against Gloucestershire with 220 not out against Northamptonshire. Cope had the satisfaction of having match figures of six for 17 in 34 overs and 25 maidens. Cope also took three for 30 and five for 23 against Surrey and four for 26 against Leicestershire. In the latter game Ray Illingworth did even better as he made top score (78) and then took six for 52 and five for 27. Yorkshire were now top of the table and had a couple of games in hand over Leicestershire, who were now second. As Yorkshire had defeated the Indians at Bramall Lane with an innings to spare, they were full of confidence, which was not entirely merited as Derbyshire had the better of a draw with them, and then rain ruined the Middlesex game at Bramall Lane after Yorkshire gained a 93-run advantage on the first innings. Doug Padgett scored 111 for Yorkshire – his first century for three seasons – and Yorkshire were now 10 points clear at the top with Kent in second place.

A full strength Yorkshire were then given a dreadful drubbing from Surrey at The Oval. After losing Edrich for 0, Ken Barrington reached a monumental 158 not out and Yorkshire were made to follow on 217 behind. Yorkshire lost by an innings and eight runs.

Yorkshire had then to be satisfied with a draw at Park Avenue with rain ruining their hopes after Nicholson had taken six for 34 and further failure was to face them when Hampshire beat them at Bournemouth by six wickets. With rain about, there were more fancy declarations and Hampshire could gain little merit in their win. The Lancashire match was played at a funereal pace at Bramall Lane where Sharpe took six catches but both sides appeared to be afraid of playing shots on a dubious pitch. Yorkshire were now in third place but were only eight points behind the two leaders with two games in hand of Leicestershire and one in hand of Kent, whom they were to play in the next match at Canterbury. Both sides were weakened because of Test match calls and Kent brought back Godfrey Evans in place of Knott. He kept wicket with his old brilliance. Kent lost Luckhurst early on when he suffered a broken hand from Trueman's bowling, but reached a respectable 223. With the pitch taking spin, Yorkshire gained a two-run lead. In the Kent second innings, Trueman and Nicholson reduced Kent to 5 for three. Kent rallied to 100. Yorkshire had little difficulty in scoring the 99 required for the loss of three wickets.

After a rain-affected draw with Derbyshire at Bradford, Yorkshire met Warwickshire and had the worst of a draw, although John Hampshire scored 102 and Nicholson took six for 50 in Warwickshire's first innings. In this match Brian Close was accused of time-wasting, a charge which resulted in him eventually losing the captaincy of the MCC side to tour the West Indies.

Nor had Yorkshire's troubles ceased as they went home to Scarborough, although they soon had Essex on the rack. Getting them all out for 87, Yorkshire built up a strong position before leg-spinner Hobbs went through the tailenders to confine their lead to 127. In the second innings Essex came back into the game when they reached 245, despite Tony Nicholson bowling splendidly to take five for 30. Set 119 to win, Yorkshire lost Boycott early on and offered little resistance to Acfield's off-spin. With ten required and still two wickets left, Hobbs snapped up the last two wickets to give Essex a 9-run win.

With four games left the positions stood as follows:

	P	W	L	D	ND	1st inn lead	Pts
Kent	25	9	2	12	2	14	152
Yorkshire	24	9	5	8	2	14	144
Leicestershire	25	7	3	12	3	15	140
Surrey	26	8	4	10	4	14	140

At Eastbourne, Yorkshire looked to be in much better form as Padgett (81 not out) guided them to 210 and then Tony Nicholson took nine wickets for 62 runs to give Yorkshire a lead of 68. Sharpe, Illingworth and Wilson all obtained half centuries to set Sussex 350 to win. Yorkshire went on to win by 83 runs. This victory placed Yorkshire back on top, but Nottinghamshire at Trent Bridge provided Yorkshire with no more than first-innings points in spite of a Padgett century and more good bowling from Nicholson. At Middlesbrough Yorkshire reached 250 thanks to Close's 98 and then Wilson took six for 31 as Warwickshire collapsed to 148. With Warwickshire set 300 to win, Wilson was again in fine form with seven for 21 as Warwickshire were shot out for 70.

Yorkshire went to Harrogate to play Gloucestershire in the last match with both Kent and Leicestershire two points ahead of them so that a first-innings lead was required for Yorkshire to win the Championship. Boycott (74) and Sharpe (75) put on 127 for the first wicket and a last wicket stand put on 64 so that Yorkshire reached 309. Gloucestershire could make little headway against Illingworth and the match was completed in two days. Illingworth followed up his seven for 58 with a second innings analysis which read 13-9-6-7.

Boycott again topped the Yorkshire averages and his 1,530 runs were made at an average of 49.35. Sharpe, Padgett and Hampshire all passed 1,200 runs and only Taylor, who averaged 20, had a poor season. Young Cope actually topped the bowling averages, his 40 wickets costing 13.82 each, while Illingworth was second with 78 at 16.52. Nicholson deservedly reached his 100 wickets and Wilson bowled very well at times. Trueman was no longer the force of old, but his 71 wickets at 22.12 each was a satisfactory return for most bowlers. Fred is not judged by normal standards. When Close was absent Trueman led the side with much enthusiasm and handled his bowlers astutely.

As expected, in the Gillette Cup, Yorkshire made progress at Cambridgeshire's expense in a 10-overs slog but the venue, Castleford, was chosen only at an hour or so's notice as Headingley and Harrogate and every other possible ground was waterlogged. Yorkshire lost by four runs in the next round at Old Trafford.

A worse start to a season could not be envisaged than Yorkshire made in 1968. Bonus points for both batting and bowling were introduced.

At Harrogate, Hampshire did complete an innings and Barry Richards made an attractive 70 but there was no time for much more and the trip to Taunton saw 176 runs scored for seven wickets, Binks bagging four victims; and there were three declarations in the match. Back at Bradford, Boycott (100) and Sharpe (78) did open with a stand of 168 and Sussex took five wickets in all as Yorkshire scored 242. In reply Sussex were 96 for seven in a game confined to one innings. Another century by Boycott (132) gave Yorkshire a first innings lead of 160 against Leicestershire after Don Wilson had taken seven for 50. They went on to an innings win. Rain ruined the Nottinghamshire match at Headingley and then an easy innings win over Warwickshire at Middlesbrough was due to a match bag of ten for 71 by Ray Illingworth and 180 not out from Boycott.

Yorkshire narrowly escaped defeat from Gloucestershire at Bristol in spite of another Boycott century (125) and a lead of 103 on the first innings. Set only 136 to win it was an innings of 45 not out by Illingworth that saved them from full eclipse as Procter crashed through the early batting as Yorkshire finished on 93 for nine.

Fred Trueman bowled at his best against Lancashire at Headingley in a lack-lustre Red Rose batting display and Yorkshire's Doug Padgett (105) and Ken Taylor (85) showed there was little wrong with the Headingley pitch. An innings victory was a mere formality.

Now in top place, Yorkshire were only three points in front of Warwickshire after the latter had completely outplayed Yorkshire at Edgbaston to win by 156 runs. It was a side lacking Boycott on Test duty and with Close injured during the game but Yorkshire almost had to follow on and a target of 307 was quite beyond their batsmen.

Yorkshire returned to winning ways against Leicestershire at

Bramall Lane with Boycott carrying his bat through the first innings for 114 all out from 297, and Illingworth (100 not out) and Hampshire (96) sharing a fourth-wicket stand of 184 in the second. Trueman with six for 20 was far too good for the Leicestershire batsmen, with ony Jack Birkenshaw (60) showing up well against his old County, who won by 143 runs. A fine win over Middlesex at Headingley was due to a fine 136 not out by Padgett as Yorkshire compiled 358 for seven declared, and the game was over in two days as Middlesex collapsed to Wilson (eleven for 59) for 59 all out and 143. Rain ruined the next two county games but Yorkshire were now 32 points ahead of Derbyshire, who were having one of their best seasons for many years.

Away from the county scene and still without the injured Close, Yorkshire under the leadership of the ever-enthusiastic Fred Trueman made the Australians follow on at Sheffield and then proceeded to beat them by an innings and 69 runs. Boycott (86) and Sharpe (47) put on 105 for the first wicket and Padgett (56) and Illingworth (69 not out) enabled Yorkshire to declare at 355 for nine. Trueman (eight for 83) and Illingworth (eight for 67) humiliated the opposition for whom the only redeeming features were fifties from Bill Lawry and Doug Walters. It was Yorkshire's first victory over the Australians since 1902.

Yorkshire then suffered defeat against Glamorgan at Bramall Lane, declarations taking place before Glamorgan set the home side 205 to win. Yorkshire were in trouble from the start and Don Shepherd's six

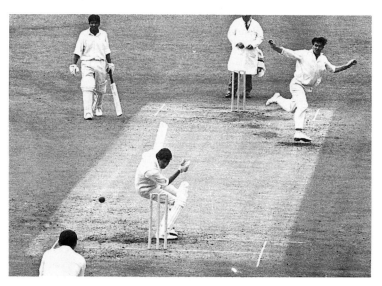

'Fiery Fred' Trueman bowling a bouncer against Kent in 1968. (NCCC)

for 40 was sufficient to give Glamorgan victory by 103 runs. Another draw at Bradford with Kent went in Yorkshire's favour and then Yorkshire claimed revenge at Cardiff with Sharpe's 114 enabling them to go on and beat Glamorgan by 10 wickets. Geoff Cope had a fine match taking seven for 42 and five for 74, with Illingworth and Boycott away on Test duty.

A low-scoring match at Bramall Lane against Worcestershire provided an excellent finish, with Illingworth taking ten for 79 in the match. In reply to Worcestershire's 99 all out Yorkshire fell to Norman Gifford (eight for 28) but Yorkshire only needed 126 to win. John Hampshire with 44 not out and Illingworth with 32 guided Yorkshire home by four wickets. Boycott was suffering from disc trouble and was unable to play again in the Championship. At The Oval Yorkshire were 257 for one at one stage with Taylor (78) and Padgett (74) helping Sharpe (125), but then a further 29 wickets fell for 351 runs with Yorkshire winning with ease by an innings and 32 runs.

At Westcliff Keith Boyce proved Yorkshire's undoing in a low-scoring game. Essex won by five wickets after taking a 65-run lead on the first innings and being set 99 to win. Nicholson took five for 59 in the Essex first innings. The weather at Trent Bridge resulted in a draw with Nottinghamshire, although Yorkshire did gain a first innings lead thanks to Phil Sharpe's 143 not out. Nicholson again bowled well in Nottinghamshire's second innings with six for 49 but there was no time to force a win. Yorkshire still had a lead of 22 points at the top but the side's performances were not those of potential Champions. Two further draws followed with Nicholson again bowling at his best with eight for 22 at Canterbury against Kent but both that and the following match were rain-affected games. Hutton and Nicholson both bowled well at Old Trafford, but facing Lancashire's 162, Yorkshire were 61 all out. In the end Yorkshire were set 253 to win and Close's 77 not out undoubtedly saved the game for his side. Some argued that he had time enough to win and that Yorkshire made no real effort; others saw it as a magnificent rearguard innings on a bowler's pitch. Yorkshire still had 21 points to spare with six games left in the Championship.

Padgett (75) and Binks (48) were mainly responsible for Yorkshire reaching 230 at Lord's and this proved far too many for Middlesex, with Don Wilson taking five for 17. He then scored a fast 45 not out to enable his side to declare and set the southerners 218 to win. At no stage did Middlesex look like reaching their target and their last four wickets all fell at 100. An innings win over Somerset at Scarborough was due to Richard Hutton's six for 56 and Illingsworth's timely 90 not out.

A rain-ruined game at Park Avenue with Derbyshire was little help to Yorkshire nor was a defeat at Worcester, although only one run separated the teams in a remarkable match. Seam and spin dismissed Worcestershire for 101, and then Yorkshire gained a lead of 25 with Close top scorer on 27. Worcestershire set Yorkshire a formidable 139 to win but Yorkshire steadily garnered the runs thanks to Hampshire (31) and Binks (34) but Trueman was lbw for 12 after a last-wicket stand had added 14.

Yorkshire had all the best of the Derbyshire match at Chesterfield but they could not quite force a win, Derbyshire still requiring 96 to win with only two wickets left. John Hampshire batted well on the first day to reach 100.

To clinch the Championship Yorkshire had to win at Hull against Surrey and when they reached 327 for nine declared, they seemed to have the game well in hand. Surrey reached 189 and Yorkshire declared at 112 for seven to set Surrey 251 to win. Surrey never looked like winning but they held on until the last two overs, when they lost their last three wickets. Don Wilson was again Yorkshire's bowling hero with five for 61. Yorkshire were therefore the Champions for the third year running and finished 14 points ahead of Kent.

There had been one or two hiccups on the way, one being the loss of Raymond Illingworth who was going to play for Leicestershire in the following year as captain. Had Yorkshire given him the longer contract that he wanted then he would no doubt have stayed with Yorkshire. But Yorkshire, with Cope in the background, did not consider that they should treat Illingworth differently to any other player. Both sides had a point, but if other counties were giving longer contracts to overseas players, then Illingworth's argument was that he was justified in thinking about his future – though no longer a young player he was still at the peak of his powers. The other problem was poor Geoff Cope himself. Some had accused him of throwing, and this plagued the remainder of his career. A man with a doubtful action is not a cheat. Cope always claimed that he was unjustly treated but at the back of a lot of people's minds was the suspicion that his faster ball sometimes looked doubtful.

Boycott just managed his 1,000 runs in all matches which was a good performance as he played in only 14 matches. His average was 77.23, while Sharpe averaged over 33 with 1,256 runs. Hampshire and Padgett also reached their thousands. Illingworth, who missed several games because of the Tests, was third in the batting averages but scored only 717 runs. He topped the bowling, however, with 105 wickets at 13.46; marginally better than Wilson, whose 107 wickets were taken at 13.49. Cope's 20 wickets cost only 14.20 and Nicholson took 87 wickets at 16.43 each. Trueman and Hutton gave good support with over fifty wickets each.

Yorkshire went out to Warwickshire at Edgbaston by four wickets in the Gillette Cup but the Colts had the satisfaction of winning the Minor Counties Championship without losing a match under the leadership of Bob Platt.

Ken Taylor retired at the end of the season in which he had received a good benefit. During the past seven seasons he had obtained only three centuries in the County Championship and his batting had been disappointing. There had never been any doubt concerning his temperament but he lacked consistency. On the other hand his bowling was never to be taken lightly while his fielding and catching were outstanding in any company. As a cover-point, he was not only brilliant but quite unspectacular in his methods. Not a tall man, he was extremely well-built, as his career as a centre-half with Huddersfield Town, then a leading side, indicated. Perhaps Taylor, like Watson, suffered because he was an outstanding footballer too; but in eight or nine regular seasons with Yorkshire, some of his innings were of the very highest calibre and his scampering between the wickets with Bryan Stott was a joy to behold. A man of many parts, he was a talented artist. He became a schoolteacher and taught art. For a time he emigrated to New Zealand and played cricket for Auckland.

Raymond Illingworth's loss to the side, in spite of the presence of Cope, was the worst loss for Yorkshire to overcome. Apart from being a top-class off-spinner, not in the class of Bob Appleyard, he showed steady improvement until he was in the forefront of that type of bowling. His record in Test cricket is very similar to his two contemporaries, David Allen and Fred Titmus, even if he did have a tendency to underbowl himself when England captain. Illingworth was a rarity. He was a success as an England captain, and if he did have that aforementioned weakness of not bowling when the heat was on or if a big hitter was at the crease it was a very minor fault. When Illingworth played for Yorkshire, he bowled to the best of his ability at all times and never shirked an issue. With the bat he was perhaps the most reliable batsman in the team (apart from Boycott) and whether runs were wanted quickly or whether he was required to block an end up, he never failed to do other than what his captain or his side required of him. By any standards Illingworth was a top-class cricketer. Undoubtedly he was the third best all-rounder that the Club had produced, allowing for the fact that Jackson did not play often enough to be considered. He had been to school at Wesley Street in Farsley, and he averaged 100 with the bat and took his wickets at two runs each. He also played soccer and he was offered trials with various football league clubs. A very astute cricket brain, his knowledge had been used to the full by his captain and friend, Brian Close. He was to miss him when Illingworth moved to the midland county.

The third player to leave Yorkshire was Fred Trueman, who had bowled his heart out over the years both for Yorkshire and England. In his last 15 full seasons he had rarely missed a match because of injury and his record compared favourably with any fast bowler in the history of the game. He was born at Stainton, very close to the Nottinghamshire border and not far from Larwood's birthplace. He was educated at Maltby Hall Modern School and joined Roche Abbey CC taking 25 wickets for 37 in his first four games. When 16 he went to play for Sheffield United and met with immediate success. He first played for Yorkshire in 1949. He also impressed as a centre-forward but was advised to drop soccer by the County Committee. A good businessman, after his retirement from the game he became well-known as a radio commentator and for a time served as the Craven representative on the Yorkshire CCC committee.

Brian Close would be leading quite a different side into the field in 1969.

Amidst all these changes, Boycott's batting and his personality were becoming ever more evident. This domination of Yorkshire's cricket by the England opener was to remain and indeed increase as the seasons passed. Some would say that the presence of such a figure was very much to the County's detriment, but others felt it was the one redeeming feature in a lack-lustre side. The truth lies somewhere in between.

Geoffrey Boycott, the eldest of three brothers, was born in Fitzwilliam and learnt his cricket with Ackworth and Barnsley, as well as at the cricket School run by John Lawrence at Rothwell. He had made his Yorkshire debut in 1962 and gained a regular place the following summer.

Of his many great innings for Yorkshire, perhaps the most outstanding was his 146 in the 1965 Gillette Cup Final, but his batting against Sobers at Park Avenue and two innings he played against Hendrick, at Headingley and Abbeydale, were just as brilliant in their way.

It is impossible not to admire his dedicated professional approach to batting and to cricket and this could be seen in the amount of time he devoted to net practice on the one hand and his immaculate turn-out on the other. He thought little of fellow cricketers who failed to live up to the high standards he set himself, and it is said that some promising batsmen, overawed by his presence in the eleven, failed to do themselves justice.

When Boycott joined the Yorkshire County Committee many people turned against him, but when present at meetings he talked a good deal of sense and he continues to do so. The name of Boycott will be to the forefront, so long as Yorkshire's cricket is the subject of the written word or conversation. Figures alone prove that he was something out of the ordinary, but they do not tell the whole truth.

THE DOWNHILL PATH

THE NEW SEASON (1969) OPENED AT SWANSEA with Yorkshire having to be satisfied with a draw after Glamorgan had been set to obtain 168 to win. The Welshmen put on 47 for the first wicket but collapsed to 91 for nine before the last pair took the score to 109 without further loss.

Chris Old, after Trueman's retirement, became a fixture in the Yorkshire side and was capped before the end of the season. He was the youngest and most talented of three sporting brothers from Middlesbrough, and was a right-arm medium-fast to fast bowler and attractive, forcing, left-hand batsman who was at his best against slow bowling. Like him, his brothers, Malcolm and Alan, both played for Middlesbrough and Alan, a rugby union international, also played cricket for Durham and appeared for Warwickshire. Chris Old also played rugger for Otley in the early 1970s. Educated at Acklam Grammar School, he captained Durham Schoolboys and played for ESCA and North of England Schools. He played regularly for Yorkshire from 1969 – first assisting them in 1966 – to 1982, but suffered many injuries which limited his appearances, as did his 46 matches for England, in which he took 143 wickets. After leaving Yorkshire, he played for Warwickshire for a time and also for Northumberland.

At Park Avenue Yorkshire fought hard on a bowler's wicket after being 48 runs behind Warwickshire on the first innings. Boycott batted through the innings for 53 not out, Hampshire (27) being the only other player to reach double figures. Warwickshire's second innings saw them collapse to 72 all out thanks to Nicholson (four for 22) and Wilson (four for 15) and Yorkshire's target of 121 seemed far from impossible. But again Cartwright bowled superbly to finish with seven for 34 (12 in the match).

A string of four draws followed, all against Northern neighbours whom Yorkshire could have been expected to beat. Old took four for 15 against Nottinghamshire in a game with three declarations while Don Wilson took four for 55 at Old Trafford in the only innings of the match. Sharpe and Close added 148 at Headingley against Leicestershire in a game in which only two wickets fell, while the Derbyshire match provided a springboard for victory at Headingley but the visitors declined a target of 161 in about 100 minutes. At the end of this game Yorkshire were in 17th and last place in the County Championship with a quarter of the curtailed 24-match programme out of the way.

Nor did matters improve at Lord's, where only Leadbeater (71) batted well when Yorkshire finished 79 in arrears, with rain preventing either side's efforts to force victory.

Barrie Leadbeater, who began his career with Yorkshire in 1966, played regularly in the side in 1969 and following a successful match in the Gillette Cup final was capped during the following winter. Born and brought up in Harehills, Leeds, he was an attractive right-hand batsman and useful slip-fielder but never lived up to his early promise. A pleasant, likeable individual, he did not possess an athletic frame, and his running – between the wickets or in the field – was not up to Yorkshire standards. Purely a batsman, he obtained only one century for the County, a disappointing performance when one remembers that he appeared in 14 seasons and qualified for a benefit which he shared with his townsman Geoff Cope. After his playing career he became a first-class umpire in 1981.

At Middlesbrough, on a fast and lively pitch ideally suited for Chris Old, Yorkshire compiled 202, with Boycott top scorer with 84. Mike Procter took six for 64 with some lively pace bowling but this paled into insignificance in comparison to Chris Old, who took seven for 20 as Gloucestershire were dismissed for 41. At their second attempt Gloucestershire reached 108 with Old taking four more wickets for 26.

Further draws were to follow with Essex and with Hampshire, against whom, Richard Hutton bowled well to take five for 54, but Yorkshire made little effort to go for the runs after losing quick wickets. Gloucestershire had revenge by five wickets at Gloucester, with Procter scoring a quick 51 not out.

Against the New Zealanders, Colin Johnson had made his first appearance for Yorkshire, scoring an attractive 61 not out. A brilliant outfielder and useful medium-pace or off-spin bowler, he was in and out of the side for ten years without gaining his county cap. He played regularly for Yorkshire in some four seasons only, but did some very useful work in the one-day game. He later captained the Yorkshire 2nd XI and could always be relied on to do his best for the Club.

At Chesterfield, Doug Padgett held Yorkshire's innings together with 64 not out but Derbyshire established a lead of 130 and Yorkshire had to fight a rearguard action to save the game. They were now level at the foot of the table with Derbyshire and Somerset but had matches in hand.

Making his first appearance in this match was Mike Bore, a left-arm fast-medium bowler of great accuracy. He played fairly regularly for Yorkshire in 1970–73 and last appeared in 1977. He took only 162 wickets for Yorkshire and they cost over 30 runs apiece but he was a hard-working member of the side and had some good performances.

He moved to Nottinghamshire in 1979 and played with them for several seasons, also leading the 2nd XI and coaching at all levels.

Yorkshire's luck changed at Bramall Lane, when Boycott was on a Test call and Close was injured. Leadbeater and Woodford ran up a first-wicket stand of 115 and Yorkshire reached 295 for nine before declaring. Worcestershire finished 134 in arrears. Yorkshire's second declaration at 149 for six left Worcestershire needing 284 to win. Yorkshire won by 119 runs. Leadbeater reached two fifties in the next match at The Oval, but rain again prevented a finish.

The next match was against Lancashire at Bramall Lane and it resulted in a remarkable finish, not entirely to Yorkshire's credit, although they obtained 12 points to Lancashire's two. Chris Old (five for 34) bowled at his best as Lancashire were dismissed for 171, but at one stage they were 94 for eight before Peter Lever scored 57 against his native county. Boycott with 80 and Hampshire with 62 enabled Yorkshire to declare at 290 for eight and Lancashire were well back in the game at 150 for two, but then collapsed and were soon all out for 183. Yorkshire were left with 65 to win in 19 overs but Higgs and Lever bowled with accuracy and Yorkshire still required one run to win with one over to go. In that over, a maiden, Higgs managed to dismiss Leadbeater, Wilson and Hutton. In spite of their disappointment, Yorkshire had risen to 14th in the Championship. The match was Doug Padgett's benefit match.

Another defeat followed at Trent Bridge, where Nottinghamshire scored 341 and 208 for five, with Sobers scoring 88 in the first innings. Yorkshire, again lacking their skipper and Boycott, were well beaten by 137 runs, although Hutton batted well with 59 not out and 56, while John Hampshire scored 93 in the first innings. Two drawn games with Somerset followed with Yorkshire on top in both games without forcing victory. At Weston, Geoff Cope took five for 49 and then Hampshire (85) nearly brought Yorkshire a win but squally showers and winds spoilt the game in the end. The other match at Headingley saw Boycott score his side's first century in the County Championship for the season. Greg Chappell with seven for 40 wrecked Yorkshire's batting on a seamer's wicket. Richard Hutton did even better with seven for 39. Somerset ended with 141 for seven, needing 235 to win.

Yorkshire finished fifth from the bottom of the table after winning one and losing three of their last six matches. It was a disappointing end to the season but a 29-run defeat at Scarborough had seen Hutton take four for 32 in Surrey's first innings and contribute 66 and 35 with the bat. In the victory at Leicester, Wilson had taken six for 36 in the home side's second innings. At Hull Northamptonshire had dealt out a

447

sound thrashing with Prideaux scoring 170 not out while Mushtaq had the remarkable figures of five for 26 and six for 41.

Boycott again headed the batting averages, but he scored only 843 runs at 38.31, closely followed by Sharpe (37.48) who did reach his 1,000 runs, as did Padgett. Close and Hampshire batted well at times and Leadbeater and Hutton both scored over 700.

Wilson headed the bowling averages with 101 wickets at 16.88 – a very creditable performance – while Old, Hutton and Nicholson gave reasonable support in taking over 50 wickets each.

In the one-day competitions, the John Player Sunday League had its first season and Yorkshire finished with seven wins and seven defeats. The Gillette Cup was won convincingly with Yorkshire defeating Norfolk, Lancashire, Surrey and Nottinghamshire – all by convincing margins – before beating Derbyshire by 69 runs in the final. Leadbeater took the honours with a well-played 76.

Chris Balderstone made his last appearance in the Yorkshire side in 1969. A sound, stylish right-hand batsman, he became an opener when he joined Leicestershire, although he could bat anywhere. He was perhaps utilised mostly by Yorkshire as a left-arm slow bowler, although he took only 37 wickets for the County at a reasonable cost of 21 runs each. Born at Longwood, Huddersfield, he began his career with Paddock and like Willie Watson, also a Paddock cricketer, was an extremely good soccer player which interrupted his advance as a cricketer. A talented inside-forward and a stylish passer of the ball he played with Huddersfield Town, Doncaster Rovers, Carlisle United and Queen of the South. In 1975 he played in a match for Doncaster Rovers at night after representing Leicestershire during the day. From 1971 to 1986 he advanced greatly as a cricketer and when he retired he had completed over 19,000 runs in first-class cricket. He also played in two Test matches. In 1980 he became chairman of the Cricketers' Association and after his retirement from the game became a first-class umpire.

After seven years of captaincy, Brian Close was granted a testimonial and was re-appointed captain. In the Club report for the season, it was stated:

> The season of 1969 will be remembered as one in which one of the major changes in the structure of County Cricket was made, namely, the introduction of the John Player Sunday League. Consquently there were three separate Competitions . . . being played, each requiring a different approach to the game.

That was a very apt summing-up of the situation of county cricket in 1969. It still holds good to-day. There are many who claim that county cricket was saved by the advent of the 40-overs Sunday

Close's team in 1969, the last great Yorkshire side. Back: Leadbeater, Balderstone, Hampshire, Old, Hutton, Nicholson, Boycott, Cope. Front: Sharpe, Binks, Close, Padgett, Wilson. (Sport and General Press Agency Ltd)

League. That is true if one accepts that the ills that had smitten county cricket since the war were to be shoved under the carpet instead of an effort being made to cure them. Another school of thought would claim that limited-overs cricket has ruined county cricket and that all grades of English cricket have fallen to astonishingly low levels, with the result that the England side at Test level needs South Africans and West Indians to compete on an even basis against even the poorest opposition.

During the winter, Jimmy Binks decided to retire too. One of the most consistent and reliable of wicket-keepers, he had kept wicket in 412 successive county matches from 1955 until his retirement and in his last season, in Brian Close's absence, he had captained the side. Binks went on to play for Lincolnshire from 1971 to 1973 but in 1978 went to the United States.

The new season began in fine style with Derbyshire well beaten by an innings and 20 runs at Bradford. Old took five for 14 and Yorkshire's reply contained Richard Hutton's first century for the County (104). An easy victory followed over Cambridge University at Fenner's.

To replace Binks, Yorkshire had introduced their second-team wicket-keeper as his natural successor in the side. Neil Smith was an able batsman, too, but in the seven matches he played in the first team in this season, luck did not go his way and at the end of May he was dropped from the side and replaced by David Bairstow. He never appeared for Yorkshire again after a fleeting appearance against the Indians in the following season, but proved to be a valuable member of the Essex side from 1973 to 1981.

Rain ruined the Surrey match at The Oval but Yorkshire were having the worst of the game and three defeats followed at the hands of Glamorgan, Lancashire and Gloucestershire.

At Bramall Lane, Cope, in a nightwatchman's role, made 50 and helped Padgett (106) put on 113 for the fourth wicket against Hampshire. Yorkshire went on to win by an innings and five runs which took them up to 11th place in the table. A further victory at Edgbaston over Warwickshire was welcome with Woodford scoring 42 and 51 in support of Padgett who made top score in each Yorkshire innings with 61 and 75. With a lead of 83 Yorkshire had difficulty in breaking the back of Warwickshire's second innings, but a three-wicket win was duly theirs.

David Bairstow had been introduced into the side in the Gloucestershire match and he caught out five batsmen behind the stumps. He kept his place for the rest of the season and showed early signs that once he had learnt discretion he would be a very capable batsman indeed. Bairstow began life as a bowler at Laisterdyke. An infectious enthusiasm made him a very good team man and later as a wicket-keeper he was good enough to assist England on several occasions and for most of his career was without peer when standing back. He was never as successful standing up. As a batsman he square cut with tremendous power and hooked and pulled well and could be relied on in a crisis. Bairstow, ever the sergeant-major and the man to spur his colleagues on, led the Yorkshire side in 1984–86 but to lead the side and to keep wicket to his old standards was too much to ask. A tendency to put on weight might have affected his keeping, too. Though he lost his place for a time during the 1988 season, this was due partly to his batting which had hit a bad spell. If one examines the figures of Yorkshire wicket-keepers, then Bairstow is in the forefront. He typifies Yorkshire cricket with his attitude and was always a popular member of the team and with the public. His benefit in 1982 was at that time a record for Yorkshire cricket. In 1982, too, he had equalled the world record number of catches taken in a match (when playing against Derbyshire at Scarborough) and in 1987 became the 22nd wicket-keeper to take 1,000 victims in first-class cricket.

Another Padgett century put Yorkshire in a strong position at Bramall Lane against Nottinghamshire, for whom Gary Sobers saved the match for his side with 144 not out. Nor could Yorkshire get the better of Leicestershire in spite of Leicestershire being 52 for six at one stage. Booth (84) and Birkenshaw (57) revived the midlands county to 184 and then dismissed Yorkshire for 131. Marner and Inman both reached centuries and Leicester set Yorkshire 319 to win, a task they never attempted.

In a heavy scoring match at Chesterfield there were three declarations before Yorkshire were set 263 to win; a target they achieved comfortably thanks to a brilliant 120 not out from John Hampshire, who had also scored 43 not out in the first innings, when Boycott had top scored with 99. Yorkshire also had the best of the Sussex match at Headingley without being able to force victory but at Leicester, Yorkshire gained a good win by 17 runs. A fine century by Hampshire (107) saved Yorkshire on the first day. Now in 10th place, Yorkshire took a lead of 217 over Kent at Sheffield, with Boycott (148) and Sharpe (108) to thank for such a satisfactory position. Kent fought hard on the last day to save the match and when all out were 75 to the good. There was not time for Yorkshire to bat again.

The next match at Colchester brought Yorkshire a victory by an innings and 101 runs. Boycott made 260 not out, his highest ever score for Yorkshire, and this enabled Yorkshire to declare at 450 for four. In Essex's follow-on Cope ran through the batting to finish with seven for 36 including the hat-trick, which earned him his cap in the following week. Yorkshire had moved up to fifth position.

In the match at Leicester, Cope's action had been photographed and a 'minor fault' had been reported to Lord's, where Yorkshire played their next match against Middlesex. Cope's position from this time onwards was never quite satisfactory. Yorkshire were badly weakened by the calls of the England v Rest of the World match at Headingley, losing Boycott, Old and Wilson, and it was due to their bowling that they took a first innings lead of 64. Dick Hutton took four for 39 which he followed up with six for 83 when Middlesex reached 250 for seven to win the match after Yorkshire had declared their second innings on 182 for five.

After the Northamptonshire match at Northampton which was a draw in Yorkshire's favour, Close scoring 128, the positions at the top showed that Yorkshire had an excellent chance in the Championship with just eight games left:

	P	W	L	D	Bonus pts	Pts
Surrey	17	5	1	11	110	160
Derbyshire	17	6	4	7	97	157
Lancashire	16	5	1	10	105	155
Glamorgan	18	6	6	6	95	155
Yorkshire	16	6	4	6	93	153

At Park Avenue, playing against the leaders, Yorkshire's Chris Old with five for 44 bowled very well to dismiss Surrey for 193. Boycott scored 77 for Yorkshire to gain a lead of 51. Surrey were dismissed for 171, Cope bowling extremely well to take six for 55. Yorkshire won without much difficulty by five wickets, skipper Close scoring 46. After this match Derbyshire took over at the top only four points ahead of Surrey and six ahead of Yorkshire. The championship was still a possibility for the young Yorkshire side.

At Trent Bridge, again with a weakened side, Yorkshire fought hard but victory was denied them in the end while striving to obtain 211 in 130 minutes. They made a good start as Close plundered 54, to follow his first innings score of 68, in some 40 minutes but Plummer's bowling compelled them to put up the shutters and they finished at 157 for seven. Hutton had taken six for 81 in Nottinghamshire's first innings of 288 all out. That draw put Yorkshire only three points behind Derbyshire, and they had two matches in hand of their neighbours with Lancashire two points ahead of them.

At Worcester, again with a weak side, Yorkshire fell behind on the first innings by 219 runs with Glenn Turner scoring 140, Tom Graveney 100 not out and Ron Headley 91. At the close Yorkshire were 164 for eight in their second innings, still 55 behind. The weather ruined the Middlesex match at Scarborough after Sharpe (120) and Boycott (64) had enabled Yorkshire to declare at 304 for seven. Middlesex replied with 183 for seven. Yorkshire were now in third place but were nine points behind leaders Glamorgan with a game in hand. Rain also ruined the game at Bristol but their main disappointment on their western tour was to lose to Somerset at Taunton by six wickets. Yorkshire had recovered to score 309 after being 179 for eight thanks to a hard-hitting 92 not out from Old. With Cope taking six for 81, Yorkshire took a six-run lead but with Yorkshire struggling in their second innings in spite of Padgett's 59 a total of 204 was treated lightly by Somerset. It was not a good performance from Yorkshire, who batted badly in good conditions in their second innings. Yorkshire were still only seven points from the top but the Lancashire match at Old Trafford put paid to Yorkshire's chances as Lancashire reached 430 for seven before declaring. Barry Wood scored 144, his second century of the season in the Roses match. In reply Yorkshire hardly forced the pace, with Boycott making 98 out of 282 for three, and though Lancashire did set Yorkshire 210 to win in two hours, they made no effort to go for the runs after losing Boycott first ball.

Remarkably, Yorkshire had dropped down to eighth place, and though their last match at Hull against Somerset was won very comfortably by an innings and 30 runs, it was felt that Yorkshire had not deserved to be there at the finish anyway. Kent finished Champions with Yorkshire having to be satisfied with fourth place, 22 points behind.

Once again Boycott headed the batting averages with 1,558 runs, average 51.93, well ahead of Hampshire who averaged 37.20 and Close 36.50. Sharpe and Padgett both completed their thousand runs and Close failed by only 51 runs and Hutton by 125. In the end the batting was adequate but the bowling, apart from Old and Hutton, was not reliable enough. Cope took most wickets (83) but Wilson fell away badly, taking only 47 at 26.50 each, and Nicholson had his worst season ever, his 65 wickets costing 29.83 each. Yorkshire were summarily dismissed from the Gillette Cup in a snow-storm at Harrogate and Yorkshire's 14th place in the Sunday League was far from satisfactory.

Brian Close had from time to time indicated that he had little liking for limited-overs cricket. He had expressed this opinion in the press and following this season, which was the worst season ever for the Club in relation to finance, it was decided to remove him from the captaincy of the Club and that his services as a player would not be required either. Such action caused great stress amongst a section of the membership which resulted in an action group being formed in order to remove the chairman of the cricket committee, Brian Sellers, who had issued a statement concerning Close. It was also decided that certain elections would be contested against sitting members of the Yorkshire committee. Wardle's sacking and Illingworth's move to Leicestershire had passed with a minimum of fuss. The Close case was rather different and was the first split within the Club to have been aired by the press to any extent. Family quarrels can be kept out of the public gaze but when the 'family' in question had shown a record loss over the season, their popular captain had been dismissed at a moment's notice, and one of their favourite grounds, Bramall Lane, was likely to disappear to make way for a gigantic soccer stand, then something had to be said, and said in public – and it was.

Furthermore, the former favourite son, Raymond Illingworth, regained the Ashes from Australia, Close was signed up by Somerset and Geoff Boycott broke his arm in Australia. Brian Sellers decided to retire after serving as chairman of the cricket committee for 13 years. Geoffrey Boycott was appointed captain of Yorkshire. The winter of discontent was giving way to a more hopeful spring.

Yorkshire started the 1971 season at Park Avenue without Boycott, still suffering with his arm, and facing Kent, the County Champions. A defeat by an innings and 92 runs, and scarcely into the third day, was a sad start. Yorkshire were also missing Nicholson and Leadbeater, while during the game Sharpe, Cope and Old all suffered injuries that were to keep them out of several subsequent games.

A three-wicket win at Middlesbrough over Warwickshire on a good batting track saw Boycott in fine form with 61 and 110 on his return to the side, and in the second innings, he and John Woodford

(101) put on 161 for the first wicket before Boycott was out after batting only 100 minutes. Mike Smith, Amiss and Kanhai all recorded centuries for Warwickshire, while Padgett made 99 in Yorkshire's first innings. Nicholson bowled well to take five for 75. Victory over Oxford University by an innings and 177 runs meant very little as the 'varsity side must have been one of the weakest ever. Hutton, Dalton and Hampshire all recorded centuries for Yorkshire.

At Hove, John Hampshire made his highest score for the County with 183 not out against Sussex, after Hutton had taken five for 54 on a seaming pitch. Yorkshire could not force victory in spite of their 181 lead on the first innings.

A draw at Chesterfield saw Barrie Leadbeater return to the team and a welcome 54 not out as Yorkshire batted consistently to declare at 344 for five. In the next game at Headingley, Yorkshire gained a creditable eight-wicket win over Middlesex with Boycott again the star with 88 and 112 not out while John Hampshire helped him win the game with 72 not out as they added 169 for victory.

On a bowler's pitch at Old Trafford, Lancashire fell to Hutton's pace. Hutton's six for 38 was followed by five for 24 as Lancashire collapsed to 75 all out in their second innings, after dismissing Yorkshire for 79 – 89 in arrears. With about three hours left Yorkshire declined the target of 165 with Boycott absent ill. Yorkshire were in 10th place in the table.

Yorkshire were without Boycott and Nicholson at Bramall Lane against Worcestershire who were always on top after Headley had given them a good start with 80. Cope took five for 95 as the visitors reached 244. Yorkshire got within 84 runs on the first innings. Worcestershire then declared at 197 for nine but Yorkshire collapsed without much fight.

The return of Boycott saw another huge innings from him – this time 169 – and Yorkshire declared at 375 for five. Nottinghamshire then collapsed twice on a good Headingley pitch and were all out for 142 and 102. In the second innings it was John Hampshire's leg-breaks that did the damage with five for 37.

The topsy-turvy form continued with Yorkshire losing at Taunton by ten wickets when lacking Boycott and Hutton on Test duty. Inevitably, Close made 102 for Somerset.

Boycott's double century in Essex became an annual event when he scored 233 out of 421 for four declared, putting on 240 with Sharpe (92) for the first wicket. Essex followed on 204 behind after Bore had taken four for 58, and he followed that up with four for 77 as Essex fought back to draw at 230 for seven. Rain ruined a possible chance of a finish at Bramall Lane against Surrey and at Lord's there was a similar result with Yorkshire managing to save the match. Boycott made 182 not out from Yorkshire's 320 all out on the first day. M. J. Smith scored 106 when Middlesex declared 16 behind with five wickets left. The ball was in Yorkshire's court but seven wickets were down for 79 when Hampshire (74) and Nicholson (33) saved the day, batting for nearly 2½ hours together.

A further century from Boycott at Scarborough against Derbyshire with Padgett (59) and Leadbeater (69) giving him support enabled Yorkshire to declare at 349 for seven. Derbyshire followed on 190 behind but yet another rearguard action saved the match. At Bramall Lane, 105 not out from Hampshire and 63 from Padgett allowed Yorkshire to declare setting Gloucestershire 201 to win in 2¼ hours. Gloucestershire lost three wickets for 11 runs before Procter (111) and Bissex (50) added 114 and they went on to win by four wickets.

Draws at Dudley and Bramall Lane followed with Yorkshire saving the game at Dudley thanks to Andrew Dalton who scored 119 not out after Worcestershire had built a big lead. At Bramall Lane against Lancashire Boycott scored another monumental century – another 169 – while Hampshire scored 83. Rain again interfered with the game after Hutton had taken five for 58 to give Yorkshire a lead of 43.

Boycott was absent again at Canterbury for the Kent match and Hutton was also away. Old took five for 70 as Kent compiled 250, but after Sharpe and Leadbeater had opened with 32, Yorkshire lost twenty wickets while 188 runs were scored. Only Dalton with 30 in the second innings was able to bat confidently against Underwood or Norman Graham on a wet wicket.

The weather completely ruined the Glamorgan match at Swansea but Phil Sharpe came good with 172 not out and Doug Padgett made 133, the two adding 301 for the second wicket. For Yorkshire Don Wilson took five for 44 but after Glamorgan had followed on the weather broke. The return with Essex at Hull provided a game that was hardly a thrill for spectators. After losing the first day to rain, Essex declared at 153 for four after tea, and then Yorkshire were bowled out for 91. Essex collapsed in their turn for 87, Don Wilson taking six for 35, thus setting Yorkshire 150 to win in three hours. On that pitch it was quite a tall order, but Hampshire (32) gave Yorkshire hope. After two run-outs, however, Yorkshire gave up the chase with two overs left and still needing 15 to win. Yorkshire were ten behind at the close with their last men at the crease.

Nicholson took five for 54 when Leicestershire were dismissed for 204 at Park Avenue and then Boycott (151) and Hampshire (95) put Yorkshire on top, but again the bad weather persisted and Leicestershire finished at 53 for two in 38 overs in their second knock, still 68 runs behind. Wilson's second innings figures read: 10-10-0-2.

At Bournemouth after Turner (132) had put Hampshire in a strong position only Boycott made any sort of a show with 40 and 111 as Yorkshire went down by eight wickets. Sainsbury took six for 14 and five for 62. It was similar at The Oval where Graham Roope notched 171 out of Surrey's 381 and then Intikhab and Pocock took seven wickets each. Boycott did make 66 in the second innings and Richard Hutton 47 not out but Yorkshire lost by an innings and 12 runs. At Edgbaston Yorkshire put up a much better fight and went down only by 22 runs in a game they ought to have won. Kanhai (135) and Jameson (95) took Warwickshire to 354 for eight declared and when Yorkshire went in to bat, six wickets fell for 45 but Boycott steered the score to 232. Boycott made 138 not out and Yorkshire saved the follow-on. Warwickshire were then bowled out for 161, Tony Nicholson taking five for 48, thus setting Yorkshire 284 to win. Boycott (84) and Lumb (65) put on 134 for Yorkshire's first wicket and at 223 for five Yorkshire were still favourites but collapsed. That defeat left Yorkshire in 16th place with one game left.

Yorkshire finished the season with an overwhelming win over Northamptonshire at Harrogate inside two days. Hutton with four for 6 in 12 overs was the chief destroyer as Northamptonshire were dismissed for 61. Then Yorkshire replied with 266 for two, with Boycott not out 124, and Sharpe 92. Boycott had become the first Englishman to complete a season with a three-figure average – 100.12. In their second innings Northamptonshire were all out for 106 to lose by an innings and 99 runs. Thus Yorkshire finished in 13th place, the lowest position in the Club's history.

For Yorkshire, Boycott had scored 2,221 runs at an average of 105.76. John Hampshire had 1,259 runs to his name at 35.97. Sharpe was third with 34.29 and Padgett also notched over 800 runs – 866 at an average of 25.47. Hutton averaged 29 but Leadbeater's average was only 23 and the rest of the batting was disappointing.

Hutton, who could certainly be classed as an all-rounder, topped the bowling averages with 63 wickets at 17.65, while Wilson took 60 at 18.25, which was good too. Nicholson's 56 wickets cost over 26 runs each as did Bore's 44, while Old and Cope were by any standards below what was expected from them.

In the Gillette Cup, Kent put Yorkshire out in the first round at Canterbury, West Indians Julien and Shepherd bowling them out for 148. Yorkshire finished 16th in the John Player Sunday League, with only Boycott and Hampshire batting with much conviction.

Perhaps Yorkshire's one ray of hope was in the Minor Counties Championship which they won very comfortably and then beat Somerset 2nd XI in the Challenge match at Harrogate. Mike Bore took twelve for 127 in that match. Platt had captained the colts side very competently but he retired at the end of the season, and Doug Padgett would captain the 2nd XI in 1972 as well as acting as coach to the Club. Padgett had been a loyal member of the side for some 20 years and he would take a lot of replacing, although his form during the last season or two had deteriorated.

So ended the worst season in the Club's history both from a playing and a financial point of view. Season 1972 would start with a new secretary. Joe Lister, a former Yorkshire player, would take the place of John Nash, who would be retiring after 40 years' service as secretary. John Temple of York would take over the cricket sub-committee's chairmanship in succession to Brian Sellers. Geoffrey Boycott had been re-elected captain. Hopefully the side would not suffer from the horrendous injury problems of the past season.

The new season opened with a new limited-overs competition on the stocks. The Benson and Hedges Cup Competition was a 55-over affair. It resulted in the County Championship fixture list being shortened to 20 matches per team from 24.

Yorkshire began with an impressive win over Gloucestershire at Middlesbrough. The pitch was always helpful to the quicker bowlers who gained a fair amount of lift. Yorkshire's 185 was mainly due to Richard Hutton (57 not out). Old on his home ground took two for 37 in support of Nicholson (five for 55) and Richard Hutton (three for 22) and followed that up with three for 4 in 10 overs and a ball. Yorkshire's lead of 60 was extended by 173 thanks to Boycott (68) and Gloucestershire fell for 97 to lose by 126 runs. Richard Lumb took five catches in the second innings.

Richard Lumb, a tall, steady opening batsman in the classic style, had appeared once for Yorkshire in 1970 and gained a regular place in the side this season. Richard Lumb was an extremely talented batsman who specialised in the straight drive and the cover drive. In all matches for Yorkshire he scored 11,525 runs at an average of over 31, including 22 centuries. In 1983 he obtained over £50,000 from his benefit. He retired from county cricket after the 1984 season and emigrated to South Africa.

A Boycott century was recorded at Taunton against Somerset in a game spoilt by the weather after Hutton and Nicholson had bowled out Somerset for 242. Boycott also scored 105 at Headingley against Lancashire and more fine bowling from Nicholson (seven for 49) ensured a 63-run lead for Yorkshire. More rain meant a draw in Don Wilson's benefit match.

At Scarborough, John Hampshire with 111 took Yorkshire to a large score of 345 for eight declared. Glamorgan were dismissed for 86 with Hutton taking five for 27 and Nicholson four for 39. When asked to bat again, Nicholson took a further five for 32 and Yorkshire gained a first-rate victory by an innings and 124 runs before lunch on the third day.

Yorkshire's chances were ruined at Lord's by adverse weather but not before John Hampshire had scored 103, and the game at Bramall Lane against Derbyshire was confined to a one-innings match from which neither side gained a point. Old had taken five for 26 when Derbyshire were dismissed for 121. The return game at Chesterfield was also drawn, but Yorkshire gained a first innings lead of 140 thanks to Tony Nicholson's five for 49. They then took eight of Derbyshire's second-innings wickets. Rain also prevented Yorkshire beating Warwickshire, who scored only 60 in reply to the home side's 266, in which Lumb made top score (70). At the close Warwickshire were still 92 runs in arrears with four wickets down in the second innings. Rain also hindered Yorkshire's efforts at Worksop where Boycott scored 100 and 75 not out against Nottinghamshire, while Old followed his five for 41 there with five for 39 in Worcestershire's second innings a Bramall Lane but once again the weather won the day. Six consecutive draws had dropped Yorkshire from a promising leader's position to a comparatively lowly sixth place.

In the Derbyshire game at Chesterfield, Howard Cooper, who had played a few times in 1971 returned to the side. A hard-working medium-fast bowler who had persistent trouble with his back during his career, he gained a regular place in the Yorkshire team in 1973 and again in 1975, continuing to assist the side until 1980.

Cope's action was causing consternation in some quarters and Johnny Wardle took him in hand for a while in an effort to cure him. He was first reported to MCC for 'alleged throwing' in 1968 and received his cap in 1970 when his action again came under scrutiny. From 1974 to 1978 he was an important and regular member of the Yorkshire side and he continued to play for the County until 1980, when he had taken 630 wickets at 24.80 each. His bowling was considered good enough to earn him an England place in Pakistan. Misfortune dogged his career in other ways apart from his bowling action and he once returned from an overseas tour following the sudden death of his father. Through all his trials and tribulations, Cope remained a sincere, honest cricketer whose cheerful character invariably overcame any immediate irritability that might rear its ugly head. After leaving Yorkshire – he shared a benefit with Barrie Leadbeater in 1980 – he played for Lincolnshire for a season or two.

At Northampton, Yorkshire were still without their skipper with a split finger, and though they were only two runs behind on the first innings, Mushtaq Mohammad followed up his score of 90 with 119 in the second innings and Northamptonshire won comfortably enough by 151 runs. Surrey at The Oval dished out an innings defeat, mainly due to Intikhab whose leg-spinners accounted for 12 wickets for 82 runs. The game finished in two days.

Those two defeats dropped Yorkshire down to ninth place but worse was to follow at Old Trafford where Lancashire won by an innings and 34 runs. This was almost entirely due to Clive Lloyd's aggressive 181 followed by Jack Simmons' off-breaks, which accounted for ten for 84.

Inevitably, rain ruined the match at Park Avenue with Sussex but with Boycott back in the side Yorkshire surprisingly beat Surrey by nine wickets.

Boycott was back to form at Leicester with 204 not out from his side's 310 for seven declared. Leicestershire made little effort to attempt to score the 226 set them in 165 minutes. Against Essex at Chelmsford the skipper held sway again, scoring 121 and 86 but Essex scored faster throughout the match and deserved their six-wicket win. Needing 154 in the final twenty overs, they were helped by Keith Fletcher who batted magnificently to score 139 not out. Yorkshire were back to winning ways at Headingley against Middlesex with Andrew Dalton playing a mature role with 128 and 49. Producing every scoring shot in the book, he played one of the best middle-order innings by a Yorkshire player for several years. Its value was proved by the fact that no other batsman in the match reached 40. Cooper and Hutton both bowled well to take eight wickets.

Yorkshire came down to earth at Bradford, losing five wickets with only ten on the board. Kent's Luckhurst soon put the visitors in front with 109 as Kent built a first-innings lead of 264. Underwood was irresistible with eight for 70 as the match was completed inside two days.

Strengthened by the return of Boycott for the last match at Southampton, Yorkshire declared at 255 for three, with Boycott scoring 105 after putting on 181 with Richard Lumb (70) for the first wicket. In a match falling foul of the weather, Hampshire scored 147 and, following on, recovered to take their score to 224 for three. The Championship table was headed by Warwickshire, while Yorkshire finished tenth after at one time looking as though they might put up a fight for the title. Regrettably injuries again interfered with the side's performances and the batting averages were a somewhat sad reflection of the team's performances.

Boycott, although playing in less than half of Yorkshire's games, again headed the batting averages with 1,156 runs, average 96.33. Hampshire was second, averaging 30.96 and scoring 805 runs, with Lumb and Leadbeater next with a modest average of 27. Sharpe scored only 370 runs, average 21.

Chris Old headed the bowling averages with 54 wickets at 17.24, just ahead of Cope, who played in only nine games, while Nicholson had 62 wickets at 19.40. Hutton took 54 at 20.53 but Wilson was very disappointing, taking only 26 at 25.61 each. Bairstow kept wicket well but his batting was still irresponsible at times, although he was beginning to show some discretion.

Yorkshire lost to Warwickshire at Headingley in the first round of the Gillette Cup. In the Benson and Hedges Cup, Yorkshire qualified for the quarter-finals, losing only to Nottinghamshire at Trent Bridge and Sussex were beaten by five wickets at Park Avenue in the quarter-final. Gloucestershire were well beaten in the semi-final at Headingley by seven wickets with Boycott scoring 75 not out but he was unfit for the final at Lord's against Leicestershire. In this game Yorkshire, who had the worst of the conditions, were restricted to 136 for nine, only Leadbeater with 32 making much progress, and Leicestershire won comfortably by five wickets with Balderstone 41 not out.

Yorkshire did well in the John Player League, finishing in fourth position only four points behind the winners Kent. At one stage they lost four matches in a row but made a good recovery towards the end of the season. Barrie Leadbeater averaged 55.00 and scored 440 runs and was well ahead of his colleagues. With the ball Tony Nicholson took 24 wickets at 11.83.

Before the end of the season, Geoff Cope, in spite of extensive practise with his changed bowling action, still failed to satisfy the TCCB and there was a further worry for Yorkshire when Tony Nicholson injured his right leg and suffered a thrombosis, from which fortunately he recovered before the start of the next season.

Rain ruined the first game of 1973 at Edgbaston where Carrick took three for 64 and Boycott began well in his third season as captain with 86.

At Worcester, Sharpe, leading the team, scored 58 and 70, and Hampshire scored 80 not out in the second innings to set Worcestershire 294 to win. They fell short with 251 for six for the match to finish an even draw.

At Headingley, the game with Hampshire was completely dominated by Gordon Greenidge who scored 196 not out and was mainly responsible for his side's seven-wicket win. Yorkshire were then beaten at Cardiff after a couple of declarations. Though they bowled out Glamorgan for 97, with Phil Carrick taking five for 24, when set 163 to win they failed dismally against off-spinner Roger Davis, who took five for 12, and were routed for 98. Phil Carrick had already taken eight for 30 at Fenner's, where Boycott chipped in with 141 not out.

Phillip Carrick, who was still only 20, had first appeared for Yorkshire in three matches in 1970 and in 1973 gained a regular place in the Yorkshire team. A left-arm slow bowler of the orthodox variety, he suffered with the increase in limited-overs cricket by modifying his methods to suit all forms of cricket. Although far from a natural right-hand batsman, by sheer guts and fortitude he overcame any technical weaknesses to make himself into a good all-rounder in the team. He coached in South Africa in the mid-1970s and 1980s and appeared for both Eastern Province and Northern Transvaal. He was elected captain of Yorkshire in 1987 and 1988 and undertook a difficult task at the most difficult time in the Club's history with a certain panache that did credit to him. He did well to keep the ship afloat when it was expected to keel over.

Boycott (101) and Lumb (114) put on 178 for the first wicket at Old Trafford against Lancashire but Yorkshire had little success after declaring with seven wickets down for 286. Lancashire came within two runs of Yorkshire's score, and then Yorkshire collapsed for 69, Peter Lee taking five for 20. Yorkshire were fortunate that the rain set in to save them from certain defeat. At Middlesbrough Yorkshire gained an impressive innings victory over Northamptonshire, thanks mainly to Chris Old who usually does well on his home ground, taking nine wickets and scoring 66. Bairstow had seven victims behind the stumps.

A further victory over Somerset by nine wickets was mainly due to Tony Nicholson who took six for 44 as Somerset collapsed. Sharpe, captaining the side with Boycott on Test duty, scored a fine 133 and Colin Johnson recorded his first century for Yorkshire to enable them to declare at 320 for nine. Carrick then took five for 41 and Yorkshire won easily by nine wickets. That victory put Yorkshire into fourth place and in the next game at Chesterfield David Bairstow was rewarded his cap. It was spoilt by more adverse weather, but not before Sharpe had recorded another century while Bairstow, in celebration, scored 53 not out. Rain was also responsible for two more draws at Gloucester and against Leicestershire at Headingley, but Yorkshire had large deficits in both matches after the first innings.

Arnold Sidebottom made his first appearance aged 19 in the Gloucestershire match but was not called upon again until the 1975 season when he gained a regular place. A right-arm medium-fast bowler, he was extremely hard-working and could get lift and movement out of a pitch when other bowlers looked innocuous. Also a very talented and stylish batsman, he could well have got into the side as an opening batsman, but he was mostly needed for his pace bowling and he lacked the stamina to fill both roles. A professional footballer of great promise, he was a member of the strong Manchester United side for several seasons. He was capped in 1980 and was certainly the best bowler in the Yorkshire ranks for several years,

461

Arnie Sidebottom in action.

and his benefit in 1988 was a deserved success. He played once in Test cricket for England *v* Australia in 1985.

Another draw at Hove followed but this was due to a good pitch and some slow batting from Yorkshire's early batsmen, but Lumb's 103 in the second innings enabled Yorkshire to set Sussex 287 to win in three hours. Sussex only narrowly failed to achieve their target, finishing on 271 for five. Boycott returned for The Oval match, where Surrey dismissed Yorkshire for 60 and 43 in what was their worst batting display for 108 years. Jackman took seven for 36 in the first innings and Pocock six for 11 in the second. Surrey's margin of victory was an innings and 165 runs and Boycott, Lumb, Leadbeater, Hampshire and Sharpe all failed to reach double figures in either innings.

Boycott at this stage was coming in for severe criticism. Certainly nothing was going right for the team, and team spirit must have been very low after the Surrey game. The next game was at Park Avenue against Nottinghamshire, who scored 248 for nine declared and then took six wickets for 51 with Boycott still at the crease. With 111 for nine on the board, Mike Bore joined his captain and they succeeded in taking the score to 219 before Boycott was run out for a fine innings of 129. The game was drawn.

Geoff Cope returned for the Derbyshire match at Bramall Lane but after his action was passed as satisfactory it was again called into question later in the season. Derbyshire were dismissed for 117 and Lumb's 51 helped Yorkshire to a first innings lead of 93, before Bolus with 138 took Derbyshire to 284 for seven declared. Yorkshire knocked off the target of 192 for the loss of six wickets.

The Lancashire match at Bramall Lane was the last first-class match to take place on the ground and it proved to be a damp squib of a game, remembered from a playing point of view for Nicholson taking four for 40 and Phil Sharpe scoring 35 and 62 not out. A sad occasion for all.

Kent at Canterbury provided another draw after Yorkshire declined a target in $3\frac{3}{4}$ hours. Moving up to Lord's, lacking Old Boycott and Nicholson, Yorkshire were dismissed for 174 with only Lumb making much headway with 67. J. M. Brearley made 134 and Radley and Smith 99 each before Middlesex declared at 410 for three. In their second innings Yorkshire were going well at 148 for two but the side collapsed after that and were all out for 190.

At Scarborough Bruce Francis made 188 not out in Essex's second innings to set Yorkshire 238 to win in 165 minutes but they were not capable of scoring quickly enough after losing three for 49 and played out time for a draw. At Headingley Surrey made 184 with Robinson taking five for 54. In reply Yorkshire could muster only 90 and Surrey were well on top with Edrich (109) helping them to 247 for three before declaring. Yorkshire, needing 342 to win, eventually reached 299 with Sharpe scoring 68, Hampshire 66 and Johnson 50.

For the last match of the season at Park Avenue, Yorkshire had a very weak side out and introduced Graham Stevenson into the side for the first time. Aged 17 he was an aggressive right-hand batsman and right-arm medium-fast bowler with a fine easy action. He began well by dismissing Brearley and Radley as his first two first-class victims and with Nicholson at his best taking five for 23, Middlesex scored only 102. Yorkshire did little better, collapsing 106 for nine declared. A 'flu bug hit the Yorkshire seamers in the Middlesex second innings which reached 211. Yorkshire required 208 to win and Colin Johnson (78) and Bairstow (56) helped the score to 192 for nine, when Middlesex were clear favourites but Cooper and Robinson levelled the scores before Selvey clean bowled Robinson in a thrilling tied match.

Stevenson became a regular member of the Yorkshire side in 1977 and was capped in the following season, but though he did play in two Test matches he never advanced to the standard expected. In some eyes he had as much natural talent as Ian Botham, but the weaknesses he had as a teenager were still with him when he left Yorkshire after the 1986 season. He then joined Northamptonshire without success. Stevenson suffered with various injuries and latterly he had a tendency to put on weight, with the result that he was not as fit as he should have been. He never received a benefit with Yorkshire.

The tie against Middlesex meant that Yorkshire finished in 14th position in the Championship table which meant that it was again the worst season in the Club's history.

The batting averages were again headed by Boycott but he missed ten out of the 20 matches while taking part in Test matches. That is a ridiculous situation and it has been one of the reasons why first-class county cricket has been steadily deteriorating over the years and has become less popular. Sharpe had a good season with the bat, scoring 1,320 runs, average 38.82, and Hampshire and Lumb did reasonably well with Hampshire missing his thousand by 75 runs and Lumb scoring 1,002 with an average of 29.47. Leadbeater had a very poor season and Hutton failed with both bat and ball.

Chris Old took 34 wickets at 18.67 to head the averages just ahead of the hard-working Nicholson, who was not always 100 per cent fit but stuck manfully to his task. He took 65 wickets at 18.95. Cooper took 39 wickets; Robinson 24 and Bore 41 at a higher cost. Cope scarcely played at all but his newly formed action was declared satisfactory at the end of the season. Neither did Wilson play often, and Carrick looked the pick of the spinners.

Yorkshire, regrettably, created history by losing to a minor county in the Gillette Cup at Harrogate. Brian Lander took five for 15 as Yorkshire struggled to 135, and Durham had plenty of overs left as they cruised home by five wickets. In the John Player League, Yorkshire had their best season to date and finished second to Kent. They bowled and fielded well throughout the season. Hampshire, with 668 runs at 55.66, was the pick of the batsmen. In the Benson and Hedges Cup, Yorkshire just failed to qualify for the quarter-finals.

There was an air of optimism within the Club, with the financial aspect a little better, and there was action to provide Sheffield with a ground to replace Bramall Lane. A fund was set up inviting businesses to pledge certain sums of money. Sir Kenneth Parkinson had become the new president in succession to Sir William Worsley, who had died at the end of 1973.

The new season (1974) saw the 100-over limit placed on the first innings of each side, but if a side could bowl out the opposition in fewer, they could claim the 'unused' overs, e.g. if a side was bowled out in 80 overs; then their opponents could bat for 120 overs. It was another form of limited-overs cricket which the far-sighted Law-makers were inflicting on a mostly unwilling membership who knew the consequences of such changes but could do little about them.

In the first match at Northampton, Richard Lumb batted throughout the 100 overs to score 123 not out, while Hutton, back in the side on a full-time basis, gave most support with 47 in 265 for eight. Northamptonshire were restricted to 250 for eight in their allocation.

Boycott fell twice to Sarfraz in this game and some lamentable Yorkshire batting saw them dismissed for 105. Northamptonshire gained a two-wicket win with Cope – now cleared to bowl with his satisfactory action – taking four for 45.

Bad weather ruined the Warwickshire match at Abbeydale Park, to make it a doleful start for Yorkshire's first match at their new home. Lancashire batted slowly at Headingley to compile 250, but Yorkshire batted even slower, with the over-rate of Lever and Shuttleworth making this a depressing match for spectators. Shuttleworth took seven for 61. Lancashire batted much better at their second attempt to reach 213 for seven declared. Set 244 in $3\frac{1}{2}$ hours, Yorkshire made no effort to win and Boycott was 79 not out at the close. It was a match in which detractors of Boycott's captaincy were given ammunition to use against him in the future. Yorkshire's 124 for three provided very poor watching to spectators, Lever and Shuttleworth would have bowled their overs so slowly anyway that Yorkshire's task would have proved impossible the fact remains that Yorkshire made no effort at any time to go for the runs. It was that attitude that rankled with members and cricket lovers whether they were Boycott's detractors or not.

Another draw followed at The Oval where Yorkshire without Boycott and Old on Test duty, made 179. Surrey were dismissed for 204, Arthur Robinson taking six for 61, and in their second innings Yorkshire batted much better to declare at 263 for seven, but Surrey made no attempt to go for the runs. A weakened side at Bath was rescued by Richard Hutton (102 not out), with Yorkshire scoring 274 for seven inside the hundred overs. Somerset's innings went on similar lines, Viv Richards batting brilliantly for 107 (his second century). Unfortunately, Yorkshire collapsed in their second knock and Somerset won easily enough by seven wickets. Dropped catches certainly helped the home side. By now Yorkshire were at the foot of the Championship table and were in dire straits.

Boycott was back to form at Sheffield with 149 not out out of 251 for four, and Yorkshire did well to bowl out Derbyshire for 152. Yorkshire set Derbyshire 299 to win in 5 hours 20 minutes. Bearing in mind the slowness of the Derbyshire batting, it was not a venturous declaration and they were never up with the clock, ending at 260 for seven.

A spinner's wicket up at Middlesbrough surprised the players with only Boycott (24 and 63) able to cope with Titmus, who took 14 wickets. Middlesex did little better against Cope (seven for 101 and two for 13) but in Norman Featherstone, Middlesex had the match-winner as he obtained a century, and Middlesex won easily by eight wickets. In similar circumstances at Leicester, off-spinner Birkenshaw bowled Yorkshire out for 108, but it was Illingworth who took the crucial wicket of Boycott. When Leicester batted Balderstone scored 83 and his side went 112 ahead. Balderstone then took four for 25 and McKenzie broke Boycott's finger, so that Leicestershire won very comfortably by seven wickets.

Geoff Cope's 43 was top score against Glamorgan at Scarborough. Yorkshire were 40 for six when Cope went out to bat and he enabled them to declare at 162 for nine. Glamorgan replied with 110 for nine before rain ruined the rest of the game. Yorkshire's misfortunes continued at Hull where, under Hampshire's captaincy, Yorkshire were dismissed for 101 with Hampshire (48) alone capable of withstanding the accurate Worcestershire attack. Worcestershire were 57 for five but Basil D'Oliveira played an epic innings of 227 in six hours and paved the way for an innings win. Only Hampshire (87) in the second innings, was exempt from criticism.

There was talk now of Boycott being removed from the captaincy and another action group was considering getting under way again. The committee denied the rumour, and with Boycott returning to lead the side at Worksop, Yorkshire gained an emphatic first Championship win of the season over Nottinghamshire by an innings and 69 runs. Smedley, another Yorkshireman, made top score in each innings for Nottinghamshire as they collapsed on a rain-affected wicket, with Denis Schofield, making his last appearance for Yorkshire and only brought in due to Nicholson's injury, taking five for 42, while Arthur Robinson took five for 27. After Yorkshire lost two early wickets, Hampshire batted superbly to make 157 not out and gave his side a lead of 156. Cope (five for 34) and Don Wilson (five for 36) bowled well to dismiss Nottinghamshire for 57. That victory was followed by another innings win over Gloucestershire at Harrogate in even more emphatic manner. Batting first Yorkshire scored 406 for eight in less than 100 overs thanks to John Hampshire (158) who has rarely batted so well. Leadbeater (60) and Bairstow (68) gave him good support and when Gloucestershire batted they were all out for 71 with newcomer Steve Oldham taking three for 7. Yorkshire won by an innings and 165 runs, and these two victories took Yorkshire up to tenth place in the table.

At Lord's a stand of 192 between M. J. Smith (105) and J. M. Brearley (163 not out) put Middlesex on top as they scored 303 for three in their allotted span of overs and Yorkshire finished 76 behind on the first innings. Middlesex then declared at 215 for five, setting Yorkshire 292 to win. Boycott did score 71 and Nicholson reached 50 but the spin attack was always on top and Yorkshire conceded defeat by 104 runs.

Steve Oldham, a right-arm medium-fast bowler, played twice for

Yorkshire in 1974, but it was 1978 before he gained a regular place in the side. Offered terms by Derbyshire, he spent four years in their side but returned to play a few games for Yorkshire in 1984. He eventually became captain of the Yorkshire 2nd XI and was employed as assistant coach to the Club.

In the Lancashire match at Old Trafford Boycott and Lumb opened with a stand of 130, but at the end of 100 overs Yorkshire had reached only 263 for six, with Hampshire scoring 63 not out. Tony Nicholson, with five for 75, caused Lancashire to collapse and they reached only 216 for nine. In the end Lancashire were set 224 to win but soon fell behind the clock and they finished at 169 for five. Defeat at Leyton followed with only Boycott (68) showing any batting form, Richard Hutton took six for 85 as Essex compiled 313 to set up a win by an innings and 19 runs. Boyce with 75 was top scorer for Essex.

The Sussex match at Headingley was played in depressing conditions with Boycott and Lumb starting the game with a stand of 104, which they repeated in the second innings. Boycott had scores of 117 and 49 not out, but there was little else to give pleasure to spectators with Sussex having even less appetite for the game in adverse conditions.

Boycott (69) and Lumb (100) again gave Yorkshire a good start at Chesterfield and they finally reached 254 for eight in their 100 overs. Derbyshire were then bowled out for 199 with Carrick bowling well to take six for 48 which he followed up with four for 69 as Derbyshire, set 267 to win, failed dismally. The Kent match which followed was noteworthy for Barrie Leadbeater finishing the Yorkshire innings on 99 not out although the Kent side combined with Cope in trying to give the Leeds batsman his first century in first-class cricket. Colin Cowdrey batted well in each innings with 122 and 57 not out but in the end rain put a win for either side out of the question after an evenly contested game.

Yorkshire's win over Surrey at Park Avenue by an innings and two runs was due mainly to a stand between Boycott (142 not out) and Hampshire (74), who added 136 for the third wicket and took Yorkshire to 343 for five in reply to Surrey's 204. Carrick bowled at his best in Surrey's second innings to take six for 43. The final game at Bournemouth was abandoned without a ball being bowled with the result that Yorkshire finished a modest 11th in the Championship.

Yorkshire had played three extra matches during the season, thrashing the two Universities and having the best of the match with the Indians, against whom Chris Old scored 116 and took seven for 88 in the match.

In his benefit year Geoffrey Boycott again headed the batting averages with 1,478 runs at an average of 59.12. No one else reached his thousand but John Hampshire, who missed several matches with injury, did score 901 runs at an average of 53, while Leadbeater scored 804 at an average of 29.77. Lumb had a mixed season but was presented with his cap at the end of August and Chris Old averaged 25 as well as heading the bowling averages with 46 wickets at 16 apiece. He was frequently missing because of Test calls, while Carrick, with 47 wickets at 17.87, improved enough to make his place secure at Wilson's expense. Cope was Yorkshire's leading wicket-taker with 77 wickets at 21.83, while Robinson and Nicholson both had their days of success. Wilson and Hutton had disappointing seasons, as also did Sharpe, and all three were playing their last seasons for Yorkshire. Sharpe, who scored only 474 runs at an average of 17.55, did catch as well as ever and maintained his catch-a-match average throughout his career.

The Gillette Cup saw Yorkshire reach the second round where once again the flashing blade of Clive Lloyd (90) proved to be their undoing, and then Peter Lever took four for 17, dismissing the two main batsmen, Boycott and Hampshire, in their thirties. Lancashire won by 32 runs.

Yorkshire finished sixth equal in the Sunday League with their crop of seven seamers all performing ably. Perhaps their best moment came at Headingley against Middlesex who were dismissed for 23. In the Benson and Hedges Cup, Yorkshire again qualified for the quarter-finals but lost to Surrey at The Oval by 24 runs.

FALSE HOPES

LACKING THREE SENIOR PLAYERS and with Boycott re-appointed for a fifth year, Yorkshire members were filled with a mixture of hope and foreboding as the 1975 season commenced. Boycott could be playing regularly for Yorkshire as he had decided to forego representative cricket. It had been increasingly obvious that continuity of leadership was a necessity for any side if its main aim was to win something, and other counties were finding this out annually and would continue to do so.

By the end of May, Yorkshire had chalked up five draws mainly because of the poor weather. Richard Lumb started well with 82 against Surrey and followed this with 51 at Dartford against Kent. Boycott scored 152 not out against Worcestershire to complete a set of centuries against all the other counties. When Worcestershire batted they declared 101 behind Yorkshire, but finally declined the target of 273 in 110 minutes. It all seemed rather pointless, as Yorkshire's hopes of bowling Worcestershire out in anything like that time seemed pretty remote. Lancashire established a 42-run lead at Old Trafford on the first innings and then Yorkshire, thanks to Boycott (92) and Leadbeater (82), were able to declare at 285 for seven. On a slow wicket Lancashire declined to attempt 244 in 165 minutes. Old scored 115 not out against Leicestershire at Park Avenue and then took five for 32 as Leicester finished 102 behind on the first innings. Rain prevented any further progress in the match.

Surprisingly, Yorkshire then thrashed Gloucestershire at Bristol by an innings and 122 runs in a game that only just went into the third day. They bowled out Gloucestershire for only 131 and then Boycott and Lumb put on 228 for Yorkshire's first wicket. Boycott scored 141, Lumb 101 and then Hampshire scored a brilliant 106 not out as he and Leadbeater (68 not out) put on 171 in an unbroken third-wicket stand. Still 215 in arrears Gloucestershire batted a little better but Cope finished with the fine figures of eight for 73.

At Scarborough, Yorkshire's scourge Norman Featherstone with 147 and 61 made top score in each innings. Middlesex made 351 for seven in 100 overs but Yorkshire finished only 23 behind thanks to Boycott's 175 not out. He put on 186 with Lumb (88) for Yorkshire's first wicket. Middlesex were dismissed for 173 and Yorkshire were left with only 196 to win, although the pitch was becoming less reliable. Yorkshire lost five wickets with only 47 on the board but got within 20 runs of victory.

Warwickshire at Edgbaston batted poorly and struggled to 158.

Yorkshire gained a lead of 98 thanks to Boycott with 66 and then Warwickshire in their second innings gave a much better display and Yorkshire were set 183 to win in 165 minutes. Boycott with 64 in an hour soon had them on the path to victory and Lumb (72 not out) guided them home for a nine-wicket win.

Another century opening stand between Boycott (61) and Lumb (59) put Yorkshire on the victory path at Abbeydale Park after Arthur Robinson had taken five for 56 in Hampshire's 174. Carrick then bowled Hampshire out a second time for 212 by taking six for 83, while Lumb added a further half-century as Yorkshire won again by nine wickets.

Then came a remarkable game against Somerset at Harrogate on a good wicket which eventually turned to spin. Yorkshire scored 387 all out in less than 100 overs thanks to a fine 115 from John Hampshire. In their 100 overs, Somerset passed this and made 423 for seven with Richards and Close adding 227 for the fifth wicket. Vivian Richards made a remarkable 217 not out and Close 91, Old (86) and Bairstow (72 not out) then added 115 for Yorkshire's fifth wicket and Yorkshire set Somerset 300 to win in two hours, a task that they never attempted. They collapsed in alarming fashion and at the close were 116 for nine with Cope taking five for 25.

A two-wicket win at Hove put Yorkshire very close to the leaders and gave hopes of finishing on top. Chris Old with five for 81 was instrumental in Sussex reaching only 228 but Yorkshire were in a poor state at 72 for five before Old (49), Sidebottom (69) and Carrick (41) gave Yorkshire a 36-run lead. Sussex made 230. Yorkshire lost eight wickets in attaining their 195 target but John Hampshire (53) and stand-in opener Cope (39) led them to a hard-earned win.

The match at Chesterfield was drawn owing to poor weather with Yorkshire only 19 runs in front with eight wickets down in their second innings. Bob Taylor took nine catches for Derbyshire. At this stage of the season, Yorkshire were 22 points behind Lancashire in fifth position.

In this match Alan Hampshire, younger brother of John, made his one and only appearance for Yorkshire.

Jim Love also made his first appearances for Yorkshire. A powerful middle-order batsman who scores very quickly when set, he has over the years met with great success in one-day matches, including the Benson and Hedges Cup Final in 1987. He gained a regular place in the Yorkshire side in 1977 and earned his cap in 1980 going on to take his benefit in 1989. A qualified coach, he has played and coached both in South Africa and Australia. An easy-going individual, he perhaps required a little more steel in his make-up to really force himself into the reckoning at Test level and his fielding and catching were not quite as good as they perhaps should have been. For Yorkshire he proved himself a valuable member of the team.

The Nottinghamshire match at Abbeydale was a remarkable game with Yorkshire leading by 101 after each side had bowled their 100 overs and gained only four wickets each in the process. Boycott, who scored 139, put on 158 for the first wicket with Lumb (54). When Nottinghamshire batted Hassan and Smedley both reached fifties in laborious fashion. Yorkshire then scored 137 for one with Lumb making 69 not out to set Nottinghamshire 239 to win. A draw was anticipated but Nottinghamshire batted so badly that they were all out for 66.

Another remarkable win at The Oval was as welcome as it was unexpected. Richard Lumb batted well to score 118, and he added 216 for the third wicket with John Hampshire, who attacked the bowling with great power and authority. The fine Oval pitch continued to assist batsmen's strokemaking and Surrey came within 15 runs of Yorkshire's 383. Geoff Cope's long bowling spell garnered five for 123. Boycott (78) and Old (65) took Yorkshire to 251 for eight before declaring and Surrey were set 267 to win in three hours. At 201 for four Surrey were on the road to victory, but hitting out before they had their eye in proved fatal to the later Surrey batsmen and they fell 35 runs short. The win placed Yorkshire back on top of the Championship table for the first time for many years. There were six matches to go for Yorkshire but the other counties had either one or two matches in hand.

Victories over Derbyshire at Scarborough and Middlesex at Lord's kept Yorkshire on top to keep the tussle very open. Howard Cooper, with six for 44, caused Derbyshire all sorts of trouble but Yorkshire were in equal trouble at 118 for seven until Carrick, with 87, helped them gain a useful lead of 86. Sharpe (61) and Page (89) took Derbyshire to 132 for one but Carrick went through the rest of the batting and finished with a remarkable eight for 72. It proved an easy victory for Yorkshire. Boycott played a brilliant 201 not out at Lord's, putting on 182 with Lumb (77). Middlesex finished only 51 short in their allotted overs in reply to Yorkshire's 376 for four, with Radley making 152 not out. Yorkshire collapsed in their second innings for 106, John Emburey taking six for 46. Cope was also successful, but Middlesex took their score to 148 for five and appeared certain of victory. Three run-outs then swung things Yorkshire's way and victory was theirs by five runs. Cope took five for 63.

At Cardiff, Cooper was again at his best as he took eight for 62 of Glamorgan's total of 192, and Yorkshire gained a lead of 95. Glamorgan were still 17 in arrears when the third day's play was washed out. Yorkshire's lead was now 14 points but the other teams in

471

contention did have a game in hand. Perhaps inevitably the Lancashire match at Headingley had to finish in a draw. Only 17 wickets fell in the three days, which contained a wretched over-rate throughout with neither side taking any risk. Lancashire made 340 for five but Yorkshire were very slow in reply and actually declared when 139 behind. Another Lancashire declaration at 191 for three setting Yorkshire 331 in 260 minutes. Not an impossible task on a plumb wicket, but Yorkshire finished on 219 for one, with Boycott 105 not out. There was little prospect of Yorkshire getting the runs with such an appalling over-rate but to score only 83 off the first 30 overs was hardly a good advertisement for cricket. Yorkshire's lead had now been cut to two points over Hampshire and the latter still had a game in hand.

Park Avenue saw Yorkshire return to winning ways with a 78-run victory over Northamptonshire. A total of 178 was a poor start, but Northamptonshire lead was only 12 runs as Cope captured six for 69. Yorkshire reached 192 in their second innings due to 71 from Boycott. Cope (four for 47) and Carrick (five for 39) then caused a collapse on a pitch that gave little help to spin. Yorkshire's lead was now one point, but Leicestershire then won their game in hand and so went 17 points ahead.

Yorkshire's last match was at Middlesbrough against Essex, whereas Leicestershire had to visit Chesterfield where they defeated Derbyshire by 135 runs and so won the Championship for the first time in their history. Yorkshire gained their win by 59 runs and so clinched the runners-up poistion; their best season since 1968. Boycott (92) and Colin Johnson (85) added 163 for Yorkshire's second wicket and with Old taking five for 57 ensured a lead of 116 for Yorkshire. Old then got on top of the Essex spin attack to score 57 not out and left Essex 327 to win. Only Neil Smith offered much resistance and he had the satisfaction of scoring a century against his old county.

The batting was certainly more reliable than for several years. Boycott as usual headed the batting averages with 1,915 runs at 73.65, while Old had a very good season when available. He averaged 43.88 with the bat, scoring 790 runs, and with the ball took 47 wickets at 21.19. A very satisfactory season for him. Lumb and Hampshire both passed their thousand runs and averaged over 40. Of the others, Johnson, Carrick and Bairstow all batted well at times.

Tony Nicholson was nominally head of the bowling averages but he was plagued by injury most of the time and was not to appear for Yorkshire again. Phil Carrick with 79 wickets at 21.17 bowled very well in tandem with Cope, who had 69 wickets at 21.86, and was free from cameras and other torments concerning his action. Cooper and Robinson both performed satisfactorily and young Sidebottom and the even younger Stevenson gave great hope for the future with their limited opportunities. Bairstow's wicket-keeping was first-rate and he showed improvement standing up to the wicket while his batting talent was beginning to manifest itself.

Yorkshire lost by one wicket in the first round of the Gillette Cup; an unbeaten last wicket stand of 25 between McKenzie and Higgs taking the visitors, Leicestershire, to victory. Yorkshire topped their group in the Benson and Hedges Cup, but at Lord's, in the quarter-final, Middlesex got home in the last over by four wickets.

In the John Player Sunday League Yorkshire finished in sixth equal position but were never in contention for the title. Boycott and Hampshire each with over 600 runs were a reliable opening pair and Squires showed his value in the one-day game with some useful innings and some brilliant outfielding. Stevenson and Cooper both took wickets at a good average and there were some very tight matches as usual. At second team level Yorkshire finished fourth in the Second Eleven Competition and went through the season unbeaten.

A peaceful winter followed the 1975 season and hopes were high for the new season. Tony Nicholson would be missed, but Yorkshire seemed to have several capable seamers particularly if they kept a fit and settled side.

The opening match at Headingley was played on the type of pitch suitable for ten-day cricket in which 1,221 runs were scored for the loss of 15 wickets. For Yorkshire, Johnson, Hampshire, Boycott and Lumb all scored centuries, and for Gloucestershire Zaheer and Sadiq did likewise.

A visit to Ilford saw Essex win by nine wickets. The Essex pace attack was too good for Yorkshire, all out 113 in their first innings, and Essex gained a lead of 211 runs. Yorkshire were bowled out again for 228 with only Lumb (118) resisting the Essex attack for long.

Five matches without a win followed, but only Surrey at The Oval gained a victory. Old returned to the side and scored 112 against Northamptonshire, and then Cooper with seven for 72 gave Yorkshire a lead of 58 as Northamptonshire reached 180. Northamptonshire were left with 216 to win in three hours, but in the end had to be satisfied with a total of 155 for eight. After the Lancashire match had been spoilt by the weather, came the defeat at The Oval in which Yorkshire had a first innings lead of 28 after John Hampshire had hit well for 133, but Surrey recovered to win by three wickets. At this stage Yorkshire were without Boycott with a broken hand and missed him until the middle of July.

The Hampshire game was notable for two important events. One was the vandalisation of the pitch after the first day which necessitated a new pitch being cut for the Monday. Hampshire had scored 391 for nine in their 100 overs. In reply Yorkshire failed to save the follow-on. In their second innings, Hampshire (87), Old (63 not out) and Johnson (62) all helped Barrie Leadbeater to take Yorkshire's total to 389 for four before declaring. The other matter of importance in the game was a century from Leadbeater, who finished with 140 not out. It was a monumental innings lasting $6\frac{1}{2}$ hours and remained his one and only century in first-class cricket. Hampshire did not attempt the target set by Yorkshire. In the next game at Abbeydale Park, Derbyshire batted very badly to score only 64. With some six hours lost to the weather Yorkshire reached 138, a lead of 74, but Derbyshire batted out the rest of the match for 174 for six in 138 overs.

In the eighth game of the season against Kent at Harrogate, Yorkshire gained their first victory when Kent were thrashed by an innings and 27 runs. Yorkshire scored 322 for seven with Hampshire (74) and Athey (70 not out) adding 104 for the fourth wicket. On a turning pitch Kent were dismissed for 114 and 181, Carrick taking eight for 101 and Cope nine for 95 in the match.

The Sussex match at Headingley was another disappointing game with Sussex making no effort to score 302 in $3\frac{1}{2}$ hours – by no means a generous declaration set by Yorkshire's skipper, Hampshire. Hampshire with 113 and 72 not out was Yorkshire's chief run-getter while in the second innings Bill Athey scored his first century for the county – 132 not out.

C. W. J. ('Bill') Athey was an attractive batsman usually going in early in the order. He had all the strokes at his disposal, if occasionally he played some injudicious ones and had a habit of getting out lbw. He was capped in 1980 and went on to play for the County until 1983, scoring 6,320 runs at a disappointing average of 28. He also fielded well at slip, could keep wicket adequately and was a useful seam bowler. For most of his early career he was a member of an unhappy side and this probably affected his form. He played grade cricket in Australia, having toured Canada at the end of the 1976 season, and later coached in South Africa and appeared for Orange Free State in 1981/82. He joined Gloucestershire in 1984 and batted very consistently from the start. He played for England on several occasions but failed to do himself justice at that level.

A disappointing display by Yorkshire at Worksop resulted in a three-wicket defeat after Yorkshire had led by 106 on the first innings. Nottinghamshire were set 260 to win and Clive Rice (95 not out) steered them to a comfortable victory. Cope took five not 104 for Yorkshire.

In the next match at Park Avenue a splendid game with Middlesex resulted in a very tight finish. Yorkshire soon lost three for 17 before, Love driving cleanly, scored 77. Yorkshire finished 22 ahead on the first innings with Geoff Cope taking six for 60 at a time when there was further speculation about the validity of his action. Yorkshire, without Lumb who had to retire injured for 17, struggled to a score of 214. Middlesex, whose Clive Radley had an arm in a sling and who had been unable to bat first innings, were set 237 to win, and at 230 for seven the game seemed as good as over, but Yorkshire won by one run. The unfortunate Radley came out to bat one-handed, but after making three was stumped off Cope by Bairstow. Cope had five for 107 and Bore four for 83. Mike Bore at this stage of his career was bowling after the fashion of Underwood on pitches that took spin. The much-needed victory shot Yorkshire up to eighth place in the table.

Somerset recovered to accumulate 259 but Boycott, back in the team after injury, Hampshire and the hard-hitting Stevenson ensured Yorkshire a lead of 31 on the first innings. When Somerset batted again, Steve Oldham took five for 47 and Yorkshire's target of 163 was comfortably attained with five wickets in hand.

In fifth position and in good heart, Yorkshire went to Edgbaston and on a good wicket batted disappointingly after Boycott had scored 71. Fortunately the tail wagged and with Stevenson knocking up 60, Yorkshire reached 318. Warwickshire batted well to reach 393 for three inside their span of 102 overs, John Whitehouse scoring 169 not out and Rohan Kanhai 111 not out in an unbroken fourth-wicket stand of 266. Apart from Carrick (52) Yorkshire batted indifferently in the second innings and were all out for 212. Warwickshire won very easily by seven wickets. A further disappointing display at Scarborough finished in a dull draw with Yorkshire failing to force the pace in their second innings and then setting an unlikely target. Carrick with 66 alone passed fifty for Yorkshire while Arthur Robinson took five for 78 in Worcestershire's first innings, for whom the Harrogate-born Boyns made the top score of the match with 95.

A stand of 228 between Phil Sharpe (126) and Alan Hill (151 not out) helped Derbyshire to 325 for five before they had to close their innings and Yorkshire were in real trouble at 46 for five. Cope, Bairstow and Stevenson (83 in 84 minutes) took Yorkshire to 251. A declaration set Yorkshire 271 in 225 minutes. Boycott scored 73 and Squires 40 not out but a slow overrate did not help Yorkshire's cause as they batted out time at 175 for four.

Geoff Boycott (141) and Jim Love (163) put on 243 for Yorkshire's second wicket at Park Avenue against Nottinghamshire. It was Love's first century for Yorkshire and he drove particularly well on a fast wicket. Yorkshire reached 415 for seven in their 100 overs and Nottinghamshire in reply made 349 for six. When Yorkshire batted again, Richard Lumb with 87 and Peter Squires (70) helped Yorkshire to a declaration score of 210 for eight which left Nottinghamshire 277 to win. Cope took five for 46 and Yorkshire's victory was never in doubt as they bowled Nottinghamshire out for 181.

A visit to Leicester saw the home team run out easy winners by 152 runs on a pitch that always had something in it for the bowlers. Leicestershire were restricted to 242 for eight but dismissed Yorkshire for 85, and though they batted better second time round to reach 227, they were well beaten.

Two separate centuries from Glamorgan's Alan Jones could not prevent a seven-wicket victory for Yorkshire at Middlesbrough on a perfect batting track in which only 21 wickets fell in the three days for 1,339 runs. David Bairstow with 106 helped to give Yorkshire a three-run lead before Glamorgan declared at 320 for three, leaving Yorkshire 318 to win in $3\frac{1}{4}$ hours. Aided by some poor Glamorgan fielding, Boycott batted extremely well to score 156 not out as Yorkshire won easily.

At Old Trafford there was always something in the pitch for the bowlers. Yorkshire obtained 260 thanks to Hampshire who made 83 and Carrick 57; Peter Lee took five for 75. Lancashire struggled even more and Yorkshire gained a lead of 93. A timely Boycott century allowed Yorkshire to declare at 174 for six and Lancashire's chances of obtaining 268 to win always seemed remote. In the end they were dismissed for 158 with Geoff Cope doing most of the damage with six for 37.

Northamptonshire, at Scarborough, did not provide the finale to the season that Yorkshire followers hoped for. Geoff Cook provided the backbone of their innings of 323 by compiling a solid 117. Yorkshire's reply was a patchy 200. Northamptonshire declared at 209 for seven and Yorkshire collapsed again to lose by 198 runs. Yorkshire finishing a disappointing eighth in the table.

The averages make interesting reading, with Boycott on top of the batting with 1,288 runs at 67.78 (but he did obtain 248 of those against Cambridge University without being dismissed). Hampshire was second with 1,303 runs at an average of 44.93. Old, who played in only eight matches averaged 41.00 and he only took 20 wickets at 23.85 each. (Remarkably, in the County Championship his figures were seven for 310; not a great contribution towards Yorkshire's cause.) Leadbeater averaged 37 but played in only ten matches, as did Love (average 30), but Lumb had a very poor season with the bat.

Robinson's 43 wickets cost 23.39 each, but Cope was the best bowler with 87 wickets at 24.58 and was rewarded with a deserved trip to India. Carrick's 59 wickets cost 32.74 each, and Cooper and Oldham took their wickets at 31 and 26 each respectively.

After beating Shropshire in the first round of the Gillette Cup,

Yorkshire fell at home to Gloucestershire by four wickets, Zaheer Abbas notching 111 for the visitors.

In the John Player League, Yorkshire fell away to 15th. Boycott, Hampshire and Lumb all had reasonable batting averages but the bowling, apart from Old and Oldham, was expensive. Nor did Yorkshire make any progress in the Benson and Hedges Cup and actually lost to the Combined Universities at Barnsley.

Soon after the end of the season. Arthur Robinson and Phillip Carrick were awarded their county caps, but Peter Squires' contract was not renewed.

Geoffrey Boycott retained the captaincy for the 1977 season with the first three games ruined by the weather. Robinson took five for 28 as Leicestershire were dismissed for 67 and Yorkshire were well in command before the weather broke again. David Steele helped Northamptonshire to a respectable 235 and at the end of the match Yorkshire were 113 for six, of which Bill Athey had scored a brilliant 85 not out.

On the lively Abbeydale track, Surrey were all out for 171 and Yorkshire took a 108-run lead. Chris Old then routed Surrey with six for 36 to give Yorkshire victory by an innings and eight runs. Yorkshire, at this stage of the season, were equal top with Northamptonshire who they were to meet in their next match.

At Park Avenue, Graham Stevenson, with five for 68, was mainly responsible for the visitors reaching only 186. Boycott (70) and Lumb (44) put on 109 for Yorkshire's first wicket but no one else got going against Mushtaq's leg-spinners and Yorkshire's lead of only 87 was soon wiped out, and with Larkins (110) in fine form Northampton-shire declared at 303 for six. Set 213 in 39 overs, Boycott (74) and Hampshire (58) put on 135 for Yorkshire's first wicket and they romped home with seven balls to spare. A further success followed at Sophia Gardens, as Glamorgan were dismissed for 149. Boycott and Lumb then put on 84 for the first wicket but the side collapsed to 149 for nine before Sidebottom (124) and Robinson (30 not out) added 144 for the last wicket and came close to beating the Lord Hawke-David Hunter stand of 149 set up against Kent at Sheffield in 1898. It remains Sidebottom's highest score in first-class cricket and he produced every stroke in the book. He has always looked a very capable batsman and with a stronger physique would undoubtedly have become a top-class all-rounder. The lead at the top was now 22 points over Middlesex, who had two games in hand.

A remarkable meeting with Colin Croft at Old Trafford did not make a lot of progress owing to the rain. Lancashire reached 270 for four in their 100 overs, and at the close of play Yorkshire were 55 for five with Croft clean bowling Boycott, Athey and Hampshire and making the ball bump and rear dangerously with a ferocity never seen before by spectators some of whose memories went back to the days of Gregory and McDonald. Perhaps fortunately for Yorkshire, rain practically ruined the rest of the game, as it did also the match with Nottinghamshire at Headingley. By now Yorkshire had dropped down to third place and this was due purely to the fact that five of their eight matches had been ruined by the weather.

Harrogate saw Somerset total 280 for nine after being 180 for eight. Cope finished with five for 75. Boycott then reached 139 not out as Yorkshire declared with six overs still to go and five runs behind. Yorkshire were soon in a strong position with Cope capturing a further six wickets for 29 runs. After Boycott (60) and Love (50) had put on 98 for the first wicket Yorkshire had to struggle to finish on top by four wickets. The Warwickshire match at Park Avenue was another victim of the weather, after Yorkshire had lost three for 28 in reply to Warwickshire's 330 for five.

At Scarborough, on a pitch generally favouring the ball, the Australians lost seven for 63 before achieving respectability with a score of 186. It looked a pretty large total when Walker trapped Boycott lbw for 0 and then went on to take five for 29 as Yorkshire could only score 75. The Aussies then made 215 for seven before declaring and left Yorkshire with 327 to win at 65 runs per hour. Yorkshire were happy to reach 233 for six at the close with Boycott scoring 103 and Love 59.

Lord's saw Yorkshire fighting for a draw with Middlesex after seemingly being on top for most of the game. Yorkshire began well by bowling Middlesex out for 256 but then Yorkshire, in spite of having eight of Middlesex's overs, could score only 244 for four. There was much criticism of Yorkshire's tactics with Boycott, dropped at the wicket overnight, struggling to find his touch and making 117. Hampshire also batted for a long time for 63 not out. Middlesex batted with freedom in their second innings to score 269 for six and so set Yorkshire 282 to win in just under four hours. Boycott (54) and Leadbeater (73) put on 122 for the first wicket in 41 overs but thereafter Yorkshire struggled and were happy to force a draw at 219 for seven. There was a lack of enterprise in Yorkshire's approach in this match.

Victory at Trent Bridge was unexpected after Yorkshire had by far the worst of the game from the start. Nottinghamshire totalled 279 for eight and in reply Yorkshire collapsed to 97 for six and it needed an attacking innings from Bairstow (65) for Yorkshire to score 200, Clive Rice taking four for 50. Batting again, P. D. Johnson (106 not out) and Mike Smedley (130 not out) put on 243 unbeaten for Nottinghamshire's second wicket and thus set Yorkshire 323 to win in

280 minutes. After helping Leadbeater (71) put on 176 for the first wicket, Boycott cut loose and made a very fine 154 before being run out. Sidebottom then came in and batted freely to obtain 57 not out and Yorkshire got home with over ten minutes to spare. It was an uplifting win, yet Yorkshire, with by far the best record in the Championship, were still only in sixth place. This was due to their lack of batting points. In some cases there was little doubt that Yorkshire should have scored quicker; but mostly their lowish position was due to the diabolical weather that has always affected the counties in the northern Pennine country, Yorkshire, Lancashire and Derbyshire – plus Glamorgan – more than anyone else in the country. Those four counties have suffered more than any others with a points system that handicaps those unable to play because of the weather. The TCCB will claim that it is the same for everyone, but it is not.

A trip to Folkestone saw Yorkshire recover from 47 for four to a respectable 236 with Sidebottom (40) and Bairstow (81) rescuing the visitors. Kent obtained a lead of 32 runs. For Yorkshire Cope and Bore took four wickets. After a 71 stand between Boycott (61) and Lumb (32) Yorkshire collapsed before Underwood and Kent won an interesting game by six wickets.

Another defeat was to follow at Abbeydale where an extremely lively pitch was reported to the authorities, but not before several Yorkshire batsmen had been injured and had to retire hurt. Middlesex collapsed to 181 all out with Cope taking the last four wickets for five runs. Yorkshire were lacking Boycott, who was now back in the Test team, and it was Daniel who caused most of the problems, taking five for 56 and also causing the retirement of Hampshire, Sidebottom and Lumb. Bairstow did put up a fight to reach 50, but Middlesex led by 18 on the first innings. Opener Smith then made a fighting 141 against the depleted home side, who were eventually set 329 to win, a task they did not get near, but Kevin Sharp did show some spirit in scoring 56, while Athey also made 36.

Kevin Sharp was born in Leeds and as a boy went to John Lawrence's Cricket School at Rothwell on Saturday afternoons. An attractive left-handed batsman, he scored 260 not out for England against West Indies Under 19s in 1978. Sharp had played once for Yorkshire in 1976 and played fairly regularly in 1977 without doing anything of note. He gained a regular place in the side in 1978 and 1979, but it was 1982 before he received his county cap. An attacking batsman when at his best, he could score all round the wicket but his overall performances tend to be a disappointment to his admirers, as his average for Yorkshire since he started, confirms. He played some innings that touched greatness, particularly on fast hard wickets, but there were other occasions when he unaccountably failed to produce

479

his best form and he got out to strokes that were unworthy of him. A very fine fielder and a useful off-spinner, he had a cheerful outlook on the game and had he maintained any consistency he would surely have reached higher honours.

At Headingley, Yorkshire lost by eight wickets to Hampshire, for whom Greenidge scored 208 out of 304, no other batsman in the Hampshire side passing 21. With a magnificent display Greenidge virtually won the game on his own. For Yorkshire, Leadbeater scored 63 and 33, Stevenson 52 and acting-skipper Cope 44 not out.

Yorkshire made little progress at Edgbaston in spite of scoring 353 for five. Boycott scored 104 and Jim Love was at his very best in his 129 which he accumulated in a fluent, dominating manner while Sharp compiled a quick 48. The weather then turned wet and a declaration by Warwickshire 149 in arrears was followed by a declaration at 188 for four by Yorkshire in which Chris Old scored 107, including his century in 37 minutes. It was without any merit and the match quite rightly faded into a draw. With three defeats preceding this match Yorkshire had dropped to ninth in the table.

Defeat at Hove saw Yorkshire in a poor light. Javed Miandad scored 111 out of Sussex's 303 for seven and Yorkshire collapsed from 160 for three to 203 all out. Yorkshire were set 333 to win and at 182 for five Yorkshire were still in the game, but after Jim Love was run out for 86 the tail collapsed and they were dismissed for 223. At New Road, Worcestershire inflicted an even worse defeat. Their score of 279 was enough for Yorkshire to lose by an innings and 79 runs. Only Hampshire (29) managed to pass twenty in either innings, Inchmore taking eight for 58 in the first innings. Yorkshire had now dropped to 12th place but as their skipper was obtaining his 100th century at Headingley at the time, their sad exploits were almost forgotten. Old was also absent, injured.

At Park Avenue, Lancashire made a good start with 302 for four, Barry Wood scoring 150 not out against his native county. Yorkshire collapsed to 234 for nine declared but there was a sensational collapse in Lancashire's second innings as they were bowled out for 108, Phil Carrick taking six for 37. He had just returned to the side after having been out through lack of form for nearly six weeks. Yorkshire, set 177 to win, reached their target thanks mainly to Richard Lumb, who had also been badly off form; he scored a sound 77.

At Bristol, the match was abandoned without a ball being bowled, and rain also spoilt Yorkshire's chances at Acklam Park against Essex after the visitors were bowled out for 108. Robinson took five for 32 and Stevenson four for 39 and then Yorkshire scored 335 for four before declaring, with Lumb again in form with 91 after adding 170 with Geoff Cope (78). Fletcher replied with 106 not out from Essex's 276 for four. Moving to Scarborough, Yorkshire finished the season with another draw which was again partly due to bad weather. Yorkshire scored 261 with only Hampshire (81) and Lumb (59) getting on top of the spinners on a very slow turner. Bore bowled very well for Yorkshire and took seven for 63 as Derbyshire were dismissed for 205. Yorkshire then replied with 219 for seven declared, John Hampshire this time making 100 not out and Derbyshire were set 276 to win. Bad light ensured an abortive finish. Twelfth position in the Championship was a disappointment after such a promising start.

Boycott was as usual top of the batting averages with 1,257 runs at 57.22, while Hampshire averaged 43 for 779 runs. Old was third but he played in less than half the matches, while Love managed an average of 30 while scoring 739 runs. Leadbeater and Lumb were both disappointing, and on the whole the batting was unreliable, especially in Boycott's absence.

Old headed the bowling averages but took only 25 wickets at 19.24 with Geoff Cope second with 56 wickets at 24.23. Robinson took 44 wickets but was disappointing, while Stevenson worked very hard for his 69 wickets but they cost him 25.68 each. Carrick fell away badly, taking only 24 wickets at 32.08 and Sidebottom took only 13 wickets. Bairstow played in every match and kept wicket well, and also played some valuable innings.

Sidebottom's four for 36 was his best performance of the season and came in the Gillette Cup against Hampshire, who reached 261. Sidebottom also got Yorkshire's top score (45) but they lost heavily by 86 runs.

Yorkshire had a dreadful time in the John Player League, finishing in 15th place, but they had more no-decision matches than any other side in the League. Boycott scored 347 runs at 38.55 and Lumb and Hampshire also played some good innings. Old took 14 wickets at 10.07 each but no one else reached as many as ten wickets, and Cope was actually second in the averages with seven at 15.28. In the Benson and Hedges Cup, Yorkshire failed to qualify for the quarter-finals.

The winter was not going to pass quietly for cricket lovers. Kerry Packer had arrived on the scene and was making his presence felt. Nearer home, Don Brennan, a member of the Yorkshire committee, criticised Geoff Boycott on the air, and other members of the committee were responsible for leaks to the press. A reform group was set up in support of Boycott. He did not join Packer and was reappointed captain of Yorkshire for the forthcoming season. At the same time Raymond Illingworth was appointed manager of the Yorkshire side; a position that would not take effect until April

1979 – a somewhat controversial move. Brennan resigned from the Yorkshire selection committee and Mel Ryan, another outspoken cricketer was not re-elected.

After an abandoned match at Park Avenue with the Pakistani tourists, Yorkshire moved to Headingley and in 100 overs Kent restricted Yorkshire to 222 for eight, with Boycott top scorer with 61. There was no further play.

At Edgbaston, Dennis Amiss compiled 127 out of Warwickshire's 307 for four, and Boycott followed suit with 115 as Yorkshire replied with 302 for six, Hampshire scoring 73. Graham Stevenson (five for 60) and Chris Old (four for 57) then bowled out the home side for 139 and victory was a possibility, although an uneven bounce had developed. Willis trapped Boycott lbw for 4 and Yorkshire had little else to offer and lost by 34 runs.

Lumb and Love and several others obtained some batting practice at The Parks against Oxford University, where amazingly Geoffrey Boycott scored nought and three. Carrick took six for 33, and Yorkshire moved up to Abbeydale Park where Derbyshire were the opposition.

A. J. Borrington with 37 led Derbyshire to 336 for seven before they declared with 99 overs gone and after a bad start (Yorkshire lacked Boycott) the home team reached 272. When Derbyshire set them 262 at 78 runs per hour Yorkshire made no effort to get the runs on a pitch that was getting slower as the game wore on.

When victory at last came to Yorkshire, it was very sweet indeed. Without Boycott and Old and played on a pitch that was reported as being unfit for first-class cricket, Lancashire were dismissed for 123 with Graham Stevenson having a wonderful time and taking eight for 65 and Bairstow taking the first five of eight catches that he would take during the game. Although Yorkshire made a dreadful start, losing four wickets with only 20 on the board, Hampshire, the acting skipper, made 54 and added 88 with the real hero of the innings, Phil Carrick, who went on to score 105, a most opportune time to make his maiden century. A total of 260 was more than enough as Lancashire were dismissed for 105. Howard Cooper took six for 26 and Steve Oldham four for 28. The victory brought Yorkshire up to sixth place in the table.

Unfortunately it did not bring a continued revival as Yorkshire were brought down to earth in their very next match at Worksop where at one stage they were 28 for six; they did at least obtain 93 with Richard Hadlee taking six for 39. In reply Nottinghamshire took their first innings to 426 for eight before declaring, with Mike Harris scoring 143. Lumb (45) and Johnson (61) helped John Hampshire, still acting skipper, who made 124, to achieve some sort of respectability, and Carrick (67) and Stevenson (47) took Yorkshire to 398. It did not prevent an easy Nottinghamshire win by eight wickets.

Two victories followed under John Hampshire. At Middlesbrough, Worcestershire were dismissed for 200. Yorkshire obtained a lead of 114 and duly gained an eight-wicket victory.

At Grace Road, Leicestershire totalled 327 for eight and Yorkshire fared as well making 322 for nine in the same number of overs. All the Yorkshire players contributed something to the total. In their second innings, Leicestershire declared at 265 for seven and Yorkshire were left 271 to win in just under three hours. Lumb (103) and Athey (87) gave them a great start by putting on 189 for the first wicket. Illingworth did take four for 68, but Yorkshire's win by four wickets was well deserved. The win put Yorkshire in fifth position.

Rain spoilt the prospects of a good finish at Park Avenue against Middlesex. Hampshire (61) added 109 with Kevin Sharp (91) and Yorkshire totalled a very useful 307. Middlesex replied with 277 and on a slow wicket which gave little help to the bowlers, Yorkshire were 194 for nine at the close of play. Intermittent showers had prevented there being any real pattern to the game.

At Harrogate, Northamptonshire scored 320 for three in their 100 overs with Larkins (118) and Steele (102 not out) adding 139 for the second wicket. At 4 for two Yorkshire were in trouble but John Hampshire (109) ensured they were only 10 behind on the first innings. Going in again Northamptonshire struggled against the spin attack of Carrick (five for 39) and Cope (four for 57) and were all out for 146, leaving Yorkshire to obtain 157 to win. Thanks to Hampshire's 76, Yorkshire won through by five wickets and moved up into third place.

Geoff Boycott returned to the Yorkshire side at Taunton after missing six weeks cricket owing to a thumb injury. The press had subjected him and his followers and detractors to volumes of publicity good and bad that boded ill for the Yorkshire team. His return at Taunton on a good wicket, saw Yorkshire score 345 for seven in their 100 overs, with Bill Athey scoring a fine 131. Somerset always found runs hard to get and finished 92 behind, with Old taking four for 45. Yorkshire set Somerset 310 to win in $3\frac{1}{4}$ hours, a task that was quite beyond them. Old took four for 50 but Somerset saved the game with only two wickets left and 157 on the board.

Another draw at Chelmsford was mainly due to poor weather, with Yorkshire struggling to score 260 for nine in 100 overs. South African McEwan then gave a brilliant batting display, scoring 149 in less than three hours, as Essex gained a lead of 122 runs. After that Yorkshire could do no other than bat out time at 186 for three.

Yorkshire were dismissed by Warwickshire for only 227. John

Hampshire batted brilliantly and became the first Englishman to reach 1,000 runs during the season. When Warwickshire batted, Amiss made 46 out of their total of 85. Chris Old did well to take six for 34 and at one stage they looked like following on. Boycott (55) and Lumb (73) put on 114 for Yorkshire's first wicket and they eventually declared at 185 for three. At 204 for three Warwickshire were going very well, but they were finally out for 264, 63 runs short of victory. Bairstow took six catches in the second innings.

Another victory followed at The Oval. Surrey were dismissed for 164, with Steve Oldham taking five for 40, but Yorkshire passed that score by only one run. The second innings saw Surrey dismissed for 155. Yorkshire's task of 155 to win was not easy on a pitch of dubious quality. Richard Lumb held the innings together with an authoritative 71 and Yorkshire's victory by five wickets was gained with just one over left.

The visit to Northampton was a sad episode which is still talked about by Yorkshire members and followers. It was Geoff Cope's last match of the season. He retired ill when batting and his bowling analysis for the match read as follows: 48-22-64-1. His action had been photographed again and further faults were found. The on-going saga had reached another low point.

But that problem had nothing to do with the famous incident which occurred when John Hampshire was batting with Colin Johnson, and both were accused of a 'go-slow'. Johnson was eventually stated to be not guilty but Hampshire was censored over his attitude. What was surprising was the fact that the president and a selector appeared on the ground at sometime or other on the fateful day's play.

Northamptonshire batted first and obtained 280 for seven in their 100 overs. Alan Lamb was top scorer with 72 and Peter Willey made 58. In reply, Geoffrey Boycott scored 113 and Bill Athey 114 and at the end of the 100 overs Yorkshire had reached 278 for three in the same number of overs; Hampshire finished with seven not out and Johnson six not out. They had added 11 runs in the last ten overs and the slow scoring was interpreted as a gesture of protest against the slow 'selfish' earlier batting, particularly by the skipper Boycott. Northamptonshire declared at 287 for five and Yorkshire made no effort to obtain 290 in 165 minutes.

Back home at Abbeydale, Boycott and Lumb (87) put on 206 for the first wicket against Glamorgan with Boycott going on to score 118 and Yorkshire reached 318 for six in their 100 overs. Glamorgan could do little against the Yorkshire spinners, J. P. Whiteley taking four for 32 on his Championship debut. Following on Glamorgan followed their first innings of 122 with 97, Carrick taking seven for 35 and

Whiteley three for 56. Glamorgan had been caught on a turning wicket but their batsmanship was somewhat injudicious to say the least. The victory was a welcome respite for the Yorkshire team and consolidated their fourth position in the table.

Peter Whiteley came into the side for Cope at Headingley against the New Zealanders. He continued to bowl his offbreaks very tidily for the rest of the season and finished second in the Yorkshire bowling averages with 22 wickets at 21.59 each. He was given an extended trial during the 1981 season without coming up to expectations and last played for Yorkshire in 1982.

The Derbyshire match at Chesterfield made very little progress because of the wet conditions. Another draw followed at Southampton in another match interferred with by inclement weather, with Yorkshire, set 132 to win, 98 for seven at the close.

Regrettably, by now the weather had broken completely and at Lord's a Gatting century was followed by Yorkshire scoring 96 all out, and at Headingley Yorkshire scored 252 for six.

At Scarborough, Nottinghamshire scored 294 for two in 100 overs and Yorkshire 325 for eight in theirs Boycott scored 129 and Jim Love had the misfortune to be lbw for 99. Nottinghamshire collapsed in their second innings for 176 and Yorkshire won by eight wickets.

The match at Old Trafford saw Yorkshire continue their improved form although Boycott was on Test duty. The Lancashire batting failed badly against Stevenson (five for 61) and Old (four for 38). Yorkshire started badly with three down for six but Old (100 not out) put Yorkshire in a winning position. Lancashire made 155 with Old at his best taking five for 47 and Yorkshire gained a deserved ten-wicket win.

The season ended with a one-innings game at Scarborough where Gloucestershire were dismissed for 161 and Yorkshire went on to gain a two-wicket victory to obtain 12 points and fourth place in the Championship.

For the first time since 1962 Geoffrey Boycott did not lead the Yorkshire batting averages. That honour went to John Hampshire, who scored 1,596 runs, average 53.20, while Boycott was second with 1,074 runs, average 51.14. Old, who played in only nine matches was third but he scored only 197 runs, average 39.40. Carrick was next with 670 runs at 35.26, while Sharp averaged 32, just ahead of Richard Lumb who scored 1,070 runs, average 31.47. Athey scored 846 runs, average 25.63, which was somewhat disappointing and Bairstow scored over 700 runs.

Old topped the bowling averages with 44 wickets at 18.34 but the leading wicket-taker was Steve Oldham, whose 53 wickets cost 25.01, just ahead of Phil Carrick with 52 wickets at 27.86 each. Stevenson and

485

Cooper were both expensive, and Cope's 32 wickets cost 24.50 each. There was some good news with regard to the latter in so much as his 'new' action had been passed by the TCCB and he would start the 1979 season with a clean sheet.

Bill Athey, who had shown all-round promise had fitted neatly into the first-slip position which had never been filled satisfactorily since Phil Sharpe had retired, while Bairstow's 71 victims had placed him at the top of the wicket-keeping charts.

In the Gillette Cup, after defeating Durham and Nottinghamshire (by one wicket) Yorkshire had the misfortune to lose to Sussex in a ten-over slog by nine runs; a game that in its presentation and performance would have been an insult to two workshop sides operating on the Military Field at Roundhay.

Yorkshire finished seventh in the Sunday League, in which Hampshire and Athey showed good batting form but the bowling was again expensive. The team failed also in the Benson and Hedges Cup, winning only one of their zonal matches. The 2nd XI finished fourth in their Competition and the Under-25 side won the final at Edgbaston, beating Essex easily by ten wickets.

But it was to be a controversial winter.

DECADENCE PREVAILS

SHORTLY AFTER THE 1978 SEASON ENDED, Geoffrey Boycott was sacked from the Yorkshire captaincy after eight seasons of mixed fortune in which Yorkshire had the worst playing record in their history. It had been a traumatic time for the former captain who had lost his mother after a long illness; he had been overlooked for the vice-captaincy of the England team in Australia and this new blow was only off-set to an extent by the fact that Boycott had been offered a new contract for two years to stay on as a player.

John Hampshire was appointed captain in his place and would work in harness with the new manager Raymond Illingworth, whose position in relation to the Boycott sacking was never clear. Even ten years later, Illingworth's reticence on the matter was summed up in the wry smile that occasionally crossed his features. I would suspect that he considered the Yorkshire committee, both officially and unofficially, as a Ship of Fools.

The Yorkshire members' reform group was soon in action, splitting the Yorkshire membership as never before. Geoffrey Boycott was interviewed on television by Michael Parkinson and attacked the committee in no uncertain terms. It was wonderful television but a tragedy as far as cricket, Yorkshire CCC and Boycott was concerned.

For months the local newspapers were full of the Boycott sacking; letters both for and against filled the letters columns. Sometimes a double page spread contained nothing else but letters and articles on the issue. There would be columns proving that Boycott's captaincy was far superior to his replacements. Then columns to the contrary. Looking back it all seemed so silly and irrelevant. It could not happen anywhere else in England. In London it would not have merited a mention. In Manchester, the Lancashire member would have read it once, turned it over in his mind and forgotten it on the morrow. In Yorkshire it went on and on . . .

After huge amounts had been spent on litigation by all parties, and Boycott agreed to carry on playing for Yorkshire under the captaincy of John Hampshire, the season finally got under way. After a John Player League fixture had been abandoned without a ball being bowled at Acklam Park, Yorkshire scored 322 for eight in 100 overs against Northamptonshire. Boycott (53) helped Lumb (113) put on 106 for the first wicket and then skipper Hampshire made 55. Northamptonshire could score only 251 for nine in their overs. Rain prevented much more progress. Nor was there much progress in the next match at Headingley where Boycott scored 151 not out from

Geoffrey Boycott in action. Boycott was England's leading batsman of the 1970s but his career at Yorkshire was one of great controversy and bitterness and it divided the membership. (Patrick Eagar)

Yorkshire's 299 for seven, an opening partnership with Lumb (69) amounting to 145. Derbyshire scored 200 for six before the weather intervened. Boycott was to the fore again at Cardiff with 58 out of Yorkshire's 200 for eight. Glamorgan had time for 87 for six. It had been a wretched start.

Seventeen overs only were bowled in the Roses match at Old Trafford and then the Nottinghamshire match at Abbeydale was abandoned without a ball being bowled. The sixth fixture at Park

488

Avenue was against Surrey and once again it was drawn. Surrey, who were set 193 to win in 140 minutes, managed to score 181 for five before running out of time.

Although the match started four hours late, Northampton provided fine weather for Yorkshire's visit. Yorkshire declared at 181 for nine, and Northamptonshire replied with 250 for four declared. Richard Lumb then made another large score, moving to 129 not out in his side's 289 for five declared. At the close Northamptonshire were 59 without loss. There was yet another draw at Edgbaston with Warwickshire recovering from 104 for six to 302 for nine in 100 overs. Yorkshire replied with 303 for seven, with Richard Lumb again in form with 118, and skipper Hampshire getting 73. At the end of the game Warwickshire were 253 for five.

A result was achieved for the first time at Worcester. Yorkshire compiled a formidable 393 for four in their 100 overs on a very good wicket with Jim Love scoring 170 not out. Worcestershire could reply only with 260 for nine. Yorkshire declared at 195 for five and thus set the home side 329 to win in 255 minutes. This they achieved without much difficulty, with their world class batsman Glen Turner scoring a brilliant 148 not out. Yorkshire had only Glamorgan below them in the league table.

A high-scoring game at Harrogate looked at first to be going Yorkshire's way when Somerset lost their first five wickets for 77 before Peter Denning pulled them round with a fine innings of 100. Then a last wicket stand took Somerset to 313, with Old taking five for 72. A stand of 288 between Boycott (130 not out) and Richard Lumb (159) enabled Yorkshire to declare at 305 for one in 92 overs, and then Somerset scored a further 308 for six before declaring, Viv Richards scoring 116. Yorkshire, with Boycott injured, played out time at 230 for five. Hampshire scored 96, and the draw took Yorkshire three positions up the table to 13th.

Yorkshire's first victory of the season came at Chesterfield, and was largely due to the batting of Geoffrey Boycott, who scored 167 out of Yorkshire's 366 for seven declared. Derbyshire had to follow-on 163 runs in arrears and laboriously reached 272 in an effort to save the match. Boycott and Lumb put on 90 for the first wicket and Boycott went on to 57 not out as Yorkshire won by nine wickets and rose to ninth.

Down at Lord's, Middlesex compiled 438 for five in 99 overs, Mike Smith scoring 137. A weakened Yorkshire side replied with 289 for eight, Lumb making 93, and after another Middlesex declaration Yorkshire were set 311 to win in four hours. After losing Lumb for 41, they were content to bat out time at 188 for seven.

Yorkshire's next match at Park Avenue against Hampshire went in the home team's favour but a last-wicket stand of 86 took Hampshire to 297 all out. Yorkshire declared at 171 for seven and Hampshire declared in their turn at 158 for four, setting Yorkshire 285 to win. Hampshire batted very slowly in their second innings and Yorkshire's required scoring rate was 120 runs per hour. A game played in poor spirit finished with Yorkshire scoring 59 for four in 43 overs.

At Worksop Nottinghamshire scored 371 for six, and Yorkshire were 6 for four at one time. They struggled to 159 all out. Boycott then held their second innings together as he carried his bat through the innings for 175 not out in a total of 360. But Derek Randall guided Nottinghamshire to an easy six-wicket win.

At Scarborough Middlesex reached 307 for nine declared, and Yorkshire made 202 on a pitch that was increasingly taking spin. Middlesex declared their second innings at 111 for six with Carrick having taken five for 32. Set 217, Yorkshire won by six wickets, Lumb finishing with 91 not out, being dropped three times.

Aided by further dropped catches at Sheffield, Yorkshire made 259 against Warwickshire, and then, caught on a rain-affected pitch, the visitors were dismissed for 35, with Graham Stevenson taking six for 14. Following on, Wawickshire made 255, insufficient to prevent a ten-wicket win for Yorkshire, for whom Phil Carrick took five for 88.

Those two victories had brought Yorkshire up to a respectable sixth in the Championship table, but winning the toss at Park Avenue against Leicestershire, Yorkshire struggled to make 211 for eight in 100 overs. The visitors put on 119 for first wicket and they went on to compile 317 for seven. Yorkshire scored 156 for five in their second innings with rain curtailing play.

The Cheltenham match against Gloucestershire was spoilt by the weather, but not before A. J. Hignell had scored 102 in Gloucestershire's score of 288 for eight. In reply Procter achieved the rarity of an lbw hat-trick as Yorkshire collapsed to 54 for five, but a stand of 135 between Boycott (95) and Carrick, who went on to score 128 not out, saved the day for Yorkshire. At Canterbury, Yorkshire had the worst of a draw with Kent who scored 345 for two in their 100 overs, with Woolmer scoring 169. Yorkshire managed only 224 in reply, and although Kent made a declaration there was no chance of a finish.

Sussex inflicted on Yorkshire a defeat by 143 runs at Hove. Sussex made 267 with Cope taking six for 37. Yorkshire struggled to 198 and after Sussex had declared at 184 for six, Yorkshire again collapsed to 110 all out.

At Headingley, Lancashire were dismissed cheaply for 155, Mr Extras with 27 being the top scorer and the best bowling came from Boycott, who took four for 14. Yorkshire replied with 322, with Boycott top scorer with 94. Clive Lloyd then scored 103 and the game appeared to be saved when Lancashire stood at 266 for seven, but they added only four more, and Yorkshire required 104 at over seven runs per over, a target they achieved.

Neil Hartley, who scored 53 not out in the run chase, was a right-hand middle-order batsman who gained a regular place in the Yorkshire side in 1980 and was capped at the start of the 1982 season. He scored over 4,000 runs for Yorkshire at the modest average of 24, and at one time was considered captaincy material for the County. Raymond Illingworth appeared to be recommending him for that post which perhaps tended to preclude him from the list of possibilities. An enthusiastic cricketer he was a real trier and team-man and in 1988 was given the captaincy of the 2nd XI, while also appearing occasionally for the first team.

Yorkshire's last match took place at Scarborough against Essex, who declared at 339 for nine, Ken McEwan scoring 124. In reply Lumb scored 110 out of Yorkshire's 329 for six declared. Essex always struggled in their second innings in which Carrick took five for 61, but Yorkshire, needing 167, always appeared to be facing defeat, with Carrick performing the best with 32. Nine wickets were down for 134 but a last-wicket stand of 33 between Stevenson (23 not out) and Cope (5 not out) took Yorkshire to an exciting victory. Yorkshire thus finished the season in seventh position.

Boycott topped the batting averages with 1,160 runs at an average of 116.00. A remarkable performance, but he played in only half of Yorkshire's matches. Richard Lumb was next with 1,465 runs at an average of 44.39. Carrick was third with 639 runs at 33.63 while Hampshire scored 880 runs at 30.34. Love, Sharp and Athey were all disappointing with the bat and both Stevenson and Sidebottom failed to reach their potential.

The bowling was the weakest point of the team, and Boycott nominally headed the bowling averages with nine wickets at 9.33, but the real leader of the averages was Chris Old with 36 wickets at 25.11. Sidebottom took only 31 wickets at 26.64, while Stevenson's 50 wickets cost 28.80. Carrick was the heaviest wicket-taker, but his 55 wickets cost 31.31 each and Cooper and Oldham both fell away. Cope was the most disappointing member of Yorkshire's attack, his 13 wickets costing 37.69 each. At the end of the season both Colin Johnson and Barrie Leadbeater were released. The former would become captain of the 2nd XI, while Leadbeater would share a benefit with Geoff Cope during the 1980 season. Chris Old, so often unavailable, was offered only a one-year contract.

In the Gillette Cup, Yorkshire were soundly defeated at Lord's by Middlesex, but in the quarter-final of the Benson and Hedges Cup, Yorkshire defeated Middlesex, also at Lord's, by four wickets. In the

Colin Johnson, captain of the Yorkshire 2nd XI, with Doug Padgett in the early 1980s.

semi-final they lost narrowly by three wickets to Essex at Chelmsford, collapsing to 173 all out after Lumb (75) and Hampshire (53) had put on 107 for the first wicket.

Yorkshire did well to finish fourth equal in the John Player League with three matches abandoned without a ball being bowled. The batting was more consistent than in other seasons while Old, Oldham and Cooper all bowled economically.

492

Financially, the Club had improved and was showing a profit, mainly due to the sponsorship efforts of the cricket manager, Raymond Illingworth. The reform group had all along been opposed to Illingworth in his new role and there was continual bickering in the press between them. So far as the majority of the membership were concerned, the sooner the new season got under way the better. Hampshire was again skipper and if Yorkshire had released such promising young players as Mallender and Boon it was because they just could not accommodate any more additions to the staff; it was a problem that Yorkshire would have to take in their stride in the years ahead.

The 1980 season opened with a draw at Leicester with Boycott (31 and 57 not out) and Lumb (56 and 45 not out) getting some good batting practice before the wet and cold weather got the upper hand completely. A win over Oxford University was meaningless, but Stevenson took five for 25 in the first innings and in the match Arnie Sidebottom, now a capped player, along with Athey and Love, had a match analysis of ten for 30. Now free from soccer ties, it was hoped that he would at last put a full season in and fulfil expectations. At Trent Bridge, a satisfying win by an innings and 47 runs was due to Stevenson's fine bowling. He followed up seven for 48 with four for 26 in the second innings.

The Roses match at Headingley saw Lancashire score 234 with Stevenson again bowling well. Bairstow captured six victims behind the stumps, and with 61 was in good form too with the bat as he and Carrick (63) took Yorkshire from 97 for six to 201 for seven and an

Cricket on the picturesque Fartown Ground, Huddersfield, in the mid-1980s.

eventual 23-run lead. Lancashire saved the game at 182 for eight, with Stevenson taking five for 71. Another draw followed at Northampton, where Northants could only muster 140 against the rampant Stevenson (four for 51). Carrick took three for 11 and also hit a splendid 131 not out while Yorkshire obtained a 200 run lead which Northamptonshire could do no more than wipe out by the end of the game with 214 for three. A similar result followed at Acklam Park against Sussex, and again Carrick was the hero with 87 in the second innings and analyses of five for 63 and three for 59.

At last a lively wicket at Abbeydale Park helped Yorkshire gain a second victory over an under-strength Kent team. Sidebottom (six for 30) shot the visitors out for 118, but at 35 for six Yorkshire were in dire straits. Acting skipper Old then made an aggressive 61 and Yorkshire went ahead by 52 runs on the first innings. Kent showed a little more fight in their second innings but Sidebottom's five for 34 proved decisive, and Yorkshire's target was 119. At 36 for five Yorkshire were in a poor position, but Jim Love, scoring 40 not out in $2\frac{1}{2}$ hours, held the batting together and Yorkshire won through by two wickets. Yorkshire had now risen to fourth position in the Championship table.

Kevin Sharp made a brilliant 100 not out against Middlesex at Lord's, dealing with the pace of Wayne Daniel and the skills of Van der Bijl without any undue difficulty. Yorkshire declared at 314 for six. After Old had taken three early wickets, Radley (136 not out) and Gatting (110) added 177 for Middlesex's fifth wicket and they declared in their turn at 328 for five. The weather had caused further hold-ups and Yorkshire batted out time at 204 for six. There was a similar result at Park Avenue against Worcestershire for whom Glenn Turner scored 115. Carrick took six for 138, and Lumb followed 118 with 51 not out.

At Harrogate, Yorkshire returned to winning ways, but at the end of the first two innings, Nottinghamshire appeared to be in the driving seat with a lead of 127 runs after Randall (166) and Clive Rice (121 not out) added 270 for Nottinghamshire's third wicket. In their second innings, Richard Lumb (97) and Bill Athey (52) put on 114 for Yorkshire's first wicket and with the tail wagging furiously a score of 317 gave Yorkshire a chance of victory. When Nottinghamshire batted Old went through the middle order with four for 38 and a 27-run victory left Yorkshire third.

Regrettably the next four matches were badly affected by the poor weather and were all drawn. At Southampton Cope took four for 69. Cope had been 'cleared' in order to bowl in what was to be his last season of first-class cricket, but at the back of his mind was the fact that he was still under suspicion. He continued to try his utmost and on this particular occasion bowled in his old form. Lumb contributed 129 and 70 at Bradford against Glamorgan in a match in which Athey and Hampshire also displayed good form. Old took five for 68 as Yorkshire took an 86-run lead but in spite of a further Yorkshire declaration there was no chance of a finish. The Essex match produced three declarations and a very good attempt at a finish. Yorkshire were set 283 to win in 205 minutes and after losing five wickets with only 90 on the board made a valiant effort and finished just ten runs from victory with nine wickets down. Surrey were dismissed for 175 at The Oval and Yorkshire were 19 runs ahead with three wickets left when the game was abandoned.

A defeat from the West Indians at Headingley by 58 runs was no surprise but it enabled Bacchus to score 164 not out. Croft bowled the visitors to success with six for 80 but Boycott, Love, Lumb and Hartley all had some batting practice.

At Scarborough, Middlesex scored 391 thanks to Roland Butcher who took toil of a weak Yorkshire attack to the tune of 179. Stevenson finished with five for 84. Yorkshire followed on 273 behind, and fared little better with five wickets down for 86 but Hampshire made a sound 67 and then Bairstow played a brilliant innings of 145 – the highest ever made by a Yorkshire wicket-keeper – and Yorkshire finally obtained 370. Middlesex had no difficulty in recording an eight-wicket win. That was Yorkshire's first defeat of the season and they were now in fourth position.

Abbeydale Park saw another unfinished match, this time with Gloucestershire, and once again Yorkshire could blame the elements. Yorkshire declared at 153 for eight. Gloucestershire in their turn at 201 for four and at the end of the match Yorkshire had scored 243 for one with Richard Lumb scoring 101 and Bill Athey 125 not out.

On an unpredictable pitch at Chesterfield, Derbyshire collapsed against Chris Old, who took six for 44. Hendrick soon had Yorkshire in trouble at 79 for seven. Then Cope (33) was joined by Stevenson, who played a very attractive innings with the wristy drives and cuts which are his speciality, and scored 111 to help Yorkshire to a 76-run lead. Derbyshire's second innings was soon in tatters at 53 for five but rallied to 314 for eight to save the match with distinction. Yorkshire remained fourth.

Somerset at Clarence Park, Weston-super-Mare, provided another in the long list of unfinished matches although this game did have its merits. Sunil Gavaskar scored 155 not out for Somerset out of his side's 276 for five on a wicket that was somewhat unpredictable and gave increasing help to the spinners. In reply Yorkshire were dismissed for 209, out of which John Hampshire scored 124. In their second innings Somerset struggled to a total of 145. Yorkshire needed 213 to win but bad light ensured that the match would finish a draw with Yorkshire 164 for four.

In this match Simon Dennis made his debut for Yorkshire. A nephew of both Frank Dennis and L. Hutton (by marriage) and a cousin of Richard Hutton, he was a left-arm fast bowler. He toured India and Australia with the English Schools side in the late 1970s. He achieved little of note for Yorkshire in 1980 but gained a regular place in the Yorkshire side in 1983. Unfortunately he proved to be injury-prone and illness and injury followed him throughout his career and, at the end of the 1988 season, he was released.

Two remarkable games against Warwickshire came next and strangely none of the eight innings was completed. In fact there were six declarations. At Edgbaston, Warwickshire declared at 251 for five and Yorkshire at 105 for one. With Monday's play washed-out Warwickshire left Yorkshire to obtain 243 in 160 minutes. This they succeeded in achieving for two wickets, thanks to Athey (114) and Love (104), who opened with a stand of 224. In the return game at Park Avenue, Yorkshire made 312 for six, John Hampshire scoring a fine 101 not out. Warwickshire were 62 behind when they declared. Yorkshire then reached 212 for five and Warwickshire were set 275 to win. They gave up the chase after Dennis had taken two early wickets and drew at 134 for five.

Yorkshire gave a disappointing display against Lancashire at Old Trafford but on an easy pitch both sides produced some good cricket. Boycott (137) and Lumb (67) set off with an opening stand of 178 towards Yorkshire's 346 for seven in their 100 overs. Lancashire replied with 310 for five and then Yorkshire declared at 265 for five with Jim Love scoring 105 not out and John Hampshire 89. Setting Lancashire 302 to win in 250 minutes was claimed to be a too-generous declaration and Hampshire came in for some criticism. It was hardly justified, though a fine game of cricket in fine weather did go Lancashire's way. With Clive Lloyd scoring 101, Lancashire finally won by three wickets, but it could have been so different if Lloyd had not been dropped when 68 and again at 70.

Yorkshire gave a far worse display in the Northamptonshire match at Headingley. They scored 200 for four declared. Northamptonshire also declared at 200, but with eight wickets down, Graham Stevenson having taken all eight wickets for 57 runs. Yorkshire then gave a woeful batting display losing six wickets for 22 runs before Sidebottom (24) and Stevenson (52) rallied them to 109. The visitors won easily by eight wickets.

In their final match of the season at Scarborough Yorkshire made a good start by compiling 338 for six, with Boycott carrying his bat for 154 not out. Derbyshire were soon in trouble, but with only half-an-hour's play being possible on the last day, struggled to 180 for seven and a draw. Yorkshire's final position of sixth was fairly satisfactory but one felt that Yorkshire should have been capable of finishing higher. Examination of the averages show that Yorkshire had four players who took part in Tests or in Prudential Cup matches. Boycott played in less than half the Championship matches and Old missed seven games and Bairstow five.

The batting was consistent all round, with Hampshire leading the way with 987 runs at an average of 51.94 marginally ahead of Boycott who scored 706 runs average 50.42. Old averaged over 40 but scored only 325 runs while Love scored 917 runs at 36.68. Lumb scored 1,223 runs average 35.97, and Bairstow also averaged over 35 in what proved to be his best season with the bat. Athey scored 1,113 runs at an average of 34.78 and Stevenson and Carrick both averaged over 32. Sharp was suffering from stress and was in and out of the 2nd XI but headed their batting averages. He was expected to be fit for the new season.

The bowling was not very penetrative, but Old did take 47 wickets at 20.36 and Sidebottom took 42 at 22.90. Stevenson did the bulk of the work with 72 wickets at 23.18 each. On the other hand the spinners Carrick (51 wickets at 32.39) and Cope (42 at 37.09) were both disappointing and Cooper also fell away. Neither Cooper nor Cope would play again; but the latter did have the satisfaction of having a quite substantial benefit in conjunction with Leadbeater.

In the Gillette Cup Yorkshire made progress against Kent at Headingley and against Hampshire at Southampton, Athey scoring 115 and 93 not out but at The Oval Yorkshire had to face Surrey in bad light. Had it been a county match there would not have been any play at all on the first day. An interpretation of the Laws to suit a one-day competition or to suit a vociferous crowd is all wrong. Yorkshire fought hard but Surrey got home by four wickets.

Yorkshire also failed in the Benson and Hedges Cup winning only one of their zonal matches; but of their three defeats, one was by one run and another by two runs.

In the John Player League, Yorkshire never recovered from a bad start in which they lost their first six matches. In the end they finished equal 14th, with only Glamorgan beneath them in the table. Ingham actually headed the batting averages with 57, and Boycott and Athey were second and third with 37 and 32. Athey scored 534 runs. Old and Sidebottom each took 20 wickets and Hartley and Stevenson performed satisfactorily.

Immediately after the season ended, John Hampshire resigned from the Yorkshire captaincy and Chris Old was appointed in his place.

The overs limitation in the first innings was to be abandoned in the new season. The number of points for a win was to be increased to 16. Full covering of pitches would be implemented. It was estimated that there had been 25 changes in the method of playing County Championship cricket since the modern Championship began in 1895.

In February, Brian Sellers died after a long illness; but there was better news prior to the season's start when Kevin Sharp was declared completely fit and ready for the first match. At the age of 22 he could expect a long cricketing life ahead of him.

Yorkshire started the 1981 season by having the best of a draw with Oxford University at The Parks. At Edgbaston, Yorkshire obtained 396 with Love in fine form with 161, putting on 160 for the third wicket with John Hampshire (64). The home side replied with 260, and Yorkshire were 112 for one at the close with Boycott 51 not out.

At Headingley, Yorkshire were comprehensively defeated by Middlesex by 81 runs. Gatting (158) put Middlesex into a good position to declare at 329 for four and a second innings 142 for nine declared set Yorkshire 265 to win. Yorkshire were never able to cope.

There was never any chance of a finished game at Old Trafford, where Jim Love scored 154 to help Yorkshire to a score of 348, to which Lancashire replied with 310 for eight. Rain also interfered with the Kent match at Dartford, where Yorkshire batted out time with 112 for five after being set 228 in $2\frac{1}{2}$ hours.

Yorkshire's misfortunes continued at Headingley against Essex who accumulated a substantial 354 for eight. Sidebottom bowled well and took four for 44. Yorkshire failed dismally against Lever (eight for 49) and only partially recovered from 16 for six to make 129. Following on, Yorkshire batted much better, with Moxon on his first appearance making a cultured 116 and putting on 122 for the first wicket with Lumb (53). Yorkshire comfortably saved the game.

Martyn Moxon played his early cricket with Monk Bretton and moved to Barnsley in 1977. A tall, orthodox opening batsman, he looked a player of class from the start and in his second match against Derbyshire also scored a century making him the first Yorkshire player to score centuries in his first two home games. Moxon earned his Yorkshire cap in 1984 and two years later made his first appearance for England. An excellent slip fielder, he unfortunately suffered with finger injuries. Apart from his various injuries, he had the misfortune to lose his father after a long illness, which was upsetting to him. A good coach and ambassador for the game, he could have a big influence on the future of English cricket.

The Gloucestershire match at Bristol did not bring any improvement in the team's performance. Gloucestershire were bowled out for 172 by Old and Sidebottom but Yorkshire still fell 42 short on the first innings. When Gloucestershire batted again, Sidebottom took five for

68 but a score of 268 on an easing pitch looked too many for the visitors, and Yorkshire lost by 117 runs. Without a win, Yorkshire were now 11th in the table.

Matters did not improve at Park Avenue where Boycott returned but he could not prevent Nottinghamshire from taking a lead of 244 on the first innings. Winning the toss, Nottinghamshire were poorly placed at 124 for six but Richard Hadlee (142 not out) dominated the rest of the innings and they were able to declare at 332 for eight. Yorkshire gave a wretched batting display and followed on, but in a defiant backs-to-the-wall exhibition, they batted out time at 355 for seven. Boycott made 124 and Love 97.

At Abbeydale Park against Derbyshire, Yorkshire were given a fine start by Richard Lumb (145) and Martyn Moxon (111) who put on 218 for the first wicket. Yorkshire went on to score 374 and on a docile pitch, Derbyshire also started well and went on to 480, but three of Yorkshire's bowlers were injured in a game that was singularly lacking in enterprise.

At Worcestershire, Yorkshire totalled 319 for seven declared, but Glenn Turner was in top form as he scored 168 putting on 231 for the second wicket with Phil Neale (102) and Worcestershire declared at 303 for three. Worcestershire were set 268 to win in $3\frac{1}{2}$ hours, and managed to get home with one ball to spare. Yorkshire were now in 15th position, without a win after nine matches, and to add to the unhappiness, Sir Kenneth Parkinson, the president of the Club since 1974, died suddenly. He had been in office during a very difficult period of the club's existence but had always done his best as a mediator between the warring factions of the Club.

At long last Yorkshire's fortunes took a turn for the better. A somewhat patchy batting display by Leicestershire at Park Avenue saw them recover from 127 for six to 249 all out. Yorkshire, too, lost early wickets but a fifth-wicket stand between John Hampshire (112) and Bairstow (84) really put them on top, and 109 runs to the good they proceeded to bowl out Leicestershire for only 194, and Yorkshire won comfortably by seven wickets, but with only one ball to spare.

At Harrogate, Surrey won the toss, batted and were dismissed for 192, but Yorkshire fared even worse and were dismissed for 157. Surrey then lost seven for 68 before recovering to a supposedly winning position with a total of 246 and lead of 281. Alan Ramage bowled very well at first and took five for 65. On a pitch that had got easier, Thomas broke through the early Yorkshire batting as they lost three for 31, but Hampshire (127) and Neil Hartley (63) put on 179 on what proved to be the turning-point of the game. Yorkshire continued to a five-wicket victory which put them back into the title race.

Alas, the revival was not sustained. At Cardiff, J. A. Hopkins compiled 116 and Glamorgan declared at 343 for six. Yorkshire then collapsed twice, only just making Glamorgan bat again. Hampshire (35 and 75 not out) was top scorer in each innings.

At Trent Bridge, Nottinghamshire put Yorkshire in to bat on a very lively pitch and the visitors were soon dismissed for 104. The pitch always gave assistance to the pace bowlers but it did not prevent Rice (172) and Randall (87) putting on 263 for the Nottinghamshire third wicket and this sealed the game as Nottinghamshire took a 250 lead on the first innings. Stevenson was the pick of the Yorkshire bowlers with five for 58. Yorkshire fared much better in their second innings with Neil Hartley completing his maiden century for the Club, but Nottinghamshire won by eight wickets. A tourist match at Abbeydale Park provided Kevin Sharp with much needed batting practice as he scored 116 out of Yorkshire's score of 275 for five against the Sri Lankans, but there was no further play due to the weather.

The Warwickshire game at Scarborough resulted in a draw with neither side earning much credit for their efforts. Warwickshire's 288 was a reasonable score, and Yorkshire scored at just three an over in a reply without much sparkle. Warwickshire were content to bat out time and compiled a further score of 296.

At Abbeydale, Somerset recovered to score 183, Simon Dennis bowling well to take five for 35, Yorkshire fell three runs behind on the first innings, and then Vivian Richards scored 153 out of his side's 349 for six declared. Apart from Love (51) and Bairstow (70), Yorkshire put up little fight and were thrashed by 167 runs.

The Hampshire match at Middlesbrough was spoilt by the weather in spite of three declarations, although Yorkshire came nearest to winning when Stevenson took five for 41 as Hampshire, at 130 for seven, still required another 134 to win at the end of the game. John Hampshire scored 118 not out in Yorkshire's second innings.

Failure to win that game meant that Yorkshire were now only three points above the bottom club Warwickshire, and 14 points behind Worcestershire in 15th place. Their often depleted side was again lacking Old and Boycott at Wellingborough, where on a sub-standard wicket seventeen wickets fell on the first day. Northamptonshire struggled to 156, and Yorkshire had lost nine wickets and were only one run ahead at one stage, but a last wicket stand between Athey (123 not out) and Sidebottom (13) took Yorkshire to a valuable 82-run lead. The Yorkshire-born Neil Mallender took six for 37 for Northamptonshire, and when the latter batted again another Yorkshireman Geoff Cook made 66 and he and Alan Lamb were largely responsible for Northamptonshire reaching 207. Sidebottom was Yorkshire's best bowler with six for 62. Kevin Sharp (70 not out) played a fine innings to take Yorkshire to victory at 126 for four.

Derbyshire began well at Chesterfield with John Wright scoring 150 and went on to total 400 in a remarkable first day's batting. In reply, and taking 16 balls more, Yorkshire in $5\frac{1}{2}$ hours batting scored 252 for four before declaring. Boycott scored 122 not out and came in for some criticism for his rate of scoring. Hampshire helped him to add 184 for Yorkshire's third wicket and scored 84. Derbyshire then declared at 151 for three, setting Yorkshire 300 to win at 88 per hour. Batting quite brilliantly they won the game with six wickets to spare and with eight overs in hand. Love scored 84 not out and Bairstow 88 not out. Yorkshire were now in eleventh position.

A below-strength team were well beaten at Lord's by Middlesex after taking 264 for nine in 109 overs before declaring. In two balls less, Middlesex replied with 366 for nine declared, and finally knocked off the 66 they wanted for the loss of four wickets.

At Headingley Yorkshire, put in to bat in the Roses match and losing six wickets for 36 recovered to reach 149, thanks to Neil Hartley (53) who played a captain's innings in adverse circumstances. Lancashire also found runs difficult to come by with five down for 79 before Clive Lloyd (145) helped them to a lead of 197. Holding took his match tally to ten wickets and Yorkshire went down by an innings and 16 runs.

In such a depressing season, there was already trouble brewing against Boycott for his absences and for his slow scoring on occasions; there were also grumblings from the reform group against Illingworth because of his manner of running the team's affairs. Boycott himself was dropped from the team for a breach of discipline by the team manager. It looked like another winter of discontent. Letters poured into the newspapers as they had previously.

The Northamptonshire game at Scarborough was a sad affair with groups of members behaving in a fashion that was quite intolerable. Remarkably Yorkshire won the game by 156 runs after being put in to bat. Yorkshire obtained a reasonable score of 287 and Northamptonshire gave a feverish batting display in getting 232. Five Northamptonshire players failed to score, and Sidebottom finished with five for 35 and skipper Old four for 53. In their second innings, Hampshire's 120 took Yorkshire to 236. Nobody did much against a rampant Stevenson, who took seven for 46 and Yorkshire won by 156 runs.

Yorkshire's problems escalated. Chairman Michael Crawford endeavoured to pour oil on troubled waters; even the sponsors declared an interest and took Illingworth's side in the dispute. The fact that Yorkshire were playing their last match of the season at Hove seemed quite irrelevant. In this game no fewer than seven players were injured at some time or another and neither Lumb nor Moxon was able to bat in Yorkshire's second innings. The Championship was at stake and until Nottinghamshire had won on the second day, Sussex were very much in the race for honours. Yorkshire were dismissed for 153 and Sussex replied with 250 for five declared, scored in very quick time. Yorkshire struggled to 198 in their second innings, putting up token resistance. Sussex went on to win easily by eight wickets and so took runner-up position in the Championship. Yorkshire finished in tenth position.

Geoffrey Boycott headed the Yorkshire averages but he played in only eight of 22 fixtures in the Championship, and scored 523 runs at an average of 43. He played in six Test matches and three Prudential matches, which accounted for 12 County Championship matches – over half the programme. This was, is and will be an idiotic way to run cricket, and has been perpetrated on the public for decades. Old, the captain, missed eight Championship fixtures which meant he played in slightly less than $\frac{2}{3}$ of the total fixtures. John Hampshire was second in the batting averages, scoring 1,425 runs at 43.18 and Bairstow, having his best season with the bat, made 1,083 runs with an average of 40.11. Love also passed his thousand and averaged 34 but Lumb, Sharp, Moxon, Hartley and Athey, especially, were all disappointing. Old and Sidebottom are both capable of better things with the bat.

Sidebottom headed the bowling averages with 47 wickets at 19.12 but he, too, missed eight Championship matches, mainly due to injury, while Old was next with 43 at 23.02 each. Dennis took 20 at 24.50. Stevenson took the most wickets, 61, but he was very expensive, as they cost him 30.44 each. Whiteley and Carrick both had very poor seasons.

In the NatWest Match – the bank had taken over from Gillette as sponsors of the Cup Competition – Yorkshire compiled 222 for six against Kent, with Hampshire scoring 63 and Bairstow 52 not out, but it was not enough. Tavare saw Kent home by six wickets with a competent 118 not out.

In the Benson and Hedges Cup Yorkshire topped their group with Love and Old prominent, but they lost at Headingley in the quarter-final to Somerset who won through by three wickets. Athey and Hampshire each scored 58 for Yorkshire but Rose (68) and Denning (66) got Somerset off to a good start with 135 for the first wicket and then Richards came in and consolidated with 47. There were one or two run-outs but the visitors won with seven balls to spare.

The John Player League saw Yorkshire finish seventh equal; they did not have much luck with the weather, four of their games being

The pavilion at Dewsbury as it is today.

'no results', a total that was not exceeded by any other county. Bairstow and Athey both batted consistently to average over 30 but few of the bowlers played enough for any clear pattern to form of their abilities.

Immediately after the end of the season, John Hampshire asked for his release from the County. It was anticipated that he would join Derbyshire. He had not found it easy as a member of the Yorkshire team to be in the establishment party opposed to the reform group, by whom he had been seen as a traitor since the Northampton incident. He left with the good wishes of the committee, while the bulk of members regretted his going whether they were pro or anti-Boycott, or pro or anti-reform group. It was a further nail in Yorkshire cricket's coffin.

September was a month to brush under the carpet as soon as possible. A further resignation from the Yorkshire committee was Eric Baines, member for Doncaster. The Club could ill afford to lose a member who was respected by all members, no matter which faction they might belong to.

A poll was taken amongst the players and resulted in support for Ray Illingworth. To expect a true and honest appraisal was optimistic and those who had a hand in it grew to realise that in due course. Solicitors on all sides were having a field day. The losers were only, and could only be, Yorkshire County Cricket Club and Yorkshire cricket. How sad it all was.

The committee set-up an in-depth enquiry into the running of the Club which used up reams of paper. What was published made some sense but to try to get anything implemented was a waste of time.

An uneasy peace was eventually established with Old retaining the captaincy and Boycott acting as his deputy. Manager Ray Illingworth would continue in harness. Sharp and Hartley were awarded their county caps before the season got under way.

The new season (1982) began at Northampton with Boycott dominating an innings of 368 for eight declared with a fine 138; he added 129 for the sixth wicket with David Bairstow (77) and then Northamptonshire were dismissed for 223. Larkins carried his bat through the innings for 118 not out and Sidebottom took five for 57. Yorkshire declared their second innings at 189 for five, and Northamptonshire were set 335 in 255 minutes. After Larkins went for 59, they gave up the chase and were 160 for four at the close. Another draw followed at Headingley where Yorkshire this time scored 380 for seven declared, with Boycott scoring 134. Glamorgan scored 322 for nine declared, and a stand of 140 between Athey (100) and Lumb (67) took Yorkshire to 248 for five before they declared, thus setting Glamorgan 307 to win in just over three hours. Glamorgan reached 112 for two and a disappointing draw.

A rain-affected draw with the Indians was distinguished by some good batting from both sides. G. A. Parkar scored 146 for the visitors who declared at 376 for five. Yorkshire declared, too, at 260 for three, after Sharp (115) and Lumb (52) opened with 127 for the first wicket. There was further batting practice for both sides without any chance of a result.

A remarkable win was gained at Edgbaston against Warwickshire, who were put in to bat and dismissed for 158 on a seamer's wicket, but for a time Yorkshire did even worse. They lost nine wickets for 143, when Graham Stevenson came out to bat. He added 149 with Boycott (79) before the latter was dismissed, at which point Stevenson had taken his score to 115 not out – it was his second century for the County. Warwickshire were then bowled out for 166, with Old taking six for 76. A nine-wicket victory was Yorkshire's just reward.

The Roses match at Headingley resulted in a draw. Lancashire, after losing early wickets, recovered to 351 for eight declared, David Hughes scoring 126 not out. Yorkshire replied with 317 for six declared, Athey making 90 and the now reliable Bairstow 70 not out. When Lancashire batted again they scored 255 for six declared and set Yorkshire 290 to win in three hours. Yorkshire made a good start with 144 for the first wicket, thanks to Boycott (68) and Lumb (72), but Croft wrecked the middle order batting and Yorkshire were content to bat out time at 197 for five.

Rain reared its ugly head at Hinckley where Leicestershire made a good start to score 329 for seven declared. Yorkshire replied with 229 for eight declared, and Leicestershire then collapsed in a quest for quick runs and Yorkshire were set 242 in 160 minutes. Boycott (56) gave them a good start but on a pitch taking more spin, Yorkshire were content to play out a draw with Athey reaching 50.

At Abbeydale Yorkshire were definitely on top of Middlesex when the game was ended 2¼ hours early. Middlesex had the upper hand after putting Yorkshire in and out again for 203. Stevenson (four for 46) was in fine form, however, and Middlesex finished 45 in arrears. In the second innings Yorkshire got the upper hand by scoring 236 for five declared, and Middlesex were 39 for two at the close.

Two further draws followed at Acklam Park against Northamptonshire and at Ilford against Essex. At Acklam, Northamptonshire put on 278 for the first wicket with Cook scoring 112 and Larkins 186 before Northamptonshire declared at 382 for three off only 81.4 overs. It was a sad exhibition of bowling by Yorkshire. Yorkshire replied with 142 for four. There was even less play at Ilford where Yorkshire scored 152 for eight before declaring. Essex were 90 for one at the finish. This Ilford game was Illingworth's first match as captain of the Yorkshire side; he had replaced Chris Old as captain following the Northamptonshire game. The timing could have been better and it caused eruption amongst the members once again.

At the age of 50, Raymond Illingworth had a big task in front of him. An abandoned match with Nottinghamshire without a ball being bowled was of no help to Yorkshire nor was the match with Derbyshire at Derby where Yorkshire scored 291 for eight at a slow rate with Love making 110 and Lumb 74 and Derbyshire replied with 473. John Wright made a fine 190 as Derbyshire hoisted 242 for the first wicket. On an easy-paced pitch, Athey (134) took Yorkshire to 200 for four and a comfortable draw. Languishing close to the foot of the table, Yorkshire were still unbeaten although they had won only one match. The Worcestershire match at Abbeydale did not change matters as a high scoring game finished slightly in Yorkshire's favour. Glenn Turner with 112 and 70 was in fine form for the visitors who were dismissed for 267, Phil Carrick bowling better than he had done for some time in taking six for 90. Boycott, with 159, helped Yorkshire to a formidable 424, with Carrick (92) helping. Boycott equalled Hutton's total of 129 centuries in this match. Towards the end of the innings Illingworth himself scored 30 and Worcestershire needed 157 to avoid an innings defeat. This was achieved without difficulty and they finished with 362 for nine declared.

Yorkshire suffered their first defeat of the season at the hands of Gloucestershire at Park Avenue. They made a bad start but Hartley (114) and Bairstow (55) added 147 for the fifth wicket, and a score of 279 seemed more than adequate when Stevenson caused a breakdown of Gloucestershire's batting at 26 for four but they reached 266 for seven and declared still 13 behind Yorkshire. After reaching 170 for four, Yorkshire collapsed to 187 all out and Gloucestershire were set 201 to win. This they achieved with five wickets to spare.

Illingworth had his first success as skipper at Headingley when Warwickshire were soundly beaten by nine wickets. Boycott with 152 not out from Yorkshire's 365 for eight declared was the main architect of victory. Simon Dennis took five for 42 as Warwickshire followed on and left Yorkshire with only 64 to get.

At Worksop, Nottinghamshire recovered well to score 329 for nine declared after being 127 for seven, due to Eddie Hemmings who scored 127 not out. Only Boycott (91) offered any resistance, and then Todd scored 117 not out in a forceful knock Nottinghamshire were able to declare at 181 for two, setting Yorkshire 305 to win. Boycott (82) and Athey (76) batted well and amidst great excitement Yorkshire went on to win by two wickets.

A wet pitch on the first day always threatened to ruin the Sussex match at Scarborough but both captains played their part with declarations and in the end Yorkshire required 251 to win in 195 minutes. Boycott was then seen at his best in scoring 122 not out and with help from Love (56) he guided his side to a six-wicket win.

The Lancashire match at Old Trafford was also ruined by the rain but not before Clive Lloyd had scored his sixth hundred against Yorkshire, a record for Lancashire. After Lancashire had made 310 for six declared, Yorkshire forfeited their innings and Lancashire declared again at 30 without loss leaving Yorkshire 341 to win. They made 142 for three in 84 overs, with Boycott making 62. At Weston, Somerset scored 388, and after Boycott (129) and Lumb (81) had put on 178 for the first wicket, Yorkshire took their score to 250 for four, after which there was no further play, with the last day being washed out.

Yorkshire scored 304 against Kent on a wicket that took a little spin, with Athey scoring 100 in $5\frac{1}{2}$ hours. With more rain about, Kent declared at 164 for three, and Yorkshire also declared at 109 for one. Set 350 to win, Kent collapsed suddenly, but bad light helped their cause, and Yorkshire still needed one wicket at the close, while Kent had 142 on the board.

A visit to Lord's began badly for Yorkshire and they were dismissed for a modest 182. Gatting (141) and Butcher (197) put on 237 for the third wicket and Middlesex finally reached 461 for five before declaring. There was time only for Yorkshire to make 75 for one in their second knock. Journeying to Dean Park, Bournemouth, Yorkshire dismissed Hampshire for 255, but with Malcolm Marshall (six for 41) bowling at his best Yorkshire finished 59 in arrears. Hampshire then declared at 167 for eight and Yorkshire were set 227 to win in 165 minutes on a wearing pitch. Both sides looked capable of winning and the match finally finished with honours even, with Yorkshire ten short but with only two wickets left.

Yorkshire finished their home programme at Scarborough against Derbyshire who were put in to bat and dismissed for only 137 thanks to Arnie Sidebottom's splendid spell of six for 31. Yorkshire took an 80-run lead, but in the second innings Derbyshire's Peter Kirsten made a fine 140 not out. Even so Derbyshire scored only 237 with Stevenson taking five for 72 and Yorkshire won comfortably enough by six wickets.

Yorkshire's last match of the season was at The Oval, where they were put in to bat. Athey and Love recorded centuries and the visitors were able to declare at 393 for eight. Surrey declared at 257 for one, and Yorkshire's 209 for seven declared set Surrey 346 to win in 220 minutes. Surrey made an effort to obtain that difficult target and finished at 294 for eight. Yorkshire ended in tenth position in the Championship but had the distinction of losing fewer matches than any other side in the competition.

Geoffrey Boycott, who missed only one match all season, finished top of the batting averages with 1,913 runs at 61.70. Moxon, who played in only two matches was next, while Athey scored 1,339 runs at 43.19, a big improvement. Love, Hartley and Bairstow all averaged 30 or more and Sharp averaged more than 29. Lumb had a poor season with 844 runs at an average of 26.37. Stevenson, Carrick and Sidebottom all averaged over 20, but Old averaged 13 with the bat and had a very thin time indeed.

Boycott actually headed the bowling averages, too, but he took only eight wickets at 10 each. Sidebottom was the most consistent bowler and he took 62 wickets, but they cost 24.80 each – a very high cost for a bowler who was virtually the spearhead. Old had 47 wickets at 26.14 but Stevenson and Carrick, who took 45 and 40 wickets respectively, took them at over 32 and over 35 runs each. Bairstow finished fourth amongst English wicket-keepers, and when his batting is taken into consideration he had few peers in the game.

In the NatWest Trophy, Yorkshire had a splendid win over Worcestershire, who had compiled 286 for five, thanks to Glenn Turner's 105. Yorkshire were in a poor position with four wickets down for 38, but Hartley (58) added 95 with Bairstow (92). Old (55 not out) helped Bairstow add 102 for the seventh wicket, and with Stevenson (28 not out) took Yorkshire to a win with three wickets and three balls to spare. In the quarter-final Essex never recovered from a score of 51 for nine and Moxon (78 not out) guided Yorkshire to a nine-wicket win. In the semi-final at Edgbaston, the Warwickshire seam attack proved too good for Yorkshire's batsmen with only Boycott (51) and Bairstow (49 not out) making much impression and 216 for nine was not enough to prevent a seven-wicket defeat.

In the Benson and Hedges Cup Yorkshire finished bottom of their section, their only success being at the hands of the Minor Counties. A veil could also be drawn over the Yorkshire side's efforts in the John Player League, in which they finished 16th and won only three matches in all.

At the end of the season, Chris Old, Peter Ingham and Steve Coverdale left the Club and Peter Whiteley's contract, which still had a year to run, was terminated in an amicable manner. Illingworth was re-appointed captain for the following season. During his term of office as team manager Illingworth had not been convincing, but there was no doubt that he had succeeded in increasing sponsorship money. He had also endeavoured to reach a better liaison between the County Club and the Leagues, with particular reference to coaching, which was in the hands of the Yorkshire Cricket Association apart from those players directly under the wing of County coach Doug Padgett.

On 17 September a tragic event took place when Neil Lloyd, a member of the Yorkshire 2nd XI from 1980 and a member of the playing staff in 1981 and 1982, died from a mysterious virus at the age of 17. A left-handed batsman of prodigious promise, he had already scored two centuries against Lancashire 2nd XI in the 1982 season and

Neil Lloyd, a promising colt who died in September 1982. He had already recorded two centuries for Yorkshire 2nd XI.

was on the verge of a first-team place. He was highly thought of in all cricket circles and there seemed little doubt that he had a great future in front of him. His father, Doug Lloyd, was one of the best wicket-keepers in the county. His death from a virus that the medical profession have been unable to give a name to was a tragedy that stunned the whole of the cricket world.

The 1983 season commenced with a slightly re-vamped Championship format, with each county playing 24 instead of 22 matches. Illingworth led his side into the field at Worcester but the game was washed out with the Worcestershire score 79 for three. The next match at Headingley saw Yorkshire with only 61 for one on the board against Warwickshire and that was followed by the Middlesex match at Lord's which had an even worse result – abandoned without a ball being bowled. The Northamptonshire match at Park Avenue did manage to get into its third innings before the inevitable occurred, and Carrick took five for 54 in Northamptonshire's first innings score of 257. Yorkshire's batting was a poor display of 157 all out.

The weather situation hardly improved but Lancashire did score 301 for four, thanks to Graeme Fowler's 156 not out and Frank Hayes' 116. Yorkshire's batting again let them down. One of the worst Mays ever to have been endured by county cricketers had drawn to a close – a month best forgotten by all.

At Acklam Park, Glamorgan 289 for nine declared, and again Yorkshire's batting failed. Yorkshire followed on and at least gained some much-needed batting practice. All the batsmen batted well and Yorkshire declared at 408 for four and set Glamorgan 245 to win in 160 minutes. Glamorgan were happy to save the game in the end at 162 for seven.

Well into June Yorkshire were firmly planted at the foot of the table with six draws. As the season wore on various excuses were invented for their low position. Yet there were only two valid reasons for it: one was the abominable weather which they shared with some of the other counties, and the other the idiotic scoring system which has always favoured the counties away from the west and north. Nevertheless there were rumblings against sections of the committee, against Illingworth and against Boycott.

Two decisions were made which were to have effects in the future. More cricket was promised to Headingley by the terms of the lease and at the same time Bradford was given an assurance that matches were to continue at Park Avenue. Also the Leeds Cricket Club disbanded and the club were not to play any more cricket at Headingley. It seemed an extraordinary move.

Yorkshire did at least have the better of the draw at Grace Road, where they struggled to pass 200 but Leicestershire could get only to within 25 of Yorkshire on the first innings. A declaration at 281 for six put Yorkshire on top: Leicestershire had to make 307 in 220 minutes. It was a task they never attempted, and they were happy to escape defeat at 193 for seven. Carrick took five for 69.

Hampshire at last provided Yorkshire with a win at Southampton. The home side struggled to reach 83 with Sidebottom in remarkable form, taking five for 6 in 8.5 overs on a pitch made for the seamers. Yorkshire passed that total without loss and reached a formidable 432 for seven before declaring. Hampshire batted much better in their second innings for 420. In the end Yorkshire won by seven wickets with only four balls to spare.

At Abbeydale Park, a substandard pitch which gave lift to the fast bowlers and turn for the spinners provided an excellent game of cricket for the spectators. Derbyshire started badly but Kim Barnett, in a typical captain's innings, drove and cut to great effect to make 95 and Derbyshire reached 225. Carrick took five for 45. Boycott (33) and Lumb (28) put on 63 for Yorkshire's first wicket but they were dismissed for 118. The Danish pace bowler Mortensen took six for 27 and proved quite unplayable, Bob Taylor securing six catches behind the wicket. Carrick in turn proved a difficult proposition with seven for 44. Set 256 to win, Yorkshire lost four wickets for 52, only Boycott remaining untroubled as he held the fort while Bairstow (44) helped him to add 90 for the fifth wicket. Sidebottom and Dennis both played their parts, but in spite of Boycott's excellent feat of carrying his bat through a completed innings for the sixth time for Yorkshire his 112 not out was not enough to take Yorkshire to victory, which went to Derbyshire by 22 runs.

An equally exciting match at Edgbaston followed, with Old taking four for 63 against his old county, who totalled 239. Warwickshire struggled even more to end 114 behind on the first innings. Stevenson took five for 35 but Yorkshire did little better in their second innings, and set Warwickshire 299 to win. Warwickshire lost six for 136 before Geoff Humpage, in a truly brilliant display on a pitch that always gave the bowlers some help, took Warwickshire to 238 before the ninth wicket fell. Amidst growing tension, Humpage continued to dominate the proceedings to reach 141 not out and gain a magnificent victory for his side.

A further defeat followed at Harrogate, where Leicestershire declared at 352 for seven on a slow easy pitch. When Yorkshire batted they showed little application to reach 251. Leicestershire then declared at 194 for five, setting Yorkshire 296 in 215 minutes. Bairstow showed his character with a second half-century, but Leicestershire bowled them out for 206 and so gained victory by 89 runs.

Another defeat by 81 runs followed at Northampton where Northamptonshire totalled 234, before Yorkshire's batting again let them down, Carrick being top scorer with 47 not out of 199. Yorkshire's final target of 272 in 260 minutes soon looked quite hopeless but Bairstow (80) showed fight and in the end Northamptonshire secured victory with just two balls left.

On a somewhat strange Headingley pitch, Sussex put in to bat by Yorkshire totalled 185 after losing seven wickets for only 87. Nick Taylor took five for 49 – his best performance for Yorkshire – and in reply Yorkshire just took a lead by making 197. Sussex's 238 left Yorkshire 227 to win in 250 minutes. Yorkshire settled for a draw at 162 for seven. There were no fewer than 14 lbw decisions during the game – a record for a match that Yorkshire took part in.

Kent had just the better of a draw at Abbeydale Park, with Yorkshire being saved by bad light. With centuries from Colin Cowdrey and Baptiste, Kent scored 424 for five declared, and despite Boycott's 101 Yorkshire were dismissed for 270. Yorkshire batted even worse in their second innings as they struggled to 121 for six in nearly four hours batting. Boycott maintained his good form at Worksop as he made 214 not out from 434 for five declared after Yorkshire had been put in to bat. Nottinghamshire scored 316 in reply at a pedestrian pace, with Carrick taking five for 69 in 43.4 overs. Yorkshire could only bat out the rest of the match on a good wicket and scored 131 for four.

By now Yorkshire had dropped to 16th in the table, but before the Lancashire match at Headingley, Simon Dennis was awarded his county cap. He took two early wickets to celebrate, but Lancashire reached 344. Moxon played a fine innings of 153 for Yorkshire, who declared at 305 for four after only 87 overs in order to make a game of it. Lancashire replied with 256 for three declared. Yorkshire, set 296 to win in $2\frac{1}{2}$ hours, made no effort to get the runs but had to struggle to avoid defeat at 90 for seven. Moxon again was top scorer with 39.

At Weston-super-Mare Yorkshire made a good start against Somerset by scoring 286, but the rate was hardly exhilarating. Somerset were even slower and no batsmen got going at all with the result that Yorkshire finished 122 ahead on the first innings. They then declared at 177 for eight, leaving Somerset with 300 to win in 245 minutes. With Richards unfit, Somerset made no effort to get the runs and were happy to bat out the rest of the day with 153 for six off 86 overs.

The western tour continued with a visit to Cheltenham College, where Gloucestershire were the opposition on the delightful ground there. Unfortunately it was the scene of what is now referred to as the 'Cheltenham Incident'. Yorkshire won the toss and batted first and lost two wickets for 50, whereupon Boycott was joined by Kevin Sharp, who batted brilliantly to obtain 121 before being run out at 274 for three. Boycott took his time in obtaining his century and it was believed before he went out to bat that he was suffering from some ailment or other. He went on to score 140 not out in Yorkshire's score of 344 for five declared in 115 overs. After he had reached his century, Boycott continued to bat very slowly. If he were fit, he should have speeded up; if not entirely fit, then he should have got himself out after reaching three figures in order that a successor could force the pace. He was reprimanded for slow scoring by Raymond Illingworth, and regrettably trouble had broken out in the Yorkshire camp once again for the County's ill-wishers to savour. Gloucestershire, on this easy paced pitch, then scored 307 for six declared. In their second innings Yorkshire made 239 for eight declared and again there was a period of unusual slowness on the part of Boycott (97) and another Yorkshire batsman. Gloucestershire were set 277 to win in 188 minutes, and got home very comfortably by five wickets. The standard of the Gloucestershire batting was vastly better than some of that earlier. Yorkshire were now at the foot of the table.

On a slow easy pitch, Yorkshire started against Nottinghamshire with a stand of 248 between Geoffrey Boycott and Ashley Metcalfe, playing in his first match for the County. Metcalfe (122) matched Boycott (163) run for run and showed great maturity as well as playing with tremendous power and timing for a player of 19 years of age. Yorkshire declared at 316 for three and in reply Nottinghamshire scored 303 for seven before declaring. Boycott scored another century in the second innings (141 not out) as Yorkshire compiled 283 for three before declaring. Nottinghamshire were set 297 in 210 minutes but only Rice (48) appeared to be interested in such a target.

The return game with Gloucestershire at Scarborough saw Yorkshire reach 333 in 111 overs. Gloucestershire were dismissed for 261 with the Yorkshire seamers generally on top. Batting again, Yorkshire tried to force the pace and eventually set the visitors 266 to win in 185 minutes. Stevenson was in good form with the ball and took three for 3 in 15 balls and Gloucestershire had to save the game, which they did at 196 for nine. Stevenson finished with five for 47.

Derbyshire batted well into the second day at Chesterfield to total 368, Carrick finishing with five for 122. Yorkshire were in immediate trouble against a powerful pace attack and only reached 160. With little else to play for in the follow-on, Yorkshire batted out the rest of the match. It was a tailor-made situation for Boycott, who finished with 169 not out.

Yorkshire's lack of success and the adverse press resulted in outspoken words from the committee members and from the team manager, who threatened to resign over the treatment he was receiving from a section of the membership. The Middlesex match at Headingley did not improve Yorkshire's position. Winning the toss they scored 293 in 110 overs. Boycott's 44 on a slow pitch was not suited to Yorkshire's requirements and it was a partnership of 133 between Sidebottom (78) and Bairstow (86) which brought Yorkshire to a reasonable score. In reply Gatting scored 100 not out as Middlesex cruised to 206 for four before declaring in less than 45 overs. Yorkshire then declared at 252 for five with Bairstow hitting out for a fine 100 not out in 112 minutes and completing his 1,000 runs for the season. Middlesex set off at a breakneck speed in their attempt to obtain 340 in 225 minutes, but rain finished the match with Middlesex 125 for two.

A poor display of batting from visitors Surrey at Scarborough resulted in their dismissal for 178. Sharp was in fine form and reached a sparkling 139 which resulted in Yorkshire gaining full batting bonus points for the first time during the season. Yorkshire took a 151-run lead on the first innings. Surrey then lost four quick wickets for only 42 runs but, with rain having already shortened the time available, they managed to draw without much trouble. Yorkshire now needed a win in their last match to have any hope of avoiding the bottom place in the Championship.

Put in on a green wicket at Chelmsford, Boycott (37) and Moxon (38) both batted well but apart from Love's 55 there was little else to offer against John Lever who took seven for 78. Facing 204, Essex soon had four down for 58 with Gooch also back in the pavilion with a bad finger. But Gooch returned and Essex finally reached a respectable 288, with Gooch making 111. Only Moxon (58) made much headway in between the showers and bad light and Essex bowled out Yorkshire again for 220. Essex finished Champions and Yorkshire bottom, yet each had lost five matches.

That last week-end was not entirely disappointing for Yorkshire because on the Sunday they succeeded in winning the John Player League for the first time. They lost only three matches during the season but by virtue of two points from an abandoned match without a ball being bowled they won the title. Boycott, Athey and Sharp all did well with the bat sharing the opening role, while Love and Neil Hartley could be relied on. Illingworth topped the bowling averages with 20 wickets at 12.95 and was most economical, proving the value of a good slow bowler in limited-overs cricket. Stevenson also bowled well with 22 wickets at 18.95 each, and the fielding and wicket-keeping was generally to be relied on.

Perhaps the success of the side in the Sunday League tended to accentuate just how badly the side did play in the Championship and the other competitions. To finish bottom of the Championship was a disgrace never envisaged either in their 75 years of almost complete domination or even in the 1970s, when the side at least had periods of success which gave great hope for the future.

Yorkshire failed to win a match in the Benson and Hedges Cup zonal matches, and in the NatWest Trophy, a comfortable victory away to Berkshire was offset by a somewhat crushing defeat at Headingley against Northamptonshire.

Once again Geoffrey Boycott headed the batting averages, with 1,941 runs at an average of 55.45. Bairstow was second with 1,102 runs, average 38.00. Sidebottom averaged 35.00 but missed seven matches and scored only 490 runs, proof enough that a higher position in the batting order would have been advantageous to the County. Moxon regained his place in the side to play in the second half of the season and he obtained 780 runs at an average of 33.91. He replaced Lumb, who had a dreadful time averaging only 23. Love completed his thousand runs and averaged 32, while Sharp played one or two good innings when he started to play regularly again. Carrick got amongst the runs, too, to average almost 30. Athey had a very poor season and appeared to lack confidence in himself and he also disappointed at slip, where he dropped too many catches and was posted to field elsewhere. He asked for his release at the end of the season and moved to Gloucestershire. Neither Stevenson nor Hartley could do anything right with the bat.

Stevenson took 56 wickets at 25.00, and Sidebottom 39 at 27.69, finishing just above Carrick who was the leading wicket-taker with 62 at 28.22. Illingworth took 32 at 29.71, and Dennis took 52 at 30.76. Those figures indicate more than the batting figures the reason Yorkshire finished at the foot of the table. Bairstow finished sixth in the wicket-keeping figures and there was no disputing the fact that he had no superior as a wicket-keeper/batsman in the country.

The 2nd XI finished second in their Championship with a batting line-up that was second to none. At this level there was no doubt that Yorkshire could compete with the rest of the country. At the senior level it was never easy for a first team competing with opposition containing top-class overseas players. During the 1983 season, 25 per cent of the batsmen who scored fifties against Yorkshire were overseas players and 40 per cent of the bowlers who took five wickets against Yorkshire were also overseas players. Not startling figures by any means, but they do spell out plainly the main reason why Yorkshire had fallen from their old pinnacle.

The two new young players introduced into the side during the past season both made an impression. Metcalfe played only in that one game against Nottinghamshire and spent the next two seasons developing in the 2nd XI until in 1986 he became a fixture in the side and was awarded his cap at the end of the season. Metcalfe quickly showed himself to be one of the best opening batsmen in the country but he still had a tendency to get out to rash shots, finding it difficult to change from one type of cricket to another. An attacking opening batsman with an orthodox style, his drives and cuts were exquisitely executed, perfect timing combining with a power not obvious in his shorter than average frame. As a fielder he lacked concentration but has improved immensely. He married a daughter of Raymond Illingworth.

Stuart Fletcher was 19 years old when he first played for Yorkshire in three matches in 1983. A right-arm medium-fast bowler he rarely tired and he showed a very steady improvement which resulted in him obtaining his cap at the end of the 1988 season.

The autumn began with Ronnie Burnet, chairman of the cricket committee, stating that David Bairstow would succeed Illingworth as captain. The latter would no longer play for the County but would continue to travel with the team, and Boycott's contract would not be renewed. The newspapers and media had a field day with this news and the County and its members were divided more than at any time in the past. A poll in the local newspaper showed that 93 per cent of the public or members believed that Geoffrey Boycott should have had one more year with Yorkshire, particularly as he had been given a testimonial.

Special meetings were held at which huge crowds attended, and the Yorkshire members voted for Boycott's reinstatement and for a vote of 'no confidence' in both the general and cricket committees. The general committee resigned, and the result was that elections would take place practically everywhere in the County. Each candidate issued

A view of the ground at Middlesbrough. S. D. Fletcher is the fielder in the deep.

his manifesto which was scrutinised in the newspapers in a manner that made a general election look singularly unimportant. Boycott himself opposed his own supporter, Dr John Turner, and not unexpectedly finished on top. Boycott was then re-instated as a player and yet still retained his place on the committee. Many regarded that as wrong. Michael Crawford, chairman of the Club for four years, resigned his position.

The other shocks on voting day saw F. S. Trueman defeated in Craven, Eric Burgin beaten in Sheffield, Ronnie Burnet beaten in Harrogate – by four votes, Bob Platt beaten in Huddersfield, Desmond Bailey beaten in the North Riding, Geoff Dennis beaten in Scarborough, and Billy Sutcliffe beaten by Tony Vann with a majority of 191 in Leeds.

Joe Lister, Secretary of Yorkshire CCC since 1972.

Reg Kirk of Hull was elected the new chairman of the Club. Further changes were Norman Shuttleworth's loss of his place on the Yorkshire committee through the fact that the Leeds club no longer had a member to serve on it as the general committee voted against making a nominee to the Leeds Board. Following that David Welch, the re-appointed treasurer, decided to resign. Welch was succeeded as Treasurer by Peter Townend, who has now served in the post for five years. The Club was in a state of unprecedented turmoil. Brian Close was elected chairman of the cricket sub-committee.

David Bairstow, the new captain, was in a state of some bewilderment but as the dust settled and the new season was about to commence, an atmosphere of common sense began to prevail. A feeling of togetherness was necessary if the Club was even to begin a revival. One small paragraph amidst all the acres of space that filled the Yorkshire papers was the good news that the Yorkshire Cricket Association was to open two new centres of excellence in the county at Northallerton and at Hoyland, and that two further such centres were planned for the future. Cricket was still going on in Yorkshire, with or without a County Cricket Club committee.

THE CURRENT SCENE

THE NEW 1984 SEASON WOULD COMMENCE for Yorkshire without Raymond Illingworth, who had been removed from his office as team manager. The Club would also be lacking Alan Ramage and Nick Taylor, whose contracts had not been renewed, as well as Bill Athey. David Bairstow would lead out a very young team at Taunton for their first match – a team that would have Geoffrey Boycott as vice-captain, now very much a veteran as well as a member of the committee.

In glorious sunshine and on a perfect batting track Bairstow won the toss and put Somerset in to bat. J. G. Wyatt (87) and Peter Roebuck (145) gave Somerset a good start and put on 246 for the first wicket, but Somerset failed to consolidate on that start and after 107 overs they declared with 298 for five on the board. Yorkshire immediately lost Boycott, and with only Moxon (61) showing any sort of form, lost eight for 163 before Sidebottom (54 not out) helped the side to a respectable 242. Somerset declared again at 249 for five, leaving Yorkshire with 306 to win in 78 overs. This time Boycott made a sound 60 and with the skipper and Jim Love both forcing the pace to make 53 each, the target was always within reach. Sidebottom and Stevenson were there at the finish and Yorkshire won with eleven balls to spare by three wickets. It was an excellent start to the season and put Yorkshiremen everywhere in good heart.

At Headingley, Yorkshire batted first against Nottinghamshire to score 301 for five declared at a good rate. Two declarations followed after a lost second day and Yorkshire set their opponents 301 to win in 77 overs. After a good start Nottinghamshire almost got them, but with two balls left Dennis clean bowled the last man Cooper and Yorkshire won a thrilling match by six runs. Dennis finished with four for 77 while the hard-working Sidebottom took four for 51. Yorkshire were second in the Championship table.

Inevitably, the weather deteriorated and the next three games were ruined by rain. Yorkshire recovered to score 188 against Lancashire, who headed them by 100 runs before declaring and capturing two Yorkshire wickets. Moxon was presented with his cap on the Saturday. Love, Sharp, Moxon and Boycott got amongst the runs at Abbeydale against Sussex but there was never a chance of anything other than a draw and the return with Somerset at Middlesbrough was notable for the fact that Jim Love scored 112 after Yorkshire had lost three wickets for 15. The tailend wagged and a score of 309 was very presentable, especially as Somerset lost six for 141 with Fletcher taking four for 24, his best performance to date. There was no time for further cricket.

While Bairstow was absent on international duties, Boycott had taken over the captaincy and Steven Rhodes had replaced his skipper behind the stumps. An outstanding wicket-keeper from the first, he was only 17 when he appeared against the Sri Lankans at Abbeydale Park for Yorkshire, but he was unable to have any activity in the game due to the wretched weather. His only appearances for Yorkshire were these two games. He went coaching in South Africa in 1982–83 and due to Bairstow's presence in the Yorkshire side, was allowed to go to Worcestershire in 1985, and quickly established his place in the side. He is also a very useful batsman with a pleasing style.

At Tunbridge Wells, Yorkshire made another good start with Boycott (59) and Moxon (110) putting on 124 for the first wicket but before they had doubled the score the Kent bowlers had wreaked havoc upon the Yorkshire batting and only a last-wicket stand of 55 took Yorkshire to 197. Kent too found runs difficult to obtain. In the second innings Boycott scored his first century of the season (104 not out) and added 185 for the fifth wicket with an aggressive Sharp (99). A target of 255 was quite beyond the home side who struggled to survive at 121 for seven as Sidebottom, bowling at his best, took six for 41.

A fine match at Basingstoke should have been won by Yorkshire but for a crucial missed chance. Yorkshire failed by just two runs to extract victory after being set 85 to win in 12 overs. Hampshire, put in to bat, made 230. Boycott (53) and Moxon (68) put on 125 for Yorkshire's first wicket and them Lumb (55) and Sharp (64) added 122 for the fourth wicket and with the tail hitting out Yorkshire reached a creditable 401. In reply Hampshire lost six for 125, but Nicholas stood firm to score 128, and Cowley (26) dropped at one, offered resistance with the result that Hampshire scored 255. Yorkshire's gallant effort to score 85 just failed.

The Derbyshire match at Harrogate provided 1,170 runs for the loss of only 22 wickets, of which total Carrick took eleven for 225 in a mammoth bowling stint of 71 overs and 2 balls. Derbyshire scored 439, batting well into the second day. In reply Yorkshire scored 352 for four in 97 overs; Boycott contributing 153 not out and Sharp 104. Carrick made Derbyshire struggle in their second innings as they scored a laborious 175 for seven, setting Yorkshire 263 to win in 50 overs. Boycott (48) and Moxon (74) put on 87 for the first wicket but after losing three middle-order batsmen for only 16 runs Yorkshire settled for a draw at 204 for six.

Yorkshire's run of six draws plummetted the County down to seventh place, but at Northampton Yorkshire gained a fine win by an innings and 34 runs on a pitch that was affected by rain and deteriorated throughout the match. A score of 329 was most satisfactory, especially when Northamptonshire lost two wickets to Sidebottom with only two on the board. They never recovered and were dismissed for 135 and when they followed on collapsed again and were finally out for 160, Carrick taking six for 32.

A stand of 265 at Trent Bridge between R. T. Robinson (169) and D. W. Randall (136) put Yorkshire in trouble against Nottinghamshire, who declared after 100 overs with 390 for five. Yorkshire made a wretched start in reply to lose five wickets for 51 but Phil Robinson (45) and skipper Bairstow (91) built Yorkshire's score up to 341 with great help from Sidebottom (49) and Dennis, who made his highest score (53 not out) for the County. Then Nottinghamshire declared at 259 for five leaving Yorkshire to get 309 in 61 overs, a target they never contemplated. Yorkshire were now in sixth position.

Yorkshire had lost Moxon injured during the Northamptonshire match, and with Sidebottom and Stevenson missing too, were at a disadvantage as they faced the strong Essex side at Headingley. Winning the toss Yorkshire struggled badly being all out for 183. Gooch and Fletcher made centuries as Essex declared at 524 for seven and dismissed Yorkshire a second time for 188.

Following this game, Yorkshire visited Telford to meet Shropshire in the first round of the NatWest Cup. Winning the toss and putting in the opposition seemed the correct decision especially as two wickets fell for only 21, but Mushtaq showed his class with 80 and Yorkshire faced a total of 229 for five. They gave a lamentable batting performance and Shropshire ran out worthy winners by 37 runs. It was the first-ever defeat in this particular competition by a first-class county, and an announcement concerning Boycott's testimonial during the play did not help to ease the defeat.

The Gloucestershire match at Park Avenue provided another remarkable game of cricket, in which only 15 wickets fell over the three days while 1,216 runs were scored. To Gloucestershire's 381 for five declared Yorkshire replied with 328 for three declared, Lumb (165 not out) adding 247 in an unbroken partnership with Neil Hartley (104 not out). Athey then scored 114 not out against his old county out of 226 for five declared and Yorkshire were set 280 to win in a minimum of 48 overs. On such a good pitch, Yorkshire knocked off the runs with nearly three overs to spare, thanks to Boycott (126 not out) who completed 45,000 runs and added 195 with Kevin Sharp, who made an aggressive 95. At the halfway stage of the season Yorkshire were in sixth position.

A stand of 260 between Richard Lumb (144) and Kevin Sharp (132) was the feature of the first day at Sophia Gardens against Glamorgan.

Yorkshire declared at 415 for nine in less than 108 overs, and then dismissed five Glamorgan batsmen for 101, but Glamorgan eventually made 357. Simon Dennis took five for 124. In their second innings Yorkshire took their score to 262 for four declared with Boycott scoring 101 not out and Glamorgan finished on 92 without loss in a tame draw that was hardly a credit to cricket.

At Lord's Yorkshire were bundled out for 121. Middlesex at 72 for three were in some trouble too, but Mike Gatting batted brilliantly for 131 not out and Middlesex declared with 303 for eight on the board. Chris Shaw in his first match took four for 68. Yorkshire batted a little better in their second innings but the home side's seamers were always on top and Middlesex knocked 22 off to win for the loss of Miller. Christopher Shaw, a very straight right-arm medium-fast bowler with a good high action, was given an extended run in 1988.

Philip Robinson also made his debut in 1984 and did well enough to finish second to Boycott at the head of the Yorkshire averages. An attacking middle-order batsman with every shot in the book, he improved his fielding to become one of the most reliable in the team. He is also a useful left-arm medium pace bowler and an above average wicket-keeper. In 1988 he won a regular place and thoroughly deserved his cap.

Yorkshire began badly at Scarborough against Worcestershire, losing Moxon to the first ball of the match, and soon had six down for 30. Bairstow hit 94 in a fighting captain's innings as Yorkshire totalled 188, which Worcestershire passed for the loss of only two wickets. They went on to score 402, Jarvis taking six for 115. Yorkshire had little difficulty in saving the game with Boycott scoring 126 not out as rain washed out play after lunch on the final day.

At Abbeydale Park, Leicestershire put on 145 for the first wicket and declared at 327 for four. Yorkshire struggled but were only 24 behind when they declared at 303 for eight. Leicestershire then scored 265 for seven declared and Yorkshire were left with 290 to win in 66 overs. On a pitch where the bounce was becoming more unreliable, Yorkshire put on 101 for the first wicket but a draw was inevitable with Yorkshire reaching 204 for six at the close.

Jarvis bowled well at Old Trafford to take six for 61 as Lancashire were dismissed for 151. Yorkshire took their score to 124 for five before the game was abandoned. At Leicester the home side needed a recovery to take their score to 206. Sidebottom took five for 39. Yorkshire headed that total by 100 runs. Going in again Leicestershire never had enough runs to declare and so they batted out time to score 363 for five. It was another poor result for cricket.

At Headingley, Warwickshire lost three wickets for 24 but Humpage went on to score 112 and Chris Old (52) helped ensure a useful score of 285 for the visitors. Sidebottom took six for 64. Yorkshire gave a poor batting display on a pitch that always had something for the seamer, and were dismissed for 153, Old taking five for 53. In the second innings Warwickshire recovered from 21 for three and were able to declare at 242 for seven. Yorkshire, set 375 to win, were never in with a chance although Boycott carried his bat through the innings for 55 not out from 183. Chris Old finished with six for 46. It was a very poor display from Yorkshire, who had now dropped to twelfth place in the table.

Yorkshire opened with Sidebottom and Metcalfe down at The Oval, but made only 175. Surrey opened with 277 through Clinton (192) and Butcher (118), Knight then scored 77 and Lynch (85) and were able to declare at 518 for five. Yorkshire batted even worse in their second knock to lose by an innings and 195 runs.

After that match, in which Boycott was out injured, Brian Close, the chairman of the cricket committee, took the responsibility of leaving Boycott out of the next match at Chesterfield. Whether he was fit or not was uncertain – there appeared to have been a lack of communication somewhere along the line. This compounded the problems facing those who run Yorkshire cricket and the press as usual evaluated, digested and fed back to the public.

The Derbyshire match was a surprise. Sharp, in $5\frac{1}{2}$ hours of fine batting, cutting exquisitely and driving with power and style, made the highest score of his career to make 173, and Yorkshire finally reached 439. Oldham spearheaded the Yorkshire attack, bowling sensibly and intelligently as Derbyshire were bowled out for 253 and 156.

The Glamorgan match at Park Avenue was played on a good pitch and Glamorgan reached 306. Boycott batted slowly to obtain 65 out of 182, but Robinson, with an aggressive 92, rescued the match from complete boredom, displaying strokes and footwork rarely seen in recent days. In their second innings Glamorgan gave another drab display with no attempt to win. Yorkshire replied with 41 without loss.

The Hampshire match on that too easy Scarborough wicket provided another draw but at least a target was set in a game that was restricted to two day's play. Hampshire scored 254 for six declared, and in 37 overs, Yorkshire reached 108 for one before declaring. Hampshire in their turn declared with 155 for two on the board setting Yorkshire 302 to win in 73 overs. Against an accurate attack they were soon behind the required rate. At 191 for eight Yorkshire could do no more than hold out for a draw with Sidebottom (28 not out) and Oldham (16 not out) taking the score from 208 for nine to 252 without further loss. There was little excitement in the Sussex game at Hove where Boycott (77) and Moxon (84) put on 149 for the first wicket before Yorkshire declared at 250 for five. Sussex in their turn declared at 202 for four but after Yorkshire had taken their lead to 146 the heavens opened at lunch-time on the last day to finish play. Yorkshire finished an unsatisfactory 14th; their one consolation being that at least it was an improvement.

An inspection of the batting averages gives no indication of the weakness of the side. Boycott again finished on top of the averages with 1,567 runs at 62.68. Robinson was second with 756 runs and an average slightly ahead of Kevin Sharp, who had his best-ever season and scored 1,445 runs at 39.05. Bairstow averaged 37.47 and Moxon was the third member of the team with a four figure aggregate at 36.28. Lumb, with a limited number of appearances, averaged 35 and Sidebottom 31. Love and Neil Hartley were both disappointing, as indeed was Metcalfe, while Carrick failed to reach a fifty in 28 innings.

The bowling tells a different story. Sidebottom was top with 63 wickets at 20.07, not sensational figures but a long way ahead of any other bowler in the side. Carrick was next in aggregate with 44 wickets at 36.50. Injuries affected the side, particularly the bowlers, some of whom seemed to be bowling on only two or three cylinders. Stevenson in particular could do little right with either bat or ball. There was little doubt that the side was not blessed with good luck, but on some occasions the side had seemed to have some sort of a death-wish, particularly in the field where some of their efforts were frankly third-rate. After a succession of captains who had no real pretensions or gift for the task, it would be churlish to criticise Bairstow, who put everything he could into his leadership and set a fine example with his attitude. With the bat he did everything and more that could have been asked of him. But there were already suspicions that keeping wicket and leading the side was asking too much of him. His keeping may or may not have deteriorated, but he finished lower in the list of wicket-keepers than in any previous season since he started with Yorkshire in 1970, when he had missed the first quarter of the season. The fielding of the side was far below average, and several of the younger players were below standard as well as the older players.

Yorkshire qualified for the quarter-finals of the Benson and Hedges Cup and won at Hove by 37 runs in a well-contested game. Moxon scored 79 and then Hartley scored a rapid 55 and thereafter Yorkshire were always on top. In the semi-final at Headingley, Yorkshire lost a thoroughly entertaining game on a perfect pitch by just three runs. Warwickshire seemed home and dry with 276 for four on the board, Kallicharran making 85, but Yorkshire came back well with Moxon (50) helping Sharp (83) in a second-wicket stand that took Yorkshire to 110 and later Bairstow and Stevenson seemed to have swung the game Yorkshire's way as they reached 263 with five wickets left. A magnificent catch got rid of the skipper for 39 and Yorkshire could add only ten more runs and they lost by three runs.

Yorkshire had a poor season in the John Player League, finishing with only one team below them but both batting and bowling averages were fairly satisfactory and many of the side's defeats were by small margins.

Boycott was given a one year's contract by the cricket committee for the next season but there was a move afoot to try and get him removed from the side. Several ex-members of the committee voiced their opinions and there appeared to be a chance of further warfare during the coming winter. Close then announced that he would resign if Boycott was not offered the captaincy and bat lower down the batting order – in other words prove that he could put the interest of the side before his own batting.

Viscount Mountgarret accepted the presidency in place of Norman Yardley, who had resigned the previous winter and he was duly elected at the AGM. Viscount Mountgarret has been without doubt a working president, being full of enthusiasm for the good of cricket and Yorkshire cricket in particular. He was a regular attender at matches and at committee meetings, was full of sound ideas and was forthright in his opinions on all aspects of Yorkshire cricket. The days of the figurehead-type president had gone, but no doubt he would have taken that role in his stride if the present state of Yorkshire cricket had not demanded a more commanding role.

In the end Reg Kirk, chairman of the Club, announced that David Bairstow would be captain as Geoffrey Boycott had indicated that he would not take on the captaincy but would be solidly behind Bairstow. Bairstow had turned down the idea that he should be captain of the side if he would cease wicket-keeping in order to allow Rhodes to take over behind the stumps. He was adamant that he would not take the captaincy on those conditions; the committee re-convened and offered the captaincy again to him without any strings attached. He accepted. A day or so later Brian Close resigned as he had indicated he would if his ideas were not implemented. Philip Sharpe and Bryan Stott also resigned from the cricket committee.

There was now a pressure group formed with various businessmen in control which in turn caused the old reform group – now renamed the 'Yorkshire Members 1984 Group' – to revive. Each side gave its opinions to the press and once again the Club, the team and its members were split asunder. Yorkshire cricket was becoming the laughing-stock of the sporting world.

As anticipated, Steve Rhodes, the reserve wicket-keeper, applied for his release in order to join Worcestershire. Yorkshire could only regret his going, being unable to give him a place in the first team. Yet another blow was to befall the club when Headingley lost its status as a regular Test match ground. They would not be staging a Test match in 1990. This was a blow to the Club's pride, and further ammunition to fire at the committee, who were accused of being neither cricketers nor businessmen and unable to negotiate with the TCCB at Lord's.

The newspapers continued to print letters and to publish tittle-tattle to a degree exceeding even the worst excesses of the past. Even Syd Fielden, a devoted friend of Boycott, at last fell out with the opening batsman over a letter and over a question of money changing hands. Whether it showed Mr Fielden or Mr Boycott in a good or a bad light this writer would not be prepared to say. But it did Yorkshire cricket little good at all.

The 'Yorkshire Cricket Devoteees' – the name adopted by the new pressure group – moved a vote of no confidence in the general committee among a series of resolutions that almost brought legal action and counter-legal action. The advice of Queen's Counsel was sought; injunctions were issued; the AGM was threatened with postponement. Rule changes would be made.

In the end the general committee won the day, but the voting was so close that neither side could gain a great deal of satisfaction from the result.

The new season was almost upon them and Tony Vann was appointed the new cricket sub-committee chairman. The only changes in the team personnel, apart from young Rhodes leaving, was the retirement of Richard Lumb, who emigrated to South Africa. The team had been on a fitness course to Catterick; they would be fit for the start of the season. Steve Oldham had been appointed bowling coach – Padgett would continue to look after the batting – and a selection committee had been formed, chaired by Tony Vann and consisting of the captain and senior pro, Geoff Boycott.

Yorkshire opened the season at Leicester in wintry conditions that contained a snow-storm on the opening day and was followed by rain and bad light. Leicestershire were dismissed for 170 and Yorkshire replied with 306 for five declared. Leicestershire had only time to score 46 without loss in their second innings.

At Headingley, Yorkshire, put in to bat by Middlesex and without Boycott, opened with Sidebottom (55), and with Robinson scoring 62, 304 for nine declared represented a pretty solid start, all the dismissed members of the side reaching double figures. Middlesex also found run-getting very easy and they declared after 74 overs with 225 for two on the board. Yorkshire then slipped to 133 all out only skipper Bairstow (33 not out) passing the twenties. Middlesex were set 215 in 60 overs and in an innings dominated by Slack (99) Middlesex appeared to be cruising home until Sharp ran out Gatting, and then Sidebottom took three quick wickets and Jarvis modded up the tail, so Yorkshire gained a thrilling two-run victory with four balls left.

Richard Blakey made his debut in this match, batting well in the first innings to make an attractive 32 and, in the absence of Bairstow in the second innings, keeping wicket and taking four catches. He went on to play in 13 other matches that season, averaged 25 and gave the impression that he could well become the best of the many young batsmen on the threshold of Yorkshire cricket. In 1986 he had limited opportunities with the first team but in the following season he scored 1,361 runs for Yorkshire at an average of 41 and at the end of the season was awarded his cap. In 1988 he lost his batting form and was dropped but soon came back to replace Bairstow behind the stumps, a position that he filled more than adequately. Whether his future is as an opener, a number three or even as a batsman/wicket-keeper further down the order, he is one of the brightest prospects in the country.

The Essex match at Abbeydale was abandoned without a ball being bowled and the Lancashire match at Old Trafford was also ruined by rain, but not before Yorkshire had recovered to reach 205 all out against West Indian Patterson, who took six for 77. Lancashire also lost quick wickets but Folley (69) and Fairbrother (1228) added 142 for the fourth wicket and in the end Lancashire reached 269. Yorkshire's second innings was 58 for four.

Against a weak Somerset attack, Yorkshire declared at 383 for four after a second-wicket partnership of 223 between Moxon (153) and Blakey (90). Somerset struggled until Vivian Richards (105) and Marks (62) added 98 for the fifth wicket and they were all out for 257. Boycott, after a long injury lay-off found his form with 114 not out and Yorkshire were able to declare at 223 for three, leaving Somerset to obtain 350 in 85 overs. After a bad start Somerset were happy to bat out time at 230 for six on an easy-paced pitch.

At Acklam Park, Hampshire made 341 for six with Chris Smith scoring 143 not out but the scoring was very slow considering that Yorkshire had lost both Jarvis and Oldham injured. When Yorkshire batted they were in some trouble despite Boycott's 114 and they collapsed from 255 for four to 283 all out. On a pitch that had turned into a slow turner, Hampshire declared at 223 for six. Yorkshire, set 282 in 215 minutes, were never really in the hunt and when rain arrived Yorkshire were in a weak position at 114 for five.

The match against the Australians at Headingley was ruined by the weather. At The Parks, Oxford University gave a good account of themselves. Jim Love (104), Neil Hartley (109 not out) and Ashley Metcalfe (109) made centuries, but despite three declarations there was not enough time to make a match of it.

Worcestershire won the toss at Harrogate and went on to score 300 for eight before declaring, thanks mainly to some poor catching and fielding from the home side. Four wickets fell for 36 when Yorkshire batted and only Boycott looked capable of staying as he obtained 105 not out of Yorkshire's 215 for seven declared. Worcestershire then scored 185 for three declared and set Yorkshire 271 to win with a minimum of 53 overs to go. Boycott batted nine overs before he got off the mark and it was obvious tht Yorkshire made no attempt to go for the runs. They finished with 124 for three with Boycott 64 not out. While the declaration might not have been a realistic one, the feeling was that Yorkshire should have made some sort of attempt to go for the target. Yorkshire by now were 15th in the Championship table.

The Leicestershire match at Park Avenue that followed was also a draw on a very good pitch where only 22 wickets fell in the three days with over 1,000 runs being scored. Yorkshire found runs difficult to come by against a keen and accurate attack and only Sharp (81) and Bairstow (77) looked to be in form. Yorkshire declared at 300 for eight in over 130 overs but when Leicestershire batted they scored more freely and reached 230 for seven in 71 overs before declaring. Yorkshire batted much better in their second innings and Bairstow came in to complete his 100 before lunch on the third day, at which point Yorkshire declared at 241 for one. Leicestershire were set 312 in four hours (or 73 overs) and made an excellent start, putting on 145 for the first wicket, after which Yorkshire went on the defensive and Leicestershire finished at 249 for six.

The match at Worcester saw Yorkshire put on 351 for the first wicket after being put in to bat, with Geoffrey Boycott scoring 184 and Martyn Moxon 168. They declared at 389 for three, and Worcestershire replied with 292 for seven before declaring, with Steven Rhodes top scorer with 58 not out. Yorkshire declared again with 194 for five to set Worcestershire 292 to win in 55 overs. They were always on target and an exciting finish saw them needing eleven off the last over. The sides finished level, with Worcestershire having lost eight wickets. Yorkshire were now two points ahead of Leicestershire at the foot of the table.

Yorkshire's first defeat of the season followed at Gloucester, where Yorkshire were put into bat and compiled 307. When Gloucestershire batted Athey (101) and Bainbridge (119) took them to 301 for six before declaring. Yorkshire then gave an abject batting display, although Moxon was unable to bat owing to injury, and Gloucestershire knocked off the runs required for the loss of only two wickets. Yorkshire's fielding had again let them down during the match.

A further defeat followed at Maidstone, where Yorkshire lacked Sidebottom as well as Moxon; the former playing in his only Test match for England. After a poor start, Kent, having been put in, recovered to 328 all out. Paul Jarvis bowled exceptionally well for Yorkshire to take seven for 105. Yorkshire replied with 300 for seven declared. Kent's Benson and Tavare then put on 232 for Kent's second wicket, each recording centuries, and Kent declared at 270 for three to set Yorkshire 299 in 66 overs. Yorkshire began disastrously with two run outs and only Love (93) offered any real resistance as Yorkshire were bowled out for 198.

Yorkshire could not look upon their defeat at Abbeydale against Surrey with much satisfaction. Surrey batted first and reached 364 in just over 100 overs, with Lynch scoring an attractive 133. Jarvis bowled well to take five for 107 but dropped catches were again of little help to the home side. Boycott carried his bat through the innings for Yorkshire scoring 55 not out of his side's 131 but the others played Gray (eight for 40) without much hope. Following on, Yorkshire fared much better but finally submitted for 280 and Surrey went to a comfortable nine-wicket victory.

That defeat placed Yorkshire quite firmly at the foot of the table, five points adrift of Worcestershire. Half the season had now gone. At Chesterfield Yorkshire won the toss and put Derbyshire in and the home side had the satisfaction of plundering a weak Yorkshire attack to the tune of 420 in 111 overs. Jarvis took five for 126 and had the

View of Abbeydale Park during the match between Yorkshire and Surrey in 1985.

satisfaction of performing the hat-trick. In reply Yorkshire were in grave danger of following on until Bairstow scored a typical century in less than three hours. Yorkshire were 147 in arrears at the end of the innings and then Derbyshire added another 218 before declaring with nine wickets down. Bairstow took eight victims behind the stumps. Rain and bad light stopped any attempt that Yorkshire might have made of scoring 366 to win and the match fizzled out with Yorkshire 21 for one.

Another pointless draw occurred at Worksop where Yorkshire's eventual target of 263 at about 5 runs an over was not attempted after Hadlee dismissed Moxon and Sharp for nought. The visit of Derbyshire to Park Avenue saw Yorkshire gain a victory at long last. The visitors could muster only 199 at just over two runs an over. With the pitch increasingly taking spin, Yorkshire were in some trouble too but Bairstow again batted splendidly to score 122 not out and so put Yorkshire on the road to victory. In their second innings Derbyshire reached only 129 and lost by an innings and 24 runs. Carrick took six for 46 and the victory shot Yorkshire up to eleventh place in the table.

Another wretched day in the field at Edgbaston was a humiliation for many of the large contingent who support Yorkshire away from home. Warwickshire's total of 456 for four declared (G. J. Lord 199) was obtained in 99 overs. Yorkshire's bowling figures are best forgotten. When Yorkshire batted a score of 228 all out was completely inadequate. Following on another bad start left Yorkshire at 156 for four but Boycott batted for five hours for his 103 not out and with Bairstow took the score to 237 without further loss.

Lancashire at Headingley was another match best forgotten as the sides compiled 327 and 328 in their first innings. Fairbrother scored his second century (147) of the season against Yorkshire and Moxon scored 127 for Yorkshire. Yorkshire had the best of the match with Surrey at The Oval for most of the game after Surrey had been put in by Bairstow. Mainly due to bad batting Surrey could total only 120. Yorkshire led by 157 on the first innings, and Surrey soon lost four for 76 but Lynch (121) and Jesty (141 not out) added 191 for the fifth wicket and Surrey finally reached 341 for eight declared and saved the game.

Kent at Scarborough toiled almost for six hours to total 217 with N. R. Taylor scoring a patient 102 not out. Shaw bowled very accurately to take five for 76 in 40 overs. Yorkshire made a hopeless effort to make a game of it by declaring at 150 for one, but torrential rain washed out the last day.

Another victory came at Swansea with the captains making a real effort to achieve a result. On a pitch taking spin from the start, Yorkshire did well to obtain 298 for nine declared with Carrick being prominent with the bat in an attacking innings of 92. On the last day Glamorgan declared at 27 for one; Yorkshire forfeited their second innings and set Glamorgan 272 to win at about $2\frac{1}{2}$ runs per over. With seven wickets down for 136, Matthew Maynard launched an attack on the bowling and reached 102 in 87 minutes, which included three consecutive straight hits for six off Carrick as he moved from 84 to 102. It was his first match for Glamorgan at the age of 19. Carrick had him caught at that score and Yorkshire won an exciting game by 34 runs to be back in eleventh spot.

After Yorkshire and Sussex had spent the majority of the first two days scoring a little over three hundred each, 552 runs were scored on the last day with Sussex trying to get 278 in a minimum of 44 overs. They always kept in contention and 21 were needed off the last over. In the end Sussex finished ten runs short with two wickets left.

Another problem had arisen during the NatWest Cup-tie at Headingley against Somerset. Yorkshire had already beaten Cheshire at Oxton by ten wickets and Neil Hartley (69) had given Yorkshire some hope of victory as he took Yorkshire to a score of 208 for eight in their 60 overs. Somerset knocked the runs off easily in the end with Vivian Richards making a brilliant 87 not out, but before that he appeared to some spectators to be walking out to a catch behind the stumps off the bowling off Shaw. In the heat of the moment a spectator (or spectators) shouted something at Richards, after which the Somerset skipper, Ian Botham, made some remark about Yorkshire's spectators subjecting Richards to racial taunts. The Yorkshire chairman Reg Kirk, in defence of Yorkshire, endeavoured to obtain a full TCCB enquiry into the matter, and a split in the Yorkshire committee between the chairman and president seemed to be imminent. The president had tried to calm down the situation by negotiating with Somerset. In the general committee a vote was held with regard to Mr Kirk's position as chairman, but peace having been made with Somerset the *status quo* was maintained.

The Northamptonshire match at Headingley consisted of 242 for five from the visitors before rain finally interfered, and this was followed by another draw at Scarborough against Nottinghamshire. Put in to bat on a pitch that eventually turned into a very easy-paced one, Yorkshire reached 262. Nottinghamshire went ahead by 39 runs before declaring with only five wickets down. Boycott, with 125 not out, then equalled Herbert Sutcliffe's record of 149 centuries but he batted too slowly, as the situation of the game demanded quick runs. Yorkshire eventually made 306 for four declared, and Nottinghamshire were set 268 in 54 overs. With Broad (72) and Randall (73) in at 163 for one, Nottinghamshire were holding the upper hand but Peter Hartley made his presence felt with five for 75. At one stage

Nottinghamshire lost four wickets for four runs, but they recovered from 208 for six to 256 for eight and either side could well have won.

At Chelmsford, Yorkshire were put in to bat by Essex on a pitch made for John Lever, who took six for 47 with all Yorkshire's batsmen struggling apart from Love. Facing 131, Graham Gooch launched an attack on the limited Yorkshire bowling and went on to score a brilliant 142. Essex made 413 for eight in less than 90 overs. With Boycott out injured, Yorkshire fared much better in their second innings with Moxon making 88, but an innings defeat was not unexpected. Yorkshire's final position of eleventh was a pretty fair summing-up of their capabilities.

Once again Boycott headed the batting averages with 1,657 runs at 75.31, while Bairstow was second with 1,163 runs at an average of 50.56, also finishing eighth in the list of wicket-keepers. Love averaged 40.73 with the bat and only just missed four figures, and Moxon, with 1,256 runs, averaged 39.25. Neil Hartley and Robinson both averaged over 30 too but there were some disappointments, particularly Sharp, who could average only 25.

Carrick headed the bowling averages with 65 wickets at 29.58 – acceptable figures in the circumstances, but they only showed up the lack of experience in the pace attack from which Jarvis and Sidebottom (especially) were absent too often with various injuries. These injuries plagued the side throughout the season and were a continuous worry to the captain, who never failed to give everything, but there were times when the off-the-field problems left him in a troublesome situation, and one could not help but think that he had too much to do.

On the one-day scene Yorkshire failed to qualify for a quarter-final place in the Benson and Hedges Cup, but in the John Player Special League, Yorkshire finished with only five sides ahead of them, although they were never really in contention. Sharp, with 546 runs, averaging 68, was in remarkable form but one wondered whether this affected his batting in the Championship, and the bowling of Oldham served as an object lesson to his younger colleagues with regard to line and length. Overall the fielding was below the standard expected and the catching close to the wicket was the weakest in the Club's history.

Soon after the end of the season, David Bairstow was re-elected captain of the Yorkshire side and Boycott was given a further one-year contract. Colin Johnson was granted an appreciation fund for the next season but he was replaced as second team captain by Steve Oldham, who was also the bowling coach for the County.

The Park Avenue ground at Bradford was heavily in debt and would face immediate closure unless an appeal for more cash from the Bradford Council was successful. It was hoped that a scheme including an indoor school would be built on the football ground which could be utilised by Yorkshire, but negotiations were already going on in this connection with a warehouse in St Michael's Lane, Leeds, opposite the Headingley ground.

The hope that a calming down period within the Club would now ensue was forlorn. A new set of rules had received committee backing, and chairman Reg Kirk, had reacted against some of these, including that allowing the dual role of player and committee member. This was particularly disturbing to the president, as the rules had been passed with only three members voting against them, and yet Mr Kirk had been urging his colleagues to support him in his attitude. Mr Kirk resigned as chairman of the committee on New Year's Eve. Before the AGM an alternative set of rules was placed before the committee, and three of the general committee voted in favour of them. Chaos appeared likely to get the upper hand, but the president made every possible effort to unify the Club, and he threatened to resign if the Club's own revised rules were not passed at the AGM.

Viscount Mountgarret won the day, with Yorkshire's membership backing the new rules, although by now apathy had set in amongst members. No doubt they were heartily sick of the bickerings that had been going on for months. One or two of the old reform group members had resigned from the committee and this resulted in a change of emphasis within the general committee. Brian Close was returned as the cricket sub-committee chairman in place of Vann, who was recognised as having performed his difficult task with some distinction, even by his detractors.

Yorkshire's new season (1986) began with a five-run victory at Taunton after both sides had forfeited an innings. Yorkshire, put in by Somerset, declared at 323 for five with Moxon (73) and Metcalfe (55) putting on 129 for the first wicket. Sharp made 96 and on the last day Somerset were required to score 324 in a minimum of 76 overs. When Roebuck (60) and Hardy (79) had taken Somerset to 185 before the second wicket fell, Somerset seemed to be in with a chance, and in spite of losing two overs due to bad light they kept going until the last over, from which they needed 16. Dredge got ten of them but was brilliantly caught off the last ball by Peter Hartley trying to hit a six and so Somerset's valiant effort failed by five runs.

At Headingley against Sussex there was a similar game, with Yorkshire forfeiting their first innings and Sussex declaring at 55 for one to set Yorkshire 251 to win. When the rain had cleared up Yorkshire were in trouble at 100 for six and it was a stand between Carrick (51) and Stevenson (58 not out), who reached his 50 off 36 balls, that took Yorkshire to a position to contemplate winning. With nine wickets down for 219, Jarvis joined Stevenson, and with the excitement growing, they got nearer the target until with a boundary that was an acceptable chance to the unfortunate Gould, Yorkshire won the day by one wicket.

With the weather being what it was, the forfeited innings became almost a rule, and traditionalists looked aghast at how contrived the game was becoming. At Chelmsford, Essex obtained 295 with Jarvis bowling extremely well to take six for 78. Two declarations later found Yorkshire needing 279 to win in 70 overs, and after losing three wickets for 10; five for 71 and eight for 120 they made an excellent revival to lose by only 26 runs. At the end, Peter Hartley had scored an excellent 87 not out. In spite of this defeat Yorkshire were in second place in the table and had a game in hand of the leaders, Lancashire.

The next match was the War of the Roses at Headingley. Batting first Lancashire were soon in trouble against Jarvis and Sidebottom and lost five for 47 before Chris Maynard (132) helped them to 296 all out. Jarvis took five for 86. Yorkshire made 314, and in their second innings Lancashire lost wickets steadily but reached 268 for seven before declaring. Dropped catches did not help Yorkshire's cause and they declined a target of 251 in 75 overs, finishing with 90 for one.

At Abbeydale Park, Alan Hill made an exceptional 172 not out and rescued Derbyshire on an easy-paced wicket, a last-wicket stand with Jean-Jacques (73) taking Derbyshire to 398. Yorkshire reached 259 for seven before declaring. Derbyshire then took their score to 140 for two before another declaration, which left Yorkshire with 280 to win in 81 overs. Apart from Boycott (69) and Bairstow (41) Yorkshire did not bat well against Michael Holding and suffered defeat by 99 runs.

Yorkshire's next match at Harrogate was spoilt by the rain, with Yorkshire making 450 for eight declared in which Sharp made 181. In reply Gloucestershire struggled to 257 for six before the third day was washed out.

On a pitch at Lord's that always had something for the bowlers, Yorkshire batted very slowly on the first day to total 276. Boycott batted for four hours and forty minutes for his 69, for which he was freely criticised but as it was the highest individual score of the game he could justify his approach. When Middlesex batted only Gatting (29) and Emburey (49) could find any sort of answer to Jarvis, who took five for 45 and Yorkshire gained a lead of 103 runs, but were then dismissed for 153, leaving the home side with 257 to win. At one stage 108 for two, they fell to the lively Jarvis who went on to take six for 47 and Yorkshire won by 69 runs. They were now second behind Essex with a game in hand.

Yorkshire were put in to bat at Worcester, and Boycott (76) and Metcalfe (108) put on 181 for the second wicket, helping Yorkshire to a total of 405. Worcestershire scored at a good rate to declare at 300 for two, and then Yorkshire scored 196 for four declared off 46 overs with runs being given freely. Worcestershire were set 302 to win in 53 overs, and as long as Hick was there Worcestershire were always in with a chance of victory. When he left for 60, they gave up the run chase and were 246 for seven at the close.

Wardown Park, Luton, staged its first first-class match between Northamptonshire and Yorkshire on a pitch that was too good for a three-day match. Northamptonshire batted first and scored 385 for four before declaring after 110 overs, with Bailey scoring an attacking 200 not out. Yorkshire lost Boycott and Sharp to Mallender with only six on the board but Metcalfe scored 151 – his second hundred in successive matches – and Yorkshire reached 314 for four before declaring. Northamptonshire then declared at 193 for seven and Yorkshire were set 265 to win in 48 overs. Boycott scored 68 and Peter Hartley hit hard to reach 54, but Yorkshire could not quite force a win and finished on 240 for eight.

Warwickshire were Yorkshire's next visitors to Headingley and with B. McMillan, a South African, making his best-ever score of 134, Warwickshire went on to score 385 off 125 overs. Yorkshire then lost early wickets before Kevin Sharp, with 114 not out took them to 300 for six before declaring. Warwickshire then declared at 201 for four. Yorkshire made a dreadful start on their way to their target of 287 in 85 overs and soon had seven wickets down for 56. Then Carrick (38 not out) and Peter Hartley (61 not out) took Yorkshire to 154 without further loss at the close.

On a wicket always assisting the seamer, Gloucestershire, put in by Yorkshire, did well to reach 246. Yorkshire gained a lead of 23 runs and this looked more than sufficient when Gloucestershire collapsed to 38 for five, but they finished with 173. Yorkshire were 20 for two and 151 to win looked a tall target when the last day was washed out. Yorkshire would have won the game well inside two days but for too many catches going to the ground.

Geoffrey Boycott reached the 150th century of his career against Leicestershire at Middlesbrough after Leicestershire had scored 314 in over 115 overs. Sidebottom took eight for 72, the best performance of his career. Yorkshire scored even slower than Leicestershire as they reached 309. Rain washed out the last morning's play and Leicestershire finished with 82 for four.

At Worksop, Nottinghamshire inflicted defeat on Yorkshire by an innings and 16 runs. Broad (122) and Robinson (105) opened with a stand of 226 before Nottinghamshire declared at 404 for three. Yorkshire were all out for 256 and 153.

Surrey provided Yorkshire with an unexpected victory at Headingley. Surrey reached 269 before Boycott, in spite of a broken bone in his hand, batted faultlessly to make 135 not out in Yorkshire's score of 307 for six declared. Surrey batted very poorly in their second innings and apart from Clinton, who carried his bat through the innings for 84 not out, could do little against Jarvis, who took seven for 55. Yorkshire won by seven wickets. Moxon, who had been disappointing for most of the season was now back in form having obtained centuries in each innings against the Indians in a game that the visitors won by five wickets.

After their defeat of Surrey, Yorkshire had moved up to sixth in the Championship and on the first day of the Kent match at Scarborough, Paul Jarvis was awarded his county cap at the age of 21. The Scarborough pitch was immaculate and Metcalfe (123) and the under-used Philip Robinson, who scored the first century of his career by compiling 104 not out, took Yorkshire to 341 for seven declared. Kent found runs easy to get and declared at 250 for two. Yorkshire then hammered 206 for two before declaring, with Robinson hitting 91 from 76 balls. Set 298 in 60 overs, Kent were never in with a chance of winning and looked likely to lose at 166 for nine, but succeeded in batting out the last ten overs to rob Yorkshire of victory.

A pitch with plenty of bounce gave the seamers a field day when Nottinghamshire visited Abbeydale Park. Peter Hartley bowled well and took six for 68 as Nottinghamshire were dismissed for 191, enough to gain a lead of 45 runs on the first innings. Nottinghamshire then declared at 188 for two after rain robbed the game of over a day's play and they were given easy runs. Yorkshire were set 234 in 54 overs and Blakey (46) and Metcalfe (108) gave them an excellent start with 117 for the first wicket. With three wickets in hand, six runs were required from the last over. Shaw was run out off the last delivery with the scores level. An exciting finish, but Yorkshire's running between the wickets veered from suicidal (three run-outs) to sluggish, otherwise they would have won easily.

Lancashire put on 79 for the first wicket at Old Trafford but were bowled out for 170. Yorkshire on an improving pitch, passed that score without loss and Moxon (147) and Metcalfe (151) went on to make a first-wicket partnership of 282. Yorkshire were able to declare with a lead of 229 and then took two wickets for 14 before the close of the second day. John Abrahams then batted 4 hours for 80 and with Fairbrother going on to score 116 not out, Lancashire saved the game by scoring 251 for six. Yorkshire had now risen to fifth position.

Leicestershire at Grace Road provided Yorkshire with a chance to improve even more in the Championship and after winning the toss they made a good start by putting on 96 for the first wicket but could reach only 216. Whitaker scored all round the wicket in an innings of 100 not out and helped Leicestershire to a 19-run lead on the first

Skipper Bairstow (left) presents Paul Jarvis with his county cap in 1986.

innings with the seamers taking all the wickets. In their second innings Yorkshire declared at 256 for seven, and Leicestershire were set 238 to win in 57 overs, a task they accomplished with ease with the two Yorkshiremen Whitaker (82 not out) and Tim Boon (78 not out) steering them home by seven wickets.

Ashley Metcalfe celebrated the award of his Yorkshire cap in the Glamorgan match at Headingley by scoring 149 out of 310 for seven declared. Yorkshire had already dismissed Glamorgan for 134. Glamorgan easily saved the game by scoring 212 for three, but the second day was almost entirely washed out by rain. A finish could not be contrived at Chesterfield where Yorkshire were dismissed for 177. A wet second day and declarations left Derbyshire with 272 to win in 70 overs. Derbyshire eventually gave up the chase and played out time at 244 for seven.

Rain also ruined the Middlesex game at Leeds where the visitors collapsed before the seam attack of Dennis (five for 71) and Fletcher (five for 90). In reply to Middlesex's 252, Yorkshire lost six for 98 before Love (65 not out) and Bairstow (42) took Yorkshire to 216 for eight declared before the weather changed. At Dean Park there was even less progress made Yorkshire scoring 212 and capturing four Hampshire wickets for 58.

Another rain-ruined game at Edgbaston resulted in a victory for Warwickshire by 54 runs after two innings had been forfeited. Warwickshire made a good start and a declaration came at 282 for two. Yorkshire thus needed 283 to win in 140 minutes plus twenty overs, but only Bairstow (57) and Peter Hartley (80) got on top of the bowling and Warwickshire clinched victory with the first ball of the last over.

The last match of the season was at Scarborough against Northamptonshire – a game that saw Yorkshire cricket at its best and at its worst. It was Geoffrey Boycott's last game for Yorkshire; a game in which he was run out in his only innings and failed by just eight runs to complete 1,000 runs during the season. Yorkshire began slowly with Boycott reaching 61 before being fourth out at 129 after which Jim Love completed a forceful century (109) while Carrick (46) helped to take Yorkshire's score to 352 for seven before the declaration. Northamptonshire collapsed against young Chris Shaw, who took five for 38 and followed on 155 in arrears. With six wickets down for 213 Yorkshire seemed to be home and dry but Yorkshireman David Ripley was still there at the close of play (they declared ten minutes early) with 134 not out and Northamptonshire had scored 422 for eight. Yorkshire's attack in the second innings looked second-rate and the fielding became ragged, in direct contrast to the side's fine effort in the first innings. Yorkshire finished tenth in the County Championship, which was perhaps a fair summing-up of their season's work.

Boycott, missing for more than half the season, again topped the batting averages at 52.35 while Metcalfe was second with 1,674 runs at 42.92; he made excellent progress but showed himself to be far from infallible against top-class bowling. Sharp had a good season, averaging 38.32, as did Robinson with limited opportunities, while Moxon, Love and Neil Hartley all had their days of success. Peter Hartley advanced as a batsman too, and Bairstow and Carrick could never be discounted with the bat.

Jarvis headed the bowling averages with 60 wickets at 22.20, with Peter Hartley second with 41 wickets at 26.70. Regrettably none of the Yorkshire pace bowlers played regularly, mainly owing to various injuries, and it must be admitted that the Yorkshire close fielding was the worst in the history of the Club. Behind the stumps Bairstow plugged away manfully but it was manifest that keeping wicket, leading the side and expecting to pull the side out of a mess with the bat was beyond even his willing capabilities. The spin attack was non-existent with Carrick ploughing a lone furrow – he bowled more overs than anyone else and always tried his best – but his overall record was inferior to his counterparts in many other counties.

In the NatWest Trophy, Yorkshire beat Cambridgeshire and Middlesex at Headingley – the latter by 20 runs after Moxon (65) and Robinson (66) had brought about a recovery – but they went out to Sussex at Headingley after the latter had compiled 213 for seven, recovering from 86 for six. When Yorkshire batted they lost five wickets for 23 and only Carrick (54) really got going. Sussex won by 88 runs. The Benson and Hedges Cup resulted in Yorkshire failing to reach the quarter-final, and in the John Player Special League, after winning their first four matches they finished a disappointing eighth. Love and Robinson were the best of the batsmen and Carrick finished on top of the bowling averages with 19 wickets at 23.63.

At the end of the season the 46-year-old Geoffrey Boycott's contract was not renewed; the decision was accepted by the membership and the Yorkshire public as inevitable. The fact that he had continued to play while still being a member of the committee had turned many of his staunchest supporters against him. Letters poured into the press in praise of him, but the threat of civil war was absent.

The Yorkshire County Cricket Club set up a programme in order to obtain £500,000 towards the development of the indoor cricket school in St Michael's Lane. The chairman of the general committee, Brian Walsh, was behind the move to have a benefit year on behalf of the Club during the forthcoming 1987 season. Before the start of the new season, the indoor school was opened with Ralph Middlebrook, cricket development officer for Leeds City Council, in charge. There were eight separate lanes for practice. Leeds City Council had put £265,000 into the school, which would cost £425,000. The County Club had launched a 'buy a brick' scheme to aid their testimonial year.

The Bradford Council purchased the Park Avenue ground from the Bradford CC for the sum of £24,000, on the undertaking that its use for cricket or other recreational purposes was a condition of the sale. Cricket had not been played on the ground during the 1986 season as the Bradford CC could not afford the upkeep, and Yorkshire's fixtures had been switched to Headingley. It was hoped that first-class cricket might return there eventually.

As expected, Phil Carrick took over the captaincy in place of David Bairstow and led out his side at Lord's to face Middlesex who made a good start by putting on 159 for the first wicket, stuttered in mid-order, but reached 292 for seven declared. Yorkshire struggled and were dismissed for 227. In their second innings Middlesex scored quickly to declare at 198 for five. Yorkshire were set 264 to win in 60

The Duchess of Kent opening the Indoor Cricket School in St Michael's Lane on 23 July 1987. From left: Ralph Middlebrook, Viscount Mountgarret, the Duchess and Brian Walsh (chairman).

overs and after Moxon (30) and Blakey (44) had given them a good start with a stand of 56, Sharp came in and played brilliantly for 75 putting Yorkshire in front of the clock and though wickets fell until Yorkshire were 202 for seven, Sidebottom (32 not out) guided the visitors to a two-wicket victory.

At Headingley, Moxon was the backbone of Yorkshire's first innings of 286 for eight declared, and in reply Hampshire collapsed and were bowled out for 148. Yorkshire collapsed in their turn on a pitch of uneven bounce and were all out for 124. Set 263 to win, Hampshire made a determined effort but in the end they lost by 15 runs. Yorkshire had made an excellent start to the season.

Their success was not confined to the first-class game as

539

Phil Carrick, captain in the late 1980s, bowling, with ex-Yorkshire opener Dickie Bird as the umpire.

Warwickshire had been beaten in the Benson and Hedges Cup by ten wickets with Moxon (93 not out) and Metcalfe (94 not out) passing Warwickshire's 208 for eight. This was followed by a 75-run win over Lancashire at Headingley with Metcalfe again in form with 84 the bowlers had little difficulty in restricting Lancashire to a total of 194. At the same venue, Kevin Sharp scored 64 not out out of 143 at Headingley against Worcestershire, who finished twelve runs short with Sidebottom taking four for 15. Scotland proved easy meat, with Yorkshire winning by seven wickets with 17 overs to spare. This time Metcalfe scored 91.

In the championship, a draw followed with Somerset at Headingley, with the visitors being held together by Peter Roebuck who played a defiant innings of 112 despite breaking his finger on a pitch of uneven bounce. Somerset were dismissed for 269 and when Yorkshire replied with 339, they had Blakey (99) and Metcalfe (66) to thank. Eventually Somerset were able to declare at 229 for nine to set Yorkshire 160 to win in 17 overs, an impossible task. Yorkshire made every effort to go for the runs but they lost seven wickets for 74 and they were happy to hold on for a draw. Yorkshire were second to Lancashire in the Championship table.

Down at Sophia Gardens, Glamorgan recovered after being put in by Carrick to total 270. On an easing pitch, Yorkshire replied with 216 for two before declaring with Blakey providing a fine 101 not out – his maiden century. In Glamorgan's second innings, a score of 226 for four declared was mainly due to runs given away by Sharp and Love in order to obtain the declaration, which required Yorkshire to score 281 to win in 66 overs. Yorkshire's batting was undistinguished after reaching 161 for five, and they were dismissed for 207.

Yorkshire had now reached the quarter-finals of the Benson and Hedges Cup and at Headingley the visitors Hampshire could score only 174 for eight on a pitch that was never easy to score on against Yorkshire's accurate seam attack. Once again Ashley Metcalfe (93 not out) took Yorkshire to victory with nearly ten overs to spare, Blakey (52 not out) adding 100 in an unbeaten second-wicket stand.

Up at Middlesbrough, Yorkshire batted badly against Nottinghamshire's strong pace attack, and Nottinghamshire's reply of 347 gave them a lead of 129 runs rain washed out the third day after Yorkshire had lost four second innings wickets for 42; they were lucky to escape with a draw. There was less play at Abbeydale. Yorkshire's score of 230 for seven declared was contrived to set Worcestershire 231 to win in 48 overs after two innings were forfeited. Even with Hick scoring 54, Worcestershire could score only 128 for five with both sides settling for a draw.

At Harrogate, Yorkshire gave a good exhibition of batting to score 393 for seven after a shortened first day because of overnight rain. Martyn Moxon (130) added 196 with David Bairstow (104). In reply Derbyshire could score only 131 and following on, batted without method or resolution and were quickly dismissed for 93. All the bowlers took wickets, and the accurate Carrick took his match analysis to five for 10 off 26 overs and a ball. It was a victory that took Yorkshire to equal top of the table with rivals Lancashire.

At Headingley, back in the Benson and Hedges Cup semi-final, Yorkshire managed to score 238 for seven against Surrey, with Moxon scoring 97 and Love racing to 40 not out off 19 balls. After that, Yorkshire's bowling was always on top and Surrey lost by 76 runs.

A drawn Championship match with Lancashire followed, which had its moments of high drama. Mendis (155) and Fowler (77) put on 153 for Lancashire's first wicket and they eventually declared at a total of 402 for three wickets. On an easy paced Old Trafford pitch, Yorkshire in reply declared at 179 for one with Moxon getting 88 not out and Metcalfe 78. Lancashire then went in and scored 96 for none declared, leaving Yorkshire with 320 to win in 79 overs. Moxon (36) helped Blakey in a second-wicket stand of 80 but after that only

Blakey stood between defeat and the Lancashire attack. He batted excellently with maturity and plenty of assurance as Yorkshire collapsed to 185 for nine before Fletcher batted out the rest of the match (17.5 overs) to ensure a draw at 223 for nine. Drama came when Simmons was upset following a possible bat-pad catch which was turned down by the umpire. Simmons accused Fletcher of cheating and the Lancashire committee imposed a week's suspension on him.

At May's Bounty, Hampshire compiled 139 without loss in a match ruined by the bad weather but back at Headingley, Essex, batting first, were dismissed for 151 with Carrick taking four for 10 on a pitch of variable bounce. When Yorkshire batted, Moxon batted with skill and resolution for 104 to help Yorkshire to 331 for eight declared. Essex were dismissed for 188, and Yorkshire went to a nine-wicket win and top place in the Championship table.

At Northampton, after the first day was lost to rain, Northamptonshire put Yorkshire into bat on a green wicket and bowled them out for 187. Only Blakey (108) could withstand the Northamptonshire pace attack in an innings that had class stamped on it throughout. Northamptonshire then declared at 138 without loss and Yorkshire totalled a further 233 for five before declaring; Northamptonshire were set 283 to win in 100 minutes plus 20 overs. Bailey (152 not out) and Capel (91 not out) in a brilliant display of stroke-play took Northamptonshire from 75 for three to their winning target with an unfinished stand of 208 in 27.3 overs.

The Kent match at Canterbury provided Jarvis with one of his best performances as he took five for 65 and reduced the home side to 200 for eight before Farbrace, the reserve wicket-keeper, made top score (75) to take Kent to 301. Yorkshire also found run-making difficult but managed to declare at 259 for seven. In their second innings, Kent were dismissed for 136. Yorkshire, requiring 178, reached 90 for one, but at 114 for five the game was in the balance and it took some aggression from Carrick (20) and the tail-enders to bring Yorkshire eventually to a two-wicket win. Yorkshire led the table with a 20 points lead over unbeaten Northamptonshire, who had three games in hand.

At Trent Bridge, Yorkshire were utterly outplayed by Nottinghamshire, on a pitch that, strange to relate, was made for the spinners. On winning the toss, Yorkshire batted but were dismissed for 160 on a pitch that turned quite considerably, although the Yorkshire batting left much to be desired. Swallow took seven for 95 but a lead of 145 runs was too much for Yorkshire's batsmen to overcome. Nottinghamshire needed 43 to win, which was a mere formality.

The final of the Benson and Hedges Cup at Lord's was against

Richard Blakey, a player with a future.

Northamptonshire, and was played on a glorious day before a capacity crowd who enjoyed a memorable day's cricket. Winning the toss, Yorkshire put the opposition in and four wickets fell to the accurate seam attack with only 92 on the board. Capel (97) and Williams (44) took the score to 212, but the innings did not blosson as well as Northamptonshire hoped, with Carrick's spell of 11 overs costing only 30 runs. In the end Northamptonshire finished with 244 for seven, with Jarvis taking four for 43. Yorkshire made a good start in

543

Phil Carrick holds aloft the Benson and Hedges Cup at Scarborough the day after Yorkshire's victory at Lord's in 1987.

reply, with Moxon scoring 45 and Metcalfe 47 as they put on 97 for the first wicket, but injudicious strokes from Metcalfe and then Blakey meant that Yorkshire slipped to 103 for three. Sharp and Love (75 not out) then added 57 and with Love settling in to his best form, Yorkshire regained the initiative. With two overs to go Yorkshire still needed ten to win, but with the scores level and one ball to go, Love had only to survive it to ensure Yorkshire victory by the fact that they had lost one wicket less than Northamptonshire. Love duly blocked the ball and earned himself the man of the match award, too. It was a good game of cricket, besides being a notable win for Yorkshire.

A visit to The Oval saw Yorkshire dismissed for only 121, and when Surrey batted Stewart quickly put them on top with a fine century (132) before Surrey declared at 303 for four. Rain prevented a finish and this was followed by a match at Hastings which was abandoned without a ball being bowled. Nor was there much progress in the Glamorgan game at Headingley where bad light and rain prevented Glamorgan getting near their eventual target of 246, being 66 short of victory with five men out at the close.

At Grace Road, on a pitch of uneven bounce, Leicestershire gave a poor display after being put in to bat and were dismissed for 131. Moxon (84) and Blakey (76) then proved that the pitch was playable and with the middle order batsmen making useful contributions, Yorkshire reached 341. A spiritless Leicestershire were then dismissed for 124 as Yorkshire won shortly after lunch on the third day.

Yorkshire now held a one point lead at the top of the table but Northamptonshire had four games in hand, a far from satisfactory situation which never occurred in the days when the counties arranged their own fixtures.

At Headingley Yorkshire again won the toss and put in Lancashire on an easy paced pitch which had been rolled more than usual owing to criticism of the pitch used for the recent Test match. Shaw bowled very accurately to take six for 64. After rain and contrived declarations, Lancashire set a target of 287 to win in 65 minutes plus the last 20 overs. Yorkshire, taking no interest in the proceedings, replied with 102 for none which reflected little credit on either side.

At Chesterfield, Yorkshire, winning the toss but lacking Moxon on Test duty, lost four wickets for 38 before Phil Robinson ((95), making his first Championship appearance of the season, enabled Yorkshire to reach a respectable 248. Derbyshire were doing little better at 222 for eight but a ninth wicket stand of 151 between Sharma (111) and Mortensen (74 not out) put the Yorkshire attack to the sword and established a first innings lead of 151. Thanks to poor light, Yorkshire managed to avoid defeat. Rain also ruined the Sussex match at Abbeydale where Yorkshire gave another poor batting display with Swallow making top score (55) out of 167. Sussex's lead was only 43, however, and when Yorkshire batted again Metcalfe scored his first century of the season (113). There was further rain after Yorkshire had declared at 239 for five.

The condition of the Taunton ground, dry as an August ground should be, was in contrast to the pitches up north. It was summer again, and when Yorkshire batted they gave a good display to total 343. Somerset also batted well to obtain 284 for four before declaring. Yorkshire were in trouble with eight down for 125 before Carrick (61) helped set Somerset a target of 246. Carrick (five for 42) then bowled well but Somerset avoided defeat at 185 for eight. A defensive attitude did not help Yorkshire's cause. In spite of the fact that Yorkshire had won only once since their great win at Lord's, they were still as high as third in the table, but they were no longer considered as Championship contenders.

The Leicestershire match at Scarborough provided another draw and a mixed display from Yorkshire. A delayed start did not help matters and a third wicket stand of 171 between Briers (104) and Whitaker (105) with some late hitting from Agnew (90) enabled the visitors to declare at 365 for eight off less than 96 overs. Agnew then took the first five wickets at which stage Yorkshire were 88 for five but Bairstow played one of his best innings to obtain 128 and Yorkshire were only 100 in arrears on the first innings. In their second innings, chasing quick runs, the visitors were able to declare at 188 for eight. Set

289 in 56 overs, Yorkshire played for a draw after Agnew had taken two early wickets and finished with 184 for five.

The pitch at Headingley was still under scrutiny during the Gloucestershire match. It played easily enough but the ball had a tendency to keep low. The first day was washed out and Moxon then fell to the first ball before Blakey settled in to make the highest score of his short career. He became the youngest player ever to score a double-century for the County as he finished with 204 not out. Both sides forfeited an innings and Gloucestershire were set 364 to win in some 103 overs, and looked like knocking them off as Athey (101 not out) and Lloyds (82) joined in a stand of 154 for the fifth wicket. But Jarvis (seven for 82) bowling superbly in indifferent light and Yorkshire managed to dismiss Gloucestershire for 319 to stay in the frame in third place.

There was now little that the side could do but sit and watch while their rivals in the Championship garnered the points and moved above them in the table. They met the MCC at Scarborough, where Metcalfe (152) and Swallow (114) obtained centuries and the former Yorkshire leg-spinner, Peter Kippax, made a rare first-class appearance to take three for 71 in the second innings for MCC. It was 25 years since he had played for Yorkshire. The visitors gained a six-wicket win. The season finished at Scarborough with a draw with

A Yorkshire Committee Team in a match in 1987.

Warwickshire, and rain and bad light having the final say on a slow pitch.

Yorkshire's final Championship position was eighth – a bitter disappointment to the members after the euphoria at Lord's. Many were convinced that Yorkshire's general unenterprising attitude since then had bordered on the unforgivable.

Moxon and Blakey topped the batting averages, and each had done very well with an average of over 40. Robinson, who played in less than a third of the matches, was next and Bairstow had done his work well, with his wicket-keeping showing an improvement, while Metcalfe, disappointing though his first-class record was, did score 1,162 runs at 32.27 – quite satisfactory for a 'bad' season. Love and Sharp were both disappointing, while one felt that the Hartleys, Sidebottom and Carrick should have done much better with the bat.

Jarvis took 77 wickets at 24.89 each to top the bowling averages and he looked the one dangerous bowler in the side. Perhaps he was overworked for one so young – he was only 22 at the end of the season – but there were times, especially with some of the youngsters injured and with Sidebottom missing a quarter of the matches, that Carrick felt he had to use him. Carrick was second in the averages with 51 wickets at 25.94, and was seldom collared. Fletcher's record was also satisfactory, but one felt that Sidebottom, with 43 wickets at 29.77, should have done better. Peter Hartley, who obtained his cap at the end of the season along with Blakey, did not have a good record, his 47 wickets costing 36.72 each, but he always worked hard, if over-bowled towards the end of the season.

In the NatWest Trophy, Yorkshire thrashed Wiltshire at Trow-bridge and handed out a nine-wicket beating to Glamorgan at Headingley, where Sidebottom took five for 27. They lost to Leicestershire at the same venue, apparently cruising home at 166 for three with 237 to make, but collapsing to 200 all out.

Yorkshire had a pretty dismal season in the Refuge Assurance League (successor to the John Player) and finished with only four counties below them. Neil Hartley finished on top of the batting averages with 40.14 and Sharp, Metcalfe, Bairstow and Love performed satisfactorily, while the seam attack bowled with a certain amount of consistency.

There was good news for Yorkshire, and Headingley in particular, with the pitch cleared for Test cricket for the immediate future, while there was a possibility of first-class cricket eventually returning to Park Avenue, where the old pavilion, a magnificent Victorian building, had been pulled down for safety reasons.

There was further good news in connection with the indoor cricket school in St Michael's Lane, which was booked throughout the winter with indoor competitions as well as with coaching. All the lanes or strips were sponsored, and help had been provided by the supporters' association which had been founded on the ebb-tide of the troubles some winters previously and had served the County admirably in a completely unbiased way which was a credit to them.

The shop, run by David Prime, was now firmly established near the scoreboard, and sold items of clothing, books and other memorabilia connected with Yorkshire cricket. Tony Vann had been partly responsible for that move, just as the new indoor school was his brainchild too. He had worked hard in connection with sponsorship and had much to do with the school in the summer being utilised by various sponsors.

Yorkshire County Cricket Club's appreciation fund had by now almost reached its target, and whatever troubles English cricket had in Pakistan in the winter of 1987–88, it was at least a relief for Yorkshire cricket not to be sunk in the depths of internal tussle.

Now that Steve Oldham had been fully established in his job as assistant coach to Doug Padgett, linking up with both the 2nd XI and with schools and junior cricket throughout the county, and with Bob Appleyard helping out with the spin department on a voluntary basis, there were mild rumblings that the County could not get all the net facilities required. It was a justifiable grouse, but only came about because of the popularity of the new school.

Phil Carrick was reappointed captain for the 1988 season which began with Yorkshire scoring 173 for one in an abandoned Benson and Hedges Cup match against Northamptonshire at Headingley. Yorkshire then faced Derbyshire, also at Headingley, in a Championship match and fell to their West Indian contingent for 161, Moxon with 79 alone withstanding the pace attack on a pitch of uneven bounce. Derbyshire scored only 170 in reply with Jarvis taking five for 49. When Yorkshire batted again they were in real trouble at 8 for three before reaching 192. Paul Newman did the damage with a remarkable eight for 29 in 16.5 overs, and Derbyshire required 184 to win. They got home easily enough by five wickets.

At Edgbaston, Yorkshire made another bad start, losing five wickets for 50 before the old stalwarts came together to add 106, Bairstow making 68 and Carrick 64, but the innings closed for 194. Warwickshire's lead was only 41, but their pace attack reduced Yorkshire to 175, and they went on to win comfortably by seven wickets.

Yorkshire found Canterbury a difficult pitch for the batsmen. They batted first and at 174 for two were in a good position but thereafter the side collapsed against the keen Kent attack to be dismissed for 244. Kent's South African batsman, Roy Pienaar, was in fine form to score

144 but Shaw (four for 56) and Jarvis (four for 75), suddenly proved unplayable as eight wickets fell for 25 and Kent's lead was only 30 in the first innings. Yorkshire struggled in their second innings and Kent needed only 104 to win, but again a collapse occurred and they were glad to see their winning total attained for the loss of only seven wickets, Paul Jarvis finishing with six for 40 on a pitch that was steadily worsening. At this stage Yorkshire were at the foot of the table and the membership was astonished that a side should continue to play so badly after the memorable win at Lord's. This season everything had gone wrong for Yorkshire, whereas in 1987 at this stage all the good luck had gone their way. On reflection, the 1987 team appeared to be at their peak at the start of the season, perhaps due to the fact that they had had a short tour of Barbados, which included a first-class game with Barbados and several one-day matches. Before the 1988 season Yorkshire had had a short spell in La Manga, which hardly conditioned the players to a difficult start to the new season.

The Hampshire match at Middlesbrough saw Yorkshire's chance of their first win spoilt by heavy showers. Hampshire were rattled out for 130, with Sidebottom taking five for 30 Yorkshire retained a lead of 109, but Hampshire drew at 149 for four.

Another draw followed at Northampton where once again the poor weather prevented a finish. Yorkshire struggled to 155 after being 82 for six, but Northamptonshire fell 25 short of this score, and in their second innings Yorkshire went on to score 228 for nine declared. Set 254 to win, Northamptonshire finished up with 192 for seven.

The Harrogate game with Surrey was also drawn after a thoroughly poor batting performance on the first day reduced Yorkshire to 18 for five before Robinson (58) helped to take the home side to 142 all out. Surrey rattled up 342 for four declared. In their second innings, against a second-string Surrey attack, Yorkshire were 310 for six declared at the close.

A trip to Fenner's should have meant batting practice for the Yorkshire side, but although they won comfortably by ten wickets, their batsmen found runs difficult to come by on a pitch that was much wetter than expected.

Warwickshire duly completed the double over Yorkshire at Headingley – the first time they had performed such a feat since 1951 – on a pitch that gave help to the pacemen until the fourth innings of the game, when it played much easier. Yorkshire made a good start but collapsed to 165 all out. Shaw (four for 17), Sidebottom (three for 25) and Dennis (three for 35) then proved to be almost unplayable as Warwickshire were all out for 81. In their second innings Yorkshire fell for only 123. While the Yorkshire batting was below standard there was no denying that the pitch was untrustworthy. Set 206 to win, Warwickshire strolled to a comfortable seven-wicket victory. Yorkshire were firmly placed at the foot of the table.

Yorkshire's batting failed again at Abbeydale Park against Essex where they were dismissed for 133. Essex did little better on a pitch that aided the pace bowler and Fletcher took eight for 58 in a fine bowling performance. At 11 for four, Yorkshire's early batting failed for a second time. Yorkshire finally scored 113, and Essex made short work of obtaining 89 for the loss of one wicket.

At last victory arrived at Hove against Sussex. The pitch gave increasing help to the pace bowlers. Batting first the home side were at one stage 161 for one but were dismissed for 299. Yorkshire's batting was again unsatisfactory and they struggled to reach 219. Jarvis (four for 21) soon made inroads into the Sussex batting and with Sidebottom taking four for 47, Yorkshire's target was only 186. The batting weakness was shown up again, however, with three players failing to score and five wickets going down for 72. Luckily Moxon stood firm and with Carrick (43) took the score to 142 before being dismissed for 61. Sidebottom with 27 not out then guided Yorkshire to a three-wicket victory which took the side off the bottom and revived a team not overloaded with confidence.

Yorkshire were fortunate to get away from Lord's without suffering an innings defeat, as the rain came to their rescue. The Middlesex catching was first-rate as Yorkshire struggled to 187 all out, with Bairstow making top score (41). Slack was in good form, scoring 144 as Middlesex took a first innings lead of 201. At the end of the game Middlesex had taken four wickets for 80. At Headingley rain again interfered with the Leicestershire match, but victory was achieved after each side had forfeited an innings. Leicestershire's Peter Willey made a laborious 104 as Carrick bowled with accuracy to take five for 46 in 33.5 overs, and Leicestershire were dismissed for 253. When Yorkshire required 254 to win, they made a fair start and Blakey, back into the side after losing form, made a valuable 51. Love (68) took over and Yorkshire got home for four wickets. It was hardly a classic win but it took Yorkshire up to 14th in the table.

At Worcester, Yorkshire fell under the spell of Hick who made a brilliant 198 before Worcestershire declared at 356 for seven. Yorkshire's poor batting form continued although they reached 302 for six before declaring. In their second innings Worcestershire obtained 215 for four declared and set Yorkshire 270 to win. Moxon batted well to compile 106 but his best support came from Robinson (33) and Yorkshire collapsed from 208 for four to 248 all out in another disappointing display.

The match with Glamorgan at Cardiff resulted in another

unsatisfactory draw caused by the rain. Yorkshire made 322 for nine declared, but the scoring rate was very slow against a modest attack. Rain followed and a Glamorgan declaration at 20 for one was followed by Yorkshire forfeiting their innings as Glamorgan were set 303 to win. Further rain and bad light ruined the game as Glamorgan finished with 179 for four. Yorkshire were now 15th in the table.

At Headingley, Yorkshire had the satisfaction of beating their great rivals in a most comprehensive manner by ten wickets. The Lancashire batsmen were always in trouble against an accurate pace attack in which Sidebottom took four for 32 and were dismissed for 154. Yorkshire were in trouble, too, and lost three wickets for 34 before Jim Love (77) and those reliable men down the order, Sidebottom (55) and skipper Carrick (37) established a lead of 139 for the home side. In their second innings, Lancashire were bowled out for 156 in an inept display. Eighteen to knock off for victory was a mere formality.

When Yorkshire were 207 for seven against Nottinghamshire at Abbeydale Park, it seemed that another batting failure was being chalked up against the Yorkshire team, but Robinson went on to score a timely 129 not out, looking his old self as soon as he had passed a fortuitous fifty. Nottinghamshire collapsed for 195 in a most uneven batting display in which Paul Johnson made 124. Hartley took five for 85, Yorkshire then compiled 119 without loss with some gifts from the Nottinghamshire skipper to induce a declaration. Nottinghamshire started well and put on 119 for the first wicket before Fletcher (four for 48) in a fiery spell reduced them to 198 for five, 64 short of their target.

An interesting match took place at Cheltenham against Gloucester-shire. Batting first, Yorkshire lost four wickets for 103 but left-hander David Byas stood firm and went on to score 112 in a stylish innings. This maiden century put Yorkshire in the driving seat and they declared at 367 for eight. Then Sidebottom, with a splendid piece of bowling, took five for 34 as Gloucestershire were dismissed for 214. Following on, the home side put on 218 for the third wicket, which virtually saved the game as they went on to 404 for six before declaring. Yorkshire were set 252 to win but batted out time at 104 for four.

A draw game against the Sri Lankans at Headingley produced centuries for Moxon and Sharp, but rain and bad light spoiled the match.

At Scarborough, Yorkshire compiled 369 for three in impressive fashion, with Moxon scoring 81, Metcalfe and Byas each 98 and Robinson 81 not out. In reply Somerset declared at 270 for eight. Yorkshire then declared at 182 for seven, to set Somerset 282 to win. At 190 for three they were well placed but they lost wickets and at the close were still 41 runs short with their last pair at the crease.

Rain interrupted the Derbyshire game at Chesterfield, where Metcalfe scored 115 and once again the out-of-form batsmen were gradually hauling themselves back after such a wretched start. Yorkshire reached a total of 301. Derbyshire then declared at 82 for three and Yorkshire at 25 for nought set the home side 245 to win in some 50 overs. Barnett followed his 64 with 109 and at 155 for one Derbyshire were in with a good chance, but their run-chase was halted and they finally finished at 216 for six.

A remarkable high-scoring match with Middlesex at Headingley saw 18 wickets fall in the four days with 1,285 runs being scored. Batting first Yorkshire accumulated 463 for three declared in almost a day and a half, with Ashley Metcalfe proving that he does at least possess the necessary qualification to concentrate by scoring 216 not out. Moxon (57), Robinson (88) and Love (70 not out) also batted well. On a feather-bed of a pitch, the crowd did not get a great deal of pleasure out of the proceedings. Middlesex also did not bat with any great freedom, but they reached 315 for six before declaring. Yorkshire then declared again at 185 without loss, Martyn Moxon obtaining 89 not out and Metcalfe 78 not out. Middlesex therefore were set 334 to win and at 285 for four appeared to be cruising home. The Middlesex batsmen then appeared to panic and some unwise strokes and some dreadful run-out mix-ups resulted in Middlesex failing by 12 runs to achieve their target with their last pair at the crease. The finish of the match could not be faulted, but the first three days were hardly a good advert for cricket.

Yorkshire's visit to Old Trafford was accompanied by weather that was dull and grey and they were soon in trouble against Allott and six wickets were down for 37. Peter Hartley then entered and played the innings of his life to score 127 not out. When Lancashire batted, the spinners came on almost immediately and Lancashire were soon in trouble against Carrick (five for 62) and the other left-arm slow bowler Paul Booth (five for 98). In their second innings Yorkshire struggled to 171 for eight but the weather won in the end.

The usual Scarborough finish – the inevitable draw – against Northamptonshire on a wicket that seemed to get better as the match went on started with a stand of 102 between Moxon (86) and Metcalfe (56). In reply to Yorkshire's 320 Northamptonshire went on to a total of 464, with Geoff Cook notching 203. Yorkshire had little also to play for except a draw and Byas on his home ground helped Moxon to put on 166 for their second wicket, making a valuable 72. Martyn went on to score 191. Yorkshire batted out time at 397 for six.

The last match of the season, a four-day match, took place at Trent Bridge and in many ways was Yorkshire's best performance of the season. Yorkshire opened with a stand of 123 with Moxon (68) and

Metcalfe (74) both in form, while Robinson was unfortunate to miss his century with a well-played 98. On a pitch that always gave some help to the fast bowlers – it was a rarity in being a good fast wicket – Yorkshire reached a total of 380. In reply Nottinghamshire lost four wickets for 106 before Stephenson (111) boosted the total. Sidebottom bowled impressively throughout and finished with seven for 89 as Yorkshire took a first innings lead of 84. Robinson was again prominent with an attractive 80 when Yorkshire batted again before Bairstow came in to thrash the Nottinghamshire bowlers to the tune of 94 not out in his best knock of the season. Yorkshire finally declared at 340 for seven with once again Stephenson being Nottinghamshire's bowling hero with seven for 117. Nottinghamshire needed 425 to win and never looked to have a chance of getting anywhere near that target except when Randall (59) and Stephenson were in harness. Franklyn Stephenson went on to complete another century (117) and completed one of the rarest doubles in the game – two separate centuries and ten wickets in the match. Fletcher was the pick of the Yorkshire bowlers with six for 74 as Yorkshire gained a deserved 127-run victory. David Bairstow, in the last match of the season, had the distinction of completing 1,000 victims for Yorkshire, after losing his place to Blakey for several matches due to loss of form, both with the bat and behind the stumps.

In what was a difficult season for Yorkshire and its players, Martyn Moxon headed the batting averages with well over 1,400 runs at an average of 44.69. By no means a success at Test level, he was disappointing only by the highest standards, as it was felt that he had the technique to become an England regular if he could put a little more steel into his batting. He also showed the ability at times to be one of the best slip fielders in the world but suffered several minor injuries that caused him to lose confidence. After a bad start Metcalfe too scored well over four figures at 37.71, and much better things will be expected of him in the future. Peter Hartley was perhaps falsely placed in third position but he proved that he can command a higher place in the batting order, even though his bowling figures were disappointing. Robinson was the third member of the side to reach four figures, and along with Fletcher he was capped at the end of the season. Carrick averaged over 30, scoring over 800 runs, and could be relied on whatever the circumstances. Love, Sharp and Blakey were all disappointing with the bat, but Blakey did improve when called upon to keep wicket and he could take that position on merit.

The bowling averages were headed by Paul Jarvis with 31 wickets at 14.00 runs each, but he missed well over half the season with a back injury which caused concern, and until he becomes 100 per cent fit his future must have a dark cloud over it. In his absence, Sidebottom, who

The Yorkshire playing staff in 1988. Back row: I. G. Swallow, P. J. Berry, P. A. Booth,
C. S. Pickles, C. Shaw, S. D. Fletcher, P. E. Robinson
Middle row: W. Morton, S. N. Hartley, M. D. Moxon, P. J. Hartley, D. Byas, S. J. Dennis,
P. W. Jarvis, N. E. Nicholson, S. Oldham, D. E. V. Padgett
Front row: A. A. Metcalfe, J. D. Love, D. L. Bairstow, P. Carrick (capt.), A. Sidebottom,
K. Sharp, R. J. Blakey

had a successful benefit season, took 63 wickets at 20.68 and certainly
looked the most dangerous bowler in the team. Fletcher, who took
only four wickets fewer at 22.17 each, worked hard at all times and
thoroughly deserved to receive his cap. Carrick took 50 wickets at a
high cost of 31.04, and suffers through having to play in a side of such
little experience. As a skipper – he was re-appointed for 1989 – he
faced up to all problems with courage and was never afraid to deal
with problems himself both on and off the field. Nature did not endow
him with alacrity in the field, and this perhaps is his greatest drawback
as skipper, although he was not afraid to field at slip or anywhere else
when needed. Both Shaw and Hartley were expensive, but Shaw tired
towards the end of the season. He has a good action and should
continue to improve while his batting showed distinct promise at
times. Bairstow had a poor season with the bat until the last match
against Nottinghamshire but he is quite capable of bouncing back into
the team, even though his years are against him.

In the Benson and Hedges Cup Yorkshire began with two matches
washed out before beating the Minor Counties, so they had to defeat
Worcestershire to have any chance of qualifying. Their batting failed

apart from Sharp (75) when facing a score of 227 for six and with Botham taking five for 41, they were defeated by 55 runs. The NatWest saw them begin with a ten-wicket win at Finchampstead against Berkshire, with Metcalfe at his best as he obtained 74 not out of the 106 needed for victory, Yorkshire actually winning with 34 overs to spare. In the second round they went out to Middlesex at Headingley, being completely outplayed after Gatting (74) had taken Middlesex to 225 for seven. Shaw bowled well to take four for 29 but Yorkshire's batting failed completely with only Bairstow (36) offering much resistance.

In the Refuge Assurance League, Yorkshire began reasonably well and were in contention for most of the season, but they fell away badly towards the end and finished a modest eighth. Fletcher and Shaw were both in good bowling form but the batting tended to be below the standard of consistency that was needed and Love and Bairstow could do little right.

The winter of 1988–89 saw the confrontation grow between the supporters of a possible move to Park Avenue – or at least a partial move with some cricket played there – and those who supported a Headingley monopoly. The future of Headingley as a Test venue (or indeed as a cricket ground) was a matter of concern. The growing popularity of rugby league and the increased crowds at Leeds matches at Headingley, together with the disenchantment of the public with soccer, could still influence the issue.

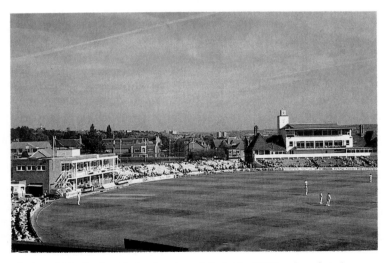

A view of Headingley, the headquarters of Yorkshire CCC, where first-class cricket has been played since 1890. Yorkshire first played there in 1891 and the first Test match to be played there was in 1899.

Yorkshire cricket is still, therefore, in a state of uncertainty which could not have been imagined by such as Lord Hawke, or the heroes of the 1930s. Yorkshire County Cricket Club has survived for 126 years – it has even survived the last 20 years, a much more difficult task than the previous hundred. It has been in the doldrums for longer than in any other period of its history. Perhaps a revival is due. Yorkshiremen will be hoping.

STATISTICAL SECTION

BIOGRAPHICAL DETAILS
OF YORKSHIRE PLAYERS

NAME AND EXTENT OF CAREER	BIRTHPLACE	DATE OF BIRTH	DATE OF DEATH
Alfred Ackroyd *1879*	Birkenshaw	29. 8.1858	3.10.1927
Spencer Allen *1924*	Halifax	20.12.1893	9.10.1978
William Reginald Allen *1921–1925*	Sharlston	14. 4.1893	14.10.1950
Joseph Ambler *1886*	Lascelles Hall	12. 2.1860	10. 2.1899
George Anderson *1863–1869*	Aiskew	20. 1.1826	27.11.1902
Paul Napier Anderson *1988*	Driffield	28. 4.1966	
Claude Esmond Anson *1924*	Bradford	14.10.1889	26. 3.1969
Charles Appleton *1865*	Hull	15. 5.1844	26. 2.1925
Robert Appleyard *1950–1958*	Wibsey	27. 6.1924	
Charles Ingram Armitage *1873–1878*	Birkby Grange	28. 4.1849	24. 4.1917
Thomas Armitage *1872–1879*	Walkley	25. 4.1848	21. 9.1922
David Leslie Ash *1965*	Bingley	18. 2.1944	
John Robert Ashman *1951*	Rotherham	20. 5.1926	
Ronald Aspinall *1946–1950*	Almondsbury	26.10.1918	
Walter Aspinall *1880*	Elland	24. 3.1858	
Frederick Thomas Asquith *1903*	Leeds	5. 2.1870	11. 1.1916
Charles William Jeffrey Athey *1976–1983*	Middlesbrough	27. 9.1957	
George Robert Atkinson *1863–1870*	Ripon	21. 9.1830	3. 5.1906
Harry Atkinson *1907*	Sculcoates	1. 2.1881	22.12.1959
Edgar Norman Backhouse *1931*	Sherriff Hutton	13. 5.1901	1.11.1936
Henry Dixon Badger *1921–1922*	Clifton, York	7. 3.1900	10. 8.1975
Alfred Brian Bainbridge *1961–1963*	Middlesbrough	15.10.1932	
Francis Edmund Baines *1888*	Eccleshall	18. 6.1864	17.11.1948
Arthur Bairstow *1896–1900*	Great Horton	14. 8.1868	7.12.1945
David Leslie Bairstow *1970–1988*	Bradford	1. 9.1951	
George Robert Baker *1884*	Malton	18. 4.1862	6. 2.1938
Robert Baker *1864–1875*	Hunmanby	3. 7.1849	21. 6.1896
John Christopher Balderstone *1961–1969*	Longwood	16.11.1940	
Alan Theodore Barber *1929–1930*	Ecclesall	17. 6.1905	10. 3.1985
Wilfred Barber *1926–1947*	Cleckheaton	18. 4.1901	10. 9.1968
Eric Scott Barraclough *1949–1950*	Bradford	30. 3.1923	
Willie Bates *1877–1887*	Lascelles Hall	19.11.1855	8. 1.1900
William Ederick Bates *1907–1913*	Kirkheaton	5. 3.1884	17. 1.1957
George William Bayes *1910–1921*	Flamborough	27. 2.1884	6.12.1960
Harold Beaumont *1946–1947*	Thongsbridge	14.10.1916	
John Beaumont *1877–1878*	Armitage Bridge	16. 9.1854	1. 5.1920
Harry Bedford *1928*	Morley	17. 7.1907	5. 7.1968
Walter Bedford *1903*	Barnsley	24. 2.1879	7.1939
John Thomson Bell *1921–1923*	Batley	16. 6.1895	8. 8.1974
John Berry *1863–1867*	Dalton	10. 1.1823	26. 2.1895
Joseph Berry *1864–1874*	Dalton	29.11.1829	20. 4.1894
Philip John Berry *1986–1988*	Saltburn	28.12.1966	
George Betts *1873–1874*	Sheffield	19. 9.1841	26. 9.1902
James Graham Binks *1955–1969*	Hull	5.10.1935	
John Binns *1898*	Leeds	31. 3.1870	8.12.1934
Harold Dennis Bird *1956–1959*	Barnsley	19. 4.1933	

NAME AND EXTENT OF CAREER	BIRTHPLACE	DATE OF BIRTH	DATE OF DEATH
Jack Birkenshaw *1958–1960*	Rothwell	13.11.1940	
Thomas James Denton Birtles *1913–1924*	Higham	26.10.1886	13. 1.1971
John Derek Hepburn Blackburn *1956*	Leeds	27.10.1924	19. 2.1987
Joseph Scott Blackburn *1876–1877*	Holbeck	24. 9.1852	8. 7.1922
William Edward Blackburn *1919–1920*	Clitheroe	24.11.1888	3. 6.1941
Wilfred Blake *1880*	Skipton	29.11.1854	
Richard John Blakey *1985–1988*	Huddersfield	15. 1.1967	
Emanuel Blamires *1877*	Bradford	31. 7.1850	22. 3.1886
George Raymonds Bloom *1964*	Aston	13. 9.1941	
Henry Bocking *1865*	Sheffield	10.12.1835	22. 2.1907
John George Boden *1878*	Birstall	27.12.1848	3. 1.1928
Benjamin Charles Bolton *1890–1891*	Cottingham	23. 9.1862	18.11.1910
John Brian Bolus *1956–1962*	Whitkirk	31. 1.1934	
Arthur Booth *1931–1947*	Featherstone	3.11.1902	17. 8.1974
Major William Booth *1908–1914*	Pudsey	10.12.1886	1. 7.1916
Paul Antony Booth *1982–1985*	Huddersfield	5. 9.1965	
Roy Booth *1951–1955*	Marsden	1.10.1926	
Michael Kenneth Bore *1969–1977*	Hull	2. 6.1947	
Peter David Borrill *1971*	Leeds	4. 7.1951	
William Edward Bosomworth *1872–1880*	Carlton Husthwaite	8. 3.1847	7. 6.1891
Isaac Henry Bottomley *1878–1880*	Shelf	9. 4.1855	23. 4.1922
Thomas Bottomley *1934–1935*	Rawmarsh	26.12.1910	19. 2.1977
William Henry Bower *1883*	Bradford	17.10.1857	31. 1.1943
William Eric Bowes *1929–1947*	Elland	25. 7.1908	4. 9.1987
Geoffrey Boycott *1962–1986*	Fitzwilliam	21.10.1940	
Thomas Brackin *1882*	Thornes	5. 1.1859	7.10.1924
Peter Beldon Brayshay *1952*	Leeds	14.10.1916	
Horace Brearley *1937*	Heckmondwike	26. 6.1913	
Donald (Vincent) Brennan *1947–1953*	Eccleshall	10. 2.1920	9. 1.1985
George Britton *1867*	Hunslet	7. 2.1843	3. 1.1910
Arthur Broadbent *1909–1910*	Armley	7. 6.1879	19. 7.1958
Wilfred Bedford Broadhead *1929*	East Ardsley	31. 5.1903	2. 4.1986
James William Brook *1923*	Ossett	1. 2.1897	3. 3.1989
Bernard Brooke *1950*	Newsome	3. 3.1930	
Peter Norman Broughton *1956*	Castleford	22.10.1935	
Alfred Brown *1872*	Old Malton	10. 6.1854	2.11.1900
John Thomas Brown Snr *1889–1904*	Driffield	20. 8.1869	4.11.1904
John Thomas Brown Jnr *1897–1903*	Darfield	24.11.1874	12. 4.1950
William Brown *1902–1908*	Darfield	19.11.1876	27. 7.1945
Thomas Brownhill *1863–1871*	Sheffield	10.10.1838	6. 1.1915
Jack Brumfitt *1938*	Guiseley	18. 2.1917	16. 3.1987
John Sydney Buller *1930*	Wortley	23. 8.1909	7. 8.1970
John Robert Leopold Bulmer *1891*	Guisborough	28.12.1867	20. 1.1917
Thomas Burgess *1895*		1861	22. 2.1922
Eric Burgin *1952–1953*	Pitsmoor	4. 1.1924	
John Burman *1867*	Bramham	5.10.1838	14. 5.1900
John Ronald Burnet *1958–1959*	Saltaire	11.10.1918	
Matthew Burrows *1880*	Chesterfield	18. 8.1855	29. 5.1893
David Cecil Fowler Burton *1907–1921*	Bridlington	13. 9.1887	24. 9.1971

NAME AND EXTENT OF CAREER	BIRTHPLACE	DATE OF BIRTH	DATE OF DEATH
Robert Claude Burton *1914*	Bridlington	11. 4.1891	30. 4.1971
Edward Banks Butterfield *1870*	Keighley	22.10.1848	6. 5.1899
David Byas *1986–1988*	Kilham	26. 8.1963	
John Lewis Byrom *1874*	Saddleworth	20. 7.1851	24. 8.1931
James William Cammish *1954*	Scarborough	21. 5.1921	1975
Phillip Carrick *1970–1988*	Armley	16. 7.1952	
Rev Edmund Sardinson Carter *1876–1881*	Malton	3. 2.1845	23. 5.1923
William Henry Cartman *1891*	Skipton	20. 6.1861	16. 1.1935
George Cawthray *1939–1952*	Brayton	28. 9.1913	
John Peter Granville Chadwick *1960–1965*	Pateley Bridge	8. 11.1934	
Albert Champion *1876–1879*	Hollins End	27.11.1851	30. 6.1909
Albert Percy Charlesworth *1894–1895*	Chapel Allerton	19. 2.1865	11. 5.1926
Brig Raleigh Charles Joseph Chichester-Constable *1919*	Great Marlow	21.12.1890	26. 5.1963
Anthony Clarkson *1963*	Killinghall	5. 9.1939	
Hugh Marsden Claughton *1914–1919*	Guiseley	24.12.1891	17.10.1980
Robert Owen Clayton *1870–1879*	Caley	1. 1.1844	26.11.1901
Henry Clegg *1881*	Dewsbury	8.12.1850	30.12.1920
Christopher Craven Clifford *1972*	Hovingham	5. 7.1942	
Dennis Brian Close *1949–1970*	Rawdon	24. 2.1931	
Robert Whiteley Collinson *1897*	Halifax	6.11.1875	26.12.1963
Howard Pennett Cooper *1971–1980*	Great Horton	17. 4.1949	
Philip Edward (Whiteoak-)Cooper *1910*	Rotherham	19. 2.1885	21. 5.1950
Geoffrey Alan Cope *1966–1980*	Leeds	23. 2.1947	
Alexander Melvin Corbett *1881*	Aston	25.11.1853	7.10.1934
Stephen Peter Coverdale *1973–1980*	York	20.11.1954	
William Coverdale *1888*	Pickering	8. 7.1862	23. 9.1934
Michael Joseph Cowan *1953–1962*	Leeds	10. 6.1933	
John Michael Cownley *1952*	Wales	24. 2.1929	
Alexander Coxon *1945–1950*	Huddersfield	18. 1.1916	
George Henry Crawford *1914–1926*	Hull	15.12.1890	28. 6.1975
Michael Grove Crawford *1951*	Leeds	30. 7.1920	
Ernest Creighton *1888*	Hemsworth	9. 7.1859	17. 2.1931
Ft Lt Harry Crick *1937–1947*	Sheffield	29. 1.1910	10. 2.1960
Ralph Crookes *1879*	Sheffield	9.10.1846	15. 2.1897
Samuel Moorhouse Crossland *1883–1886*	Leeds	16. 8.1851	11. 4.1906
Arthur Crowther *1905*	Leeds	1. 8.1878	4. 6.1946
William Cuttell *1864–1871*	Sheffield	28. 1.1835	10. 6.1896
Andrew John Dalton *1969–1972*	Horsforth	14. 3.1947	
Thomas Darnton *1864–1868*	Stockton-on-Tees	12. 2.1836	25.10.1874
Kenneth Richard Davidson *1933–1935*	Calverley	24.12.1905	25.12.1954
Joseph Dawes *1865*	Hallam	14. 2.1836	
Edwin Dawson *1863–1874*	Dalton	1. 5.1835	1.12.1888
William Arthur Dawson *1870*	Bradford	3.12.1850	6. 3.1916
Albert George Day *1885–1888*	Dewsbury	20. 9.1865	16.10.1908
Frank Dennis *1928–1933*	Holbeck	11. 6.1907	
Simon John Dennis *1980–1985*	Scarborough	18.10.1960	
David Denton *1894–1920*	Thornes	4. 7.1874	16. 2.1950
Joseph Denton *1887–1888*	Thornes	3. 2.1865	19. 7.1946

NAME AND EXTENT OF CAREER	BIRTHPLACE	DATE OF BIRTH	DATE OF DEATH
Harry Dewse *1873*	York	23. 2.1836	8. 7.1910
George Deyes *1905–1907*	Sculcoates	11. 2.1878	1.1963
Robert Douglas Dick *1911*	Middlesborough	16. 4.1889	14.12.1983
Arthur Dobson *1879*	Ilkley	22. 2.1854	17. 9.1932
Arthur Dolphin *1905–1927*	Wilsden	24.12.1885	23.10.1942
Joseph Stanley Douglas *1925–1934*	Bradford	4. 4.1903	27.12.1971
Alonzo Drake *1909–1914*	Parkgate	16. 4.1884	14. 2.1919
John Drake *1923–1924*	Tong Park	1. 9.1893	22. 5.1967
Jeremiah Driver *1889*	Keighley	16. 5.1861	10.12.1946
Theodore Seton Dury *1878–1881*	Ripley, Harrogate	12. 6.1854	20. 3.1932
William Lord Dyson *1887*	Halifax	11.12.1857	1. 5.1936
Wilson Earnshaw *1893–1896*	Morley	20. 9.1867	24.11.1941
David Eastwood *1870–1877*	Lascelles Hall	30. 3.1848	17. 5.1903
Ronald Eckersley *1945*	Bingley	4. 9.1925	
Frederick William Elam *1900–1902*	Hunslet	13. 9.1871	19. 3.1943
John Ernest Ellis *1888–1892*	Sheffield	10.11.1864	1.12.1927
Samuel Ellis *1880*	Dewsbury	23.11.1851	28.10.1930
John Emmanuel Elms *1905*	Pitsmoor	24.12.1874	1.11.1951
Thomas Emmett *1866–1888*	Crib Lane	3. 9.1841	30. 6.1904
Albert Farrar *1906*	Brighouse	29. 4.1884	25.12.1954
Michael Carruthers Fearnley *1962–1964*	Horsforth	21. 8.1936	7. 7.1979
William Dixon Featherby *1920*	Goodmanham Lodge	18. 8.1888	23.11.1958
Kenneth Fiddling *1938–1946*	Hebden Bridge	13.10.1917	
Alfred Firth *1869*	Dewsbury	3. 9.1847	16. 1.1927
Rev Edgar Beckwith Firth *1894*	Malton	11. 4.1863	25. 7.1905
Edward Loxley Firth *1912*	Hope, Derbyshire	7. 3.1886	8. 1.1949
Jack Firth *1949–1950*	Cottingley	27. 6.1918	7. 9.1981
Horace Fisher *1928–1936*	Featherstone	3. 8.1903	16. 4.1974
Samuel Flaxington *1882*	Otley	14.10.1860	10. 3.1895
Stuart David Fletcher *1983–1988*	Keighley	8. 6.1964	
William Fletcher *1891–1892*	Leeds	16. 2.1866	1. 6.1935
Charles William Foord *1947–1953*	Scarborough	11. 6.1924	
Ernest Foster *1901*	Bramley	23.11.1873	16. 4.1956
Thomas William Foster *1894–1895*	Birkdale, Lancs	12.11.1871	31. 1.1947
Joseph Frank *1881*	Helmsley	27.12.1857	22.10.1940
Robert Wilson Frank *1889–1903*	Pickering	29. 5.1864	9. 9.1950
George Freeman *1865–1880*	Boroughbridge	28. 7.1843	18.11.1895
Paul Antony Gibb *1935–1946*	Brandsby	11. 7.1913	7.12.1977
Charles John Gifkins *1880*	Thames Ditton	19. 2.1856	
Fairfax Gill *1906*	Wakefield	3. 9.1883	1.11.1917
Keith Gillhouley *1961*	Huddersfield	8. 8.1934	
Alfred Goulder *1929*	Darnall	16. 8.1907	
Andrew Greenwood *1869–1880*	Lascelles Hall	20. 8.1847	12. 2.1889
Frank Edwards Greenwood *1929–1932*	Birkby	28. 9.1905	30. 7.1963
Luke Greenwood *1864–1874*	Lascelles Hall	13. 7.1834	1.11.1909
Charles Henry Grimshaw *1904–1908*	Armley	12. 5.1880	25. 9.1947
Irwin Grimshaw *1880–1887*	Farsley	4. 5.1857	18. 1.1911

NAME AND EXTENT OF CAREER	BIRTHPLACE	DATE OF BIRTH	DATE OF DEATH
Stell Haggas *1878–1882*	Keighley	18. 4.1856	14. 3.1926
Schofield Haigh *1895–1913*	Berry Brow	19. 3.1871	27. 2.1921
Brian Hall *1952*	Morley	16. 9.1929	27. 2.1989
Charles Henry Hall *1928–1934*	York	5. 4.1906	11.12.1976
John Hall *1863*	Nottingham	11.11.1815	17. 4.1888
Louis Hall *1873–1894*	Batley	1.11.1852	19.11.1915
Harry Halliday *1938–1953*	Pudsey	9. 2.1920	27. 8.1967
Charles Halliley *1872*	Earlsheaton	5.12.1852	3.1929
Arnold Hamer *1928*	Huddersfield	8.12.1916	
Alan Wesley Hampshire *1975*	Rotherham	18.10.1950	
John Hampshire *1937*	Goldthorpe	5.10.1913	
John Harry Hampshire *1961–1981*	Thurnscoe	10. 2.1941	
William Edward Harbord *1929–1935*	Manton, Rutland	15.12.1908	
Charles Henry Hardisty *1906–1909*	Horsforth	10.12.1885	2. 3.1968
Herbert Silvester Hargreaves *1934–1938*	Cinderhill	23. 3.1913	
William Harris *1884–1887*	Greasborough	21.11.1861	23. 5.1923
George Puckrin Harrison *1883–1892*	Scarborough	11. 2.1862	14. 9.1940
Harold Harrison *1907*	Horsforth	24. 1.1885	11. 2.1962
William Hendy Harrison *1888*	Shipley	27. 5.1863	15. 7.1939
Herbert William Hart *1888*	Hull	21. 9.1859	2.11.1895
Philip Richard Hart *1981*	Seamer	12. 1.1947	
Harry Edmonson Hartington *1910–1911*	Dewsbury	18. 9.1881	16. 2.1950
Peter John Hartley *1985–1988*	Keighley	18. 4.1960	
Stuart Neil Hartley *1978–1988*	Shipley	18. 3.1956	
Anthony George Hatton *1960–1961*	Whitkirk	25. 3.1937	
Lord Martin Bladen Hawke *1881–1911*	Willingham, Lincs	16. 8.1860	10.10.1938
Harry Hayley *1884–1898*	Heath	22. 2.1860	3. 6.1922
William John Haywood *1878*	Upper Hallam	25. 2.1841	7. 1.1912
John Hicks *1872–1876*	York	10.12.1850	10. 6.1912
James Higgins *1901–1905*	Birstall	13. 3.1877	19. 7.1954
Allen Hill *1871–1882*	Newton, Kirkheaton	14.11.1843	29. 8.1910
Henry Hill *1888–1891*	Dewsbury	29.11.1858	14. 8.1935
Lewis Gordon Hill *1882*	Bradford	2.11.1860	27. 8.1940
Edward Theodore Hirst *1877–1888*	Newhouse, Huddersfield	6. 5.1857	26.10.1914
Ernest William Hirst *1881*	Newhouse, Huddersfield	27. 2.1855	24.10.1933
George Herbert Hirst *1891–1929*	Kirkheaton	7. 9.1871	10. 5.1954
Thomas Henry Hirst *1899*	Lockwood	21. 5.1865	3. 4.1927
Geoffrey Hodgson *1964*	Huddersfield	24. 7.1938	
Isaac Hodgson *1863–1866*	Bradford	15.11.1828	24.11.1867
Philip Hodgson *1954–1956*	Todmorden	21. 9.1935	
William Edgar Newman Holdsworth *1952–1953*	Armley	17. 9.1928	
Gideon Holgate *1865–1867*	Sawley	23. 6.1839	11. 7.1895
Percy Holmes *1913–1933*	Oakes	25.11.1886	3. 9.1971
Norman Frederick Horner *1950*	Queensbury	10. 5.1926	
Theodore Hind Hoyle *1919*		19. 3.1884	2. 6.1953

NAME AND EXTENT OF CAREER	BIRTHPLACE	DATE OF BIRTH	DATE OF DEATH
Bennett Hudson 1880	Sheffield	29. 6.1852	11.11.1901
David Hunter 1888–1909	Scarborough	23. 2.1860	11. 1.1927
Joseph Hunter 1878–1888	Scarborough	3. 8.1855	4. 1.1891
Leonard Hutton 1934–1955	Fulneck	23. 6.1916	
Richard Anthony Hutton 1962–1974	Pudsey	6. 9.1942	
Roger Iddison 1863–1876	Bedale	15. 9.1834	19. 3.1890
Raymond Illingworth 1951–1983	Pudsey	8. 6.1932	
Peter Geoffrey Ingham 1979–1981	Sheffield	28. 9.1956	
Rt Hon Sir Frank Stanley Jackson 1890–1907	Chapel Allerton	21.11.1870	9. 3.1947
Samuel Robinson Jackson 1891	Sheffield	15. 7.1859	19. 7.1941
Thomas Alec Jacques 1927–1936	Cliffe	19. 2.1905	
Frederick Jakeman 1946–1947	Holmfirth	10. 1.1920	18. 5.1986
Brian James 1954	Darfield	23. 4.1934	
Paul William Jarvis 1981–1988	Redcar	29. 6.1965	
Colin Johnson 1969–1979	Pocklington	5. 9.1947	
Joseph Johnson 1936–1939	South Kirkby	16. 5.1916	
Mark Johnson 1981	Gleadless	23. 4.1958	
Jonathan Joy 1864–1867	Preston Bottoms	29. 9.1826	27. 9.1889
Albert Judson 1920	Cullingworth	10. 7.1885	8. 4.1975
Haven Kaye 1872–1873	Huddersfield	11. 6.1846	24. 1.1892
Lt Col Harold Swift Kaye 1907–1908	Mirfield	9. 5.1882	6.11.1953
William Geoffrey Keighley 1947–1951	Nice, France	10. 1.1925	
George Kennie 1927	Bradford	17. 5.1904	
Sam Kilburn 1896	Dalton	16.10.1868	25. 9.1940
Norman Kilner 1919–1923	Low Valley	21. 7.1895	28. 4.1979
Roy Kilner 1911–1927	Low Valley	17.10.1890	6. 4.1928
Anthony Mountain King 1955	Laughton	8.10.1932	
Peter John Kippax 1961–1962	Huddersfield	15.10.1940	
Wlliam Whiteley Lancaster 1895	Scholes	4. 2.1873	
Charles Whittington Landon 1878–1882	Bromley, Kent	30. 5.1850	5. 3.1903
Rev William Law 1871–1873	Rochdale, Lancs	9. 4.1851	20.12.1892
Barrie Leadbeater 1966–1979	Harehills	14. 8.1943	
Edric Leadbeater 1949–1956	Huddersfield	15. 8.1927	
Harry Leadbeater 1884–1890	Scarborough	31.12.1863	9.10.1928
Gerald Arthur Buxton Leatham 1874–1886	Hemsworth Hall	30. 4.1851	19. 6.1932
Roland Sutcliffe Leather 1906	Leeds	17. 8.1880	31. 1.1913
Charles Lee 1952	Rotherham	17. 3.1924	
Frederick Lee 1882–1890	Baildon	18.11.1856	13. 9.1896
George Henry Lee 1879	Almondsbury	24. 8.1854	4.10.1919
Herbert Lee 1885	Taylor Hill, Huddersfield	2. 7.1856	4. 2.1908
James Edward Lee 1867	Dewsbury	1838	2. 4.1880
Col Alfred Digby Legard 1910	Scarborough	19. 6.1878	15. 8.1939
Edward Ibson Lester 1945–1956	Scarborough	18. 2.1923	
Maurice (registered as Morris) Leyland 1920–1947	New Park, Harrogate	20. 7.1900	1. 1.1967
Lewis Linaker 1909	Paddock, Huddersfield	8. 4.1885	17.11.1961
Benjamin Lister 1874–1878	Birkenshaw	9.12.1850	3.12.1919
Joseph Lister 1954	Thirsk	14. 5.1930	

NAME AND EXTENT OF CAREER	BIRTHPLACE	DATE OF BIRTH	DATE OF DEATH
Sir Kenelm Arthur Lister-Laye *1928*	Kensington, London	27. 3.1892	28. 2.1955
Ephraim Lockwood *1868–1884*	Lascelles Hall	4. 4.1845	19.12.1921
Henry Lockwood *1877–1882*	Lascelles Hall	20.10.1855	18. 2.1930
Joe Thomas Lodge *1948*	Skelmanthorpe	16. 4.1921	
James Derek Love *1975–1988*	Headingley	22. 4.1955	
George Emanuel Lowe *1902*		12. 1.1878	15. 8.1932
Frank Anderson Lowson *1949–1958*	Bradford	1. 7.1925	8. 9.1984
Edward Lumb *1872–1886*	Dalton	12. 9.1852	5. 4.1891
Richard Graham Lumb *1970–1984*	Doncaster	27. 2.1950	
Major Arthur William Lupton *1908–1927*	Bradford	23. 2.1879	14. 4.1944
George Goulton Lynas *1867*	Coatham	7. 9.1832	8.12.1896
George Gibson Macaulay *1920–1935*	Thirsk	7.12.1897	13.12.1940
Francis Prest McHugh *1949*	Leeds	15.11.1925	
Amos Marshall *1874*	Yeadon	10. 7.1849	3. 8.1891
Alan Mason *1947–1950*	Addingham	2. 5.1921	
Edmund Maude *1866*		31.12.1839	2. 7.1876
Ashley Anthony Metcalfe *1983–1988*	Horsforth	25.12.1963	
William Henry Micklethwait *1911*	Rotherham	13.12.1885	7.10.1947
Willie Middlebrook *1888–1889*	Morley	23. 5.1858	26. 4.1919
Charles Augustus Midgley *1906*	Wetherby	11.11.1877	24. 6.1942
Frank William Milligan *1894–1898*	Farnborough, Hants	19. 3.1870	31. 3.1900
Arthur Mitchell *1922–1945*	Baildon	13. 9.1902	25.12.1976
Frank Mitchell *1894–1904*	Market Weighton	13. 8.1872	11.10.1935
George Derek Monks *1952*	Sheffield	3. 9.1929	
Robert Moorhouse *1888–1899*	Berry Brow	7. 9.1866	7. 1.1921
Henry Mosley *1881*	Kildwick	8. 3.1852	29.11.1933
Arthur Motley *1879*	Osmondthorpe Hall	5. 2.1858	28. 9.1897
Joseph Thomas Mounsey *1891–1897*	Heeley	30. 8.1871	6. 4.1949
Martyn Douglas Moxon *1981–1988*	Stairfoot	4. 5.1960	
Hubert Myers *1901–1910*	Yeadon	2. 1.1875	12. 6.1944
Matthew Myers *1876–1878*	Yeadon	12. 4.1847	8.12.1919
John Edward Naylor *1953*	Thurcroft	11.12.1930	
John Thomas Newstead *1903–1913*	Marton-in-Cleveland	8. 9.1877	25. 3.1952
Anthony George Nicholson *1962–1975*	Dewsbury	25. 6.1938	3.11.1985
Neil George Nicholson *1988*	Danby, Whitby	17.10.1963	
William Oates *1874–1875*	Wentworth	2. 1.1852	9.12.1940
William Farrand Oates *1956*	Aston	11. 6.1929	
Christopher Middleton Old *1966–1982*	Middlesbrough	22.12.1948	
Stephen Oldham *1974–1985*	High Green	26. 7.1948	
Edgar Oldroyd *1910–1931*	Healey	1.10.1888	29.12.1964
Charles Oyston *1900–1909*	Armley	12. 5.1869	15. 7.1942
Douglas Ernest Vernon Padgett *1951–1971*	Bradford	20. 7.1934	
George Hubert Padgett *1952*	Silkstone	9.10.1931	
John Padgett *1882–1889*	Scarborough	21.11.1860	

NAME AND EXTENT OF CAREER	BIRTHPLACE	DATE OF BIRTH	DATE OF DEATH
Cecil Harry Parkin 1906	Eaglescliffe, Durham	18. 2.1886	15. 6.1943
John Parratt 1888–1890	Morley	24. 3.1859	6. 5.1905
John Wesley Parton 1889	Wellington, Salop	31. 1.1863	30. 1.1906
Harry Eyre Pearson 1878–1880	Attercliffe	7. 8.1851	8. 7.1903
John Henry Pearson 1934–1936	Scarborough	14. 5.1915	
Edmund Peate 1879–1887	Holbeck	2. 3.1855	11. 3.1900
Robert Peel 1882–1897	Morley	25. 6.1857	12. 8.1941
Joshua Hudson Penny 1891	Yeadon	29. 9.1856	29. 7.1902
Christopher Stephen Pickles 1985–1988	Mirfield	30. 1.1966	
David Pickles 1957–1960	Halifax	16.11.1935	
George Pinder (Hattersley) 1867–1880	Ecclesfield	15. 7.1841	15. 1.1903
Robert Kenworthy Platt 1955–1963	Holmfirth	26.12.1932	
David Pollard 1865	Lascelles Hall	7. 8.1835	26. 3.1909
George Pollitt 1899	Chickenley	3. 6.1874	
Charles Henry Prest 1864	York	9.12.1841	4. 3.1875
Joseph Merritt Preston 1885–1889	Yeadon	23. 8.1864	26.11.1890
Thomas Pride 1887	York	23. 7.1864	16. 2.1919
Peter Pullan 1884	Guiseley	29. 3.1857	1901
Sir Everard Joseph Reginald Henry Radcliffe 1909–1911	Hensleigh, Devon	27. 1.1884	23.11.1969
Alan Ramage 1979–1983	Guisborough	29.11.1957	
James Rhodes Stanley Raper 1936–1947	Bradford	9. 8.1909	
Eric Raymond Rawlin 1927–1936	Rotherham	4.10.1897	11. 1.1943
John Thomas Rawlin 1880–1885	Greasborough	10.11.1856	19. 1.1924
Elisha Barker Rawlinson 1867–1875	Yeadon	10. 4.1837	17. 2.1892
Joseph Redfearn 1890	Lascelles Hall	13. 5.1862	14. 1.1931
George William Armitage Render 1919	Dewsbury	5. 1.1887	17. 9.1922
Arthur Cecil Rhodes 1932–1934	Headingley	14.10.1906	21. 5.1957
Herbert Edward Rhodes 1878–1883	Hennerton, Berks	11. 1.1852	10. 9.1889
Steven John Rhodes 1981–1984	Bradford	17. 6.1964	
Wilfred Rhodes 1898–1930	Kirkheaton	29.10.1877	8. 7.1973
William Rhodes 1911	Bradford	4. 3.1883	5. 8.1941
John Alan Richardson 1936–1947	Sleights	4. 8.1908	2. 4.1985
Henry Riley 1895–1900	Thackley	17. 8.1875	6.11.1922
Martin Riley 1878–1882	Cleckheaton	5. 4.1851	1. 6.1899
William Ringrose 1901–1906	Ganton	2. 9.1871	14. 9.1943
Arthur Leslie Robinson 1971–1977	Brompton, Northallerton	17. 8.1946	
Edward Robinson 1887	Honley	27.12.1862	3. 9.1942
Emmott Robinson 1919–1931	Keighley	16.11.1883	17.11.1969
Ellis Pembroke Robinson 1934–1949	Denaby Main	10. 8.1911	
Henry Robinson 1879		12. 5.1858	14.12.1909
Philip Edward Robinson 1984–1988	Keighley	3. 8.1963	
Walter Robinson 1876–1877	Greetland	29.11.1851	14. 8.1919
Edward Roper 1878–1880	Richmond	8. 4.1851	27. 4.1921
James William Rothery 1903–1910	Staincliffe	5. 9.1877	2. 6.1919

NAME AND EXTENT OF CAREER	BIRTHPLACE	DATE OF BIRTH	DATE OF DEATH
Joseph Rowbotham *1863–1876*	Sheffield	8. 7.1831	22.12.1899
Horace Rudston *1902–1907*	Hessle	22.11.1878	14. 4.1962
Melville Ryan *1954–1965*	Huddersfield	23. 6.1933	
Louis Ryder *1924*	Thirsk	28. 8.1900	24. 1.1955
George Savile *1867–1874*	Methley	26. 4.1847	4. 9.1904
Dennis Schofield *1970–1974*	Holmfirth	9.10.1947	
Emanuel Scott *1864*	Birkenshaw	6. 7.1834	3.12.1898
Herbert Amos Sedgwick *1906*	Richmond	8. 4.1883	28.12.1957
Arthur Sellers *1890–1899*	Keighley	31. 5.1870	25. 9.1941
Arthur Brian Sellers *1932–1948*	Keighley	5. 3.1907	20. 2.1981
William Allan Shackleton *1928–1934*	Keighley	9. 3.1908	16.11.1971
Kevin Sharp *1976–1988*	Leeds	6. 4.1959	
Rev Charles Molesworth Sharpe *1875*	Codicote, Herts	6. 9.1851	25. 6.1935
Philip John Sharpe *1958–1974*	Shipley	27.12.1936	
Christopher Shaw *1984–1988*	Hemsworth	17. 2.1964	
James Shaw *1896–1897*	Linthwaite	12. 3.1865	22. 1.1921
Ernest Richard Sheepshanks *1929*	Arthington	22. 3.1910	31.12.1937
Donald Arthur Shepherd *1938*	Whitkirk	10. 3.1916	
William Shotton *1865–1874*	Lascelles Hall	1.12.1840	26. 5.1909
Arnold Sidebottom *1973–1988*	Barnsley	1. 4.1954	
Robert Sidgwick *1882*	Embsay Kirk, Craven	7. 8.1851	1934
Stephen Silvester *1976–1977*	Hull	12. 3.1951	
Edward Thornhill Beckett Simpson *1889*	Crofton	5. 3.1867	20. 3.1944
Rev Herbert Marsh Sims *1875–1877*	Mount Tavy, Devon	15. 3.1853	5.10.1885
William Slinn *1863–1864*	Sheffield	13.12.1826	19. 6.1888
Thomas Frank Smailes *1932–1948)*	Ripley	27. 3.1910	1.12.1970
Kenneth Smales *1948–1950*	Horsforth	15. 9.1927	
Alfred Farrer Smith *1868–1874*	Birstall	7. 3.1847	6. 1.1915
Ernest Smith *1888–1907*	Morley	19.10.1869	9. 4.1945
Ernest Smith *1914–1926*	Barnsley	11. 7.1888	2. 1.1972
Fred Smith *1911*	Idle	26.12.1885	
Fred Smith *1903*	Yeadon	18.12.1879	20.10.1905
George Smith *1901–1906*	Boston Spa	13. 1.1876	16. 1.1929
John Smith *1865*	Yeadon	23. 3.1833	12. 2.1909
Neil Smith *1970–1971*	Dewsbury	1. 4.1949	
Rodney Smith *1969–1970*	Batley	6. 4.1944	
Walker Smith *1874*	Bradford	14. 8.1847	1900
William Smith *1865–1874*	Darlington	1.11.1839	19. 4.1897
Gerald Arthur Smithson *1946–1950*	Spofforth	1.11.1926	6. 9.1970
James Smurthwaite *1938–1939*	Guisborough	17.10.1916	
Abram Sowden *1878–1887*	Great Horton	1.12.1853	5. 7.1921
Dick Squire *1893*	Cleckheaton	31.12.1864	28. 4.1922
Peter John Squires *1972–1976*	Ripon	4. 8.1951	
Harry Cecil Stanley *1911–1913*	Rotherham	16. 2.1888	18. 5.1934
Lt Col Ronald Thomas Stanyforth *1928*	Chelsea, London	30. 5.1892	20. 2.1964
Barry Stead *1959*	Leeds	21. 6.1939	15. 4.1980
Edwin Stephenson *1863–1873*	Sheffield	5. 6.1832	5. 7.1898
John Stewart Stephenson *1923–1926*	Brough	10.11.1903	7.10.1975

NAME AND EXTENT OF CAREER	BIRTHPLACE	DATE OF BIRTH	DATE OF DEATH
Graham Barry Stevenson *1973–1986*	Ackworth	16.12.1955	
William Bryan Stott *1952–1963*	Teadon	18. 7.1934	
Peter Michael Stringer *1967–1969*	Leeds	23. 2.1943	
Stephen Stuchbury *1978–1981*	Sheffield	22. 6.1954	
Frank Howe Sugg *1883*	Ilkeston, Derbys	11. 1.1862	29. 5.1933
Walter Sugg *1881*	Ilkeston, Derbys	21. 5.1860	21. 5.1933
Joseph Hubert Baron Sullivan *1912*	York	21. 9.1890	8. 2.1932
Herbert Sutcliffe *1919–1945*	Summer Bridge	24.11.1894	22. 1.1978
William Herbert Hobbs Sutcliffe *1948–1957*	Pudsey	10.10.1926	
Ian Geoffrey Swallow *1983–1988*	Barnsley	18.12.1962	
Thomas Tait *1898–1899*	Langley Moor, Durham	7.10.1872	6. 9.1954
John Tasker *1912–1913*	South Kirkby	4. 2.1887	24. 8.1975
Geoffrey Tattersall *1905*	Ripon	21. 4.1882	29. 6.1972
Henry Storm Taylor *1879*	Scarborough	11.12.1856	16.11.1896
Harry Taylor *1924–1925*	Idle	18.12.1900	28.10.1988
John Taylor *1880–1881*	Pudsey	2. 4.1850	27. 5.1924
Kenneth Taylor *1953–1968*	Huddersfield	21. 8.1935	
Nicholas Simon Taylor *1982–1983*	Holmfirth	2. 6.1963	
Tom Launcelot Taylor *1899–1906*	Headingley	25. 5.1878	16. 3.1960
Herbert Thewlis *1888*	Lascelles Hall	31. 8.1865	30.11.1920
John Thewlis Snr *1863–1875*	Kirkheaton	30. 6.1828	29.11.1899
John Thewlis Jnr *1879*	Lascelles Hall	21. 9.1850	9. 8.1901
A. Thornton *1881*		20. 7.1854	19. 4.1915
Dr George Thornton *1891*	Skipton	24.12.1867	31. 1.1939
George Thorpe *1864*	Sheffield	20. 2.1834	2. 3.1899
Joseph William Threapleton *1881*	Pudsey	20. 7.1857	1918
Henry James Tinsley *1890–1891*	Welham Grange, Malton	20. 2.1865	10.12.1938
Richard John Andrew Townsley *1974–1975*	Castleford	24. 6.1952	
Anthony David Towse *1986*	Bridlington	22. 4.1968	
Frederick Sewards Trueman *1949–1968*	Scotch Springs, Stainton	6. 2.1931	
John Tunnicliffe *1891–1907*	Pudsey	26. 8.1866	11. 7.1948
Alban Turner *1910–1911*	Darton	2. 9.1885	29. 8.1951
Brian Turner *1960–1961*	Sheffield	25. 7.1938	
Cyril Turner *1925–1946*	Wombwell	11. 1.1902	19.11.1968
Francis Irving Turner *1924*	Barnsley	3. 9.1894	18.10.1954
Cecil Thomas Tyson *1921*	Brompton-by-Sawdon	24. 1.1889	3. 4.1940
Charles Edward Ullathorne *1868–1875*	Hull	11. 4.1845	3. 5.1904
George Ulyett *1873–1893*	Pitsmoor	21.10.1851	18. 6.1898
John Usher *1888*	Staincliffe	26. 2.1859	10. 8.1905
Jack Van Geloven *1955*	Leeds	4. 1.1934	
Henry William Verelst *1868–1869*	Claughton, Cheshire	2. 7.1846	5. 4.1918
Hedley Verity *1930–1939*	Headingley	18. 5.1905	31. 7.1943
Abraham Waddington *1919–1927*	Clayton, Bradford	4. 2.1893	28.10.1959

NAME AND EXTENT OF CAREER	BIRTHPLACE	DATE OF BIRTH	DATE OF DEATH
Saul Wade *1886–1890*	Farsley	8. 2.1858	5.11.1931
Edward Wainwright *1888–1902*	Tinsley	8. 4.1865	28.10.1919
Walker Wainwright *1903–1905*	Rotherham	21. 1.1882	31.12.1961
William Robert Wake *1881*	Sheffield	21. 5.1852	14. 3.1896
Ashley Walker *1863–1870*	Bradford	22. 6.1844	26. 5.1927
Clifford Walker *1947–1948*	Huddersfield	26. 6.1919	
Thomas Walker *1879–1880*	Holbeck	3. 4.1854	28. 8.1925
George Waller *1893–1894*	Pitsmoor	3.12.1864	11.12.1937
Lamplough Wallgate *1875–1877*	Norton, Malton	12.11.1849	9. 5.1887
Herbert Walton *1893*	Scarborough	21. 5.1868	1930
Albert Ward *1886*	Waterloo, Leeds	21.11.1865	6. 1.1939
Frederick Ward *1903*		31. 8.1881	28. 2.1948
Humphrey Plowden Ward *1920*	Amotherby, Malton	20. 1.1899	16.12.1946
Thomas Arthur Wardall *1884–1894*	Eston Junction	19. 4.1862	20.12.1932
John Henry Wardle *1946–1958*	Ardsley	8. 1.1923	23. 7.1985
John Shaw Waring *1963–1966*	Ripon	1.10.1942	
Seth Waring *1870*	Keighley	4.11.1838	17. 4.1919
William Arthur Irving Washington *1900–1902*	Wombwell	11.12.1879	20.10.1927
Haworth Watson *1908–1914*	Barnoldswick	26. 9.1880	24.11.1951
William Watson *1939–1957*	Bolton-on-Dearne	7. 3.1920	
Brian Wilkes Waud *1863–1864*	Selby	4. 6.1837	30. 5.1889
Charles Webster *1863–1868*	Ecclesall	9. 6.1838	6. 1.1881
Harry Haywood Webster *1868*	Handsworth	8. 5.1844	1914
John West *1868–1876*	Little Sheffield	16.10.1844	27. 1.1890
Francis John Whatmuff or Whatmough *1878–1882*	Wilsden	4.12.1856	3. 6.1904
Charles Henry Wheater *1880*	Hunmanby	4. 3.1860	11. 5.1885
Sir Archibald Woollaston White *1908–1920*	Tickhill	14.10.1877	16.12.1945
John Parkin Whitehead *1946–1951*	Uppermill	3. 9.1925	
Lees Whitehead *1889–1904*	Birchen Bank	14. 3.1864	22.11.1913
Luther Whitehead *1893*	Hull	25. 6.1869	16. 1.1931
John Peter Whiteley *1978–1982*	Otley	28. 2.1955	
Charles Percival Whiting *1914–1920*	Dringhoe	18. 4.1888	14. 1.1959
Joseph Fry Whitwell *1890*	Saltburn	22. 2.1869	6.11.1932
William Fry Whitwell *1890*	Stockton-on-Tees	12.12.1867	12. 4.1942
Anthony John Anstruther Wilkinson *1865–1868*	Mount Oswald, Durham	28. 5.1835	11.12.1905
Frank Wilkinson *1937–1939*	Hull	23. 5.1914	26. 3.1984
Henry Wilkinson *1903–1905*	Huddersfield	11.12.1877	15. 4.1967
William Herbert Wilkinson *1903–1910*	Thorpe Hesley	12. 3.1881	4. 6.1961
Ambrose Causer Williams *1911–1919*	Darfield	1. 3.1887	1. 6.1966
Benjamin Birdsall Wilson *1906–1914*	Scarborough	11.12.1879	14. 9.1957
Rev Clarence Eustace Macro Wilson *1896–1899*	Bolsterstone	15. 5.1875	8. 2.1944
Donald Wilson *1957–1974*	Settle	7. 8.1937	
Evelyn Rockley Wilson *1899–1923*	Bolsterstone	25. 3.1879	21. 7.1957
Geoffrey Wilson *1919–1924*	Potternewton	21. 8.1895	29.11.1960
George Arthur Wilson *1936–1939*	Harehills	2. 2.1916	

NAME AND EXTENT OF CAREER	BIRTHPLACE	DATE OF BIRTH	DATE OF DEATH
John Wilson *1887–1888*	Hoyland	30. 6.1857	11.11.1931
John Victor Wilson *1946–1962*	Scampston	17. 1.1921	
Major John Philip Wilson *1911–1912*	Gilling	3. 4.1889	3.10.1959
Arthur Wood *1927–1946*	Fagley	25. 8.1898	1. 4.1973
Barry Wood *1964*	Ossett	26.12.1942	
Christopher Harland Wood *1959*	Manningham	23. 7.1934	
George William Wood *1895*	Huddersfield	18.11.1862	4.12.1948
Rev Hugh Wood *1879–1880*	Sheffield	22. 3.1855	31. 7.1941
J. H. Wood *1881*			
Ronald Wood *1952–1956*	Ossett	3. 6.1929	
John Douglas Woodford *1968–1972*	Little Horton	9. 9.1943	
Frank Ellis Woodhead *1893–1894*	Woodthorpe	29. 5.1868	25. 8.1943
William Henry Woodhouse *1884–1885*	Bradford	16. 4.1856	4. 3.1938
Alfred Wormald *1885–1891*	Morley	10. 5.1855	6. 2.1940
Sir William Arthington Worsley *1928–1929*	Hovingham	5. 4.1890	4.12.1973
Lewis Franklin Wrathmell *1886*	Kirkheaton	22. 1.1855	16. 9.1928
Robert Wright (Ward) *1877*	Adwalton	19. 7.1852	1891
Thomas John Wright *1919*	North Ormesby	5. 3.1900	
Norman Walter Dransfield Yardley *1936–1955*	Barnsley	19. 3.1915	
James Yeadon *1888*	Yeadon	10.12.1861	30. 5.1914

The following appeared for Yorkshire First Eleven, but only in non-first-class matches:

NAME AND EXTENT OF CAREER	BIRTHPLACE	DATE OF BIRTH	DATE OF DEATH
Hugh Barber *1898*		5. 7.1877	7. 9.1969
A. C. Berry *1890*	Dewsbury	30. 3.1865	25.12.1951
Stuart Bottomley *1975*			
W. Carter *1918*			
P. B. Coates *1896*		20. 6.1877	
W. Copestake *1898*			
Albert Cordingley *1898*	Bradford	13. 5.1871	30. 4.1945
Frederick Crabtree *1893*	Baildon	10. 3.1867	28.11.1893
Arthur Pearson Crosland *1890*	Huddersfield	10.12.1862	24. 2.1948
Fred Crowther *1890*	Birstall	22. 1.1857	
Archibald Willis Dixon *1888*	Ecclesall	8. 2.1870	23. 5.1935
Thomas Henry Fearnley *1900*	Wharfedale	1869	9. 4.1942
Gerald A. Hare *1956*	Bradford	14. 5.1936	
Alfred Edward Dryden Harrison *1886*	Sculcoates	19. 3.1856	
Leonard Robert Havers *1890*	Norwich	17. 2.1863	22.11.1928
Edward Hawden *1889*	Hunslet	20.12.1861	29. 1.1944
T. Hayes *1898*		1874	3. 1.1952
John Horsfall *1888*	Huddersfield	4.11.1867	25. 8.1930
Preston Ineson *1890*	Dewsbury	5. 5.1867	11.10.1939
Thomas Lancaster *1891*	Dalton	11. 2.1863	12.12.1935
Edwin Legard *1957*	Barnsley	23. 8.1935	
John Littlewood *1887*	Scissett	12. 5.1852	22. 3.1932
Robert Needham *1893*		1865	1945
Walter Nicholson *1892*	Otley	13. 4.1861	18. 9.1914

NAME AND EXTENT OF CAREER	BIRTHPLACE	DATE OF BIRTH	DATE OF DEATH
Harold Ostler *1891*	Hull	17. 5.1865	12.1910
Francis Thomas Prentice *1941*	Knaresborough	22. 4.1912	10.7.1978
Edward Priestman *1883*	Thornton Dale	10.12.1861	23. 3.1933
John Edward Shilton *1883*	Horbury Junction	2.10.1861	27. 9.1899
Edmund Skilbeck *1890*	Malton	21. 5.1860	4.1898
Charles Smith *1885*	Calverley	24. 8.1861	2. 5.1925
William Sykes *1876*			
H. Taylor *1878*		1857	
Fred Thewlis *1876*	Huddersfield	16. 5.1853	17.10.1927
Friend Thewlis *1876*	Huddersfield	19. 7.1857	1925
Thomas Thewlis *1876*		13. 6.1852	1929
Alfred Tinsley *1887*	Welham, Malton	12. 3.1867	25. 9.1933
William Towler *1889*	Burnley	12.11.1866	6.11.1952
C. S. Wilson *1918*			
Harry Wilson *1900*		1873	13. 8.1906
Harry Burton Wilson *1889*	Manchester	22.12.1856	22. 9.1927
Walter Wordsworth *1891*	Thurgoland	19. 5.1868	23.12.1939

YORKSHIRE CAPTAINS

1863–1872	R. Iddison	1931–1932	F. E. Greenwood
1873	J. Rowbotham	1933–1947	A. B. Sellers
1874	L. Greenwood	1948–1955	N. W. D. Yardley
1875	J. Rowbotham	1956–1957	W. H. H. Sutcliffe
1876–1877	E. Lockwood	1958–1959	J. R. Burnet
1878–1882	T. Emmett	1960–1962	J. V. Wilson
1883–1910	Hon M. B. (Lord) Hawke	1963–1970	D. B. Close
1911	E. J. Radcliffe	1971–1978	G. Boycott
1912–1914	Sir A. W. White	1979–1980	J. H. Hampshire
1919–1921	D. C. F. Burton	1981–1982	C. M. Old
1922–1924	G. Wilson	1982–1983	R. Illingworth
1925–1927	A. W. Lupton	1984–1986	D. L. Bairstow
1928–1929	W. A. Worsley	1987–1988	P. Carrick
1930	A. T. Barber		

CAREER RECORDS OF YORKSHIRE PLAYERS 1863–1988

Name	Inns	No	Runs	HS	Avge	100s	Runs	Wkts	Avge	Best	5wI
A. Ackroyd	1	1	2	2*	—	0	7	0	—	—	—
S. Allen	2	0	8	6	4.00	0	116	2	58.00	2/116	0
W. R. Allen	32	10	475	95	21.59	0			.		
J. Ambler	7	0	68	25	9.71	0	22	0	—	—	—
G. Anderson	31	6	520	99*	20.80	0					
P. N. Anderson	1	0	0	0	0.00	0	47	1	47.00	1/47	—
C. E. Anson	2	0	27	14	13.50	0					
C. Appleton	6	1	56	18	11.20	0					
R. Appleyard	122	43	679	63	8.59	0	9903	642	15.42	8/76	54
C. I. Armitage	5	0	26	12	5.20	0	29	0	—	—	—
T. Armitage	84	8	1053	95	13.85	0	1596	106	15.05	7/26	10
D. L. Ash	3	0	22	12	7.33	0	22	0	—	—	—
J. R. Ashman	1	1	0	0*	—	0	116	4	29.00	2/42	—
R. Aspinall	48	8	763	75*	19.07	0	2670	131	20.38	8/47	—
W. Aspinall	3	0	16	14	5.33	0					
F. T. Asquith	1	0	0	0	0.00	0					
C. W. J. Athey	246	21	6320	134	28.08	10	1003	21	47.76	3/38	—
G. R. Atkinson	38	8	399	44	13.30	0	1146	54	21.22	6/19	1
H. Atkinson	2	0	0	0	0.00	0	17	0	—	—	—
E. N. Backhouse	1	0	2	2	2.00	0	4	0	4	0	—
H. D. Badger	4	2	6	6*	3.00	0	145	6	24.16	3/38	—
A. B. Bainbridge	10	0	93	24	9.30	0	358	20	17.90	6/53	2
F. E. Baines	1	0	0	0	0.00	0					
A. Bairstow	24	10	69	12	4.92	0					
D. L. Bairstow	579	110	12507	145	26.66	8	192	6	32.00	3/25	0
G. R. Baker	11	1	42	13	4.20	0					
R. Baker	5	1	45	22	11.25	0	43	0	—	—	—
J. C. Balderstone	81	6	1332	82	17.76	0	790	37	21.35	4/31	0
A. T. Barber	54	3	1050	100	20.58	1	0	0	—	—	—
W. Barber	495	48	15315	255	34.26	27	404	14	28.85	2/1	0
E. S. Barraclough	4	2	43	24*	21.50	0	136	4	34.00	2/39	0
W. Bates	331	12	6499	136	20.37	8	10692	637	16.78	8/21	36
W. E. Bates	167	15	2634	81	17.32	0	57	2	28.50	1/8	0
G. W. Bayes	24	11	165	36	12.69	0	1534	48	31.95	5/83	1
H. Beaumont	46	6	716	60	17.90	0	236	9	26.22	4/31	0
J. Beaumont	8	2	44	24	7.33	0	50	2	25.00	1/7	0
H. Bedford	5	1	57	24	14.25	0	179	8	22.37	6/91	1
W. Bedford	2	1	38	30*	38.00	0	117	2	58.50	2/38	0
J. T. Bell	8	1	125	54	17.85	0					
John Berry	32	2	492	78	16.40	0	149	8	18.62	4/26	0
Joseph Berry	4	0	68	30	17.00	0					
P. J. Berry	3	2	31	23*	31.00	0	229	5	45.80	2/35	0
G. Betts	4	1	56	44*	18.66	0					
J. G. Binks	587	128	6745	95	14.69	0	66	0	—	—	—
J. Binns	1	0	4	4	4.00	0					
H. D. Bird	25	2	613	181*	26.65	1					
J. Birkenshaw	42	7	588	42	16.80	0	1819	69	26.36	7/76	3

Name	Inns	No	Runs	HS	Avge	100s	Runs	Wkts	Avge	Best	5wI
T. J. Birtles	57	11	876	104	19.04	1	20	0	—	—	—
J. D. H. Blackburn	2	0	18	15	9.00	0					
J. S. Blackburn	11	1	102	28	10.20	0	173	7	24.71	2/19	0
W. E. Blackburn	13	6	26	6*	3.71	0	1113	45	24.73	5/17	4
W. Blake	3	0	44	21	14.66	0	17	1	17.00	1/17	0
R. J. Blakey	92	13	2563	204*	32.44	4	68	1	68.00	1/68	—
E. Blamires	2	0	23	17	11.50	0	82	5	16.40	3/42	0
G. R. Bloom	1	0	2	2	2.00	0					
H. Bocking	2	0	14	11	7.00	0					
J. G. Boden	1	0	6	6	6.00	0					
B. C. Bolton	6	0	25	11	4.16	0	252	13	19.38	5/40	1
J. B. Bolus	179	18	4712	146*	29.26	7	407	13	31.30	4/40	0
A. Booth	36	16	114	29	5.70	0	1684	122	13.80	6/21	6
M. W. Booth	218	31	4244	210	22.69	2	11017	557	19.17	8/47	41
P. A. Booth	26	6	178	33*	8.90	0	1470	34	43.23	5/98	1
R. Booth	76	28	730	53*	15.20	0					
M. K. Bore	78	21	481	37*	8.43	0	4866	162	30.03	7/63	4
P. D. Borrill							61	5	12.20	2/6	0
W. E. Bosomworth	7	1	20	7	3.33	0	140	9	15.55	2/5	0
I. T. Bottomley	12	0	166	32	13.83	0	75	1	75.00	1/17	0
T. Bottomley	7	0	142	51	20.28	0	188	1	188.00	1/46	0
W. H. Bower	2	0	10	5	5.00	0					
W. E. Bowes	257	117	1251	43*	8.93	0	21227	1351	15.71	9/121	103
G. Boycott	674	111	34570	260*	57.85	103	665	28	23.75	4/14	0
T. Brackin	6	0	12	9	2.00	0					
P. B. Brayshay	3	0	20	13	6.66	0	104	3	34.66	2/48	0
H. Brearley	2	0	17	9	8.50	0					
D. Brennan	221	66	1653	47	10.66	0					
G. Britton	2	0	3	3	1.50	0					
A. Broadbent	5	0	66	29	13.20	0	252	5	50.40	3/71	0
W. B. Broadhead	2	0	5	3	2.50	0					
J. W. Brook	1	0	0	0	0.00	0	0				
B. Brooke	4	0	16	14	4.00	0	191	2	95.50	1/64	0
P. N. Broughton	5	2	19	12	6.33	0	365	16	22.81	6/38	1
A. Brown	3	0	9	5	3.00	0	47	3	15.66	2/17	0
J. T. Brown	568	41	15762	311	29.90	23	5183	177	29.28	6/52	4
J. T. Brown (Darfield)	32	3	333	37*	11.48	0	2071	97	21.35	8/40	8
W. Brown	2	1	2	2	2.00	0	84	4	21.00	3/61	0
T. Brownhill	20	3	185	25	10.88	0					
J. Brumfitt	1	0	9	9	9.00	0					
J. S. Buller	2	0	5	3	2.50	0					
J. R. L. Bulmer	2	0	0	0	0.00	0	79	1	79.00	1/51	0
T. Burgess	2	1	0	0*	0.00	0					
E. Burgin	10	3	92	32	13.14	0	795	31	25.64	6/43	2
J. Burman	2	1	1	1*	1.00	0					
J. R. Burnet	75	6	889	54	12.88	0	26	1	26.00	1/8	0
M. Burrows	10	0	82	23	8.20	0					
D. C. F. Burton	130	15	2273	142*	19.76	2					
R. C. Burton	2	0	47	47	23.50	0	73	6	12.16	3/11	0
E. B. Butterfield	2	0	18	10	9.00	0	64	0			
D. Byas	26	0	592	112	23.68	1					

Name	Inns	No	Runs	HS	Avge	100s	Runs	Wkts	Avge	Best	5wI
J. L. Byrom	4	0	19	11	4.75	0					
J. W. Cammish	1	0	0	0	0.00	0	155	3	51.66	2/56	0
P. Carrick	427	81	8021	131*	23.18	3	23998	797	30.11	8/73	34
E. S. Carter	21	2	210	39*	11.05	0	104	8	13.00	3/23	0
W. H. Cartman	8	0	116	49	14.50	0					
G. Cawthray	6	0	114	30	19.00	0	304	4	76.00	2/64	0
J. P. G. Chadwick	9	3	106	59	17.66	0	67	2	33.50	2/58	0
A. Champion	23	4	148	29	7.78	0	17	1	17.00	1/10	0
A. P. Charlesworth	12	1	241	63	21.90	0					
R. C. J. Chichester-Constable	1	0	0	0	0.00	0	6	0	—	—	—
A. Clarkson	8	1	80	30	11.42	0	92	5	18.40	2/14	0
H. M. Claughton	6	0	39	15	6.50	0	176	3	58.6	1/27	0
R. O. Clayton	115	23	992	62	10.78	0	2478	153	16.19	8/66	13
H. Clegg	8	1	63	25*	9.00	0					
C. C. Clifford	12	4	39	12*	4.87	0	666	26	25.61	5/70	1
D. B. Close	811	102	22650	198	31.94	33	23489	967	24.29	8/41	40
R. W. Collinson	3	0	58	34	19.33	0					
H. P. Cooper	107	29	1159	56	14.85	0	6327	227	27.87	8/62	4
P. E. Cooper	2	0	0	0	0.00	0					
G. A. Cope	249	89	2241	78	14.00	0	15627	630	24.80	8/73	33
A. M. Corbett	2	0	0	0	0.00	0					
S. P. Coverdale	4	0	31	18	7.75	0					
W. Coverdale	2	0	2	1	1.00	0					
M. J. Cowan	84	48	170	19*	4.72	0	6389	266	24.01	9/43	13
J. M. Cownley	2	1	19	19	19.00	0	119	1	119.00	1/16	0
A. Coxon	182	33	2747	83	18.43	0	9528	464	20.53	8/31	24
G. H. Crawford	8	0	46	21	5.75	0	541	21	25.76	5/59	1
M. G. Crawford	2	0	22	13	11.00	0					
E. Creighton	8	2	33	10	5.50	0	181	10	18.10	4/22	0
H. Crick	10	0	88	20	8.80	0					
R. Crookes	2	1	2	2*	2.00	0	14	0	—	—	—
S. M. Crossland	6	2	32	20	8.00	0					
A. Crowther	2	0	0	0	0.00	0					
W. Cuttell	27	6	271	56	12.90	0	596	36	16.55	6/48	2
A. J. Dalton	31	2	710	128	24.48	3					
T. Darnton	22	1	314	81*	14.95	0	349	12	29.08	3/63	0
K. R. Davidson	46	5	1331	128	32.46	2					
J. Dawes	9	2	93	28*	13.28	0	196	5	39.20	2/24	0
E. Dawson	25	1	224	20	9.33	0					
W. A. Dawson	2	0	0	0	0.00	0					
A. G. Day	10	0	78	25	7.80	0					
F. Dennis	100	28	1332	67	18.50	0	4517	156	28.95	6/42	5
S. J. Dennis	62	24	338	53*	8.89	0	5548	173	32.06	5/35	4
D. Denton	1058	61	33282	221	33.38	61	957	34	28.14	5/42	1
J. Denton	24	1	222	59	9.65	0					
H. Dewse	2	0	14	12	7.00	0	15	0	—	—	—
G. Deyes	24	4	44	12	2.20	0	944	41	23.02	6/62	3
R. D. Dick	1	0	2	2	2.00	0	37	2	18.50	1/3	0
A. Dobson	3	0	1	1	0.33	0					
A. Dolphin	446	157	3325	66	11.50	0	28	1	28.00	1/18	0

Name	Inns	No	Runs	HS	Avge	100s	Runs	Wkts	Avge	Best	5wI
J. S. Douglas	26	8	125	19	6.94	0	1310	49	26.73	6/59	2
A. Drake	244	24	4789	147*	21.76	3	8623	479	18.00	10/35	29
J. Drake	4	1	21	10	7.00	0	117	1	117.00	1/44	0
J. Driver	4	1	24	8	8.00	0					
T. S. Dury	24	1	329	46	14.30	0	21	0	—	—	—
W. L. Dyson	4	0	8	6	2.00	0					
W. Earnshaw	7	3	44	23	11.00	0					
D. Eastwood	51	2	591	68	12.06	0	349	11	31.72	3/58	0
R. Eckersley	1	1	9	9*	—	0	62	0	—	—	—
F. W. Elam	3	1	48	28	24.00	0					
J. E. Ellis	15	6	14	4*	1.55	0					
S. Ellis	3	0	12	9	4.00	0					
J. E. Elms	2	0	20	20	10.00	0	28	1	28.00	1/20	0
T. Emmett	483	65	6315	104	15.10	1	15441	1208	12.78	9/23	92
A. Farrar	1	0	2	2	2.00	0					
M. C. Fearnley	4	2	19	11*	9.50	0	133	6	22.16	3/56	0
W. D. Featherby							12	0	—	—	—
K. Fiddling	24	6	182	25	10.11	0					
A. Firth	1	0	4	4	4.00	0					
E. B. Firth	1	0	1	1	1.00	0					
E. L. Firth	4	0	43	37	10.75	0					
J. Firth	8	5	134	67*	44.66	0					
H. Fisher	58	14	681	76*	15.47	0	2621	93	28.18	6/11	2
S. Flaxington	8	0	121	57	15.12	0					
S. D. Fletcher	56	22	294	28*	8.64	0	5394	170	31.72	8/58	3
W. Fletcher	10	2	100	31*	12.50	0	222	9	24.66	4/45	0
C. W. Foord	34	16	114	35	6.33	0	3412	126	27.07	6/63	5
E. Foster	1	0	2	2	2.00	0	27	0	—	—	—
T. W. Foster	20	5	138	25	9.20	0	952	58	16.41	9/59	5
J. Frank	2	0	10	7	5.00	0	17	1	17.00	1/10	0
R. W. Frank	29	4	390	92	15.60	0	9	0	—	—	—
G. Freeman	54	2	752	53	14.46	0	2079	209	9.94	8/11	24
P. A. Gibb	54	7	1545	157*	32.87	2	82	3	27.33	2/40	0
C. J. Gifkins	3	0	30	23	10.00	0					
F. Gill	4	0	18	11	4.50	0					
K. Gillhouley	31	7	323	56*	13.45	0	1702	77	22.10	7/82	3
A. Goulder	1	0	3	3	3.00	0	90	3	30.00	2/21	0
A. Greenwood	165	12	2755	91	18.00	0	9	0	—	—	—
F. E. Greenwood	66	8	1458	104*	25.13	1	36	2	18.00	1/1	0
L. Greenwood	84	12	885	83	12.29	0	1615	85	19.00	8/35	6
C. H. Grimshaw	75	7	1219	85	17.92	0	221	7	31.57	2/23	0
I. Grimshaw	194	14	3354	129*	18.63	4					
S. Haggas	47	3	478	43	10.86	0					
S. Haigh	687	110	10993	159	19.05	4	29289	1876	15.61	9/25	127
B. Hall	2	0	14	10	7.00	0	55	1	55.00	1/55	0
C. H. Hall	22	9	67	15*	5.15	0	1226	45	27.24	6/71	2
J. Hall	2	0	4	3	2.00	0					
L. Hall	483	58	9999	160	23.52	10	876	22	39.81	4/51	0
H. Halliday	279	18	8361	144	32.03	12	3119	101	30.88	6/79	2
C. Halliley	5	0	27	17	5.40	0					
A. Hamer	2	0	3	3	1.50	0	64	1	64.00	1/18	0

Name	Inns	No	Runs	HS	Avge	100s	Runs	Wkts	Avge	Best	5wI
A. W. Hampshire	2	0	18	17	9.00	0					
J. Hampshire	2	0	5	5	2.50	0	109	5	21.80	2/22	0
J. H. Hampshire	724	89	21979	183*	34.61	34	1108	24	46.16	7/52	2
W. E. Harbord	21	1	411	109	20.55	1					
C. H. Hardisty	55	5	991	84	19.82	0					
H. S. Hargreaves	20	6	51	9	3.64	0	1145	55	20.81	5/93	1
W. Harris	8	2	45	22	7.50	0	18	0			
G. P. Harrison	91	26	430	28	6.61	0	3477	232	14.98	7/43	12
H. Harrison	1	1	4	4*	—	0	39	2	19.50	2/15	0
W. H. Harrison	6	1	12	7	2.40	0					
H. W. Hart	2	0	6	6	3.00	0	32	2	16.00	2/19	0
P. R. Hart	5	0	23	11	4.60	0	140	2	70.00	1/22	0
H. H. Hartington	10	4	51	16	8.50	0	764	23	33.21	5/81	1
P. J. Hartley	72	20	1323	127*	25.44	1	5285	154	34.31	6/68	4
S. N. Hartley	199	27	4193	114	24.37	4	2052	42	48.85	4/51	0
A. G. Hatton	1	1	4	4*	—	0	202	6	33.66	2/27	0
Lord Hawke	744	91	13197	166	20.20	10	16	0	—	—	—
H. Hayley	12	1	122	24	11.09	0	48	0	—	—	—
W. J. Haywood	2	0	7	7	3.50	0	14	1	14.00	1/14	0
J. Hicks	25	3	313	66	14.22	0	17	0	—	—	—
J. Higgins	14	5	93	28*	10.33	0					
A. Hill	222	25	1695	49	8.60	0	6961	537	12.96	7/14	39
H. Hill	27	2	337	34	13.48	0					
L. G. Hill	2	0	13	8	6.50	0					
E. T. Hirst	33	2	328	87*	10.58	0					
E. W. Hirst	3	0	33	28	11.00	0	3	0	—	—	—
G. H. Hirst	1052	129	32057	341	34.73	56	44806	2484	18.03	9/23	174
T. H. Hirst	1	1	5	5*	—	0	27	0	—	—	—
G. Hodgson	1	0	4	4	4.00	0					
I. Hodgson	35	14	164	21*	7.80	0	1537	88	17.46	6/63	3
P. Hodgson	6	2	33	8*	8.25	0	648	22	29.45	5/41	1
W. E. N. Holdsworth	26	12	111	22*	7.92	0	1598	53	30.15	6/58	2
G. Holgate	19	0	174	38	9.15	0					
P. Holmes	699	74	26220	315*	41.95	60	124	1	124.00	1/5	0
N. F. Horner	4	0	114	43	28.50	0					
T. H. Hoyle	2	0	7	7	3.50	0					
B. Hudson	4	0	13	5	3.25	0					
D. Hunter	687	326	4239	58*	11.74	0	43	0	—	—	—
J. Hunter	213	61	1183	60*	7.78	0					
L. Hutton	527	62	24807	280*	53.34	85	4221	154	27.40	6/76	4
R. A. Hutton	292	45	4986	189	20.18	4	10254	468	21.91	7/39	17
R. Iddison	108	15	1916	112	20.60	1	1540	102	15.09	7/30	4
R. Illingworth	668	131	14986	162	27.90	14	26806	1431	18.73	9/42	79
P. G. Ingham	14	0	290	64	20.71	0					
F. S. Jackson	328	22	10371	160	33.89	21	9690	506	19.15	7/42	25
S. R. Jackson	2	0	9	9	4.50	0					
T. A. Jacques	20	7	162	35*	12.46	0	1786	57	31.3	5/33	2
F. Jakeman	16	2	262	51	18.71	0					
B. James	5	3	22	11*	11.00	0	228	8	28.50	4/54	0
P. W. Jarvis	89	30	788	47	13.35	0	6859	260	26.38	7/55	13
C. Johnson	152	14	2960	107	21.44	2	265	4	66.25	2/22	0

Name	Inns	No	Runs	HS	Avge	100s	Runs	Wkts	Avge	Best	5wI
J. Johnson	3	2	5	4*	5.00	0	27	5	5.40	5/16	1
M. Johnson	4	2	2	2	1.00	0	301	7	43.00	4/48	0
J. Joy	5	0	107	74	21.40	0	5	0	—	—	—
A. Judson							5	0	—	—	—
H. Kaye	14	0	117	33	8.35	0					
H. S. Kaye	25	1	243	37	10.12	0					
W. G. Keighley	51	5	1227	110	26.67	1	18	0			
G. Kennie	2	0	6	6	3.00	0					
S. Kilburn	1	0	8	8	8.00	0					
N. Kilner	73	7	1253	112	18.98	2					
R. Kilner	478	46	13018	206*	30.13	15	14855	857	17.33	8/26	39
A. M. King	1	0	12	12	12.00	0					
P. J. Kippax	7	2	37	9	7.40	0	279	8	34.87	5/74	1
W. W. Lancaster	10	0	163	51	16.30	0	29	0			
C. W. Landon	13	0	51	18	3.92	0	74	0			
W. Law	7	0	51	22	7.28	0					
B. Leadbeater	236	27	5247	140*	25.10	1	5	1	5.00	1/1	0
E. Leadbeater	94	29	898	91	13.81	0	5657	201	28.14	8/83	7
H. Leadbeater	10	2	141	65	17.62	0	11	0	—	—	—
G. A. B. Leatham	18	5	61	14	4.69	0					
R. S. Leather	2	0	19	14	9.50	0					
C. Lee	4	0	98	74	24.50	0					
F. Lee	183	10	3706	165	21.42	3					
G. H. Lee	2	0	13	9	6.50	0					
H. Lee	6	0	20	12	3.33	0					
J. E. Lee	3	0	9	6	3.00	0					
A. D. Legard	5	0	50	27	10.00	0	26	0	—	—	—
E. I. Lester	339	27	10616	186	34.02	24	160	3	53.33	1/7	0
M. Leyland	720	82	26181	263	41.03	62	11079	409	27.08	8/63	10
L. Linaker	2	0	0	0	0.00	0	28	1	28.00	1/28	0
B. Lister	10	1	26	6*	2.88	0					
J. Lister	4	0	35	16	8.75	0					
K. A. Lister-Kaye	2	1	13	7*	13.00	0	64	1	64.00	1/30	0
E. Lockwood	363	29	7758	208	23.22	6	2227	135	16.49	6/26	3
H. Lockwood	27	2	408	90	16.32	0	37	0			
J. T. Lodge	3	0	48	30	16.00	0	17	0			
J. D. Love	373	56	9999	170*	31.54	13	815	10	81.50	2/0	0
G. E. Lowe	1	1	5	5*	—	0					
F. A. Lowson	404	31	13897	259*	37.25	30	15	0	—	—	—
E. Lumb	23	4	311	70*	16.36	0					
R. G. Lumb	395	30	11525	165*	31.57	22	5	0	—	—	—
A. W. Lupton	79	15	668	43*	10.43	0	88	0	—	—	—
G. G. Lynas	3	1	4	4*	2.0	0					
G. G. Macaulay	430	112	5717	125*	17.97	3	30554	1774	17.22	8/21	125
F. P. McHugh	1	0	0	0	0.00	0	147	4	36.75	2/16	0
A. Marshall	2	0	2	2	1.00	0	11	0			
A. Mason	19	3	105	22	6.56	0	1473	51	28.88	5/56	1
E. Maude	2	0	17	16	8.50	0					
A. A. Metcalfe	14.8	9	4769	216*	34.30	12	154	3	51.33	2/18	0
W. H. Micklethwait	1	0	44	44	44.00	0					
W. Middlebrook	27	7	88	19*	4.40	0	895	50	17.90	5/59	1

Name	Inns	No	Runs	HS	Avge	100s	Runs	Wkts	Avge	Best	5wI
C. A. Midgley	6	2	115	59*	28.75	0	149	8	18.62	2/13	0
F. W. Milligan	113	10	1879	74	18.24	0	2736	112	24.42	7/65	3
A. Mitchell	550	69	18189	189	37.81	39	291	5	58.20	3/49	0
F. Mitchell	125	5	4104	194	34.20	10	16	1	16.00	1/16	0
G. D. Monks	1	0	3	3	3.00	0					
R. Moorhouse	320	45	5239	113	19.05	3	1283	43	29.83	3/20	0
H. Mosley	4	0	1	1	0.25	0	34	3	11.33	3/12	0
A. Motley	2	1	10	8*	10.00	0	135	7	19.28	4/48	0
J. T. Mounsey	147	21	1963	64	15.57	0	476	13	36.61	3/58	0
M. D. Moxon	211	15	7546	191	38.50	17	832	12	69.33	1/6	0
H. Myers	289	46	4450	91	18.31	0	7095	282	25.15	8/81	11
M. Myers	39	4	537	49	15.34	0	20	0	—	—	—
J. E. Naylor							88	0	—	—	—
J. T. Newstead	128	17	1791	100*	16.13	1	5555	297	18.70	7/10	13
A. G. Nicholson	267	125	1667	50	11.73	0	17296	876	19.74	9/62	40
W. G. Nicholson	4	1	47	16	15.66	0					
W. Oates	13	7	34	14*	5.66	0					
W. F. Oates	3	0	20	9	6.66	0					
C. M. Old	262	56	4785	116	23.22	5	13409	647	20.72	7/20	24
S. Oldham	39	18	212	50	10.09	0	3849	130	29.60	5/40	2
E. Oldroyd	509	58	15891	194	35.23	36	1658	42	39.47	4/14	0
C. Oyston	21	8	96	22	7.38	0	872	31	28.12	3/30	0
D. E. V. Padgett	774	63	20306	161*	28.55	29	208	6	34.66	1/2	0
G. H. Padgett	7	4	56	32*	18.66	0	336	4	84.00	2/37	0
J. Padgett	9	0	92	22	10.22	0					
C. H. Parkin	1	0	0	0	0.00	0	25	2	12.50	2/23	0
J. Parratt	2	0	11	11	5.50	0	75	1	75.00	1/12	0
J. W. Parton	2	0	16	14	8.00	0	4	1	4.00	1/4	0
H. E. Pearson	7	5	31	10*	15.50	0	90	5	18.00	3/37	0
J. H. Pearson	3	0	54	44	18.00	0					
E. Peate	226	61	1793	95	10.86	0	9986	794	12.57	8/5	68
R. Peel	514	42	9378	210*	19.86	6	20954	1334	15.70	9/22	100
J. H. Penny	1	1	8	8*	—	0	31	2	15.50	1/7	0
C. S. Pickles	5	2	55	31*	18.33	0	443	6	73.83	2/31	0
D. Pickles	40	20	74	12	3.70	0	2062	96	21.47	7/61	4
G. Pinder	198	44	1639	57	10.64	0	325	19	17.10	4/56	0
R. K. Platt	103	48	405	57*	7.36	0	6389	282	22.65	7/40	10
D. Pollard	2	0	3	3	1.50	0	19	0	—	—	—
G. Pollitt	1	0	51	51	51.00	0					
C. H. Prest	4	0	57	31	14.25	0					
J. M. Preston	135	11	1944	93	15.67	0	3283	180	18.23	9/28	8
T. Pride	1	0	1	1	1.00	0					
P. Pullan	1	0	14	14	14.00	0	5	0	—	—	—
E. J. R. H. Radcliffe	89	13	826	54	10.86	0	134	2	67.00	1/15	0
A. Ramage	22	9	219	52	16.84	0	1649	44	37.47	5/65	1
J. R. S. Raper	4	0	24	15	6.00	0					
E. R. Rawlin	10	1	72	35	8.00	0	498	21	23.71	3/28	0
J. T. Rawlin	36	2	274	31	8.05	0	258	11	23.45	4/35	0
E. B. Rawlinson	68	5	991	55	15.73	0	62	5	12.40	4/41	0
J. Redfearn	1	1	0	5	5	5.00	0				
G. W. Render	1	0	5	5	5.00	0					

Name	Inns	No	Runs	HS	Avge	100s	Runs	Wkts	Avge	Best	5wI
A. C. Rhodes	70	19	917	64*	17.98	0	3026	107	28.28	6/19	5
H. E. Rhodes	16	1	269	64	17.93	0					
S. J. Rhodes	2	1	41	35	41.00	0					
Wilfred Rhodes	1195	162	31075	267*	30.08	46	57634	3598	16.01	9/28	252
William Rhodes	1	1	1	1*	—	0	40	0	—	—	—
J. A. Richardson	12	2	308	61	30.80	0	90	2	45.00	2/23	0
H. Riley	5	1	36	25*	9.00	0	54	1	54.00	1/17	0
M. Riley	28	1	361	92	13.37	0	10	0	—	—	—
W. Ringrose	66	9	353	23	6.19	0	3224	155	20.80	9/76	9
A. L. Robinson	69	31	365	30*	9.60	0	4927	196	25.13	6/61	7
Edward Robinson	2	1	23	23*	23.00	0					
Emmott Robinson	455	77	9651	135*	25.53	7	19645	893	21.99	9/36	36
E. P. Robinson	253	46	2597	75*	12.54	0	15141	735	20.60	8/35	43
H. Robinson	2	0	5	4	2.50	0	20	1	20.00	1/20	0
P. E. Robinson	106	13	3192	129*	34.32	2	139	0	—	—	—
W. Robinson	14	1	151	68	11.61	0					
E. Roper	7	1	85	68	14.16	0					
J. W. Rothery	236	18	4614	161	21.16	3	44	2	22.00	1/18	0
J. Rowbotham	162	9	2624	113	17.15	3	37	3	12.33	3/37	0
H. Rudston	30	0	609	164	20.30	1					
M. Ryan	149	58	682	26*	7.49	0	9466	413	22.92	7/45	12
L. Ryder	2	1	1	1	1.00	0	151	4	37.75	2/75	0
G. Savile	7	0	140	65	20.00	0					
D. Schofield	4	4	13	6*	—	0	112	5	22.40	5/42	1
E. Scott	1	0	8	8	8.00	0	27	2	13.50	1/6	0
H. A. Sedgwick	5	2	53	34	17.66	0	327	16	20.43	5/8	1
A. Sellers	91	1	1677	105	18.63	2	149	2	74.50	2/28	0
A. B. Sellers	437	51	8949	204	23.18	4	653	8	81.62	2/10	0
W. A. Shackleton	6	0	49	25	8.16	0	130	6	21.66	4/18	0
K. Sharp	288	26	7596	181	28.99	11	751	12	62.58	2/13	0
C. M. Sharpe	1	0	15	15	15.00	0	17	0	—	—	—
P. J. Sharpe	666	71	17685	203*	29.72	23	140	2	70.00	1/1	0
C. Shaw	58	27	340	31	10.96	0	41.01	123	33.34	6/64	3
J. Shaw	3	0	8	7	2.66	0	181	7	25.85	4/119	0
E. R. Sheepshanks	1	0	26	26	26.00	0					
D. A. Shepherd	1	0	0	0	0.00	0					
W. Shotton	4	0	13	7	3.25	0					
A. Sidebottom	220	53	3777	124	22.61	1	12046	485	24.83	8/72	17
R. Sidgwick	13	0	64	17	4.92	0					
S. Silvester	7	4	30	14	10.00	0	313	12	26.08	4/86	0
E. T. B. Simpson	3	0	11	10	3.66	0					
H. M. Sims	10	1	109	35*	12.11	0					
W. Slinn	14	3	22	11	2.00	0	742	48	15.45	6/19	4
T. F. Smailes	339	42	5686	117	19.14	3	16593	802	20.68	10/47	39
K. Smales	19	3	165	45	10.31	0	766	22	34.81	5/44	2
A. F. Smith	49	4	692	89	15.37	0					
E. Smith (Ossett)	21	5	169	49	10.56	0	1090	46	23.69	6/40	2
E. Smith (Morley)	234	18	4453	129	20.61	2	6278	248	25.31	7/40	14
F. Smith (Idle)	1	0	11	11	11.00	0	45	2	22.50	1/12	0
F. Smith (Yeadon)	19	1	292	55	16.22	0					
G. Smith	1	0	7	7	7.00	0	62	0	—	—	—

578

Name	Inns	No	Runs	HS	Avge	100s	Runs	Wkts	Avge	Best	5wI
J. Smith	3	0	28	16	9.33	0	72	6	12.00	3/49	9
N. Smith	11	5	82	20	13.66	0					
R. Smith	8	3	99	37*	19.80	0					
Walker Smith	9	0	152	59	16.88	0					
William Smith	19	3	260	90	16.25	0					
G. A. Smithson	60	5	1449	169	26.34	2	84	1	84.00	1/26	0
J. Smurthwaite	9	5	29	20*	7.25	0	237	12	19.75	5/7	1
A. Sowden	11	0	137	37	12.45	0	22	0			
D. Squires	2	0	0	0	0.00	0	25	0	—	—	—
P. J. Squires	84	8	1271	70	16.72	0	32	0	—	—	—
H. C. Stanley	13	0	155	42	11.92	0					
R. T. Stanyforth	3	0	26	10	8.66	0					
B. Stead	3	0	8	8	2.66	0	115	7	16.42	7.76	1
E. Stephenson	61	5	803	67	14.33	0					
J. S. Stephenson	19	2	182	60	10.70	0	65	0	—	—	—
G. B. Stevenson	217	32	3856	115*	20.84	2	13254	464	28.56	8/57	17
W. B. Scott	309	19	9168	186	31.61	17	112	7	16.00	4/34	0
P. M. Stringer	17	8	101	15*	11.22	0	696	32	21.75	4/10	0
S. Stuchbury	3	2	7	4*	7.00	0	236	8	29.50	3/82	0
F. H. Sugg	12	4	80	13*	10.00	0					
W. Sugg	1	0	9	9	9.00	0					
J. H. B. Sullivan	2	0	41	26	20.50	0	43	0	—	—	—
H. Sutcliffe	864	96	38530	313	50.16	112	381	8	47.62	2/16	0
W. H. H. Sutcliffe	273	34	6247	181	26.13	6	152	6	25.33	2/23	0
I. G. Swallow	23	7	256	34*	16.00	0	1372	29	47.31	4/52	0
T. Tait	3	1	7	3	3.50	0					
J. Tasker	43	4	586	67	15.02	0					
G. Tattersall	2	0	26	26	13.00	0					
H. Taylor	13	0	153	36	11.76	0					
H. S. Taylor	5	0	36	22	7.20	0					
J. Taylor	13	1	107	44	8.91	0					
K. Taylor	505	35	12864	203*	27.37	16	3680	129	28.52	6/75	1
N. S. Taylor	6	1	10	4	2.00	0	720	22	32.72	5/49	1
T. L. Taylor	122	10	3933	156	35.11	8					
H. Thewlis	4	1	4	2*	1.33	0					
J. Thewlis Snr	80	3	1280	108	16.62	1					
J. Thewlis Jnr	4	0	21	10	5.25	0					
A. Thornton	4	0	21	7	5.25	0					
G. Thornton	4	0	21	16	5.25	0	74	2	37.00	1/13	0
G. Thorpe	2	1	14	9*	14.00	0					
J. W. Threapleton	1	1	8	8*	—	0					
H. J. Tinsley	13	0	56	15	4.30	0	57	4	14.25	3/15	0
R. A. J. Townsley	4	0	22	12	5.50	0	0	0	—	—	—
D. A. Towse	1	0	1	1	1.00	0	50	3	16.66	2/26	0
F. S. Trueman	533	81	6852	104	15.15	2	29890	1745	17.12	8/28	97
J. Tunnicliffe	773	57	19477	243	27.20	22	401	7	57.28	1/6	0
A. Turner	16	1	163	37	10.86	0					
B. Turner	4	2	7	3*	3.50	0	47	4	11.75	2/9	0
C. Turner	266	32	6132	130	26.20	2	5320	173	30.75	7/54	4
F. I. Turner	7	0	33	12	4.71	0					
C. T. Tyson	5	2	232	100*	77.33	1					

Name	Inns	No	Runs	HS	Avge	100s	Runs	Wkts	Avge	Best	5wI
C. E. Ullathorne	46	8	283	28	7.44	0					
G. Ulyett	624	31	14351	199*	24.20	14	8225	460	17.88	7/30	21
J. Usher	2	0	7	5	3.50	0	31	2	15.50	2/11	0
J. van Geloven	2	1	17	16	17.00	0	224	6	37.33	3/46	0
H. W. Verelst	4	1	66	33*	22.00	0					
H. Verity	294	77	3898	101	17.96	1	21353	1558	13.70	10/10	141
A. Waddington	250	65	2396	114	12.95	1	16201	835	19.40	8/34	51
S. Wade	112	20	1440	74*	15.65	0	2520	134	18.80	7/28	7
E. Wainwright	549	30	11130	228	21.44	18	17949	1007	17.12	9/66	59
W. Wainwright	36	3	648	62	19.63	0	582	19	30.63	6/49	1
W. R. Wake	3	0	13	11	4.33	0					
A. Walker	16	1	138	26	9.20	0	74	1	74.00	1/65	0
C. Walker	9	2	268	91	38.28	0	71	2	35.50	1/25	0
T. Walker	22	2	179	30	8.95	0	7	0	—	—	—
G. Waller	4	0	17	13	4.25	0	70	4	17.50	2/10	0
L. Wallgate	2	0	3	3	1.50	0	17	1	17.00	1/17	0
H. Walton	1	0	5	5	5.00	0	135	5	27.00	3/93	0
A. Ward	7	1	67	26	11.16	0	1	0	—	—	—
F. Ward	1	0	0	0	0.00	0	16	0	—	—	—
H. P. Ward	1	1	10	10*	—	0					
T. A. Wardall	76	3	1141	112	15.63	3	667	30	22.23	5/13	1
J. H. Wardle	418	57	5765	79	15.96	0	27917	1539	18.13	9/25	117
J. S. Waring	27	15	137	26	11.41	0	1122	53	21.16	7/40	2
S. Waring	1	0	9	9	9.00	0					
W. A. I. Washington	62	6	1290	100*	23.03	1					
H. Watson	35	11	141	41	5.87	0					
W. Watson	430	65	13953	214*	38.22	26	75	0			
B. W. Waud	10	1	165	42	18.33	0					
C. Webster	5	1	30	10	7.50	0					
H. H. Webster	3	0	10	10	3.33	0					
J. West	64	13	461	41	9.03	0	853	53	16.09	5/3	3
F. J. Whatmough	11	1	51	20	5.10	0	111	5	22.20	3/58	0
C. H. Wheater	4	1	45	27	15.00	0					
A. W. White	128	28	1457	55	14.57	0	7	0	—	—	—
J. P. Whitehead	38	17	387	58*	18.42	0	2610	96	27.47	5/31	2
Lees Whitehead	172	38	2073	67*	15.47	0	2408	99	24.32	6/45	3
Luther Whitehead	4	0	21	13	5.25	0					
J. P. Whiteley	38	17	231	20	11.00	0	2410	70	34.42	4/14	0
C. P. Whiting	10	2	92	26	11.50	0	416	15	27.73	5/46	1
J. F. Whitwell	2	0	8	4	4.00	0	11	1	11.00	1/11	0
W. F. Whitwell	14	2	67	26	5.58	0	518	25	20.72	5/56	1
A. J. A. Wilkinson	6	0	129	53	21.50	0	57	0	—	—	—
F. Wilkinson	14	1	73	18*	5.61	0	590	26	22.69	7/68	1
H. Wilkinson	75	3	1382	113	19.19	1	121	3	40.33	2/28	0
W. H. Wilkinson	192	14	3812	103	21.41	1	971	31	31.32	4/23	0
A. C. Williams	14	10	95	48*	23.75	0	678	30	22.60	9/29	2
B. B. Wilson	308	12	8053	208	27.50	15	278	2	139.00	1/16	0
C. E. M. Wilson	13	3	256	91*	25.60	0	257	12	21.41	3/31	0
D. Wilson	502	85	5788	83	13.88	0	22626	1104	20.49	7/19	46
E. R. Wilson	72	18	902	104*	16.70	1	3106	197	15.76	7/32	12
G. Wilson	94	14	983	70	12.28	0	11	0	—	—	—

Name	Inns	No	Runs	HS	Avge	100s	Runs	Wkts	Avge	Best	5wI
G. A. Wilson	25	5	352	55*	17.60	0	138	1	138.00	1/5	0
J. Wilson	5	1	17	13*	4.25	0	165	12	13.75	3/28	0
J. P. Wilson	14	1	81	36	6.23	0	24	1	24.00	1/20	0
J. V. Wilson	724	75	20548	230	31.66	29	313	3	104.33	1/3	0
A. Wood	481	80	8579	123*	21.39	1	33	1	33.00	1/33	0
B. Wood	7	2	63	35	12.60	0					
C. H. Wood	4	1	22	10	7.33	0	319	11	29.00	4/39	0
G. W. Wood	2	0	2	2	1.00	0					
H. Wood	16	1	156	36	10.40	0	212	10	21.20	2/35	0
J. H. Wood	1	0	14	14	14.00	0					
R. Wood	18	4	60	17	4.28	0	1346	51	26.39	8/45	3
J. D. Woodford	61	2	1204	101	20.40	1	185	4	46.25	2/20	0
F. E. Woodhead	8	0	57	18	7.12	0					
W. H. Woodhouse	13	0	218	63	16.76	0					
A. Wormald	11	3	161	80	20.12	0					
W. A. Worsley	50	4	722	60	15.69	0					
L. F. Wrathmell	2	0	18	17	9.00	0					
R. Wright	4	1	28	22	9.33	0					
T. J. Wright	1	0	12	12	12.00	0					
N. W. D. Yardley	420	56	11632	183*	31.95	17	5818	195	29.83	6/106	2
J. Yeadon	6	2	41	22	10.25	0					

RESULTS OF ALL INTER-COUNTY FIRST-CLASS MATCHES 1863–1988

Year	DY	EX	GM	GS	HA	KT	LA	LE	MX	NR	NT	SM	SY	SX	WA	WO	CA	P	W	L	D	T	Pos
1863											WL		DW					4	2	1	1		
1864						W					WL		DL				LL	7	2	4	1		
1865						DL					LL		LL				LD	8	0	6	2		
1866											DL						l	3	0	2	1		
1867						WWW							WW				WW	7	7	0	0		
1868						W			WL		WL		LW					7	4	3	0		
1869											LW		WW				W	5	4	1	0		
1870						WW					WD		WW					6	5	0	1		
1871						WL					LW		DW					6	3	2	1		
1872			L			LL			W		LLD		LW					9	2	6	1		
1873		LL				WW			L		LDW		WWWW					12	7	4	1		7th
1874		LL				WL			WD		WW		WWWW					12	8	3	1		4th
1875		WL				LW			DW		LW		WW					10	6	3	1		4th
1876		LD				WW			WD		DL		WW					10	5	2	3		3rd
1877	WD	DL					LL		WD		LD		LD					12	2	5	5		7th
1878	WL	WD					LD		LL		WL		WWWW					14	7	5	2		6th
1879	LL	WD		WL	LW				WW		DW		WD					14	7	4	3		6th
1880	WW	DL		DL	DD				WL		LW		DW					14	5	4	5		5th
1881	WD	LD		WW	LL				WW		WD		WWWW					16	10	3	3		3rd
1882	WW	WL		WL	DL				LW		LW		DW	WW				16	9	5	2		3rd
1883	DW	DW		WW	WW				WD		DL		WD	LW				16	9	2	5		2nd
1884	WW	WW		WW	WL				DD		LL		DD	WL				16	8	4	4		3rd
1885	WD	WD		LD	DW				WL		DW		WW	DD				16	7	2	7		2nd
1886	WW	DW		DL	LD				DW		LD		LL	DD				16	4	5	7		4th
1887	WW	DW		WD	DW				LD		DD		LL	WD				16	6	3	7		3rd
1888		WD		DW	DW				LL		DW		LL	WW				14	6	4	4		2nd
1889		LW		LL	LL				LD		LD		LL	LW				14	2	10	2		7th
1890		WL		WD	DL				WD		LD		DW	WW				14	6	3	5		3rd
1891		WW		LD	LL				WL			LL	WL	LL	LW			16	5	10	1		8th
1892		DD		WD	WL				WL			DD	LD	LL	WW			16	5	5	6		6th
1893		WW		WW	WW				LL				DW	WW	WL			16	12	3	1		1st
1894	WL	WW		WW	W	WWD	LW		WW				WW	WW	LL	WW	DD	24	16	4	4		2nd
1895	LW	WL	WL	WL	DW	LD	WW		WW				DW	WL	LW	WD	WD	26	14	7	5		3rd
1896	DW	WL	WW	DW	WW	WW	WW		WD				DL	WW	DL	WD	DW	26	16	3	7		1st
1897	WW	LL	WL	WW	WW	DL	WD		DD				DD	WW	WD	WL	DW	26	13	5	8		4th
1898	DW	WW	DW	WW	WL	DW	WW		WL				DD	WW	WW	WD	WW	26	16	3	7		1st
1899	WW	WL	WW	WD	WL	LD	WW		LD			DW	WD	DD	DD	WW	WD	28	14	4	10		3rd
1900	DW	WW	WW	WW	WD	DD	WW		WW			DD	WW	DD	WD	DD	WD	28	16	0	12		1st
1901	WWWW	WW	WW	WW	WD	WW	WD		WW				WL	DD	WD	DD	WW	28	20	1	7		1st
1902	DD	DW	WW		WW	WD	D		WW				WD	LW	DD	DD	WDW	25	13	1	11		1st
1903	WD	WD	WW		WD	DW	WW		LW			WW	LD	LW	LL	DW	DD	26	13	5	8		3rd
1904	DW	WD	DD	WW	D	DD	DD		LD			WD	WW	WD	DD	WL	DD	27	9	2	16		2nd
1905	WL	WD	WW	WD	LW	LW	DW		WD				WWWW	WW	DD	DW	WW	28	18	3	7		1st
1906	WW	WD	DL	WW	WW	WW	WD		DL				WW	WW	WW	WD	WW	28	17	3	8		2nd
1907	W	WW	WW	DD	DD	DW	DW		DW			D	WW	DD	LW	WD	LL	26	12	3	11		2nd
1908	WW	DD	WW	WD	DW	WD	WD		WD			WD	DW	WD	WW	DD	DW	28	16	0	12		1st
1909	WW	WW	WW	WW	LD	WW			DD			DW	WD	DD	WL	DD	DW	26	12	4	10		2nd
1910	WW	LD		DW	LL	DL	DL		WL			WL	DD	WD	DW	WL	LL	28	10	7	11		8th
1911	WW	LD		WL	DL	WD	WL		LD			DL	WWWW	LD	WW	WL	WW	28	14	8	6		7th
1912		DW	WW	DW	DW	WD	WW		LW			DD	WW	DW	D	DD	DDWD	27	13	1	13		1st
1913		WW	WL	WD	DD	LLW	DW		DW			DL	DW	WW	LW	WD	WW	29	16	5	8		2nd
1914	WW	WD	WW	DD	LL	DDW	DD		DW			WW	DW	WW	LL	WD	DW	29	14	4	11		4th
1919	WD	DW	WW	WD	DD	LD	DW		WD			WW	LD		WD	LD	WW	26	12	3	11		1st
1920	WWWW		WD	LW	DL	WD	WD		DL			WW	WD		LL	DL	WWWW	28	15	6	7		4th
1921	WW	WD	WW	DW	LW	DD	WD		LD			WW	LD		WW	WWWW		26	16	3	7		3rd
1922	WD	DD	WWWW	WWWW	LW	WW	WD		DW			WW	LW	DD	WWWW	WD		30	19	2	9		1st
1923	WWWW	WWWW	WWWW	DW	DW	DW	WW		WW			WW	LD	WW	WD	WD	WWWW	32	25	1	6		1st
1924	WD	DW	WW	WD	DW	DD	LD		WW	LD		WW	WD	WW	LD	WW	DW	30	16	3	11		1st

Year	DY	EX	GM	GS	HA	KT	LA	LE	MX	NR	NT	SM	SY	SX	WA	WO	CA	P	W	L	D	T	Pos
1925	WW	DD	DW	WW	WD	DW	DD	WD	WD	WW	WD	WW	WD	WW	WW	WW	WW	32	21	0	11		1st
1926	DD	WW	WW	WW	DW	DD	DD	WD	WD	DW	DD	D	WD	WD	WW	WD	DW	31	14	0	17		2nd
1927	DD	WD	WD	WW	DD	D	LD	DD	LD	WW	DD	WD	WD	DW	LD	WD		31	10	3	18		3rd
1928	WW	DW	DW		DD	DD	DD	WD	WD	DW	DD		DD	DD	DD	DW		28	8	0	20		4th
1929	DD	WW	DW		WD	WL	DD	DD	DW	DW	WD		DD	DL	DW	DW		28	10	2	16		2nd
1930	D	WD	DD	WD	WW	LW	DD	WD	DW	W	DD	WW	LD	DD	WD			28	11	2	15		3rd
1931	WW	WW	LW		DW	DW	DD	DW	WD	WD	DW	WW	WD	W	WD			27	16	1	10		1st
1932	W	WW		WW	LW	W	LW	WW	WD	WW	WD	WW	WW	DW	DD			26	19	2	5		1st
1933	WD	WW	WW	WW	DD	WL	WD	WW	WW	WW	DW		WD	LL	DW	WD		30	19	3	8		1st
1934	WD	WL	DD	LL	WD	DW	WD	WL	LW	WW	DD		DW	LD	DL	WW		30	12	7	11		5th
1935	DW	WL	DW	WW	WW	WW	DW	DW	DW	WW	DD		WD	WD	DW	WW		30	19	1	10		1st
1936	DD	DW	WD	DD	DW	WL	DD	DD	DW			DD	WW	DD	DW	LW		30	10	2	18		3rd
1937	WW	WW	DW	WW	WW	WW	WL	DW	LDW		DD		WD	DW	DW	WW		29	19	2	8		1st
1938	WW	WW	WW	DW	DW	DW	WW	WW	WL	WW	DD		WL	DW	WD	WD		30	20	2	8		1st
1939	WD	WL	WW	LL	WW	WW	WW	WW	WW	WD	DD		WD	WW	WW	LW		30	20	4	6		1st
1945						D												1			1		
1946	W	W	WW	DW	WL	WW	DD	DD	WD	W	WD	D	WW	L	WW	W		26	17	1	8		1st
1947	D	D	WW	LL	DD	LD	DD	DW	DL	W	LD	W	LD	L	WW	W		26	8	7	11		7th
1948	DD	WD	D	L	W	W	DD	L	WD	WW	WD	DD	WW	WL	L	WD		26	11	4	11		4th
1949	WW	DD	W	W	W	W	DD	W	DD	WD	DD	WW	WL	WD	W	LW		26	14	2	10		1st
1950	LW	WD	D	DW	DW	W	LD	W	WD	DD	DW	WW	DW	WW	DD	W		28	14	2	12		3rd
1951	WD	DW	W	WD	WW	W	DD	W	DD	DD	WW	WW	DD	DD	LL	L		28	12	3	13		2nd
1952	WL	W	DD	WW	W	WW	DD	WW	DW	D	WW	DW	LW	D	WD	WW		28	17	2	9		2nd
1953	LW	D	DL	DW	W	WD	DD	DL	DD	L	DL	DD	LD	D	WD	WD		28	6	6	16		12th
1954	DL	WW	D	WW	WW	D	DW	T	DL	WW	LD	WD	WD	DW	D			28	13	3	11	1	2nd
1955	WW	WW	L	WW	LW	W	WD	WW	WL	WW	DW	WW	LW	LW	WW	W		28	21	5	2		2nd
1956	LD	L	DD	WL	D	DD	LD	DD	DD	W	WD	WW	LL	D	WW	LW		28	8	7	13		7th
1957	WL	W	LW	DL	W	WD	DD	DW	WD	D	WW	WW	LD	W	DD	WD		28	13	4	11		3rd
1958	DW	DW	D	LD	DD	W	LDL	D	DD	DL	D	WW	WL	WL	DD			27	7	6	14		11th
1959	DW	WW	W	DL	WL	W	LWD	W	WW	DL	WD	DL	LL	WW	DW	W		29	15	7	7		1st
1960	WW	DL	WL	WD	WD	WD	LL	WW	DD	WL	WW	WD	WD	LW	WW	WD		32	17	6	9		1st
1961	DW	WW	WD	LW	DWD	DL	WD	WL	LL	WW	WW	WD	DD	WD	WD	WW		33	17	5	11		2nd
1962	WD	DW	LW	WW	WD	WW	WD	WD	DL	LD	WD	WD	DD	DW	WL	DD		32	14	4	14		1st
1963	WW	D	WW	DD	L	DW	WD	WW	LD	W	DD	WD	DD	W	WW	DL		28	13	3	12		1st
1964	DD	W	WW	DW	W	LW	DW	DD	WD	D	WW	DD	DL	D	LD	DW		28	11	3	14		5th
1965	DD	DW	L	WD	LD	W	DW	W	DD	WL	DW	WW	LD	DD	DD	D		28	9	4	15		4th
1966	WW	WD	W	WD	DD	W	WW	W	DW	LL	WW	WW	LD	LD	WL	D		28	15	5	8		1st
1967	DD	L	DW	WW	L	DW	D	W	LD	W	WD	LD	WL	W	DW	WW		26	12	5	9		1st
1968	DD	L	LW	DD	D	DD	WD	WW	WW	D	DD	DW	WW	D	WL	WL		28	11	4	13		1st
1969	DD	D	D	WL	D	D	DD	DW	DD	L	DL	DD	DL	L	L	W		24	3	6	15		13th
1970	WW	W	L	LD	W	L	LD	DW	LD	D	DD	LW	DW	D	W	D		24	8	5	11		4th
1971	DD	DD	D	L	L	LL	DD	D	WD	W	W	L	DL	D	WL	LD		24	4	8	12		13th
1972	DD	L	W	W	D	L	DL	D	DW	L	D	D	LW	D	D	D		20	4	5	11		10th
1973	DW	D	L	D	L	D	DD	D	LT	W	D	WL	D	D	D			20	3	5	11	1	14th
1974	DW	L	D	W		D	DD	L	LL	L	W	L	DW	D	D	L		19	4	7	8		11th
1975	DW	W	D	W	W	D	DD	D	LW	W	W	D	DW	W	W	D		20	10	1	9		2nd
1976	DD	L	W	D	D	W	DW	L	W	DL	LW	W	L	D	L	D		20	6	6	8		8th
1977	DD	D	W		L	L	DW	D	DL	DW	DW	W	W	L	DD	W		21	6	5	10		12th
1978	DD	D	W	D	D	D	WW	W	DL	WD	LW	D	W	D	LW	W		22	10	3	9		4th
1979	DW	W	D	D	D	D	DW	D	DW	DD	L	D	D	L	DW	L		21	5	3	13		7th
1980	DD	D	D	D	D	W	DL	D	DL	DL	WW	D	D	D	WD	D		22	4	3	15		6th
1981	DW	D	L	L	D	D	DL	W	LL	WW	DL	L	W	L	DD	L		22	5	9	8		10th
1982	DW	D	D	L	D	D	DD	D	DD	DD	W	D	W	WW	D			21	5	1	15		10th
1983	LD	D	D	LD	W	D	DD	DL	D	DL	DD	D	D	DL	D			23	1	5	17		17th
1984	DW	L	DD	W	DD	D	DD	DD	L	W	WD	WD	L	DD	L	D		24	5	4	15		14th
1985	DW	L	W	L	D	LD	DD	W	D	D	DD	D	LD	D	D	DD		23	3	4	16		11th
1986	LD	L	D	DD	D	D	DD	DL	WD	DD	LD	W	W	W	DL	D		24	4	5	15		10th
1987	WD	W	LD	W	WD	W	DD	WD	W	L	DL	DD	D	D	D	D		23	7	3	13		8th
1988	LD	L	D	D	D	L	WD	W	DD	DD	DW	D	D	W	LL	L		22	4	6	12		13th

RESULTS OF SUNDAY LEAGUE MATCHES 1969–1988

Year	DY	EX	GM	GS	HA	KT	LA	LE	MX	NR	NT	SM	SY	SX	WA	WO	P	W	L	D	T	Pos
1969	W	L	W	L	L	W	A	L	L	W	W	L	L	W	A	W	14	7	7			8
1970	L	W	L	L	L	W	L	W	D	W	L	D	L	W	L	L	16	5	9	2		14
1971	L	L	L	A	L	L	L	W	L	W	L	A	L	W	W	W	14	5	9			15
1972	W	L	W	W	L	L	W	W	W	W	W	W	W	A	L	L	15	10	5			4
1973	W	W	W	L	W	L	L	L	W	W	W	L	W	W	W	L	16	11	5			2
1974	W	W	L	D	L	W	W	L	W	W	W	W	L	A	L	A	15	8	6	1		6=
1975	W	W	W	W	L	L	L	W	W	L	L	W	W	L	L	W	16	9	7			5=
1976	L	L	W	W	W	L	W	L	W	L	W	L	L	L	L	L	16	6	10			15
1977	L	W	L	D	L	L	W	L	D	D	D	L	A	L	A	W	14	3	7	4		13=
1978	L	A	L	A	L	W	L	W	W	W	W	L	L	L	W	W	14	7	7			7
1979	W	W	W	L	L	A	D	A	L	W	W	L	W	W	W	A	13	8	4	1		4=
1980	W	W	L	W	W	L	L	L	L	W	W	L	L	L	L	L	16	6	10			14=
1981	W	L	L	D	W	L	L	W	D	W	L	W	L	A	A	W	14	6	6	2		7=
1982	W	L	A	W	L	W	D	L	L	L	T	L	L	L	L	L	15	3	10	1		16
1983	W	A	L	W	W	D	W	W	W	W	L	L	A	W	W	W	14	10	3	1		1
1984	W	L	L	W	L	W	L	W	L	W	L	W	L	L	L	L	16	6	10			13=
1985	A	L	L	L	W	W	A	W	D	L	L	W	W	L	A	W	13	6	6	1		6
1986	L	W	W	L	L	A	D	W	L	L	W	W	W	L	T	W	13	7	6	1		3
1987	L	L	L	L	A	W	L	D	W	W	L	L	W	A	W	L	14	5	8	1		12=
1988	D	W	L	L	L	W	L	W	W	A	W	L	W	L	W	L	15	7	7	1		8

RESULTS IN BENSON AND HEDGES CUP 1972–1988

1972 First in Group North; *Quarter-Final*: beat Sussex; *Semi-Final*: beat Gloucestershire; *Final*: lost to Leicestershire

1973 Third in Group North

1974 Second in Group North; *Quarter-Final*: lost to Surrey

1975 Second in Group North; *Quarter-Final*: lost to Middlesex

1976 Third in Group D

1977 Third in Group D

1978 Fifth in Group D

1979 Second in Group D; *Quarter-Final*: beat Middlesex; *Semi-Final*: lost to Essex

1980 Fourth in Group B

1981 First in Group B; *Quarter-Final*: lost to Somerset

1982 Fifth in Group A

1983 Fifth in Group B

1984 Second in Group A; *Quarter-Final*: beat Sussex; *Semi-Final*: lost to Warwickshire

1985 Third in Group B

1986 Third in Group B

1987 First in Group B; *Quarter-Final*: beat Hampshire; *Semi-Final*: beat Surrey; *Final*: beat Northamptonshire

1988 Fourth in Group B

RESULTS IN GILLETTE CUP/ NATWEST TROPHY 1963–1988

1963   *1st Round*: beat Nottinghamshire; *Quarter-Final*: lost to Sussex
1964   *1st Round*: bye; *2nd Round*: lost to Middlesex
1965   *1st Round*: bye; *2nd Round*: beat Leicestershire; *Quarter-Final*: beat Somerset; *Semi-Final*: beat Warwickshire; *Final*: beat Surrey
1966   *1st Round*: bye; *2nd Round*: lost to Somerset
1967   *1st Round*: bye; *2nd Round*: beat Cambridgeshire; *Quarter-Final*: lost to Lancashire
1968   *1st Round*: bye; *2nd Round*: lost to Warwickshire
1969   *1st Round*: beat Norfolk; *2nd Round*: beat Lancashire; *Quarter-Final*: beat Surrey; *Semi-Final*: beat Nottinghamshire; *Final*: beat Derbyshire
1970   *1st Round*: lost to Surrey
1971   *1st Round*: bye; *2nd Round*: lost to Kent
1972   *1st Round*: lost to Warwickshire
1973   *1st Round*: lost to Durham
1974   *1st Round*: bye; *2nd Round*: beat Hampshire; *Quarter-Final*: lost to Lancashire
1975   *1st Round*: bye; *2nd Round*: lost to Leicestershire
1976   *1st Round*: beat Shropshire; *2nd Round*: lost to Gloucestershire
1977   *1st Round*: bye; *2nd Round*: lost to Hampshire
1978   *1st Round*: beat Durham; *2nd Round*: beat Nottinghamshire; *Quarter-Final*: lost to Sussex
1979   *1st Round*: bye; *2nd Round*: beat Durham; *Quarter-Final*: lost to Middlesex
1980   *1st Round*: bye; *2nd Round*: beat Kent; *Quarter-Final*: beat Hampshire; *Semi-Final*: lost to Surrey
1981   *1st Round*: lost to Kent
1982   *1st Round*: bye; *2nd Round*: beat Worcestershire; *Quarter-Final*: beat Essex; *Semi-Final*: lost to Warwickshire
1983   *1st Round*: beat Berkshire; *2nd Round*: lost to Northamptonshire
1984   *1st Round*: lost to Shropshire
1985   *1st Round*: beat Cheshire *2nd Round*: lost to Somerset
1986   *1st Round*: beat Cambridgeshire; *2nd Round*: beat Middlesex; *Quarter-Final*: lost to Sussex
1987   *1st Round*: beat Wiltshire; *2nd Round*: beat Glamorgan; *Quarter-Final*: lost to Leicestershire
1988   *1st Round*: beat Berkshire; *2nd Round*: lost to Middlesex

GROUNDS USED BY YORKSHIRE 1863–1988

Centre	Ground		Occasions and Opponents
Bradford	Great Horton Road also known as Easby Road	First	22, 23, 24 June 1863 *v* Nottinghamshire
		Last	10, 11, 12 August 1874 *v* Lancashire
	Horton Park Avenue	First	13, 14, 15 June 1881 *v* Kent
		Last	31 July, 1, 2 August 1985 *v* Derbyshire

Centre	Ground		Occasions and Opponents
Dewsbury	Dewsbury and Savile Ground	*First*	25, 26, 27 July 1867 *v* Cambridgeshire
		Last	17, 18, 19 May 1933 *v* Essex
Halifax	Thrum Hall, Hanson Lane	*First*	30, 31 July 1888 *v* Gloucester
		Last	10, 11, June 1897 *v* Kent
Harrogate	St George's Road	*First*	16, 17 August 1894 *v* Leicester
		Current Ground	
Holbeck (Leeds)	Recreation Ground	*First*	9, 10, July 1868 *v* Lancashire
		Last	26, 27, 28 August 1886 *v* Derbyshire
Hull	Argyle Street	*First*	12, 13, 14 June 1879 *v* Surrey (only match)
	The Circle, Anlaby Road (Now used by Yorkshire for Sunday League matches)	*First*	10, 11, 12 July 1899 *v* Somerset
		Last	6, 8, 9 July 1974 *v* Worcester
Hunslet (Leeds)	Woodhouse Hill Ground	*First*	12, 13 July 1869 *v* Cambridge (only match)
Horsforth	Hall Park Ground	*First*	13, 14, 15 August 1885 *v* M. B. Hawke's XI (only match)
Leeds	Headingley Grounds	*First*	24, 25, 26 August 1891 *v* Kent
		Current ground	
Huddersfield	St John's Ground, Fartown	*First*	28, 29, 30 August 1873 *v* Nottinghamshire
		Last	17, 18, 19 August 1955 *v* Gloucestershire
Middlesbrough	Swatter's Carr, Linthorpe Road	*First*	19, 20, 21 September 1864 *v* Kent
		Last	2, 3 September 1867 *v* Lancashire
	West Linthorpe Road	*First*	20, 21, 22 July 1882 *v* Australians (only match)
	Acklam Park	*First*	28, 30, 31 July 1956 *v* Glamorgan
		Current ground	
Scarborough	Queen's Cricket Ground, Castle Hill	*First*	7, 8, 9 September 1874 *v* Middlesex
		Last	30, 31 August, 1 September 1877 *v* MCC
	North Marine Road Ground	*First*	2, 3, 4 September 1878 *v* I Zingari
		Current ground	

586

Centre	Ground		Occasions and Opponents
Sheffield	Bramall Lane	*First*	27, 28, 29 August 1855 *v* Sussex
		Last	4, 6, 7 August 1973 *v* Lancashire
	Abbeydale Park	*First*	22, 23, 24 May 1974 *v* Warwickshire
		Current ground	
Wakefield	College Ground (believed to be College Grove)	*First*	13, 14, 15 June 1878 *v* Sussex (only match)
York	Bootham Crescent	*First*	9, 10 June 1890 *v* Kent (only match)

TEAM RECORDS

(1) HIGHEST AND LOWEST SCORE FOR YORKSHIRE AGAINST EACH COUNTY

Opponents	Highest	Year	Lowest	Year
Derbyshire	662 *at* Chesterfield	1898	44 *at* Chesterfield	1948
Essex	555-1 dec *at* Leyton	1932	31 *at* Huddersfield	1935
Glamorgan	579-6 dec *at* Huddersfield	1925	83 *at* Sheffield	1946
Gloucestershire	504-7 dec *at* Bradford	1905	35 *at* Bristol	1959
Hampshire	585-3 dec *at* Portsmouth	1920	23 *at* Middlesbrough	1965
Kent	559 *at* Canterbury	1887	30 *at* Sheffield	1865
Lancashire	590 *at* Bradford	1887	33 *at* Leeds	1924
Leicestershire	660 *at* Leicester	1896	47 *at* Leicester	1911
Middlesex	575-7 dec *at* Bradford	1899	43 *at* Lord's	1888
Northamptonshire	548-4 dec *at* Harrogate	1921	64 *at* Northampton	1959
Nottinghamshire	562 *at* Bradford	1899	32 *at* Sheffield	1876
Somerset	549-9 dec *at* Taunton	1905	73 *at* Leeds	1895
Surrey	704 *at* The Oval	1899	26 *at* The Oval	1909
Sussex	681-5 dec *at* Sheffield	1897	42 *at* Hove	1922
Warwickshire	887 *at* Birmingham	1896	49 *at* Huddersfield	1951
Worcestershire	560-6 dec *at* Worcester	1928	62 *at* Bradford	1907

(2) HIGHEST AND LOWEST SCORE AGAINST YORKSHIRE BY EACH COUNTY

Opponents	Highest	Year	Lowest	Year
Derbyshire	491 *at* Bradford	1949	20 *at* Sheffield	1939
Essex	524-7 dec *at* Leeds	1984	30 *at* Leyton	1901
Glamorgan	357-9 dec *at* Cardiff	1984	48 *at* Cardiff	1924
Gloucestershire	528 *at* Cheltenham	1876	36 *at* Sheffield	1969
Hampshire	521-8 dec *at* Portsmouth	1927	36 *at* Southampton	1898
			36 *at* Leeds	1904
Kent	493 *at* Tonbridge	1914	39 *at* Sheffield	1882
			39 *at* Sheffield	1936
Lancashire	509-9 dec *at* Manchester	1926	30 *at* Holbeck	1868
Leicestershire	458 *at* Hull	1937	34 *at* Leeds	1906
Middlesex	527 *at* Huddersfield	1887	45 *at* Huddersfield	1879
Northamptonshire	464 *at* Scarborough	1988	15 *at* Northampton	1908
Nottinghamshire	492-5 dec *at* Sheffield	1949	13 *at* Nottingham	1901
Somerset	630 *at* Leeds	1901	35 *at* Bath	1898
Surrey	560-6 dec *at* The Oval	1933	31 *at* Holbeck	1883
Sussex	566 *at* Sheffield	1937	20 *at* Hull	1922
Warwickshire	536-7 dec *at* Birmingham	1929	35 *at* Birmingham	1963
			35 *at* Sheffield	1979
Worcestershire	456-8 *at* Worcester	1904	24 *at* Huddersfield	1903

(3) HIGHEST SCORES IN LIMITED-OVERS MATCHES

John Player/Refuge Assurance League	263-8 *v* Surrey at Bradford	1985
Benson and Hedges Cup	317-5 *v* Scotland at Leeds	1986
Gillette Cup/NatWest Trophy	317-4 *v* Surrey at Lord's	1965

(4) LOWEST SCORES IN LIMITED-OVERS MATCHES

John Player/Refuge Assurance League	74 *v* Warwickshire at Birmingham	1972
Benson and Hedges Cup	114 *v* Kent at Canterbury	1978
Gillette Cup/NatWest Trophy	76 *v* Surrey at Harrogate	1970

INDIVIDUAL BATTING RECORDS

(1) DOUBLE-CENTURIES IN FIRST-CLASS MATCHES

Score	Batsman	Opponents	Venue	Year
341	G. H. Hirst	Leicestershire	Leicester	1905
315★	P. Holmes	Middlesex	Lord's	1925
313	H. Sutcliffe	Essex	Leyton	1932
311	J. T. Brown	Sussex	Sheffield	1897
302★	P. Holmes	Hampshire	Portsmouth	1920
300	J. T. Brown	Derbyshire	Chesterfield	1898
285	P. Holmes	Nottinghamshire	Nottingham	1929
280★	L. Hutton	Hampshire	Sheffield	1939
277★	P. Holmes	Northamptonshire	Harrogate	1921
275	P. Holmes	Warwickshire	Bradford	1928
271★	L. Hutton	Derbyshire	Sheffield	1937
270★	L. Hutton	Hampshire	Bournemouth	1947
270	H. Sutcliffe	Sussex	Leeds	1932
269★	L. Hutton	Northamptonshire	Wellingborough	1949
267★	W. Rhodes	Leicestershire	Leeds	1921
263	M. Leyland	Essex	Hull	1936
260★	G. Boycott	Essex	Colchester	1970
259★	F. A. Lowson	Worcestershire	Worcester	1953
255★	H. Sutcliffe	Essex	Southend-on-Sea	1924
255	W. Barber	Surrey	Sheffield	1935
250	P. Holmes	Warwickshire	Birmingham	1931
248	W. Barber	Kent	Leeds	1934
247	M. Leyland	Worcestershire	Worcester	1928
243	J. Tunnicliffe	Derbyshire	Chesterfield	1898
235	H. Sutcliffe	Middlesex	Leeds	1925

★not out.

Score	Batsman	Opponents	Venue	Year
234*	H. Sutcliffe	Leicestershire	Hull	1939
233	G. Boycott	Essex	Colchester	1971
232*	G. H. Hirst	Surrey	The Oval	1905
232	H. Sutcliffe	Surrey	The Oval	1922
230	H. Sutcliffe	Kent	Folkestone	1931
230	J. V. Wilson	Derbyshire	Sheffield	1952
228	E. Wainwright	Surrey	The Oval	1899
228	H. Sutcliffe	Sussex	Eastbourne	1928
224*	P. Holmes	Essex	Leyton	1932
223*	J. V. Wilson	Scotland	Scarborough	1951
221	D. Denton	Kent	Tunbridge Wells	1912
220*	P. Holmes	Warwickshire	Huddersfield	1922
220*	G. Boycott	Northamptonshire	Sheffield	1967
218	G. H. Hirst	Sussex	Hastings	1911
216*	A. A. Metcalfe	Middlesex	Leeds	1988
214*	W. Watson	Worcestershire	Worcester	1955
214*	G. Boycott	Nottinghamshire	Worksop	1983
214	G. H. Hirst	Worcestershire	Worcester	1901
213	H. Sutcliffe	Somerset	Dewsbury	1924
212	H. Sutcliffe	Leicestershire	Leicester	1935
211*	M. Leyland	Lancashire	Leeds	1930
210*	R. Peel	Warwickshire	Birmingham	1896
210*	M. Leyland	Kent	Dover	1933
210	M. W. Booth	Worcestershire	Worcester	1911
209*	D. Denton	Worcestershire	Worcester	1920
209	P. Holmes	Warwickshire	Birmingham	1922
208	E. Lockwood	Kent	Gravesend	1883
208	B. B. Wilson	Sussex	Bradford	1914
207*	G. Boycott	Cambridge University	Cambridge	1976
206*	R. Kilner	Derbyshire	Sheffield	1920
206	H. Sutcliffe	Warwickshire	Dewsbury	1925
205	H. Sutcliffe	Warwickshire	Birmingham	1933
204*	M. Leyland	Middlesex	Sheffield	1927
204*	G. Boycott	Leicestershire	Leicester	1972
204*	R. J. Blakey	Gloucestershire	Leeds	1987
204	A. B. Sellers	Cambridge University	Cambridge	1936
203*	P. J. Sharpe	Cambridge University	Cambridge	1960
203*	K. Taylor	Warwickshire	Birmingham	1961
203	J. T. Brown	Middlesex	Lord's	1896
203	H. Sutcliffe	Surrey	The Oval	1934
202	H. Sutcliffe	Middlesex	Scarborough	1936
201*	G. Boycott	Middlesex	Lord's	1975
201	W. Rhodes	Somerset	Taunton	1905
201	L. Hutton	Lancashire	Manchester	1949
200*	D. Denton	Warwickshire	Birmingham	1912
200*	H. Sutcliffe	Worcestershire	Sheffield	1935
200	H. Sutcliffe	Leicestershire	Leicester	1926

72 in all, of which H. Sutcliffe (16), P. Holmes (9), G. Boycott (7), L. Hutton (5) and M. Leyland (5) account for 42.

*not out.

(2) CENTURIES IN LIMITED-OVERS MATCHES

(a) John Player/Refuge Assurance League

Score	Batsman	Opponents	Venue	Year
119	J. H. Hampshire	Leicestershire	Hull	1970
118*	J. D. Love	Surrey	Leeds	1987
118	C. W. J. Athey	Leicestershire	Leicester	1978
115*	A. A. Metcalfe	Gloucestershire	Scarborough	1984
114*	J. H. Hampshire	Northamptonshire	Scarborough	1978
114	K. Sharp	Essex	Chelmsford	1985
112*	K. Sharp	Worcestershire	Worcester	1985
111*	J. H. Hampshire	Sussex	Hastings	1973
108*	G. Boycott	Northamptonshire	Huddersfield	1974
108	J. H. Hampshire	Nottinghamshire	Sheffield	1970
106*	J. H. Hampshire	Lancashire	Manchester	1972
104*	G. Boycott	Glamorgan	Colwyn Bay	1973
104*	J. D. Love	Nottinghamshire	Hull	1986
101	R. G. Lumb	Nottinghamshire	Scarborough	1976
100*	J. H. Hampshire	Warwickshire	Birmingham	1975
100*	J. D. Love	Gloucestershire	Gloucester	1985

(b) Benson and Hedges Cup

Score	Batsman	Opponents	Venue	Year
142	G. Boycott	Northamptonshire	Northampton	1980
118*	J. D. Love	Scotland	Bradford	1981
106*	M. D. Moxon	Lancashire	Manchester	1986
106	G. Boycott	Northamptonshire	Bradford	1984
105*	K. Sharp	Scotland	Leeds	1986
103*	D. L. Bairstow	Derbyshire	Derby	1981
102	G. Boycott	Northamptonshire	Middlesbrough	1977

(c) Gillette Cup/NatWest Trophy

Score	Batsman	Opponents	Venue	Year
146	G. Boycott	Surrey	Lord's	1965
115	C. W. J. Athey	Kent	Leeds	1980
110	J. H. Hampshire	Durham	Middlesbrough	1978

(3) CARRYING BAT THROUGH A COMPLETED FIRST-CLASS INNINGS

Batsman	Score	Total	Opponents	Venue	Year
G. R. Atkinson	30*	73	Nottinghamshire	Bradford	1865
L. Hall	31*	94	Sussex	Hove	1878
I. Grimshaw	36*	182	Kent	Maidstone	1881
L. Hall	124*	331	Sussex	Hove	1883
L. Hall	128*	285	Sussex	Huddersfield	1884
L. Hall	32*	81	Kent	Sheffield	1885
L. Hall	79*	285	Surrey	Sheffield	1885
L. Hall	37*	96	Derbyshire	Derby	1885

*Not out.

Batsman	Score	Total	Opponents	Venue	Year
L. Hall	50*	173	Sussex	Huddersfield	1886
L. Hall	74*	172	Kent	Canterbury	1886
G. Ulyett	199*	399	Derbyshire	Sheffield	1887
L. Hall	119*	334	Gloucestershire	Dewsbury	1887
L. Hall	82*	218	Sussex	Hove	1887
L. Hall	34*	104	Surrey	The Oval	1888
L. Hall	129*	461	Gloucestershire	Clifton	1888
L. Hall	85*	259	Middlesex	Lord's	1889
L. Hall	41*	106	Nottinghamshire	Sheffield	1891
F. S. Jackson	59*	162	Cambridge University	Cambridge	1897
W. Rhodes	98*	184	MCC	Lord's	1903
J. W. Rothery	53*	258	Worcestershire	Worcester	1907
W. Rhodes	85*	152	Essex	Leyton	1910
P. Holmes	145*	270	Northamptonshire	Northampton	1920
H. Sutcliffe	125*	307	Essex	Southend-on-Sea	1920
P. Holmes	175*	377	New Zealanders	Bradford	1927
P. Holmes	110*	219	Northamptonshire	Bradford	1929
H. Sutcliffe	104*	170†	Hampshire	Leeds	1932
H. Sutcliffe	114*	202	Rest of England	The Oval	1933
H. Sutcliffe	187*	401	Worcestershire	Bradford	1934
H. Sutcliffe	135*	262	Glamorgan	Neath	1935
H. Sutcliffe	125*	322	Oxford University	Oxford	1939
L. Hutton	99*	200	Leicestershire	Sheffield	1948
L. Hutton	78*	153	Worcestershire	Sheffield	1949
F. A. Lowson	76*	218	MCC	Lord's	1951
W. B. Stott	144*	262	Worcestershire	Worcester	1959
D. E. V. Padgett	115*	230	Gloucestershire	Bristol	1962
G. Boycott	114*	297	Leicestershire	Sheffield	1968
G. Boycott	53*	119	Warwickshire	Bradford	1969
G. Boycott	182*	320	Middlesex	Lord's	1971
G. Boycott	138*	232	Warwickshire	Birmingham	1971
G. Boycott	175*	360	Nottinghamshire	Worksop	1979
G. Boycott	112*	233	Derbyshire	Sheffield	1983
G. Boycott	55*	183	Warwickshire	Leeds	1984
G. Boycott	55*	131	Surrey	Sheffield	1985

43 Instances in all, of which L. Hall (14 times), G. Boycott (8) and H. Sutcliffe (6) account for 28 between them.

*Not out
†Denotes completed innings in which ten wickets did not fall as one batsman was absent ill.

(4) CARRYING BAT THROUGH A COMPLETED LIMITED-OVERS INNINGS

(a) John Player/Refuge Assurance League

Batsman	Score	Total	Opponents	Venue	Year
G. Boycott	73*	161–7	Leicestershire	Scarborough	1969
B. Leadbeater	73*	181–4	Kent	Canterbury	1969

*Not out.

Batsman	Score	Total	Opponents	Venue	Year
G. Boycott	104★	186-5	Glamorgan	Colwyn Bay	1973
G. Boycott	108★	186-6	Northamptonshire	Huddersfield	1974
J. H. Hampshire	100★	217-3	Warwickshire	Birmingham	1975
J. H. Hampshire	92★	200-1	Gloucestershire	Scarborough	1975
G. Boycott	82★	205-2	Somerset	Glastonbury	1976
K. Sharp	112★	215-5	Worcestershire	Worcester	1985

(b) Benson and Hedges Cup

Nil

(c) Gillette Cup/NatWest Trophy

Nil

★Not out.

(5) CENTURY IN EACH INNINGS OF A FIRST-CLASS MATCH

Scores	Batsman	Opponents	Venue	Year
107 and 109★	D. Denton	Nottinghamshire	Nottingham	1906
111 and 117★	G. H. Hirst	Somerset	Bath	1906
133 and 121	D. Denton	MCC	Scarborough	1908
128 and 115	W. Rhodes	MCC	Scarborough	1911
126 and 111★	P. Holmes	Lancashire	Manchester	1920
107 and 109★	H. Sutcliffe	MCC	Scarborough	1926
111 and 100★	H. Sutcliffe	Nottinghamshire	Nottingham	1928
126 and 142	E. I. Lester	Northamptonshire	Northampton	1947
197 and 104	L. Hutton	Essex	Southend-on-Sea	1947
125★ and 132	E. I. Lester	Lancashire	Manchester	1948
165 and 100	L. Hutton	Sussex	Hove	1949
103 and 137	L. Hutton	MCC	Scarborough	1952
103 and 105	G. Boycott	Nottinghamshire	Sheffield	1966
163 and 141★	G. Boycott	Nottinghamshire	Bradford	1983
123 and 112★	M. D. Moxon	Indians	Scarborough	1986

★Not out.

(6) CENTURY ON DEBUT FOR YORKSHIRE

Score	Batsman	Opponents	Venue	Year
100†	C. T. Tyson	Hampshire	Southampton	1920
157★	P. A. Gibb†	Nottinghamshire	Sheffield	1935
116	M. D. Moxon‡	Essex	Leeds	1981
122	A. A. Metcalfe	Nottinghamshire	Bradford	1983

★Not out.
†Having already made first-class debut.
‡Second innings.

(7) 2,000 FIRST-CLASS RUNS IN A SEASON FOR YORKSHIRE

Batsman	Matches	Inns	NO	Runs	HS	Avge	100s	Year
H. Sutcliffe	29	41	5	2883	313	80.08	12	1932
L. Hutton	26	44	6	2640	269★	69.47	9	1949
L. Hutton	28	45	6	2448	271★	62.76	8	1937
H. Sutcliffe	27	35	5	2418	228	80.60	11	1928
P. Holmes	35	49	9	2351	315★	58.77	6	1925
H. Sutcliffe	28	33	8	2351	230	94.04	9	1931
L. Hutton	29	44	5	2316	280★	59.38	10	1939
D. Denton	33	52	2	2258	172	45.16	8	1905
G. H. Hirst	32	44	3	2257	157	55.04	8	1904
H. Sutcliffe	34	48	8	2236	235	55.90	7	1925
G. Boycott	18	25	4	2221	233	105.76	11	1971
P. J. Sharpe	36	62	8	2201	138	40.75	7	1962
M. Leyland	31	44	4	2196	210★	54.90	7	1933
H. Sutcliffe	32	47	3	2183	212	49.61	8	1935
G. H. Hirst	32	53	6	2164	169	46.04	6	1906
D. Denton	32	55	4	2161	137★	42.37	6	1911
D. E. V. Padgett	35	60	8	2158	161★	41.50	4	1959
P. Holmes	30	45	6	2144	302★	54.97	7	1920
A. Mitchell	34	49	10	2100	158	53.84	6	1933
P. Holmes	31	40	4	2093	275	58.13	6	1928
D. Denton	36	51	4	2079	221	44.23	6	1912
L. Hutton	19	31	2	2068	270★	71.31	10	1947
F. A. Lowson	31	54	5	2067	141★	42.18	5	1950
H. Sutcliffe	32	52	5	2054	189	43.70	4	1937
W. B. Stott	32	56	2	2034	144★	37.66	3	1959

★Not out.

INDIVIDUAL BOWLING RECORDS

(1) HAT-TRICKS FOR YORKSHIRE IN FIRST-CLASS MATCHES

Bowler	Opponents	Venue	Year
G. Freeman	Lancashire	Holbeck	1868
G. Freeman	Middlesex	Sheffield	1868
A. Hill	United South XI	Bradford	1874
A. Hill	Surrey	The Oval	1880
E. Peate	Kent	Sheffield	1882
G. Ulyett	Lancashire	Sheffield	1883
E. Peate	Gloucestershire	Moreton-in-Marsh	1884
W. Fletcher	MCC	Lord's	1892
E. Wainwright	Sussex	Dewsbury	1894
G. H. Hirst	Leicestershire	Leicester	1895
J. T. Brown	Derbyshire	Derby	1896

Bowler	Opponents	Venue	Year
R. Peel	Kent	Halifax	1897
S. Haigh	Derbyshire	Bradford	1897
S. Haigh	Somerset	Sheffield	1902
H. A. Sedgwick	Worcestershire	Hull	1906
G. Deyes	Gentlemen of Ireland	Bray	1907
G. H. Hirst	Leicestershire	Hull	1907
J. T. Newstead	Worcestershire	Bradford	1907
S. Haigh	Lancashire	Manchester	1909
M. W. Booth	Worcestershire	Bradford	1911
A. Drake	Essex	Huddersfield	1912
M. W. Booth	Essex	Leyton	1912
A. Drake	Derbyshire	Chesterfield	1914 (4 in 4)
W. Rhodes	Derbyshire	Derby	1920
A. Waddington	Northamptonshire	Northampton	1920 (4 in 5)
G. G. Macaulay	Warwickshire	Birmingham	1923
E. Robinson	Sussex	Hull	1928
G. G. Macaulay	Leicestershire	Hull	1930
E. Robinson	Kent	Gravesend	1930
H. Verity	Nottinghamshire	Leeds	1932
H. Fisher	Somerset	Sheffield	1932 (all lbw)
G. G. Macaulay	Glamorgan	Cardiff	1933
G. G. Macaulay	Lancashire	Manchester	1933 (4 in 5)
M. Leyland	Surrey	Sheffield	1935
E. P. Robinson	Kent	Leeds	1939
A. Coxon	Worcestershire	Leeds	1946
F. S. Trueman	Nottinghamshire	Nottingham	1951
F. S. Trueman	Nottinghamshire	Scarborough	1955
R. Appleyard	Gloucestershire	Sheffield	1956
F. S. Trueman	MCC	Lord's	1958
D. Wilson	Nottinghamshire	Middlesbrough	1959
F. S. Trueman	Nottinghamshire	Bradford	1963
D. Wilson	Nottinghamshire	Worksop	1966
D. Wilson	Kent	Harrogate	1966
G. A. Cope	Essex	Colchester	1970
A. L. Robinson	Nottinghamshire	Worksop	1974
P. W. Jarvis	Derbyshire	Chesterfield	1985

(2) HAT-TRICKS IN LIMITED-OVERS MATCHES

(a) John Player/Refuge Assurance League

Bowler	Opponent	Venue	Year
P. W. Jarvis	Derbyshire	Derby	1982

(b) Benson and Hedges Cup

Nil

(c) Gillette Cup/NatWest Trophy

Nil

595

(3) NINE WICKETS IN AN INNINGS

Analysis	Bowler	Opponents	Venue	Year
10-10	H. Verity	Nottinghamshire	Leeds	1932
10-35	A. Drake	Somerset	Weston-super-Mare	1914
10-36	H. Verity	Warwickshire	Leeds	1931
10-47	T. F. Smailes	Derbyshire	Sheffield	1939
9-12	H. Verity	Kent	Sheffield	1936
9-22	R. Peel	Somerset	Leeds	1895
9-23	T. Emmett	Cambridgeshire	Hunslet	1869
9-23	G. H. Hirst	Lancashire	Leeds	1910
9-25	S. Haigh	Gloucestershire	Leeds	1913
9-25	J. H. Wardle	Lancashire	Manchester	1954
9-28	J. M. Preston	MCC	Scarborough	1888
9-28	W. Rhodes	Essex	Leyton	1899
9-29	A. C. Williams	Hampshire	Dewsbury	1919
9-34	T. Emmett	Nottinghamshire	Dewsbury	1868
9-36	E. Robinson	Lancashire	Bradford	1920
9-39	W. Rhodes	Essex	Leyton	1929
9-41	G. H. Hirst	Worcestershire	Worcester	1911
9-42	R. Illingworth	Worcestershire	Worcester	1957
9-43	H. Verity	Warwickshire	Leeds	1937
9-43	M. J. Cowan	Warwickshire	Birmingham	1960
9-44	H. Verity	Essex	Leyton	1933
9-45	G. H. Hirst	Middlesex	Sheffield	1907
9-48	H. Verity	Essex	Westcliff-on-Sea	1936
9-48	J. H. Wardle	Sussex	Hull	1954
9-59	T. W. Foster	MCC	Lord's	1894
9-59	H. Verity	Kent	Dover	1933
9-60	H. Verity	Glamorgan	Swansea	1930
9-62	H. Verity	MCC	Lord's	1939
9-62	A. G. Nicholson	Sussex	Eastbourne	1967
9-66	E. Wainwright	Middlesex	Sheffield	1894
9-69	G. H. Hirst	MCC	Lord's	1912
9-76	W. Ringrose	Australians	Bradford	1905
9-121	W. E. Bowes	Essex	Scarborough	1932

(4) FIFTEEN WICKETS IN A MATCH

Analysis	Bowler	Opponents	Venue	Year
17-91	H. Verity	Essex	Leyton	1933
16-35	W. E. Bowes	Northamptonshire	Kettering	1935
16-38	T. Emmett	Cambridgeshire	Hunslet	1869
16-112	J. H. Wardle	Sussex	Hull	1954
15-38	H. Verity	Kent	Sheffield	1936
15-50	R. Peel	Somerset	Leeds	1895
15-51	A. Drake	Somerset	Weston-super-Mare	1914
15-56	W. Rhodes	Essex	Leyton	1899
14-63	G. H. Hirst	Leicestershire	Hull	1907
15-100	H. Verity	Essex	Westcliff-on-Sea	1936
15-123	R. Illingworth	Glamorgan	Swansea	1960
15-129	H. Verity	Oxford University	Oxford	1936

(5) SIX WICKETS IN A LIMITED-OVERS MATCH

(a) John Player/Refuge Assurance League

Analysis	Bowler	Opponents	Venue	Year
7-15	R. A. Hutton	Worcestershire	Leeds	1969
6-14	H. P. Cooper	Worcestershire	Worcester	1975
6-18	D. Wilson	Kent	Canterbury	1969
6-36	A. G. Nicholson	Somerset	Sheffield	1972

(b) Benson and Hedges Cup

Analysis	Bowler	Opponents	Venue	Year
6-27	A. G. Nicholson	Minor Counties (North)	Middlesbrough	1972

(c) Gillette Cup/NatWest Trophy

Analysis	Bowler	Opponents	Venue	Year
6-15	F. S. Trueman	Somerset	Taunton	1965

(6) 125 WICKETS IN A SEASON

Bowler	Runs	Wkts	Avge	Year	Bowler	Runs	Wkts	Avge	Year
W. Rhodes	3054	240	12.72	1900	E. Wainwright	1795	157	11.43	1894
W. Rhodes	3497	233	15.00	1900	W. Rhodes	2008	156	12.87	1920
G. H. Hirst	3089	201	15.36	1906	R. Peel	2234	155	14.41	1895
G. G. Macaulay	2986	200	14.93	1925	M. W. Booth	2697	155	17.40	1914
R. Appleyard	2829	200	14.14	1951	W. Rhodes	2233	155	14.40	1919
H. Verity	2761	199	13.87	1935	S. Haigh	1770	154	11.49	1902
H. Verity	2455	189	12.98	1939	W. E. Bowes	2106	154	13.67	1935
H. Verity	2332	185	12.60	1936	W. Rhodes	2473	153	16.16	1899
H. Verity	2777	185	15.01	1937	G. H. Hirst	2560	150	17.07	1895
G. G. Macaulay	2282	184	12.40	1924	F. S. Trueman	1908	150	12.72	1960
W. Rhodes	2118	174	12.17	1902	E. P. Robinson	2164	149	14.52	1946
J. H. Wardle	2815	172	16.30	1950	J. H. Wardle	2733	148	18.46	1948
G. H. Hirst	2788	171	16.30	1901	H. Verity	2059	146	14.10	1932
W. Rhodes	2420	169	14.31	1903	J. H. Wardle	2196	146	15.04	1956
G. H. Hirst	2442	169	14.44	1907	R. Kilner	1815	143	11.99	1923
H. Verity	2147	169	12.70	1931	W. Rhodes	1982	141	14.05	1898
J. H. Wardle	3204	169	18.95	1952	G. G. Macaulay	2219	141	15.73	1933
W. E. Bowes	2454	168	14.60	1932	R. Appleyard	2018	141	14.31	1954
H. Verity	2136	168	12.71	1933	A. Waddington	2334	140	16.67	1920
M. W. Booth	3094	167	18.52	1913	F. S. Trueman	2072	140	14.80	1955
E. Peate	1837	165	11.13	1882	G. H. Hirst	2162	138	15.66	1910
W. Rhodes	2587	164	15.77	1907	H. Verity	1952	137	14.24	1938
G. H. Hirst	2240	164	13.65	1908	R. Peel	1689	134	12.60	1894
G. G. Macaulay	2217	163	13.53	1923	R. Kilner	1744	134	13.01	1924
S. Haigh	2196	161	13.63	1906	E. Peate	1631	133	12.26	1881
S. Haigh	2331	160	14.56	1900	G. G. Macaulay	2148	133	16.15	1926
J. H. Wardle	2442	159	15.35	1955	R. Peel	1690	132	12.80	1890
W. Rhodes	2478	158	15.68	1905	A. Waddington	2090	132	15.83	1922
A. Drake	2418	158	15.30	1914	E. Peate	1514	131	11.55	1880

Bowler	Runs	Wkts	Avge	Year	Bowler	Runs	Wkts	Avge	Year
J. T. Newstead	2089	131	15.94	1908	F. S. Trueman	1999	129	15.49	1954
G. H. Hirst	2418	130	18.60	1911	W. Rhodes	1672	128	13.06	1921
G. G. Macaulay	1785	130	13.73	1922	W. Rhodes	1460	127	11.49	1923
G. G. Macaulay	2375	130	18.26	1927	J. H. Wardle	2742	126	21.76	1953
W. E. Bowes	2372	130	18.24	1933	S. Haigh	1508	125	12.06	1912
A. Coxon	2399	129	18.59	1950	T. F. Smailes	2187	125	17.49	1936

HIGHEST WICKET PARTNERSHIPS

(1) IN FIRST-CLASS MATCHES

FIRST WICKET (Qualification 250 runs)

555	P. Holmes and H. Sutcliffe v Essex at Leyton	1932
554	J. T. Brown and J. Tunnicliffe v Derbyshire at Chesterfield	1898
378	J. T. Brown and J. Tunnicliffe v Sussex at Sheffield	1897
351	G. Boycott and M. D. Moxon v Worcestershire at Worcester	1985
347	P. Holmes and H. Sutcliffe v Hampshire at Portsmouth	1920
323	P. Holmes and H. Sutcliffe v Lancashire at Sheffield	1931
315	H. Sutcliffe and L. Hutton v Leicestershire at Hull	1937
315	H. Sutcliffe and L. Hutton v Hampshire at Sheffield	1939
309	P. Holmes and H. Sutcliffe v Warwickshire at Birmingham	1931
290	P. Holmes and H. Sutcliffe v Middlesex at Leeds	1928
288	G. Boycott and R. G. Lumb v Somerset at Harrogate	1979
286	L. Hutton and F. A. Lowson v South Africans at Sheffield	1951
282	M. D. Moxon and A. A. Metcalfe v Lancashire at Manchester	1986
281*	W. B. Stott and K. Taylor v Sussex at Hove	1960
279	P. Holmes and H. Sutcliffe v Northamptonshire at Northampton	1919
274	P. Holmes and H. Sutcliffe v Somerset at Hull	1923
274	P. Holmes and H. Sutcliffe v Gloucestershire at Gloucester	1927
272	P. Holmes and H. Sutcliffe v Leicestershire at Hull	1925
268	P. Holmes and H. Sutcliffe v Essex at Leyton	1928
267	W. Barber and L. Hutton v Kent at Leeds	1934
265*	P. Holmes and H. Sutcliffe v Surrey at The Oval	1926
264	G. Boycott and R. G. Lumb v Gloucestershire at Leeds	1976
253	P. Holmes and H. Sutcliffe v Lancashire at Sheffield	1919

SECOND WICKET (Qualification 250 runs)

346	W. Barber and M. Leyland v Middlesex at Sheffield	1932
343	F. A. Lowson and J. V. Wilson v Oxford University at Oxford	1956
333	P. Holmes and E. Oldroyd v Warwickshire at Birmingham	1922
314	H. Sutcliffe and E. Oldroyd v Essex at Southend-on-Sea	1924
305	J. W. Rothery and D. Denton v Derbyshire at Chesterfield	1910
302	W. Watson and J. V. Wilson v Derbyshire at Scarborough	1948
301	P. J. Sharpe and D. E. V. Padgett v Glamorgan at Swansea	1971
288	H. Sutcliffe and A. Mitchell v Lancashire at Manchester	1939
280	L. Hall and F. Lee v Lancashire at Bradford	1887
266*	K. Taylor and D. E. V. Padgett v Oxford University at Oxford	1962
261*	L. Hutton and J. V. Wilson v Scotland at Hull	1949

*Not out.

260	R. G. Lumb and K. Sharp *v* Glamorgan *at* Cardiff	1984
258	H. Sutcliffe and E. Oldroyd *v* Kent *at* Folkestone	1931
253	B. B. Wilson and D. Denton *v* Warwickshire *at* Birmingham	1912

THIRD WICKET (Qualification 250 runs)

323★	H. Sutcliffe and M. Leyland *v* Glamorgan *at* Huddersfield	1928
301	H. Sutcliffe and M. Leyland *v* Middlesex *at* Lord's	1939
258★	J. T. Brown and F. Mitchell *v* Warwickshire *at* Bradford	1901
252	D. E. V. Padgett and D. B. Close *v* Nottinghamshire *at* Nottingham	1959

FOURTH WICKET (Qualification 250 runs)

312	D. Denton and G. H. Hirst *v* Hampshire *at* Southampton	1914
299	P. Holmes and R. Kilner *v* Northamptonshire *at* Harrogate	1921
271	B. B. Wilson and W. Rhodes *v* Sussex *at* Bradford	1914
259	A. Drake and G. H. Hirst *v* Sussex *at* Hastings	1911
258	J. Tunnicliffe and G. H. Hirst *v* Hampshire *at* Portsmouth	1904

FIFTH WICKET (Qualification 200 runs)

340	E. Wainwright and G. H. Hirst *v* Surrey *at* The Oval	1899
329	F. Mitchell and E. Wainwright *v* Leicestershire *at* Leicester	1899
276	W. Rhodes and R. Kilner *v* Northamptonshire *at* Northampton	1921
273	L. Hutton and N. W. D. Yardley *v* Hampshire *at* Bournemouth	1947
245★	H. Sutcliffe and W. Barber *v* Northamptonshire *at* Northampton	1939
217	D. B. Close and R. Illingworth *v* Warwickshire *at* Sheffield	1962

SIXTH WICKET (Qualification 200 runs)

276	M. Leyland and E. Robinson *v* Glamorgan *at* Swansea	1926
233	M. W. Booth and G. H. Hirst *v* Worcestershire *at* Worcester	1911
229	W. Rhodes and N. Kilner *v* Leicestershire *at* Leeds	1921
225	E. Wainwright and Lord Hawke *v* Hampshire *at* Southampton	1899
217★	H. Sutcliffe and A. Wood *v* Worcestershire *at* Sheffield	1935
214	W. Watson and N. W. D. Yardley *v* Worcestershire *at* Worcester	1955
205	G. H. Hirst and S. Haigh *v* Nottinghamshire *at* Sheffield	1901
200	D. Denton and G. H. Hirst *v* Essex *at* Bradford	1902

SEVENTH WICKET (Qualification 150 runs)

254	W. Rhodes and D. C. F. Burton *v* Hampshire *at* Dewsbury	1919
247	P. Holmes and W. Rhodes *v* Nottinghamshire *at* Nottingham	1929
215	E. Robinson and D. C. F. Burton *v* Leicestershire *at* Leicester	1921
185	E. Wainwright and G. H. Hirst *v* Gloucestershire *at* Bristol	1897
183	G. H. Hirst and H. Myers *v* Leicestershire *at* Leicester	1905
180	C. Turner and A. Wood *v* Somerset *at* Sheffield	1936
166	R. Peel and I. Grimshaw *v* Derbyshire *at* Holbeck	1886
162	E. Wainwright and S. Haigh *v* Somerset *at* Taunton	1900
161	R. G. Lumb and C. M. Old *v* Worcestershire *at* Bradford	1980
160	J. Tunnicliffe and D. Hunter *v* Worcestershire *at* Worcester	1900
157★	F. A. Lowson and R. Booth *v* Worcestershire *at* Worcester	1953
154★	G. H. Hirst and J. T. Newstead *v* Nottinghamshire *at* Nottingham	1908

★Not out.

EIGHTH WICKET (Qualification 150 runs)

292	R. Peel and Lord Hawke *v* Warwickshire *at* Birmingham	1896
192★	W. Rhodes and G. G. Macaulay *v* Essex *at* Harrogate	1922
180	W. Barber and T. F. Smailes *v* Sussex *at* Leeds	1935
165	S. Haigh and Lord Hawke *v* Surrey *at* The Oval	1902
163	G. G. Macaulay and A. Waddington *v* Worcestershire *at* Leeds	1928
159	E. Smith and W. Rhodes *v* MCC *at* Scarborough	1901
152	W. Rhodes and J. W. Rothery *v* Hampshire *at* Portsmouth	1904
151	W. Rhodes and Lord Hawke *v* Somerset *at* Taunton	1905

NINTH WICKET (Qualification 150 runs)

192	G. H. Hirst and S. Haigh *v* Surrey *at* Bradford	1898
179	R. A. Hutton and G. A. Cope *v* Pakistanis *at* Bradford	1971
176★	R. Moorhouse and G. H. Hirst *v* Gloucestershire *at* Bristol	1894
173	S. Haigh and W. Rhodes *v* Sussex *at* Hove	1902
167	H. Verity and T. F. Smailes *v* Somerset *at* Bath	1936
162	W. Rhodes and S. Haigh *v* Lancashire *at* Manchester	1904
161	E. Smith and W. Rhodes *v* Sussex *at* Sheffield	1900

TENTH WICKET (Qualification 100 runs)

149	G. Boycott and G. B. Stevenson *v* Warwickshire *at* Birmingham	1982
148	Lord Hawke and D. Hunter *v* Kent *at* Sheffield	1898
144	A. Sidebottom and A. L. Robinson *v* Glamorgan *at* Cardiff	1977
121	J. T. Brown and D. Hunter *v* Liverpool and District *at* Liverpool	1894
118	Lord Hawke and D. Hunter *v* Kent *at* Leeds	1896
108	Lord Hawke and L. Whitehead *v* Lancashire *at* Manchester	1903
108	G. Boycott and M. K. Bore *v* Nottinghamshire *at* Bradford	1973
107★	G. G. Macaulay and W. R. Allen *v.* Nottinghamshire *at* Nottingham	1921
106	A. B. Sellers and D. V. Brennan *v* Worcestershire *at* Worcester	1948
103	A. Dophin and E. Smith *v* Essex *at* Leyton	1919
102	D. Denton and D. Hunter *v* Cambridge University *at* Cambridge	1895

(2) IN LIMITED-OVERS MATCHES

(a) John Player/Refuge Assurance League

FIRST WICKET (Qualification 150 runs)

201	J. H. Hampshire and C. W. J. Athey *v* Leicestershire *at* Leicester	1978
190	G. Boycott and R. G. Lumb *v* Nottinghamshire *at* Scarborough	1976
186	G. Boycott and J. H. Hampshire *v* Gloucestershire *at* Scarborough	1975
160	G. Boycott and J. H. Hampshire *v* Warwickshire *at* Birmingham	1973

SECOND WICKET (Qualification 150 runs)

164★	G. Boycott and C. W. J. Athey *v* Worcestershire *at* Worcester	1981
154★	J. H. Hampshire and B. Leadbeater *v* Sussex *at* Hastings	1973

THIRD WICKET (Qualification 125 runs)

141★	G. Boycott and C. M. Old *v* Somerset *at* Glastonbury	1976
132★	G. Boycott and C. W. J. Athey *v* Northamptonshire *at* Tring	1986
127	S. N. Hartley and P. E. Robinson *v* Leicesterhire *at* Middlesbrough	1986

★Not out.

FOURTH WICKET (Qualification 125 runs)

138*	K. Sharp and P. E. Robinson *v* Leicestershire *at* Leicester	1985

FIFTH WICKET (Qualification 100 runs)

150*	S. N. Hartley and J. D. Love *v* Hampshire *at* Middlesbrough	1983
130*	A. A. Metcalfe and D. L. Bairstow *v* Surrey *at* The Oval	1986
114	K. Sharp and D. L. Bairstow *v* Essex *at* Chelmsford	1985

SIXTH WICKET (Qualification 100 runs)

110	B. Leadbeater and C. Johnson *v* Nottinghamshire *at* Hull	1972
105	S. N. Hartley and D. L. Bairstow *v* Warwickshire *at* Scarborough	1984

SEVENTH WICKET

76	J. C. Balderstone and J. G. Binks *v* Hampshire *at* Southampton	1969

EIGHTH WICKET

64	D. L. Bairstow and A. Sidebottom *v* Sussex *at* Scarborough	1976

NINTH WICKET

88	S. N. Hartley and A. Ramage *v* Middlesex *at* Lord's	1982

TENTH WICKET

50*	P. Carrick and S. Oldham *v* Warwickshire *at* Scarborough	1984

(b) Benson and Hedges Cup

FIRST WICKET (Qualification 150 runs)

211*	M. D. Moxon and A. A. Metcalfe *v* Warwickshire *at* Birmingham	1987
166	M. D. Moxon and A. A. Metcalfe *v* Nottinghamshire *at* Leeds	1988

SECOND WICKET (Qualification 125 runs)

148*	G. Boycott and C. W. J. Athey *v* Combined Universities *at* Oxford	1980
147*	G. Boycott and R. G. Lumb *v* Kent *at* Canterbury	1976

THIRD WICKET (Qualification 100 runs)

146	G. Boycott and K. Sharp *v* Nottinghamshire *at* Bradford	1984

FOURTH WICKET

91*	J. H. Hampshire and C. M. Old *v* Minor Counties (North) *at* Scunthorpe	1975

FIFTH WICKET (Qualification 100 runs)

114	B. Leadbeater and C. M. Old *v* Sussex *at* Hove	1976
100*	J. H. Hampshire and D. L. Bairstow *v* Warwickshire *at* Leeds	1980

SIXTH WICKET

71	D. L. Bairstow and G. B. Stevenson *v* Warwickshire *at* Leeds	1984

SEVENTH WICKET

149*	J. D. Love and C. M. Old *v* Scotland *at* Bradford	1981

EIGHTH WICKET

48*	J. D. Love and P. J. Hartley *v* Surrey *at* Leeds	1987

*Not out.

NINTH WICKET
41   K. Sharp and P. W. Jarvis *v* Worcestershire *at* Leeds   1987

TENTH WICKET
80★ D. L. Bairstow and M. Johnson *v* Derbyshire *at* Derby   1981

(c) Gillette Cup/NatWest Trophy

FIRST WICKET (Qualification 150 runs)
161   M. D. Moxon and A. A. Metcalfe *v* Wiltshire *at* Trowbridge   1987
160★ G. Boycott and M. D. Moxon *v* Cheshire *at* Oxton   1986

SECOND WICKET (Qualification 150 runs)
202   G. Boycott and C. W. J. Athey *v* Kent *at* Leeds   1980
192   G. Boycott and D. B. Close *v* Surrey *at* Lord's   1965
159   G. Boycott and D. B. Close *v* Surrey *at* The Oval   1969

THIRD WICKET (Qualification 100 runs)
115   R. G. Lumb and J. H. Hampshire *v* Shropshire *at* Wellington   1976
101   P. J. Sharpe and D. E. V. Padgett *v* Nottinghamshire *at* Scarborough   1969

FOURTH WICKET (Qualification 100 runs)
142★ C. W. J. Athey and J. D. Love *v* Hampshire *at* Southampton   1980
106   J. H. Hampshire and R. G. Lumb *v* Durham *at* Middlesbrough   1978

FIFTH WICKET (Qualification 100 runs)
95   S. N. Hartley and D. L. Baistow *v* Worcestershire *at* Leeds   1982

SIXTH WICKET
59   J. H. Hampshire and D. L. Bairstow *v* Kent *at* Canterbury   1981

SEVENTH WICKET
102   D. L. Bairstow and C. M. Old *v* Worcestershire *at* Leeds   1982

EIGHTH WICKET
50   G. Boycott and J. G. Binks *v* Sussex *at* Hove   1963

NINTH WICKET
32   D. L. Bairstow and C. M. Old *v* Warwickshire *at* Birmingham   1982

TENTH WICKET
29★ R. Illingworth and A. G. Nicholson *v* Warwickshire *at* Birmingham   1968

WICKET-KEEPING RECORDS

(1) SIX DISMISSALS IN AN INNINGS

Keeper	Total	Ct	St	Opponents	Venue	Year
D. L. Bairstow	7	7	0	Derbyshire	Scarborough	1982
J. Hunter	6	6	0	Gloucestershire	Gloucester	1887

★Not out.

Keeper	Total	Ct	St	Opponents	Venue	Year
D. Hunter	6	5	1	Surrey	Sheffield	1891
D. Hunter	6	6	0	Middlesex	Leeds	1909
W. R. Allen	6	2	4	Sussex	Hove	1921
J. G. Binks	6	5	1	Lancashire	Leeds	1962
D. L. Bairstow	6	6	0	Lancashire	Manchester	1971
D. L. Bairstow	6	6	0	Warwickshire	Bradford	1978
D. L. Bairstow	6	5	1	Lancashire	Leeds	1980
D. L. Bairstow	6	6	0	Derbyshire	Chesterfield	1984

(2) EIGHT DISMISSALS IN A MATCH

Keeper	Total	Ct	St	Opponents	Venue	Year
D. L. Bairstow	11	11	0	Derbyshire	Scarborough	1982
J. Hunter	9	9	0	Gloucestershire	Gloucester	1887
A. Dolphin	9	8	1	Derbyshire	Bradford	1919
D. L. Bairstow	9	9	0	Lancashire	Manchester	1971
G. Pinder	8	2	6	Lancashire	Sheffield	1872
D. Hunter	8	2	6	Surrey	Bradford	1898
A. Bairstow	8	7	1	Cambridge Univ	Cambridge	1899
A Wood	8	8	0	Northamptonshire	Huddersfield	1932
D. L. Bairstow	8	8	0	Lancashire	Leeds	1978
D. L. Bairstow	8	7	12	Derbyshire	Chesterfield	1984
D. L. Bairstow	8	6	2	Derbyshire	Chesterfield	1985

(3) EIGHTY DISMISSALS IN A SEASON

Keeper	Total	Ct	St	Year
J. G. Binks	107	96	11	1960
J. G. Binks	94	81	13	1964
A. Wood	89	75	14	1934
J. G. Binks	88	80	8	1963
J. G. Binks	86	70	16	1962
A. Dolphin	82	52	30	1919
A. Wood	80	57	23	1935

(4) EIGHT-HUNDRED DISMISSALS IN A CAREER

Keeper	Total	Ct	St	Career
D. Hunter	1190	863	327	1888–1909
J. G. Binks	1044	872	172	1955–1969
D. L. Bairstow	1004	874	130	1970–1988
A. Wood	855	612	243	1927–1946
A. Dolphin	828	568	260	1905–1927

Note: These figures include some catches taken in the field.

FIELDING RECORDS

(1) FIVE CATCHES IN AN INNINGS

Fielder	Catches	Opponents	Venue	Year
E. P. Robinson	6	Leicestershire	Bradford	1938
J. Tunnicliffe	5	Leicestershire	Leeds	1897
J. Tunnicliffe	5	Leicestershire	Leicester	1900
J. Tunnicliffe	5	Leicestershire	Scarborough	1901
A. B. Sellers	5	Essex	Leyton	1933
D. Wilson	5	Surrey	The Oval	1969
R. G. Lumb	5	Gloucestershire	Middlesbrough	1972

(2) SEVEN CATCHES IN A MATCH

Fielder	Catches	Opponents	Venue	Year
J. Tunnicliffe	7	Leicestershire	Leeds	1897
J. Tunnicliffe	7	Leicestershire	Leicester	1900
A. B. Sellers	7	Essex	Leyton	1933
E. P. Robinson	7	Leicestershire	Bradford	1938

(3) FIFTY CATCHES IN A SEASON

Fielder	Catches	Year
J. Tunnicliffe	70	1901
P. J. Sharpe	70	1962
J. Tunnicliffe	61	1895
J. Tunnicliffe	60	1904
J. Tunnicliffe	59	1896
J. V. Wilson	57	1955
J. V. Wilson	54	1961
J. V. Wilson	53	1957
J. V. Wilson	51	1951

(4) FIVE-HUNDRED CATCHES IN A CAREER

Fielder	Catches	Career
J. Tunnicliffe	665	1891–1907
W. Rhodes	572	1898–1930
D. B. Close	564	1949–1970
P. J. Sharpe	525	1958–1974
J. V. Wilson	521	1946–1962
G. H. Hirst	500	1891–1929

TEST CAREER RECORDS OF YORKSHIRE PLAYERS 1877–1988

Name	Country	Years	Matches	Runs	Avge	Wkts	Avge	c/st
R. Appleyard	England	1954–1956	9	51	17.00	31	17.87	4
T. Armitage	England	1877	2	33	11.00			
C. W. J. Athey	England	1980–1988	23	919	22.97			13
D. L. Bairstow	England	1979–1981	4	125	20.83			12/1
W. Barber	England	1935	2	83	20.75	1	0.00	1
W. Bates	England	1882–1887	15	656	27.33	50	16.42	9
J. G. Binks	England	1964	2	91	22.75			8/–
M. W. Booth	England	1913–1914	2	46	23.00	7	18.57	
W. E. Bowes	England	1932–1946	15	28	4.66	68	22.33	2
G. Boycott	England	1964–1982	108	8114	47.72	7	54.57	33
D. V. Brennan	England	1951	2	16	8.00			–/1
J. T. Brown	England	1894–1899	8	470	36.15			7
D. B. Close	England	1949–1976	22	887	25.34	18	29.55	24
G. A. Cope	England	1977	3	40	13.33	8	34.62	1
A. Coxon	England	1948	1	19	9.50	3	57.33	
D. Denton	England	1905–1910	11	424	20.19			8
A. Dolphin	England	1921	1	1	0.50			1/–
T. Emmett	England	1877–1882	7	160	13.33	9	31.55	9
P. A. Gibb	England	1938–1946	8	581	44.69			3/1
A. Greenwood	England	1877	2	77	19.25			2
S. Haigh	England	1899–1912	11	113	7.53	24	25.91	8
J. H. Hampshire	England	1969–1975	8	403	26.86			9
Lord Hawke	England	1896–1899	5	55	7.85			3
A. Hill	England	1877	2	101	50.50	7	18.57	1
G. H. Hirst	England	1899–1909	24	790	22.57	59	30.00	18
P. Holmes	England	1921–1932	7	357	27.46			3
J. Hunter	England	1884–1885	5	93	18.60			8/3
L. Hutton	England	1937–1955	79	6971	56.67	3	77.33	57
R. A. Hutton	England	1971	5	219	36.50	9	28.55	9
R. Illingworth	England	1958–1973	61	1836	23.24	122	31.20	45
Hon F. S. Jackson	England	1893–1905	20	1415	48.79	24	33.29	10
P. W. Jarvis	England	1988	4	76	19.00	12	34.83	
R. Kilner	England	1924–1926	9	233	33.28	24	30.58	6
E. Leadbeater	England	1951–1952	2	40	20.00	2	109.00	3
M. Leyland	England	1928–1938	41	2764	46.06	6	97.50	13
F. A. Lowson	England	1951–1955	7	245	18.84			5
G. G. Macaulay	England	1923–1933	8	112	18.66	24	27.58	5
F. W. Milligan	England	1899	2	58	14.50			1
A. Mitchell	England	1933–1938	6	298	29.80			9
F. Mitchell	England and South Africa	1899–1912	5	116	11.60			2
M. D. Moxon	England	1986–1988	9	437	27.31			10
C. M. Old	England	1972–1981	46	845	14.82	143	28.11	22
D. E. V. Padgett	England	1960	2	51	12.75			
E. Peate	England	1882–1886	9	70	11.66	31	22.00	2
R. Peel	England	1884–1896	20	427	14.72	102	16.81	17
W. Rhodes	England	1899–1930	58	2325	30.19	127	26.96	60

Name	Country	Years	Matches	Runs	Avge	Wkts	Avge	c/st
P. J. Sharpe	England	1963–1969	12	786	46.23			17
A. Sidebottom	England	1985	1	2	2.00	1	65.00	
T. F. Smailes	England	1946	1	25	25.00	3	20.66	
G. A. Smithson	England	1948	2	70	23.33			
R. T. Stanyforth	England	1927–1928	4	13	2.60			7/2
G. B. Stevenson	England	1980–1981	2	28	28.00	5	36.60	
H. Sutcliffe	England	1924–1935	54	4555	60.733			23
K. Taylor	England	1959–1964	3	57	11.40	1		
F. S. Trueman	England	1952–1965	67	981	13.81	307	21.57	64
G. Ulyett	England	1877–1890	25	949	24.33	50	20.40	19
H. Verity	England	1931–1939	40	669	20.90	144	24.37	30
A. Waddington	England	1920–1921	2	16	4.00	1	119.00	1
E. Wainwright	England	1893–1898	5	132	14.66			2
J. H. Wardle	England	1948–1957	28	653	19.78	102	20.39	12
W. Watson	England	1951–1959	23	879	25.85			8
C. E. M. Wilson	England	1899	2	42	14.00			
D. Wilson	England	1964–1971	6	75	12.50	11	42.36	1
E. R. Wilson	England	1921	1	10	5.00	3	12.00	
A. Wood	England	1938–1939	4	80	20.00			10/1
N. W. D. Yardley	England	1938–1950	20	812	25.37	21	33.66	14

BIBLIOGRAPHY

Association of Cricket Statisticians: *First-Class Matches 1864–1897*
—— Journals (VY)
—— *Yorkshire Cricketers 1863–1895*
P. Bailey, P. Thorn, P. Wynne-Thomas: *Who's Who of Cricketers* (Newnes, 1984)
Robert Brooke: *The Collins Who's Who of First-Class Cricketers* (1985)
W. Duthoit: *Yorkshire Cricketer's Guide for 1878*
Lord Hawke: *Recollections and Reminiscences* (Williams Norgate, London 1924)
Rev. R. S. Holmes: *History of Yorkshire County Cricket 1893–1903* (Archibald Constable 1904)
J. M. Kilburn: *History of Yorkshire County Cricket 1924–1949* (Yorkshire CCC, 1950)
Frederick Lillywhite: *Cricket Scores and Biographies* Vols 1–4
—— *Cricketer's Guides* (annual series 1847–1866)
James Lillywhite: *Cricketers' Annuals* (1872–1900)
John Lillywhite: *Cricketer's Companions* (1865–1885)
MCC: *Cricket Scores and Biographies* Vols 5–15
A. W. Pullin: *History of Yorkshire County Cricket 1903–1923* (Pickersgill Chorley 1924)
Peter Thomas: *Yorkshire Cricketers* (D. Hodgson, 1973)
A. A. Thomson: *Cricket my Pleasure* (Museum Press 1953)
—— *Hirst & Rhodes* (Epworth Press 1959)
—— *Hutton & Washbrook* (Epworth Press 1963)
Yorkshire Cricketers' Guide & West Riding Cricketers' Guides and Handbooks (VY)
Yorkshire CCC Year Books 1893–1988

ACKNOWLEDGEMENTS

THE AUTHOR gratefully acknowledges the assistance of the following in providing the statistical material for this book:

R. D. Wilkinson and the Yorkshire County Cricket Club, and the Association of Cricket Statisticians, among whom he would especially like to thank Philip Baily, Robert Brooke, Philip Thorne and Peter Wynne-Thomas.

The author and publishers would also like to thank the Yorkshire CCC and its officials for their assistance in allowing access to photographs, minutes and other materials.

Thanks also go to John Featherstone for his help with regard to photographs, and to the following, who also assisted with pictures:

C. F. Stansfield
Wombwell Cricket Lovers' Society
Marylebone Cricket Club
Nottinghamshire County Cricket Club
A. Wilkes & Son
Central Press Photos Ltd.
Patrick Eagar

A.W. 1989

INDEX

617